The HISTORY of the EVANGELICAL UNITED BRETHREN CHURCH

The HISTORY of the EVANGELICAL UNITED BRETHREN CHURCH

J. Bruce Behney & Paul H. Eller

EDITED BY
Kenneth W. Krueger

Abingdon   Nashville

The History of the Evangelical United
Brethren Church

Copyright © 1979 by Abingdon

Library of Congress Cataloging in Publication Data
BEHNEY, J BRUCE.
  The history of the Evangelical United Brethren
Church.
  Includes index.
  1. Evangelical United Brethren Church—History.
I. Eller, Paul Himmel, 1905-   joint author.
II. Krueger, Kenneth W. III. Title.
BX7556.A4B43   289.9   79-14738

ISBN 0-687-17206-3

MANUFACTURED BY THE PARTHENON PRESS AT
NASHVILLE, TENNESSEE, UNITED STATES OF AMERICA

CONTENTS

EDITOR'S FOREWORD......7

AUTHORS' FOREWORD......9

PREFACE......11

Chapter I   HISTORICAL BACKGROUND......15

Chapter II   UNITED BRETHREN BACKGROUND TO 1800......29

Chapter III   EVANGELICAL BEGINNINGS TO 1816......67

Chapter IV   THE FOUNDING OF THE UNITED BRETHREN CHURCH, 1800–1815......97

Chapter V   THE CHURCH OF THE UNITED BRETHREN IN CHRIST, 1815–1841......113

Chapter VI   THE EVANGELICAL ASSOCIATION, 1816–1840......131

Chapter VII   THE UNITED BRETHREN CHURCH, 1841–1890......153

Chapter VIII   THE EVANGELICAL ASSOCIATION, 1840–1890......189

Chapter IX   UNITED BRETHREN: CRISIS, DEVELOPMENT, EXPANSION, 1889–1921......225

Chapter X   UNITED BRETHREN: CHANGES IN A CHANGING WORLD, 1920–1946......255

Chapter XI   THE EVANGELICAL ASSOCIATION AND THE UNITED EVANGELICAL CHURCH, 1891–1922......283

Maps and Photographs......315

Chapter XII   EVANGELICALS FROM UNION TO UNION, 1922–1946......331

97063

Chapter XIII   THE EVANGELICAL UNITED BRETHREN
              CHURCH, 1946–1968......*357*
EPILOGUE......*393*
NOTES......*397*
INDEX......*413*

EDITOR'S FOREWORD

For if you have been cut from what is by nature a wild olive tree, and grafted, contrary to nature, into a cultivated olive tree, how much more will these natural branches be grafted back into their own olive tree (Romans 11:24).

From the troubled land of Germany in the eighteenth century came the immigrants to Pennsylvania seeking a new life. They were mostly the dispossessed and the poor. Some of them arrived as indentured servants, repaying their creditors for the ship passage with human bondage for as long as seven years. They were classified as outcasts and serfs.

Successive waves of German immigration followed in the eighteenth and nineteenth centuries. In this soil the seed of the gospel was planted by the early founders and circuit riders of the Evangelical and the United Brethren movements.

As Wesley preached to the down-and-outers of England whom the Church of England neglected, so Philip William Otterbein, a co-founder of the United Brethren Church, and Jacob Albright, the founder of the Evangelical Church, ministered to those persons whom the "respectable" churches did not reach.

The roots of these branches are similar. They were influenced by German pietism, which stressed a warm "heart" faith and a personal relationship with God through a first-hand experience of Christ.

While Luther emphasized justification by faith and Calvin stressed the sovereignty of God, the founders of the United Methodist movement proclaimed Christian assurance. "It is the Spirit himself bearing witness with our spirit that we are children of God," testified both Wesley after his heart-warming experience at Aldersgate in 1738 and Albright after his conversion in 1791 (Romans 8:16).

With assurance came a sense of joy, optimism, and confidence

7

inspired by the Holy Spirit. Sanctification, a Wesleyan doctrine, is a note of expectation—the Christian is expected to grow. The United Methodists shared the bold and optimistic belief that perfect love to God should be our constant goal and is expressed in our compassion for others.

Not many of these early followers were "wise according to worldly standards, not many were powerful, not many were of noble birth" (I Corinthians 1:26). We might call all three branches of United Methodism branches from a wild olive tree, grafted by God into his church universal.

It is important that the history of two of these branches be added to the three volumes *The History of American Methodism* (Nashville: Abingdon Press, 1964). We are fortunate that two reputable scholars from the Evangelical United Brethren heritage— Dr. J. Bruce Behney of the former United Brethren Church and Dr. Paul H. Eller of the former Evangelical Church—have carefully and skillfully summarized this story.

KENNETH W. KRUEGER, *Editor*

AUTHORS' FOREWORD

In the following pages we have endeavored to present a brief, responsible history of the Evangelical United Brethren Church and its antecedents. The history begins in the eighteenth century in Pennsylvania, Maryland, and Virginia and terminates in the union of the Evangelical United Brethren Church with the Methodist Church to form the United Methodist Church. This union was accomplished in the first General Conference of the United Methodist Church held in Dallas, Texas, in 1968.

Within restricted limits the broad panorama of the life of the Evangelical United Brethren Church is sketched with some attention to personalities in leadership roles but major attention to positions and achievements articulated in official decisions. Although in a communion where leadership and authoritative bodies are elected such decisions may not be presumed to express the mind of everyone, they may be presumed to represent the consensus of the denomination. History, as life itself, is comprehensive, embracing thought and action, both of which must be evaluated in relation to the contemporary and changing milieu.

The limitations of these pages are freely acknowledged—the omission of certain aspects of church life such as the growing appreciation and understanding of the meaning of worship and the restricted references to personalities who promoted new positions and undertakings. Vapid generalizations and direct endeavors to plumb the denominational psyche are avoided. These limitations and avoidances may be ascribed to the decisions of the writers and the prescriptions placed upon them. Nor is this a detached, "objective" study. Indeed, that would be impossible because the writers freely confess their esteem and affection for the Evangelical United Brethren Church. They view with disciplined pride the record of Christian service rendered while not unmindful of events (such as schisms) which a later generation can only deplore.

A person and a church are distinguished by the memories they keep. The past as recorded in these pages serves as a ground for the grateful recognition of our predecessors. They believed that their lives fit into a story of dignity and purpose as they sought to interpret and implement the unfathomable riches of the graces of Christ. Thus they inspired a later generation to be no less sensitive and responsive to the signs of the times and the claims of Christian discipleship as interpreted by the Holy Spirit.

The constructive criticisms of many who remain nameless have been incorporated in these pages. However the Rev. Kenneth W. Krueger, serving the writers as counselor, contributed criticism and guidance during the years when this book was being written. His work must be recognized with particular mention and gratitude.

The authors also wish to acknowledge the assistance of Dr. John H. Ness, Jr., executive secretary of the United Methodist Commission on Archives and History, in selecting and permitting the use of many of the illustrations in this book. Garrett-Evangelical Theological Seminary permitted the use of several pictures from their collection.

The writers by original assignment shared the work by using the date of 1890 as the point of division. J. Bruce Behney wrote the material preceding that date, and Paul H. Eller wrote the material following that date.

J. Bruce Behney
Paul H. Eller

PREFACE

In the United States there are more than two hundred and fifty denominations, no two of which are precisely the same in all particulars. Some are distinguished by unique rites, some by singular doctrinal or behavioral emphases, and some by their church governments. The singular character of the Evangelical United Brethren Church was distinguished by none of these. Through many years of the nineteenth century its use of the German language marked it off from the body of American Methodism, but well before the end of the century that singularity was rapidly disappearing. This church was always flexible enough to meet new circumstances in a changing world—in missionary operations, in educational programs, in administration, in ways of worship, and in creedal expression. Though it was not the first to experiment in novelties in any of these areas, neither was it the last to alter its ways in the face of changing times. Its modest numerical size made for a warm familial relation in the church and its work.

Believing the divine Spirit gave a knowable witness in the hearts of the redeemed, it also held that the Spirit gave guidance and energy for new undertakings and for a never-ending growth in grace through an intimate, liberating, and invigorating relationship with God. Through Christ, lives could be transformed. The Spirit's witness with its message of forgiveness and acceptance brought religious feelings of joy and satisfaction, but never in the sense that sinlessness had been achieved, for if God's Spirit were faithfully and obediently followed, new aspects of the spiritual life and new understandings of God's ways for men would be discovered. Religion was held to be a meaningful and vital aspect of life not fully accomplished by an initial religious experience, nor by baptism, nor by church membership. From the first, Evangelical United Brethren were emphatic that while religious life began in the moment when Christ's mastery was accepted, it did not end there; for that mastery brought divine graces which expanded consciousness and prompt-

11

ed undertakings, personal and social, in ethical living, in personal character, in brotherly love, in good will and justice.

Without major concern for sophisticated theology or dreams of grandeur, but with energy and with dollars this church through its years strove to proclaim its understanding of the gospel. It did not send missionaries everywhere in the world but sent them to selected locations. It was a lower middle class, northern, white church, and it did little for deprived and ethnic minorities in America apart from several efforts among mountaineers and Spanish and Italian Americans. However, as concern was sensitized and means were available, this church seriously and productively witnessed to its understanding of Christian discipleship as a way of life initiated by God's grace at the moment of commitment to Christ, nurtured by attendance upon the means of grace, by reflecton upon God's word, and by responsiveness to the Holy Spirit. It sought not the "good old days" of the past, but to be a useful instrument in the hands of God in the continuing present. While little of this may be claimed as genuinely singular, all this taken together constituted the singularity of the Evangelical United Brethren Church.

The HISTORY
of the
EVANGELICAL
UNITED
BRETHREN
CHURCH

he Evangelical United Brethren Church came into existence when the Church of the United Brethren in Christ and the Evangelical Church were united on November 16, 1946. The two uniting denominations began in 1800 and 1803 respectively. At the time of the foundings their people were of German origin living in Pennsylvania, Maryland, and Virginia. The course of events leading to the foundings had begun many years earlier in Germany, Switzerland, and Holland, as well as in the New World.

SETTLEMENTS IN PENNSYLVANIA

The immigration of German people into the New World began in 1683 in response to the invitation of the English Quaker proprietor of Pennsylvania, William Penn (1644–1718). Penn wished to provide a place where people who were persecuted for their religious faith could find refuge. His own co-religionists, the English Quakers, came first in 1682. They were followed the next year by Quakers from Holland and the first Germans, who were Mennonites coming from Krefeld and Krisheim. Mennonites continued to arrive throughout the remainder of the seventeenth and into the eighteenth century. In the eighteenth century other religiously oppressed sects began to arrive. Among them were the German Baptists or "Dunkers" beginning in 1719, the Schwenckfelders in 1734, and the Moravians in 1740.

HISTORICAL BACKGROUND

In 1703 people of the German Lutheran Church began to arrive in Pennsylvania, and in 1712 came members of the German Reformed Church. Their main reason for migrating was not religious persecution but escape from poverty.

As the eighteenth century proceeded, Scotch-Irish and English Presbyterians and Anglicans also came. As these different religious and national groups settled in Pennsylvania, they tended to accumulate in three "bands" of settlements. The Quakers and Anglicans settled mostly in the eastern part of the colony along the west bank of the Delaware River. The second band, exclusively German, was immediately west of the English, extending to the west bank of the Susquehanna River. The third band was composed of Scotch-Irish along the Susquehanna from its northeastern branch southward through Pennsylvania into Maryland and the Virginia (Shenandoah) Valley. Obviously these overlapped, but the predominant group gave each area a distinctive quality or character which can be discerned to the present day.

GERMAN SECTS AND CHURCHES IN PENNSYLVANIA

The German groups fell into two classifications: the sect groups and the church groups. The former were the Mennonites, Dunkers, Schwenckfelders, and Moravians; the latter were the German Lutherans and German Reformed. The distinction between the two classifications went back to their homeland.

The Lutheran and the Reformed Churches, along with the Roman Catholic Church, had legal recognition as state churches in the various German states after the Thirty Years' War ended in 1648. They were organized as unified bodies with formally accepted ritualistic practices, established doctrines, and ordained clergy.

The sects, as that word implies, were regarded as groups which had separated from the churches. Their emphasis was upon individual religious life, with little stress on formal doctrine and organization. They emphasized Bible study and careful moral application of the gospel. In their home states they were granted no legal recognition.

The early United Brethren and Evangelical movements had their roots in all these German religious groups, both in the churches and in the sects.

The Mennonites

The Mennonites under the judicious leadership of Menno Simons (1492–1559) sprang from a movement called Anabaptism that developed among Protestants in Switzerland and the western provinces of Germany, especially the Palatinate, beginning in 1521. The Anabaptists accepted the Reformers' stress upon Bible study but with freedom of individual interpretation. They felt that true religious belief and practice should be free from all external domination, ecclesiastical and governmental. They renounced warfare and all other forms of violence and the taking of oaths. Most of them affirmed baptism of believers only (adult baptism) and the necessity to follow the moral and devotional precepts which they derived from the study of the life of Jesus. Because many had repudiated the baptism they had received as infants within the Roman Catholic Church, they submitted themselves to baptism as adults, thereby bringing upon themselves the derisive name "Anabaptists" or "Rebaptizers."

During the first decade of their existence, the 1520's, they had leaders of local groups who were vigorous but modest and self-disciplined. However, their practice of "rebaptizing" brought condemnation from the Roman Catholic, Lutheran, and Reformed Churches. They were cruelly persecuted, often killed by burning at the stake or drowning, the latter in horrible mimicry of baptism by immersion which many, but not all, practiced.

By the 1530's many of the judicious leaders had been killed, leaving a fanatical group to lead some of the Anabaptists into violence and rebellion. In 1534 they gained possession of and fortified the city of Münster. An army made up of Roman Catholic and Lutheran soldiers under the leadership of the Roman Catholic Bishop of Münster recaptured the city and ruthlessly eradicated the fanatical leaders, leaving the Anabaptists in confusion and terror. It was then that Menno Simons, a converted Roman Catholic priest, began to gather some of the leaderless Anabaptists into a movement which reaffirmed their original beliefs and practices. His followers henceforth were called Mennonites. Their mode of adult baptism was by pouring.

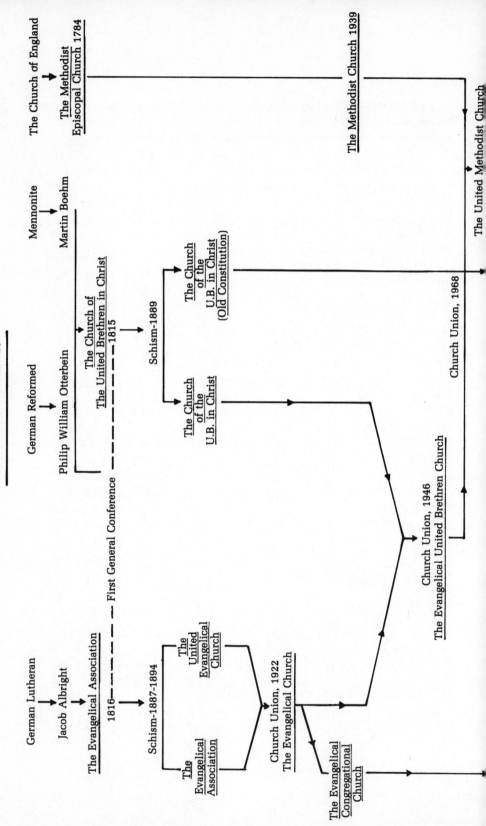

ECCLESIASTICAL BACKGROUNDS

The Church of England

The Methodist
Episcopal Church 1784

The Methodist Church 1939

Mennonite

Martin Boehm

German Reformed

Philip William Otterbein

The Church of
The United Brethren in Christ
1815

Schism-1889

The Church
of the
U.B. in Christ
(Old Constitution)

The Church
of the
U.B. in Christ

First General Conference

Church Union, 1968

The United Methodist Church

German Lutheran

Jacob Albright

The Evangelical Association

1816

Schism-1887-1894

The
United
Evangelical
Church

The
Evangelical
Association

Church Union, 1922
The Evangelical Church

The Evangelical
Congregational
Church

Church Union, 1946
The Evangelical United Brethren Church

Persecution continued to be their lot in spite of their peace-loving, forgiving spirit. Therefore in 1683, after a century and a half of torment, they accepted the offer of religious shelter in Pennsylvania.

Most of them had been farmers in their homeland. After arriving in Philadelphia they spread westward into the present Lancaster County area where they developed rich, productive farms. They prospered also in their religious life because their practice of selecting ministers from the congregation by lot always provided them with leadership.

In 1693 in Switzerland a division occurred among the Mennonites. Jacob Ammann led a group away from the main body. He declared religious practices should be more severe in personal conduct and relationships and that the group should withdraw from all "worldly" practices, such as wearing stylish clothing and jewelry and trimming beards. He also repudiated houses of worship, requiring that worship be held in members' homes. According to Ammann, worship should consist of informal Bible study, preaching, and singing without instruments. His followers came to be called Amish after the leader's name. They influenced the main body of Mennonites to some degree, especially in the wearing of plain clothing, which came to make them, and also the Dunkers, to be quite visible in their distinctiveness.

The first Amish came to Pennsylvania in 1714. They settled in Berks County but spread into neighboring counties as the colonial years passed.

German Baptists, or Dunkers

The next group to arrive in Pennsylvania were the German Baptists, or "Dunkers." This name was derived from the German word tunken, "to dip," because they practiced adult baptism by immersion only. Furthermore, baptism was to be in a flowing stream (living water) face forward three times in recognition of the Trinity.

The German Baptists sprang from groups within the Lutheran and Reformed Churches who were influenced by the pietistic movement, which called for deep inner devotion and saintly living. Pietism had ancient roots, but as a movement within Protestantism it began under the influence of a Lutheran minister named Philipp Jakob Spener (1635–1705). Against bitter opposition he repudiated

"Protestant scholasticism," that is, reducing Christianity to intellectual premises, doctrines, rules, and creeds, and urged the acceptance of Christianity as a mystical religion of the heart which prompts striving for moral perfection and engaging in evangelism and missions.

In spite of the opposition, Pietism gained a following of ministers and lay people within the Lutheran and Reformed Churches. Many small groups were formed for prayer, Bible study, and mutual helpfulness, each of which was given the name *collegium pietatis.*

In 1708 in Schwarzenau, Germany, a Lutheran named Alexander Mack and a *collegium pietatis* of which he was the leader, withdrew from the church. They formed a congregation which engaged in Bible study and spontaneous prayers. Like the Mennonites they repudiated violence, the taking of oaths, and external domination. They practiced strict moral living. In worship they celebrated the *Agape* or the "Love Feast" and a ceremony of footwashing.

In 1719 the first of these people came to Pennsylvania. In 1729 Mack came with another group. Like the Mennonites, many Dunkers had been farmers in Germany. They also started farming in the Lancaster County area and prospered. They formed congregations and called ministers from among their own fellowship.

The Schwenckfelders

The Schwenckfelders derived their name from their first leader, Kaspar Schwenckfeld (1489–1561). Their homeland was Silesia, an eastern state of Germany. They were not directly related to the Anabaptists, who were largely to be found in the western states of Germany and neighboring areas, but held some similar beliefs. They held the Bible to be authoritative but only as it is interpreted by the Holy Spirit in the heart of the believer. Thus the Bible becomes "the living Word." All religious rites were to be celebrated inwardly only. The Lord's Supper and baptism were "celestial" and not to be celebrated as external ceremonies with materials such as bread, wine, and water. This position granted a large measure of religious autonomy to the individual, but as a consequence it provoked much dissension within the group because of personal differences.

After suffering persecution in Silesia these people fled to

Saxony where Count von Zinzendorf granted them shelter on his estates. In 1734 they began to immigrate to Pennsylvania. They settled mostly in the present areas of Bucks, Montgomery, Lehigh, and Berks Counties. Their fortunes wavered, due partly to their tendency toward quarrelsomeness. They were slow to form congregations. Leadership was judged to lie in the heads of the individual families. Eventually a congregation was formed in 1782 and the first church building erected in 1790. In quite recent times the Lord's Supper and adult baptism have become formal celebrations in more traditional form.

The Moravians

In origin the Moravians antedated all the other German Protestant groups who immigrated to Pennsylvania. Their movement began with the ministry and thought of John Hus (ca. 1373–1415), a minister and rector of the University of Prague in Bohemia. In much of his thought and leadership he was the forerunner of Martin Luther. He was excommunicated twice by the Roman Catholic Church and at the Council of Constance, which met from 1414 to 1417, was condemned to be burned at the stake for heresy.

Following his death many Bohemians declared their loyalty to his teachings, especially his criticism of Roman Catholic practices and claims to power. After much persecution in Bohemia they fled to the province of Moravia, from which they derived their commonly used name (they actually called themselves Unitas Fratrum or "Unity of Brethren" or "United Brethren").

Persecution pursued them in Moravia. Therefore in 1722 they accepted the invitation of the wealthy Lutheran Count von Zinzendorf to find shelter on his estates in Saxony. By this time much radicalism, common in their years in Bohemia and the cause of bitter internal strife, had yielded to quiet, pietistic, religious devotion and a stress on a life of peace, nonviolence, evangelism, and social consciousness.

They still suffered bitter opposition, so in 1733 a group accepted an invitation to migrate to the colony of Georgia in America. In 1740 a group from Herrnhut (the town built on Zinzendorf's estate) and another group from Georgia settled in Pennsylvania in towns they named Nazareth and Bethlehem. Count von

Zinzendorf, who had been Lutheran, joined them in 1741. He became a member of their fellowship and served them as bishop. With this leadership as his basis he attempted to bring about a grand union of all German religious groups in Pennsylvania into one body to be called "The Congregation of God in the Spirit." He failed because the other German groups, after considering the proposal in several meetings, were prompted by leaders in America and in the homeland to remain aloof from such unprecedented action.

As colonial years passed, the Moravians had distinctive success in evangelizing and pacifying Indians in Pennsylvania. Although this was a noble accomplishment, it brought great tragedy to the Indians during the French and Indian and the Revolutionary Wars. In both wars the Christian, peace-loving Moravian Indians were massacred by the warring forces.

The Moravians contributed greatly to American religious life in the development of moving worship forms and beautiful hymnody.

The Lutheran and the Reformed Churches

The story of the settlement of German Lutherans and Reformed in Pennsylvania is quite different from that of the sects. In both cases the Lutheran and Reformed people came to America to escape the miserable economic conditions in their homeland.

Beginning in 1529, following the Diet of Speyer, the Holy Roman Empire placed heavy restraints on all Protestant groups. This action led to a series of wars which lasted over a century. They concluded in the Thirty Years' War which was ended in 1648 by the Peace of Westphalia. It granted recognition in certain German states to the Roman Catholic, the Lutheran, and the Reformed Churches, respectively.

The Thirty Years' War left Germany devastated. Historians estimate that due to killing, disease, and starvation the population dropped to one-third of what it had been before the war.

Even this was not the end of war and devastation. During the second half of the seventeenth century France, which had prospered greatly during the Thirty Years' War by preying upon the war-torn Germans, continued military raids into the Palatinate area. The wars of the Spanish Succession (1701–1713) followed. They were fought mostly on German territory. Then came a war involving Sweden, Poland, and Russia which spilled over into Germany. This was followed by the War of the Austrian Succession, known in England and America as King George's War (1744–1748). And last came the Seven Years' War (1756–1763) involving Prussia and other European powers, including England and France, who were already fighting in America in the French and Indian War (1754–1763).

These wars kept the states of Germany in economic ruin. Lutheran and Reformed people began to look to the New World for refuge. Their poverty required many of them to gain ship passage by yielding themselves to the practice of indenture, selling years of individual personal servitude to ship captains or other wealthy investors.

When they arrived in the New World, their servitude was sold to American landowners or tradesmen, who required them to serve the stated number of years with no remuneration other than food, clothing, and shelter, much of which was very poor. Such servitude often lasted as many as seven years, at the end of which freedom was granted. Even as free people they were still poor. Hence, they could not strike out immediately on their own in a trade or farming. Most had not been farmers in their homeland and had no knowledge for that kind of work. It took a long time for them to become established.

Religiously their lot was just as desperate. In America there was a lack of ministerial leadership. They could not freely choose religious leaders from among their lay members as the sects did because theological education and formal ordination were required for preaching and administering the sacraments.

Several Lutheran and Reformed ministers had come to Pennsylvania, but with few exceptions they were inferior. They had been failures or even worse in the homeland. Their coming to America was virtually banishment from their home churches. The more able Lutheran and Reformed ministers in Germany remained there in spite of the economic situation because as ministers in state-supported churches, they were favored by the guarantee of salaries.

Conditions in Pennsylvania finally improved for both church groups. A young Lutheran minister, Henry Melchior Muhlenberg (1711–1787), came to Pennsylvania in 1742 and spent the remaining years of his life organizing churches and establishing theological training schools to educate American-born Lutherans for the ministry. In 1748 he formed the first American Lutheran Synod. He personally served several churches as pastor and also spent much time traveling among Lutheran Churches supervising their activities, overseeing the young pastors who were coming out of the schools, and organizing local church schools for general education. Thus the religious fortunes of the Pennsylvania Lutherans took a decided turn upward.

The story of the German Reformed Churches is similar. After years of very poor economic conditions and suffering from inept and corrupt ministerial leadership, the fortunes of the Reformed Churches in Pennsylvania were enhanced by the coming of a German Reformed minister, Michael Schlatter (1716–1790) in 1746. After surveying the situation he gathered four worthy ministers and twenty-seven lay leaders in 1747 to form the Pennsylvania Coetus (sometimes called the Philadelphia Coetus). A coetus was a ministerial organization subordinate to a larger Reformed organization, the synod. In organizing the Pennsylvania Coetus, Schlatter established a Pennsylvania organization subordinate to the North and South Holland Synods. These synods delegated the guidance of and responsibility for the Pennsylvania Coetus to a local branch of the Dutch Reformed Church, the Amsterdam Classis. This classis appointed a Board of Deputies to have the direction of the Pennsylvania Coetus as its immediate responsibility. The Pennsylvania Coetus was to make annual reports to the Amsterdam deputies and to consult them whenever any serious issue called for a decision.

This arrangement continued until the independence of the American Colonies. The formation of the new nation brought about the separation of many American organizations from their European connections. This happened to the Pennsylvania Coetus when in 1798 it was granted independence from Dutch control and took the status of a synod in its own right. It was thereafter called the Pennsylvania Synod.

Schlatter believed that European help was desperately needed in two areas, financial and ministerial. In 1751 he went to Holland to appeal for this help.

Holland had scarcely been affected by the wars which had devastated Germany. Therefore the Dutch Reformed Church was able to lend aid to the German Reformed people in America. It responded to Schlatter's plea by granting an annual sum of two thousand guldin for five years to be used to better the conditions in the German Reformed Churches in America. It also commissioned

Schlatter to enlist six young German Reformed clergymen to take to America as a nucleus of sincere and competent ministers. Schlatter visited German Universities until he found the six young men. Among them was Philip William Otterbein. They arrived in New York on July 28, 1752. They were greeted there, instructed, and encouraged by Henry Melchior Muhlenberg. Then they went to Philadelphia where they received calls from needy and leaderless congregations. Otterbein was called by the Reformed congregation in Lancaster, a frontier town of about two thousand people, seventy miles west of Philadelphia.

Schlatter gave further supervision to the colonial Reformed Churches. He organized church schools for the general education of the children. Unfortunately some church leaders became bitterly critical of his work, probably out of jealousy. This led him to discontinue this great service to the American churches.

General Religious Conditions

By the latter part of the American colonial period the German groups discussed above, all of whom contributed later to the United Brethren and Evangelical movements, were well established. However, this does not mean that all German colonials in Pennsylvania, Maryland, and Virginia were in favorable religious circumstances—far from it. While most held nominal relationship to some religious group, especially Lutheran or Reformed, the great majority were without vital religious connections because they were outside the reaches of the established congregations. The time was ripe for a religious movement which would intimately affect the lives of many Germans, especially those who were not touched by an effective religious ministry. Conditions were still primitive in the smaller towns as well as on the open frontier. Many people were deprived of hearing the gospel from one year's end to the next.

To give an indication of the German population and religious statistics in Pennsylvania at the end of the colonial period, the following table has been compiled for the year 1770. Some of the statistics are exact, the rest are calculated estimates, based on statements by W. F. Dunaway in the second edition of his book, *History of Pennsylvania*.

Total population of Pennsylvania 300,000
Total German population 100,000

Mennonites: Church population 4,000, meeting houses (congregations) 42, ministers (ordained according to Mennonite form) 15
Dunkers: Church population 1,500, congregations 14, ministers (ordained according to Dunker form) 8
Schwenckfelders: Population 300, congregation 1 (1782)
Moravians: Population 2,500, congregations 14
German Lutherans: Population 60,000, congregations 63
German Reformed: Population 30,000, congregations 106

The German people who settled in Maryland and the Virginia Valley were in even more remote regions than most of the Germans in Pennsylvania. In Maryland a tradition of religious freedom going back to the original Roman Catholic proprietor, Lord Baltimore, allowed the German and other religious groups to be undisturbed by governmental authority. In Virginia, which had the Anglican Church legally established, all other religious groups had no stated rights. However, this did not affect the religious groups in the Virginia Valley because that area was remote from the eastern seaboard center of political authority. In general the religious conditions of the Germans in these areas were similar to those in Pennsylvania.

THE GREAT AWAKENING

Religious life throughout the American Colonies had fluctuated during the colonial period of American history. By the beginning of the eighteenth century it had fallen to low ebb. A radical upswing occurred when the Great Awakening began in New Jersey in the 1720's under the preaching of a pietistic Dutch Reformed minister, Theodore Frelinghuysen (1691–1747). It spread into New England where the great Congregationalist preacher and theologian, Jonathan Edwards (1703–1758), became the main leader.

Under other leadership it swept southward and affected all English-speaking churches. A leading figure was George Whitefield, a close associate of John Wesley.

The Great Awakening reached its peak during the 1730's and 1740's. The Colonies were greatly revived. However, the Great Awakening ran its course and ended by 1760.

The Germans were affected very little by the Great Awakening, probably because the leaders of the Awakening did not include Germans.

After 1760 the religious life in the Colonies declined sharply. By the time of the Revolutionary War only about five percent (one in twenty) of the colonial population openly professed religious faith or admitted church relationship. Yet it was during this desperate time that the preaching of several German ministers began in Pennsylvania.

CHAPTER II

T he two religious developments among the Germans in the eighteenth century, the one under Philip William Otterbein and Martin Boehm, the other under Jacob Albright, culminated in distinct denominations in 1800 and 1803, respectively.

By that time a second great religious revival was sweeping America. In distinction from the Great Awakening, which had ended abruptly in 1760, it has been called the Second Awakening.

Religious conditions in America between 1760 and near the end of the century were at the lowest level in American history. The picture looked hopeless. Professor William Warren Sweet in his book *The Story of Religion in America* states that Episcopalian Bishop Madison of Virginia believed that the church was too far gone ever to be revived. It was asserted that the church and its Christian profession would end as soon as the members of the older generation passed away.

The reasons given for this low state of affairs are several. (1) The basic Calvinistic authoritarian theology, stressing God's sovereignty and man's low spiritual condition, gave way to religious-philosophical deism which affirmed an absent God and man's inherent rational nature and competence. (2) The political subjection to an absent royal crown was supplanted by the idealism of the power of "the voice of the people," stressing freedom from any form of tyranny. (3) The rigors of a universal moral code, to which all are

UNITED BRETHREN
BACKGROUND TO 1800

subject, gave way to the affirmation of individual freedom of decision. (4) The general struggle for survival by violent action during and after the Revolutionary War bred a spirit of lawlessness.

Much of the antireligious development was a manifestation of the painful reappraisal which Americans had to make in every phase of life—political, economic, and industrial, as well as religious. Periods of basic transitions always have some negative effects. What appears to be destructive has often been the result of adjustment to a new day. The freedoms won in the successful struggle for political independence were reflected in religious freedom too. The greatest positive indication of this was the declaration of religious freedom in the constitutions of the several states and the principle of separation of church and state in the first amendment of the national constitution.

It was during this period of upheaval that the German and Methodist revivalists were vigorously serving as harbingers of a new era of religious life in America.

When the change came on a national scale, it was profound. It was manifested in the eastern colleges where previously religion had been scorned. At the beginning of the new century students had their attention directed toward things spiritual by devout teachers and administrators. From the schools the interest spread through the churches and the communities in the east. The result was a revival of religion, quiet, deep, and fervent, with little outward emotional expression.

In 1797 a revival began in the new territories west of the Appalachians, in Kentucky, Tennessee, Ohio, and thence into Indiana, Illinois, and Missouri. Relatively few congregations had been established in these areas. Most people had been living a lonely frontier life. The revival therefore took free expression as itinerant Presbyterian, Methodist, and Baptist preachers moved about holding camp meetings to which came hundreds of religiously and socially starved people. They usually met in forest groves where the people found shelter in hastily erected rough booths and tents. The camp meetings often lasted a week or more.

Preaching was spontaneous and vigorous. The sermons were based on uncritical interpretations of the Scriptures with realistic descriptions of the glories of heaven and the fiery torments of hell. Many people were converted in meetings which resounded with shouting, singing, and cries of spiritual agony or victory.

These two forms of revivalism, the "eastern" and the "western," although quite different, formed the Second Awakening. Its positive effects have remained, with several periods of renewal, to the present day.

The German revival movements, which culminated in the United Brethren and Evangelical Churches, antedated the Second Awakening, but coincided with it as they entered their denominational phase. The beginnings of the United Brethren and Evangelical Churches were the result of several causative factors: religious (theological-pietistic), nationalistic (German), and cultural (pioneer-agricultural).

These factors, dealt with in the previous chapter, in themselves would not have mechanically resulted in the rise of two new denominations. The human factor, in the form of leaders and followers, fashioned the causes into actual accomplishments.

In the case of the United Brethren, one leader is judged to be most responsible—a German Reformed pastor named Philip William Otterbein.

PHILIP WILLIAM OTTERBEIN

Philip William Otterbein (1726–1813) was born in Dillenburg, Nassau, Germany. Dillenburg, a town of about three thousand people, was the seat of the government of the state of Nassau, with the castle, the court of the ruling count, on a hill overlooking the town.

The birth date of Otterbein was June 3, 1726, as the following statement found in the Dillenburg German Reformed Church record attests:

> To John Daniel Otterbein, prime preceptor of the Latin School, and Mrs. Wilhelmina Henrietta [Otterbein] were born twins on the third of June early in the morning at two o'clock. The elder is a son, and the second is a daughter. Both were baptized on the sixth of June; godfather for the son was Philip William Keller, steward to the court [and a close relative of the Otterbein family]; the godmother of the second, the wife of Mr. John Martin Keller, butler to the court. The son was named Philip William and the daughter Anna Margaret.

Although the full name of Philip William was given to the son, his family called him William,[1] and he usually signed his name

William Otterbein or W. Otterbein. Henceforward in this work he will be referred to as William Otterbein.

The Otterbein Family[2]

John Daniel Otterbein, William's father, remained the prime preceptor (principal) in the Latin school until 1728 when he resigned in order to accept the position of pastor of two Reformed Churches in the neighboring towns of Fronhausen and Wissenbach. He had qualified for ordination by studying in the academy in Herborn, a town three miles south of Dillenburg. The Herborn Academy had university status. John Daniel Otterbein remained in the work of the ministry until his death on November 14, 1742.

The Otterbeins had a total of ten children. Of this number six sons and one daughter, Philippine Margaretha, grew to maturity. All six sons became German Reformed ministers. Philippine Margaretha married a German Reformed minister, Pastor Schaller.

The six Otterbein brothers received their theological education in the Herborn Academy. They all rendered most commendable service to German Reformed churches. Next to William, probably the most distinguished was George Godfrey. In addition to serving several pastorates he wrote a three-volume exposition of the Heidelberg Confession, several devotional books, and several books dealing with religious instruction and with the practice of the Christian life. After William came to America, he used some of these materials in schools which he founded.

Much of the credit for the remarkable ministerial service rendered by the Otterbein brothers and sister must be given to their mother, Henrietta, who after the death of her husband moved with her family to Herborn where living was cheaper and where the academy was available for her children's education. In his late years William paid great tribute to his mother for her spiritual and intellectual guidance. Certainly her responsibilities were heavy in rearing her family as a widow. At the father's death the eldest son, a teacher, was twenty years old. His earnings were half the amount his father's had been. It is probable that Henrietta depended on his salary for family support. William was only sixteen when his father died. After he began his ministerial service, he also contributed financially to the family's welfare.

Otterbein's Education

Herborn Academy was a school of the German Reformed Church with a high reputation for its departments of medicine, law, and theology.

Theologically the academy was of the Calvinistic tradition, but with modification in the direction of the moderate and heart-warming tone of the Heidelberg Confession. One of the founders of the Herborn Academy was Kaspar Olevianus (1536–1587), co-author with Zacharia Ursinus (1534–1583) of this confession. By Otterbein's day the academy had come to be influenced by the pietistic spirit and a Calvinism, modified by Johann Koch (Latin-*Coccejus*) (1603–1669) who, following the thought of Olevianus, taught the doctrine of the "Two Covenants," the covenant of works and the covenant of grace. Both covenants are of divine origin. Human activity can take place only within their bounds. Yet, contrary to the rigid determinism of Calvinism, the doctrine of the covenants holds that a person has responsibility in choosing to be subject to one or the other. This granted a real measure of religious freedom.[3]

Throughout his ministry Otterbein showed the influence of Calvinistic thought in its warm expression in the Heidelberg Confession, the doctrine of the covenants, and the depth of religious feeling and moral rectitude of Pietism. These influences came upon him from every member of his family and from the religious spirit of his theological teachers in the Herborn Academy, especially Professors John Henry Schramm, Valentine Rau, and John Eberhart.

After completing the standard theological course at Herborn in 1747, Otterbein accepted a position as tutor to a noble family in the Duchy of Berg, about one hundred miles north of Herborn. In 1748 he returned to Herborn and passed the required examination for ordination on May 6, 1748. He took further studies in the academy, and on June 13, 1749, he presented himself for ordination. He was given a certificate of ordination signed by his teacher-friend, John Henry Schramm.[4]

Ministry in Germany

Otterbein accepted a call to share in a joint ministry with two other ministers, one of whom was one of his revered teachers, Dr. Valentine Rau, serving three churches, one in Herborn, one in Burg, and one in Ockersdorf. Otterbein had primary responsibility for Ockersdorf. He quickly gained a reputation for vigorous, direct preaching, especially stressing regeneration. In Ockersdorf he organized Bible study and prayer groups after the manner of the *collegia pietatis*. Because this involved direct lay participation, including spoken prayers, some parishoners expressed vigorous disapproval. They thought only ordained ministers should utter audible, extemporaneous prayers.

At the end of three years of service in Ockersdorf, Otterbein was urged by Michael Schlatter to join the group of young German Reformed ministers to serve in America. With the tearful but earnest approval of his mother Otterbein accepted the call. He appeared before the Amsterdam Classis for examination and was approved. He set sail for America with his five associates on April 15, 1752, arriving in New York on July 28.

Early American Ministry

Two days after their arrival the six young German Reformed pastors traveled to Philadelphia where they were received into the fellowship of the Pennsylvania Coetus which Michael Schlatter had organized five years earlier. Several German Reformed congregations had already been formed in Pennsylvania and Maryland, but most were without regular ministerial leadership. In addition, in sparsely settled areas there were German Reformed people not affiliated with any congregations but also in need of pastoral care.

When it became known that the six young pastors had arrived, the congregations immediately issued calls. Otterbein accepted a call from the congregation in Lancaster and made the journey westward over seventy miles of rough wagon trail. He served the Lancaster church for six years from 1752 to 1758. Following that pastorate he served two churches in the area of Tulpehocken, Pennsylvania, from 1758 to 1760, the church in Frederick, Maryland, from 1760 to 1765, and the church in York, Pennsylvania, from 1765 to 1774. This constituted his early ministry. His last pastorate was in Baltimore from 1774 to 1813.

While serving these early pastorates Otterbein also responded to the needs of people living in remote areas. To do so he traveled on horseback or, where there were passable roads, by carriage. Such places were Pequea, Reading, Oley, Conewago, Lebanon, Paradise,

Bermudian, and Kreutz Creek in Pennsylvania and Antietam, Pipe Creek, and Middletown in Maryland.

Otterbein always served under the guidance of the coetus. His standing within that fellowship grew. Occasionally the coetus held its annual sessions in other places besides Philadelphia. It met several times in Lancaster. Otterbein occasionally served as the presiding official and also was named on a committee assigned to the duty of mediating disputes which arose occasionally.

As Otterbein entered into the service of the congregations, he generally found immediate problems due to former poor ministerial leadership or no leadership at all. It was not easy to bring religious order and discipline into such situations. This disturbed him, especially in Lancaster and Frederick. In Lancaster he finally solved the problem by having the members approve a "covenant" which he drew up, thereby pledging their orderly response.[5] In Frederick a cantankerous faction even locked the church door against him one Sunday in order to prevent his preaching. This did not deter him. He simply took those of the congregation who were not rebellious out into the cemetery and, using a tombstone as a pulpit, preached to them in the open air. The rebellious group were thereby shamed, and such disorder did not occur again.

Some of the protests he had to face were from members who disapproved of his emphatic preaching and open form of worship. In each place he organized a prayer and study group, the *collegium pietatis*, which he had used in the church at Ockersdorf. This called for lively lay participation to which the more staid members of his churches objected.

The deep pietistic spirit of his earlier ministry was greatly enhanced in 1754 while he was at Lancaster. One Sunday he preached on a favorite theme, "God's Grace." After the service a parishioner questioned him about the meaning of grace. To the parishioner's surprise Otterbein answered, "Advice is scarce with me this day," and abruptly turned away. His problem was that, genuine though his religious convictions were, he needed a more vital inner assurance. Otterbein went into a quiet room where after fervent prayer he suddenly experienced the inner assurance of God's grace. His preaching, which had been fervent before, now became much more confident and convincing. He also turned away from traditional formalities. No longer did he read his sermons as though they were essays. His preaching was given in the form of direct witness to the people. Formerly he had worn a silk robe when he preached; now he laid that aside.

Otterbein was a theological preacher. This is shown in a sermon he preached in 1760 in Germantown, Pennsylvania. He had prepared the sermon carefully. It was judged to be so basic a declaration of the Christian faith that the Dunker printer, Christopher Saur, published it in 1763. For many years the sermon was lost, but in 1963 Dr. Arthur C. Core discovered it in the Library of Congress as item 9471 in the Charles Evans Bibliography. The sermon was in German. After its discovery it was translated into English by the Rev. Ehrhart Lang and was published in Dr. Core's book, *Philip William Otterbein*.[6] This is the most theologically definitive work of all of Otterbein's extant writings.

The sermon is entitled "The Salvation-Bringing Incarnation and the Glorious Victory of Jesus Christ over the Devil and Death." The text used is Hebrews 2:14–15. The progression of thought may be summarized under the following statements:

1. The biblical God is one of judgment and love.

2. Man is of basically sinful nature. The concept of original sin is to be affirmed but not to the exclusion of man's responsible freedom. (Thus the extreme Calvinistic doctrine of unconditional predestination is repudiated.)

3. The damning effect of sin is physical and spiritual death. Sinful man is under Satan's control. This causes a life of fear.

4. Man is unable in himself alone to gain spiritual life.

5. Therefore, God has intervened on man's behalf in the incarnation of Christ.

6. The meaning of the cross is in the fact that Jesus atoned for man's sin by dying, thus symbolizing the necessity for every man to join with Christ in dying to sin through suffering. (This was a key doctrine in Otterbein's thought. Salvation always involves participating in the sufferings of our Lord.)

7. Christ's death brings reconciliation of man to God.

8. This becomes complete when, by having "Christ in us," we are reconciled to God.

9. Salvation is God's gift to man, but it requires a broken and contrite heart.

10. Through God's grace man in this life "can be free" (not, necessarily, "is free") from sin.

11. This requires determination and effort on man's part.

12. A man can be conscious that he has been redeemed.

13. The unconverted will be lost as "an unsaved worm in hell."

14. The converted person dies to sin, grows in grace, and is promised "the more glorious" state in heaven.

15. Therefore the sinner should repent and believe the gospel.

Otterbein's ministry also included the building of churches. In 1753 at Lancaster he led in the building of a spacious church to replace the log church which had been used for seventeen years. The new building served the congregation for nearly a century. A record was kept of its cost—1,018 pounds. Items listed in this cost were "foundation, stones, poles, kegs of nails, masonwork, boards, shingles, window frames, wine and rum together with three barrels of beer."[7] A new church was also built in Frederick, Maryland, in 1764 near the end of Otterbein's pastorate there.

When Otterbein accepted the Frederick pastorate, a problem of relationship to the Pennsylvania Coetus was raised. When the coetus was organized by Michael Schlatter, the Amsterdam Classis directed it to deal only with congregations in Pennsylvania. This left nine Maryland congregations without supervision. However, without taking official action, the coetus gradually expanded its influence by giving guidance to those congregations in Maryland which called ministers who earlier had served pastorates in Pennsylvania under its direction. Since Otterbein had been a member of the coetus, when he went to Frederick, that church also received its guidance. As the years passed, this process brought other Maryland churches into affiliation with the coetus.[8]

On April 19, 1762, while Otterbein was in Frederick, he married Susan LeRoy (anglicized to "King"). Apparently Otterbein met her while he served the two churches at Tulpehocken where her family, French Hugenots, had settled. The Hugenots were French Calvinistic Protestants who came under persecution in France when the Edict of Nantes of 1598, which had granted Protestants in France a measure of security, was revoked in 1685. Hence, many migrated to America. Susan's family had arrived in 1754. They established farms and prospered. An uncle had arrived in 1752 and settled at Penn's Creek in the Buffalo Valley of Pennsylvania near Lewisburg. He was tomahawked and burned during an Indian raid in 1755.[9] Through his death and later the deaths of her father and a brother Susan inherited about fifteen hundred dollars.

At the time of their marriage Otterbein was thirty-five years old and Susan was twenty-six. Tragically, after only six years Susan died on April 27, 1768, after a lengthy illness. There is no record that children were born to the union. Otterbein did not remarry.

Apparently when Otterbein came to America in 1752 he did not intend to spend the rest of his life here. In 1757 and again in 1758 he announced his intention to return to Germany. Each time he had to postpone the journey because of the hazards of travel due to the war between England and France.

In 1770 while he was serving the church in York he again announced his intention to return to Germany. However, the York congregation urged him not to resign his pastorate but to take a leave of absence for one year, visit Germany, and then return to York. This he decided to do.

When he reached home, his mother and five brothers were still living. His sister had died in 1754. Four of the brothers were serving pastorates. The fifth, John Charles, had become a teacher in the Herborn Academy. His mother made her home with John Charles until her death in 1778. In 1771 Otterbein returned to York.

Meeting with Martin Boehm

It was during Otterbein's pastorate at York that an event occurred which proved to be one of the decisive factors in the eventual formation of the United Brethren Church. A great meeting had been called by a Mennonite preacher, Martin Boehm, to be held at Whitsuntide on the farm of Isaac Long in Lancaster County about two miles from the town of Neffsville. The precise year has not been established with certainty; however A. W. Drury, after careful research, set the year in the period from 1766 to 1769.[10] It is commonly believed to have been held in 1767.

Great meetings had been taking place in rural areas since the first one was held in 1724.[11] The members of the Church of the Brethren, especially, were active in holding them. An announcement would be spread abroad that a great meeting would be held at some available place, a farm or a grove. People from many miles around would come bringing with them provisions to last several days. They spent the nights in nearby homes or barns or in hastily erected rude shelters. Preachers of different denominations attended the great meetings and preached wherever they could get a crowd to gather about them within voice range. Often several preached at the same time at different places within the great meeting area. The great meetings were heavily attended because they afforded people who lived in lonely, remote places the opportunity to hear the gospel and to enjoy social contacts. Most of the people attending were German, although English-speaking people, both ministerial and lay, also attended.

Otterbein decided to attend the great meeting which Martin Boehm had called. He went not in his capacity as a preacher but to enter into the joyous fellowship the meeting afforded. When he arrived, two men were preaching, one a "Virginia preacher" in the orchard of the farm, the other Martin Boehm on the threshing floor of the large barn.

The barn had been built in 1753. It still stands and has been in constant agricultural use. Its gable ends were constructed from the stone which had been cut from outcroppings on the farm. The rest of the barn was constructed from the heavy timber cut in the vicinity. The barn is 108 feet in length.

Otterbein listened intently to Martin Boehm's preaching. He heard witness to the gospel which corresponded very closely to his own spiritual experiences and struggles, especially the "assurance experience" he had in Lancaster in 1754. Hence, he was greatly moved. At the end of Boehm's sermon Otterbein went forward, embraced Boehm and exclaimed, *"Wir sind Brüder!"* ("We are Brethren!"). Thus began a comradeship which lasted until Boehm's death in 1812.

It has been claimed that before Otterbein, Boehm, and the Virginia preacher parted company they entered into a formal agreement of union which determined their subsequent activities. There is no direct evidence to support this. They probably met at later meetings during the following two decades and discussed many religious matters including those on which they differed, such as the mode and meaning of baptism. This conjecture is based on the fact that when they met in conferences beginning in 1789, there was no indication of tension on such points.

MARTIN BOEHM

Martin Boehm (1725–1812) is usually regarded as second only to Otterbein in leading the movement which eventuated in the founding of the Church of the United Brethren in Christ. Indeed, if all facts were known, it may be that his contribution would be seen to be as great as Otterbein's because it was under Boehm's itinerant, evangelistic ministry that a religious movement developed among the Germans, largely in Lancaster County, which was known as the "Boehm Revival."

Martin Boehm was born November 30, 1725, the son of Jacob Boehm, a Swiss-German Mennonite, who came to America in 1715 to escape the constant threat of persecution in the homeland. He settled in the Pequea area of Lancaster County where he prospered by blacksmithing and farming. In due time he was able to purchase a rich farm of 381 acres.[12] He married Barbara Kendig, also a Mennonite. Their youngest child was Martin.

The family belonged to a Mennonite congregation. Martin received religious training in the Mennonite tradition "and in due time, by baptism and partaking of the Lord's Supper became a member of the Mennonite church."[13]

Boehm accepted the distinctive religious beliefs the Mennonites derived from the New Testament. Religious assurance comes from the knowledge of the life, death, and resurrection of Jesus Christ. Worship and Bible study are to be undertaken under the guidance of the Holy Spirit. Daily life is to be lived by following Jesus' moral precepts especially as they are given in the Sermon on the Mount. Swearing of oaths and all forms of violence, including warfare, are repudiated. Baptism is to be administered only to understanding believers by the mode of "pouring."

When Boehm grew to manhood, he took possession of 181 acres of his father's farm and built a substantial home. As he prospered, he purchased other parcels of land until he owned four hundred acres.[14]

In 1753 Boehm married a nineteen-year-old Mennonite girl named Eve Steiner. They had eight children.[15] The youngest was Henry, who became a leader in the Methodist movement and a traveling companion and confidant of Bishop Francis Asbury. At the age of ninety-one Henry Boehm wrote his Reminiscences upon which much information of his father's life is based.

It was probably in the year 1758 that Boehm was chosen by lot to be a minister in his local Mennonite congregation.[16] He was appalled at this action, feeling quite unfitted for the task. Nevertheless, he felt it his duty to accept.

As a newly chosen minister among a group of senior ministers he found his duties at first consisted only in expressing words of exhortation at the end of the sermon preached by one of his older colleagues. To his dismay he found himself stammering in confusion. He tried to rectify this by memorizing passages of scripture. This went awry when under the tension of the occasions, his memory failed him.[17] He asked himself, "Why is it so?" His continuing failures led him to say, "You pray for grace to teach others the way of salvation, and you have not prayed for your own salvation." This led him to conclude that he was "lost."

One day while he was plowing, his spiritual agony reached its climax. "Lost, lost," his heart kept saying, even though he paused for prayer each time he reached the end of the furrow. Finally, midway across the field he dropped to his knees and cried out, "Lord, save, I am lost." Immediately the words of Jesus came into his mind, "I am come to seek and save that which is lost." He later said, "In a moment a stream of joy was poured over me." He sprang to his feet and rushed to his house to tell his wife. Later his wife had a similar experience of assurance.

Boehm eagerly looked forward to the services of the coming Sunday because now he had something to say. With great fervency he related to the congregation the miracle of the past week's experience. Apparently other members of the congregation found his story to be the answer to their own spiritual quest. They burst into tears and shouts of joy.

The report of Boehm's testimony became widespread. Other Mennonite congregations invited him to speak to them. Thus began the "Boehm Revival."

In 1761 when Bishop Hostetter, the head of the congregation, died, Martin Boehm was advanced to the office of bishop.[18]

Boehm's earnest desire to testify to his faith more and more led him into itinerant ministry. He preached in many Mennonite churches but also in less formal places, including homes and open crossroads. His reputation extended beyond the bounds of Lancaster County.

In 1761 he responded to an unusual call to visit the Virginia Valley. Mennonite congregations had been organized there also. Some of the effects of the Great Awakening had penetrated at that late date due largely to the preaching of George Whitefield and the influence of evangelistically-minded Baptists. The more staid Mennonite leaders feared the effects upon their people. Hearing of

Boehm's stress upon evangelism, and trusting him as a Mennonite bishop, they invited him to visit them to guide them in responding to the situation. His assistance was effective, resulting in the acceptance among Mennonite congregations of a more vigorous form of religious expression.

While visiting Virginia, Boehm responded to individual cases of spiritual need. A young girl had become greatly disturbed by the revival preachers' declaration of personal sinfulness and the hopelessness which is its consequence. She had become melancholy over her feeling of being lost, and no one seemed to be able to give her comfort. Boehm met her and shared his own earlier feelings and the triumph he had experienced. He repeated the words of Jesus which had given him his assurance, "I am come to seek and save that which is lost." The girl responded with great joy and comfort.[19]

Out of Boehm's Virginia evangelistic ministry came a number of religious leaders, both German and English, who followed his itinerant example. They even traveled into Pennsylvania where they were known as "Virginia preachers."

Martin Boehm's son Henry in his *Reminiscences* gives a sketch of Boehm's continuing itinerant ministry. Christian Newcomer, Henry Spayth, and Bishop Asbury, Boehm's contemporaries, also recorded recollections of Boehm's work. However, the combination of these accounts gives only a brief and partial record of his work in the latter part of the eighteenth century. Later effects of his ministry attest that it was very significant.

Boehm did not win the approval of all who knew him. The sort of ministry he exemplified was bound to bring negative criticisms and reactions. This was so even within the fellowship of the Mennonites. In spite of their generally admirable religious, moral, and social life, the fact that many had become economically and religiously established led them to complacency and the inclination to resist change. The Boehm Revival thus held a threat for them. Furthermore, Boehm's ministry reached beyond Mennonite bounds. It brought him into close relationship with preachers of other groups, an example of which was the growing relationship with Otterbein, a German Reformed minister.

The Mennonites remembered that back in their homeland they had been persecuted by governments of states where the German Reformed Church was the only legally recognized religious body. On the other hand, the Reformed people regarded the Mennonites and the other sects as fanatical and politically irresponsible. In light of these feelings it is remarkable that Boehm and Otterbein could develop their uninhibited mutual esteem.

Boehm and Otterbein in personal appearance and other characteristics were quite different. Boehm was short and stout with a flowing beard. He wore the plain clothing typical of the Mennonites.[20] Otterbein "was tall, being six feet high, with a noble frame and commanding appearance. He had a thoughtful open countenance, full of benignity, a dark bluish eye that was very expressive. . . . He had a high forehead, a double chin, with a beautiful dimple in the center. His locks were gray, his dress parsonic."[21]

Boehm had little formal education, although he had improved himself by independent study. Otterbein had university training. Boehm owned a large estate and thereby wielded considerable community influence. Otterbein owned no property although his wife had inherited money from the estates of her uncle, father, and brother, which Otterbein later inherited from her. Boehm had a large family and maintained a happy home. He greatly enjoyed acting as host to many visitors, as many as one hundred at a time when a great meeting was held near his place. Otterbein's family life lasted but six years, due to his wife's early death. He lived in church parsonages.

The intimacy of Boehm with people of other religious traditions and his enthusiastic declaration of the gospel finally caused a break with the Mennonites. About the year 1775 Mennonite leaders not in sympathy with Boehm's revival movement declared that there was real danger of a division among the Mennonites. To prevent it they felt they had to deal firmly with Martin Boehm. They held a conference in which they examined and seriously criticized his views and activities. A record of the conference was made and has been preserved.[22] After spelling out the accusations against Boehm, the record states that he was admonished three times to renounce his deviations and errors. Each time Boehm refused, replying with counter-accusations and statements of self-defense. Therefore the decision was reached that "the church could no longer retain Boehm and his followers . . . as brethren, and that they should be excluded from the communion and the counsel of the brotherhood . . . ."[23] The exact date of the excommunication was not recorded. John Funk, who preserved this record, places it between 1775 and 1780.

The charges leveled against Boehm can be summarized into five statements; (1) Boehm participated "in forming a union and associating with men (professors) [sic] which allow themselves to walk on the broad way, practicing warfare, and the swearing of oaths"; (2) "He maintained that Satan was a benefit to men"; (3) He said "that faith cometh from unbelief, life from death, and light out of darkness"; (4) "On one occasion he said, . . . 'The Scriptures might be burned'"; (5) He said "That the old men (Bishops and ministers, or men) [sic], lay so much stress upon the ordinances, viz., baptism and communion . . . (that) the people are thereby led only to the devil and not to God."[24]

Accusations 1 and 5 had some justification inasmuch as Boehm worked with ministers who were of other traditions and held other concepts. This does not prove, however, that he compromised his own beliefs and practices. Accusations 2, 3, and 4 most likely are the result of misunderstanding or misrepresenting statements Boehm had made.

Boehm preached the gospel wherever it would be heard. He had unusual ability to preach expository sermons, interpreting the Scriptures simply, clearly, and forcefully. His preaching was almost entirely in German, although, according to his son Henry, he had good command of the English language both in speaking and reading. He accumulated a small library of relogous works in German and English. He especially delighted in reading the published sermons of John Wesley. In his travels he was frequently joined by other preachers, some of them Methodist lay preachers. Relations with the Methodists throughout the remainder of his life were close and cordial.[25] His preaching journeys reached beyond Pennsylvania into Maryland, Delaware, and Virginia.

In 1783 Boehm sold two large portions of land to his son Jacob. In 1791 a parcel of this land, almost an acre in size, was given to the Methodists for the erection of a chapel and for a burial ground. Just who gave the lot is not certain. Henry Boehm said that his brother Jacob gave it.[26] Bishop Asbury referred to the building as "Father [Martin] Boehm's Chapel."[27] However, deeds drawn up dealing with the property indicate that the one-acre parcel was part of a tract that Jacob Boehm (one of Martin's sons) sold to Christian Herr on December 3, 1791. The next day Mr. Herr sold the one-acre lot to the Methodists for five pounds. It is probable that this record of selling and transfer of deeds was a legal necessity and that the one-acre property actually had been given to the Methodists by the Boehms.

After coming into posession of the lot and erecting a chapel, the

Methodists organized a "class" which worshipped there. Limited capacity led them to restrict attendance to their own group. Boehm's wife and children therefore joined the Methodist class. Although Boehm did not formally join, he was given special recognition so that when he was at home he could worship there. He often did, even to the extent of preaching and leading in communion services.

Nine trustees were appointed to care for the property. The names of Martin Boehm and his son Jacob are given first on the list. This seems to indicate that the Boehms maintained direct interest and a measure of control over the property.[28]

OTTERBEIN'S BALTIMORE MINISTRY

In 1773 Otterbein received a call from a congregation in Baltimore. Until 1771 there had been only one German Reformed Church in that city. It had been served by John Christopher Faber, who had been ordained in Germany. He was not a member of the coetus. Dissatisfaction arose in the congregation because some members found fault with Faber's preaching as uninspiring and also charged him with careless ministerial conduct.

This dissatisfied group had come to know a German Reformed lay preacher, Benedict Schwope (1730–1810), who was preaching at Pipe Creek, an area about twenty miles northwest of Baltimore and a few miles west of the present town of Westminister. Schwope preached vigorously after the manner of the traveling ministers. He and Otterbein became close friends and co-laborers. Schwope's itinerant ministry occasionally brought him to Baltimore. The dissatisfied group in the Baltimore church heard him and requested Faber to resign so that Schwope could become the new pastor. This caused division in the congregation. Although neither Faber nor Schwope was a member of the Pennsylvania Coetus, both factions appealed to it to resolve the division. The coetus attempted to do so, proposing several solutions, none of which satisfied both parties. Therefore the dissatisfied group separated from the "old" congregation, formed a "new" congregation and called Schwope to be its pastor early in 1771. Schwope accepted. Immediately the new congregation bought several lots on Howard's Hill, a short distance from the water front of the Patapsco Estuary, and erected a building in which they began to worship in October 1771.

For several years the coetus strove for a reunion of the two congregations. It urged both Faber and Schwope to resign their pastorates so that a new minister could be called who could bring about reconciliation. Faber resigned in 1771. In 1773 Schwope announced his intention to resign and did so in 1774. Meanwhile he had met the standards required by the coetus for ordination. He was ordained and became a member of the coetus in 1774, attending a number of its sessions in the following years.

When in 1773 Schwope announced his intention to resign the new Baltimore pastorate, he urged the congregation to extend a call to Otterbein to become its pastor. It did so. Otterbein, who had shown interest in Schwope's work in Baltimore and was sympathetic with the new congregation's spirit, was inclined to accept. However, he decided to consult the coetus first. It rendered an opinion not favoring Otterbein's desire to accept the call. Therefore, Otterbein informed Schwope and the new congregation of his decision to reject it. Schwope was persistent. In the meantime he had become acquainted with Francis Asbury, the Methodist lay preacher who, under John Wesley's direction, had come to America in 1771 and had been preaching in the Baltimore area. Schwope and Asbury became close friends because of the similarity in their Christian convictions and in their form of ministry. Although Asbury and Otterbein had not yet met, Schwope persuaded Asbury to write to Otterbein urging him to reconsider the Baltimore call. Otterbein, after much prayerful thought, early in 1774 decided to accept in spite of the disapproval of the coetus. He gave as his reasons that the new congregation, irreparably separated from the old congregation, would be without leadership in a critical time of its beginning and that the Baltimore pastorate would give him the opportunity to bring the evangelistic form of preaching to the German people in that rapidly growing port city. When Otterbein began his ministry there, Baltimore had a population of nearly 6,000.[29]

The reason for Asbury's keen interest in the matter was twofold. First was his personal friendship with Schwope. Second was the fact that on June 22, 1772, at the invitation of the new congregation, Asbury and another of Wesley's missionaries to America, Joseph Pilmoor, gathered forty Methodists into the new congregation's meeting house on Howard's Hill to organize the first Baltimore Methodist Society.[30] The Society met frequently in the meeting house for two years until it built its own chapel on Lovely Lane in 1774. Thus a close, cordial relationship had developed between the members of the new congregation and Asbury and the early Methodists in Baltimore.

The old congregation had been called the German Reformed Church in Baltimore. After the division it was called the First German Reformed Church. The new congregation regarded itself as within the German Reformed denomination but held its desire to be free in its devotional expressions and in evangelistic minstry; therefore it took the name "The German Evangelical Reformed Church."

For years the question of the control or ownership of the property was a vexing problem. Although the congregation accepted direction from the coetus, it regarded itself as independent of German Reformed denominational control and ownership. This was challenged many times until in 1840 and 1842 appeals were made to the civil courts. The decision finally rendered was that the church was independent and not owned by the German Reformed denomination.

Therefore the congregation had a unique status. It was affiliated with the German Reformed Church and directed by the coetus in many official actions but only with its free consent. After the Church of the United Brethren in Christ was formed, the congregation entered into relationship with it and accepted ministers appointed under the practice of its itinerant system. Nevertheless, the congregation still claimed independence. It maintained this nebulous relationship until, by its own decision, it entered into regular relationship with the Pennsylvania Annual Conference of the Evangelical United Brethren Church in 1949.[31]

The Baltimore congregation was Otterbein's last pastorate. It began on May 4, 1774, when he was nearly forty-eight years old. It ended at his death on November 17, 1813, a pastorate of thirty-nine and one-half years.

Otterbein's service in Baltimore was successful from the start, although he had to contend with problems of disorganization and individual assertiveness within the congregation. The coetus, which had advised against his acceptance of the call, recorded in its minutes of May 11, 1775, "after mature deliberation [it is deemed] advisable for Dom. [Pastor] Otterbein to continue his ministry in the congregation in Baltimore. It appears from the report that his labors are blessed and the opposing party [the old congregation] is becoming quiet."

The growth in membership in the congregation was steady but not exceedingly rapid. The size was not recorded at the beginning of Otterbein's ministry there. However, in the minutes of the coetus in 1783, 1788, and 1791 the membership by families was 32, 44, and 60, respectively. If it can be estimated that each family represented five persons, the membership by persons would have been 160, 220, and 300.

When Otterbein assumed the pastorate of the Baltimore church, the congregation was worshipping in the small frame building which had been erected on Howard's Hill in 1771. One year after Otterbein began his ministry there the building was either enlarged or replaced. In 1785 an entirely new edifice was erected of brick and stone. It has remained in constant use to the present day and is known for its architectural design. The church is sixty-five feet long and forty-eight feet wide. It has a high steeple which was not on the building originally but was added later. It is the oldest church structure in Baltimore and is highly regarded for its historical heritage. A small parsonage was also built at the same time. The total cost was six thousand dollars. It is believed that Otterbein contributed a portion of this cost out of the inheritance which he had received at his wife's death. In recent years the sanctuary has been completely refurbished.

The nature of Otterbein's ministry was similar to that which he rendered in his previous pastorates. His preaching was dynamic. He spoke directly to his people's needs and emphasized personal commitment. To this end he organized three "classes" within the congregation, two for the men and one for the women. Their purpose was through frequent devotional meetings to serve as a leaven to the whole congregation, building and sustaining a vital form of religious life. The classes in a sense were small congregations within the whole congregation.

Even though the church made progress, Otterbein and the classes felt the need to strengthen and stabilize the church and its members by establishing a book of order covering every phase of the congregation's life. It was entitled "The Church Book of the Evangelical Reformed Church." Paramount in its contents was a section entitled "The Constitution and Ordinances of the Evangelical Reformed Church of Baltimore, Maryland, 1785." This material can be found in several sources, including Dr. Arthur C. Core's book, Philip William Otterbein.[32] In this publication the constitution and ordinances require five printed pages. It consists of twenty-eight main articles, with Article 8 requiring eight sub-articles. Issues dealt with are the organization of the congregation; the moral character and conduct of minister and lay members; worship times and forms; relation to Christians of other religious bodies; qualifications for participation in the sacraments; pastoral duties; maintaining a German school; evangelistic and missionary activities in Pennsylvania, Maryland, and Virginia; holding and conveying of "all deeds, leases, and other rights concerning the property of [the] church"; suspending of persons guilty of immorality; resolving any divisive issues which may arise among members; and the reading of the constitution and ordinances before the congregation on every New Year's Day.

Two issues not made explicit in the above listing deserve special examination because they give unusual insight into the thought and spirit both of the congregation and also of Otterbein himself who, doubtless, was the leader in composing the Church Book.

The first (Article 6) reads, "Persons expressing a desire to commune with us at the Lord's table, although they have not been members of our church, shall be admitted by consent of the Vestry" and (Article 7) "Forasmuch as the differences of people and denominations end in Christ,—(Rom. x:12, Col. iii:11]—and availeth nothing in him but a new creature—(Gal. vi:13-16)—it becomes our duty, according to the gospel, to commune with, and admit to the Lord's table, professors, to whatever order, or sort, of the Christian Church they belong."

This reveals an ecumenical spirit which was rare in that day when radical expressions of exclusiveness among Christian bodies were the rule. Certainly Otterbein held no spirit of divisiveness based upon a feeling of religious superiority.

The second (Article 13) reads, "no preacher can stay among us who teacheth the doctrine of predestination, or the impossibility of falling from grace. . . . "

This article shows that Otterbein had rejected the traditional German Reformed Calvinistic view that the salvation or damnation of a human soul lay solely within the absolute, sovereign will of God and that the individual person could not affect his eternal destiny by any effort or expression of his will.

Otterbein's obvious rejection of the extreme Calvinistic doctrine of predestination did not receive approval from a number of his fellow German Reformed ministers. In 1788 he learned that the pastor of the old congregation, Nicholas Pomp, a basically good minister, had taken sharp exception to his position. Pomp's attitude probably was conditioned by ill feeling which still survived between the two congregations. He wrote a letter to the Holland deputies, officials of the Amsterdam Classis, who were appointed to give special attention to the activities of the Pennsylvania Coetus and the ministers within its fellowship. In the letter Pomp told the deputies that Otterbein was in error concerning the doctrine of predestination and, further, that he denied the doctrine completely.

Upon learning that Pomp had made these charges to the deputies, Otterbein wrote to them on July 15, 1778, defending and explaining his position. He said, "to tell the truth I cannot side with Calvin in this case. I believe that God is love and that he desires the welfare of all his creatures. . . . I believe in election, but cannot persuade myself that God has absolutely and without condition predestined some men to perdition."[33] In this statement Otterbein revealed that he repudiated the doctrine of "double predestination" held by Calvin and earlier Christian theologians. It teaches that from eternity and before creation God, by his eternal, absolute, sovereign will, determined the salvation or damnation of every human being, with no human conditions affecting the decision. In contrast, Otterbein believed that every person is freely responsible to accept or reject salvation in Christ. Furthermore, Article 13 of the Church Book clearly states that a person who has accepted Christ still remains free either to grow in grace or to turn away again. Thus Otterbein also repudiated the Calvinistic doctrine of the "perseverance of the saints" or "eternal security." This doctrine teaches that God guards whoever is granted salvation in Christ against any possibility of falling from grace.

In summation, Otterbein believed in personal religious freedom and its corollary, human responsibility.

The Church Book served the congregation well and made clear the position it held on relevant matters. Although it had been made primarily for use by the Baltimore congregation, for years it served as a guide for the larger fellowship of the early United Brethren denomination.

The congregation, wishing to guard its independence, applied for incorporation under the laws of the State of Maryland. The

Church Book was a basis for the application. The appeal was successful, and a charter was granted in 1798. The Articles of Incorporation gave the church a legal basis to support its existence and service. The conditions of property ownership and organizational responsibility were spelled out.

Article 10 of the charter stated, "The church is to establish and maintain a German school as soon as possible. . . . " The purpose was not only to give religious catechetical instruction but to teach children the rudiments of a general education. This was a practice carried out in many churches in lieu of public education. Otterbein had supported church-sponsored schools in his previous parishes, especially at Lancaster. He saw the close relationship between the ability of lay people to read and their study of the Bible. The Articles of Incorporation established more firmly the Baltimore church's educational enterprise.

Otterbein was concerned about the physical welfare of people not only in his church but in the community, where he saw many instances of poverty. He brought relief to individual families by getting a horse and wagon, canvassing the neighborhood stores for food and clothing, and then personally distributing these materials to the needy.

As a childless widower Otterbein had a lonely home life. He lived in a small parsonage beside the church. His love of flowers was satisfied by growing them in the churchyard. He was relieved of many household chores by women servants. He kept a cow in a stable nearby. He liked good food and, as was the common custom among the German people, he drank beer and smoked a pipe. In religious observances he regularly engaged in private devotions. On Fridays he fasted until noon. In the afternoon he taught a weekly catechetical class.[34]

Otterbein spent much time in study. He had a sizeable library of religious books. He probably wrote much in the area of religion. However, comparatively few of his writings are extant. One tradition has it that shortly before his death, out of unwarranted personal modesty, he destroyed many of his writings.[35] Very likely many of his communications to parishoners and other friends simply were not preserved.

The most important of all his extant literary works is the sermon of 1760 (see pages 22, 23). In addition are twelve letters written to personal friends, to churches, and to the Holland deputies; two brief sermon outlines; and his last will and testament. All are to be found in Dr. Core's book, *Philip William Otterbein.*

Two matters in these writings are especially interesting because they reveal something of Otterbein's spirit. The first is in a letter to a cousin in Richmond, Virginia, responding to the news that his cousin's wife and daughter had perished in a theater fire on December 26, 1811. The letter contains little condolence but rebukes his cousin for allowing his family to patronize the theater. He wrote, ". . . do you see and feel that terrible evil, the sin, that brought this evil upon you? Awake, my dear cousin, awake."

Second, in two brief letters he answered theological questions. On the meaning of justification and sanctification and their relationship he gave the analogy of Pharaoh's releasing Joseph from prison and then enrobing "him in kingly apparel and [setting] him a prince over the whole land of Egypt." Otterbein also stated, "He that denies the possibility of living without sin, denies God. . . . " As for justification, it and "pardon of sin are one." As for the meaning of faith, it can be gained by observing children as they "perform the duties the mother enjoins, and who live meantime without caring for bread. . . . " As to church discipline, it is justified by Matthew 18. As to the doctrine of the millennium, the belief in a literal earthly rule by Christ is to be rejected. As to the work of the anti-Christ as set forth in the Scriptures, it is presently being accomplished. "The prophecies will be fulfilled and they are fulfilling from day to day, and you [Otterbein's correspondent] may live to see great things. . . . But what to do now? . . . 'Be ye also ready.'"

The Development of the Revival Movement

Otterbein's acceptance of the Baltimore pastorate did not bring an end to his itinerant preaching. Since the coetus gave no attention to most of the churches in Maryland and Virginia, Otterbein and other German Reformed ordained and lay preachers paid them occasional visits. The leaderless conditions of groups of people who came to hear these preachers led to the organization of "classes," after the manner of Methodist practice. A class was a small group of lay people who gathered together under local lay leadership for sharing their Christian witness and engaging in Bible study and prayer. The preachers who visited occasionally were concerned that these classes be given effective guidance.

The Pipe Creek Meetings

In 1882 Professor J. H. Dubbs, a historian of the German Reformed Church, discovered in the St. Benjamin's Church at Pipe Creek, Maryland, the minutes of five semiannual meetings held by these traveling preachers.[36] Because the minutes were found at Pipe Creek, the meetings have been given that name, although only the first two were held there. The others were held at Frederick, Baltimore, and John Ranger's home (location unknown). The dates were May 29, 1774; October 2, 1774; June 12, 1775; October 15, 1775; and June 2, 1776, respectively. Six preachers attended each meeting, namely, William Otterbein (whose name was always listed first, as though he were the leader), William Hendel (Otterbein's brother-in-law), Jacob Weimer, Frederick Henop, Daniel Wagner, and Benedict Schwope, who served as secretary..

Whether later meetings were held is not known. Item 13 of the minutes of June 2, 1776, states, "On Sunday, October 20, we will meet again at Canawaken at Jacob Wilt's." Francis Asbury, while on one of his periods of ministry in Maryland, recorded in his *Journal* under the date of October 11, 1777, "I attended and spoke at the half-yearly meetings of the Germans and on the Lord's Day (October 12). I returned to the meeting of the Germans where brother Shadford and myself both spoke." This notation would seem to imply that the meetings continued for some years beyond the date of the last extant minutes. It may be that the disruption caused by the Revolutionary War brought them to an end sometime after 1777.

In the minutes of the first Pipe Creek meeting a statement of purpose is given in Item 5:

> The ground and object of these meetings [of a number of classes named in items 1, 2, 3, 4, and 5] is to be, that those united may encourage one another, pray and sing in unison, and watch over one another's conduct. At these meetings they are to be especially careful to see to it that family worship is regularly maintained. All those who are thus united are to take heed that no disturbances occur among them, and that the affairs of the congregation be conducted and managed in an orderly manner.[37]

The bulk of the minutes reports the progress in Christian growth and living among the people visited or regularly served by the six ministers. Twelve places are named, all of them in Maryland except

Conewago, Pennsylvania. In addition to the six ministers present at the meetings eighteen names are mentioned as local lay class leaders. Among them was one destined to become very prominent in the early United Brethren Church, George Adam Geeting.

Not all the reports were favorable. In some instances it was noted that contention existed among the people. This disturbed the brethren who were concerned that all "affairs of the congregation be conducted and managed *in an orderly manner.*"

A statement in the minutes of June 12, 1775, referring to the men present as "the United Ministers," is significant because of setting a precedent in later establishing the denominational name.

Otterbein and the Methodists

The part Francis Asbury played in urging Otterbein to accept the call to the Baltimore pastorate was the first step in the development of a long and cordial relationship between the two men. They met for the first time when Otterbein came to Baltimore on May 4, 1774.

Asbury was born in 1745. Thus Otterbein was his senior by nineteen years. Asbury was English; Otterbein was German and could speak only broken English. In spite of these differences the men became close friends. In his *Journal* Asbury makes many cordial references to Otterbein and also to Martin Boehm and other German preachers. Asbury was in Baltimore many times and entered into friendly conversations with Otterbein on their mutual dedication to the work of evangelism.

They differed at one point. Asbury was very aggressive in establishing orderly rules and, once the Methodist *Discipline* and Articles of Religion were adopted, regarded them as having weighty authority. Otterbein also was a man of order, as witnessed by his developing the Church Book for his congregation. However, Otterbein did not impose his authority in a weighty manner either as pastor of his congregation or later as bishop of the United Brethren Church. When Bishop Asbury preached the sermon at the funeral of Martin Boehm in 1812, he took the occasion to express his disappointment that neither Otterbein nor Boehm had been sufficiently authoritative, and said he wished that they had followed the Methodist *Discipline.*

In spite of this difference in attitude, Asbury and Otterbein showed great mutual esteem. When Asbury was ordained to the superintendency on December 26, 1784, at the first American Methodist General Conference (the "Christmas Conference"), he requested the participation of Otterbein in the ceremony of the laying on of hands. It was a moving experience for both the German Reformed minister and the English Methodist.

The intimacy of Otterbein and Asbury led to many occasions when they and their respective colleagues joined forces in evangelistic work—one group preaching in German, the other in English. However, in spite of this close fellowship in purpose and labor, the German and the English Methodist movements did not coalesce. Two reasons are given: the difference in language and the difference in concepts of authority.

The German Revivalists

The meeting between Otterbein and Boehm in Isaac Long's barn in 1767 led to the expansion of the movement among the Germans which had been called the Boehm Revival. It spread throughout southeastern Pennsylvania, Maryland, and Virginia.

The Revolutionary War caused a lessening of activity because of the dangers and difficulties of travel, but after the war ended, the movement gained new vigor. Other preachers, mostly Reformed and Mennonite, joined in the work. Their preaching was spontaneous and impassioned.

On the other hand there were preachers who turned away from this free expression of the faith. Reformed ministers who did not share in the pietistic spirit held aloof. Of the four "United Ministers" of the Pipe Creek meetings who were still living at the end of the war, only Otterbein and Schwope were participants in the revival.

In a historical preface in the United Brethren *Discipline* in 1815 it is stated that "at great meetings Otterbein held at times conferences with the preachers who were present . . . [in which] he placed before them the importance of the preacher's office, how necessary it was to use all earnestness in the work of saving souls."[38] How many of these conferences were held is not known. However, the historical statement in the *Discipline* of 1815 says that in these meetings some of the revival preachers, many of whom were laymen, "were accepted by one or another of the [ordained] preachers and by them designated to the preacher's office."[39] Thus it would seem that these conferences assumed the responsibility of commissioning lay participants to serve as evangelistic preachers. A historical note in the *Discipline* of 1817 says, "It was resolved to hold a conference of all the preachers, in order to take into consideration, how, and in what manner they might be most useful."[40]

Conferences of 1789 and 1791

This resolution led to the holding of conferences in 1789 and 1791 which were more formal. The first probably met in Otterbein's parsonage in Baltimore. The second met in the home of a layman, John Spangler, eight miles east of York. No minutes of the meetings are extant, but two historians of the United Brethren Church, Henry Spayth, writing in 1819 and 1850, and John Lawrence, writing in 1860, both depending on prior sources, give a total list of twenty-two preachers who were in attendance at the meetings or who were regarded by those in attendance as members of the fellowship. The church background is known of all but four of these men. Ten—William Otterbein, George A. Geeting, Adam Lehman, John Ernst, John George Pfrimmer, Henry Weidner, Henry Baker, Frederick Schaffer, Christian Crum, and Benedict Schwope—were of the Reformed Church; six—Martin Boehm, Christian Newcomer, John Neidig, Martin Crider, John Hershey, and Simon Herre—were Mennonite; Abraham Troxel was Amish; Christopher Grosh was Moravian. The four whose religious affiliation is not known were Benedict Sanders, G. Fortenbach, Daniel Strickler, and J. Hautz. Of the ten Reformed preachers only Otterbein, Geeting, and Schwope had been formally ordained.

Since no minutes of these meetings are extant, we do not have primary sources giving the precise actions taken. Certainly under the leadership of Otterbein and Boehm the resolution to expand evangelistic efforts was strengthened. It is likely that reports were given of the work being done and that mutual counsel was shared.

Later speculation, not based upon clear evidence, has claimed that in these two conferences men were assigned to definite appointments, a confession of faith drawn up, a list of disciplinary rules formally adopted, and annual conference or even denominational organization accomplished. Rather, in light of the clear fact that denominational organization was not achieved until 1800, it is justifiable to regard these two conferences as early steps leading toward those accomplishments. It has also been assumed that other conferences of this sort were held later in the decade of the 1790's, but no direct evidence supports the assumption.

EARLY LEADERS

In the list of preachers attending the conferences of 1789 and 1791 are the names of four men whose contributions to the movement leading to and culminating in the formation of the United Brethren Church were outstanding. They were George Adam Geeting, John Neidig, John George Pfrimmer, and Christian Newcomer.

George Adam Geeting

George Adam Geeting[41] (1741–1812) was born in Germany in the town of Niederschelden, ten miles from Dillenburg, Otterbein's birthplace. In German his name was spelled Güthing. He was given a good education in Latin and the German classics. He came to America in 1759 and settled in the area of the Little Antietam Creek near Keedysville, Maryland, where he probably began to farm on land owned by an earlier immigrant, Conrad Snively. He married and became the father of ten children. His wife died in 1802. Later he remarried.

When Otterbein was the pastor of the church in Frederick from 1760 to 1765, he preached occasionally at Antietam. Geeting heard him and was greatly influenced. In 1760 Geeting decided to open a school and built a small schoolhouse on Snively's farm. He taught there several years. In 1777 he bought a farm and built a house upon it. The farm probably had been a part of the Snively farm on which the schoolhouse had been built. Through Otterbein's occasional visits into the area a class was formed which met in the schoolhouse. Because he was well educated, his Christian neighbors persuaded Geeting to be the class leader and to read sermons from a book in the Sunday services. He did it so effectively that Otterbein determined Geeting could preach sermons of his own. At Otterbein's suggestion, while Geeting was leading in prayer one Sunday, Jacob Hess reached over to the pulpit desk and removed the sermon book. After recovering from his astonishment at finding the book gone, Geeting extemporaneously preached a very effective sermon. Thus began his preaching ministry which led Henry Boehm to say that he "was the most eloquent" among the early United Brethren.[42]

Geeting took his religious responsibilities seriously. About 1774 he built a chapel beside the schoolhouse as a more proper place for worship. This became known as the Geeting Meeting House. The date of 1774 has been questioned, but if it is correct, then it was the first church building to be erected by anyone who became a leader in the United Brethren Church. Great meetings were held in and about the meeting house.

Because Geeting showed so much promise as a preacher, in 1783 William Otterbein and William Hendel "laid hands upon him" as one set aside for the preaching ministry. Geeting, whose religious background was German Reformed, desired full ordination. Therefore in 1788 he applied to the Pennsylvania Coetus for examination and ordination. Although some of the members claimed that Geeting was "fanatical," the coetus formally ordained him. He attended a number of its annual sessions in the years following.

Unfortunately those who opposed Geeting as fanatical pressed further charges against him. The issue reached a climax in 1798, the year the relations between the coetus and the Holland synods ended and the coetus became a synod in its own right. It considered the charges against Geeting and issued a warning to him about the matter. By 1804 the charges were expressed as "disorderly conduct." No charge was made against his ability as a preacher or his moral character. The synod voted on the proposition that he be dismissed. The vote was twenty to seventeen in favor of dismissal. Thus his relation to the synod ended in 1804; however in the meanwhile he had become an influential leader in the United Brethren movement.

Before and after the founding of the United Brethren Church in 1800 Geeting traveled extensively as a preacher, going to Pennsylvania, Virginia, West Virginia, Kentucky, and at least once to Ohio. He continued to serve the class which was meeting in the Geeting Meeting House. He established new preaching appointments. Outstanding among these was the organization of the St. Paul's congregation in Hagerstown in 1790. He served the early United Brethren conferences as secretary.

Toward the end of June 1812 he and his wife went to Baltimore to visit the aging Otterbein. Suddenly Geeting became very ill. They promptly set out on their journey home, normally requiring two days. On the second night they stayed in an inn owned by a friend,

Mr. Snyder, at Ridgeville. During the night Geeting worsened. He died before noon the next day, June 28, at the age of seventy-one.

John Neidig

John Neidig (1765–1844) was born to a German Reformed family in the Tulpehocken area. When he was five years of age, the Neidig family moved to a farm at Paxtang, two miles east of Harrisburg. There John came into fellowship with the Mennonites.

When Neidig was twenty-five years old, he was chosen by lot to be a preacher in the local Mennonite church. His conscientious acceptance quickly led to a warm experience of assurance which was reflected in his preaching. While some of his religious brethren were helped by it, opposition arose in the Mennonite congregation against him. Gradually he drew away and began to preach in the area as an independent preacher. People were converted and regarded him as their leader. They came to be known as "Neidig's People." In 1793 they built a church at Oberlin, a mile south of Paxtang. This was the second church to be built by people who later were related to the United Brethren Church. Neidig himself contributed about eighteen pounds to its cost and worked about sixteen days breaking stone and lime. A record of contributions of time, money, and materials by other people was kept. It includes an item of six gallons of whiskey contributed to the workmen by one generous brother. In the record of these contributions a name is used for the people of the congregation, *Die Vereinigten,* or "The United [People]." For years the congregation followed an independent existence, but in 1840 it united in full measure with the Pennsylvania Conference of the United Brethren Church.

Neidig continued his itinerant preaching while also serving as pastor of the Oberlin church. He attended several of the early United Brethren Conferences. In the conference of 1801 he was named, along with nine others, as "willing to take charge of a circuit and preach at the appointed places." In 1828 he became the pastor of the Baltimore Evangelical Reformed church and served three years. Then he returned to the Paxtang area and lived there until his death.

Persons who heard him preach commented on the beauty and simplicity of his speech, his gentle nature, and his convincing earnestness.

John George Pfrimmer

John George Pfrimmer (1762–1825) was born in Alsace, which then was a province of Germany. He was well educated in general studies and in medicine and surgery. He served a period of time as a surgeon in the French Navy during which time he engaged in combat and received a sword slash across his face. In 1788 he and his wife came to America. At first they settled in the Tulpehocken area, but three years later they moved to a home north of Harrisburg. In the years following he served in the capacities of teacher, evangelist, hymnist, physician, surgeon, farmer, miller, and circuit judge.

He began to preach immediately after he was converted in the German revival movement in 1790. He set up a weekday school in his home in which he gave children training in general studies as well as in religion. For about ten years the area of his preaching was along the Susquehanna River between Harrisburg and Lewisburg. A favorite place was near Milton under a tree on the east bank of the river. The people who gathered to hear him were given the name "Pfrimmer's People."[43] Pfrimmer participated in the great meetings of the 1790's and so was frequently in the ministerial company of Otterbein and Boehm. Sometime during this decade he was ordained irregularly as a German Reformed minister.

About the year 1801 Pfrimmer moved into western Pennsylvania. He preached in Somerset, Westmorland, and Washington Counties. His itinerant preaching and his irregular ordination provoked a sharp dispute with German Reformed ministers in the area. In 1806 they carried the matter to the synod, which took action repudiating his claims and refusing to acknowledge his ministerial status.

In 1800 he participated in the founding of the United Brethren Church. However, some difficulty arose, probably over Pfrimmer's reluctance to be subject to action by the conference. In 1801 the conference recorded, "a letter was read from Rev. Pfrimmer, and it was resolved to make no answer. . . . " In 1802 action was taken "that we write to Pfrimmer that for the present we will have nothing to do with him." It seems that Pfrimmer, making an irregular claim for ministerial standing among the Reformed ministers, offended both them and the United Brethren.

Whatever the trouble with the United Brethren was, it must have been rectified by 1805 because in the minutes of that year an item reads, "Pfrimmer received permission to preach among us."[44]

In 1808 Pfrimmer moved with his family to a farm in the southeast territory of Indiana several miles east of the present city of Corydon. In addition to farming he also served as an independent traveling minister, a physician—traveling as far as forty miles to attend patients— and as a common pleas judge under the appointment of the territorial governor, General William Henry Harrison. He also was employed to supervise the operation of Harrison's mills.

A bill of sale recorded in the deed book of Harrison County states that in 1811 Pfrimmer purchased two slaves, a mother and her mulatto child, for four hundred dollars.[45] The purpose of the purchase is not known. When in 1821 the United Brethren Church took action forbidding slave ownership among the members, Pfrimmer favored that action. It is not beyond the bounds of possibility that after buying the slaves he gave them their freedom, as many people of good spirit were doing.

In 1810 an Annual Conference of the United Brethren Church was organized in Ohio, the Miami Conference. In 1814 Pfrimmer applied for and was given membership in it. He was formally ordained in 1815. His leadership abilities were recognized so that the conference chose him to be "assistant" to Bishop Newcomer, the successor to Bishops Boehm and Otterbein, and he was chosen to be the superintendent of the district of southeastern Indiana and northern Kentucky. He served the Miami Annual Conference as its secretary, compiling and thereby preserving its minutes from its beginning in 1810. He wrote hymns and was appointed by the conference to examine the hymn book the brethren in the east had adopted.

Perhaps his most distinctive contribution was the establishment in 1820 of a Sunday school in the log church near Corydon, built on land owned by his son. The church has been known as Pfrimmer's Church. This was the first Sunday school to be established in the United Brethren Church.

Pfrimmer died on September 25, 1825. He was buried in the cemetery beside the Pfrimmer Meeting House.

Christian Newcomer

Ranking in importance with Otterbein and Boehm in United Brethren history was Christian Newcomer (1749–1830). We know more of his life and ministry than of any other United Brethren leader because he kept an extensive journal in which he recorded his own activities, contemporary activities in the United Brethren Church, and many public events.

The journal was "transcribed, corrected, and translated" and published in 1834 by John Hildt, a member of the Baltimore Church, under the title *The Life and Journal of the Rev'd Christian Newcomer, Late Bishop of the Church of the United Brethren in Christ*.

The first few pages of the *Journal* are Newcomer's brief account of his early life. The major part deals with events from October 27, 1795, to March 4, 1830. A copy of the *Journal* is in the Library of Congress where it has served to establish definite dates and events of early national history.

Newcomer was reared in a Mennonite family on a farm in eastern Lancaster County, Pennsylvania, one and one-half miles south of the present town of Bareville. In due time he inherited the farm and became a farmer even though he had earlier learned the carpenter's trade.

When he turned his mind toward religious matters, he analyzed his condition in the light of two "principles," man's evil state and personal transgressions as over against the forgiving mercy of God. He had several climactic religious experiences. Once as a boy, plowing in the fields, he dropped to his knees in anguished prayer. As a young man he faced death twice, by having a peach pit lodge in his throat and by suffering a severe case of measles. Each time he appealed to God, pledging to give himself to Christian witness. Each time shyness intervened, holding him back from preaching.[46]

On March 31, 1772, he married. His note on the matter seems not to indicate a fervent romantic feeling: "I had to seek a housekeeper, which I found in Miss Elizabeth Baer, and entered with her into a state of matrimony."[47] However, when she died thirty-nine years later, he showed his mature affection as he wrote, "This evening at 6 o'clock my dear companion departed this life, and resigned her immortal spirit into the arms of Jesus her Savior. Peace be to thy ashes: for many years thou hast been a staff and comfort unto me; soon we shall be reunited where parting will be no more."[48] Christian and Elizabeth Newcomer had four children, Andrew, Jacob, David, and Elizabeth. After his wife's death he made his home with Andrew.[49]

The continual urging by his friends to preach troubled Newcomer greatly. In 1775, to escape the issue, he sold his farm in Lancaster County and moved to another he had bought at Beaver Creek, Maryland, seven miles south of Hagerstown in Washington County. Shortly afterward he became seriously ill "with a fever" which was so severe that he was deprived of all bodily feeling and movement, although his mind remained clear. He believed he was dying. Again he cried out for divine help. The illness subsided. It left him with the determination no longer to fight the call to preach.

Shortly after his recovery he came under the itinerant preaching of Otterbein and Boehm and resolved to throw aside his inhibitions and go forth to preach. The probable date for the beginning of his itinerant ministry is 1777.

No precise record of the first eighteen years of his ministry has been kept, although his name appears in the lists of the conferences of 1789 and 1791.

In 1795 he began to record his activities in the *Journal*. Using his farm home in Washington County, Maryland, as his base, he rode many times on horseback, usually with one or two companions, in four different areas or "circuits": (1) north into Pennsylvania west of the Susquehanna as far as Tyrone, Mount Union, and Lewisburg, then across the river to the eastern side, south through Lancaster County, and then to his home; (2) east in Maryland toward Baltimore and then back to his home; (3) south into the Virginia Valley and back to his home; and (4) beginning in 1799, westward into southwestern Pennsylvania. He made this journey five times, thus crossing the Allegheny Mountains ten times. In 1810, when he was sixty-one years old, he extended the western trips and usually rode through Wheeling, across southern Ohio, into Kentucky as far as Lexington, through Louisville into southeastern Indiana, to Dayton, Ohio, and through north central Ohio to Akron, through Pittsburgh and Bedford and back to his home. This journey he made nineteen times, once each year until 1829—except 1811, the year his wife died. Thus he crossed the Alleghenies on these extended trips thirty-eight times, making a total of forty-eight crossings. He usually left on these extended trips in early spring and returned home in midsummer in time to take his grain cradle and help harvest the grain crops on his farm. He took the last trip in 1829 when he had reached the age of eighty. When he returned, he complained that after working for a while in the fields, he had to say, "Alas, my strength soon failed, and I was obliged to desist."

Newcomer traveled on the other three circuits many times each year. He traveled through rain, sleet, and snow. He usually tried to find frontier homes in which he could spend the nights, but sometimes had to sleep on the ground with his saddle for a pillow, even in inclement weather.

On his first recorded journey in 1795 he dismounted as he was following a steep trail up a mountain north of Mercersburg, Pennsylvania. The horse broke away, leaving him fearful that he would be stranded as night was falling. Great was his relief when he reached the top of the mountain and found the horse waiting.

In 1826 Newcomer made the only journey northward through Pennsylvania and New York to Niagara Falls and southern Ontario.

A typical record of the strenuousness of all his journeys is indicated by the following selected items from his last trip in the summer of 1829 when he was eighty.

> April 16—Today we rode on horseback 40 miles. . . . April 22—Rode 46 miles today. . . . May 21—Rode 45 miles. . . . June 3—Rode 40 miles. . . . June 8—Rode 52 miles. . . . June 24 [one day from home]—this day my horse appeared to know that he was not far from home, he traveled with uncommon speed and spirit; I rode more than 40 miles.

A conservative estimate of the direct distance on this last journey westward would be twelve hundred miles. However, Newcomer did not travel on direct lines between the towns and cities named but took digressing trails to small villages and farm homes. Therefore it is more likely his journey extended to two thousand miles. An attempt to estimate the total mileage Newcomer traveled on horseback on all his circuits has reached the figure of one hundred and fifty thousand miles—all between his age of forty-six and eighty-one years.

Marvelous as Newcomer's journeys were, they were important only because they were necessary to carry on his ministry. This took place mostly after the founding of the United Brethren Church in 1800 and is dealt with in the next chapter. It may be summarized here by listing his forms of service as preacher, evangelist, pastor, bishop, organizer of Annual and General Conferences, ecumenist, and author of disciplinary and doctrinal statements.

A problem is presented by a record kept in the courthouse at Hagerstown, county seat of Washington County, Maryland, in Record Book K, page 425, where a bill of sale dated September 18, 1797, states that Newcomer bought a Negro girl named Patience, about twelve years old. The bill of sale states that Newcomer and his heirs and assigns should own the girl until she reached the age of thirty, when she was to be declared free; and, if she have offspring, the girls be owned until age twenty-five, and the boys until thirty, when they should be set free.

No reference to these matters is found in Newcomer's *Journal*. No matters are recorded at all between September 8 and September 19, 1797. On those two dates the statements read, "September 8— . . . I rode home and found my family well. September 19—I left home on a journey to Virginia."

At no place in the whole *Journal* does Newcomer mention owning a slave. However, on August 1, 1806, he recorded, "Rode to Hagerstown for medicine for a servant girl who lived with us. On my return home she was very low, and about midnight departed this life." If this reference is to the Negro girl, Patience, then it appears that she died at the age of about twenty-one, and in lieu of the mention of offspring, she probably had none.

This whole matter is in conflict with Newcomer's known opposition to slavery. In 1821 with Bishop Newcomer presiding, the United Brethren General Conference condemned slavery and forbade ownership of slaves by any member of the church. As to Newcomer's use of the term "servant girl," it is found again in his entry on January 31, 1830, when it could not have meant slave girl.

Newcomer showed interest in black people and betrayed no prejudice against them. Several times he preached to Negro congregations. On March 24, 1811, he preached in an "African meeting-house" to a congregation of about one thousand.

As with Pfrimmer's purchase of two slaves, it is possible that Newcomer did what other antislavery people did where the law permitted, that is, bought slaves in order to give them their freedom. Whether Newcomer did this or whether in 1797 he owned a slave and therefore at that time condoned slavery but later repudiated it, we do not know.

Newcomer's last trip was a short one to Boonsborough, Maryland, on March 1, 1830. On the way home on March 2 his horse stumbled, throwing him heavily to the ground. His injuries were serious. They included four fractured ribs, one of which pierced his lung. He was able to reach home where he was attended by a physician who reduced the fractures and firmly advised uninterrupted confinement to bed. When the physician returned the next day, he found Newcomer kneeling by his bed in ecstasy, clapping his hands and shouting, "Hallelujah to the Lamb which sitteth upon the throne!" With some difficulty he was returned to bed. His condition worsened. On March 12 he arose from his bed, knelt beside it in prayer, and then quietly lay down again and breathed his last. Newcomer was buried in the Beaver Creek cemetery near his home on March 14, 1830. About one thousand people attended his funeral.[50]

he Evangelical Association originated mostly in the same areas of Pennsylvania, Maryland, and Virginia as the United Brethren, but several decades later. By 1800 Otterbein had preached forty-eight years in America, Martin Boehm forty-two, George Adam Geeting twenty-eight, and Christian Newcomer twenty-three. By 1800 Jacob Albrecht (Albright), the founder of the Evangelical Association, had been engaged in Christian witness nine years, the last four in active preaching. His three most important associates did not begin to preach until several years after 1800: John Walter in 1802, George Miller in 1805, and John Dreisbach in 1807.

JACOB ALBRIGHT

The founder of the Evangelical Movement was Jacob Albright (1759–1808). Attempts to formulate Albright's genealogy have been difficult because of the lack of precise information. Earlier historians have been at variance on several points and thus have proposed differing accounts of his lineage. Possibly the most defensible is based on the following information.

In a letter written on March 2, 1938, by the noted Evangelical historian, Raymond W. Albright, to the Rev. Robert S. Wilson, editor of the Church Center Press, Myerstown, Pennsylvania, after Albright had returned from a research trip to Germany in 1937, he states

EVANGELICAL BEGINNINGS TO 1816

"while in Germany I set a few agencies to work trying to trace the [Albrecht] family in Germany and less than a month ago I have sufficient evidence to convince me that the family originated in Coburg and that Johannes [Albrecht] was married there to his wife Anna in 1724."

In the passenger list of the ship *The Pink Johnson*, which arrived in Philadelphia from Germany on September 19, 1732, appear the names of Johannes and Anna Albrecht and the names of five Albrecht children, three girls and two boys, Jacob and Lodawick (Ludwig).[1] For years Evangelical historians have believed that Jacob Albright, born in 1759, was the child of Johannes and Anna. If this be so, the above statements would indicate that he was born thirty-five years after his parents' marriage in Coburg and twenty-seven years after they arrived in America, which is quite improbable.

It is more likely that the Albrecht children on board *The Pink Johnson* were children born to Johannes and Anna, and that Jacob, one of the two sons, was the father of his namesake, born in 1759. Thus Johannes and Anna would have been the grandparents rather than the parents of the founder of the Evangelical Association.

It is fairly well established that the Albright family settled in a farming district called Fuchsberg (Fox Mountain) in the present Montgomery County, three miles north of Pottstown, Pennsylvania. Their American church affiliation is indefinite, but it is believed that they were affiliated with the Lutheran Church in New Hanover and later with one in Pottstown.[2]

Reared in a German-speaking family, Albright was given the rudiments of a general education and learned to cypher and read and write in the German language. He also learned to speak English well enough to communicate with English neighbors. When he began his ministry, he studied the Lutheran catechism, the Bible, a hymnal, and a biblical commentary, all written in German.[3]

When the Revolutionary War broke out, Albright was seventeen years old. His older brother Ludwig was killed in the war. Jacob entered the Pennsylvania milita and served as a drummer in Captain John Witz's company, composed largely of volunteers from Berks County. He may have engaged in combat, but this is not certain. In the latter years of the war he served as a guard of captured Hessian soldiers at Reading under a Sergeant Eisenbiss.

In 1785 Albright married Catherine Cope. She was a member of the Reformed Church. Shortly after the marriage Albright bought a

120-acre farm at Hahnstown in eastern Lancaster County. The farm adjoined one owned by a Fry family. The two farms were separated by a creek on which the Fry family had a grist mill.

Albright's farm was fertile and productive. Also on the farm were valuable limestone and clay deposits. Albright used the clay to make bricks and tile. He developed a good business and, because of his trustworthiness in the trade, was known as "the Honest Tilemaker." He prospered. At his death he left an estate of four thousand dollars, at that time a sizeable amount.

Albright and his wife united with the Bergstrasse Lutheran Church. He was to confess later, however, that at that time he was indifferent to the religious life.

It is believed that six children were born into the home. In 1790 tragedy struck. "Several" of his children died in an epidemic of dysentery. Of the children who survived him, only one, David, had children. In direct line of descent from David was the late Evangelical historian, Dr. Raymond W. Albright, great great-grandson of Jacob.

Albright's Conversion

The deaths of the children in 1790 came as a severe blow. Albright wondered whether their deaths were punishment upon him for his indifferent religious life. He consulted three devout men. The first was the Rev. Anthony Houtz, an evangelistically-minded German Reformed minister of Harrisburg. He had conducted the funeral services of the children. The second was Isaac Davies (or Davis), a Methodist lay preacher who farmed nearby. The third was Adam Riegel, another neighbor and an associate of Otterbein and Boehm. In the summer of 1791 Albright attended a prayer meeting in Riegel's home. He poured out his soul before God and received a glorious conversion experience. He is quoted as testifying, " . . . all fear and anxiety of heart disappeared. Joy and blessed peace inbreathed my breast. God gave witness to my spirit that I had become a child of God."[4]

Albright now accepted opportunities to testify to his personal faith. He was so certain of its genuineness that he sometimes became critical of others. He told a Dunker that he should not depend merely upon the traditional rigors of the Dunker Church, but that he must be born again.[5]

Albright desired close Christian fellowship, therefore, he joined a Methodist class which was meeting in the home of his neighbor Isaac Davies. He preferred this affiliation to one with a similar German group because he found the Methodists to be more orderly. However, he found difficulty in worshipping with the Methodists because he had so little proficiency in English. He studied to correct this difficulty but achieved only moderate success.

Call to the Ministry

Albright's friends urged him to launch out as an itinerant preacher. In spite of the fact that the Methodists had granted him an exhorter's license in 1796, which gave him the privilege of speaking in class meetings, he felt that because his education was limited and his ability to preach was untested he should not do it. Thus he resisted the call but found no rest day or night as he brooded upon it. He began to lose weight. He said,

> For such indecision and procrastination God punished me with severe illness, a constant increasing pain of body went through all my nervous system . . . . What I endured in body, soul, and spirit during this illness is difficult to describe. In time of such sensation of being completely forsaken, I cried out so bitterly, that all who were near me and saw and heard me turned away from me in horror and frightfulness.[6]

The struggle finally ended in victory. He again found God putting a flood of joy into his soul. As he began to go about the area preaching, he felt three things were necessary to make him acceptable. First was a greater acquaintance with the scriptural message. Second was long periods in meditation and prayer. Third was rigid morality. This meant bodily discipline. Hence, he said, "I fasted for weeks at a time. As a result my body became feverish and burning to such a degree that I had to bathe in cold water, to cool off the fever that raged within."[7] This description of his bodily condition indicates that the tuberculosis which brought about his untimely death in 1808 had already begun.

Ministry

Albright began preaching late in 1796. He probably preached his first formal sermon in a neighboring nondenominational church known as the Flickinger Church.[8] Later he held revivals in this church in which the children of Adam Riegel, who in 1790 and 1791 had been his counselor, were converted.[9] Gradually he allowed his Methodist affiliations, including his exhorter's license, to lapse.[10]

Albright preached in Montgomery County among Schwenckfelder people. At first he was heard gladly, but later opposition was raised against him. However, one of the Schwenckfelders, David Schultz, welcomed him into his home, and Albright used it a number of times as a place to preach. His influence was felt in the community many years after his death.

In the first four years of his preaching ministry (1796–1800) Albright traveled in Lancaster, Dauphin (including Lebanon), Berks, Bucks, Montgomery, and Northampton Counties. Later his journeys reached north to Northumberland County, west of the Susquehanna River into York and Cumberland Counties, and south into Maryland and the Virginia Valley. He preached at many places, in church buildings, schoolhouses, homes, barns, on street corners, in open fields and woods, and outside churches where the doors were shut against him. His sermons were "methodical, convincing, conclusive" although "somewhat argumentative and remonstrant."[11] In vigorous terms he chided Lutherans, Reformed, Dunkers, and Mennonites, cautioning them not to rely for their salvation on their churches' traditions, forms, and ceremonies, rather than on a change of heart.

This brought about angry and dangerous opposition. On October 8, 1797, at the dedication of a Reformed church in Schaefferstown, Pennsylvania, which Otterbein's friends, Wagner, Hendel, Geeting, and Newcomer also attended, Albright mounted a pile of lumber nearby and preached a sharply convicting message. Several ruffians attacked him. He might have been seriously injured but for the intervention of a burly friend named Maise who picked him up bodily and carried him away. In 1799 in the same town he again was attacked and so cruelly beaten that he could scarcely mount his horse and ride two miles to a farm owned by a friend, Jacob Zentmoyer, who called a physician and cared for him for two weeks until his wounds had healed.[12]

Perhaps an even heavier burden for Albright to bear was the lack of sympathy the members of his family showed toward his call. His wife apparently resented his absences from home. These absences required her and the children to carry on the firing of the brick and tile which he had molded and then left for them to finish. He once said, "It makes a person feel sad, to go out in the world to preach repentance and conversion, when one's family is yet unconverted, but I still have hope for my [daughter] Sarah.[13] He grieved because his son David led an intemperate life. However, although Albright did not live to see it, his wife, David, and Sarah fulfilled his wish and eventually became affiliated with the Evangelical Association.

Albright's relation to the Bergstrasse Lutheran Church deteriorated. A pamphlet published in 1876 by S. S. Henry, pastor of that church, on the occasion of the church's sesquicentennial celebration, contains the statement:

> During the pastorate of Henry Moeller (1790–1797) we find the name of the notorious Jacob Albright among the communicant members of the congregation. He afterward left the Lutheran Church and became a fanatic. He connected himself with the Methodist Church in the state of New York, whither, as it is reported, he had fled to escape the arm of justice.[14]

Implications in this statement can be challenged. That Albright was called a fanatic reflects the attitude of the Lutheran Church toward free, itinerant, lay preaching. The reference to his flight to New York to escape justice can easily have been the result of gossip based on extended absences from home and his wife's displeasure. The known record of his life leaves no period when he could have been away from his ministry because of such an interruption. There are no hints of such an episode in the writings of his associates, George Miller and John Dreisbach.

These and other matters could be resolved if his journal were extant. That he kept such a journal and urged his associates to do the same is known.[15] We must depend upon other contemporary sources for information about his life and many related matters. These tell that he was a man of courage, resolution, and action. His forthright denunciation of sin and sinful men could sting hearers into reprisals. Yet this harshness did not really portray the man whose heart burned with love toward Christ and toward his neighbors for whom he wanted salvation. Those who understood him in this way regarded him as one whose face "shone as it had been the face of an angel."[16]

In personal appearance he was described as "spare, thin, of light complexion, with steady, keen, frank, honest, blue eyes, high forehead, a finely chiseled intelligent face."[17]

In the first four years of his itinerant ministry Albright gained converts at many places. At times he would gather with several of them for "pentecostal meetings." The first of these was held in the home of Peter Walter, near Quakertown, Pennsylvania. Five of his new Christian friends met with him there, probably in 1799.

Albright began to realize that a means should be devised to conserve the results of his ministry. He saw that many converts lapsed into their old careless ways after he had moved on. Therefore, in 1800 he gathered a number of converts in three places and formed three classes after the manner of the Methodist class to which he had belonged. These classes were begun in the homes of Peter Walter near Quakertown, Samuel Liesser, two miles east of Barto in Berks County, and George Phillips in Monroe County. Each man served as class leader of the group meeting in his home, and the classes were called by their names, Walter's, Liesser's, and Phillips'. Rolls were not kept, but an estimate of members of the classes would be fifteen to twenty in each. The classes met on Sundays and Wednesday evenings for worship and Bible study.

The three classes did not include all persons who had been converted under Albright's preaching by that time. There were converts in other places some of whom formed the nuclei of classes which were organized later. It has been estimated that by the end of 1800 there were altogether about two hundred persons who had been converted under Albright's preaching.

Out of these first three classes came a number of young men who became associates of Albright in his itinerant ministry, including John Walter, Abraham Liesser, and Alexander Jameson. Other young preachers were to follow. Three among them stood out above the rest, John Walter, George Miller, and John Dreisbach.

John Walter

John Walter (1781–1818) was born in Berks County, a member of the large family of Peter Walter. In 1801 he offered his services to Albright, at first not as a preacher, but as a tile-making apprentice. He was accepted and moved into the Albright home. He learned rapidly. This gave Albright greater freedom to go on his preaching journeys, leaving the business to be conducted by Walter.

Because he had been converted under Albright's preaching, Walter witnessed to people who came to the Albright home for business reasons. Although he had almost no formal education and could scarcely read or write, he was very effective in his witnessing.

After serving as a tile-maker apprentice for one year, in 1802 he joined Albright on his travels. He sensed his lack of formal learning and plunged diligently into the task of self-education. He was so successful that not only did he become a very effective and fluent traveling preacher but also a competent writer. In 1810 he gathered and published a collection of fifty-six German hymns, several of which he had written, under the title A Brief Collection of Old and New Spiritual Songs (English translation). It found use among German religious groups beyond the bounds of the Evangelical Association.

On August 8, 1808, Walter married Christena Becker, of a family which was prominent in the Evangelical movement. He and his wife established their home on a farm in northern Lancaster County near the town of Cocalico. As he traveled, he wrote remarkable letters to his wife revealing his deep religious devotion and his literary ability.

Two unusual events occuring during his traveling ministry reveal the nature of his experiences. In 1805 on a journey to an appointment in the home of John Thomas in Mifflin County he lost his way as night fell. In a chilling rain he plunged into a dense thicket where he became literally stuck in the branches and rocks. The waiting congregation stayed in the Thomas home until ten o'clock and then, disappointed, started for their homes. Walter, hopelessly lost, began to shout for help, and the people heard the voice in the distance. They went toward it, found and released Walter, and took him to the Thomas home where he thereupon preached a two-hour sermon!

Another time in 1805 he had an appointment to preach in a schoolhouse near the town of New Berlin. Persons who opposed the "fanatical Albright preachers" got there first and closed and barred the schoolhouse door. Walter thereupon preached to a crowd outside the building. As he reached the climax of his sermon, he cried out, "God has opened for himself a door in New Berlin." At that moment the schoolhouse door suddenly sprang open with a loud noise. Later it was found that a clamp had worked loose. However, the people declared that a miracle had occurred. This gave undergirding to Walter's preaching in the area. The result was a vigorous revival leading to the establishing of another class and the development of New Berlin as a center of Evangelical organization and service.

Walter's life was strenuous. His exposure to the hardships of travel and inclement weather took its toll. In 1813 he showed definite signs of tuberculosis. He discontinued his travels, although continuing his preaching near his home. Thus he prolonged his life until late in 1818. He died at the age of thirty-seven on December 3 in his home near Jonestown, Pennsylvania, to which his family had moved. He was buried in a cemetery near that town. His wife moved back to the Becker homestead at Kleinfeltersville, Pennsylvania. She died in 1868, fifty years after her husband's death.

THE CONFERENCE OF 1803

By 1803 the number of classes had increased to five. They all were located in the southeastern section of Pennsylvania, east of the Susquehanna River. On November 3 Albright and two assistants, Peter Walter and Samuel Liesser, called a conference of class leaders and members to meet in the Liesser home in Berks County. George Miller, a new convert, served as secretary and recorded that the persons attending the conference numbered "40, most of them blessed [converted] souls." Three significant actions were taken. First, they declared that they were a new ecclesiastical organization. Second, they declared the Scriptures to be the guide and rule of faith. Third, on November 5 they took action with respect to Albright as follows:

> In this year [1803] it was resolved that this association should establish a church substance and elected Jacob Albright as elder preacher. He was ordained and given the right to govern all meetings. . . . They gave him a certificate [which confirmed this action].[18]

No clear description is given to the nature of the ordination, whether by a formal ceremony of "laying on of hands" or a procedure less formal. Paul H. Eller has judged it to have been "ordination by resolution rather than ordination by rite."[19]

The importance of the Conference of 1803 can scarcely be exaggerated. Paramount is the fact that the brethren regarded themselves not as a loose fellowship, but as a distinct organization. Whether they regarded the action as the formation of a new denomination cannot be said, but subsequent events support this interpretation. Hence the claim is made that the Evangelical Association had its formal beginning in 1803.

The ordination of Albright must have given him great satisfaction because he had always favored proper order. The exhorter's license given him by the Methodist class had supported his right to preach but gave him no further recognition. The ordination set him aside as a "full" preacher, the only one so far in the Evangelical movement, and therefore its recognized leader.

Prior to the conference, Albright, accompanied by Walter and Liesser, had moved northwestward and had opened preaching places in Mifflin and neighboring counties.[20] In his capacity as the leader of the movement, at the Conference of 1803 Albright sent Walter and Liesser into that area to expand the work. The work prospered even as it did in the southeastern part of the state. Since these areas were rather distinct, the area southeast of the Susquehanna River was called the old circuit, and the area further north and west of the River was called the new circuit. The former embraced Dauphin, Lancaster, Lebanon, Schuylkill, Berks, Lehigh, Monroe, Bucks, and Montgomery Counties. The new circuit was in Northumberland, Juniata, Mifflin, Snyder, and Union Counties, with the town of New Berlin as the center of the work in this area. As the Evangelical preachers on the new circuit established preaching places and classes, the area expanded. By 1810 it was bounded by a line beginning near Lewisburg, running westward to Lemont, southward to Bedford, eastward to York and Harrisburg, and northward to the starting point. The plan of itinerant preaching for Walter and Liesser and other preachers, including Albright, was that this boundary should be followed four times each year.

In 1810 the new circuit had become so large that it was divided and a third circuit formed. It embraced the territory west of the Susquehanna River and south of the Juniata River into Maryland and Virginia.

The three circuits were often called by names derived from their areas. Thus the old circuit was called the Lancaster or Schuylkill Circuit, the new the Northumberland or Union Circuit, and the third the Franklin Circuit.

George Miller

In the conference of 1803 a new name became prominent, that of George Miller (1774–1816) who served the conference as secretary.

Miller was born in Pottstown, Pennsylvania, of Lutheran parents. Shortly after his birth his family moved to Alsace Township where his father farmed and operated a grist mill. At an early age George learned the work of milling. He joined his brother John in that work and in the construction of mills after his father died in 1785, leaving them to support the family.

Miller's mother was very devout. She encouraged her children to give serious attention to religious matters, especially Bible reading. She was greatly pleased when her son George bought a Bible with two dollars she had given him to buy a pet sheep.

When Miller was in his twelfth and thirteenth years, he suffered severely from inflammation in his limbs and knee joints. He described the illness in the story of his life written in 1815 when he was approaching his death.[21] During his ministry, even though he appeared to be rugged, he experienced occasions of sudden weakness and shortness of breath. In 1968 Dr. Homer D. Cassel, physician and medical consultant for the Evangelical United Brethren Board of Missions, having studied Miller's description of his lifelong illness, expressed the opinion that Miller had suffered rheumatic fever as a child and had been left with a permanently damaged heart, the eventual cause of his death.

When he was in his teens, Miller took a thorough catechetical course in the Lutheran Church. He expressed gratitude many times for this instruction. He was confirmed in the Trinity Lutheran Church in Reading in 1789.[22] In spite of this training Miller's religious conviction fluctuated. In his religious quest he found the book *The Foundation of True Christianity* by Joseph Alleine very helpful.

In 1800 he married Magdalena Brobst. They lived on a farm he had bought in Brunswick Township in Berks County. He built a grist mill beside the home. He prospered so that he was able to buy a larger farm at Allemangel, near Reading. Here he and his brother Solomon, who had married Magdalena's sister and lived on an adjacent farm, engaged in milling together.

Miller first met Albright and heard him preach in 1798. In 1802 he heard him again and was persuaded that Albright bore the true message. After consulting with him and gaining a vital experience of assurance Miller decided to become one of Albright's followers. In 1803 he joined the Albright preachers.

This brought difficulties. When his father-in-law, Michael

Brobst, a Revolutionary War veteran, learned of Miller's decision to go out on preaching journeys, he accused him of laziness for not keeping at his farming and milling. Once in one of his frequent fits of temper he tried to do Miller physical harm by running him down with his horse. Miller escaped with minor injuries. People in the vicinity of his home showed their anger at this member of the fanatical Albright preachers. They damaged his mill, ruined the mill race, and refused to pay him for milling their grain. Appeal to the local justice of the peace was in vain.

Nevertheless, in 1805 Miller began a very vigorous and successful traveling ministry. Under Albright's assignment he had great success in a revival in the Lancaster-Lebanon area centering in Kleinfeltersville. In 1806 he was assigned to the new circuit where his work as evangelist and organizer brought rapid and permanent growth. He was the most effective of Albright's assistants.

Miller was troubled with occasional spells of sudden physical weakness which required that he lie down immediately. When riding horseback, he would have to dismount and lie on the ground until his strength returned. On Christmas evening 1808 he preached in a Methodist home in Lost Creek Valley on the new circuit. That night he dreamed that he was struggling in an impenetrable thicket which caused him to fight for his breath. In the dream an angel approached and pressed a hot stone die on his chest causing great pain. He awoke to find these symptoms to be real. Although the next day he felt somewhat recovered, he decided to journey home. After reaching home safely he no longer went forth on preaching journeys. He preached at nearby places and attended the Annual Conferences, which began in 1809, where he gave sage counsel.

Miller's illness did not prevent him from engaging in literary work. In the Conference of 1807 Albright had been commissioned to prepare a set of Articles of Faith and a *Discipline*. His early death prevented him from carrying out this task. Thereupon Miller assumed the responsibility. He took the Methodist *Discipline* and Articles of Faith as they had been translated into German by Dr. Ignatius Römer of Middletown, Pennsylvania, and with slight modifications of the Articles of Faith and more extensive modifications of the *Discipline* he formulated the Evangelical *Discipline*. This work was adopted by the Annual Conference of 1809. It comprised a book of seventy-five pages and contained, besides the

Articles of Faith and the rules of discipline, "doctrinal essays taken from the writings of [John] Wesley and Fletcher on 'Christian Perfection,' 'Predestination.' 'Final Perseverance of the Saints,' and a dissertation against 'antinomianism.'"[23]

Miller also drew up a list of rules to govern the conducting of conferences. In 1811 he completed a biography of Albright. In the same year he completed *Practical Christianity*, a book which provides rich insight into early Evangelical doctrine, forms of worship, and practical application of the gospel. The book was first printed in 1814, reprinted in 1844, and translated into English in 1871.

Shortly before his death, at the urging of friends he wrote his autobiography. In spite of constant chest pain he completed this very valuable work in four weeks. He asserted the authenticity of his biographical account by writing, "In part I copied it from my papers, and partly from memory, and I know, as also my conscience testifies, that I have written the truth."[24]

Miller's health had been steadily declining. In his last months he suffered great pains in his chest, apparently the result of deteriorating heart action and not tuberculosis, as some accounts have said.[25]

DEVELOPMENT OF THE CHURCH

The years 1805, 1806, and 1807 had brought rapid development in the church. George Miller was responsible for much of this. He made progress in places where even Albright met with indifferent success. In 1805, using the home of George Becker near Kleinfeltersville in south Lebanon County as his base, he carried on a revival movement in Lebanon and Lancaster Counties which led to the formation of several new classes.

In the meanwhile Albright and Walter developed the work in the new circuit. They had a series of meetings in the Penns, Buffalo, and Dry valleys.

In May 1806 Albright called an assembly of the preachers. A number of matters were resolved. George Miller was given the status of a "full" and "traveling" minister which only Albright and Walter had held. There were other preachers who preached only in places near their homes and so were called "local" preachers.

This distinction between the two kinds of preachers became significantly important.

An unhappy event occurred at the assembly. Alexander Jameson, who traveled as an assistant to Albright and Walter, expressed dissatisfaction over the fact that he had not received very much money for his work. Small sums had been gathered by the men, but when the money was distributed among them to help in defraying expenses and paying family obligations, Jameson felt he did not receive a fair share; therefore he withdrew from the fellowship. This prompted the men to give more serious attention to financial matters. Several, such as Albright and Miller, who owned farms, were financially independent. To help the others it was decided to solicit gifts and establish a "subsidiary fund" from which money could be drawn to give support to those in need. Some of the money was donated to other poor people.

Before the assembly concluded, it was decided to begin holding regular annual sessions of the Albright brethren. They set the next year, 1807, for the first.[26]

Albright, as usual, appointed the several preachers to travel in one or the other of the circuits. Miller was sent to the new circuit where again he carried on vigorous and successful evangelistic work. In addition he showed himself to be especially effective in organization. Building on the work Albright and Walter had begun the previous year, he organized ten new classes.

In October 1806, as they were traveling on the new circuit, Albright, Walter, and Miller came together in the home of Martin Dreisbach in Buffalo Valley in Union County. After discussing the progress of the work the three men decided to place into a written "covenant" an expression of their purpose "still more earnestly to prosecute the work of the Lord" and to maintain personal loyalty to one another.[27]

In early 1807 Albright reassigned Miller to the old circuit. He reassumed leadership of the revival he had begun there in 1805, especially in Lebanon and Lancaster Counties. The work centered in the Muehlbach area, named after the Muehlbach Creek, which forms the boundary of those counties. The area includes the towns of Cocalico, Kleinfeltersville, and Schaefferstown. Another center of revival was Millersville. The Becker Class in Kleinfeltersville was strengthened.

An important result of the Millersville revival was the

conversion and recruitment of John Erb (1787–1858), who became a faithful member of the traveling preachers.

In April 1807 a "pentecostal" meeting was held near Millheim on the new circuit. During the meeting John Dreisbach, seventeen years old, stepped forward to offer himself for ministerial service. He was given a preaching license and appointed to be the assistant to George Miller. During the year he also served with Albright.

In the summer of 1807 the preachers traveled among appointments in Bedford, Somerset, and Cambria Counties, carrying on the work there more vigorously than at any time since it has been begun several years earlier.

On November 13, 14, 15, 1807, the Annual Conference, which had been announced in the assembly of 1806, convened. It was to be the first of a series of Annual Conferences. It differed from the meetings of 1803 and 1806 because it was the intention to have all preachers in attendance and also as many class leaders as possible.

The conference was held in the home of Samuel Becker in Kleinfeltersville. The roll consisted of Albright, who had been ordained as an elder; Walter and Miller, who held the rank of traveling or full ministers; Jacob Fry (or Frey) and John Dreisbach, who were called "preachers on trial"; Charles Bisse, Solomon Miller (George's brother), and Jacob Philips, who were called local preachers; and twenty class leaders.

It was announced that the formal membership of the church, including the preachers and the members of the classes, was 220. This did not include several hundreds who had responded to the preachers but were living in places where no classes had been formed.

The most important action taken by the conference was bestowing the title of Bishop upon Albright by a majority vote. Thus the leadership which was tacitly attributed to him in 1803 when he was ordained became more formal.

Questions have been raised as to the validity of this action and whether the title was recognized significantly by Albright's followers. The fact that he lived only six months after becoming a bishop lends difficulty to assessing the recognition of his episcopal status among his brethren. However, several contemporary references to Albright as bishop support his episcopal status. Dreisbach called him by that title on several occasions.[28]

In light of the service Albright had rendered to the church in the years prior to the conference and in the six months afterward, it appears that the title conveyed the significance of "overseer," a meaning which has been traditional in the history of Christianity. Hence, it is proper to speak of Albright as the first bishop of the Evangelical Association.

It is probable that the brethren wished to honor Albright with this title before he would have to discontinue his work, as his rapidly worsening health indicated he would have to do. In view of this, the conference also took action designating George Miller as elder, thereby indicating that he would be regarded as the main leader if and when Albright had to relinquish his duties.

The conference also took action to have a formal *Discipline* prepared for its future use. It was deemed proper to assign the task to Bishop Albright, who had advised that the church should assume the episcopal form of church government.[29] However, Albright's health did not permit him to carry out the task, and it was later assigned to George Miller, who presented the completed work to the Annual Conference of 1809.

Lastly, the conference issued newly printed licenses to at least two of the preachers present, one to John Dreisbach as minister on trial and one to Samuel Liesser, formerly a class leader. Facsimiles of those licenses are printed in R. W. Albright's *History of the Evangelical Church*. These facsimiles show Albright's name in his own handwriting.

In the licenses the name "the Newly-formed Methodist Conference" is used. This reflects Albright's continuing consciousness of Methodist influences. However, the word "conference" indicates that the title was not used as a denominational name. The choosing of a denominational name did not occur until 1816.

Albright's Last Months

As the Annual Conference ended, Albright again assigned the preachers to serve on the two circuits. Walter and Dreisbach were sent to the old circuit and Miller and Fry to the new.

It was evident in the Annual Conference of 1807 that Albright was very ill. Nevertheless he did not discontinue his work. In the middle of the winter of 1807–1808 he reached the home of a Lutheran, Peter Raidabaugh, near Linglestown, east of Harrisburg, and asked for a night's lodging. When he was recognized as the "fanatical" preacher, the request was granted reluctantly. Albright next asked for the privilege of preaching in the home. Again with some hesitation this was granted. A number of neighbors gathered in the home that evening. Albright preached very effectively. His emphasis was on one of his favorite themes, personal sanctification, the responsibility and the possibility of living a life cleansed by God from all unrighteousness. This message sounded strange to the listeners, most of whom were Lutherans who had been catechized to believe that, although God forgives sinners, as fallible people they continue to be sinners as long as they live. Some of Albright's hearers could not accept his message, but others did, including Raidabough.

In delivering this message Albright gave emphasis to the Wesleyan doctrine of sanctification. In the biography of Jacob Albright, written by Miller after Albright's death, he is seen as stressing this doctrine again and again. By God's grace a converted person can be sanctified, that is, be made holy or pure, in heart and mind. The process is both instantaneous, at the moment of conversion, and gradual as it grows and penetrates deeper and deeper into the convert's new being in Christ.

As much as Albright stressed sanctification, he apparently had recognized a danger in this doctrine, that of spiritual pride. At no place in the biography is he quoted as saying by word or action that he had achieved moral and spiritual perfection. Rather the stress is upon constant striving, with the hope that further growth in grace is to be achieved.[30]

As the result of Albright's stress on sanctification, it became central in the preaching of his followers. Dreisbach constantly warned against either surrendering the doctrine or perverting it. The degree of emphasis was a point of difference between the early Evangelicals and the early United Brethren.

On Easter Sunday in 1808 a general or pentecostal meeting was held in the home of John Brobst, the brother-in-law of George Miller, in Albany Township in Berks County. Although this was not an Annual Conference, Albright, meeting the preachers, made a change in their assignments, with Walter and Fry going to the old circuit, and Miller and Dreisbach to the new.

After the meeting ended, the brethren traveled to Raidabaugh's, near Linglestown, to hold another meeting. Albright was barely able to make the journey, and when the meeting was held, he was too weak to take an active part. After the meeting he left for his home at

Hahnstown, about forty miles away. Because of his feeble condition he was accompanied by two of the brethren. He got only as far as Kleinfeltersville, fifteen miles from home, when he felt he could go no further. He stopped at the home of George Becker where a room was always kept in readiness for a traveling preacher. As he was received, he said to his hosts, "Have you my bed ready? I have come to die."[31]

He lingered for several weeks and died on May 18, 1808, at the age of 49. No member of his family was at his bedside. His wife and daughter arrived too late to exchange farewells.[32]

Albright was buried in the Becker burial grounds on the eastern edge of Kleinfeltersville. A rough headstone was placed over the grave, giving his name and the dates of his birth and death.

In 1850 the Evangelical Association, as a fitting memorial, erected a church near the grave and named it the Albright Church. Faulty construction required its rebuilding in 1860. In recent years a prominent stone marker was erected beside the church.

No religious writings of Albright remain. Nevertheless his basic religious emphases can be reconstructed from information given in the writings of his contemporaries. While he gave great emphasis to the doctrine of sanctification, it was only part of a well-rounded theological system. A summary of his religious emphases can be set forth in the following propositions: (1) the God of the Bible is the true God; (2) he sent Jesus Christ to save men; (3) men are helpless in their sins, and no self-righteousness or ritualistic ceremony can redeem them; (4) sinful men are not so completely separated from God but that they can repent and call upon God for salvation; (5) faith in Jesus Christ, the Son of God, will be answered by God's saving grace; (6) this is revealed in the cross of Christ; (7) one who is touched by this grace will live a godly or sanctified life; (8) sanctification is a promise which should be claimed by all saved men.

In spite of the decision in 1806 to hold a conference annually beginning in 1807, no conference was held in 1808, probably because of the death of Albright.

It appears that Miller assumed the leadership as had earlier been planned. However, this did not last long because at Christmas 1808, Miller suffered a severe heart attack which brought his itinerant ministry to an end. Walter also was beginning to decline in health. Of the three most effective assistants of Albright, only John Dreisbach was left to carry on the leadership of the Evangelical movement.

JOHN DREISBACH

John Dreisbach (1789–1871) was born on a farm owned by his father, Martin Dreisbach, located in Buffalo Valley about ten miles west of Lewisburg. The Dreisbach family were faithful members of the Reformed Church. Martin Dreisbach had donated seven and one-half acres of the farm for a community cemetery and as a site of a church which was built as a place of worship for the Reformed and Lutheran people of the area. A Reformed minister, Jonathan Rawhouser, served the church from 1790 to 1792. Thereafter for a number of years it was the place where early United Brethren preachers, John George Pfrimmer, Christian Newcomer, George Adam Geeting, and Dietrich Aurand held meetings.

Early in 1807 Albright assigned John Dreisbach to be the assistant to George Miller. He was in this service only one and one-half years when Miller had to discontinue his itinerant ministry because of ill health. With Albright's death in 1808 and Miller's and Walter's decline in health, the story of the Evangelical Association largely centered in Dreisbach's leadership until his own break in health occurred in 1821.

Dreisbach's influence was renewed after his recovery a year later, but, although he performed many kinds of service, his precarious health, which seemed largely to be a nervous ailment, kept him from becoming the main leader again.

Dreisbach's greatest services to the church in his vigorous years were largely of two kinds: directing the church as it grew and expanded and beginning and promoting the work of publishing religious materials.

In the Annual Conference of 1809 it was decided that Dreisbach and John Walter should be advanced to the status of elder. Miller had been granted that status in 1807. It was also decided that all three men should be ordained by the laying on of hands. This was done during a great meeting held in the home of Henry Eby near Lebanon in 1810.

Dreisbach served as secretary of the Annual Conference from 1809 to 1812. He presided over the Annual Conferences of 1813 and 1814. In 1814 he was elected as the first presiding elder. In that capacity he presided over the first General Conference in 1816.

As Dreisbach led in the church's work he was influential in

recruiting young ministers. Two, Matthias Betz and Henry Niebel, became very prominent.

Mathias Betz (1782–1813) was born in Millheim, a town on the new circuit. He was converted under Miller's preaching in 1806. In 1809 he was granted a license to preach. He was very effective in gaining converts. Among them was John Seybert of Manheim, Lancaster County, who was destined to become the second bishop of the Evangelical Association in 1839. Tragically, Betz's ministry was ended by his early death from pneumonia in 1813.

Henry Niebel (1784–1877) was the second outstanding preacher to begin his work during Dreisbach's years of leadership. The two men became brothers-in-law by marrying daughters of a prominent church member, Abraham Eyer, of Winfield, south of Lewisburg. Niebel had been serving as a teacher in Winfield and boarded in the Eyer home. His future father-in-law gave him the spiritual guidance which led to his conversion and entrance into the ministry. He received a license to preach in 1809. Thereafter he and Dreisbach worked very closely together. In 1815 he was elected the second presiding elder. In 1819 he had a break in health. Ten years later he reentered the work and gave leadership to the church, especially in Ohio, where it had extended by that time. His ministry lasted sixty-eight years.

Dreisbach's Ministry

Dreisbach learned what hardship was as he traveled extensively in his supervisory work. He endured the rigors of inclement weather, irregular and uncomfortable lodging, poor food, and on more than one occasion physical violence. As early as 1808 he had a difficult experience as he was leading in a prayer service in the home of Peter Walter, the father of John Walter, near Jonestown in Lebanon County. Because threats had been made, the meeting was held with windows bolted and doors shut. Nevertheless, a group of ruffians shouting, "Kill the priest!" broke into the home, smashed the furniture and set upon the worshippers with fists and clubs. Their primary target was Dreisbach. However, in the melee the lights were extinguished. In the darkness Dreisbach dropped to the floor and escaped from the house leaving the ruffians pounding the worshippers and each other. Several of the worshippers were painfully injured. Suit was brought against the rowdies. They were tried in a Harrisburg court, pronounced guilty, and assessed a substantial sum of money as damages. However, the brethren declared they did not wish to accept the award. The attackers were surprised at this indication of forgiveness and in shame changed their hostile spirit.

In 1810 a very significant event occurred in Dreisbach's life. Three separate accounts of this, closely related in detail, still remain. On August 2 as he was traveling southward along the Susquehanna River he met Bishop Asbury of the Methodist Episcopal Church and his companion, Henry Boehm, son of Martin Boehm, one of the founders of the United Brethren Church. They traveled together all day until they arrived at the home of a Mr. Folke, north of Harrisburg, where they spent the night. Dreisbach said that Bishop Asbury urged him to break his relations with the Evangelical brethren and join the Methodist Church. He told him there were several reasons he should do this. (1) If Dreisbach were to join the Methodists, he would be assigned to travel for a year with a Methodist preacher, Jacob Gruber, from whom he could learn to be more fluent in English (although Dreisbach could speak and write in German and English) and for which he would be paid a salary. (2) By becoming Methodist, Dreisbach could render greater service while at the same time he would be guarded against "becoming self-exalted." (3) Since "the German language could not exist much longer in this country," for Dreisbach to restrict his preaching to the Germans in the German language was not farsighted.

Dreisbach replied that he felt if he were to leave the Evangelicals for the Methodists he would do the former a great disservice and would be yielding to self-interest. He proposed another plan which would take care of the matter on a more inclusive scale. As he stated in 1855 in an *Evangelical Messenger* article, he said to Bishop Asbury:

> Grant us to labor among the Germans; to have German Circuits, districts and conferences; the supervision of the latter to be one of your Bishops: this being granted, we venture to state that we shall come over as a community, to a man. [Dreisbach stated further] however the answer we received from the Bishop on this proposal, was, that it would be *inexpedient.*

Although all three accounts were written many years after the event, while differing on details of sentence order and construction, they tell essentially the same story. Most likely all three, including that of Dreisbach, relied upon an original account which Dreisbach wrote in his *Journal* at the time of the event. (It is known that the *Journal* covering this period of Dreisbach's ministry was extant until at least 1894 but has since been lost.)[33] Therefore, the three cited accounts may be taken as authentic.[34]

It is strange that Asbury made no mention of the encounter or the proposal in his *Journal* under the date of August 2, 1810. However, he recorded that he and Henry Boehm spent that night at Folke's which note ties the accounts together.

It is also a puzzling fact that although Bishop Asbury had many contacts with members of the Evangelical movement, he makes no mention of them anywhere in his *Journal*. This stands in contrast to his several references to United Brethren names and events. That the encounter with Dreisbach did not cause Asbury to be offended is seen in that before they parted on August 3, 1810, Asbury made a gift to Dreisbach of Fletcher's "Portrait of St. Paul."[35]

In 1811 Dreisbach married Catherine, the eldest daughter of Abraham Eyer. They had two children, Salome and Elizabeth. Catherine contracted tuberculosis and died in the spring of 1815. In 1817 Dreisbach married a sister of Catherine, Fanny. They had nine children. Dreisbach spoke frequently of his great love for the sister-wives and of the selfless way each had helped him in his work.

The Annual Conference of 1812 sent Dreisbach and Robert McCray to investigate the possibility of opening a new circuit in New York state. In 1807 Christian Wolf, an uncle of Dreisbach and a convert under Miller in 1806, had moved to Seneca County, New York, and had begun work as a local preacher. Other Germans had moved there from the Susquehanna Valley.

Dreisbach and McCray were disappointed in the smallness of the work. They returned to recommend that it would be inexpedient to establish a circuit there. However, when Dreisbach made a second trip into the same area in 1816, he found that Wolf had expanded the work and had organized several classes, thereby making the work permanent. Before he returned, Dreisbach traveled to the western part of the state, across the Niagara River into Canada as far as Burlington to survey that territory for later inclusion in the Evangelical Association. In the Annual Conference of 1816 the work in New York was called the Lake Circuit.

In 1814, after Dreisbach was elected presiding elder over the entire church, the Annual Conference instructed him to supervise the work by traveling on horseback over its whole extent four times each year. By this time a total of seven circuits had been formed, namely, Lancaster, Schuylkill (which together had earlier comprised the old circuit), Union (which had been the new circuit), Somerset, Bedford, Franklin (formerly the third circuit, extending into Maryland and Virginia), and York. The traveling responsibilities were enormous. Roughly the whole area embraced a rectangle in Pennsylvania, extending westward from Easton to Lock Haven, southwestward to Johnstown and Somerset, eastward to Philadelphia, and northward to Easton, with the extension into Maryland and Virginia. The perimeter of this area is about eight hundred miles, the territory about thirty-thousand square miles.[36] Dreisbach valiantly attempted to carry out the assignment, but obviously could not fulfill the task of traveling over the whole church area four times each year.

Dreisbach continued his supervision until 1821 when a combination of physical and nervous ailments caused a serious break in health. This brought an end to his leadership in the church although his services continued for many more years.

Dreisbach also had deep interest in printed materials produced for use in the church. From the beginning of his ministry in 1806 at the age of seventeen he had the ability to speak, read, and write in both German and English because his father, a prosperous farmer, had been able to give his children good schooling. After he entered the ministry, he studied the Scriptures diligently and carefully read the writings of Thomas à Kempis, Martin Luther, John Calvin, John Wesley, and others.

John Dreisbach was the most prolific writer among the early Evangelicals. Having experienced difficulty in giving instruction in the faith to new converts, including children, without written aids, he published a Catechism in 1809. With Henry Niebel he published a German hymnbook entitled Das Geistliche Saitenspiel ("The Spiritual Psaltery"). He published thirty-five hymns in German, some of which he had composed. The others he had translated from English. In 1815 he and Niebel revised, corrected, and enlarged the Discipline which Miller had written in 1808–1809.

As Dreisbach looked to the future, he realized that the work would become more firmly established among the people if they had literature to use to supplement the hearing of the Word. Therefore, he believed the church should have a printing press. He was so firmly convinced of this that he decided to purchase one with his own money. He had come into possession of part of his father's farm. Because he was constantly away from home, he rented out the land and collected rent annually. On November 30, 1815, and again in January 1816 he made trips to Philadelphia and with the rent money bought a press, type, ink, and bookbindery at a total cost of $440.58. This was more than he had anticipated so he had to borrow money to return home. He took the press to New Berlin and set it up in a shop which had been built, also at his own expense, for $96. In this same year, 1816, the Evangelical brethren erected their first church building on the same lot. Neither structure exists today, but a stone marker stands on the spot.

Dreisbach recovered a measure of health by 1822. He still had nearly a half century of life before him. From 1822 to 1828 he served as a preacher and as superintendent of the press in New Berlin. In 1827 he entered state politics on the Jacksonian ticket and served in the Pennsylvania state legislature representng Union County. He served on the legislative committee dealing with vice and immorality and was held in high regard. However, when he ran for reelection in 1829, he found that his popularity in Union County had dropped sharply because the candidate for governor on the Jacksonian ticket, George Wolf, openly favored an English public school system, which did not please the Germans, and was a member of the Masonic Order, which was in popular disfavor. Dreisbach opposed all secret societies, yet he supported Wolf because of loyalty to Jacksonianism. Hence he was not reelected.

In 1831 Dreisbach moved with his family to Pickaway Township in Pickaway County, Ohio. An uncle, Henry Dreisbach, had been a leader of German people who had moved into that area from the east in 1804, and had laid out the town of Circleville, Ohio, to which many Germans came. John Dreisbach lived there most of the remainder of his life. He served as a local preacher except on three occasions when he attempted to return to the work of a traveling preacher—on the Lancaster (Ohio) and Pickaway Circuits in 1851, in Dayton in 1853, and on the Chillicothe Circuit in 1854. He found that he could not maintain the vigor that these assignments required.

His last effort at denominational service occurred in 1854–1857 when he was editor of the denominational periodical the *Evangelical Messenger*, published in Cleveland. Again precarious health brought this work to an end.

DENOMINATIONAL ACTIVITY

In the Annual Conference of 1809 names used to designate the association were *Die sogenannten Albrechts* and *Die soggenannten Albrechtsleute*, which translate literally into "The so-called Albrights" and "The so-called Albright's people." The German term *sogenannt* does not denote disparagement as does its English equivalent "so-called." A proper translation of the full names would be, "Those Designated as Albright's People." These German names had been used commonly from the beginning. They appeared on Evangelical documents as convenient names.[37] The permanent denominational name, The Evangelical Association, was not chosen until the General Conference of 1816.

The minutes of the Annual Conference of 1810 mention ordination to the diaconate for the first time, as they record that J. Erb and M. Metz were ordained to the office of deacon. The minutes of 1812 stated that "John Erb was ordained Elder." Other men in subsequent conferences were first ordained as deacons and two or three years later as elders. Thus the Evangelical Association from as early as 1812 recognized the two levels of ordination.

The issues of salary payments which had arisen in 1806, when Alexander Jameson withdrew from the fellowship in dissatisfaction over the matter, was given serious attention. Money had been collected, and in 1810 each traveling preacher received $35. In 1812 that amount was increased to $50. To deserve their individual share of the money collected each year the preachers had to "render . . . an accurate account of all their receipts and expenditures" of the year. Of this collected "subsidiary fund" $30.80 was given to a poor widow, Maria Griffeson.[38]

During the years 1812 to 1816 twenty-six young men were accepted as new preachers. This was a good number. Very strict personal moral standards were required, so strict that a number of the men who had been accepted were later discharged. Even Jacob Fry was "expelled on account of immoral conduct" two years after he had joined the preachers. It appears that he had engaged in an overly ardent courtship. He married the young lady, and in 1819 he was readmitted to the fellowship.

In the Annual Conference of 1814 Dreisbach was elected to the office of presiding elder with responsibility to oversee the work of the whole church. The task was enormous, which leads to the question, "Why was he not elected bishop?" inasmuch as the *Discipline* made provision for that office and defined its responsibilities. No reason was ever recorded. However, speculation has been made that two reasons prevented the election of a bishop until 1839, when John Seybert became the second person to hold the office. The first is that Francis Asbury of the Methodist Episcopal Chu..ch nad assumed that title and set the example of severe authority. Neither the Evangelicals nor the United Brethren wished to have that established in their churches. Second, the time was early in national history, when political centralized authority was held in low esteem.

It was soon seen that adequate supervision of the whole church by one man was impossible. Therefore, it was decided to elect a second presiding elder. In the Annual Conference of 1815 Henry Niebel was chosen. These two brothers-in-law proposed that the territory of the church be divided into two districts: the Canaan District comprised of the Franklin, York, Lancaster, and Schuylkill Circuits, to be served by Dreisbach; and the Salem District comprised of the Union, Center, and Somerset Circuits (the Center Circuit embraced the territory east and west of Lewisburg), to be served by Niebel.

The Annual Conference of 1816 dealt with several important matters. It was held in the barn of Abraham Eyer, the father-in-law of both Dreisbach and Niebel, near Winfield, Pennsylvania. The barn still stands and is regarded as a shrine of the church.

The conference met June 11–13. Its first item of business was to consider the expansion of the church into two neighboring states, Ohio and New York. Over the previous decade followers of the Evangelical movement had moved into Ohio. They settled into two centers. One was in Stark, Tuscarawas, Wayne, and Richland Counties. The other was in the Scioto River Valley in the south-central part of the state where the United Brethren had begun work a decade earlier.

The Annual Conference of 1816 decided to regard these two areas as "Missions"; the first was given the name the Canton Mission and the second the Scioto Mission. Later these missions were referred to as districts.

A vigorous preacher, Adam Hennig, was assigned to travel over the Canton Mission. He did so, preaching in many places, trying to cover the area, which had a perimeter of four hundred miles, every four weeks. He held a great meeting in 1818 and expanded this the following year into a midwest-type camp meeting.

The Scioto Mission did not grow as rapidly. The first preacher sent there was Frederick Shauer, who felt the work was unneeded because of the presence of the United Brethren. Therefore, he resigned from the Evangelical Association and joined the United Brethren. In 1817 two brothers, John and Adam Kleinfelter, arrived to carry on the work.

The Annual Conference of 1816 raised the standards for new preachers. It was decided that a local preacher, that is, one who had been received by the Annual Conference to begin preaching, should be required to serve for six years before he became eligible to apply for ordination as deacon, and that his application had to be accompanied by written statements of endorsement from twelve itinerant ministers. John Dreisbach and Henry Niebel were directed to prepare new printed license forms. In carrying out the assignment Dreisbach prepared an official seal to be stamped on the forms. The seal, symbolizing the nature and spirit of the Evangelical Association, was accepted so widely that it was used on many Evangelical materials throughout the history of the Association.[39]

The Annual Conference took action to put into use the printing press which Dreisbach had purchased the previous winter. A Book Commission comprised of seven men, including Dreisbach, was established.

Several other matters remained to be decided which the Annual Conference felt were so important that they should be dealt with, not by the rank and file of all the preachers assembled, but by a smaller group of mature ministers who would be effective in representing the other preachers as well as the whole church. The issues were: (1) appointing a director of the printing press, (2) choosing a more effective name for the church, and (3) attempting a union with the United Brethren. Twelve men were chosen to carry out this responsibility. Among them were Dreisbach and Niebel. Thus came the call for the first General Conference.

THE GENERAL CONFERENCE OF 1816

The first General Conference was held in the home of Martin Dreisbach October 14–16, 1816. John Dreisbach served as chairman; Henry Niebel as secretary.

The conference chose Solomon Miller, brother of George Miller, as superintendent of the new printing facilities. He accepted and served four years.

The second item was the selection of a new official name for the denomination. The two previously used, "The Newly-Formed Methodist Conference" and "The So-called Albrights," were obviously inappropriate. Therefore, the General Conference changed the name to The Evangelical Association, which was maintained until 1922.

The third item dealt with the proposal that the Evangelical Association and the United Brethren Church should unite. This was not the first time this matter had been proposed. In 1813 both groups sent representatives to a meeting held in John Walter's home on November 11 to 13. In the part of Dreisbach's *Journal* which is still extant (1813 to 1817) under the date of November 12, 1813, he stated,

> We . . . sought ways to unite fully both denominations of the Evangelicals and the United Brethren in Christ, and then began to prepare Articles of Faith for the Discipline, in which we all agreed. But with reference to ministers, we did not agree. We, the Evangelicals, held firmly that . . . only itinerant ministers in good standing shall be privileged to vote in annual and general conferences. . . . They desired . . . that we receive all their ministers who are in full standing in such relation [that is, with power to vote], even though they are not all itinerating. . . . We . . . were unable to agree, and so we adjourned.

This statement reveals clearly the difference in policy between the two groups with respect to the rating of ministers, a distinction which was held throughout the history of the two denominations. The Evangelicals always held clear and precise distinctions among the ranks of the ministers effecting their privileges and responsibilities. The United Brethren were much less precise.

The action of the General Conference of 1816 again brought consideration of union to the fore. Twelve representatives from each denomination met on February 14, 1817, in the home of one of the

United Brethren, Henry Kumler, near Greencastle, Pennsylvania. The result was the same, and for the same reason. When the Evangelical brethren urged that precise ministerial standards be held in the united church, the United Brethren delegates, led by Christian Newcomer, claimed that they had no power to commit their church to such an agreement.

Apparently the difference provoked temporary ill-will. Dreisbach states in his *Journal* under that date, "From our [the Evangelical] delegation . . . some did not consider them [the United Brethren] as good and pure as ourselves, and so there were accusations also against us as proud, and not sincere loving people."

It would appear from this statement that there was an undertone of feeling which indicated the difference of emphasis upon the doctrine of sanctification. Both groups accepted the doctrine, but the Evangelicals stressed it much more than did the United Brethren.

The conference ended on a happier note. Dreisbach stated, "We closed the conference with the suggestion, exhortation and promise to love one another, despite our differences and to pray for one another and to honor and treat one another at all times as Christians."

Because this conference did not achieve its objective, but nevertheless ended in the expression of love, it has been referred to as the Social Conference of 1817.

n September 25, 1800, a group of thirteen or fourteen German preachers, the followers of William Otterbein and Martin Boehm, gathered for a conference in the home of Frederick Kemp and his son Peter, one mile west of Frederick, Maryland. Actions taken there and subsequent events point to this conference as the formal beginning of the United Brethren Church.

In the first place, minutes were kept of this meeting which was the first in a line of uninterrupted annual meetings. George Adam Geeting was usually the secretary of these meetings. In 1812 he gathered all the minutes of the previous annual meetings into one compilation. He entitled them "Protocol of the United Brethren in Christ," thereby signifying that the delegates in attendance had formed a corporate body.

CHURCH ORGANIZATION

The First Bishops

Although in the minutes of 1800 there is no mention of a formal choosing of leaders, in the minutes of 1802 Otterbein and Boehm are referred to as "our superintendents . . . who are appointed." The word "superintendents" in the original German was *Eldesten*, which literally translated means "elders." That the word held more

THE FOUNDING OF THE UNITED BRETHREN CHURCH, 1800–1815

meaning than the word elders usually connotes is seen in later titles applied to Otterbein and Boehm.

In John Hildt's translation of Newcomer's *Journal*, under the date of May 21, 1805, the two men are referred to as "Presidents." Since the original German manuscript of the *Journal* is not extant, it is impossible to determine whether that was the term Newcomer used, or whether Hildt used the same designation in his English translation as was given the new nation's chief official.

Clearer evidence that Otterbein and Boehm were chosen as bishops in 1800 comes from two sources. First, Henry Boehm, son of Martin Boehm, attended the 1800 session. He says on page fifty-five of his *Reminiscences*, " . . . they elected bishops for the first time. William Otterbein and Martin Boehm (my father) were unanimously chosen." Second, the preliminary historical statement of 1815 in the first United Brethren *Discipline*, speaking of the conference of 1800, says, "They elected William Otterbein and Martin Boehm as superintendents or bishops."[1] The term bishop is used several times in that statement to refer to Otterbein and Boehm and their first successor in that office, Christian Newcomer.

Inasmuch as the titles bishop and superintendent are used interchangeably, it would appear that the title bishop connoted the work of superintendency. This would correspond to the meaning of the original New Testament term *episcopos* which also is usually translated "bishop." Thus to the United Brethren the term bishop connoted primarily the administrative and supervisory function rather than the sacerdotal.

The Denomination's Name

In the original German minutes, written by Geeting, the church is referred to as "the United Brethren in Christ." However, he had first written *Brüderschaft*, which means Brotherhood, but either he or some unknown person crossed out the syllable *schaft*, which left *Brüder* or Brethren. Later in the same minutes the term *Brüderschaft* is used. At a third place in the same minutes he states that the men were referred to as "the United" until 1800. This term may have been in use ever since the Pipe Creek meetings where the term "the United Ministers" was used.

Other later references to the church call it "The Society (*Gemeinde*) of the United Brethren in Christ," the "*Gesellschaft*"

(Association) and the "*Gemeindschaft*" (Society or Fellowship). The first time the word church (*Kirche*) is found is in an item in the minutes of 1814 of the Miami Annual Conference. The *Discipline* of 1816 refers to The United Brethren in Christ. The earliest extant document which has the name in full form, the Church of the United Brethren in Christ, is the flyleaf of the English translation of Newcomer's *Journal*, published in 1834. In spite of the fact that the full title was in common use thereafter, it was not until 1890, when the Board of Trustees of the church was incorporated under that denominational name, that it became legal.

All the above uses echo the words of William Otterbein at the great meeting in Isaac Long's barn in 1767 when he embraced Martin Boehm and exclaimed, "*Wir sind Brüder*"—We are brethren!"

Membership

In each of the annual minutes from 1800 to 1812 Geeting, the secretary, gave the list of the persons attending. Altogether fifty-three names are listed. However, many of these were not regarded as preachers. In 1812 Geeting listed only twenty-six who "are authorized to perform all services of God's house."

The reference to the men who were "authorized to perform all services of God's house" raises the question of meaning. It is certain that the word authorized did not mean ordained because Newcomer and two other brethren were the first to be formally ordained, an event which occurred in 1813. Apparently Geeting's statement of 1812 means that action was taken in the Annual Conferences supporting the itinerant ministry of some of the brethren. Later similar statements include the granting of preaching licenses to those who were "authorized."

According to item 8 in the minutes of 1802 the suggestion was made that a numbering be made of all people associated with all the circuits and classes. The suggestion met with disfavor and was defeated by a vote of nine to three. For years there was a feeling that church members should not be counted or numbered. It was probably based on the disobedience of King David in numbering Israel (II Sam. 24; I Chr. 21:1-8). This feeling persisted in the church so that it was not until 1857 that the church made an accurate count of its membership.

Translation of the Methodist Discipline

No reference is made to the matter in the minutes of 1800, but an item in the *Journal* of Henry Boehm states that a suggestion was made that the *Discipline* which the Methodists had formulated in 1784 be made available to the United Brethren. To this end, he states, "Father Otterbein made a move to get the Methodist Discipline translated [into German]. They all agreed to it."[2] The matter was not carried out at once, but a Dr. Ignatius Römer was employed to do it in the years 1807 and 1808. The United Brethren apparently made little use of it. The Evangelical ministers, on the other hand, adopted the translation for their use.

General Observations of the Minutes

The minutes of the meetings from 1800 until 1815 reveal a warm and cordial spirit prevailing among the brethren. This doubtless reflects the attitudes of Otterbein and Boehm and other preachers such as Newcomer, Geeting, and Christopher Grosh, who were the leaders when Otterbein and Boehm were absent. There were a few exceptions to this spirit of harmony. In 1808 a dispute arose among three of the brethren. Apparently it was resolved by the withdrawal of one of them from the fellowship.

A number of basic interests were recorded in the minutes. Each member reported on his year's activities, including his own spiritual progress. Stress was placed on preaching earnest and vital but not lengthy sermons. Participation in great meetings and camp meetings was urged. One or two days of fasting and prayer per year were to be observed by the whole church. Division of the ministerial work, both as to geographical areas and ministerial appointments, was made. The territory served in Pennsylvania, Maryland, and Virginia was divided into districts and these, in turn, into circuits. A preacher was appointed to each circuit, and a superintendent was appointed over each district. By 1814 the superintendent was called the presiding elder.

Item 6 of the minutes of 1812 provided that "a single preacher shall yearly receive eighty dollars and a married preacher one hundred and sixty dollars and also expenses." A further note gives an indication that the money was to be solicited by each preacher as he traveled about.

Newcomer's Emerging Leadership

When the church was organized in 1800 Otterbein was seventy-four years old and Boehm nearly seventy-five. Their activity in the first half of the decade belies their ages, but this was soon to change. Otterbein attended the conferences of 1800, 1802, 1803, and 1805. Boehm attended all but two of the conferences up to 1809. When both bishops were absent, leadership was taken over by Geeting, Newcomer, and Christopher Grosh. More and more the name of Newcomer became the most prominent.

Item 18 of the minutes of 1802 states that "when one of our superintendents dies, namely Otterbein or Martin Boehm, . . . then shall another always be chosen in his stead."

In harmony with this action, after the death of Martin Boehm on March 23, 1812, the conference of May 5, 1813, chose Christian Newcomer to serve as bishop for one year. After Otterbein died on November 17, 1813, the conference of May 14, 1814, reëlected Newcomer, this time for a term of three years.

Newcomer was the logical choice. His itinerant ministry had begun about 1777. The extensiveness of his travels and some of his achievements have already been given. Outstanding among them was the formation of the Miami Annual Conference in 1810.

THE MIAMI CONFERENCE

The reason Newcomer extended his journeys westward into Ohio, Kentucky, and Indiana beginning in 1810 was that after the Revolutionary War many Americans migrated westward to avoid the intermittent economic recessions. They had learned that beyond the Appalachian Mountains there were great expanses of cheap, fertile land on which they could settle and establish new homes.

The Germans moved westward through southwestern Pennsylvania. As Newcomer followed them, this was the route he traveled. He was eager to extend his work because he had known many of the German settlers and was troubled that by going westward they had severed their family and religious ties and were without pastoral care. A number of the German itinerant ministers were in this migration.

Newcomer visited a number of these old friends in their frontier homes and towns. Going westward, he traveled through southern

Ohio to Cincinnati and Newport, Kentucky. On August 13, 1810, as he was returning, he met with a group of the brethren who had gathered in the home of Michael Kreider near the town of Chillicothe, Ohio. He recorded in his *Journal*, "Today I held a little conference with the Brethren; 15 preachers (How I write?—preachers! indeed!—we are not worthy the appellation) were present."

Minutes of the meeting have been preserved.[3] A list of fifteen names, including Newcomer's, is given. They are listed under three categories: nine full ministers or elders, four preachers, and two exhorters. Of the nine full ministers four had been licensed by the conference in the east. The other five apparently were granted licenses in some unrecorded manner, probably by these four. The four preachers and two exhorters probably were granted recognition in the same way. The minutes of the meeting record no formal actions but consist of affirmations of Christian faith and statements of spiritual relations to one another.

Because subsequent meetings were held annually, except in 1811, as Newcomer traveled through the area, the meeting of 1810 is regarded as the beginning of the Miami Annual Conference. Its territorial extent reached from the Pennsylvania–Ohio line across Ohio to northern Kentucky and southeastern Indiana. Within this large territory there were five areas of German settlement: along the Muskingum River; in the Scioto and Hocking River valleys; in the vicinity of Cincinnati and Newport, Kentucky; in the Great Miami River valley; and in southeastern Indiana.

When Newcomer reported to the conference in the east that the Miami Annual Conference had been formed, the action was given full approval, and he was instructed to continue his leadership there.

In 1812 as Newcomer made his second extended journey westward, it became apparent that the extent of the Miami Annual Conference and the distances to be traveled by the preachers attending the conference sessions were too great; two conference sessions were held, one near Germantown, Ohio, and the other near Lancaster.[4] The combined minutes were regarded as comprising the record of one session of the Miami Annual Conference. However, this divided Annual Conference obviously did not prove satisfactory. Therefore, only one session was held each ensuing year with the place of meeting alternating between the two centers. The conference was divided into two districts, the Scioto and the Miami, with a district superintendent appointed over each. The matter of distance to travel to the conference sessions still remained a problem which increased as the conference grew in size. Hence, in 1818 the conference divided, with the eastern section becoming the Muskingum Annual Conference. In 1825 the Scioto area was separated to become the Scioto Annual Conference. Further adjustments were made in subsequent years.

The First Ordinations

As stated above, the Miami Conference minutes of 1810 classified the members as "full ministers," "preachers," and "exhorters." None had been ordained. Even Newcomer, though he had the status of a full minister, was unordained. By the time of the meeting in August 1813 it was felt that full ministerial status should be made more distinct. Therefore, the Miami Annual Conference on August 27 took action to approve "the matter of writing a letter to Father Otterbein . . . asking him to ordain, by the laying on of hands, one or more preachers, who afterward may perform the same for others."

The letter reached the aged and infirm Otterbein in late September 1813. Newcomer visited him soon thereafter. It was decided that Otterbein should ordain Newcomer, Joseph Hoffman, and Frederick Shaffer. On October 2, after a solemn period of worship and meditation, Otterbein, with the assistance of a Methodist elder, William Ryland, ordained the three men, the first to be ordained in the United Brethren Church.

The Last Years of Boehm and Ottebein

Although in advanced years when the Unted Brethren Church was founded in 1800, Martin Boehm was still very active and remained so until shortly before his death early in 1812. He continued his itinerant ministry, traveling and preaching in the company of Newcomer or Geeting or other brethren. In 1800 he made a journey on horseback into Virginia. During the years as bishop he served mostly in southern Pennsylvania east and west of the Susquehanna River. He attended all the conferences from 1800 until his death except those in 1806, 1808, 1810, and 1811.

Boehm's preaching was always simple but rich in spirituality and warmth of love. He centered much of it in the interpretation of the life and ministry of Jesus. Newcomer was much affected by his preaching and relates that many times at the communion services held during the great meetings Boehm was called on for the sermon.

Martin Boehm and the Methodists were on intimate terms. His name was on the membership list of the Methodist class which met in "Boehm's Chapel." His son Henry states that Martin Boehm "found great comfort in meeting with the brethren [of the Methodist class]." There was a later claim that Boehm came into full affiliation with the Methodists and relinquished his relationship with the United Brethren. It was based on a remark of Bishop Asbury's in the memorial sermon for Boehm. Henry Boehm's *Reminiscences* report that Asbury said it was late in life that Martin Boehm joined the Methodists. However, the statement is ambiguous and does not mean that Boehm surrendered his United Brethren relationships. Until his death the United Brethren cited him as one of their two bishops. For Boehm to be on intimate terms with the Methodists meeting in Boehm's Chapel and also to be a bishop in the new United Brethren Church caused no conflict in his spirit of fellowship.

On March 31, 1812, Asbury brought to a close a Methodist Conference held at Leesburg, Virginia. He informed his traveling companion, Henry Boehm, that he had a prompting to go at once to the Boehm homestead in Lancaster County, even though it meant canceling scheduled engagements and required a four-day journey. The two men set out but were still one day's journey away when the word reached them that Martin Boehm had died on March 23 after a six-day illness. On Sunday, April 5, Asbury preached a memorial sermon in Boehm's Chapel, paying Boehm great tribute and also commending Boehm's associates, Otterbein, Newcomer, and others for the work they accomplished among the Germans.[5] Boehm was buried beside the chapel.

Otterbein's active leadership in the conferences ended earlier than Boehm's. He last attended and presided in 1805. This has led to the claim that he severed his relations with the United Brethren at that time. Not so. He remained in constant contact with the United Brethren until his death in 1813. A copy of the conference minutes was sent to him annually for his criticisms and approval. Geeting's visit in June 1812 is an instance of this. Otterbein's absence from conference sessions after 1805 was due to his infirmities.

Arguments have been given that Otterbein never was a primary leader of the United Brethren Church, but rather a minister in full and exclusive relationship with the Reformed Church. Such arguments have been based on the following facts: he never renounced his status as a Reformed minister and a member of the synod; in his lifetime his congregation kept its Reformed connections even though they were tenuous; his theological views were in harmony with the Heidelberg catechism; his practice of holding prayer and inquiry meetings was traditional in many Reformed churches; his pietism was common, although not universal, in the Reformed Church; his last attendance at a meeting of the synod was in 1806, one year *after* his last attendance at a United Brethren conference. His name remained on the synod roll without his objection to the end of his life.

On the other hand, replies have been that Otterbein's evangelistic work surpassed the work of Reformed preachers; his leadership outside the Reformed Church from the Pipe Creek meetings on did not have the formal approval or direction of the Reformed Church; his acceptance of the office of bishop in the United Brethren Church indicated a break with the Reformed Church; criticism by such Reformed ministers as Nicholas Pomp alienated him; he criticized the Reformed ministers for spiritual blindness; his attendance at synod meetings in later life was very sporadic, as the last meetings he attended were in 1791, 1797, 1800, and 1806, and the reason he attended in 1806 was simply that it was held near his home in Baltimore.

These arguments are not convincing so far as they attempt to show that Otterbein held to one group to the exclusion of the other. If the question is asked, "Was Otterbein a minister of the Reformed Church until his death?" the answer is, "Yes," and if the question is asked, "Was Otterbein a formally chosen leader, a bishop, in the new United Brethren Church until his death?" the answer again is, "Yes." He was one who held high the office of Christian minister and interpreted it broadly enough so that it transcended denominational exclusiveness. In a day when ecumenicity was an unknown term, he was ecumenical. Even the last hours of his life and his funeral confirm this. On his deathbed he received the ministry of a Lutheran pastor, J. D. Kurtz, who also preached his funeral sermon. A Methodist minister, William Ryland, preached in English. The graveside ceremonies were conducted by an Episcopal rector,

George Dashields. It is a sad fact that word of his terminal illness and his death did not reach any of his United Brethren followers in time for them to arrive before his death and burial. Christian Newcomer, who had been ordained by Otterbein one month earlier, had gone to New Berlin, Pennsylvania, and other places to preach and did not receive the news of Otterbein's passing until November 24, seven days after the death occurred. Otterbein was buried in the churchyard of the Baltimore church.

On March 24, 1814, just two years before his own death, Francis Asbury conducted a service in memory of Otterbein during the session of the Methodist Baltimore Annual Conference. In his euology he said, "Forty years have I known the retiring modesty of this man of God: towering majestic above his fellows in learning, wisdom, and grace, yet seeking to be known only of God and the people of God."[6]

RELATIONS WITH THE METHODISTS

Relations between leaders of the early American Methodists and the United Brethren had been close and cordial ever since 1773 when Asbury urged Otterbein to accept the Baltimore pastorate. Genuine personal affection developed as leaders of both movements came more and more into close contact and engaged in coöperative efforts of evangelism.

One significant difference in spirit lay at the point of emphasizing conformity to an official church discipline and recognition of centralized authority. The Methodists were strict on these points; the United Brethren under Otterbein and Boehm were less so. In the Christmas Conference of 1784 the Methodists had adopted a discipline and a set of Articles of Faith, much of which Wesley had prescribed.[7] At Asbury's urging the United Brethren in their first conference of 1800 gave attention to this matter, and Otterbein himself made the motion that the Methodist *Discipline* be translated into German. When this was finished in 1808, it had little effect upon United Brethren action. The only disciplinary guide the early United Brethren used was the Baltimore Church Book of 1785.

At least one United Brethren leader did not favor this lack of formal denominational standards—Christian Newcomer. Already in 1803 Newcomer had indicated that he desired close union with the Methodists.[8] In March 1809 the Methodist Baltimore Annual

Conference requested Newcomer to carry to the United Brethren a statement of the Methodist desire for close union. In the proposal it was urged that the United Brethren adopt a formal discipline in order to make such union easier to attain. The United Brethren in the Conference of 1809 held aloof from the proposal, much to Newcomer's dismay. Indeed, he stated that this attitude almost led him to withdraw from the United Brethren.[9] As he criticized the action, he stated the main reason why it was taken: " . . . my brethren were of the opinion that [adopting a discipine and rules of order] was unnecessary; that the word of God [the Bible] was all-sufficient."

The Methodist communication of March 1809 was the first in an exchange of fourteen letters between the Methodist Baltimore and Philadelphia Annual Conferences and the United Brethren. The correspondence has been preserved.[10] Although all the letters stress the spirit of Christian love and fellowship between the two groups, the Methodist letters clearly state that no union can occur until the United Brethren adopt a formal discipline. Newcomer was so anxious for this to occur that by 1813 he had drawn up a discipline, hoping it could serve to bring about a union with the Methodists as well as a union with the Evangelical Association,[11] but it did not accomplish this purpose.

Therefore, in the last letter from the Methodists, dated March 22, 1814, an abrupt statement is given: " . . . we must keep in view the items specified in a former letter from this [the Baltimore] conference as terms of union [the adoption of a discipline by the United Brethren] . . . . [Since it has not occurred] we think it unnecessary to continue the ceremony of annual letters, etc." This brought to an end the efforts toward union.

The abrupt dismissal by the Methodists of the possibility of union may have been too hasty. Item 8 of the United Brethren conference minutes of May 5, 1813, states, "Resolved that the Confession of Faith and Evangelical Discipline of the United Brethren in Christ shall be printed." No information is given directly stating the origin of this confession and discipline, but it is believed that they were the work of Christopher Grosh and Christian Newcomer, respectively, because when they appeared in print in 1814, they bore the signatures of these men. The documents consist of one printed page of doctrine expressed in five articles and two and one-half pages of "Rules of the United Brethren in Christ."[12]

The Miami Annual Conference objected to this action of

adopting a confession and discipline in its meeting of August 23, 1814, with the statement, "The present order [or discipline] of the Church was taken under consideration and protested against," an action all the more surprising because Newcomer was presiding. Apparently the objection was based on the fact that the Eastern Annual Conference had taken the action and had expected the Miami Annual Conference to accept it even though it had not been consulted.

This conjecture is supported by the next item in the Miami Annual Conference minutes. It called for a conference to meet which would represent every district—a total of nine—of the church. It named the place where the delegates should assemble, Abraham Troxel's in Westmoreland County, Pennsylvania, and set the date for June 1815. Thus came the call for the first General Conference of the United Brethren Church.

THE FIRST GENERAL CONFERENCE

The first General Conference of the United Brethren Church was held from June 6 to 10, 1815. It met in a schoolhouse which had been erected in 1810 by a Mennonite, John Bonnet, on land owned by a United Brethren preacher, Abraham Troxel. It was commonly referred to as the Bonnet Schoolhouse. Both the Mennonites and the United Brethren used it for worship, sometimes holding services jointly. The location is one and one-half miles east of Mount Pleasant, Pennsylvania. The schoolhouse no longer stands, but its site is shown by a marker on the south side of the present State Route 31.

Fourteen delegates representing the nine districts were present. Christian Newcomer, who had been elected bishop by the eastern conference in 1813 and again in 1814, presided.

The minutes of the conference are very brief and reveal little of the action taken. Only one item is distinct, and that is that Newcomer received considerable negative criticism, probably because he had presided over the Eastern Annual Conference when the Confession of Faith and the Discipline were adopted without consulting the Miami Annual Conference. A paragraph also states that Bonnet, who was present as a guest, brought severe charges of untruthfulness against Newcomer. It is likely these were based on Bonnet's feeling that in his leadership before and during the conference Newcomer had betrayed the Mennonite spirit. However, after a day of strife over these matters, harmony was brought about through prayer.

The most important item in the minutes reads, "The Confession of Faith and the Discipline were considered, in some respects enlarged, some things omitted, on the whole improved, and ordered printed."

The best insight into the nature and accomplishments of the conference is gained by studying the Confession of Faith and the discipline, which comprise a relatively lengthy document. In A. W. Drury's *Disciplines* it requires fourteen printed pages. It is divided into three main parts: a historical statement, "The Confession of Faith of the United Brethren in Christ" in "Section First," and seven "Sections" dealing with definitions and rules.

The Confession of Faith is stated in seven brief paragraphs. The first four follow the order and statements of the Apostles' Creed, and are quite traditional except for the omission of reference to Mary as a virgin. The remaining three cite the Bible as the source of all Christian beliefs concerning man, his sinful nature, and the means of salvation, and state that "outward means of grace," baptism and the Lord's Supper, are to be observed "according to the command of the Lord Jesus; the mode and manner, however, shall be left to the judgment of everyone"—a statement that clearly indicates a compromise between delegates of Mennonite and Dunker background and those of Reformed. The final statement, "Also the example of feet-washing remains free to everyone," reflects the Dunker influence.

In the statement a very brief reference is made to a doctrine which had become very prominent in the Methodist Church and the Evangelical Association, namely sanctification. In the statement of faith of 1813 the matter was dealt with in part of a single sentence, ". . . we through [the Holy Ghost] must be sanctified and receive faith, thereby being cleansed from all filthiness of the flesh and spirit." In the Confession of Faith of 1815 the reference is even briefer, " . . . we are [through the Holy Ghost] enlightened; through faith justified and sanctified."

The sections dealing with definitions and rules can be summarized by the use of the headings: "Of the General and Annual Conferences"; "Of the Election and Ordination of a Bishop and His Office and Duty"; "Of the Presiding Elders: Their Election, Office, and Duty, and Ordination"; "Of the Method of Receiving Preachers, and Their Office and Duties"; "Of the Immoral Conduct of Preachers, and How They Are to Be Dealt With"; "Of Members in General."

Paramount in these definitions and rules is the clear implication of the structure of authority in the church. It rests ultimately in the local "society" and then is expressed upward through the local (unordained but licensed) preachers, the ordained elders, the presiding elders, and the bishops. The local societies or congregations send the itinerant local (unordained) preachers and the elders (ordained preachers) as their delegates to the Annual Conferences in which both the local preachers and the ordained elders have the privilege of voting. They have the responsibility of electing the presiding elders (district superintendents) and the delegates to the General Conferences. In turn these delegates at the General Conferences elect the bishop or bishops for a four year term, with succeeding terms of service depending upon reëlection.

It can be seen that the structure of authority bears resemblance to the national representative system, which doubtless served as model for the organization of the church.

A very important consequence of holding the first General Conference was that thenceforth it was the highest court of appeal or decision in the Church.

The General Conference of 1815 by recognizing the two existing Annual Conferences as of equal rank, thereby opened the denomination to further expansion as the Annual Conferences grew and as new Annual Conferences were formed.

It appears that the General Conference of 1815 also took action approving the publication of a denominational hymnbook. Prior to 1815 attention had been given to collections of German hymns to be used in worship services. The first was published in 1795, before the denomination was founded; the second was published by George Adam Geeting in 1807 by order of the Annual Conference of that year.[13]

Apparently the Miami Annual Conference did not have these publications for use. In 1814 it took action referring the approval of a collection of hymns to the General Conference. No record of the matter is found in the conference's actions, but apparently it was referred back to the Miami Annual Conference. The 1816 minutes of that Annual Conference list the "expenses and receipts" in the publication of the hymnbook. Thus a hymnbook was available for use throughout the entire church.

The General Conference of 1815 took action that General Conferences should meet thereafter every four years. It aso took action decreeing the election of bishops every four years. However, in 1815 no election of a bishop was held because in 1814 Newcomer had been elected by the Eastern Annual Conference to serve three years, running that term to 1817. To bring these two four-year actions into harmony the second General Conference was held in 1817. After that session and until the last United Brethren General Conference was held in 1945, preceding union with the Evangelical Church, all the General Conferences were held quadrennially without interruption.

he period from the first General Conference in 1815 until the adoption of a church constitution in 1841 is the time when the Church of the United Brethren in Christ took on clearly defined denominational form. This is seen in the consolidation of denominational structure, in numerical and geographical expansion, and in the religious life of the people.

THE CONFERENCES

The *Discipline* of 1815 in defining the governmental structure of the United Brethren Church provided for three categories of conferences, Quarterly, Annual, and General.

The Quarterly Conference represented the church at the local level. It centered in a local class or congregation or several classes or congregations located within a limited area, functioning as a unit, and being served by a minister. In order to deal with local issues the persons chosen for certain responsibilities in the local unit, together with the minister, were to meet four times each year under the direction of a presiding elder. The Quarterly Conference planned all local services and functions, including recommending young men for the ministry.

The Annual Conference was comprised of "all the elders and preachers who have received a written permission [license]." As the

THE CHURCH OF THE UNITED BRETHREN IN CHRIST, 1815–1841

designation indicates, the conference was held annually. The term Annual Conference also came to designate the geographical area from which the delegates came and the organization of which they were a part.

The sessions of the Annual Conference were to be presided over by a bishop, if one be present, or an elder chosen from among the elders who were in attendance. The Annual Conference had jurisdiction over the congregations and classes in matters involving their interrelationship and joint actions.

The General Conference represented and acted as the highest authority of the entire denomination. The *Discipline* of 1815 provided that it was to be comprised of two elders from each district in the several Annual Conferences. These elder-delegates were chosen by the local "societies," that is congregations or classes, from among the elders of the respective districts. The General Conference was to be held every four years.

The Ministry

The *Discipline* of 1815 provided rules for the filling of all ministerial categories: bishop, presiding elder, elder, and preacher.

The bishop was to be elected in the General Conference by majority vote of the elder-delegates from among their own number. His election was for a term of four years with the possibility of reëlection in subsequent General Conferences. In case the extent of duties demanded it, more than one bishop could be elected.

The duties of the bishop were largely administrative. He was to preside over the sessions of the General Conference and also over the sessions of the Annual Conferences, if he was able to attend. Along with two presiding elders of his own choosing he was to appoint "the traveling preachers to their various circuits." He was to appoint presiding elders and designate the districts in which they were to travel and preside over Quarterly Conferences. He was to "travel throughout the bounds of the various [annual] conferences, and to have in spiritual things the oversight of all the societies."

In the General Conference of 1817 two bishops were elected, Christian Newcomer and Andrew Zeller. Thereafter the sucession of bishops until 1841 was as follows: 1821–1825, Newcomer and Joseph Hoffman; 1825–1829, Newcomer and Henry Kumler, Sr.; 1829–1833, Newcomer (d. 1830) and Henry Kumler, Sr.; 1833–1837,

Henry Kumler, Sr., Samuel Hiestand, and William Brown; 1837–1841, Henry Kumler, Sr., Samuel Hiestand (d. 1838), and Jacob Erb.

In the *Discipline* of 1815 it was decreed that a ceremony of ordination by the laying on of hands be imposed upon the persons elected to the office of bishop. It is likely Newcomer was not made subject to this ceremony, probably because he had served as bishop two years before the rule was adopted. However, in the General Conferences of 1817 and 1821 Andrew Zeller and Joseph Hoffman were ordained to the bishopric.[1]

In the quadrennium of 1821–1825 the significance of the rite of ordination to the office of bishop came under examination. It was pointed out that by this time all elders in the church had been ordained in the line beginning with Otterbein's ordination of Christian Newcomer, Frederick Schaffer, and Joseph Hoffman in 1813. Since ordination conveys the full and indelible characteristics of the call to ministry, a second ordination could carry no meaning. Furthermore, a separate ordination to the office of bishop, if it conveyed distinctive significance, would grant to its recipient lifelong tenure in that office. This would stand in contradiction to the practice of electing a man to the office of bishop for only a four-year term at a time, with no guarantee that reëlection would take place.

In light of these considerations the General Conference of 1825 took the following action: "Resolved, that as a newly elected Bishop has already been consecrated and ordained as an elder, by the laying on of hands, a second laying on of hands is deemed unnecessary inasmuch as we find it not in the Scripture."

Of the two men who had been ordained to the office of bishop, Joseph Hoffman caused the church consternation. He was not reëlected in 1825 and for some years removed himself from the fellowship. However, he appeared at the General Conference of 1845 with a group of supporters and by virtue of ordination to the office of bishop in 1821, demanded recognition as a presiding officer of the conference. It was necessary for the conference to take special action repudiating his claim "on the ground that the church long since abrogated the ordination of Bishops as Presiding Officers."

Throughout the remainder of its existence as a distinct denomination the United Brethren Church recognized and practiced only one ordination, that to the rank of elder in the church. All forms of full ministerial service rested upon this one ordination.

The second category within the hierarchy of the ministry was that of presiding elder. The designation was used unofficially as early as 1812. In the minutes of the Eastern Annual Conference of that year the term "district" was used for an area within the conference bounds, and two "elders" were appointed to oversee it.[2] In the Eastern Annual Conference of 1814 the term was used again, with the further statement that Christian Hershey be elected "presiding elder" over it. In the same year the Miami Annual Conference named nine districts from which delegates should be selected to participate in the first General Conference. The nine districts comprised the entire church.

Thus the General Conference of 1815, accepting the divisions of territory called districts, decreed that the bishop, with the approval of the conference, should "elect" the elders who were to supervise the work in these districts.

The duties of the presiding elder included traveling "the district assigned him, and [preaching] as often as he can," having oversight of the traveling and local preachers on his district, calling quarterly and great meetings, administering the Lord's Supper, holding Quarterly Conferences, after consulting the bishops "[exchanging] the traveling ministers on his district," giving a financial report periodically to the bishop, and distributing money among the preachers—eighty dollars per year to a single man and twice that amount to a married man.

The elder was a man who had served at least two years as a preacher on probation and then, having been found worthy, been ordained by the bishop assisted by at least one presiding elder. The elder's duties were to preach, baptize, solemnize marriages, assist the presiding elder in administering the Lord's Supper, conduct public divine worship, hold class meetings, and "help in the election of leaders." He was to take offerings for the traveling preachers and the poor.

The preacher was one who served under the approval of the Annual Conference, looking forward to ordination and reception as a member into the Annual Conference after probation. He was to respond correctly to a series of questions which tested his Christian beliefs and manner of life. He was to preach the Christian message, to guide souls toward Christian commitment, and to engage in pastoral duties, especially in visiting the sick.

The distinctions drawn among the four categories of the

ministry did not nullify the fundamental fact that all ministers had one common duty and purpose. It was to declare and make effective the message of the church, which is the Christian gospel. This was what imposed unity among the preachers. It was regarded as the foundation on which the church structure rested. Therefore, the interrelations among the categories of ministry were judged to be unifying and essential.

This form of organization and structure, worked out in the General Conference of 1815, was given the name "the itinerant plan" because every minister, whatever his rank, agreed to be adaptable to the form of service to which he was appointed or elected, and literally to travel to and within the area where his service was to be given.

Thus the structure of ministry in the United Brethren Church was itinerancy. The General Conference of 1815 decreed that no authority within the church, not even the General Conference, may take any action "which shall abolish or do away with the itinerant plan." Throughout the history of the United Brethren Church this decree was never modified.

GROWTH AND EXPANSION

It is possible to trace with accuracy the territorial expansion but not the numerical growth of the United Brethren Church from 1815 to 1841 because the action taken in the conference of 1802 against keeping numerical rolls still held. Numerical records of church membership were not kept in the first five decades of United Brethren history. The first accurate numbering was made in 1857.

Nevertheless, estimates have been made of membership in the years beginning in 1810. At that time it is estimated that there were ten thousand members. A general decline in membership in American churches following the crest of the Second Awakening was felt in the United Brethren Church, so that the estimate for 1820 is only nine thousand. Then a decided upswing occurred bringing the estimated membership to twenty thousand by 1835. By 1841 the membership was probably about twenty-five thousand.[3]

The territorial expansion of the church moved from the area of the "Old" or Eastern Annual Conference through southwestern Pennsylvania into the new states and territories west of the Appalachians.

At the time of the General Conference of 1815, two Annual Conferences constituted the church: the Eastern and the Miami. Division and realignments brought the total of Annual Conferences to nine by 1841. They were (1) the Hagerstown (or Virginia), embracing the Maryland counties of Allegany and Washington and the Shenandoah Valley; (2) the Harrisburg (or Pennsylvania), embracing all church area in Pennsylvania east of the eastern slope of the Allegheny Mountains, and Frederick County and Baltimore, Maryland; (3) the Allegheny, embracing all church territory from the crest of the Alleghenies to the Ohio–Pennsylvania state line; (4) the Muskingum, largely in the Muskingum Valley, Ohio, and north to Lake Erie; (5) the Scioto, in south central Ohio; (6) the Miami in southwestern Ohio and northern Kentucky; (7) the Sandusky in northwestern Ohio; (8) the Indiana in the eastern part of Indiana; and (9) the Wabash in western Indiana and eastern Illinois.

The division of the Eastern Annual Conference into the Pennsylvania and Virginia Annual Conferences in 1831 and a later (1846) division of the Pennsylvania Conference into Pennsylvania and East Pennsylvania Annual Conferences, provoked a dispute among the three as to which one could claim to be the first or original Annual Conference, all three resting their cases on the fact that part of the Old or Eastern Conference lay within their areas. The issue was never resolved to everyone's satisfaction.

LIFE IN THE CHURCH

The United Brethren Church had its religious and doctrinal roots in pietism and, through Otterbein, in modified Calvinism. The former was influential because in the evangelistic efforts of the ministers the claim for certainty of salvation was based upon the inner experience of conversion and the continuing work of the Holy Spirit in the heart. As the early preachers, most of whom had minimal schooling, engaged in preaching, they gave testimony to their own religious experience.

In preparation for preaching or when challenged by critics, as William Nauman points out, the preachers affirmed three bases for the validity of their experiential claims: the Bible, common sense, and the good works which result from Christian experience.[4]

The Bible was carried by all the preachers. It was a bottomless well of inspired and infallible truth, testifying to the ways God deals with his people. Proof texts were always available to support testimony.

Common sense was simply the use of good, calm judgment based upon experience in general and what is learned through observation of the natural world which God created. As the great number of the German people in America lived close to the soil, they found it good. Nature declares God's power, goodness, and righteousness.

The fact that good works spring up wherever the Holy Spirit is in the heart supports the claims of the Christian faith. Good fruits prove validity. Good works are of the nature of charitable deeds and moral rectitude.

With this confidence the United Brethren (as well as the Evangelicals) were prepared for whatever joys or sorrows the demands of their ministry would bring. However, they were painfully aware that three theological claims which stood in contrast to their own views were being promulgated by the Deists, the Universalists, and the strict Calvinists. It was necessary to respond to each. First, the Deists and the atheists denied the existence of an intimate God. The pietistic experience of the Holy Spirit in the heart answered them. Second, the Universalists claimed that the same destiny of eternal salvation is guaranteed to all men. The answer to them was that all men are sinful and only those who repent and call upon the mercy of God as revealed in Christ will be saved. Third, the Calvinists' doctrine of God's unconditional predestination of "the elect" for salvation and the "non-elect" for damnation was answered by the assertion that "whosoever will" can be saved and whosoever willfully rejects God's free gift of salvation to all men will be lost.

The doctrinal assertions of the preachers had their counterpart in the acceptance of the same gospel by the lay people. This was spelled out in Section Eight of the *Discipline* of 1815. The doctrinal certitude of ministers and lay people alike led to the problem of what should be done about members who violated the moral standards implied in the doctrinal beliefs. The General Conference of 1815 made provision for this. Warnings should be given to offenders, and if these be not heeded, expulsion from the fellowship would follow. Since moral standards were held high, there were offenders who had to be dealt with. In the early years these were rare, but they increased in number as the membership grew.

One very suprising case was that of John Hildt. He had been

prominent in the early history: a lay (class) leader under Otterbein in the Baltimore church; a minister in the Eastern Annual Conference beginning in 1817 and secretary of that conference; a delegate in the General Conferences of 1825 and 1829; compiler, translator, editor, and publisher of Newcomer's *Journal*; and church pioneer in Ohio. Nevertheless the Muskingum Annual Conference in 1838 took the following action: "Resolved, that John Hildt be expelled from this Conference for unchristian conduct, and disrespectful behavior."

In 1831 the Virginia Annual Conference "agreed after due deliberation . . . that Reverend Conrad Weast should quit selling liquor, and preach more than he has been doing; if not, his license shall be demanded and be member of the United Brethren in Christ no longer."

The worship life in the church continued much as it had been in the first fifteen years of denominational history. Services were held most often in the homes in which the traveling ministers visited, with the neighbors invited to attend. It frequently happened that after a group of committed Christians became established a meeting house was built. The brethren still held great meetings and camp meetings with preachers and people of other churches participating, especially the Evangelicals and the Methodists. Baptism was practiced with the mode and form left to the discretion of the persons involved. Occasionally the rite of footwashing was practiced, due to the influence of a number of Dunkers who were affiliated. Caution was expressed in the *Discipline* of 1825 warning against extreme emphasis on insisting on this rite, "It is not becoming any of our preachers to traduce any of his brethren where judgment and understanding in this respect are different from his own."

The German language was used almost exclusively by all the preachers at the beginning of United Brethren history, although a few, like Newcomer, occasionally preached in English. Nevertheless quite early a change began to take place. The General Conference of 1817, after revising the *Discipline*, ordered that the original be printed in German and a translation into English also be published. One hundred English copies were made. In the 1820's General and Annual Conferences had two secretaries, one German and one English. By 1837 the English language had become predominant. The General Conference of that year was conducted in English. It ordered the *Discipline* to be printed primarily in English and then in

German. Six thousand copies of the English *Discipline* were made and two thousand of the German translation.

By the middle of the nineteenth century the English language was used in every area of the church's life except in three new Annual Conferences in Pennsylvania, Ohio, and Indiana. These conferences gradually declined in membership and finally were absorbed into the English conferences in their areas. The Ohio German Annual Conference was the last to exist. It was discontinued in 1930.

Education of children in religious and general learning subjects was a practice in the United Brethren Church from its beginning. Schools supported by congregations were opened at several places. Otterbein was a strong supporter of the church-supported as well as the "Charity" or nonchurch schools.

Geeting was a teacher by profession and opened a school on his farm near Antietam, Maryland. Pfrimmer did the same in his home north of Harrisburg and again when he moved into southwestern Pennsylvania and into southeastern Indiana.

The basic purpose of instruction in the church schools was to enable children to gain understanding of the Christian faith. Teaching them to read was to enable them to read the Bible and other religious materials. The *Discipline* of 1817 required the preachers to "gather [the children] as often as practicable and profitable; converse with, instruct and exhort them in and to that which is good . . . that they may learn to know their Creator and Redeemer in their youth." Subsequent *Disciplines* repeated this requirement with modifications making the item more explicit and earnest.

Although in the first two decades of United Brethren history there were no explicit educational standards for men entering the ministry, references were made to the excellence of Otterbein's theological and biblical proficiency which stood as an example for others to attain by Bible study and reading.

In order to provide materials for study and inspiration the church established the first printing press in 1834, printing and distributing the denominational periodical, the *Religious Telescope*. In 1841 the General Conference instructed the publishing agent, William Hanby, to prepare a list of books for ministerial study. He recommended a total of seventeen books, including the Bible. The other books ranged through biblical studies, English grammar, elocution, church history, histories of Rome and England, philosophy, chemistry and psychology.[5]

MINISTERIAL SALARIES

The financial support of ministers was not a serious matter at the beginning of the church's history. The outstanding leaders—Otterbein, Boehm, Geeting, and Newcomer—all had support either from inheritance, as with Otterbein, or productive farms. However, apparently a few of the early brethren were not as fortunate. They appealed for help but got no response. An item in the minutes of 1802 reads, "A proposal was made relating to the collecting of a sum of money for poor preachers. Nothing, however, was done." In 1807 positive action was taken. The conference decreed that "as a rule . . . a married preacher shall receive per year forty pounds, and a single preacher twenty-four pounds." In 1812 the amount was given in American currency, "A single preacher shall yearly receive eighty dollars and a married preacher one hundred and sixty dollars and also expenses." The money was to be collected by the preachers as they traveled or in the congregations they served.

This system did not work well. On only a few occasions was sufficient money raised. Therefore, the Eastern Annual Conference organized a Benevolent Society in 1821, and charged it with raising money for the "support of the traveling, aged or worn-out preachers."[6] In 1829 the Benevolent Society of the Eastern Annual Conference was united with a similar society which had been started in the Scioto Annual Conference in 1826 to form a denominational Benevolent Society.

The work of the Benevolent Society was not very successful. The funds were to be raised by charging membership fees or through direct gifts to the fund. Not all the gifts reached the Society because some of the ministers regarded the gifts as presented to them personally, and so kept them. After several futile attempts to reorder its organization and methods of collecting funds, the Benevolent Society was dissolved in 1853.

SOCIAL ISSUES

Temperance

The use of alcoholic beverages, including distilled liquor, was common among the German people, including the early preachers.

On the property of Peter Kemp, where the first Annual Conference was held in 1800, was a still run by the Kemp family. Indeed, some of the early brethren took grain there to be distilled.[7]

Nevertheless, opposition developed quite early against the use of "ardent spirits." In the *Discipline* of 1814 Article 11 states, "Every member shall abstain from strong drink, and use it only on necessity as medicine."[8] In the *Discipline* of 1839 it was stated that "Should any Exhorter, Preacher, or elder . . . be engaged in the distillation or vending of ardent spirits," and continue after a proper procedure of admonition and warning, he shall "for the time not be considered a member of this church."[9] This action was made broader in 1841 by including laymen in the prohibition.

Sabbath Observance

The *Discipline* of 1814 ruled that "Every Member shall abstain from ordinary occupations on Sunday, buying or selling, but spend time in devotion, in singing spiritual songs to the [honor] and glory of God."[10] All subsequent *Disciplines* repeated this rule.

Taking Oaths

The influence of members in the United Brethren ministry who had been Mennonite and Dunker caused the feeling that the swearing of oaths in legal procedures should not be practiced, since Jesus had said, "Swear not at all." A statement in the *Discipline* of 1833 held that "the mode of testifying to the Truth, when thereto required to do so in a legal form *by way of affirmation* [italics added] is on us solemnly, conscienciously [sic] and fully binding before God and man to tell the truth, the whole truth and nothing but the truth."[11] This did not absolutely rule out the swearing of oaths by any or all members of the church. This rule was continued with only minor verbal changes throughout United Brethren history.

SLAVERY

While slavery, as it developed in America following the invention of the cotton gin in 1793, became an established institution and affected every area of life, including the religious, it did not have profound effect upon the early United Brethren Church.

Very few United Brethren people owned slaves. Only two cases of slave ownership among the United Brethren are known, those of Christian Newcomer and John George Pfrimmer, and they may have been benign efforts to give freedom to the three slaves involved.

In the General Conference of 1821 the United Brethren took the following action:

> Resolved that in no sense of the word shall slavery in whatsoever form it may exist, be tolerated in our church, and that no slaveholder, making application for membership, shall be received, and that if any member be found to possess slaves, he cannot remain a member, unless he manumit his slaves as soon as notified to do so by the annual coءference; that no member shall have the privilege of selling any of his slaves; that it shall be in the power of the annual conference to say whether a slave holder as a member of our church shall have the privilege of hiring out any of his slaves and for how long a time; but in no case shall the annual conference have the power of granting to any slaveholder the privilege of hiring out or holding any of his slaves for any longer time than until such slave shall by his labor have remunerated his master for raising or purchasing him.

The United Brethren Church never retreated from this position.

Nevertheless the slave question led to a bitter struggle in the church, not between anti-slavery and pro-slavery members, but between extreme anti-slavery people or abolitionists and anti-slavery people who hoped to have the national issue eventually settled amicably.

The struggle was caused by the abolitionist position which William Rhinehart, editor of the *Religious Telescope*, took and expressed in editorials. He demanded that slaves be given their freedom at once. This brought a protest from members of the church in Virginia. The state of Virginia had adopted laws prohibiting manumission of slaves and forbidding the printing and dissemination of abolitionist materials. Rhinehart replied in editorials directly attacking these Virginia laws with scathing comments on "The Gag Law of Virginia."

Serious attempts were made to end the bitter controversy by ordering the *Religious Telescope* to close its columns to the discussion of slavery. Rhinehart proposed a compromise. The discussion should continue but writers, including himself, should refrain from using hard expressions in contradicting other points of view.

This suggestion was approved by the trustees of the *Religious Telescope*, but objections to this "gag rule" were raised. Rhinehart resumed his extreme position and finally in 1839 under pressure resigned his editorship.

The General Conference of 1841 decreed that the *Religious Telescope* should forbid any further controversy on slavery but supported the printing of factual news items on the subject. In 1845 the General Conference relaxed this action by allowing the *Religious Telescope* to publish various views but directed the editor, David Edwards, to keep the debate under control.

Secret Societies

Society in America by the third decade of the nineteenth century seemed to be dividing between the rich, aristocratic class and the common working class. In the tensions arising between the two the Masonic Order came under severe criticism as the representative of the affluent class. It semed to embody everything the common people feared. Because of its restricted membership and secret oath it was judged to be anti-democratic and potentially oppressive. Reports were circulated claiming that opponents of the Masons were assassinated. Many religious people came to repudiate the Order because they believed that secret society oaths violated the Christian principle of speaking openly and affirmatively. Therefore in both religious and political circles a strong anti-Masonic spirit prevailed.

The first action of the United Brethren Church concerning the Masons was taken by the Miami Annual Conference in 1826. Its minutes, stating that several members belonged to the Masons, urged them to withdraw from that order and forbade any other members to join. In 1827 the Eastern Annual Conference took action disapproving membership in the Order and decreeing that, if in the future any church members joined it, "they thereby lock themselves out of the conference and the church."

The issue came to a climax in the General Conference of 1829 which passed a resolution stating:

. . . in no way or manner nor in any sense of the word, shall Free Masonry be approved or tolerated in our church; and that should any of our church members, who may now be a Free Mason, continue to attend their lodges, or as a Free Mason attend and take part in their processions; or if he joins the Free Masons, such member, by such an act excludes himself from membership in our church.

The General Conference of 1833 inserted a condensed statement of this action into the *Discipline*. In the General Conference of 1841 a similar statement was inserted as Section Twenty-fifth, and a briefer, more inclusive statement in the new constitution, which was Section Second, Article II, part of paragraph 7: "There shall be no connection with secret combinations," thereby making the prohibition to apply to all secret orders. This issue was destined to have dire consequences in later years.

PUBLICATIONS

The need for certain printed materials began in the first decade of United Brethren history.[12] In 1808 George Adam Geeting published a German hymnbook. In the years following other hymnbooks were published.

Beginning in 1815 the *Disciplines* were printed. The *Discipline* of 1817 was first printed in German, and two years later a revision was printed in German and English. Thereafter, the *Disciplines* were printed in both languages.

In 1834 Newcomer's *Journal* was published. John Hildt, a lay leader in Otterbein's church in Baltimore and after 1829 a traveling preacher in the Muskingum Annual Conference, visited Newcomer on December 16, 1829. The two men began to collate the many fragmented pages of Newcomer's diary which he had begun to keep in 1795. After Newcomer died in 1830 Hildt continued to work at the task for four years. He first had to arrange the German script into proper sequence. Then he translated it into English and edited it. He occasionally omitted what he judged to be irrelevant material and rewrote obscure items.

The work of Hildt, although subject to criticism because of some of his editing, was one of the greatest services ever rendered to the study of United Brethren history. Unfortunately, after the *Journal* was published, Newcomer's German manuscript, the German collation, and the original English translation were lost. In 1964 after patient searching the Rev. D. Homer Kendall found that at least eighty-two copies of Hildt's publication of the *Journal* are extant.[13]

To meet the need in the church for periodical materials the Miami Annual Conference published *Zion's Advocate* from 1829 to 1831.

All the above publications were printed on commerical presses.

Early in 1834 William Rhinehart (1800–1861), a minister in the Virginia Annual Conference, printed the *Union Messenger* on a press which he owned. In the meantime a movement was underway to establish a denominational publishing house. This culminated in the location of a "Printing Establishment" under the direction of the Scioto Annual Conference in Circleville, Ohio. It began operating in May 1834. William Rhinehart was called from Virginia to assume direction of the press and to publish a denominational periodical. Rhinehart responded, bringing with him some of his printing equipment as well as his list of subscribers to the *Union Messenger*. The work began at once, and the first issue of the denominational periodical *Religious Telescope* was published on December 31, 1834.

The *Religious Telescope* began as a biweekly publication with 1,197 subscribers. Its subscription price was $1.50 per year. It was a struggle for a number of years to collect the money from subscribers. From the beginning it was printed in English. It continued with certain modifications but without interruption until 1946 when, at the time of the union of the United Brethren and the Evangelical Churches, it was combined with the *Evangelical Messenger* to form the *Telescope-Messenger*.

A protest from members still using the German language led to the publishing of a German periodical in Baltimore by the Rev. (later Bishop) John Russell, beginning in 1840. It was called *Die Geschäftige Martha (The Busy Martha)*.

Other materials flowed from the United Brethren Publishing House. In 1840 the need was felt for the publication of a history of the denomination. The assignment of the work was given to Henry G. Spayth (1788–1873), who had joined the United Brethren ministers in 1812 and had served in several capacities, especially as secretary at Annual and General Conferences, and as compiler and editor of United Brethren *Disciplines*. By 1850 he had completed the *History of the Church of the United Brethren in Christ* up to 1825. It is a wealth of information of early denominational history. In 1850 William B. Hanby added a supplement, or Part II, bringing the history up to 1850. The combined work was published in 1851.

INTERDENOMINATIONAL RELATIONS

The cordiality which had been expressed between the United Brethren and the Methodists and Evangelicals in earlier years continued through exchanges of fraternal delegates in conferences, associations in great meetings, and sharing in preaching services.

In 1829 the General Conference received a communication from leaders who were in the process of forming a new denomination to be called the Methodist Protestant Church, proposing a union of the two churches. The General Conference gave considerable attention to it and then replied expressing deep, brotherly affection to the Methodist Protestant Church and appreciation for its proposal. However, the proposal was declined with the following reasons: the General Conference was not prepared to make such a decision because the proposal had come too late for preliminary study; there was no rubric in the Discipline dealing with church union; and "in a case of such importance we do not consider prudent to act without special instructions from our constituents upon the subject."[14]

This rejection of the proposal of union, while couched in proper terms, may seem to have the ring of unreality about it. The fact that it was dismissed so summarily has led to speculation that there were more serious reasons behind the decision. First, the encouraging development in growth and expansion of the denomination led to the feeling that the United Brethren would gain no advantage by the union.[15] Second, because the Methodist Protestants had not adopted resolutions ruling out slavery and membership in secret societies, the United Brethren would not consider favorably the proposal of union.[16]

A CONSTITUTION FOR THE CHURCH

In the Disciplines, as they were issued after each General Conference, there were a historical statement, a Confession of Faith, and thereafter a number of sections defining the several levels of conferences, the several levels of the ministry with their respective duties, the membership in general, specific definitions and rules dealing with slavery, the taking of oaths, alcoholic beverages, forms and ceremonies, and lastly, several doctrinal articles.

Leading up to the General Conference of 1837 there was agitation to abstract the rules of procedure and authority from the different sections of the *Discipline* and combine them into a "constitution" to be placed in the *Discipline* immediately after the Confession of Faith. William Rhinehart, editor of the *Religious Telescope*, set himself to the task of drawing up the constitution.

Rhinehart presented the constitution to the General Conference of 1837. It is obvious that he was influenced by the U.S. Constitution because the introductory statement begins, "We as members of the Church of the UNITED BRETHREN IN CHRIST, in order to retain a *perfect union,* . . . ."

Two new items were inserted. First, a *pro rata* selection of delegates to General Conference was set, providing for one delegate for each five hundred church members in the several Annual Conferences, instead of electing delegates by districts.

The second was Section II, Article IV, stating that the constitution could be amended "by a vote of two thirds of" the General Conference. Formerly the *Discipline* could be changed at every point by majority vote of the General Conference.

This constitution was approved and adopted.

In the quadrennium following, serious questions about the constitution were raised throughout the church and objections made to some of its items. Its author William Rhinehart had become embroiled in several controversies through articles which he and others wrote for the *Religious Telescope*, which he edited. Bitter opposition developed against him, forcing him to resign his editorship in 1839. This unhappy state of affairs was reflected thereafter in the tendency of the church to ignore completely the constitution of 1837 which he had written, as though it had never been adopted.

Therefore, when the General Conference of 1841 convened, it appointed a committee to form a constitution. After one day's work the constitution of 1841 was presented and adopted. It was inserted in the *Discipline* as Section Second.

This constitution differed from the constitution of 1837 at three points. First, the *pro rata* system for determining the number of delegates to General Conference was omitted. Second, while the former rule against Freemasonry was repeated as an item in the latter part of the *Discipline*, a rule was also inserted in the constitution excluding membership in any "secret combination." Third, Article IV of the constitution read, "There shall be no alteration of the foregoing constitution, unless by request of two-thirds of the whole society."

Article IV was to be the center of controversy of interpretation for years to follow, and finally it was one of four issues which brought about the division of the church in 1889. The main problem was to interpret the phrase "*request* of two-thirds of the *whole society*" (italics added). In the German translation the word request was rendered *stimmenzahl*. This clearly means "vote," but it was the original English form and not the German translation which was valid.

Another provision of the constitution of 1841 also harbored future difficulties. It is, "No rule or ordinance shall at anytime be passed, to change or do away with the Confession of Faith as it now stands; nor to destroy the itinerant plan." How could this harmonize with Article IV which appears to provide for change?

In spite of these problems the church operated under this constitution for forty-eight years.

Conclusion

It is obvious that the United Brethren Church from 1815 to 1841 was faced with two purposes. The first was to continue the ministry of evangelism together with pastoral and other functions of ministry. This required commitment and dedication to the divine call and to human spiritual needs. The second was the necessity to develop orderliness and regularity through denominational organization so that gains be preserved and coördinated future efforts be made. Bringing these two into proper relationship was not easy.

*T*he first conference sessions of the Evangelical Association had been held at the call of Jacob Albright in 1803 and 1806. Beginning in 1807 and without interruption thereafter except in 1808, regularly scheduled conference sessions were held annually. They were attended by all the preachers of the church who were of three classifications: ordained elders, ordained deacons, and ministers on trial.

THE MINISTRY

In early records no explanation is found giving the distinctions among these ministerial classifications. However, since the three classifications are mentioned for the first time in the Annual Conference minutes of 1810, one year after the Evangelical brethren had adopted a *Discipline* based on the Methodist *Discipline*, it is likely the distinctions and the ordination ceremonies were derived directly from it.

From the beginning of Dreisbach's ministry to the German people in 1807 he carried the Methodist *Discipline* of 1805 which defined the minister on trial as one who had received the first license to preach. After several years of proving his worth, the minister would be voted by the Annual Conference to be ordained to the rank of deacon. The deacon's duties were described as: "1. To baptize and

THE EVANGELICAL ASSOCIATION, 1816–1840

perform the office of matrimony in the absence of the elder. 2. To assist the elder in administering the Lord's Supper. 3. To do all the duties of a traveling preacher." After at least two years as deacon he was ordained to the eldership, which conveyed upon him the responsibility of performing all forms of ministerial service.

This ministerial structure prescribed two forms of ordination, to the diaconate and to the eldership. The forms were quite similar, each depending upon the candidate's record of worthy character and service and a satisfactory test of his religious beliefs and convictions. Both ordinations were "by the laying on of hands."

The first ordinations to the eldership, following the death of Albright, were of George Miller, John Walter, and John Dreisbach in 1810 by the decision of the conferences of 1807 and 1809. All subsequent ordinations were in the line beginning with these three men.

The first reference to the office of deacon is found in the minutes of the Annual Conference of 1810, "The following were the preachers . . . [who were] received into full connection and ordained (to the office of) deacon, J. Erb and M. Betz." [1]

In many of the conference minutes the title "local preacher" is found. This title was given to any preacher within the three classifications who because of age, ill health, or family responsibilities, gave up the traveling ministry but thereafter gave his services o classes or congregations near his home. Thus he was said to "locate." He still attended the conferences and maintained the ministerial standing he had achieved. The church depended heavily upon these local preachers for service and stability. In the conference of 1820 there were thirty-two itinerant ministers (elders, deacons, ministers on trial) and fifty local preachers.[2]

The *Discipline* of 1817 clearly provided for the election of a bishop. However, from the time of the death of the first bishop, Jacob Albright, in May 1808, after he had served in that office for only one-half year, no one was elected bishop until 1839. This stands as an odd fact because all the *Disciplines* contained a description of the office and duties of the bishop and, until 1830, provided a ritual for his ordination.

After his election as presiding elder in 1814, John Dreisbach served in all respects, except in name, as bishop. Had his health permitted, he might have been advanced to that office.[3]

The practice of relying upon presiding elders for primary

leadership continued until 1839. By that time the expansion of the church and the fact that there were nine presiding elders with no one of them officially preeminent led to the decision to elect a bishop. Therefore the General Conference of 1839 elected John Seybert as the second bishop in Evangelical history.

THE ANNUAL CONFERENCE

Until 1827 there was but one Annual Conference. It embraced the entire church. Although all ministers, whatever their classification, were expected to be in attendance at its sessions, the vote on issues before the conference was restricted to the ordained elders, both active and retired.[4]

By 1816 the Annual Conference had expanded westward through western Pennsylvania into Ohio and northward into New York. From early years it also included the extension into Maryland and the Shenandoah Valley of Virginia. The conference was divided into circuits, which were modified from time to time.

With the expansion of the church it became necessary to group the circuits into two districts with a presiding elder as superintendent over each. This occurred in 1815 when Henry Niebel was elected as a second presiding elder to serve in that capacity with his brother-in-law, John Dreisbach. To define their respective geographical areas of superintendency the circuits were grouped into two districts—the Canaan District and the Salem District. Dreisbach supervised the former. It included the Franklin, York, Lancaster, and Schuykill Circuits. This constituted all the work in the southern part of the church, including Maryland and Virginia. The Salem District, supervised by Niebel, included Union, Centre, and Somerset Circuits—the northern and western part of the church. Within one year the work in New York (the Lake Mission) became a part of the Canaan District, and the new work in Ohio (the Canton and Scioto Missions) became part of the Salem District. Adjustments were made in these areas at different times. The presiding elders attempted to visit every appointment in their districts four times each year.

By 1827 the work in Ohio had so developed that it seemed expedient to form a separate Annual Conference. In 1828 a third presiding elder was chosen to give it supervision. With the organization of the new conference in Ohio, called the Western Conference, the old conference was called the Eastern Conference. For a number of years the Western Conference was held subordinate to the Eastern. It was required to meet at least three weeks prior to the Eastern Conference's annual session so that it could submit its minutes for endorsement and inclusion in the minutes of the Eastern Conference. It also had to submit a financial accounting to the Eastern Conference.

In turn the Eastern Conference guaranteed that a sufficient number of preachers would be supplied as needed to fill the Western Conference appointments and that all Western Conference preachers would share in the regular and subsidiary salary payments.

This arrangement continued with some modifications until 1839 when all dependence was ended because the growth of the Western Annual Conference had made it self-sufficient.

In 1839 the Eastern Conference divided into two Annual Conferences, the East Pennsylvania and the West Pennsylvania. The conference hitherto called Western was renamed the Ohio Annual Conference. Throughout the whole church there were nine districts.

The Annual Conferences expanded their territories beyond their earlier bounds to include missions in Waterloo and Black Creek, Canada; New York City; Dansville and Buffalo, New York; and westward through Indiana to Wheeling (near Chicago) and Mt. Carmel, Illinois. In 1836 and 1837 bands of Evangelical Association members from Warren, Pennsylvania, moved to Des Plaines, Naperville, and Moline, Illinois, and formed classes in each place. Among those who settled at Des Plaines was the Esher family whose son, J. J. Esher (1828–1901) was to become a very influential bishop in the second half of the century.

In 1817 the membership of the Evangelical Association was set at 1,493. By 1820 it had reached 1,992, but then a decline set in so that by 1823 it was 1,854. Apparently there were tensions among the brethren, reflected in Dreisbach's nervous disorder and decline in health in 1820–1821. Apathy seemed to descend especially in the area east of the Susquehanna River. This was reversed by a revival which began in Orwigsburg, Pennsylvania, in 1823 and spread throughout the area. Steady growth occurred thereafter so that by 1839 the total membership was 7,859.[5] Of this number 3,653 were in the Ohio Annual Conference.[6]

THE GENERAL CONFERENCES TO 1839

During the period from 1816 to 1839 General Conferences were held seven or eight times. The early *Discipline* did not require that

General Conferences should be held at regular intervals. The first General Conference in 1816 was held because there were matters of special importance which, it was judged, could be dealt with only by a select group of experienced elders. Twelve of these were chosen by the Annual Conference of June 1816 to convene later in October as a General Conference.

The second General Conference in 1820 was held jointly with the Annual Conference, with all ordained elders as voting members. At least twice thereafter the Annual and General Conferences were held jointly, but the record is not always clear. In 1827 the minutes state that the session was a joint meeting of the Annual and General Conferences, but a note was appended by W. W. Orwig, a prominent elder, which said, "This was not intended to be a General Conference."[7] However, accepting this as a General Conference, General Conferences were held in 1816, 1820, 1826, 1827, 1830, 1835, 1836, and 1839, with those of 1820, 1826, and 1827 held jointly with the Annual Conference.

MINISTERIAL SALARIES

Financial support for traveling preachers was a serious problem. A few of the preachers had independent sources of support. Albright owned a farm and a tile-making business. Dreisbach owned a farm which he rented to tenants. Most of the others lived on the level of abject poverty. Attempts were made in the early years to raise funds to pay salaries. In 1804 the annual salary paid was $15.30. In 1816 one preacher received the princely sum of $92.48.[8] In 1820 each preacher received $36.30 plus traveling expenses.[9]

After several tentative but unsuccessful plans were made to improve the situation the General Conference of 1835 approved the organization of a "Charitable Society" "for the purpose of creating and establishing a fund for the relief of itinerant superannuated ministers, their wives, and children, widows and orphans of the Evangelical Association." The society was formed with nine trustees, all Pennsylvania citizens. It was incorporated in Pennsylvania by act of the General Assembly and given the title, "The Charitable Society of the Evangelical Association." Its center was in Orwigsburg, Pennsylvania.

The Charitable Society got off to a good start by receiving two substantial gifts: $4,312 from John Seybert, a sum he had quietly collected over several years, and $3,150 from Sister Kugler of Adams County. Other substantial gifts came in, sometimes in the form of farm produce.

The giving to the "Charity Fund" apparently stimulated gifts given for direct support of the traveling ministers. In 1841 for the first time the East Pennsylvania Annual Conference was able to pay its itinerant preachers the sum which had been specified several years earlier—$60 for an unmarried preacher and $105 for a married preacher plus traveling expenses and $15 for each child under fourteen.[10]

Some of the traveling preachers did not have homes of their own. John Seybert, serving as presiding elder in the East Pennsylvania Annual Conference in the early 1830's, arranged to have several parsonages built in his, the Salem, district.[11] This prompted a resolution in his conference in 1838 "that upon each charge a parsonage shall be erected, if practicable."

MORAL STANDARDS

The combination of the pietistic spirit and the emphasis upon the doctrine of sanctification led the Evangelical brethren to set rigid standards of moral conduct for the ministers. At every Annual Conference each preacher was subjected to a careful examination of his life and conduct. If accusations were made against him, he would either have to justify himself or be severely censored or dismissed. Dismissals were all too frequent. In 1832 ten preachers were dismissed—"three for not preaching, three for unchristian conduct, one for . . . tolerating unchristian behavior in his family, one for unpeaceful conduct towards his relatives and one because of inefficiency; also one itinerant for dishonest transaction."[12] Charges were made at different times against erring brethren, leading to dismissals for "gross offenses," "immoral conduct," "distilling brandy," "uncharitable expressions against our disciplinary management," "promulgat[ing] doctrines contrary to the word of God," and "unmerciful treatment of a poor widow." In 1818 a rule was passed stating, "Resolved that none of our ministers be allowed to wear gloves during Summer, nor to use silver-plated bridle bits or stirrups, or loaded whips, and in no case to adorn their person with large watch keys."[13]

In 1863 the aging and saintly Dreisbach, addressing the General Conference, lamented that so many promising young men had been lost to the ministry because of petty charges and urged that a spirit of love and helpfulness instead of censoriousness be expressed should a brother display weakness.

RELIGIOUS VITALITY IN THE CHURCH

The Second Awakening among the American churches brought a high level of religious vitality during the first two decades of the nineteenth century. Thereafter a decline set in, possibly because of a sense of tranquility as American political and economic life became somewhat stabilized and secure following the final adjustment of relations between the United States and its two European threats, England and France. A low point of religious life was reached in the early 1820's. The trend then changed. New stirrings of religious fervor in America developed through the intellectual-emotional preaching of men like Lyman Beecher, Asahel Nettelton, and the great Presbyterian-Congregationalist revivalist-theologian, Charles G. Finney. Both the Evangelical Association and United Brethren Church experienced the decline and subsequent revival of religious life in this period.

In the Evangelical Association the decline was most evident in the area of the Old Circuit, east of the Susquehanna River, centering in Lancaster and Lebanon Counties. The decline was not as evident in the area of the New Circuit, centering in the town of New Berlin. In 1805 and 1806, respectively, George Miller had held vigorous revivals on these two circuits. It may be that the establishing of the printing press in New Berlin in 1816, thus making it the most active center of the Evangelical Association, is what caused that area to be more stable.

Nevertheless, the overall membership of the Evangelical Association declined. It was feared that the religious life of the denomination was expiring.

The trend took a sudden turn in 1823 when a revival began in the town of Orwigsburg in Schuylkill County. Work had been done there in earlier years, but it had not been very successful. Even Albright had preached there but had been warned to leave the area and not return. Most of the people were Reformed and Lutheran. They looked upon the enthusiastic Methodist and Evangelical preachers as "Strawelers" because of their "fanatical" practices and doctrines. The emphases of the revivalists upon fervency in conversion and worship and upon the doctrine of sanctification stood in sharp contrast to the Augustinian-Lutheran-Calvinistic stress upon man's basic and incurably sinful nature.

Following the teachings of Albright and his early associates, the Evangelicals preached that the sanctifying power of God enables a converted person to resist sin successfully. However, man's redemption and sanctification are not accomplished automatically or unconditionally. They require constant diligence. It is quite possible for a sanctified person to lapse into sin. Dreisbach's *Journal* is replete with digressions in which he confessed that he was tormented by temptations and prayed for power to thrust sin aside. He never claimed that he had achieved moral perfection, although he always had it before him as his goal. This interpretation of the saved life seemed intolerable to the staid Lutherans and Reformed.

The first sign of things to come occurred in Orwigsburg in 1817 when Daniel Focht, the owner of a forge, was converted under the preaching of two Evangelical preachers, Adam Kleinfelter and Moses Dehoff. He opened his property for a camp meeting and supported the circuit rider John Breidenbach as he preached there.

In 1823 a young itinerant deacon, John Seybert, was appointed to the Schuylkill Circuit. He announced a preaching service to be held in a schoolhouse, three miles from Orwigsburg. When he arrived, he found the schoolhouse locked. A Negro named Mr. Wilson had come to attend the service with a group of other people. He invited Seybert and the people into his nearby humble home. The invitation was accepted. Seybert preached a moving sermon on the text, "He came unto his own, and his own received him not." (John 1:11 KJV).

This combination of circumstances was the impetus which began the new revival. Meetings were held again in Wilson's home, in a nearby hotel, and in other homes and buildings. Forty persons were converted and a new class formed. Among the converts was William Orwig (1810–1889), destined to become an Evangelical historian, editor, and bishop. Several whole families were converted, among them the Hammer and Reifschneider families. Three converts, Samuel Richart, and the brothers Joseph and Jacob Saylor, became effective Evangelical preachers.

In 1825 Seybert was appointed to the York Circuit. His coming touched off a revival there. It spread into Lancaster County, and in the decade following it spread westward into Ohio and as far west as

Illinois. In 1833 Seybert went into the Erie and Warren, Pennsylvania, areas where the Evangelical movement had not hitherto reached, with the same consequences.[14] Other Evangelical preachers were doing similar work in Berks, Lebanon, and Lehigh Counties.

Sometimes the worshippers were subjected to violence. At Womelsdorf, Pennsylvania, members of other German churches tried to break up a camp meeting with rocks, clubs, and pitchforks, and when emotional seizures caused converts to fall to the earth, the intruders tried by force to revive them by pouring water on them and even by having a doctor "bleed" them, that is, by the old practice of phlebotomy.

In Lebanon a Mennonite named Felix Light opened his chapel, known as Light's Meeting House, to the use of both the Evangelicals and United Brethren. Out of the Evangelical work came a Lebanon class, which in turn was the forerunner of several Evangelical congregations in that city.

In 1829 W. W. Orwig and Charles Hammer preached in a Schwenckfelder neighborhood in Lehigh County. At first they were treated harshly, but they made progress. Out of that revival came the Yeakel family from which sprang Reuben Yeakel (1827–1904), preacher, editor, historian, and bishop.

The revival movement initiated a new concept of "protracted" meetings. Hitherto great meetings, camp meetings, and single revival meetings were announced to begin and end at set times. However, it was found that some penitents found themselves still in spiritual distress when the meeting ended. Therefore it was decided not to announce a precise time of ending but to "protract" the meetings until all seekers after salvation were satisfied. Consequently the meetings continued until this was accomplished, even though it meant an extension for days or even weeks.[15]

Unfortunately the membership of the Evangelical Association did not increase as significantly as the large number of converts in the meetings would indicate. The stress on gaining conversions to Christ mitigated against emphasis upon bringing the converts into affiliation with established classes or congregations. Many of the revival preachers were content to gain converts in the meetings and then move on, leaving the new Christians without stable pastoral care. The membership count of 7,859 by 1839 is far short of the total which might have been reached if the converts had been conserved.

Furthermore, a few leaders disapproved of all formal church

activity. John Hamilton, a young Evangelical preacher, deplored the development of congregational and denominational structure. He denounced the use of creeds, confessions of faith, ceremonies and rituals, and urged that the Evangelical movement return to the simplicity of its early years under Albright's leadership. He felt that any formal actions or doctrinal expressions tended to cause divisiveness among Christians. He regarded them as latter-day expressions of the divisive sects in Corinth—those loyal to Apollos, to Paul, and to Cephas.[16] His efforts were judged to be disruptive. Therefore he was dismissed from the Evangelical ministry in 1831 "because he had . . . promulgated unscriptural doctrines" and "made an attempt to cause a schism in the Association."[17] Thereupon he attemped to form a band of dissatisfied Evangelical ministers apart from the Association. The attempt, after gaining temporary success, ended in failure.

Another disruptive brother, George Kimmel, was dismissed because he threatened to cause a schism by teaching that Jesus' example of washing the disciples' feet should be a mandatory practice.[18] Throughout subsequent history the Evangelical Association repudiated this rite. The United Brethren, who had several preachers of Dunker background, permitted footwashing wherever it was desired.

A third troublesome case was that of James Bruer (Brewer) who had the conviction that while achieving perfection (sanctification) in this life is possible and should be sought for, when it was achieved, the subject would no longer be related to this world of sin and error but "would be called from time to eternity." Bruer was not dismissed for this irregular teaching, but was "called to an account for it, . . . and died shortly afterward. . . , it is hoped, in the triumphs of faith."[19]

MINISTERIAL WITNESS AND LEARNING

The content of the preaching by the Evangelical preachers closely resembled that of the United Brethren and Methodists. The stress was upon personal Christian experience. This bore with it the implications of personal sinfulness, helplessness, and certain damnation if redemption does not intervene. The good news was that God promises redemption in Christ which is marked in the heart in a climactic and sudden conversion expressed in the joyful consciousness of release from the hold of sin. In turn this leads to the assurance that life can be lived in moral purity which can and should reach perfection. Thus sanctification is a cardinal doctrine.

The Evangelical brethren were not theological scholars and, in the early decades, saw little value in formal theological study. Yet when they were opposed by criticism and animosity from people of cynical, even atheistic, viewpoints they rallied in defense of their views.

The Bible was the textbook of the Evangelicals. Some of the preachers thought that it need not be supplemented by any other printed helps. However, several leaders undertook serious study of devotional and theological works. A great favorite was the *Imitation of Christ* by Thomas à Kempis. John Seybert throughout his ministry subjected himself to solid theological study and was instrumental in getting preachers and lay people under his jurisdiction to do the same. Printed materials from the publishing establishment in New Berlin, especially the denominational periodical *Der Christliche Botschafter*, gave opportunity both to study and to write religious articles.

MISSIONARY EFFORTS

From the very beginning the Evangelical Association was motivated by the evangelistic, that is, the missionary nature of true Christian faith. All evangelistic preaching was mission work. This was why the church expanded from its original area into new places like New York City, upper New York state, Canada, and westward into Ohio, Indiana, Michigan, and Illinois.

A need was felt for carrying on this missionary work in a more vigorous and purposive manner. John Seybert and W. W. Orwig, editor of *Der Christliche Botschafter* from 1836 to 1843, collaborated in stirring the church to action.

Orwig had received a letter from a Canadian correspondent in which he pleaded, "But, dear Brother! shall we, because we are too poor to give a teacher a sufficient support, . . . on that account . . . suffer and starve [spiritually]? Will ye Pennsylvanians . . . who have plenty and to spare . . . let us suffer in the wilderness, without any pity?"[20] Orwig published this letter in the *Botschafter*. Its effect was to cause the Eastern Annual Conference to organize a missionary society in 1838. In turn the General

Conference, meeting in 1839, made the missionary cause to be denominational by organizing the Missionary Society of the Evangelical Association of North America. All ministers were automatically regarded as members. A contribution of $2.00 or $25.00 made a church member a "subscriber" for a year or for life, respectively. The name "Parent Society" was often used because the denominational society embraced societies organized in smaller divisions of the church. John Seybert served as the first president of the society governing board, which had twenty-two members. The missionaries sent out into new areas were to receive salaries on the same scale as the active itinerants of the church.

CHRISTIAN EDUCATION

In 1809 John Dreisbach published a catechism which he had translated from English into German. He felt that the Christian message should be spread by the printed page, especially to children. When the printing press was established in New Berlin in 1816, materials were published for this purpose.

The spread of study materials prompted the organization of church schools. The first one to be established in Evangelical history was in 1832 in an Evangelical church in Lebanon, Pennsylvania.[21]

In 1835 the General Conference decreed "wherever practicable German Sabbath Schools are to be organized and conducted in the congregations of our Evangelical Association, and that it be made the duty of every Evangelical preacher in charge to strive earnestly to carry out this purpose."[22] Shortly thereafter Sunday schools were started in Philadelphia, New Berlin, Upper Milford in Lehigh County, Orwigsburg, Des Plaines, and Berlin in Ontario.

Some ministers opposed the church school movement, either fearing education as stultifying or, according to some indications, because it added responsibility to already overworked ministers. In the church schools the basic secular subjects of spelling and reading, as well as religious materials, were studied.

The church school movement called for regularization. Therefore in 1836 the Rev. Adam Ettinger published a well-thought-out set of rules to use in the New Berlin church school. The rules defined the duties of the superintendent and teachers for gathering a "serviceable library" and for providing necessary funds. To support the rules and make them effective the New Berlin Sunday School

Society was formed. It became a model for other Sunday schools throughout the denomination.

LANGUAGE

In all these developments the problem was raised about the use of the German or English language. In 1830 John Hamilton, preaching in the Virginia-Maryland-Cumberland Valley area, where English was making rapid inroads among the Germans, urged that the church should rapidly move in the direction of predominantly English usage. He believed that exclusive use of German forced too narrow a pattern on the church's forms, ceremonies, and organization. A number of the young ministers agreed. However, because Hamilton urged the abolishment of organization and formal doctrinal statements he was dismissed from the Evangelical Association.

Opposition by older ministers to all that Hamilton advocated brought a move to curb the use of English in all areas of the church's activities in spite of the fact that there already were a number of English-speaking congregations. The General Conference of 1830 took action "that no more preachers shall be received into the traveling connection who are not somewhat proficient in the German language."[23] This action might have been prompted by the trend in the United Brethren Church to move toward preference for English usage, thus reducing its ministry among German-speaking people.

However, the rule favoring the use of German was not absolute. One of the rules of the New Berlin Sunday school stated, "Should it not be possible to teach in German, then do so in English."[24] In 1834 the General Conference took action conferring authority "upon each annual conference to organize within its bounds, whenever it may be deemed advisable, an English conference, to consist of ten or more English preachers."[25] Nevertheless the German language was given priority over English. This had a restrictive effect upon the growth of the church for the remainder of the century.[26]

PUBLICATION

The printing press installed by John Dreisbach in New Berlin, Pennsylvania, in 1816 at his own expense immediately rendered the church valuable service in publishing religious materials.[27] George Miller (not to be confused with the early ministerial associate of Jacob Albright) was the printer. Solomon Miller, brother to the early George Miller, was named to be manager of the establishment. Book agents were appointed in the circuits to receive printed materials and distribute them to the churches. Two songbooks were published, Das Geistliche Saitenspiel (The Spiritual Lyre) and Die Geistliche Viole, the latter for camp meeting use.

In 1818 a book committee was appointed to decide which books should be published.

A serious error in judgment was made in 1819 when the book committee decided to print Luther's German New Testament with marginal notes. The project was far too great for the small press and too costly to permit sales at moderate price. The result was that the printing press faced bankruptcy. Under Dreisbach's reluctant leadership the press was leased to the printer, George Miller, and in 1828 it was sold to him. Miller continued to print materials for the church on a contract basis. This change in the status of the press distressed Dreisbach greatly. It was a contributing factor in his weakened health and withdrawal from prime leadership in the church.

After nearly a decade the issue of a denominationally owned printing establishment again was raised. There was opposition to the proposal based on the experiences with the first press, but the General Conference of 1836 voted to establish a new and superior press and bindery in New Berlin. Funds were raised, and the project was accomplished at a cost of $3,500. A large two-story building, formerly a tavern, was purchased to house the press and to provide living quarters for the family of the printer, Solomon Miller, and the family of the manager, book agent, and editor, W. W. Orwig.

Under wise management this second printing establishment flourished. Religious books and Sunday school aids—including spelling books and Sunday school tickets to be used as inducements toward attendance and study—flowed from the press.

The most significant publication was Der Christliche Botschafter, begun on the old press and expanded on the new. It was the main denominational periodical. Adam Ettinger was the first editor. Its first issue appeared in January 1836. At first it was published monthly, but success in distribution and readership prompted issuing it bimonthly in 1839. In 1837 W. W. Orwig became the editor.

He was an accomplished writer. The success of the publication was due largely to his work. He used the *Botschafter* as a forum for many contemporary religious discussions and to promote the work in missions and Christian education.

The General Conference of 1839 decided that a history of the Evangelical Church should be written and published. The matter was referred to Editor Orwig with the appointment of three others to gather materials for him to use as sources for the history. The plan did not work well. Hence, in 1854 Orwig was commissioned to undertake the project alone. He did so and in 1858 published an exceptionally well-written history of the church up to 1845. He designated the work Volume I and gave the explanation that he contemplated a second edition in which he would include materials not available when he wrote volume I and would also make necessary corrections to his first work.[28] Apparently he was not able to fulfill this intention.

THE DISCIPLINE

The first *Discipline* was formulated by George Miller and printed in 1809. It contained an introductory statement, twenty-six Articles of Faith (the twenty-five of the Methodist articles plus another "On the Last Judgment, and God's Righteous Sentence, Rewards and Punishments"), and directions for personal conduct and the activities of church officials and organization. To this were added four doctrinal essays.

The 1817 edition of the *Discipline* was revised by George Miller, John Dreisbach, and Henry Niebel and was expanded considerably. It was divided into four chapters: (1) a brief history of the church, the Articles of Faith, and rules for Christian life and worship, (2) organization and procedures of the conferences and a statement on Christian perfection, (3) a set of rituals for ordination, baptism, the Lord's Supper, and marriage and rules for dealing with transgressors, and (4) the temporal concerns of the church, such as salary support, publication, and erection of churches.

The Articles of Faith were reduced in number from twenty-six to twenty-one. The articles omitted included four which were directed against Roman Catholic beliefs and practices (supererogation, purgatory, withholding the cup from the laity in communion, and clerical celibacy) and one dealing with the swearing of oaths in legal transactions.

In the *Disciplines* of 1809 and 1817 among a list of offenses of man against man was a statement condemning slavery. Members of the church are "to avoid . . . supporting traffic in human beings through which slavery is either established or carried on." In the General Conference of 1839 the prohibition of slavery was made completely explicit. It stated that no member of the Evangelical Association "shall be allowed under any pretence or condition whatsoever the holding of slaves or the trafficking in the same."

Revisions of 1830

In the General Conference of 1830 the *Discipline* was revised at several points. Changes were made in the terminology of the Articles of Faith, the main one being the removal of the term sacraments because it was commonly used as an expletive of profanity. In its place the terms baptism and the Lord's Supper were used. The tenure of bishops was limited to two four-year terms (although the church had no bishops at this time), and the ritual for the ordination of bishops was removed, leaving the church with two levels of ordination—the diaconate and the eldership. The General Conferences were to be held every four years. This did not become effective until 1839. Thereafter General Conferences were held quadrennially.

The Discipline of 1839

The *Discipline* of 1839 made four very significant modifications with respect to the character and powers of the General Conference.

First, membership in General Conference was limited by electing one out of every four itinerant elders in the church. The former practice of granting membership to all itinerant elders had made the sessions unwieldly because of their growing numbers.

Second, setting the time and place for each subsequent meeting of the General Conference should be determined by any one of three methods which, in descending order of preference, were: (1) "the Bishop or Bishops in conjunction with the consent of the majority of the [General] conference"; (2) a majority vote of the General Conference if no bishop were present; or (3) action of "the oldest annual conference."

Third, "the general conference shall have power, to make rules and arrangements for . . . [the] society under the following restrictions,"

(1.) The General Conference shall have no power, to alter, detract from, or add to any of our Articles of Faith [except Article XII dealing with the recognition of civil authority].

(2.) It shall have no power to alter any rules or forms of our church Discipline (the rules of our temporal economy being excepted) unless such alterations are previously recommended by two thirds of the members of all the annual conferences, who may be present at the sessions of the same; whereupon the general conference shall have the power by three fourths of the majority of their votes to alter any of our rules or forms, excepting the Articles of Faith.

Fourth, a new regulation provided for a bishop to serve as the presiding officer at each General Conference. If no bishop be present, then a presiding elder should be chosen to preside; if no presiding elder be present, then the choice should be from the elders present.

The third of these four modifications, with its two restrictive rules, was very significant because for the first time the General Conference had limitations placed upon its powers.

These four new regulations were set into Chapter II, Section IV of the *Discipline*, supplementing or modifying former descriptions of the nature and duties of the General Conference. Because of the limitations placed on the order and power of all future General Conferences, Chapter II, Section IV of the *Discipline* came to be referred to as the "Constitution of 1839," although the word constitution was not inserted into the *Discipline*.

The *Discipline* of 1839 set forth several rules dealing with four social issues. (1) Lavishness of dress was disapproved because "splendid apparel is always expensive, and we may become spendthrifts in clothing as well as in eating and drinking." This rule especially warned against wearing "gold or pearls, or costly array." (2) Article XIX of the Articles of Faith (which had been in effect since the first *Discipline* of 1809) added the statement, "we believe that wars and bloodshed are not agreeable to the Gospel and Spirit of Christ." (3) Chapter III added the statement, "None of our members shall be allowed to make or prepare, or deal in, or use as a drink, spiritous or intoxicating liquors, except as medicine." (4) A statement, already referred to in this chapter, prohibited members of the church from dealing in slavery "under any pretence or condition whatsoever."

BAPTISM

From its beginning the Evangelical Association had no problem with the sacrament of baptism. Infant as well as adult baptism was practiced, and all methods or modes of baptism were permitted. In his *Journal* under the date of September 10, 1836, John Seybert, at that time a presiding elder, stated that he had baptized seven persons: "Three were baptised under water [immersion] and the other four with water [sprinkling]. . . . The baptism of the Holy Ghost came down upon all [seven]."[29]

However, a question was raised as to whether circumstances ever warranted a second baptism. In 1829 the Western Annual Conference faced the issue because one of its ministers had knowingly baptized a person who had been baptized as an infant. The conference took unanimous action forbidding this to occur again because neither the *Discipline* nor the New Testament gives warrant for it.[30]

This did not end the matter. It was referred to the General Conference of 1839. It cautioned against frequent practice of rebaptism and forbade any preacher to advocate it, but held that where a person who had been baptized as an infant desired to be baptized as an adult, it could be done.[31]

ELECTION OF A BISHOP: JOHN SEYBERT

The expansion of the Evangelical Association both in territory and program caused the delegates in the General Conference of 1839 to realize that the church's organization in Annual Conferences under the leadership of several presiding elders was too decentralized. Therefore, they decided to elect a bishop to act as prime leader of the denomination. They chose John Seybert, a truly great man of the church.

John Seybert was born July 7, 1791, in Manheim, Pennsylvania. He died January 4, 1860, near Flat Rock, Ohio.

Seybert's father, Henry, had been a German mercenary soldier in the British army during the Revolutionary War. He was captured and imprisoned in Lancaster, Pennsylvania. After the war he was "redeemed" by a Mr. Schaffner, whom he served for three years, the term required by the redemption. In 1790 he was married by Dr. Henry M. Muhlenburg to Susan Kreuzer. Two of their four sons grew to maturity, John and David.

The family was Lutheran. John was confirmed in that faith. He received an elementary education in German and English but did not become fluent in the latter.

The family prospered. When the father died in 1806, he left his family a farm near Manheim and other possessions.

One year after the father's death, the mother deserted her sons and entered the religious-community sect called the Rappites at Harmony, Pennsylvania. The Rappites dominated the mother and attempted to gain possession of the family's property, thereby depriving the sons of their inheritance. Their efforts failed, but this action permanently alienated David from his mother. John maintained contact with her until he preceded her in death.

Although John had been confirmed as a Lutheran in his boyhood, he was careless in his way of life until he was nineteen. On June 21, 1810, he attended a revival held by an Evangelical itinerant, Matthias Betz, in Manheim. Before the meeting ended he was converted.

Immediately he showed great zeal for the faith. Hence, the class which met in Manheim chose him as leader. He was so vigorous in promoting Bible study that a class in Mt. Joy, eight miles south of Manheim, persuaded him to be their class leader also.

Seybert caught the attention of John Dreisbach, who brought him into the ministry as a preacher on trial in 1819 and appointed him as an itinerant to the Lancaster Circuit. To serve more effectively Seybert began a strenuous discipline of study of biblical and theological works, which he followed throughout the remainder of his long ministry.

In 1822 Seybert was advanced to the status of deacon. He served successively churches in York, in the Union Circuit near Lewisburg, and in the Ohio Conference. While in Ohio he developed a deep love for the "West." However, while traveling through swampy areas of Ohio, he contracted malaria which kept him in precarious health the rest of his life.

In 1823 he was appointed to the Schuylkill Circuit, and by his preaching at Orwigsburg, Pennsylvania, began the revival which swept throughout the denomination. In 1824 he became an ordained elder.

In 1825, to his dismay, he was elected a presiding elder with responsibility in the Canaan District, the area largely east of the Susquehanna River, south into Virginia, and north into New York.

In 1833 he asked to be relieved of the responsibility of presiding elder so that he might go into the area of Erie and Warren, Pennsylvania, where the Evangelical Association had not reached. In one year's time he was very successful in making that area a stronghold of the church.

In 1834 he was again elected presiding elder and served the following five years in several districts, preaching in camp meetings, churches, homes, courthouses, and schools, sometimes against open hostility of people opposed to the "fanatics."

The expansion of the Evangelical Association, both in territory and through the activities of the Charitable and Mission Societies, led the church to adopt a greater centralization of leadership in 1839. At the General Conference of that year Seybert was elected bishop, the first Evangelical leader to hold that office since the death of Bishop Jacob Albright in 1808. Seybert accepted the office only after much prayer and self-study.

This new responsibility required Seybert to travel extensively all over the expanding church in general ministry and in presiding at all conferences. He traveled by carriage where roads were adequate, otherwise on horseback, and sometimes by walking. The far points of his visits included New York City, southern New Jersey, Philadelphia, the Shenandoah Valley, southwestern Pennsylvania, St. Louis, eastern Iowa, northern Illinois, Milwaukee, Detroit, Waterloo in Canada, Buffalo, and the Mohawk Valley in New York state. At the end of 1850 he summarized his extensive travels in that year as follows:

> In Pennsylvania, one hundred and six days; in New York, fifty days; in Ohio, sixty days; in Michigan, eleven days; in Indiana, thirty-four days; in Illinois, eighty-one days; in Canada, only three days; in Wisconsin, fourteen days; in Maryland, six days; total three hundred and sixty-five days.[32]

Seybert faced many difficulties. Once he traveled on an eighteen-mile journey through the swampland of central Ohio with a postman, who acted as his guide, but who had an annoying practice of frequently blowing a loud horn to summon people who lived in their primitive shacks along the postal route. In November 1835 he walked on a two-day round trip journey from Waterford Works, New Jersey, to Philadelphia, twenty-eight miles each way, through mud, rain, and storm, in order to hold a meeting in Philadelphia and make pastoral visits.

Seybert was frugal in his habits, thereby accumulating about $6,000, most of which he bequeathed to organizations of the church.[33] Twice he rescued persons he didn't even know from debtor's penalties. One was a widow threatened with the loss of her modest home. Seybert bought it and gave it back to her. A poor weaver, the father of a large family, was having his loom confiscated. It was the only means of livelihood for the family. Seybert heard of the trouble, bought the loom and sent it back to the weaver who did not even know who his benefactor was.

Seybert was very much concerned about the study life of the ministers. Whenever he traveled by carriage, he took with him many books and study materials from the publishing establishment in New Berlin. He distributed these materials among the preachers and their churches.

Seybert never married and consequently had to endure false, vicious rumors and accusations as he ministered to women. In spite of his unmarried status he worked hard to get adequate support for preachers with families.

Seybert's preaching was not judged to be dynamic. However, he was an effective preacher because of his clarity and thoughtful simplicity.

He enjoyed pastoral work. Although in his later ministry he could have traveled by train, he continued his previous methods of travel because thereby he could stop to minister to people in need all along his route. One day in 1833 he rode on horseback all day to the home of friends. In the evening he walked with them on an eight-mile round trip to a prayer meeting. After returning at midnight he immediately walked up a steep one-mile mountain trail to bring spiritual solace to a troubled man, returning to his hosts' home in early morning.

In dealing with his ministers Seybert was rigorous but scrupulously fair. He was very critical of any form of carelessness or negligence. He rebuked them for irregularities. Once he came unexpectedly upon several ministers who were smoking. They tried to brazen it out by inviting him to engage in their conversation. Seybert refused, saying, "I can't stand this, it smells as if hell were not far off."[34] He was in demand as a lecturer on temperance at Evangelical and interdenominational assemblies.[35]

Seybert excelled as an administrator. He was foresighted in denominational leadership, but the work soon became too much of a burden. Therefore, in 1843 the General Conference elected a second bishop, Joseph Long (1800–1869), who also had an illustrious career. Although they divided the work, it continued to mount so that in 1859 W. W. Orwig was elected as a third bishop.

In his last years of service Seybert spent most of his time in the western area. He continued his extensive travels although incipient malaria forced him to discontinue the work for weeks at a time. Under these circumstances he fumed with impatience and often resumed his work before he had recovered sufficient strength. This led to an increasing weakness of body.

In the fall of 1859 he was performing his duties in Illinois. On November 7 he started a trip through Indiana and Michigan and into Ohio. The weather was stormy with icy rain. On December 20 he reached the home of Isaac Parker near Flat Rock, four miles west of Bellevue, Ohio. He was so weary rest gave him no relief. On the morning of January 4, 1860, he arose and joined the Parker family at breakfast. Then he moved to a lounge and shortly afterward, commenting on death, said, "So I too will fall asleep," and passed away moments later. He was buried two days later in the cemetery at Flat Rock.

Seybert, a small man in physical stature, was a giant in the Christian church. This is seen not only in the magnitude of his labors but in the simple grandeur with which he witnessed to the grace of God in Christ. This is reflected in the sheer massiveness of his life's service, which has been summarized as follows:

> In these forty years he traveled per horse, one hundred and seventy-five thousand miles, preached about nine thousand eight hundred and fifty times, made about forty-six thousand pastoral visits, held about eight thousand prayer and class meetings, besides visiting at least ten thousand sick and afflicted ones.[36]

he fifth to the ninth decades, inclusive, of the nineteenth century in America were vigorous and dynamic, but darkened by the tragedies of slavery, the Civil War, and the agonies of postwar reconstruction. Population growth was phenomenal. In 1840 the population was seventeen million. By 1890 it was sixty-three million. This growth was due in large measure to immigration first from the northern nations of Europe including Germany and after the Civil War from the central and southern European nations. The storied promises of the United States lured many of these people who endured low economic conditions, periodic famines, and religious oppression in their homelands.

The Cultural Setting

The religious life during these decades was lively with enthusiastic evangelistic and missionary action. Beginning about 1810 missionary movements developed in the churches, causing the Congregationalist, Baptist, Presbyterian, and Methodist Churches to engage in mission at home and abroad. The home field included evangelistic work on the eastern seaboard and in the eastern midwest area. As territories were opened for settlement west of the Mississippi all the way to the Pacific coast, Protestant missionaries followed the migrants.

THE UNITED BRETHREN CHURCH, 1841–1890

The German immigrants tended to settle in the northern tier of states. Most of these people were Lutheran, Reformed, and Roman Catholic. Both the United Brethren Church and the Evangelical Association accepted opportunities to expand their work among them.

During this period religious zeal which had been invigorated by the Second Awakening and the revivals of the 1820's and 1830's was periodically renewed by a series of evangelistic movements. In the late 1850's there was the "Laymen's Revival." A revival in the churches directed toward the armed services, north and south, took place during the Civil War. In the last two decades of the century came the revival in which Dwight L. Moody and Ira D. Sankey were the leading figures.

The social and political issues were weighty during this period. Beginning with the Jacksonian era of the late 1820's there developed a great and vigorous demand for the rights of the common man competing with the demands of the established interests of developing business and industry and the conservative complacency of the eastern seaboard "culture."

Hovering over the developments in American life was the dark shadow of slavery. Before this period, although slavery was an established institution, there was general disapproval of this evil. In the 1830's and 1840's the disapproval declined, especially in the south, because of the economics and agricultural effects of "King Cotton."

The churches found slavery to be the most devastating social problem they had been called upon to face. Their dealing with it, in both the North and the South, was tragically inept, causing divisions in the Presbyterian, Methodist, and Baptist churches, some of which still prevail.

The problem of war itself disturbed the churches, especially those which had a tradition of Christian pacifism. In the 1840's temperance became a live social issue.

Following the Civil War the great force of labor became effective politically and economically. The reconstruction period following the war was the propitious time for the rise of the labor movement. Along with it was the development of great concentrations of capitalistic wealth and power, exemplified in the appearance of the great giants of the economy such as Rockefeller, Morgan, Carnegie, and Vanderbilt.

The period was also typified by an emphasis on higher education, especially the establishment of denominational colleges. The churches felt that it was their responsibility to guide learning in such a way as to keep the intellectual climate conducive to the claims of the Christian faith. Theological seminaries were established not only to prepare religious leaders but to maintain the distinctiveness of the individual denominations which sponsored them. The educational spirit had always been vigorous in the Congregational, Presbyterian, and Episcopal Churches, but beginning in the 1830's it became part of the denominational life and programs of the Methodist, Baptist, and other free denominations.

CHURCH GROWTH, EXPANSION, AND ORGANIZATION

In 1841 the membership of the United Brethren Church was about 25,000. It was distributed among nine Annual Conferences. The geographical expansion of the denomination thereafter is indicated on the accompanying maps.

By 1861 the membership had grown to 94,453.[1] This included members in a small mission in Massachusetts, which was designated an Annual Conference in 1862, but which soon passed out of existence. It also included mission stations in eastern Tennessee carried on by the Virginia Annual Conference and two mission conferences in California and Oregon. By 1889 the membership of the church was declared to be "not less than 207,800."[2] Geographical expansion was not great after 1861, although the church moved into new territory in Nebraska, Colorado, Kentucky, and Tennessee, and expanded its areas in Oregon, California, and Ontario in Canada.

By 1889 the denomination was divided into forty-nine Annual Conferences. Size of the conferences varied considerably from the smallest (Colorado) with 632 members to the largest (Miami) with 9,920. Three others exceeded 9,000; four were between 8,000 and 9,000; four were between 7,000 and 8,000; twenty-one were between 2,000 and 7,000; the remainder were under 2,000.[3]

BISHOPS' DISTRICTS

Before 1849 the men who were elected bishops were not assigned to districts of the denomination. All were regarded as bishops of the church and served in whatever area it was temporarily expedient. In 1849 the General Conference appointed a stationing committee for assigning each bishop to a defined district. Three districts were named: the East (east of the Ohio-Pennsylvania state line), the Middle (eastern and northern Ohio through northern Indiana), and the West (southwest Ohio through southern Indiana, Illinois, into Iowa). Bishops Jacob Erb (1804–1883), David Edwards (1816–1876), and Jacob John Glossbrenner (1812–1887), respectively, were assigned to these districts.

In 1857 a fourth district was organized to embrace all the remaining German-speaking churches which previously had been located within the Ohio and Indiana German Annual Conferences. In 1865 the German District was discontinued. The German-speaking churches were all placed within the Ohio German Annual Conference, which was part of a newly-named Ohio District.

In 1861 the Pacific District, embracing the California, Oregon, and Walla Walla Annual Conferences, was organized.

In the years following, the bishops' districts were rearranged several times. They became five in number, four east of the Rocky Mountains, and the Pacific District. They were served by as many bishops. The practice was to make complete changes of the assignments of bishops at each General Conference, and in the quadrennium of 1885 to 1889 every year to rotate the bishops serving the four districts east of the Rockies. The reason for the quadrennial rotation was that each bishop was a bishop of the whole church and would be enhanced in that relationship by serving successively in each of the districts. The reason for the annual rotation was that by 1885 the church was being torn by several issues. To prevent a bishop from unduly imposing his own opinions on these issues on a district he was not permitted to remain there too long! Obviously this frequent rotation of a bishop's location imposed great hardship upon him and his family.

Membership in General Conferences

In 1841 the General Conference changed the method of selecting delegates. Formerly, one delegate was chosen from each presiding elder's district in the whole denomination. Henceforth, three delegates were to be chosen from each Annual Conference without reference to presiding elder districts. This identical representation from each Annual Conference, regardless of its size, prompted modifications (each one strongly resisted by the smaller Annual Conferences) until in the General Conference of 1881 a standard was adopted by a 60 to 57 vote granting two delegates to Annual Conferences which had 3,000 or fewer members, three delegates to conferences which had from 3,000 to 5,000 members, and four delegates to conferences having more than 5,000 members.[4]

LAY REPRESENTATION

Membership in General and Annual Conferences had been restricted to the clergy. In 1853 petitions reached the General Conference asking for lay representation in all conferences, claiming that since the laity were responsible for many local church activities and financial support, they should be granted representation.

When the issue was considered with reference to lay representation in the General Conference, it was immediately seen to be blocked by the constitutional statement (Section Second, Article IV), "There shall be no alteration of the foregoing constitution, unless by request of two thirds of the whole society." General Conference membership was defined within the constitution as consisting only of elders. Therefore to effect lay membership in General Conference would require the successful use of Article IV. For the first time use of that article was seen to be virtually impossible.

Lay membership in the Annual Conferences was another matter because Annual Conference membership was not defined in the constitution (Section Second) but in the Discipline (Section Fourth). Hence it did not come under the rule (Section Second, Article IV). Items in the Discipline could be changed by a simple majority vote in General Conference.

Even so there was resistance against permitting lay representation in Annual Conferences, which blocked modification of the disciplinary statement until 1877. Action taken by the General Conference of that year states, "Any Annual Conference may receive into its body one layman from any charge in its bounds, whenever two-thirds of its members shall . . . decide to do so."[5]

The Miami Annual Conference took immediate action to admit lay delegates. Allegheny Annual Conference did not do so until 1886.

This new action raised another question. Might lay delegates be women? Pennsylvania Annual Conference in 1878 restricted the delegates to men. Other conferences, without taking formal action, did the same.

Henceforth, after an Annual Conference took the proper action, its membership was made up of all the ordained and licensed preachers and one layman from each charge. General Conference membership remained all clerical until a new constitution was adopted in 1889.

MINISTERIAL QUALIFICATIONS

In 1841 the General Conference set forth a regular procedure to be followed by persons desiring to become ministers in full standing. Three steps were prescribed. First, the candidate had to be approved as a Quarterly Conference licentiate by a two-thirds vote of a class or congregation. He had to give "satisfactory evidence of his . . . call, experience, soundness of doctrine, and attachment to our church and government."[6] Second, after holding that status for at least one year and passing a prescribed doctrinal examination, he was received as a member of the Annual Conference on probation. Third, after three years of probation, if judged worthy by a majority vote of the Annual Conference, he was approved for ordination as an elder.

It was recommended that the candidate spend the three years of probation in studying selected books which included the Bible, general history, church history, philosophy and logic, grammar and elocution, and theology. William Hanby (1808–1880), who served the church as editor, historian, hymn writer, and bishop, in an article on preaching in the September 1, 1841 issue of the *Religious Telescope* gave advice to preachers, urging them to show discretion in their elocution by not "thumping the Bible on the desk [pulpit] as though [they] intended to tear it to pieces—Good people do not like to see the Book of Good (sic) abused."

The General Conference of 1853 expanded and made mandatory the "study course" program, arranging the order in which the books should be read, and requiring that the candidate write essays on the contents of the books.

Standards of morality were held on a high level. Conferences dismissed ministers who engaged in business irregularities, indiscrete personal conduct, and arrogance. Personal vanity in the wearing of jewelry, "the making of artificials [wigs] . . . and the cutting and wearing of the hair—most especially our *ministers and their families*, they being ensamples to the flock," should be avoided.[7]

Furthermore, ministers should never "electioneer" in aspiring for a church office. In 1849 one brother was required to ask forgiveness for forging, altering, opening, and resealing bills of election.[8]

Ministerial salaries were extremely low at the beginning of the period. The General Conference of 1841 set the annual salaries of all elders, including bishops, at one hundred dollars and traveling expenses for a single man, and two hundred dollars, traveling expenses, and "house rent not exceeding forty dollars for a married man."

In the quadrennia following, with the national economic conditions constantly changing, the salary schedules were changed frequently. In 1885 the General Conference set the bishop's salary at fifteen hundred dollars. In the Miami Annual Conference the salaries of the two presiding elders were respectively $725.23 and $729, and the salaries of the itinerants ranged from $93 to $1600, the range being due to cost of living in different places and to sizes of enrollments.[9]

WOMEN IN THE MINISTRY

Early in the period the question was raised whether women should be received into ministerial standing. Several cases arose and were dealt with individually. In the Scioto Annual Conference of 1841, Sister S. Copeland declared that she had "impressions" that she was prompted by the Holy Ghost to teach, preach, and exhort, and requested the conference to grant her "a permit . . . to do such work as assigned her." The conference declared itself unable to give a satisfactory judgment, but "advised [her] to exercise according to her gifts and callings in promoting the cause of Christ on earth."[10]

Two years later another woman, Sister L. P. Clemens, made a similar petition to the Scioto Annual Conference with the response of the conference that "she could not be heard."[11] Sister Clemens carried her petition to the General Conference of 1845, which dismissed it because "she is not a member of the Church [or] of the Annual Conference, and we do not think the Gospel authorizes the introduction of females into the ministry in the sense in which she requests it."[12]

In 1847 Charity Opherel petitioned the White River Annual Conference for approval to preach. Without taking action implying a basic policy, the conference voted to give her a "vote of commendation to liberate to [to have the freedom to engage in] public speaking." Because the conference did not thereafter include her in the list of recognized preachers the "vote of commendation" apparently did not imply recognition as a preacher of the church.

Mrs. Lydia Sexton was granted a Quarterly Conference license to preach in 1851. When she applied for advancement to the status of an Annual Conference licentiate in 1859 in the Illinois Annual Conference, the presiding bishop, David Edwards, ruled that there was no authority in the United Brethren Church for licensing a woman.[13]

As the decades passed this negative attitude changed. In the General Conference of 1889, action was taken as follows:

> Whenever any godly woman presents herself . . . for authority to preach the gospel among us, she may be granted license, provided she complies with the usual conditions required of men who wish to enter the ministry of our church. When such person shall have passed the required examination before the regular committees, she may, after the usual probation, be ordained.[14]

Worship

Worship practices remained simple during the first two decades of the period. Emphasis was placed on preaching and exhortation. Gradually the quality of preaching became more sophisticated due to the measures of scholarly preparation of the preachers. Many preachers studied diligently. Others felt that a general acquaintance with the Scriptures was the only study needed.

The purpose of preaching was basically evangelistic, that is, winning people to Christ or maintaining in the faith those already won.

Lay participation in worship through personal testimony, prayer, and hymn singing gave opportunity for vigorous religious expression. Hymnbooks were published periodically. Hymnbooks with the music as well as the words were first published in 1874.

The General Conference of 1861, while urging hearty hymn singing, and "the cultivation of vocal music," also stated, "we . . . kindly forbid the introduction of choirs into any of our churches,"[15] apparently believing that choirs tend to rob congregational singing of spontaneity. The General Conference of 1865 also banned the use of musical instruments.

However, a trend was underway which brought reaction against the banning of choirs and musical instruments. To use them need not reduce spirituality in worship. Even the old Otterbein Church in Baltimore had a choir and an organ. Therefore the General Conference of 1869 toned down the prohibition by asserting, "We hereby earnestly advise our societies to avoid introduction of choirs and instrumental music into their worship."[16] With the prohibition removed, many churches organized choirs and installed instruments.

THEOLOGICAL ISSUES

Controversy over Depravity

The Confession of Faith of 1817 stated, "We believe [in] . . . the fall in Adam." In 1841 this was supplemented by a question to be asked of candidates for the ministry, "What is your knowledge of . . . depravity . . . ?" At once there were ministers who objected to the implication of this question, namely, John Calvin's affirmation of the doctrine of the total depravity of human nature. After heated debate the General Conference of 1853, by vote of twenty-three to nineteen, stated the question even more emphatically, "Do you believe in the doctrine of natural, hereditary, total [later changed to 'complete'] depravity as held by the church?" but with an explanatory note by Bishop Glossbrenner defining the key terms in language more moderate than strict Calvinism.

This did not satisfy those who believed that no person, however sinful, is ever totally depraved. He never reaches the point of depravity where of his own volition he cannot call upon God for forgiveness.

During the ensuing quadrennium depravity became the center of vigorous, even acrimonious, debate between "total depravity" men and "partial depravity" men. The debate came to its climax in the General Conference of 1857 with such vehemence that many feared the church would be divided. Finally the matter was consigned to a committee for further study and the formation of a revised question.

The committee recommended that the question be changed to read:

> Do you believe that man, abstract of [later changed to "apart from"] the grace of our Lord Jesus Christ, is fallen from original righteousness and is not only entirely destitute of holiness, but is inclined to evil, and only evil, and that continually; and that except a man be born again he cannot see the kingdom of God?[17]

The genius of this question lies in the phrase "abstract of the grace of our Lord Jesus Christ." The total depravity men could accept it because they interpreted it to mean, "Since man is abstract of the grace of our Lord Jesus Christ, he is fallen, etc." The partial depravity men could accept it because they interpreted it to mean, "*If* man would be abstract of the grace of our Lord Jesus Christ, he would be fallen, etc., but actually he is not thus abstract."

Hence, in the ambiguity of the phrase "abstract of the grace of our Lord Jesus Christ," which ambiguity was not unintentional, agreement on acceptance of the question was possible. The motion to adopt this new question lacked but one vote of unanimous approval. The tension was broken and the conference arose to sing the doxology.

When in 1889 a new Confession of Faith consisting of thirteen articles was adopted, the exact content of the question was reproduced in Article VIII with only the substitution of "We believe" for "Do you believe?"

Baptism, Footwashing, and the Lord's Supper

There is no indication that in the first decades of United Brethren history there was any controversy over the meaning and form of baptism. This is remarkable because the first church leaders, Otterbein, Boehm, Geeting, Newcomer, and Grosh came from various church traditions: Reformed, Mennonite, and Dunker. The Reformed recognized all modes of baptism but practiced sprinkling almost exclusively and baptized infants as well as adults. The Mennonites baptized only adults (believers) by pouring. The

Dunkers baptized only adults by trine immersion in a flowing stream. The brethren apparently agreed that in working together they would not raise the issues in baptism which would separate them, even though each one followed his own preference. This conciliatory spirit is revealed in a statement Henry Spayth made of Boehm's attitude, "Boehm [a Mennonite] would witness the baptism of an infant by Otterbein [Reformed] with benignity of countenance, and love beaming in his eyes; but lest he might offend his Mennonite brethren and kinsmen in the flesh, Boehm himself baptized none but adults."[18] Spayth also said the church founders "did not view [baptism] in the light of a saving ordinance."[19]

There were ministers in the United Brethren Church who did not regard the matter of baptism in so broad a spirit. In the General Conferences of 1853, 1857, and 1861 demands were made that the church take a precise and definite stand in prescribing an exact interpretation of the meaning and mode of baptism. Each time the controversial issue was avoided by action to table it. No attempt was made after 1861 to deal with it in General Conference.

The disciplinary clause dealing with baptism also had a statement recognizing the "example" of footwashing. The practice was challenged several times in the General Conferences, but no action was ever taken to abolish it.

The sacrament of the Lord's Supper was affirmed many times without any controversy over its significance. From the early days of the great or "Sacramental" meetings the emphasis consistently was upon the sacrament as a memorial to the crucified and risen Lord, with stress laid upon the strengthening power of the Holy Spirit.

SOCIAL ISSUES

Temperance

The *Discipline* of 1841 contained a rule which forbade the "distilling and vending of ardent spirits" by anyone in the church. It is to be noted that the use was not included in the prohibition, and also there was no reference to fermented liquors.

In 1845 the first modification was made by prohibiting the use of "ardent spirits." In 1873 the prohibition was made all inclusive by changing the term "ardent spirits" to "intoxicating beverages," thereby forbidding all phases of manufacturing, vending, and using intoxicants as beverages. Two more prohibitory steps were taken later. In 1881 a rule was passed forbidding church members to sign petitions being circulated to permit dispensing of liquor, to rent a building in which liquor would be sold, or to become bondsmen for persons engaged in the liquor business. Lastly, in 1877 the General Conference forbade the use of "fermented and intoxicating wines for sacramental purposes." In the General Conferences, beginning in 1881, resolutions were passed calling for "constitutional prohibition . . . in every state of this great domain." After the Woman's Christian Temperance Union was organized in 1873, General Conferences passed resolutions commending the work of the Union.

Tobacco

The use of tobacco early came in for implied criticism and disapproval. A resolution passed by the Muskingum Annual Conference in 1847 stating that those "who occupied that side of the house [the sanctuary of the church in which the conference was meeting] generally occupied by females; refrain from chewing tobacco while seated there; or they shall be under painful necessity of removing the nauseous juice before the females occupy the pews."

For years similar resolutions were made at the beginning of Annual and General Conference sessions. In 1877 the General Conference adopted an extensive statement condemning tobacco as "narcotic poison," "injurious," causing "perplexing and painful diseases," deadly, "inconvenient, offensive and unclean," "intrusion upon the rights of others," a violation of the scriptural admonition of cleanliness, an "evil habit and example," and stating that individuals and corporations should be forbidden to allow its use in places of "public conveyance and entertainment" so that nonusers be spared exposure to "the filthy and nauseating saliva and sickening fumes."[20]

GAMBLING

Several other social and moral issues were dealt with in various conferences. Gambling "in whatever shape it may appear," including betting on United States presidential elections, was denounced by the Scioto Annual Conference in 1841. The General Conference of 1881 passed the following resolutions:

Resolved, 1. That dancing is unbecoming the profession of faith in Christ Jesus, ...
2. That all games of chance should be discountenanced. . . .
3. That horse-racing and walking-races, and the practice of betting thereon, should be condemned. . . .
7. That we deprecate and oppose the frequent violations of the Sabbath in all the different departments of life.[21]

Divorce

For decades occasional charges of immoral conduct were brought against ministers. These accusations were not spelled out, but sexual improprieties were implied, including marital infidelity.

In 1877 the General Conference gave attention to the growing problem in society of the violation of marriage vows and the consequent rise in divorce actions. Its reaction was put forth in several resolutions stating that divorce is justifiable only when one of the parties is guilty of infidelity, and that ministers "should not solemnize the marriage of persons who have been divorced from others for any offense other than adultery or fornication."[22]

Women's Rights

The growing spirit in America to recognize the rights of women as expressed in the women's suffrage movement was reflected indirectly in the General Conference of 1881 as it dealt again with the issue of temperance. In general discussion of the purposes of the Woman's Christian Temperance Union and the National Women Suffrage Association, organized in 1869, the conference showed general approval of both movements and tended to regard them as interrelated. However, the conference did not record specific action with respect to the women's suffrage movement.

SLAVERY AND THE CIVIL WAR

After its repudiation of slavery in 1821 the United Brethren Church never modified its position. Except for Maryland and Virginia the United Brethren Church was in northern territory, where slave holding had become rare. However, the slave issue became serious in the area of the Virginia Annual Conference (which included the state of Maryland). In response to northern abolitionist agitation the state of Virginia passed laws forbidding the manumission of slaves and refusing distribution of antislavery literature.

Although a rule had been passed forbidding inflammatory articles on slavery to appear in the *Religious Telescope*, the editorial policy of that periodical was known to be antislavery, and so its distribution was curtailed in Virginia.

When the War Between the States broke out, the church members in Virginia were caught in an intolerable situation. With few exceptions they were antislavery in attitude, but they had to avoid giving offense to the Confederate authorities. This was extremely difficult.

The boundary between North and South allowed the members of the Virginia Annual Conference who lived in Maryland to maintain normal relationships with the denomination. Not so with those living in Virginia. At first some ministerial members felt that it would be necessary to declare a break with the church in the North and form a southern United Brethren Church.

Fortunately this was prevented by Bishop J. J. Glossbrenner who, when the dividing line was drawn between North and South, decided to stay with the Virginians and give them administrative and pastoral leadership.

As the result of his influence the Virginia section of the Virginia Annual Conference did not declare itself independent of the denomination. Each section of the conference met in separate sessions throughout the war and recorded in its minutes brotherly affection for those who were separated from them by the battle lines, always including them in their prayers.

The integrity of Bishop Glossbrenner was recognized by both warring sides. In 1864 they both granted him safe passage through the lines, enabling him to attend and preside over the Maryland section of the Virginia Annual Conference and then return to Virginia.

When the war finally ended, both divisions of the Virginia Annual Conference came together in a spirit of joyful reunion.

The duration of the war fell precisely between the General Conference sessions of 1861 and 1865. During the war the great section of the church in the north gave full support to the Union and upheld President Lincoln by prayers and by resolutions of loyalty.

The General Conference convening on May 11, 1865, in Iowa received word of the final surrender of the Confederacy. There were many expressions of great joy, but also expressions of bitterness against "that scoundrel," Jefferson Davis, and other southern leaders. Bishop Glossbrenner was in attendance. At first he was coldly received by some bitter anti-South brethren. He was given an opportunity to describe his work of preventing the division in the Virginia Annual Conference from becoming permanent and of his administrative and pastoral leadership in Virginia during the war. A resolution expressing approval of his heroic work was passed by the conference with but two dissenting votes.

Thus the war ended without leaving the United Brethren Church divided.

The Civil War required the church to examine its stand on armed conflict. Through its heritage of Mennonite, Moravian, and Dunker Christian pacifism the General Conference of 1849 had approved by a vote of twenty-one to one with several abstentions the following action: "Resolved, that we believe that the spirit that leads men to engage voluntarily in national warfare is unholy and unchristian and ought not to be tolerated by us."[23] In light of the fact that the Mexican War had so recently ended by which the United States had wrested territory from its southern neighbor, which was popularly regarded as a great achievement, this total denunciation of "national warfare" was courageous and startling.

The horror of the Civil War and the general feeling in the North that it had been fought for the righteous purpose of ending the evil of slavery caused the church to modify the resolution of 1849. Therefore, the General Conference of 1865 passed a new resolution which ended with the statement, "We believe it to be entirely consistent with the spirit of Christianity to bear arms when called upon to do so by the properly constituted authorities of our government for its preservation and defense."[24] Agressive warfare was still ruled out. This position was maintained throughout the remainder of the history of the United Brethren Church.

Ecumenicity

Proposal of Church Union

In 1843 about six thousand members of the Methodist Church withdrew from that denomination to form the Wesleyan Methodist Connection (or Church). By 1855 their numbers had grown to about twenty thousand. They believed that the Methodist Church did not take a clear and unequivocal stand against slavery, intemperance, war, and secret societies. Because the United Brethren Church and the Wesleyan Methodists held similar positions on these matters, a proposal was made by both churches that they should unite. W. J. Shuey of the United Brethren Church stated in the *Religious Telescope*. "Their theology is the same [as ours]. They preach alike, they occupy the same positions as to secrecy [secret societies] and slavery.They all possess in a measure the spirit of Christ . . ."[25].

There was one significant difference between the two churches. The Wesleyan Methodist Church had not retained the itinerant system. Advocates of the union in both churches believed that this was an adjustable matter.

Invitations were extended to other churches to consider entering the proposed union. In an "Unofficial Union Convention" held in Dayton, Ohio, on May 10, 1855, representatives were present from the United Brethren, Evanglical, Wesleyan Methodist, Free Presbyterian, Free Will Baptist, and Congregational denominations. Resolutions were passed calling for close relations among these churches and their clergy, and setting May 1856 as the time for holding a convention to form a plan of union.

Enthusiasm among the United Brethren for this proposed union apparently declined as fast as it had arisen. A representative of the Wesleyan Methodist Church made a stirring plea for the union in the General Conference of 1857. The conference responded by appointing a committee to "correspond with any religious denomination on the subject of Christian Union."[26]

In the General Conference of 1889, S. C. Breyfogel of the Evangelical Association expressed the hope that the two denominations, which had contemplated union in 1814 and 1817, might still be united, if not upon earth, then surely and "finally in the spacious harbor of heaven."[27] Since both churches were facing denominational rupture, the possibility of the union of the two groups immediately perished.

Ecumenical Activities

· The General Conference of 1873 received a communication from the newly formed American Evangelical Alliance inviting United Brethren representatives to attend a meeting in New York in

October of that year. The stated purpose of the Alliance was to allow American churches of evangelical spirit to enter into close fellowship so they could speak with a united voice on matters dealing with public morality, Bible reading in public schools, evangelization of newly arrived immigrants, separation of church and state, and related matters.

The General Conference sent twenty-five delegates to the meeting. No immediate results were accomplished. The greatest effect of the alliance lay in setting a precedent for the later forming of Protestant ministerial alliances and councils.

In 1881 the General Conference responded to an invitation from the executive committee of the Ecumenical Methodist Conference to send delegates to a meeting to be held in London. The General Conference was cautious about what it feared was an implication that the United Brethren Church was regarded as "a Methodist body." However, when it was made plain that the invitation was based on the recognition that the United Brethren Church in "religion, doctrine, experience, and methods of ecclesiastical work, as well as church polity" resembled the churches which constituted the Ecumenical Methodist Conference, it was decided to send two delegates. Thus was begun the United Brethren participation in an association which in 1951 was renamed World Methodist Council.

MISSIONS

By their very nature the United Brethren Church and the Evangelical Association were missionary.[28] Both churches regarded declaring the Gospel to needy people as their fundamental task. This was their purpose in the eastern areas where the churches began. It continued to be their task as the frontier moved westward until it eventually reached the Pacific coast. However, recognition of the necessity to take the gospel to foreign lands was slow in coming.

The rise of modern foreign mission programs and organizations occurred first in the Congregational Church in the formation of the American Board of Commissioners for Foreign Missions in 1810. The Presbyterian, Baptist, and Methodist Churches followed this example in the following two decades.

It was inevitable that the challenge would reach the United Brethren. In the General Conference of 1841 it was decided to form a missionary Society and to construct a constitution for its governance. However, the planning proved to be inadequate. The society was not denominational in the sense that it was part of the program of the whole church, but rather was a centralizing organization serving to interrelate the work of automonous local church and Annual Conference missionary societies which sprang up and received their support from individual personal, congregational, or Annual Conference memberships. The society did not flourish. Its only significant accomplishment was supporting the organization of a group of settlers under the leadership of T. J. Conner of Indiana. They moved to the Willamette Valley of Oregon in 1853. The party consisted of ninety-eight persons in sixteen families. The project was regarded as missionary because they included among their purposes the evangelization of earlier settlers and the Indians in the area. In due time the settlement became the nucleus of the Oregon Conference.

The General Conference of 1853 regarded this enterprise as not sufficiently effective and therefore reorganized the society and drastically revised its constitution. The change was so complete that a new formal name was given: the Home, Frontier, and Foreign Missionary Society. To distinguish it from the prior society, the latter was referred to thereafter as the Parent Missionary Society.

The new society was truly denominational, embracing the whole church and receiving its support from the whole church. Local and Annual Conference societies continued but had their standing only as they were related to the denominational organization.

The society, as its name implies, was committed to the expansion of the church in the home areas and on the frontier. Its first act was to send a missionary to Missouri.

The African Mission

In its first regular annual meeting in June 1854 the society decided to enter foreign missionary work by opening a field of service in Africa. On January 23, 1855, three men sailed for Sierra Leone, West Africa. They were W. J. Shuey, a Cincinnati preacher who was later to serve the church in many other ways, D. C. Kumler, a physician and preacher, and D. K. Flickinger, a preacher in Dayton, Ohio.

These men found living conditions in Sierra Leone extremely

hazardous. In June 1855 Shuey and Kumler returned home because of ill health. Flickinger remained behind in spite of the debilitating climate, and after overcoming difficulties of health and native hostilities, finally in 1857 established a missionary base at Shenge. Illness sent him back to America in 1857, but he later returned to Africa with other missionary volunteers. He returned home a second time and was made executive secretary of the society. Thereafter his work was administrative.

Other volunteers went to Africa, but the problem of health usually brought a speedy end to their services. By 1869 all missionaries had returned to America, leaving the missionary work which had been established at Shenge under the capable leadership of a native preacher, J. A. Williams. The toll of missionaries raised the question as to whether white people could live and work in Africa. This led to the proposal that American Negroes might find the work possible. Fortunately an American Negro married couple was available to enter and carry on the work, Mr. and Mrs. Joseph Gomer of Dayton, Ohio.[29]

Joseph Gomer was born in Ann Arbor, Michigan. He received basic education in a Quaker school. During the Civil War he served as a cook in the Union Army. After honorable discharge he traveled by riverboat to Dayton, Ohio, and got employment as a carpet layer. On the riverboat he met a young widow, Mary Green, a gifted singer. When they reached Dayton, they were married.

In Dayton they became members of the Third United Brethren Church, a small Negro congregation which had been begun in 1858 by the Miami Annual Conference as a missionary project.[30] It was disbanded in 1883.

The Gomers were lay leaders in the congregation. When the question was raised whether American Negroes could be sent to Africa for missionary work, the Gomers volunteered. The urgency for United Brethren leadership in the mission station at Shenge prompted the board of the society to send them even though they had little by way of educational preparation or denominational involvement to recommend them. They sailed in January 1871. No more fortunate decision of the board was ever made.

Their work in Sierra Leone was phenomenal. Their race made them acceptable to the African natives. Mr. Gomer was an effective preacher, pastor, and organizer. Mrs. Gomer rendered services through singing and teaching. The work was not easy. The Gomers also had problems of health but were able to withstand them. Native customs which conflicted with Christian standards were a greater problem. Polygamy was common. When a native man, husband of several wives and father of numerous children, was converted, what should thereafter be his relation to the wives and the several sets of children? Gomer dealt with such problems judiciously and won native confidence.

The Gomers had three furloughs in America the first in 1876 when after some hesitation the Miami Annual Conference granted him ordination. Gomer died on the mission field in 1892. Mrs. Gomer returned to America in 1894 and died in 1896. They were the persons most responsible for establishing the mission in Sierra Leone.

Two other negro missionaries, the Rev. and Mrs. J. A. Evans, went to Sierra Leone and did excellent work in assisting the Gomers.

A native-born African, David Flickinger Wilberforce, came to America at the age of fifteen. After studying in the Dayton, Ohio, public schools and one year in Union Biblical Seminary, he returned to Africa in 1876. He was the main leader in building and directing a training school at Shenge, thus developing native leadership.

Toward the end of the century American white missionaries, including unmarried women, went to Sierra Leone and did effective work in evangelism, teaching, and medicine. The area of service moved into the back country of Sherbro and as far inland as Kono. In 1883 the Congregational Church turned over its missionary work in the Mendi district to the United Brethren.

Native preachers entered the work with marked success. By 1883 sixteen native men, led by Tom Tucker, rendered very effective service. The African Missionary Annual Conference was organized around this group.

D. K. Flickinger

Although ill health had ended the African missionary work of David K. Flickinger, he continued his interest in missions. As secretary of the Home, Frontier, and Foreign Missionary Society he faced several great problems, namely, recruiting missionaries, inspiring interest in mission work throughout the church, and raising funds to keep the work alive. This last was his biggest problem. By 1885 the society had accumulated a debt of $40,000, for which Flickinger received unjustly severe criticism. The General Conference of 1885 felt that Flickinger's status as secretary of the society was not great enough to enable him to face these issues. Against his better judgment the conference voted to create the office of missionary bishop and to confer its duties and prerogatives upon him. He served in this capacity for one quadrennium.

The German Mission

In light of the debt the United Brethren Church owed to Germany, the homeland of a number of its early leaders and many lay people, the General Conference of 1869 proposed mission work in that country. Under the leadership of the Rev. Christian Bischoff, who had been born and reared in Bavaria but had come to America and was a member of the Ohio German Annual Conference, a congregation was begun in his native town of Naila. Against opposition from state religious authorities the work made slow progress but it moved beyond Bavaria into other areas. In 1880 it was regarded as the German Mission District, and in 1883 the German Missionary Conference. In 1884 J. Sick, also from the Ohio German Conference, succeeded Bischoff as the mission leader, and in 1887 Edward Lorenz succeeded him.

Although the work made some progress, it did not thrive. In 1905 it was given over to the Methodists.

Women's Missionary Association

Although the Home, Frontier, and Foreign Missionary Society represented all the members of the United Brethren Church, a protest arose that the women of the church did not have sufficient influence in the missionary program. The secretary of the society, D. K. Flickinger, agreed and urged that the women should press for greater recognition. In the Ohio German, the California, and the Miami Annual Conferences women's societies or "branches" were organized which eventuated in the formation of the Women's Missionary Association in 1875. The association declared that it was not its purpose to compete or enter into conflict with the denominational society, but it proposed to choose its own fields of missionary work and to send missionaries directly into those fields.

After cordial negotiations with the board of the denominational society it was agreed that the Women's Missionary Association should maintain its autonomy but work under the supervision of the board and that each should support the other in program and finances.

The Women's Missionary Association began its first work in the town of Rotifunk, Sierra Leone. A girls' school was established there, and the Mary Sowers Home was erected to provide girls refuge from the nefarious practice of being sold into child marriage. Other schools for girls were established as the work spread to other towns.

The cooperative relationship between the Women's Missionary Society and the denominational board continued throughout the remainder of United Brethren history.

EDUCATION

Sabbath Schools

In 1849 a communication was received by the General Conference from the American Sabbath School Union calling for participation of the church in their program. The conference responded by adopting a resolution which read:

> Resolved that we labor to have Sabbath Schools organized throughout the church.
> Resolved that all our ministers, . . . do all consistently in their power to organize Sabbath Schools in our Society wherever practicable.
> Resolved that our Printing Establishment furnish the church . . . with books of suitable character for Sabbath Schools.[31]

To enhance and promote the Sabbath school movement the printing establishment published a biweekly periodical, *The Children's Friend*, beginning in 1854.

Not all preachers favored the Sabbath school movement. Some felt that it was an attempt to substitute education for evangelism. Nevertheless the movement went forward. In 1865 the General Conference adopted the constitution and bylaws of an organization to be known as the Sabbath-school Association of the United Brethren in Christ. It provided for a denominational organization headed by a superintendent, treasurer, and secretary. It called for financial undergirding, publication of study materials, the organization of local Sabbath schools, the holding of conventions, and the proper selection and training of teachers.

The greatest leader in the early Sabbath school movement was Isaac Crouse of Ohio who served in effect as executive secretary of the Association from 1865 to 1877. Much of the development of Christian education in the denomination has been due to his early leadership.

In June 1872 the Association introduced the use of the "National Series of Bible Lessons," later called the "International Uniform Lessons." This brought an ecumenical dimension into the Christian education work. In 1873 the printing establishment began to publish Our Bible Teacher for the assistance of United Brethren teachers.

In 1877 Crouse was succeeded by Colonel Robert Cowden, who served as executive secretary of the Association for thirty-six years and earned recognition as a truly great denominational leader. Two significant developments enhancing the Sabbath school work occurred during Cowden's years of service. First, following the example of a program developed by the Chautauqua (New York) Normal Union, a school for training teachers and leaders, the United Brethren Church organized the Bible Normal Union in 1886. It issued diplomas to those who completed a prescribed course. Second, the Home Reading Circle was organized in 1887, providing for a three-year reading course.

Colleges

No institution of higher learning had been established in the United Brethren Church during the first generation of its history. By 1840 some leaders expressed the need to establish a college. They were concerned because young members of the church were enrolling in colleges of other denominations for advanced education, including ministerial preparation, and then changing their church memberships to the denominations which supported those colleges, and so were lost to the United Brethren Church.

On the other hand, strong opposition to college education and the establishment of a college was immediately expressed. William Rhinehart, editor of the Religious Telescope, and John Russell (1799–1870), pastor of the old Otterbein Church in Baltimore and later a bishop in the church, vigorously opposed the proposal. Although Rhinehart favored public education, the idea of having candidates for the ministry go to college and also to theological seminary for their training led him to write, "Don't you see that three or seven years is too long a period to doom a pious youth to Christian theology?"[32]

Rhinehart's successor as editor of the *Religious Telescope*, William Hanby, felt and wrote quite otherwise. Other church leaders supported the establishment of colleges. Among them the most forceful and influential was Lewis Davis (1814–1890). Largely self-educated and a lover of learning, he pressed for the establishment of colleges and a denominational theological seminary and was largely responsible for both accomplishments in the United Brethren Church.

The matter of establishing a college came to a climax in the General Conference of 1845. Although this conference elected Russell as a bishop, it yielded to the urging of Lewis Davis and others and took the following action: "Resolved that proper measures be adopted to establish an Institution of Learning. Resolved, therefore, that it be recommended to the attention of the annual conferences, etc., avoiding irredeemable debts."[33]

The Scioto Annual Conference took action at once. It invited the neighboring Muskingum and Sandusky Annual Conferences to join it in establishing a college. Although they hesitated, due to presiding Bishop John Russell's opposition, the Scioto Annual Conference appointed a committee of three men, William Hanby, Jonathan Dresbach, and Lewis Davis, then a presiding elder, to proceed with the project. They purchased the Methodist Blendon Young Men's Seminary, located in Westerville, Ohio, for $1300, and opened it on September 1, 1847, as Otterbein University. Among its first students, eighty-one in number, were twenty-nine women. Otterbein was the second American school to enroll women on the college level on equal standing with men.[34]

In the university's first years Lewis Davis served as field agent. In 1850 he became its president and served in that capacity, with a one-year interlude, until 1871, when he became the "senior professor" (the equivalent of dean) of the newly opened Union Biblical Seminary. Hence he has been designated the Father of Higher Education in the United Brethren Church.

In 1850 a second college, Mount Pleasant College, was opened by the Allegheny Annual Conference in Mount Pleasant, Pennsylvania, the site of the first two General Conferences. However, a heavy debt was incurred, making its continuation impossible. In 1858 its meager resources were transferred to Otterbein University.

The third college to be opened, Lebanon Valley College, in Annville, Pennsylvania, began in 1866. It also had financial difficulties and had to face serious opposition. It nearly perished in 1867 when John Russell, whose service as bishop had ended in 1861, preached a one-hour sermon in the Annville church against formal higher education. He took as his text a phrase from I Corinthians 8:1, "Knowledge Puffeth Up." Immediately one-fourth of the student body, which had reached one hundred, withdrew from the school.

That it did not perish was due to the fact that the East Pennsylvania Annual Conference granted it vigorous support.[35]

Between the years 1850 and 1890 a total of twenty-six colleges and academies or "seminaries" were founded, but all in due time were discontinued or were united with other institutions. The two which contributed most were Philomath College in Oregon and York College in Nebraska.

Russell's Biblical Chair

Apparently John Russell's opposition to college education was based on his feeling that it was gained in an environment separated from the everyday world. College graduates therefore were poorly prepared for facing the demands and problems of life. This would be especially true of young men preparing for the ministry in a college setting which was quite different from the context of the church. That he did not oppose ministerial education within a church environment was shown when in 1868 he announced that he was giving $10,000 as a fund to endow a "Biblical Chair." The sum was to be invested by the Home, Frontier, and Foreign Missionary Society at six percent interest. The income was to be used to provide a salary of from $100 to $125 to an established minister who would take under his care one or two young men, white or Negro, from the East Pennsylvania, Pennsylvania, or Virginia Annual Conferences and teach them in a one- or two-year course biblical studies, English or German, writing, and arithmetic. The program was to be under the direction of a committee appointed by the Pennsylvania Annual Conference. It was to choose a qualified pastor-teacher and apply the remainder of the annual interest to the personal needs of the students. If any money was left over, it should be used by the Missionary Society.

In addition to their study the students were to spend at least two hours a day in manual labor and three weeks in the summer on farms during haymaking and grain harvest.

Russell stated that this endowment should be maintained for forty years, after which the principal should be used by the Missionary Society at the rate of $1000 per year in mission work in the United States until it was exhausted.

No applicants ever came forth to take advantage of the Russell Biblical Chair. The forty years expired in 1908, and the money was added to the assets of the Missionary Society.[36]

Union Biblical Seminary

The General Conference of 1869 responded to a rising call for an institution for the special education of persons preparing for the ministry. Young people had been enrolling in theological seminaries of other denominations and eventually entering their ministry. Led by Henry Garst, a future president of Otterbein University, after a comparatively brief discussion of the matter, the conference passed the following resolution:

> Resolved, that the Board of Education be instructed to devise and adopt a plan for the founding of a biblical institute to be under the control of the General Conference; and said Board is hereby instructed and empowered to take measures to raise funds and locate such institution, and proceed with its establishment.[37]

The resolution indicates that the conference had already established a Board of Education for the entire educational enterprise of the church. The president of the board was Lewis Davis.

The board acted promptly. In 1870 it voted to establish a seminary in Dayton, Ohio. On October 11, 1871, Union Biblical Seminary was opened in four classrooms and a lecture room in the new Home Street Church, which was still under construction. The opening had been delayed by a windstorm in July which had blown off the partly constructed roof. In 1873 the church was renamed the Summit Street Church.

The seminary operated under an executive committee with Bishop Glossbrenner as chairman. The Rev. John Kemp served as general agent.

The facilities of the seminary were meager. Its first catalog said, " . . . there are a few valuable books in the library at present." By 1876 the catalog could state, "There are several hundred valuable books in the library at present."

The seminary's greatest asset was its early teachers. Lewis Davis was "senior professor," teaching systematic and practical theology until his retirement in 1885. George A. Funkhouser, a graduate of Western Theological Seminary in Pittsburgh, was professor of Greek exegesis and sacred and church history until 1912. Josiah P. Landis, the pastor of the Home Street Church, a graduate of Lane Theological Seminary in Cincinnati, taught part time as professor of Hebrew and homiletics. In 1880 he became a full-time teacher and taught until 1934. In 1880 this group of excellent teachers was joined by the great church historian and theologian, Augustus W. Drury, who taught from that date until 1934. Other men who taught during the first two decades of the seminary's history were Rudolph Wahl, Hebrew Exegesis, 1874, and George Kiester, Hebrew Exegesis and Biblical History, 1874–1880.

When the seminary opened on October 11, 1871, eleven students were enrolled. In 1874 the first class to be graduated numbered eight. By 1890 one hundred twenty-nine had been graduated. In 1883 the first woman, the wife of a student, was graduated. In 1887 the first unmarried woman who had prepared for full-time church vocation was graduated.

In 1879 the seminary moved into a newly constructed, large, three-story brick building at First Street and Euclid Avenue in Dayton. The building, costing $10,000, was built on a five-acre lot given by the general agent, John Kemp.

The teachers were not only conscientious scholars; they were unusually progressive in thought and methods. They were fully aware of developments in the fields of biblical interpretation and scientific investigation and the implications for Christian theology. Their insights were poorly understood by certain church leaders (who referred to the seminary as a "preacher factory"), but they held to the highest standards of teaching and interpretation. They brought high regard to the seminary from the most advanced authorities on theological education. They were warm-hearted and set before their students and the church high standards of Christian commitment. In 1909 the name was changed to Bonebrake Theological Seminary.

Publishing Interests

The denominational publishing house which had been established in Circleville, Ohio, in 1834 had rendered important service to the church in publishing the *Religious Telescope* and Henry Spayth's *History of the United Brethren Church*. It also published other materials and distributed books and literature published by other agencies.

Because Circleville was within the bounds of the Scioto Annual Conference, that conference was given the responsibility of supervising the work of publication.

Several serious problems faced the group of three publishing house trustees appointed by the Scioto Annual Conference. The first was a large debt that had been accumulating from the very beginning. A stated purpose of the publishing house was to gain profits which were to be used "to assist the itinerant superannuated and indigent preachers and their families."[38] Unwise business policies prevented the earning of profits. The main injudicious practice was trying to encourage the sale of the *Religious Telescope* and all other materials by extending credit. A large portion of the credit granted was never honored.

Another problem gradually evolved from the fact that Circleville was not a good location. As a small town it offered few facilities which could be used to supplement the equipment of the publishing house, and it was not strategically located for easy distribution of the published materials.

Last, the publishing house was required to publish a German periodical which never had enough subscribers to be profitable. The periodical was *Die Geschäftige Martha (The Busy Martha)*. It was discontinued in 1842 but was succeeded in 1846 by *Der Deutsche Telescop*, later renamed *Der Fröliche Botschafter (The Joyful Messenger)*, which remained in publication until 1930.

The difficulties of being located in Circleville led to the decision by the General Conference of 1853 to move the facilities to Dayton, Ohio. Moving the equipment by canal boat to Columbus, then to Xenia by railroad, and then to Dayton by Conestoga wagons, and relocating it in buildings on the northeast corner of Main and Fourth streets with added equipment cost the church $30,000.

The relocation was fortunate. Distribution of materials was greatly increased. Wiser business methods came into use. Larger buildings were built, and newer and much larger presses were installed. In 1881 it was announced that the debt was finally liquidated. One year later a dividend of $5000 was declared. It was used to offer support to superannuated ministers and the families of deceased ministers. By 1885 the net value of the publishing house was set at $220,358. In the quadrennium of 1881–1885 the volume of business exceeded one-half million dollars.[39]

In addition to the periodicals already mentioned, the publishing house produced many other materials for denominational use. The list included periodicals and Sunday school studies for children, intermediates, and adults. In 1874 *Hymns for the Sanctuary and Social Worship* was published, the first hymnbook to be printed by the Church having the musical scores as well as the texts. In 1883 the *United Brethren Yearbook* appeared.

Several outstanding men were largely responsible for the success of the publishing house. Solomon Voneida and W. J. Shuey served as publishing agents from 1853 to 1861 and 1864 to 1897 respectively. John Lawrence, Daniel Berger (both of whom became authors of histories of the United Brethren Church), Milton Wright, and J. W. Hott were editors of the *Religious Telescope* successively from 1852 to 1889. Edmund S. Lorenz served as editor of English and German hymnbooks from 1878 to 1891. He collaborated with Isaiah Boltzell in publishing twelve collections of German hymns which were so popular within and beyond the membership of the United Brethren Church that "hundreds of thousands of these song books were sold all over the United States."[40]

CONTROVERSY AND DIVISION

In the General Conference of 1841 a constitution was adopted and inserted into the *Discipline* as Section Second. It gathered together a number of rules and regulations, some of which formerly had been scattered throughout the *Discipline*, and set them into a category different from all other regulations by including as Article IV of the constitution the provision, "There shall be no alteration of the foregoing constitution, unless by request of two-thirds of the whole society." All other rules and regulations in other sections of the *Discipline* were modifiable by a simple majority vote of the General Conference.

The questions became: What do the phrases "request of" and

"the whole society" mean? Does "request" mean "vote count" as
Stimmenzahl in the German translation of the Discipline connotes?
What is meant by "the whole society"? Does it mean literally all the
members of the United Brethren Church? Does it mean the official
representatives of the entire membership of the church, such as the
General Conference? Does the phrase "by request of two-thirds of the
whole society" mean that any revision of the constitution requires
that two-thirds of the entire membership must spontaneously and
simultaneously rise up and make a request?—an obvious impossibility. Does it mean that the General Conference, representing the
whole society, may modify the constitution by a two-thirds majority
vote? Does it mean that an authority such as the General Conference,
by a majority vote may submit a recommendation upon which the
entire membership of the church must vote with a two-thirds
majority required to approve? Or, might it be a two-thirds majority of
the members voting?

Obviously, before any modification of the constitution could
take place, the precise meaning of Article IV had to be determined.
The matter was debated vigorously but fruitlessly in one General
Conference after another. In 1873 the General Conference adopted a
method by which, it was hoped, the proper interpretation could be
made. It commissioned the Board of (four) Bishops to decide the
matter and report the decision in the Religious Telescope. However,
the bishops could not arrive at a unanimous decision, probably
because at least one, being opposed to any modification of the
constitution, thwarted unanimous agreement.

Among the regulations in the constitution, and therefore under
Article IV, were three which came to be the centers of much dispute
in the five decades after 1841. They were:

Article I—. . . [The membership in General Conference] shall
consist of Elders . . . [but not laymen].

Article II, Section 4—No rule or ordinance shall at anytime be
passed, to change or do away with the Confession of Faith as it now
stands; . . . .

Article II, Section 7—There shall be no connection with secret
combinations, ...

Lay Delegates in General Conferences

The General Conference of 1877 had voted to grant the right of
Annual Conferences to include lay members in their membership. It

could do so because the rule concerning membership in the Annual Conferences was not in the constitution but in another section of the *Discipline*.

On the other hand, membership in General Conferences was determined by Article I of the constitution. Therefore, to permit lay membership in the General Conferences required a change in the constitution which could be accomplished only "by request of two-thirds of the whole society."

The demand that laymen be members of the General Conferences had become strident after the middle of the nineteenth century.

The Confession of Faith

Although the Confession of Faith itself comprised Section First of the *Disciple* and therefore was not a part of the constitution, the rule in the constitution, Article II, Section 4, made the confession subject to change only "by request of two-thirds of the whole society."

The Confession of Faith had consisted not of numbered and entitled articles, as in the Methodist and Evangelical *Disciplines*, but in a brief essay statement. It set forth the primary doctrines of the faith but did not include certain other related doctrines. The limitation in the coverage of Christian doctrine led to an increasing demand that the confession be entirely reconstructed.

Secret Societies

By far the most troublesome issue in the life of the church was the question whether church members could also be members of secret combinations or secret societies such as the Free Masons. The General Conference of 1825 had taken a rigid stand ruling out secret society membership, and a rule to this effect had been placed in the *Discipline*. In 1841 the rule was continued as a separate item in the *Discipline*, as heretofore, but was also inserted in the constitution as part of Article II, Section 7. This made modification of the rule against membership in secret societies a matter for "request of two-thirds of the whole society."

The absoluteness of the antisecrecy rule caused various problems. For example, for tactical reasons some temperance societies maintained secret membership lists; therefore the rule forbidding membership in secret societies ruled out participation.

As the middle decades of the nineteenth century passed, some prominent members of the church felt that membership in secret societies was not inconsistent with Christian commitment. Hence, there were occasional cases of persons who defied the rule and thereby gave the Annual Conferences the unpleasant choice of either dismissing them from church membership or winking at the violation.

Beginning in 1869 petitions were brought to the General Conferences requesting modification of the antisecrecy rule. The General Conferences rejected the petitions with declining majorities. This caused sharp disagreement among the members of the General Conferences and the formation of two factions: the "radicals," who favored strict enforcement of the antisecrecy rule, and the "liberals," who desired modification. Milton Wright became the leader of the radicals both in his capacity as editor of the *Religious Telescope* from 1869 to 1877 and as bishop in two nonconsecutive quadrennia, 1877–1881 and 1885–1889. When his successor as editor of the *Religious Telescope* took a position leaning toward the liberals, Milton Wright published an independent antisecrecy periodical, the *Richmond Star*, from 1882 to 1885 in his home in Richmond, Indiana. Other efforts were made to prevent a swing toward the liberal view.

Nevertheless the proportion of liberals grew rapidly in the 1880's, and the demand for reinterpretation of the antisecrecy rule increased. The stated attitude of the liberals was not to eliminate completely the antisecrecy rule but to express it not as forbidding membership in secret societies but as placing the issue upon the judgment of individual members with a statement calling for caution.

A New Constitution

As these three issues became increasingly more pressing, it became apparent that the constitution would have to be changed at these points—especially so as to end the confusion over the phrase "by request of two-thirds of the whole society." Dealing with each of these issues in effect required a whole new constitution. The General Conference of 1885 decided by a majority vote, with a vocal minority firmly objecting, to appoint a Church Commission on the Confession of Faith and Constitution comprised of the board of six bishops and twenty-one other members to be chosen from the General Conference membership. The commission was instructed to formulate a new constitution containing a rule providing for lay membership in General Conferences and another rule on secret societies as well as to formulate a new Confession of Faith.

After these matters were prepared, the commission was to submit them to the membership of the whole church with the stipulation that a majority of two-thirds of all votes cast would be necessary for adoption.

The commission carried out its assignment with Bishops Milton Wright and John Dickson refusing to participate. Immediately after the adjournment of the General Conference of 1885 the commission spent seven days formulating a new constitution and a new Confession of Faith.

The newly formulated Confession of Faith consisted of thirteen numbered and entitled paragraphs.

As to lay membership in General Conferences, the commission proposed the rule, "General Conference, . . . shall consist of elders and laymen elected in each annual conference district throughout the church."[41]

The new rule with reference to membership in secret societies did not prohibit such membership but warned against membership in secret orders "which infringe upon the rights of those outside their organization, and whose principles and practices are injurious to the character of their members, [and] are contrary to the word of God . . . . "[42]

In the proposed new or amended constitution the rule for making changes, displacing the rule "by request of two-thirds of the whole society," read:

> Amendments . . . may be proposed by any General Conference—two thirds of the members elected thereto concurring—which amendments shall be submitted to a vote of the membership of the church, ...
> A majority of all the votes cast upon any submitted amendment shall be necessary to its final ratification.[43]

Because of the seriousness of these constitutional changes, their adoption would be in effect adopting a new constitution. Therefore, it was deemed that there were four issues altogether: (1) a new constitution, (2) lay delegates in General Conferences, (3) membership in secret combinations, and (4) a new Confession of Faith.

In the ensuing three and one-half years these proposals were disseminated throughout the church in order to prepare the members to vote. Many articles for and against the proposals appeared in the church periodicals.

In November 1888 the commission presented these four issues in the form of a ballot to the members of the entire church who at this time numbered about 200,000. The vote as reported to the General Conference of 1889 was as follows:

For the new constitution...................... 50,685   against—3,659
For lay delegates.................................. 48,825   against—5,634
For the section on secret
    combinations.................................... 46,994   against—7,298
For the new Confession of Faith.......... 51,070 against—3,310[44]

The General Conference of 1889

The General Conference of 1889 convened in York, Pennsylvania, on May 9, 1889. The next day the commission presented its report. On Saturday, May 11, the conference debated the report, adopting it at the end of the day by a vote of 110 to 20. It was announced that when the conference convened on Monday morning, May 13, it would be operating under the new constitution.

Bishop Wright and others protested strenuously, claiming that the whole action was in violation of the constitution of 1841. Bishop Dickson also had opposed the action, but the overwhelming vote of the church members convinced him to support the changes.

In spite of attempts to assuage the feelings of the radicals, which they took to be condescending, when the conference came into session on May 13, Bishop Milton Wright and fifteen conference delegates withdrew. The next day they were denounced and declared to be "no longer ministers or members of the Church of the United Brethren in Christ."[45] Alternate conference delegates were named to replace them.

Bishop Wright and those who had withdrawn with him rented a meeting place in York and "reconvened" the General Conference claiming that, since they were operating under the original constitution of 1841, and the majority group had illegally violated it, they were the true Church of the United Brethren in Christ. They recognized fourteen other persons as members of the conference, and with the total of thirty persons proceeded to fill offices and carry out the business of the conference. As by legal action they later were forbidden the name of the Church of the United Brethren in Christ they referred to themselves as The United Brethren Church (Old Constitution).

Thus the tragic event of the division of the church was accomplished. The writer was told by the late Bishop A. R. Clippinger that in conversation with Orville and Wilbur Wright, the inventors of the airplane and sons of Bishop Milton Wright, they told him that had there been less impetuosity in moving toward modifications of the old constitution and more regard and respect for those who opposed the changes, a few more years of time would have brought resolution to the problems without denominational rupture.

*I*n 1839 the membership of the Evangelical Association was given as 12,065. By 1887 it was 138,668. During this five-decade period the growth was steady but not rapid. The gain was made almost entirely from among people of German origin. As the German people settled across the country, especially in the northern tier of states, the Evangelical Association restricted its ministry to them. Thus few English-speaking people were found in the church. This accounts for the modest growth.

On the accompanying map the geographic expansion of the church is shown during this period.

By 1840 the church was made up of three Annual Conferences: East Pennsylvania, including southeastern Pennsylvania, missions in New York City and westward in New York state to Buffalo and in the Waterloo area of Ontario, Canada; West Pennsylvania, including circuits in Maryland, Virginia, and Pennsylvania west of the Susquehanna to the Ohio line; and Ohio, including everything west of Pennsylvania with circuits in Ohio, Indiana, Illinois, southern Michigan, and southern Wisconsin.

By 1890 there were twenty-one Annual Conferences in the United States, one in Canada, one in Germany, and one in Switzerland.

THE EVANGELICAL ASSOCIATION, 1840–1890

Authority in the Church

The General Conference

Begining in 1839 the General Conference met every four years, giving a means for regular appeal for final decisions in the church. Heretofore the meetings of General Conferences had been irregular. The holding of quadrennial sessions gave regularity to processes of decision and action. This was heightened in 1839 by establishing a formal way of choosing delegates proportionately from all areas of the church, as stated in the Discipline, "The General Conference (is to) consist of one member for every four members of each Annual Conference, who are to be elected from the Elders by the majority votes of the said Annual Conference."[1] In 1855 the proportion was changed to one General Conference delegate for every seven Annual Conference members. In 1867 the proportion was changed again to one delegate for every ten members in the Annual Conference.[2]

In the General Conference of 1867 action was passed giving the General Conference judicial power for deciding issues of dispute or legality anywhere within the structure and workings of the church. It set forth in the Discipline the following statement:

> The General Conference is the supreme law in the Church, it shall decide upon the legality of all acts of Annual Conferences . . . ; and in its judicial capacity it shall decide, render verdict, and declare judgment only on such cases as are lawfully brought before it for adjudication.
> It shall have power to make such rules and regulations as will enable it to execute the powers conferred upon it.[3]

This action did not delegate to the General Conference new powers or methods to initiate new legislation, but it confirmed the powers it already had to regulate all decisions of all bodies within the church so as to preserve unity and prevent conflict.

The Bishops and Denominational Officers

The hesitation in electing a bishop from 1808, the year of Bishop Albright's death, until 1839, when John Seybert was chosen to be the second bishop in Evangelical history, was due to the fear that the office of bishop would accumulate inordinate power. Seybert himself shared this fear. When in 1859 the General Conference proposed strengthening the office of bishop, Bishop Seybert strenuously opposed it.[4] Furthermore, the bishops themselves were made subject to disciplinary provisions in case of misconduct.[5]

As the years passed, questions arose as to what should be the prerogatives in General Conferences of officials of the church who had not been elected as delegates but whose expertise made it desirable for them to engage in conference discussions and decisions. Such officials were editors, executive secretaries of societies, and even the bishops themselves. In 1867 the General Conference granted all privileges to such officials, including the right to vote.[6]

This action was not accepted without protest by some delegates because they still feared episcopal domination. This was especially true of many delegates from the Annual Conference east of the Ohio-Pennsylvania line. As late as 1879 these delegates favored withdrawing from the bishops all General Conference privileges except the responsibility to preside. This probably reflected eastern opposition to Bishop J. J. Esher of Illinois who was forceful in his leadership and had been engaged several times in controversies with eastern church leaders.

Incorporation and Property Ownership

In 1832 the Eastern Conference, at that time the center of power and administration in the church, commissioned "A. Ettinger and Jacob Hammer . . . to obtain an act of incorporation from the Commonwealth of Pennsylvania for the Evangelical Association."[7]

This was accomplished, but it did not include a provision granting the local churches individual legal powers, which raised a question as to the legal ownership and control of church property. The General Conference of 1867, under the rights held through the denominational incorporation, decided that all church property was owned by the denomination. Therefore, as for the local church properties, the congregations had only the responsibility that they be "used, kept, maintained and disposed of . . . for the use of the ministry and membership of the Evangelical Association of North America, subject to the discipline . . . of said Church or Association."[8]

The statement of incorporation gives the denominational name as the Evangelical Association. In the General Conference of 1871 petitions were considered asking for a change of name, especially changing "Association" to "Church." It was felt that the word association connoted too loose a structure. The conference laid the issue on the table. When it arose again in 1875, the result was the same. The General Conference of 1879 again considered it and by a vote of 69 to 9 sent it as a recommendation to the Annual Conferences for their endorsement (according to the disciplinary rule dealing with changes)—recommending that the name become the Evangelical Church of North America. The Annual Conferences repudiated the action by a substantial vote. In the East Pennsylvania Annual Conference the vote was typical: "Affirmative 9, Negative 74."[9]

THE MINISTRY

From 1840 to 1890 there were three levels of ministry in the Evangelical Association: (1) local preacher or itinerant minister on trial, (2) deacon, (3) elder. To be received into the first level required approval and acceptance by an Annual Conference. A local preacher had to remain on that level for six years and bring to each session of the Annual Conference written testimonies of commendations from two elders of his district. The itinerant minister on trial had to do the same but for only two years. Then the candidate could be voted to the level of deacon by the Annual Conference and ordained to that standing by the bishop. After serving satifactorily for two years as deacon, the candidate could then be voted to the highest ministerial level of elder by the Annual Conference and be ordained to the eldership by the bishop.

Educational attainment was not involved in this procedure. Three standards were the basis for reaching full standing: good character, assurance of a divine call, and evidence of natural ability.

Bishop Seybert was not satisfied with these standards. He believed in and personally practiced diligent study of good works on religion and theology. On many of his episcopal journeys by carriage he started from the publishing establishment in New Berlin with a trunkful of books and other study materials to distribute to preachers. His spirit led the General Conference of 1843 to appoint him as the chairman of a committee to "prepare a course of study for our junior preachers and for candidates for the ministry."[10] This constituted a step forward, but no authority made such study a requirement. As late as 1889 there were still no rules requiring study, although statements in the *Discipline* implied that it was expected.[11] To progressive members of the clergy this condition was unfortunate.

John Dreisbach in 1845 submitted an article to *Der Christliche Botschafter* entitled "Teachers and Preachers Should not Be Ignorant," and followed it with a recommendation to General Conference in 1847 calling for the establishment of a seminary for training young ministers. The General Conference acted favorably, but the Annual Conferences did not. Arguments were raised against such formal education that it would result in cold religion of the head, putting an end to the stress upon the inner religious life. The opposition perceived such spiritual sterility among the denominations that had "preacher-factories."

Itinerancy

Itinerancy, a method of appointing preachers to ministerial tasks, arose in the beginning of the Evangelical Association out of necessity. As the term implies, it is the system of appointment of preachers by the bishop and presiding elders to circuits requiring travel, first from former to new circuits and second among the different preaching stations comprising their circuits. This system was especially effective in ministering to scattered congregations.

By the middle of the nineteenth century the eastern section of the church had become relatively stabilized. Many stations had become sufficiently strong to require a minister's full-time service, and so he did little "traveling" while serving such an appointment. Yet he was frequently moved to new appointments, which required that he and his family periodically had to travel to the new station. Hence, the term itinerancy continued to be used to describe the method by which the preachers were moved from one assignment to another.

The bishops and presiding elders also were involved in itinerancy. In both cases responsibilities of supervision of the churches of the Annual Conferences or districts required extensive travel. They also were subject to assignments by General or Annual Conference action from one area or district to another.

Corresponding to this willingness of the clergy to itinerate was the obligation of the churches, districts, or bishops' areas to receive the persons assigned.

As the result of this itinerant system it was possible to guarantee to every church or district or area that it would always be granted ministerial leadership.

Even though in the East the itinerant system had achieved a measure of stability, in the open spaces of the Midwest and Far West the assignments required strenuous and even dangerous travel. Rev. M. J. Muller, presiding elder in Kansas in 1861, who traveled 720 miles on one quarterly round of his district, gave a description of some of his itinerant experiences.

> I met with [hospitality] wherever I came. One night, however, I was entertained all alone, out on the open prairie. A piece of dried bread and three eggs, which I had with me, served for supper, and my buggy cushions and great coat a bed, down in the grass by the side of my buggy. I had a far better time of it than in many of the small smothering cabins along the road, where bugs and fleas are your night long associates.[12]

In August 1862 an Indian uprising in Minnesota took one thousand lives including three itinerant preachers and the members of their classes. On other occasions an itinerant, Lewis Seder, was shot and tomahawked; N. Mus had his tongue cut out, but escaped death; August Nierens, after surviving one day of Indian attack, was caught by surprise and shot to death the next day.[13]

Tenure

For seven decades it had been the custom to permit a preacher or a presiding elder to serve an appointment only a limited length of time. A disciplinary rule read: "No preacher shall be permitted to remain more than two years successively on one circuit, station or mission, nor any Presiding Elder more than four years on one district."[14]

Over the years an increasing protest was raised against this restriction, resulting in harsh debate in General Conferences. Finally in the General Conference of 1871 the rule was changed to permit preachers to serve for three years at the most. This was judged to be such a radical change that the compiler of the minutes added, "Thus, beloved, the happy [?] hour has finally come in which this long and much debated question has been determined."[15]

Even three years seemed to be too restrictive, so that the tenure was extended several times thereafter. In 1934 the observing of a time limit of service was completely discontinued.

Ministerial Responsibility

Each issue of the *Discipline* included a long section detailing ministerial duties. The *Discipline* of 1860 devoted twenty pages to a question-and-answer form of discussion. Along with the many instructions on preaching, pastoral duties, celebration of the sacraments, etc., were also admonitions on ministerial conduct and dedication. Jesting was castigated; lengthy preaching along with "unabating loudness" should be avoided; interviews with the female sex should be circumspect; and sixteen out of twenty-four hours should be spent awake and engaged in employment.[16]

LIFE IN THE CHURCH

The Laity

In spite of occasional assertions of acceptance of democratic principles in the procedures of the General and Annual Conferences, the Evangelical Association throughout the period under discussion never granted membership to lay representatives, and all decision making was the prerogative of only the ordained elders. The lower ranks of the clergy, while attendants at the Annual Conferences, had no privileges.

The laity were instructed by the actions of conferences that they should be circumspect in their behavior. Frivolous and careless conduct should be avoided especially in matters of pleasures and amusements. Picnics, fairs, and cakewalks were repudiated. Fancy dress, jewelry, and other inordinate displays of wealth were condemned. Marriage should be only with believing partners, and warnings were to be seen in such biblical matrimonial ventures as those of Samson and Solomon.[17]

Worship

The custom of the Evangelical Association in devotional meetings was to stress reading of scripture, preaching the gospel, fervent singing of hymns, and uttering earnest prayers. Spontaneity was typical.

However, as local churches became more settled and younger, more highly trained ministers gained in numbers, greater sophistication in worship became the pattern. This disturbed the ministers who remembered the days of greater freedom.

Camp meetings were still held, but even in these, many felt, the earlier fervency had abated. Charges were made that the young preachers often used the camp meetings to put on display their refined gifts of eloquence. They chose subjects and texts which were calculated to impress the hearers with their profundity. One young preacher, for instance, chose to preach on Ezekiel 17:3, "A great eagle with great wings, long-winged, full of feathers, which had divers colors, came unto Lebanon, and took the highest branch of the cedar."[18] Often these young preachers engaged in "levity and unseemly jesting."

In spite of these instances of violations of the camp-meeting spirit, the camp-meeting movement was effective, especially in the East. Many times the emphasis was centered in "holiness," which resulted in extreme emotionalism. Crowds numbering up to twelve thousand attended. Some camp meetings lasted as long as ten days.[19]

Leaders such as Bishops Orwig and Esher urged that worship services in the churches should be conducted with propriety. The Scriptures always should be read and good hymns sung with vigor and dignity. Hymns should always be sung thoughtfully, and certainly never should there be sung "senseless and absurd choruses to irreverent tunes." Preaching should be fresh and vital. There should be no preaching based on borrowed skeletons of sermons because that results in violation of the gospel, being only dry and theoretical.[20]

Bishops Long and Esher stated that "we perceive careless often noisy walking in and out, irreverent conversation, frivolous talking before and after service, and other unbecoming behavior, whereby the sanctity of the place is impaired, and in many instances, the good effects of the services neutralized."[21]

These negative criticisms of worship practices are not to be taken as indications of the predominant mood. Much the greater part of Evangelical worship was true expression of the acceptance of God's redeeming grace with a complementing emphasis upon a disciplined godly life.

Sabbath Observance

The Evangelical Association stressed the sacred obligation to remember the Sabbath (Sunday) to keep it holy. Many General Conferences adopted resolutions deploring the growing tendency in American society to violate the Sabbath. The General Conference of 1867 adopted the following statement:

> The day of the Lord is, according to the Holy Scriptures, a day of rest from all temporal business and is to be kept *holy*, . . . to the honor of the Lord and the physical and spiritual benefit of man. . . . All vain pleasure-seeking on this day, as rioting, dancing, excursions, drinking, etc., together with temporal business, are entirely forbidden as direct transgressions of the divine law. . . . "[22]

Jubilee

As the year 1850 approached, the East and West Annual Conferences proposed a celebration of the half century of the Evangelical movement, counting from the year 1800 when Jacob Albright organized the first "classes." As proper recognition, four projects were proposed: (1) observe a day of thanksgiving, (2) establish a memorial to Jacob Albright, (3) begin foreign missionary work, and (4) establish a seminary.

October 17 was chosen for the day of thanksgiving because in October 1796 Albright began his itinerant ministry. The memorial was to be a chapel built within a few feet of Albright's grave in Kleinfeltersville, Pennsylvania. Difficulty was experienced here because as the foundation was being laid, a severe rain storm weakened it so that the finished structure almost at once began to disintegrate. Ten years later a completely new building was erected, which stands to the present day as a fitting monument. Foreign mission work was begun in the opening of a German mission field in late 1850. In 1852 a "high school" called "Albright Seminary" was opened in Berlin, Somerset County, Pennsylvania.

Language

The determination of the Evangelical Association in the first four decades to confine its preaching and publishing almost exclusively to the German language began to change after 1843. In that year the General Conference, recognizing that some churches and preachers were using English, provided for the organization of English Annual Conferences where ten or more closely grouped English-speaking preachers were serving.[23]

The conference also made provision for publishing materials in the English language and the translation and publication of the *Discipline* of 1844 in English. Other English publications were set forth in subsequent years. Once the movement got underway, the trend toward English usage developed so rapidly with the Annual Conferences changing over to English that the German-speaking people protested. To guarantee that their integrity be maintained, in 1875 three German Annual Conferences, Atlantic, Erie, and Iowa, were organized to embrace the German-speaking preachers and congregations.

SOCIAL AND ETHICAL ISSUES

Slavery

The opposition to slavery which the Evangelical Association had earlier expressed did not change. In the church's periodicals the only dispute over slavery was not between pro and antislavery parties, but between those who contributed articles of bitter abolitionist spirit and those who felt that a more judicious position would ultimately be more effective. Actually only a few congregations were located in areas where slavery was commonly practiced, namely those in the Shenandoah Valley and the Baltimore area. Even in these places German people rarely held slaves.

The Civil War

During the Civil War the church gave staunch support to the Union. The General Conference of 1863 met at the time when the horror of the war had been amply demonstrated and the uncertainty of its outcome was causing deep apprehension. Slavery, the war it caused, and the horrible loss of life and property were declared to be due to the power of Satan. The southern seceders were his tools, and therefore the use of "every proper measure" to suppress the rebels was fully warranted. President Lincoln was given full support and commended for issuing the Emancipation Proclamation.[24]

The conference also took action recommending that the Board of Missions should "adopt suitable measures to bring (the negroes) the glad tidings of spiritual freedom, in the Gospel of Jesus Christ."[25] This resolution was not carried out during or after the war because of limited financial resources.

The churches in the Shenandoah Valley had been listed among the churches of the Pittsburgh Annual Conference until 1861 when they were removed from the list.[26] A brief notation in the minutes of the Pittsburgh Annual Conference simply says the "Shenandoah Circuit in Virginia is abandoned."[27]

After the war ended, the Evangelical Association joined the demand of many northern political leaders that just retribution be required of the South. Within a set of seven resolutions the General Conference of 1867 declared

> . . . the Congress of the United States has introduced with praiseworthy zeal and precedence a reconstruction for the South which promises a lasting peace. We regard this measure as being wise, statesmanlike, just and humane, giving no reason of just complaint to the South . . . .
>
> Resolved, that we deplore that President Johnson opposes this congressional measure of pacification and regulation, and tries to render it ineffective. . . . [28]

The Civil War also brought change in the official stance the church had previously assumed, namely that "wars and bloodshed are not agreeable to the Gospel and Spirit of Christ."[29] This article was reaffirmed in later *Disciplines*, but the General Conference of 1863, in resolutions dealing with the war declared, " . . . it is the imperative duty of our Government, to use the sword entrusted to it of God, . . . and it is the holiest duty of every citizen, faithfully to support the Government in the important duties devolving upon the same."[30]

Liquor and Tobacco

A declaration made in 1839 forbidding the using, making, and selling of spiritous liquors remained the church's position throughout its history. Hence, when organizations were formed to oppose the liquor traffic, such as the Pennsylvania State Temperance Union and the Woman's Christian Temperance Union, the church gave them its support.

The church also constantly opposed the use of tobacco in any form because of the crudity involved, the danger to good health, and the financial wastefulness. The East Pennsylvania Annual Conference passed the resolution "that it is the sense of this Conference that no person addicted to this evil should hereafter be received into the Itinerant Ministry."[31]

Marriage and Divorce

The church's stance on marriage and divorce was always to stress the sanctity of the former and to deplore the latter. Its attitude is reflected in the statement, ". . . none of our members ought to seek a divorce upon any other pretence [than adultery], and it shall not be permitted that our preachers marry such as want to re-marry but are not divorced legally by the word of God."[32]

Insurance

Several Evangelical churches were destroyed in the great Chicago fire of October 8 and 9, 1871. When the General Conference convened on October 12, the loss was central in the minds of many delegates. They immediately decided that the church should insure all its property against fire. To save money they decided to organize the Evangelical Fire Insurance Company. However, they later discovered that the laws governing such independent companies involved requirements too intricate for a church to fulfill. Hence, in 1875 the idea was abandoned.

It is strange that while the church gave such attention to fire insurance, it reacted negatively against the development of life insurance companies. They were referred to as "Speculative Life Insurance Companies," and regarded somewhat as a form of gambling. The East Pennsylvania Annual Conference assigned a committee to study the twin evils of life insurance and Mormon polygamy! Its report said that life insurance companies, evaluating personal life in dollar terms, tended "to obliterate all feeling of love and respect, thus rending the strongest and tenderest ties of humanity." Mormon polygamy was also declared an offense.[33]

Secret Societies

In contrast to the United Brethren Church, which so strongly opposed membership in secret societies that the issue became a prominent factor in dividing that church in 1889, the Evangelical Association never permitted the issue to become predominant. In the General Conference of 1847 John Dreisbach proposed an action which would prohibit such membership. The proposal was adopted, but by the next day Dreisbach had learned that the proposal also forbade membership in secret prohibition and other worthy societies. Therefore at his urging the action was rescinded.[34]

This did not give approval for members to join "oath-bound" societies. At different times after 1847 attempts were made to deny church memberhip to members of secret societies, but the disapproval was not put into law, largely because to do so would have required a change in the long-accepted standards for church membership.

THEOLOGICAL ISSUES

When the first Evangelical *Discipline* was written in 1809, it included the twenty-five Articles adopted by the Methodists at the Christmas Conference in 1784 plus a twenty-sixth Article, "Of the Last Judgment," which, strangely enough, was not included among the Methodist Articles. Later the Evangelical Association made some adjustments in the Articles, deleting those portions which were merely negative responses to unacceptable doctrines, such as the doctrines of purgatory, celibacy, and repudiation of oath taking. By these adjustments and by combining the contents of related Articles the Evangelical Association reduced the number to twenty-one.

Sanctification

The Methodist Articles of Religion did not include one dealing with sanctification, nor did the Evangelical Articles, even though the doctrine of sanctification reflected the spirit of the church more than did some of the approved Articles.

In the Evangelical *Discipline*, where all doctrinal matters were placed in Chapter I, Section II, a separate treatise on sanctification comprised one subsection of five or six pages in successive *Disciplines*, depending on the size of the print.

In the *Discipline* of 1844 the treatise claimed that it should be the purpose of every Christian to attain to complete holiness in this life in which "all self-will and selfishness must be subdued," to "gain the victory over any temptation the moment that it may present itself," and to "love God with all his heart, with all his mind, and with all his strength." "Sin, as it were, has lost all its power against such a one." "The flesh, the world and Satan are under his feet and he rules over his enemies; yet with watching, and not slumbering." "That such a state is attainable, even in this life, is very evident, because Christ and his Apostles exhort thereto." Yet once attained it may be lost, but renewed striving may reattain it. "Experience has moreover taught that, ordinarily, the state of Christian perfection is attained gradually, by an upward course of life . . . ; however, under this graduation this work is perfected in the soul, sooner or later, by a sudden and powerful influence of grace and outpouring of the divine Spirit." Therefore, in every case holiness is "attained gradually" and is also "instantaneous." "This grace is called *Sanctification*." Even though man can attain to Christian perfection, he is still finite and less than God. Hence, in spite of his attainment he can still "grow and increase yet more and more in grace, and proceed from one glory to another." Sanctification does "not take away the natural infirmities of man" such as bodily weakness, and "weakness of understanding, of memory, of judgment and of mind," which do not constitute sin.[35]

This doctrinal statement appeared in only slightly modified form in all *Disciplines* until 1962.

The Dispute

On January 16, 1856, an article appeared in *Der Christliche Botschafter*, signed by "An Old Evangelical," who undoubtedly was W. W. Orwig, in which the Evangelical interpretation of sanctification was given, but which ended with this statement:

> Those who professed religion were summoned to seek santifica-
> tion—and were assured that, if they did not obtain sanctification, then
> they would not be able to see the Lord—Someone may wonder what my
> opinion may be concerning the fate of those who die without entire
> santification. That is clear: they will inevitably be lost.—A partially
> sanctified person will as little come to heaven as one who is altogether
> impure.—Then will all the justified, who have not obtained entire
> sanctification, be lost? Undoubtedly![36]

This concluding statement carried three most disconcerting declarations. First, God's work of justification was insufficient for salvation. Second, therefore sanctification as a second and distinct work of grace was the absolute *sine qua non* of eternal salvation. Thirdly, justification and sanctification are not basically inter-related.

Many of the leading brethren of the church were astounded at this interpretation of "Wesleyan" sanctification. Even though Orwig was held in high regard, they could not allow such an extreme view to go unchallenged. The challenge was not slow in coming, and that from another prominent Evangelical leader, Solomon Neitz (1821–1885), a man who served the church in the capacities of pastor and district superintendent in the East Pennsylvania Annual Conference, agent for Union Seminary, special representative to the German mission field, secretary and treasurer of the Charitable Society, member of the Board of Publication, author of the *Life of Bishop John Seybert* and several other books, and delegate to General Conferences from the East Pennsylvania Annual Conference in all sessions from 1851 to 1879. Although largely self-taught he was a distinguished pulpit orator and theologian, judged by Dr. Philip Schaff, who heard him preach, as the leading German orator in America.[37]

In February 1857 Neitz published a pamphlet on "Christian Sanctification According to Apostolic Teaching." In it he not only replied to Orwig's extreme statement (which Orwig later deemphasized), but set forth an interpretation of sanctification quite different from the traditional "Wesleyan" view.

Neitz, following Pauline statements, taught that justification and sanctification are not two but are one act of God in human redemption. It is a free gift of God. It cannot be obtained by human effort, although the Christian will constantly strive to live a virtuous life. Justification-sanctification is imputed to a man—it is not earned, not even by Christ-assisted effort. Even the saved man retains the "root of evil" originally implanted within him. Therefore, he must depend solely upon God's continuing, pardoning grace to be kept in the state of justification-sanctification. Neitz stated bluntly, "My view is not Wesleyan, but it is biblical."[38]

Neitz's pamphlet raised a torrent of criticism from many sources, with articles appearing in *Der Christliche Botschafter* and the *Evangelical Messenger*. Amidst the furor, Orwig's extreme statement—that only entirely sanctified souls will be received into heaven and all others will be eternally lost—was forgotten.

Francis Hoffman, who along with Neitz served as a presiding elder of the East Pennsylvania Annual Conference, felt that the issue should be settled on the East Pennsylvania Annual Conference floor. He invited Orwig, a member of the Central Pennsylvania Annual Conference, to appear before the East Pennsylvania Annual Conference, which was held in February 1859, and refute Neitz's interpretation. Many members listened to Orwig and Neitz, both theologians of repute, with considerable complexity of mind. At the end of the dispute Neitz spoke with regret that such a controversy was begun. His fellow Annual Conference members accepted his promise that he would no longer press the issue and voted to support him in his well-intentional if poorly understood statement. This infuriated Orwig, who wished for a unanimous rejection of Neitz's views.

Therefore, Orwig brought the matter before the General Conference of 1859. He obtained the floor even before the roll call had been completed or the bishop's message had been read and offered a resolution repudiating Neitz's views and calling for Neitz and any followers he may have to be silenced on the matter of sanctification. A whole day was taken for Orwig's statements and for arguments pro and con. When Neitz responded, he first pointed out that charges against any preacher are to be heard and acted upon only by his own Annual Conference and that judgment upon him was not the prerogative of a General Conference. Bishop Long ruled otherwise and bade the hearing to proceed. Neitz then restated his interpretation of sanctification. Finally a resolution was passed stating that Neitz was not in harmony with the Evangelical position. No other action was taken, which Neitz interpreted to mean that he was judged to be undeserving of censure. This seemed to be corroborated by the fact that he was appointed to several high denominational responsibilities. On the other hand, later in the conference session Orwig was elected bishop.

A contributing factor in Orwig's vigorous opposition to Neitz was the charge that Neitz had joined the Masonic Order, which Orwig strongly opposed.[39]

Although many in the East Pennsylvania Conference, in which Neitz was the presiding elder of the Lehigh District, were dubious about his interpretation of sanctification, they were still more offended by Orwig, from another Annual Conference, taking the initiative in opposing him. Hence, in the quadrennium of

1859–1863, although the dispute had quieted, they conspired to bring to an end Orwig's service as bishop. When the balloting began in the General Conference of 1863, Orwig quickly saw that his reelection would not occur. It was obvious that Neitz hoped to replace him. He was accused of electioneering, a practice specifically forbidden in the Evangelical Association. Orwig threw his support to a young churchman from Illinois, J. J. Esher, who won the election over Neitz by a narrow margin. In subsequent General Conferences Esher and Neitz competed for the bishopric, but Neitz was always defeated.

Esher was known to support the Evangelical or Wesleyan doctrine of sanctification. Because rivalry for election to the bishopric was strong, personal antagonism developed between the two men.

Neitz again stirred up the controversy by having a sermon presenting his interpretation of sanctification published in June 11, 1867, in The Lehigh County Patriot, a secular newspaper. Orwig took the matter to the General Conference of October 1867, meeting in Pittsburgh. Holding Neitz's sermon in his hand, he took the whole third day of the conference to refute it sentence by sentence. Neitz replied heatedly, calling Orwig's repeated claims of basic love to him as hypocritical. He infuriated Orwig's supporters by using theological terminology they could neither match nor understand.

The conference appointed a commission to study the whole controversy and bring a final recommendation. The next day the commission reported that while Neitz "makes use of terms, phrases and figures of speech of which we decidedly disapprove . . . it appears that he does not design to teach doctrines essentially different from those held by our church, and therefore we unanimously recommend his acquital."[40]

This report was followed by another which spelled out the Evangelical interpretation still further. When Neitz rose to speak, it was feared his words would precipitate another bitter discussion. To the joy of all, his words were supportive of the report. The venerable Bishop Joseph Long, who was presiding and was known to be strongly anti-Neitz in the dispute, praised the action, and the conference secretary concluded the written record by adding, "Well might here and there a hearty 'Praise God!' be heard."

The battle was not over. Following the conference Neitz still showed reluctance to accept the "final" decision. Thereupon the two bishops, Long and Esher, brought episcopal pressure to silence him.

He responded by composing in the "Pennsylvania Dutch" dialect a doggerel entitled "Sporadisches" ("Sporadic Verses") in which he referred to the two bishops by their first names, and had "Simon" (Peter) at "heaven's gate" order them to take their sanctification "trifles" on getting into heaven "back to Cleveland" (the location of the publishing house) and "On your life, bring't not again, but bring me Solomon [Neitz] along."[41]

He asked his friend Rudolph Dubs to print it in *Der Christliche Botschafter*, of which Dubs was editor. In spite of the fact Dubs favored the Evangelical interpretation of sanctification, and therefore on that issue sided with Bishops Long and Esher, he published the doggerel. Expressions of personal outrage were immediate. Thereafter Long and Esher regarded Dubs as a common enemy along with Neitz.

In the years following, the Evangelical or Wesleyan doctrine of sanctification was generally accepted. Two opponents of it and the "un-Wesleyan" connotations of the Articles of Faith, T. G. Clewel, an editor of the *Evangelical Messenger*, and Daniel B. Byers, a presiding elder of the Illinois Annual Conference, received rebukes. Clewel responded by leaving the Evangelical Association. Byers consented to remain silent.

The ultimate effects of the controversy were expressed in personal animosities, even after several of the early leaders had passed away. They left a permanent cleavage among their successors. In 1871 Reuben Yeakel and in 1875 Rudolph Dubs and Thomas Bowman were elected bishops and joined Esher in the episcopacy. The four men were divided, not in beliefs, but in inheritance of the divisive spirit of the earlier struggle. Esher, Yeakel, and Bowman stood out as antagonists of Rudolph Dubs (with the aroma of "Sporadisches" still permeating the air). Church leaders were classified according as they favored one party or the other. In 1879 Yeakel yielded his episcopal office to become principal of the seminary in Naperville, Illinois, leaving Esher and Bowman to be the antagonists of Dubs.

Thus was formed the main factor leading to later denominational division.

During the latter years of the century the stress on sanctification turned toward celebrations of holiness. Members of the Evangelical

Association had participated in the formation of the National Holiness Association in 1867 in Vineland, New Jersey, and a number of Evangelical Holiness Camp Meetings were held, especially in the eastern part of the church.

Some Evangelical leaders criticized them as extravagant expressions of holiness convictions. Bishop Long responded to such criticisms in 1867 by saying "I should think that if such meetings are held in the fear of God and for the purpose of seeking and promoting holiness, one should rejoice over it and co-operate, but if they degenerate, then the contrary should be done."[42]

In spite of the holiness meetings the issue of sanctification, especially as an instantaneous second work of grace followed by a gradual growth from glory to glory, while always affirmed by the Evangelical Association, declined in emphasis in the last quarter of the nineteenth century.[43]

EDUCATION

Christian Education

The Sunday school movement in the Evangelical Association began in 1832 in the Evangelical Church of Lebanon, Pennsylvania, later named the St. Paul's Evangelical Church. The movement thereafter spread rapidly over the denomination so that by 1859 there were 389 schools with 17,651 pupils.

The early educational methods were unorganized and crude. Oftentimes it seemed that the main reason for the Sunday schools was to get children off the streets.[44] However, the purpose was deeper, namely, to lead the children to Christian commitment. This was achieved by basic teachings, then moving to memorizing Bible verses and catechetical questions and answers, and then dealing with moral issues.

Singing was very important. It was often spontaneous and confused. To correct this, song books containing the verses and designated meter appeared, which gave greater orderliness. Musical instruments were rarely used.

The Sunday school work was mostly done under lay leadership, which made the efforts in the local schools to be of greatly varying effectiveness. In the General Conference of 1859 the denominational Sunday School and Tract Society was organized, which set up guidelines and teaching methods and prompted the publishing establishment to provide adequate study materials.

Interest in Sunday school work began to reach beyond the borders of the denomination. Evangelical representatives attended and participated in interchurch Sunday school conventions. This brought progressive ideas and methods which were passed on to the local Sunday schools through denominational publications.

The next step was accepting the International Uniform Sunday School Lessons in 1875 by order of the General Conference. The lessons had first appeared two years earlier.

Nevertheless Sunday school work was still sporadic due to the varying abilities of the laity in the local churches and to the varying support given by the local pastors. In many churches the work was not even undertaken, but this was rectified when in 1875 the General Conference took action that "in each of our societies there shall be formed a Sunday school, which shall meet . . . under the charge of the preacher in charge." It was provided that the officials of the Sunday school, the superintendent, teachers, etc., will be under the preacher's direction. The conference also authorized publishing improved Sunday school literature and a periodical, *The Sunday School Teacher.*

In 1883 the General Conference authorized the publication of ten textbooks for teachers, entitled "The Evangelical Normal Series," based upon interdenominational Chautauqua Normal-class textbooks. In the series were study books on such subjects as "Books of the Bible," "Church History," and "History of the English Bible."[45]

Young People's Society

Six months before Francis E. Clark launched the Christian Endeavor Society, the Evangelical church in Dayton, Ohio, on September 13, 1880, organized a local young people's society "for the Glory of God and the Good of Men." The originator was the local pastor, C. F. Hansing. Other local churches followed the example, and shortly the church entered into participation in the interdenominational Christian Endeavor Society.

Colleges

Few of the early Evangelical leaders had formal education although several, such as Dreisbach, Seybert, Neitz, and Orwig, through the discipline of wide, prudent study, attained high intellectual and literary accomplishments. The General Conference of 1843 made a recommendation that "candidates for the ministry . . . take proper measures to store their minds with as large amount of useful information as they possibly can, or to endeavor to become learned and literary men."

This statement spurred W. W. Orwig, John Dreisbach, and others to write articles for the denominational periodicals supporting the idea of establishing schools of higher learning. On the other hand it also spurred others to denounce higher learning as inimical to evangelical piety and intellectual humility. In response to a call from John Dreisbach to establish a "seminary" for the study of "general science" came objections that this could lead to theological seminaries or "preacher factories."

In 1847 the General Conference steered a middle ground and approved the establishing of "high schools." This received approval by Annual Conferences and the general church membership.[46]

The action resulted in establishing a "high school" called Albright Seminary in Berlin, Somerset County, Pennsylvania, in 1857. It was a start, but its progress was not good. In 1858 it united with a similar school, Greensburg Seminary, in Greensburg, Ohio. Unfavorable circumstances caused by the Civil War brought insurmountable financial problems. Bishop Joseph Long tried desperately to maintain the school by purchasing it with his personal funds, but in 1865 it was sold at serious financial loss to Bishop Long.

By 1890 the Evangelical Association had opened two other short-lived schools, Blairstown Seminary, in Blairstown, Iowa (1867–1873), and La Fayette College, later called Dallas College, in Dallas, Oregon (1890–1914). Only three schools begun before 1890 achieved permanence.

Union Seminary

In 1854 the West Pennsylvania Annual Conference opened Union Seminary (first progenitor of Albright College in Reading, Pennsylvania) on a six-acre lot in New Berlin, Pennsylvania, the old Evangelical publishing center and site of the first Evangelical church building. Two agents who had much to do with the enterprise were

W. W. Orwig and Solomon Neitz, destined to be opponents on the doctrine of sanctification. The school opened in January 1856 with Orwig as first president. Courses taught included mathematics, natural sciences, ancient languages and literature, English, book-keeping, vocal and instrumental music, and primary-school teaching. At first the entire course of studies required three years. In 1859 a "classical collegiate" course was added. Enrollment in 1859 was 264, including both men and women.

The Civil War brought reversal so that in 1863 the school had to be closed. Two years later it was reopened but continued under precarious circumstances. In 1880 a theological department was added. In 1887 the school was renamed Central Pennsylvania College.

Schuylkill Seminary

The East Pennsylvania Annual Conference opened a school in Reading, Pennsylvania, on August 19, 1884. It was given the name Schuylkill Seminary. Colonel J. H. Lick of Lebanon, Pennsylvania, gave a gift of $24,000 with the request that the school be moved to Fredericksburg, Pennsylvania, and relocated on eight acres of land which he also contributed. This was done, but almost at once the new location was found to be unsatisfactory because of its remoteness. Therefore, the school was returned to Reading in 1902 where, after subsequent institutional and denominational unions, it became the present Albright College.

Plainfield (North Central)College

In 1862 a school was opened in the small town of Plainfield, Illinois, and named after that town. It was sponsored by the Illinois and Wisconsin Annual Conferences. J. J. Esher, to be elected bishop in 1863, was the most effective leader in establishing the school. In 1864 it was renamed Northwestern College.

In 1870 it was moved to Naperville, Illinois, because of the greater accessibility of that town. By 1871 enrollment was 185. Thereafter the college flourished. In 1926 it was renamed North Central College to make it distinct from other colleges which had assimilated "Northwestern" into their names.

Union Biblical Institute
(Evangelical Theological Seminary)

The old fear of establishing a theological seminary or "preacher factory" continued for many years against the hopes of such men as Dreisbach, Seybert, Long, and Orwig. Finally, because the above named seminaries or colleges were unable to prepare missionaries for that developing program, the breakthough took place.

In 1867 T. G. Clewel, editor of the *Evangelical Messenger,* proposed to the General Conference the following resolution: "Resolved, That all rules in our discipline and all General Conference resolutions conflicting with the (present) report of the committee on education (recommending establishing biblical institutes) be hereby annulled."[47]

The term biblical institutes was used to designate ministerial educational institutions. After sharp debate the resolution was adopted, but with the general feeling that the biblical institutes were for one purpose only, the training of missionaries.

In 1873 representatives from the Annual Conferences supporting Northwestern (North Central) College joined in a "confederation" to lay plans to open the Union Biblical Institute. The school opened for its first classses in the fall of 1876 with eight men enrolled.[48]

Two men were preeminently responsible for the successful development of the institute, J. J. Esher and Reuben Yeakel. Esher, who had begun his service as bishop in 1863, was a member of the "confederation." In anticipation of the opening of the institute he was appointed the first solicitor and "principal" in 1875. Two years later he resigned the principalship. Reuben Yeakel, who had been serving since 1871 as a bishop, was chosen to be the second principal and a member of the faculty. He served in these three capacities, bishop, principal, and teacher, for four years. In 1879 he relinquished the bishopric but continued to serve as principal and teacher until 1883 when he became assistant editor of *Der Christliche Botschafter.* Thereupon Bishop Esher again served as principal.[49]

The offerings in the institute at first consisted of a two-year curriculum. The subjects were almost entirely biblical: biblical geography, biblical natural history, biblical chronology, biblical antiquities, biblical history, biblical exegesis, introduction to the Holy Scriptures, and systematic theology.

Four men out of the original eight who enrolled in 1876 were graduated after completing the two-year course in 1878.

To make the theological training better rounded, courses in church history, church discipline, homiletics, and pastoral theology were added, and, although a two-year curriculum was continued, full completion of the ministerial studies required three years, thus the institute became a full-fledged theological seminary. Hence, the name was changed in 1909 to the Evangelical Theological Seminary.

The academic and religious life in the seminary was maintained on a high level. Members of its faculty engaged in scholarly theological writings, especially in the fields of biblical, historical, and theological studies. The seminary had a very positive effect upon the church's life and ministry.

Missions

Missionary work as a formal program was late and slow in getting underway.[50] However, the evangelistic spirit of the Evangelical Association had always made it a mission church as it expanded from the Eastern Conference westward.

As the year 1850 approached, marking the passing of one-half century since Jacob Albright organized the three original "classes," a cry went up urging the celebration of that year as a Jubilee Year, with special emphasis to be placed upon missionary effort both at home and abroad.

Home and Frontier Missions

Emphasis upon home and frontier missions simply meant intensifying the work the church was already doing and applying more formal and organized effort. Hence, specific centers out of which "missionary points" would grow were designated. In 1851 twenty-eight missionary points, mostly in the Midwest and Far West, were listed. By 1885 the number had grown to 443.[51]

The dates and places where missionary points were first established indicate the expansion of the home and frontier work:

Nebraska, 1858; California and Oregon (with the missionaries traveling by way of Panama), 1864; Kansas, 1866; South Dakota, 1870; Texas, 1880; Colorado, 1881; and Washington, 1884. In 1886 work was begun in Florida under the East Pennsylvania Annual Conference Society.

Evangelistic work in Ontario, Canada, begun by Christian Wolf in 1807, spread westward after very slow development to reach Berlin (now Kitchener) by 1838. The work thereafter expanded more rapidly so that in 1863 Bishop Joseph Long organized the Canada Annual Conference with Kitchener as the center.

As the Canadian provinces were opened in western Canada, the Evangelical Association began to show interest there, especially in southern Manitoba, because of its proximity to Evangelical work in Minnesota and the Dakotas. A Manitoba mission was begun in 1882 by the Minnesota Annual Conference with Rev. A. C. Schmidt as missionary. In 1884 the newly formed Dakota Annual Conference assumed responsibility for the work. From this beginning Evangelical work spread northward and westward in Canada in the following decades.[52]

Foreign Missions

The cry for the development of missionary work included interest in carrying the work abroad. Leaders of the East Pennsylvania Annual Conference declared that the most appropriate place to begin would be in the area from which so many members of the church had derived their heritage, namely, Germany. The conference proposed a "provisional" board, made up of a bishop and one representative from each Annual Conference to plan work in that country, with the Parent Missionary Society, which had been practically dormant since its formation in 1839, supervising. In turn it chose a Board of Missions to carry out the work.

The work got underway at once. On January 6, 1851, the family of John C. Link reached Stuttgart, the capital city of the province of Wurttemberg. There they were welcomed by Sebastian Kurtz, who had been a farmer in York County, Pennsylvania. After his conversion in 1845 he had gone to Germany on his own initiative to preach the word.

With Kurtz' help and guidance Link got a mission underway in

Stuttgart. Although the state church attempted to discourage his work, Link was unusually successful and within one year had a society of 130 people.

Other missionaries, among them John Nickolai and J. P. Walport, came to help in the work. In 1859 Walport built a church in Plochingen, the first one to be built in a foreign country by the Evangelical Association.

In spite of opposition from the established church, the work in Germany flourished. In 1863 the redoubtable Solomon Neitz was sent to inspect the work being done. His effective preaching in the German language won wide recognition for himself and the work. In 1865 Bishop J. J. Esher arrived and organized the German Conference. By this time there were seven American missionaries and several native preachers and other workers engaged in the effort, with sixty-four preaching places.

The work continued to spread—to Switzerland, Alsace, north and northeast into the areas of Baden, Dresden, and by 1888 even to Berlin. An Annual Conference was organized in Switzerland in 1880.

Because of this spread of the work it became necessary to establish two supporting institutions, a publishing house in Stuttgart in 1875 and Reutlingen Theological Seminary in 1877.

In 1881 it was reported that a total of fifty-eight Americans were employed in the European work.[53]

Financial problems prevented the early beginning of mission work in "heathen" areas. However, in 1863 the General Conference decreed that as soon as funds were available work should be begun in India. This did not occur.

Finally in 1875 it was felt that new missionary work could be started, not in India as originally planned, but in Japan. In October 1876 the Rev. Halmhuber, a native of Switzerland who first spent several years in the United States to study the English language, Miss Rachel Hudson, a member of the faculty of the Millersville (Pa.) State Normal School, and the Rev. Frederick C. Krecker, M. D., and his family of Lebanon, Pennsylvania, were sent to Japan. They were welcomed by the Rev. and Mrs. J. Carrell, Canadian missionaries in Yokohama, and worked under their guidance until they became acquainted with the new country and had studied the Japanese language. In 1877 they gained their first convert, the young Japanese man employed to teach them the Japanese language.

Dr. Krecker practiced medicine and did evangelistic work in Tokyo. Mrs. Krecker began a school of religion in their home. Miss Hudson, utilizing her teaching ability, opened a day school in Tokyo. Through her work the missionaries soon learned that the most effective method of conducting missionary work in Japan was through schools. Halmhuber went to Osaka to begin missionary work there.

These missionaries found opposition from a people suspicious of foreigners. They were handicapped by laws restricting the purchase of land for homes, schools, and churches. However, by their obvious humility and dedication they gradually overcame these problems, and progress was made. By 1879 a class had been organized in Tokyo.

In 1880 Jacob Hartzler, a former editor of the *Evangelical Messenger*, was sent to Japan to be mission superintendent. He sent back favorable (perhaps too favorable) reports. He reported nine preaching stations, twenty-six full members, and one hundred and fifty Sunday school scholars. A year later he sent a still more optimistic report.

Then came a series of devastating reversals. In 1882 Halmhuber had to give up the work because of cholera and a nervous collapse. Before leaving Osaka he sold the mission appointments and facilities to the Cumberland Presbyterians, thus discontinuing the Evangelical work there. In 1883 Dr. Krecker died after contracting typhoid fever from a poor Japanese mother whom he was treating.[54] His family returned home in 1885. In 1884 Miss Hudson, after frequent illnesses, returned home.

Although other missionaries had arrived, the loss of these pioneers was calamitous. Superintendent Hartzler in 1885 reported to the General Conference that 112 members were lost, 6 by death, 26 by expulsion, and 70 by withdrawal, as over against only 12 newly received.[55]

In December 1884 Bishop Esher had been sent to Japan to survey the work. He reported on the reversal but also stated that not all was lost, that faithful workers were still in the field, and that headway had been made in gaining converts. Another reporter stated that Esher ordained a convert to the diaconate.[56]

After his return in the fall of 1885 Esher made a lengthy report to the Board of Missions in which he clearly blamed Superintendent Hartzler for the reversals. He indicated that he was a poor administrator and that he could not maintain cordial relationships with the missionaries. He accused Henry Hartzler, editor of the *Evangelical Messenger* and brother of Superintendent Jacob Hartzler, of having edited out of the letters he had sent from Japan the unfavorable references regarding mismanagement.

Esher's report to the Board was printed in the German language in *Der Christliche Botschafter*. Henry Hartzler printed it in the English *Evangelical Messenger* only after pressure was placed upon him to do so.[57]

Thus a harsh controversy began. Superintendent Hartzler had his defenders. A series of bitter articles appeared in the two periodicals. Those in *Der Christliche Botschafter* generally were in sympathy with Esher; those in the *Evangelical Messenger* generally sided with Superintendent Hartzler.

Thus antagonisms which had originated during the sanctification controversy were heightened.

To reverse the downward trend of the mission work in Japan the superintendency was discontinued and a mission committee was appointed to give oversight to the work. It was successful. In 1887 a training school was opened called the Mission Seminary of the Evangelical Association in Tokyo. Because the Japanese people were (and still are) a highly literate society, it was found that printed materials were very effective in promoting the gospel. The Bible was translated into Japanese by interdenominational scholars and published in 1888.

In spite of growing personal antagonisms Hartzler still held a high position in the estimation of American missionaries in Japan. In 1886 he was named president of the Japanese branch of the Evangelical Alliance, an international and interdenominational organization dedicated to emphasizing basic Christian teachings and freedom of religious expression and propagation. The Japanese branch of the· Alliance contributed· much to the change of ·attitude of the Japanese government toward Christian mission and freedom.

The Women's Missionary Society

On November 11, 1839, a group of women formed the Women's Missionary Society of Immanuel Evangelical Church in Philadelphia. Their purpose was to gather funds to aid the Eastern Annual

Conference in carrying on missionary or evangelistic work within the conference.

The mission interests, stimulated by the Jubilee Year, spurred women's groups in many other local churches to form similar societies. The General Board of Missions of the denomination looked upon this movement as potentially rebellious. The women repudiated such judgment, stating that their purpose was to solicit funds to support denominational mission work.

The organization of local women's societies continued until 1883, when with the approval and encouragement of the General Conference the Women's Missionary Society was formed, embracing all local and Annual Conference societies. A constitution was adopted in 1884. Thereafter the society gave generous and steady support to the missionary enterprise of the Evangelical Association.

Flat Rock Children's Home

The Jubilee emphasis upon missions stimulated the church to provide for the shelter and care of needy children. Several Annual Conferences made plans to establish orphanages with special encouragement from the General Conference of 1863.[58]

The Ohio Conference proceeded at once to establish an orphanage. In 1865 a farm was donated by George Weiker of Bellevue, Ohio, for this purpose, and in 1868 the Ebenezer Orphan Institution of the Evangelical Association of North America was opened at Flat Rock, Ohio. The cumbersome name was soon supplanted by the name the Flat Rock Children's Home.

Discipline was strict, but the children who were admitted were provided with wholesome physical, educational, and spiritual advantages. A bell was rung for rising in the summer at 5:00 A.M. and in the winter at 6:00. It was also rung at mealtime. This evoked the comment, "This bell has the peculiar quality, that it does not sound half so sweet so early in the morning as it does when calling for meals."[59]

Because the Flat Rock Home flourished and its facilities became more and more adequate, other attempts at establishing orphanages were redirected toward supporting it. Thus it became the orphanage serving the whole denomination.

ECUMENICAL ISSUES

Discussions with the Methodists

Over the years many cordial relationships between Evangelical and Methodist preachers and leaders had been established. Hence, in 1859 William Nast of the Methodist Church appeared before the Evangelical General Conference and, while guarding against making a direct appeal for church union, which he favored, urged a "close relationship." He pointed out that the Methodists had developed considerable work among the German people who had been immigrating to the United States in large numbers. Therefore, the two churches were engaging in similar work. Also, since the two churches closely shared similar doctrines and discipline, closer cooperation would be appropriate.

The Civil War interrupted immediate specific planning for some sort of closer relationship, but after the war ended, Nast, leading a Methodist delegation, renewed the plea. The Evangelical Association responded in kind and appointed Rudolph Dubs to lead a delegation to the Methodist General Conference of 1868 to express the Evangelical attitude.

This was misunderstood to be a definite gesture toward working out a specific plan of action leading toward union. Two proposals were made: one of organic union of the two churches, and another, less drastic but still startling, of transferring all Methodist German work to the Evangelical Association and all Evangelical Association English conferences to the Methodists.

Although both the proposals were idealistic and had such initial attraction as, for once, to gain the mutual approval of Esher, Dubs, Orwig, and Neitz, subsequent sober thought brought out the sheer impossibility of getting favorable actions if the proposals would be presented to the General Conference, the Annual Conferences, and the total membership, as would be required by the *Discipline*.

Therefore, by 1879 all proposals to bring about Methodist–Evangelical Association union or basic adjustments in their denominational cooperative programs came to an end. However, the General Conference of 1879 received an invitation to join in the formation of an International Ecumenical Methodist Conference. Although the Evangelical Association pointed out that it did not regard itself as a subsidiary body of the Methodist Church, it expressed its pleasure in receiving the invitation. "Bishop R. Dubs and D. B. Byers were appointed a committee to represent [the Evangelical Association] at the Ecumenical Conference of Methodism."[60] The growing dissension among Evangelical leaders prevented the carrying out of the participation of representatives of the Evangelical Association.

Two Other Proposals of Church Union

The previous chapter discussed the proposal that six American denominations, including the Evangelical Association and the United Brethren Church, should be united into one body; the initial enthusiasm for accomplishing such union swiftly subsided and perished.

In the previous chapter is also given the serious proposal made in 1883 to achieve union of the Evangelical Association and the United Brethren Church. The discussion began with what appeared to be favorable prospects. However, the proposal never went beyond the resolution that was expressed by the Rev. J. H. Becker of the United Brethren Church to the Evangelical General Conference of 1877 that the two denominations move toward "co-operative union." Both denominations were suffering internal tensions, which led in each case to denominational division. The possibility of organic union perished during that time of turmoil.

PUBLICATION INTERESTS

The second printing establishment which had begun in New Berlin, Pennsylvania, in 1836 made considerable progress. It began to publish the first denominational periodical, Der Christliche Botschafter, in 1836.

With the start of a trend toward English usage the need for an English periodical equivalent to the German became evident. Hence, on January 8, 1848, appeared the first issue of the Evangelical Messenger. Both periodicals during the ensuing year had the same editor, Nicholes Gehr.

The two periodicals were used in parallel ways to accomplish several services to the church: (1) as news magazines giving information about the church; (2) as means for instructing church members in religious beliefs; (3) as means for the discussion of relevant and debatable issues; (4) as means for sending communications to individuals of the church, such as notifying persons or congregations that books were being sent, or that money was owed the printing establishment; (5) to announce meetings of conferences or camp meetings, etc; (6) to solicit funds for different interests; (7) to carry on personal or group controversies; (8) to promote mission and educational interests.

In due time it became evident that the small community of New Berlin was not suitable for the development of the publishing work. It had no railroad facilities, no significant business enterprises, and no daily mail service. Furthermore, the publishing agent, the printers, and the editors and their families were all living in accommodations provided for them in the establishment building. The intimacy caused personal tensions to develop.

Hence the General Conference of 1851 approved a move to Cleveland, Ohio. This was done in April 1854. A three-story building had been erected there at a cost of $14,500.

The move greatly enhanced the services of the establishment. Reli$_{\jmath}$iou. materials poured from the presses. The work expanded so rapidly that by 1874 another building was erected adjacent to the first and in 1878 an addition made to it. In 1884 the first building was replaced by a new one which was much more spacious.

The equipment also changed radically. John Dreisbach's press of 1816 was small and of wooden frame. It was replaced in 1836 by a larger press, powered by hand, constructed with a metal frame. In the latest developments in Cleveland the presses were large and ran by steam power.

In 1852 the establishment did business amounting to $7,059. In 1875 it exceeded $300,000.

The printing establishment increased its publication of periodicals. The three most significant were Der Christliche Kinderfreund (The Christian Children's Friend); The Living Epistle, a "holiness" periodical; and its German equivalent Das Evangelische Magazin. Sunday School periodicals were also printed in German and English. Two very important historical books were published, Das Leben und Wirken des Seligen Johannes Seybert (The Life and Works of the Sainted John Seybert), by Solomon Neitz in 1862 and Albright and His Co-Laborers, in German and English editions, by Reuben Yeakel in 1882.

When the printing establishment was relocated in Cleveland in 1854, the Ohio Annual Conference was given the responsibility of overseeing its work. In 1859 the General Conference assumed the responsibility, and thereafter the establishment was subject to a denominational Board of Publication, composed of seven men. This number was changed several times thereafter.

It was unfortunate that two controversies which arose in the church, the dispute over sanctification and the dispute over the mission work in Japan, were carried on largely in the columns of *Der Christliche Botschafter* and the *Evangelical Messenger*. The controversies led to dismissal of editors and appointing of replacements, to church trials of denominational leaders, to civil court suits, and to the circulating of divisive materials printed on independent presses.

These difficulties tended to overshadow the great service rendered by the printing establishment, whose contribution to the life and work of the Evangelical Association was incalculable.

THE DENOMINATIONAL RUPTURE

Tension which had been developing in the Evangelical Association for three decades came to a climax in the General Conference of 1887. Each of these tensions has already been discussed. A listing includes (1) geographical sectionalism; (2) the use of the English language versus German; (3) growth of episcopal authority; (4) rivalries for the office of bishop with attendant personal and party divisions; (5) the tendency toward democracy among members of longer American heritage versus the tendency toward centralized authority of those of later immigration; and (6) disputes over such matters as appointment of representatives of the denomination to interdenominational activities.

In the General Conference of 1887 the clash of opinions showed how deep a rift had developed in the church. The main issue was the continuing quarrel between Bishop Esher and H. B. Hartzler, editor of the *Evangelical Messenger*, which had begun over the problem of the Japanese mission. Thereafter Hartzler had subjected material submitted by Esher for publication to "unholy" treatment. For this continuing offense the Board of Publication demanded Hartzler's resignation. He refused, and the matter was brought to the General Conference. A bitter debate resulted which in effect placed Hartzler on trial. It lasted thirteen days, usurping time which was needed for other important matters. It ended in a vote of the delegates to dismiss Hartzler from his editorship because of "unchristian conduct, official misconduct and grievous official offense as Minister and Editor in our Church." The vote for dismissal was fifty-seven to forty-seven, a figure which represented the relative strength of the "majority" and "minority" parties.

Although few other important issues were dealt with, the debate was interrupted in order to hear an address by a United Brethren fraternal delegate. The address prompted the General Conference to commend the United Brethren for "their efforts to forward our common and glorious Christianity."[61]

The time for adjourning the conference was rapidly approaching. It was decided that the next session should begin on the first Thursday of October 1891. When the attempt was made to decide where it should be held, another dispute broke out. Since there was not enough time to decide the matter, the conference referred the responsibility for determining the place to the Board of Publication. Shortly after the adjournment of the conference the board named Indianapolis as the place of meeting.

This action brought a strong protest from the Eastern Annual Conference delegates, most of whom were in the minority group. They reminded the conference that the *Discipline* of 1839 named three ways that the places for the General Conferences should be decided: (1) by the bishops with the consent of the majority of the members of the General Conference; (2) in the absence of a bishop, by a majority vote of the members of the General Conference; and (3) by decision made by the oldest Annual Conference (which the delegates from the Eastern Annual Conference declared to be their conference).

Because methods (1) and (2) had not been used, the Eastern Annual Conference later chose Philadelphia, a decision the majority refused to accept.

The approaching division of the church became constantly more evident. Several attempts were made to prevent it. Groups of lay people urged that the incumbent bishops (J. J. Esher; Thomas Bowman, who sided with Esher; and Rudolph Dubs) resign so that younger, less involved men might be chosen to take their places. The bishops rejected the suggestion.

In 1890 H. K. Carroll, religious editor of the *New York Independent*, and other prominent non-Evangelical leaders offered their services as mediators. Many ministers and lay people urged that their services be accepted, but when it was suggested that the issues be compromised or arbitrated, Bishop Esher responded, "Compromise is unthinkable. We have nothing to arbitrate."

During the quadrennium the majority party, led by Esher and Bowman, ordered Dubs to stand trial according to an old provision of the *Discipline*.[62] The trial was held in his absence, and he was declared deposed. Dubs and his supporters summoned Esher and Bowman to similar trials. They refused to respond, and they were declared deposed. Dubs heeded the action against him enough to discontinue his service as bishop throughout the remainder of the quadrennium. Esher and Bowman completely disregarded the action taken against them.

When October 1891 arrived, Esher and Bowman summoned the General Conference to meet in Indianapolis. The majority group responded. Dubs summoned the General Conference to meet in Philadelphia. The minority responded. Each claimed to be the true General Conference of the Evangelical Association. Delegates in each place sent greetings to the other group and expressed hope that the denomination might still remain undivided. Their hopes were in vain.

The division had been accomplished. The majority group retained the original denominational name, the Evangelical Association. The minority, because of subsequent legal actions, took a new name, the United Evangelical Church.

Fortunately, as succeeding years passed and new leaders were chosen, regret over the division became strong in both churches. This led to a reunion of the two denominations in 1922 under the name, the Evangelical Church.

*M*en are never wholly products of their environment, but they must forever reckon with it," writes Howard Mumford Jones.[1] The severed parts of the Church of the United Brethren in the last decade of the nineteenth century lived in times marked by bitter contentiousness and turbulence in America and were themselves infected with them.

After 1890, immigrants came to this country in greater numbers than ever before. While the earlier immigrants had come predominantly from northern Europe, after 1890 immigration hailed chiefly from southern and western Europe. Italians, Hungarians, and Poles flocked to this country, concentrating in the burgeoning cities where they became dynamic factors in the emerging industrial, economic, and political life.

Intense struggles erupted in the American scene. The organization of the American Federation of Labor in 1885 prompted the formation of the National Association of Manufacturers in 1895, and the divergent economic and social forces met in brutal and bloody confrontation. In the steel industry at Homestead, Pennsylvania, in July 1892 there was a bitter strike. Two years later the American Railway Union called the Pullman strike which was suppressed judicially by a federal court and forcibly by federal troops. A painful depression paralyzed the nation's economy in 1893, and the ensuing hard times provoked street riots in many cities and the

UNITED BRETHREN: CRISIS, DEVELOPMENT, EXPANSION, 1889-1921

march of Jacob S. Coxy and his "army" upon Washington. In the political arena there were furious debates issuing in political divisions. In 1890 in Kansas the Populist Party was launched by people dissatisfied with both Democrats and Republicans. Its platform in 1892 was a strange amalgam of things prophetic and things incredible, advocating: free coinage of silver, nationalization of the transportation and communications industries, a graduated income tax, prohibition of land ownership by aliens, a shorter working day, and a restriction of immigration. While this party never won significant strength nationally, it was victorious in several midwestern states, and it did contribute to the defeat of the Democratic Party in the 1896 and 1900 national elections.

If affairs were tempestuous on the domestic scene, they were no less so in foreign relations. In 1891 Italy was affronted by the lynchings of three Italian citizens in New Orleans. The next year the American and British governments were in tense controversy regarding rights over the seal herds in the waters off Bering Strait. In 1894 the United States responded to the appeals of rebels against Queen Liliuokalani in Hawaii. When Britain and Venezuela were at loggerheads in 1895 over territorial boundaries, the United States moved in, invoking the Monroe Doctrine to settle the issue.

The sinking of the *Maine* and the loss of 270 sailors led promptly to America's declaration of war against Spain in 1898. After a brief conflict, Spain relinquished her claims to Cuba, ceded Puerto Rico to the United States for protection, and for $20,000,000 granted the United States the right to occupy the Philippines. At the outbreak of hostilities, America had transported Emilio Aguinaldo, an insurrectionist, to the Philippines to organize an uprising against the Spanish, but angry that the peace had not accomplished Philippine independence, Aguinaldo organized armed resistance against the Americans which persisted in open or guerilla warfare until well into the twentieth century.

The religious life of the nation was shaken by issues from various quarters. More conservative Christians were affronted by the theological liberalism championed by such distinguished divines as Lyman Abbott and Washington Gladden. They were scandalized by the theories and contentions of the new sciences as they were appalled by the pronouncements of higher criticism. They gleaned some satisfaction from the heresy trials such as the one which issued in the dismissal of Charles A. Briggs from the faculty of Union

Theological Seminary and his suspension from the Presbyterian ministry. Led by Walter Rauschenbusch, a growing corps sensing the biblical concern for the social dimensions of life in terms of love and justice began to proclaim the "social gospel." Vigorous opposition issued from those who held that the social gospel concerned itself with matters not properly the concern of the church. Moved by the perils they found in these theological, critical, and social positions, there were those in many denominations who found satisfaction in the emerging militant and fundamentalist reaction.

CHURCH OF THE UNITED BRETHREN IN CHRIST (OLD CONSTITUTION)

In this turbulent decade the Church of the United Brethren in Christ was enmeshed in the bitter throes of church division, which after the separation evoked even stronger feelings than the differences leading to it. On May 13, 1889, the United Brethren General Conference in York, Pennsylvania, by a vote of 110 to 20, adopted the rewritten Confession of Faith and the revised constitution, both of which had been overwhelmingly upheld by a referendum in the local churches. At this juncture, sixteen delegates withdrew to the Park Opera House to do business as the only lawful session of the General Conference of the church.

This smaller body affirmed that those delegates who had approved changes in the confession and constitution had "thereby vacated their seats as members of the Church of the United Brethren in Christ."[2] Fourteen additional persons were seated with them as delegates from nine Annual Conferences. Under the leadership of Bishop Milton Wright the following pastors were elected to the episcopacy: N. Y. Barnaby, H. Floyd, and H. J. Becker. While contending they were the true Church of the United Brethren in Christ, this group added the words "Old Constitution" to its name. Later legal action caused them to change the name to The United Brethren Church (Old Constitution). Its constituency numbered about 20,000.

Immediately it was recognized that "to inspire confidence and faith among the people"[3] prompt legal steps were imperative. Bishop Milton Wright was named supervisor of litigation, and on July 26, 1889, a suit for the possession of the printing establishment was filed before the Common Pleas Court in Montgomery County, Ohio. In December the court's verdict denied the claim. This verdict was upheld by the circuit court and by the Supreme Court of Ohio. An appeal was made to the federal court, and on May 24, 1897, Judge William Howard Taft rendered his decision, denying the plaintiffs any claims upon the establishment. Undaunted, they took their case to the United States Court of Appeals where, on March 7, 1899, Judge H. H. Lurton declared the appellants were without grounds for contest. While it is reported that this dreary litigation cost the United Brethren $35,500 and the Old Constitution another $10,000[4] there is good reason to believe that these sums were but a fraction of the actual cost. Rebuffed by the courts, Bishop Milton Wright remained irreconcilable: "We have been robbed of millions of dollars."[5]

While the court battles for the printing establishment were raging, scores of suits over local church properties were initiated in at least seven states, but only in Michigan, where state laws upheld the right of majorities in local churches in the control of their properties, were the plaintiffs successful. However, this decision was reversed in the higher courts. Elsewhere, Bishop Wright lamented, properties were lost to men who had betrayed everything the church stood for. By 1900, after a decade of litigation, the Church of the United Brethren in Christ (Old Constitution) turned to more creative and fruitful efforts.

Denied any claims upon the printing establishment, the Old Constitution Church first rented quarters in Dayton for their publications until May 2, 1917, when a four-story structure in Huntington, Indiana, was dedicated. In addition to serving publications, this building provided offices for the general denominational agencies.

Previously in Dayton in 1885 a group who viewed with alarm the proposals to modify the Confession of Faith and the constitution had begun publishing The Christian Conservator. At the schism in 1889 this became the official periodical of the Old Constitution Church, heralded for its purpose to "conserve and maintain the distinctive principles of United Brethrenism."[6] The publications of the Missions and Christian Education Departments were combined with it in 1954, and the enlarged periodical was called The United Brethren.

The first General Conference of the Old Constitution Church in 1889 organized a Domestic, Frontier and Foreign Missionary Society and elected a secretary and a board of directors for it, but this society had neither funds nor a missionary field. The church's Women's

Missionary Association rallied to the cause, but funds came slowly; nevertheless money accumulated, and on November 4, 1897, Mary Mullen arrived in Danville, Sierra Leone, where foundations were laid for a prosperous mission. A projected enterprise at Momaling, Sierra Leone, was thwarted by violent native uprisings in the spring of 1898, and instead, work was undertaken in the Imperrah area. Also from 1898 to 1931 there was a missionary program among the Chinese in Portland, Oregon.

Hopes for overseas medical services, first expressed in 1905, were not realized for two decades because funds were lacking. Following the appointment of doctors and nurses, a hospital near Mattru, Sierra Leone, was dedicated in 1950. In Honduras mission work was initiated in 1945. While at first it was confined to English-speaking people, it soon began to minister to Spanish-speaking people and now serves them exclusively. Almost simultaneously a mission was established in Jamaica.

Preceded by meetings in Annual Conferences during 1890, on May 14, 1891, a denominational Women's Missionary Association was organized. Allied with the Domestic, Frontier and Foreign Missionary Society, in January 1897 it began the publication of the *Missionary Monthly*.

After the uncertainties in the days of United Brethren division, the Old Constitution Church won the allegiance of one college: Hartsville in Indiana. In 1898 Central College was established in Huntington, Indiana. Two years later a disastrous fire destroyed the buildings at Hartsville, and the resources from Hartsville were transferred to Huntington. In 1917 Central College was renamed Huntington College. A school for the education of ministers is now also in operation on this college campus.

The Sabbath school work was placed under the supervision of the Board of Missions in 1901; eight years later a secretary and a board of managers were elected for it. *Gems of Cheer*, promoting Sunday school work, appeared in 1918; in 1950 this publication was renamed *Contact*. Youth work received new impetus in 1897 when the Young Peoples Christian Association was officially endorsed. Four years later the name was changed to the United Brethren Christian Endeavor Society, and in 1905 a secretary was elected for it. Then in 1921 the General Conference merged the Sunday school and Christian Endeavor operations into a Department of Christan Education whose activities were promoted in a new publication,

The United Brethren Magnet. Besides its services within the denomination, this department found profit and satisfactions in participating in such interchurch agencies as the National Sunday School Association, the International Society of Christian Endeavor, and the National Association of Evangelicals. The Old Constitution Church is now called the Church of the United Brethren in Christ. Currently it reports a membership of 26,409.

CHURCH OF THE UNITED BRETHREN IN CHRIST

Facing the stern realities of the secession, the Church of the United Brethren in Christ, a body of 204,492 members, in 1889 took two protective measures. Legal incorporation was acquired for the denomination, and local congregations were urged to do the same. Secondly, disciplinary measures were provided for dealing with "seceding members," clerical and lay.

Ecclesiastical Structure

From their beginning, United Brethren strove primarily to persuade men to acknowledge Christ as their Savior, after which reception into church membership followed with the affirmative answers to five simple questions.[7] In 1913 children were made eligible for church membership upon their confession and with parental consent.[8] The designated duties of church membership remained relatively constant, including the obligations to witness to the Christian faith, observe the Sabbath, obey government, support the Sunday school, and contribute to the church. For years, like many denominations with a pietistic inheritance, there was a hankering after the "perfect church" which expressed itself in the exhortations to eschew fashionable and costly array and jewelry.

The lowliest ecclesiastical unit among United Brethren was the class, one or more of which might constitute a charge or station. It consisted of three or more persons who met weekly; it elected a class leader, who exercised spiritual guidance, and a class steward, who collected money and provided the elements for the celebration of the Lord's Supper, "always securing if at all possible unfermented wine."[9] With changing circumstances in the passing years, the role of the class diminished and ultimately disappeared. By 1917 church members made their contributions through the "envelope system."

In 1893 the Official Board supplanted the Official Meeting. Its duties, under the pastor's leadership, were to handle the financial obligations of the church.

Despite the growing importance of the Official Board, the supreme authority in the local church was the Quarterly Conference, chaired by the presiding elder or in his absence the pastor. Its membership increased with the years as organizations and services multiplied. It was amenable to the Annual Conference, which was composed of ordained clergy, licentiates, and laymen if the local churches had chosen to elect them. The Annual Conference through its agents and agencies promoted its own programs as well as those of the denomination. The capstone of the United Brethren Church structure was the General Conference, composed of clergy and laity. Lay delegation on the Annual Conference level encountered no strong objection, but on the General Conference level its implementation was debated and amended for many years. The issue at stake was not whether laymen were qualified to sit in General Conference nor whether women could serve in this capacity, for in 1897 seven of the sixty-two lay delegates were women.[10] The issue at stake was how many lay people should sit in this conference, and how this number should be equitably distributed among the Annual Conferences. Quadrennially new formulas were adopted until the matter was resolved by the provision for equal clerical and lay representation in General Conference.

To strengthen denominational organization, in 1901 the church treasurer was made treasurer of seven major auxiliaries, and in 1917 the term of office for members of major boards was extended from four to eight years.

Confession and Constitution

The confession of thirteen articles, overwhelmingly approved by the vote in local churches and adopted by the 1889 General Conference, supplanted the previous confession of seven paragraphs. While there was no substantive alteration in theological positions, the new confession was more comprehensive in scope and more precise in expression than its predecessor and was kept by the United Brethren to and through the union with the Evangelicals in 1946.

The constitution, similarly approved in the local churches and adopted by General Conference, had much in common with its predecessor, affirming proprietory rights of the denomination over church properties and the ultimate authority of the General Conference. Nevertheless, there were significant changes. Replacing the cloudy language regarding the amendability of the constitution, the new document precisely specified the measures by which it could be changed. It granted General Conference "full control" of six major denominational auxiliaries. Replacing the earlier rule forbidding church members to affiliate with "secret combinations" (fraternal orders), this constitution was permissive: only societies which infringed upon the rights of any man or were injurious to Christian character were to be shunned.[11]

Orders, Ministers, and the Ministry

While among United Brethren there was a single order of ministry, the eldership, other ministries such as those of exhorter and class leader were recognized. Both the latter had been most effective in the nineteenth century, but changes in American social and church life led to the discontinuance of the exhorter in 1909, and the class leader's role steadily diminished.

In 1889 United Brethren provided for a Quarterly Conference preacher. This individual was licensed by the Quarterly Conference after passing an examination and receiving a vote of approval. After one year in this capacity he was eligible for recommendation to the Annual Conference for licensure. After 1915 the role of the Quarterly Conference preacher markedly declined, occasioned in part by changed circumstances in the church and in part by the developing cultural life of society where increasingly the professionally trained minister was preferred.

Applicants, male or female,[12] for Annual Conference license were orally examined as to goals and purposes and then committed to the course of study program. Beginning with 1897 the applicant was required to have completed a high school course, but there is clear evidence that some conferences winked at this rule. Nevertheless, by 1909 there were those boldly asserting that the proper preparation for the ministry was a full college and seminary course, but years passed before this ideal was achieved.

The Annual Conference licentiate, following a three-year probationary period, completion of the course of study, examination by a bishop, and a confirming vote of the conference, was eligible for ordination as an elder and entrance upon an unqualified ministry in the church.[13] As appreciation for formal theological study increased, in 1921 graduates from Bonebrake Theological Seminary or an equivalent theological course were exempted from specified subjects in the course of study in establishing academic eligibility for ordination. Elders served the church in administrative posts and in specialized ministries, but the great majority were pastors of churches.

The presiding elder in 1889 was an elder elected by the Annual Conference, usually annually and normally only one for the conference. He presided at Quarterly Conferences and camp meetings and gave general superintendance to pastors and congregations. The presiding elder became the conference superintendent in 1913. To aid him in his responsibilities, the conference elected two elders and two laymen, who with the superintendent constituted a Council of Administration to which pastors reported quarterly.[14]

Bishops in this church were not a distinct order of ministry but were elders elected by General Conference for four-year terms of administrative service, they were eligible for reelection. In 1901 the stationing of bishops upon their districts was delegated to a committee of three from each episcopal district. Though the initial three-year time limit for a pastor's service on a given parish was amended, the bishop with the counsel of the superintendent annually appointed preachers to their places of service. To meet the growing conviction that the total operations of the church deserved better integration, the bishops were allied with the Board of Missions in supervising overseas mission. Later the officers of all the major church auxiliaries were directed to meet with the bishops annually for consultation and for planning their programs.

Course of Study

The course of study, offered in both the English and German languages, was the instrument for the nurture and instruction of those preparing for the ministry. To achieve greater uniformity and quality, in 1897 a grading scale was devised for the examiners in the Annual Conferences, and the faculty of Union Biblical Seminary was appointed to draft the questions to be asked of the licentiates.[15] Upon the emergence of the deaconess program, a two-year course was fashioned for those entering this ministry. The secretary of the conference committee supervising the course in 1913 was charged to fulfill the functions of a registrar, keeping an accurate record of each student's performance through the course. In 1921 Bonebrake Theological Seminary was authorized to provide a correspondence course leading to a diploma from that institution, which could be a partial alternative to the course of study.

For many years this course was a major and invaluable instrument for the instruction of the majority of the clergy of this church. A later, better schooled, and more sophisticated generation is prone to see the elementary and limited dimensions of the course. Yet it must be remembered that the clergy who received this instruction ministered to people whose education for the most part was just as elementary and limited. However, the educational standards in America were rapidly rising, and with the twentieth century the utility of the course had passed its zenith as a growing number of ministerial candidates were college graduates and matriculating in the theological seminary.

Deaconess Movement

Impressed by similar movements in other American denominations, the General Conference in 1897 gave official approval for deaconess service, embracing visitation, evangelization, and humanitarian Christian efforts. Annual Conferences were empowered to organize boards, including at least three women on each, to supervise the certification and services of the deaconesses. Four years later the deaconess work was more clearly structured. The candidate was to be recommended and licensed by the Quarterly Conference; she was exempted from "perpetual vows" and was to have a uniform "to distinguish and protect her." Serving in a local church, she was under the supervision of the pastor; that church was responsible for her support. After completing the course of study and two years of service, she was eligible for consecration and a permanent license. City associations of clergy and Annual Conferences were empowered to found deaconess homes.[16]

While the deaconess movement won the approval of General Conference, it never won substantial support in the general church; it was given formal approval but little more. At no time during its brief span of existence did it reach any significant stature.

Witnessing for Christ in the U.S.A.

The missionary operations of this church in 1889 were under the supervision of the Home, Frontier and Foreign Missionary Society, with B. F. Booth, secretary. There were branch societies in each Annual Conference, and each elected a representative to serve on the General Board of Directors.[17] The pyramiding opportunities in America and overseas and the complexities of administering numerous and varied programs, together with the belief of some that missionary funds were not being equitably dispersed, led to the decision in 1905 to supplant the Home, Frontier and Foreign Missionary with two societies—the Home Missionary Society and the Foreign Missionary Society. The former was dedicated to missionary endeavors in the United States both within and apart from the Annual Conferences, to evangelism, and to church erection. E. F. Whitney was the first secretary of the Home Society. Annual Conferences organized branch societies, and boards and local churches appointed committees to further the work of home missions.

The Home Society and its programs were widely heralded and won gratifying responses in terms of both interest and financial support. Local churches supported the cause with special Thanksgiving and prayer services during November. Sunday schools celebrated "Missionary Day." Organized Bible classes and individuals rallied to support the Home Society. Previously the Women's Missionary Association had been occupied almost exclusively in overseas programs but it too rallied to this cause and was awarded representation on the Board of Control.

In 1912 property was purchased at Velarde, New Mexico, forty miles north of Santa Fe, and there a day school and a Sunday school under the supervision of a missionary were opened to serve Spanish Americans and Indians. At nearby Santa Cruz a second school was opened, and in 1917, a third at Alcalde. These endeavors won the enthusiastic and generous support of the entire denomination, and the work prospered. Far less glamorous, but no less significant, the Home Society gave assistance to Annual Conferences and local churches in situations of need and opportunity in numerous rural and urban communities.

An unprecedented thrust was initiated in 1909 when the secretary published suitable texts on "present great social questions." Four years later the Home Society was relieved of its responsibilities for evangelism and authorized to establish a "bureau of social service and reform" and also a commission on "rural life problems." By this action this church entered a distinctly new phase of its life and witness.

The Church Erection Society, formed for "aiding feeble churches in the erection of houses of worship,"[18] was legally an independent agency, though the personnel of its board was identical with that of the missionary board. Initially it was restricted to making loans to congregations involved in building or rebuilding programs; in 1893 a Donation Fund was established from which outright grants could be made. Support for the Church Erection Society was penurious, its problems multiplied and frustrated; its secretaries in 1889 and 1893 resigned.[19]

A reorganization of procedures and a more generous support are apparent after 1897. New regulations involved the Annual Conference with the congregation in securing a loan. A Parsonage Fund and a Lot Fund were established to assist churches in erecting manses or securing real estate. Thanks to improved procedure and support, the society proudly reported it had been able to render assistance to 470 church and 29 parsonage buildings projects.[20]

Upon the dissolution of the Home, Frontier and Foreign Missionary Society, the Church Erection Society was integrally allied with the Home Society. With the growth of the nation, calls for aid multiplied, requiring the exercise of sound judgment, involving justice as well as sympathetic understanding. While an earlier generation because of inclination and necessity sought to erect churches plain and neat, their children began to sense the need for dignity, beauty, and proper appointments in God's House. By 1922 the Erection Society was offering architectural counsel for the construction of worthier sanctuaries for worship.

In the World

The Foreign Missionary Society, created in 1905, was under the direction of a board and superintended by a secretary, S. S. Hough, who was also charged with the promotion of programs, the solicitation of money, and the recruitment of missionaries. Annual Conferences organized conference branches, and local churches appointed missionary committees to promote overseas missions and gather funds. The overseas operations of the Women's Missionary

Association were more closely related to those of the society, and the Women's organization was awarded representation on the society's board.[21] Administratively, the Society was empowered to name mission superintendents, to gather missionaries into Mission Councils, and to cultivate the organization of Mission Conferences which would mature to the status of Annual Conferences.[22]

The new mood developing in missionary administration is apparent in the declaration in 1913 that the supreme aim of the church's programs was to establish self-supporting native churches and that, upon the request of a Mission Council, authority be granted for cooperation and federation with mission programs of other denominations. To further the supervision of overseas operations, the office of a foreign missions bishop was created, and the Rev. A. T. Howard was elected to fill it. The office was discontinued in 1921 when an associate secretary was authorized for the board, but because funds were lacking, no appointment was made for several years.

United Brethren in 1889 were supporting missionary programs in Canada, Germany, and Sierra Leone and were on the threshold of establishing one in China. General Conference in 1905 granted its Ontario Conference authority to negotiate and effect a union with the Congregational churches in Canada. This was done without delay. In Bavaria, Germany, where work had begun in 1869 and a Mission Conference had been formed in 1893, the work languished. The church preferred to employ resources elsewhere; in 1905 the operations in Germany were transferred to the Methodist Episcopal Church.

Sierra Leone

The mission in Sierra Leone suffered with the schism in the American church in 1889, but even more disastrously in 1898 in the native uprising allegedly prompted by the resurgence of superstition and by British colonial measures to collect taxes and to suppress the slave trade.[23] Before disorders subsided, numerous buildings had been vandalized or destroyed, and seven missionaries had been martyred.

The latter calamity evoked deep compassion and renewed commitment among United Brethren, spurring them to greater generosity for the reestablishment and expansion of the mission. In

1902 the Martyrs Memorial Church was dedicated in Rotifunk, Sierra Leone, honoring the missionaries who had been massacred. October 4, 1904, Albert Academy was opened in Freetown. In 1906 the Hatfield-Archer Dispensary opened its doors in Rotifunk. That same year the Women's Association opened a Boys' Home in Tiama and a Girls' Home in Moyamba. The latter in 1926 gave rise to the Harford School for Girls. Through the years the operations spread from the initial centers to adjacent communities and among different tribes, but unquestionably it was the heroic episode of missionary martyrdom which gave this mission field a place of endearment in the hearts of United Brethren.

China

While the passions of the schism were raging in the American church, in 1889 the Rev. George Sickafoose, Moy Ling, Austia Petterson, and Lillian Shaffner sailed to locate a mission in the vicinity of Canton. The arrival of Regina M. Bigler, M.D., in 1892 was an eventful day, for she began a service in medical and evangelistic activities which lasted thirty-two years. A dispensary was opened in Canton in 1893. Evangelistic work was undertaken in adjacent Sam Tong and Siu Lam. Medical services begun in 1911 led to the erection of the Ramsburg Memorial Hospital.

From the beginning, Canton was the center of this mission. In this teeming city in 1901 a Girls' Boarding School was opened which later was transferred to Siu Lam, where it became the Miller Seminary for Girls. The mission prospered, in 1905 reporting the activities of its two dispensaries, the fourteen day and boarding schools, and the thirty-eight organized churches with their 1,429 members. A Foundlings' Home was opened in 1907. January 5, 1908, a Mission Conference was organized which reported, in addition to the western missionaries, twenty Chinese helpers.

Their oneness in purpose and in Christ led to trustful ventures in interchurch programs. In 1911 United Brethren began their support of Canton Christian College, a middle school maintained by seven mission bodies, and in 1914 of Union Theological Seminary. United Brethren missionaries and those of the American Board, the London Missionary Society, and the Scandanavian Alliance in 1919 formed a federation which aspired to the formation of a United

Church of Christ in China, but some years were to elapse before this goal became a reality.

Japan

In December 1895 George Iris and U. Yoniyama, both members of First United Brethren Church, Dayton, returned to Tokyo for evangelistic efforts, but early prospects quickly collapsed, and the Foreign Society decided to send a missionary to Tokyo to teach English, to promote Sunday school work and evangelism, and to superintend. In 1898 the Rev. A. T. Howard arrived in Tokyo. Three years later the Nihombashi church was dedicated, hailed as the first United Brethren sanctuary in Japan. In 1902 the Japan Mission Conference was organized, which in 1908 included six missionaries, fifteen Japanese pastors and evangelists, and thirteen organized churches with a membership of 381.

An ecumenical spirit was expressed in several ways by this mission. In 1900, following negotiations, it began to provide one teacher at Doshisha University, Kyoto. It accepted the comity arrangement to work in Chiba Ken and Shiga Ken. Early in the century it joined with four other denominational missions in seeking the creation of one Japanese Christian Church, but that was an idea whose time was still to come.

Puerto Rico

Following the Spanish-American War many American Christians, inspired both by patriotism and evangelistic zeal, clamored for the establishment of missions among those newly released from Spanish sovereignty. By comity arrangements the United Brethren were awarded an area centering at Ponce, Puerto Rico. There the first missionaries, the Rev. and Mrs. H. H. Huffman, arrived July 28, 1899. Within a year a church was organized in Ponce, and evangelistic work began in Juana Dias in 1901 and in Tauco in 1907. The skills and propensities of some of the missionaries led to singularly fruitful measures such as P. W. Drury's labors with printing: the initial modest publication evolved into an interdenominational periodical, *Puerto Rio Evangelico,* which had a wide reading and influence in the island. The emerging ecumenical spirit was expressed in 1916 when United Brethren joined in the cooperative Evangelical Union of Puerto Rico. Then in 1931 United Brethren and

Congregational Christian Churches formed the United Evangelical Church of Puerto Rico. In Santo Domingo, Dominican Republic, the United Brethren worked under the Church Board for Christian Work in Santo Domingo.

Philippines

Though some United Brethren were content with the foundation of a mission in Puerto Rico, others vigorously contended for another in the Philippines, and the Women's Association responded to their appeals. Using money gathered in their Silver Anniversary Memorial campaign, they sent two missionaries in 1901 who worked in three provinces in northwestern Luzon by comity agreement: Ilocos North, Ilocos South, and LaUnion. Dire difficulties quickly emerged. Opposition, even hostility, was relentless, stemming from native superstition and obscurantist Romanism. Within two years the missionaries had withdrawn. The arrival of the Rev. H. W. Widdoes in 1903 marked the beginning of a vigorous program centered in San Fernando. A church was organized in 1904, additional missionaries came from the States, capable Filipinoes were enlisted, and in 1908 a Mission Conference was organized. A Young Women's Training School was initiated in 1910, but it was 1920 before it was adequately housed. The mission prospered, and in 1920 it was acclaimed the most rapidly growing mission of the denomination.

Apart from the enterprise in Sierra Leone, United Brethren overseas missions were initiated between 1889 and 1910. The recognized needs of the world and of America, coupled with a clearer conception of missionary responsibility and of Christian stewardship, led this church in trustful obedience to the Lord's commission into these courageous endeavors. The vocabulary of success is of limited use in appraising Christian enterprise, but of the earnest, faithful obedience demonstrated in these undertakings there can be no question.

Women's Missionary Association

Initially the Women's Missionary Association with its conference branches and local societies worked harmoniously but separately from the Home, Frontier and Foreign Missionary Society.

Though its operations were almost exclusively overseas, after the creation of the Foreign and Home Societies in 1905, the Association was awarded representation on both boards, and in 1913 the representation was increased.[24]

In the thirty years since its formation in 1875, the Women's Missionary Association had moved into many new, creative, and fruitful activities. Sound literature, wise pedagogical techniques, and patient cultivation combined to produce a broad missionary enthusiasm. As the work and worth of the Association was recognized, it was brought into integral relations with the Home and Foreign Societies and made a partner in the administration of the denomination's total missionary program.

Sunday School and Youth Work

In 1889 the United Brethren Sabbath school operations were managed by an elected secretary and directors. The secretary, Robert Cowden, was charged with the organization and maintenance of Sunday schools "wherever praticable." Officially, Sabbath schools became Sunday schools in 1905,[25] but before that time innovations had been introduced such as the Home Department, the cradle roll, and the annual observance of Children's Day.

A Congregational pastor, Francis H. Clark, in 1881 in Portland, Maine, drew young people into a Society of Christian Endeavor. The example was infectious, and rapidly similar societies were organized in many denominations and many places. A large number of these banded together in an interdenominational Christian Endeavor Society with Clark as president. United Brethren were uncommitted to Christian Endeavor, but they were convinced of the worth of youth work in the church. Reputedly, the first young people's society in the denomination was formed in March 1883 in Mt. Pleasant, Pennsylvania. Others followed, and in 1888 those in the Allegheny Conference banded themselves into a conference organization. Aware of these developments and confronted with numerous recommendations, the General Conference of 1893 authorized the creation of a Young People's Christian Union and a Department of Young People's Work as well as the publication of a periodical promoting this work. The Young People's Union was intended for "mutual helpfulness, for stimulating church loyalty and an intelligent interest in various church enterprises."[26] The

Department was placed under the control of a council. The periodical, The Young People's Watchword, began publication in September of that year. Rules for union auxiliaries in the Annual Conferences and for local societies were drafted. Junior societies appeared in 1894 and also prospered. In 1908 when suspicions of Christian Endeavor had diminished, the Young People's Christian Union became the Young People's Christian Endeavor Union.

Men's work, or the Brotherhood as it was later called, began about 1909 and was widely heralded as a most promising movement. It was inspired in part by similar organizations in other denominations and in part by those who were impressed by the achievements of the Women's Missionary Association. The Brotherhood was intended to cultivate personal piety and denominational loyalty and to encourage participation in activities for social, civic, and industrial betterment.[27]

At first these various programs—for Sunday schools, for youth societies and for men—operated independently. The General Conference of 1909 determined there should be a unified denominational program. The preceding structures were abolished, and a Department of Sunday Schools, Brotherhood, and Young People's Work was created. The new department was placed under the direction of a board with Robert Cowden as secretary. Assessments and offerings from Sunday schools, youth societies, Brotherhoods, and churches provided its support. Branch departments in the Annual Conferences, each with its officers, implemented the new department's concerns in conference programs.

The integrative process was extended in 1913 with the formation of the Religious Education Council, consisting of representatives of this department, the Home and Foreign Missionary Societies, the Women's Missionary Association, the Christian Stewardship Commission, and Bonebrake Theological Seminary. Its assignment was "to consider and correlate all plans for such education proposed by these several departments."[28]

A further unifying step by which this department and the Board of Education would be consolidated was proposed in 1917 but was not enacted until 1929. However, the department enthusiastically promoted effective educational measures: teacher training, the Otterbein Standard Training Course, and vacation and weekday schools of religious education.

Higher Education

Colleges

Otterbein College began its life in Westerville, Ohio, in 1847 and from the first has grown consistently. Lebanon Valley College, Annville, Pennsylvania, was founded in 1866. For twenty years after 1890 its future was uncertain, but since 1910 it has grown steadily. Shenandoah Seminary in Dayton, Virginia, became Shenandoah Collegiate Institute and School of Music in 1902, but small enrollments and meager support clouded its future.

In the Midwest there were numerous locations and relocations of institutions. Leander Clark College, Toledo, Iowa, was founded in 1889, but after a decade began to languish and in 1917 was merged into Coe College, Cedar Rapids, Iowa. Lane University was established in LeCompton, Kansas, in 1865 but subsequently was removed to Holton, where it became Campbell College. Problems continued to harrass the school, and in 1913 it was merged into Kansas City University, Kansas City, a Methodist Protestant school. Gibbon Collegiate Institute, Gibbon, Nebraska, was acquired in 1886 and in 1890 relocated in York as York College. It too was belabored with financial difficulties, but grow it did, even though slowly. After three years of planning and efforts, in 1905 Indiana Central College in Indianapolis was launched upon its impressive career.

Union Biblical Seminary—Bonebrake Theological Seminary

Union Biblical Seminary, Dayton, Ohio, was the only ministerial training school of the United Brethren, and it was the only educational institution over which the General Conference exercised "full control." By 1893 when an entrance examination was required, the seminary offered two programs: (1) the regular course for the college graduate requiring the study of Greek and Hebrew and leading to the degree, Bachelor of Divinity, and (2) the English course for others, with no language requirements, which led to a diploma. Courses multiplied—a postgraduate reading course, a missionary course, a deaconess course, and a German-English course—but by 1922 most of these had disappeared, leaving only the regular and English courses.

For many years the seminary was obliged to contend with the large number of people in the church who were either openly opposed to formal theological education or just as openly indifferent to it. Nevertheless seminary enrollment grew slowly. The seminary moved from its first location in the basement of the Summit Street Church to a commodious, three-story brick building of its own where it continued to grow. In 1909 because of a substantial gift of Kansas farm land Union Biblical Seminary was renamed Bonebrake Theological Seminary to honor the donor's five great uncles, and a new campus site in the Dayton View section of the city was purchased. Years elapsed during which campus and building plans were drafted and funds were collected, but upon the erection of three buildings at the new site the seminary moved to its new campus in 1923.

Board of Education

The United Brethren concern for Christian higher education found expression in the Board of Education which, in 1893, was charged with: (1) gathering and administering funds to assist needy candidates preparing for the ministry or missionary service, (2) discouraging impetuous and unsound efforts to launch new schools, and (3) encouraging a more generous support for established denominational schools.[29] General Conference gave the board more precise authority in 1897, and four years later it was counseling colleges in financial and academic affairs. Special days were introduced into the church calendar on which offerings were to be received in the congregations for the support of the colleges. Through the influence of the board denominational support for the colleges and the seminary was materially increased.

While the colleges enjoyed increasing enrollments, they were handicapped with outgrown facilities and clamored for more support from the denomination. Further, there were persisting complaints that the educational funds were not being distributed equitably among the schools. To meet these circumstances, the General Conference of 1913 created a new Board of Education, awarding it the status of a major department of the church. Dr. W. E. Schell was elected its secretary. Among the duties assigned the new board were: (1) to "determine the number of colleges and academies," (2) to assign supporting conferences to each institution and, as necessary, to alter the allocations, and (3) to establish the standards for colleges granting the bachelor's degree.[30] During the following eight years the Board of Education worked tirelessly for the cause of Christian higher education, resulting in broader popular interest in it and in improved standards in the education institutions.

The Printing Establishment

The publishing house in 1889 at the corner of Main and Fourth Streets, Dayton, occupied the site of the first United Brethren printing plant in Dayton. Through the years the building on that site was enlarged several times, and adjacent property on Fourth Street was acquired. In 1915, in lieu of a number of alternatives, the printing plant was relocated at West Fifth and Perry Streets. The denominational offices remained in the old building at Main and Fourth Streets. That building was replaced with a fourteen-story building, and in 1924 it was capped with a seven-story tower and hailed as the world's tallest reinforced concrete building.[31] The printing establishment was from its foundation dedicated to publications but found itself engulfed in a maze of real estate transactions and construction contracts and obligations until it was obliged to make a clear separation of its printing operations from all others.

In 1889 W. J. Shuey served the church as publishing agent. The major denominational periodicals were: *The Religious Telescope* with I. E. Kephart as editor and *Die Fröliche Botschafter* with William Mittendorf as editor. The diminishing patronage of the German periodical led to its transfer to the supervision of the Ohio German Conference in 1901, and in 1924 it was discontinued. In 1889 Daniel Berger edited the Sabbath school literature. The *Young Peoples' Watchword*, with H. F. Shupe as editor, appeared in 1893. *The Missionary Visitor* replaced *The Searchlight* in 1895 as a missionary publication. *The Otterbein Hymnal* was issued in 1890 and *The Sanctuary Hymnal* in 1914. In addition to these publications, there were numerous educational and promotional magazines and releases that flowed from the denominational presses.

There were theologically minded churchmen who wrote, but their publications were few. Undoubtedly the most productive was Bishop Jonathan Weaver, whose books served as denominational standards: his *Christian Doctrine* (1889), *Practical Comments on the Confession of Faith* (1892) and *Christian Theology* (1900) had no rivals. His most able successor was Dr. A. W. Drury whose *outline of Doctrinal Theology* (1914) was revised, enlarged, and republished in 1926. Through these years the theological position was predominantly that of conservative, biblical pietism which only marginally reckoned with the newer scientific knowledge and the newer theological issues which were making their impact upon traditional positions.

The Christian Life and Way

The United Brethren Church in 1889 continued the inherited positions of its past which held that Christianity was not so much an intellectual affirmation as it was a way of life initiated in an experience of conversion. Religion was individualistic, immoderately so—individuals were offered and found salvation in a conversion experience and individuals were summoned to the Christian way of life. Pietistic perfectionism prompted United Brethren toward the concept of the perfect church.

There were precise norms for individual Christian practice. Divorce was permissible only upon the grounds of adultery, and one divorced was ineligible for the ministry. Sunday was a holy day—this church made an official protest when it was proposed that the World Exposition in Chicago be opened on a Sunday.[32] When the protest was ignored, the denominational exhibits were withdrawn. Regarding temperance, members were forbidden to make, sell, or use alcoholic beverages (except for medical purposes) or to lease any property for these purposes. Members were exhorted to abstain from the use of tobacco.

These positions continued in the twentieth century and with new measures. The last Sunday in November became Temperance Sunday when pastors proclaimed the gospel grounds for abstinence. In 1905 a Temperance Commission was formed to promote the cause and to collaborate with like groups in other denominations. A paragraph in the *Discipline* captioned "Sabbath Observance" cautioned against the demands and temptations of urban and industrial life which threatened God's Day. In 1901 "the open saloon, the beer-garden, the baseball game, the social dance, "excursion trains," and "the increasingly prevalent apathy of the masses to attendance upon the public service of the church" were denounced.[33]

Meanwhile in the church there were those who, while not repudiating the older moral norms, felt more strongly impelled to speak out in Christ's Name against the manifestations of corruption and greed and the inhumanity of industrialization. They were more distantly separated in thought than in years from the United Brethren of 1893 whose simplistic solution for social injustices was an intimate association with Jesus. Increasing numbers came to believe that the individualistic, pietistic prescriptions—good as they were—were alone incapable to remedy social evils. Rauschenbusch's social gospel appealed to many.

The episcopal message of 1909 spoke with unprecedented decisiveness, denouncing the unwarrantable poverty-line existence of millions and the raw selfishness of the contending forces, capital and labor. "The Church does not stand for the present social order."[34] This General Conference approved the report of the Committee on Moral Reform which began with Rauschenbusch's declaration: "The social crisis is the over-shadowing problem of our generation." The report went on to urge that pastors familiarize themselves with current social movements, that churches practice brotherhood in local affairs, and that youth societies study current social issues.[35]

This mood issued in the adoption of a social creed by the General Conference, an affirmation unquestionably inspired by the social creed of the Federal Council of Churches. Its pronouncements were decisive:

Inasmuch as existing social and industrial conditions call for wise and firm leadership from the churches, the Church of the United Brethren in Christ stands

For equal rights and complete justice for all men in all conditions of life:

For the protection of the family . . . uniform divorce laws, proper regulations of marriage and proper housing:

For the fullest possible development of every child:

For the abolition of child labor:

For the regulation of the conditions of toil for women . . . :

For the abatement and prevention of poverty:

For the protection of the individual and society from the social, economic and moral waste of the liquor traffic:

For the protection of the worker from dangerous machinery . . . :

For the . . . protection of workers from the hardships of enforced employment:

For suitable provision for old age . . . and those incapacitiated by injury:

For the rights of employees and employers alike to organize: for adequate means of conciliation and arbitration in industrial disputes:

For the release from employment one day in seven:

For the gradual and reasonable reduction of the hours of labor . . . :

For a living wage as a minimum in every industry and for the highest wage that each industry can afford:

For a new emphasis upon the application of Christian principles to the acquisition and use of property, and for the most equitable division of the products of industry that can be ultimately devised.[36]

This social creed marked a new chapter in the life of the United Brethren Church, separating the earlier day with its almost exclusive accent upon personal morality when the Christian responses to poverty and social injustices were prayers and alms. Earlier thinking added to the call to individual Christian living the presumption that society stood in need of overhauling, even Christianizing, and that Christian men and the church bore responsibilities for achieving this end. The new outlook reflected in the social creed was not the fruit of reflective utopianism, idealistic philosophy, or sheer humanitarianism, but of a deeper understanding that every man under God is precious and deserving of justice. God's redemption is available for individuals and for social relations. The world is his by creation, and by dedicated efforts, human society may be shaped into his Kingdom, or at least into something approximating it.

The social creed of 1909 spoke only on American domestic affairs. Within five years came World War I, which United Brethren declared a grim and awe-full manifestation of human sinfulness. Without ecclesiastical ties to people in Germany, conferences unhesitatingly passed patriotic resolutions affirming loyalty to the American government and to the cause of liberty, justice, and democracy. While the conflict was "truly the high festival of Hell" and costly in terms of lives and dollars, there was the conviction that "America ought and will lead the way to the world organization for peace."[37]

Toward the redemption of the American social order, the ballot was hailed as the proper instrument of the Christan citizen for achieving the improved social and political democracy. For twenty years the church called consistently for an intelligent, earnest, conscientious Christian citizenship to penetrate civic and social affairs.[38]

Even if society bore some responsibility for those in need, the church was not exempt from obligations to aid the distressed, and thus philanthropic agencies were launched. In 1903 an orphanage was opened at Quincy, Pennsylvania. A decade earlier an old people's home began operations at Mechanicsburg. These two were merged in 1913, and the Quincy Home and Orphanage became their successor. On an extensive tract of 4,005 acres near Lebanon, Ohio, which was acquired from a dying Shaker community for $325,000, Otterbein Home began its ministry in 1913. Through the sale of some of its acres and support from the denomination, the initial heavy debt was somewhat diminished, new buildings and services were provided, and the home provided a compassionate ministry for children and the elderly. On a twenty-acre site near Los Angeles, the Baker Home for Retired Ministers was founded in 1911. Its restriction of residency to retired clergy limited the development of this home. The Beatrice United Brethren Hospital, Beatrice, Nebraska, was the sole endeavor of this kind in the church, and though accounted a general institution of the church about 1913, its life was brief. All these efforts are properly understood as expressions of the developing social consciousness in the church.

Ministerial Pensions

In 1889 ministerial salaries were deplorably low, and a minister retired normally only because of broken health or advanced age. Concomitant with the rising sensitivity to social concerns was the issue of ministerial aid. The Ministerial Relief Bureau was formed in 1909. To its treasury the printing establishment was to contribute $5,000, and churches were summoned to give on the basis of five cents per member. From the bureau the retired minister would receive what the treasury would "justify."[39] However, contributions were very small, nor were all the Annual Conferences eager or even willing to participate. A quadrennium later an assessment was levied on such conferences as elected to participate. A directive in 1917 for an improved plan for ministerial aid and for a campaign for funds went unheeded because of the more assertive claims advanced by other auxiliaries of the church. The Ministerial Relief Bureau was abolished in 1921, supplanted by the Ministerial Pension and

Annuity Plan. Under its provisions there were two categories of membership, the contributory and the noncontributory, both sharing in the support given by the general church. The minister electing contributory membership paid an annual premium based on his age and salary; upon retirement his pension was larger. The plan did operate, but again funds remained dismally small, and the actual assistance to the superannuated was miserably minimal.

Emerging Auxiliaries and Boards

The Historical Society in 1889 was structured for the collection and preservation of records and artifacts, but it was niggardly supported and it accomplished little. In 1920 its life centered in a room which the printing establishment awarded it on an upper floor where its modest collection was available to the interested and persistent inquirer.

From their early nineteenth-century beginning, United Brethren labored zealously for a primary purpose: to proclaim Jesus Christ and invite men to accept him as Lord. But as the older revivalism which centered in a decisive religious experience as the hallmark of the true Christian began to diminish in effectiveness and as new agencies and methods began to appear, another consideration was advanced. While the whole church could not be relieved of its responsibility for evangelism, some smaller unit could promote it with greater effectiveness. Accordingly, in 1905 an Evangelistic Committee was created in the Home Missionary Society. Eight years later the Home Society was relieved of its supervision, and a denominational Commission on Evangelism was formed.[40] This commission assisted pastors in the employment of evangelists, recruited evangelists, encouraged evangelistic work in the churches, and participated in the Federal Council of Churches' Commission on Evangelism.

The combination of Christian faith and current needs gave powerful promptings to the promotion of Christian stewardship. Missionary programs, church erection, and educational institutions needed and deserved enlarged support, and commitment to Christ was interpreted to involve personal resources as an integral part of the whole life surrendered to Him. In 1905 a Christian Stewardship Commission was created, which after 1909 had its own secretary. Literature was disseminated exhorting churches to accept apportionments and budgets and individuals to accept the "weekly system of giving." Succeeding the Christian Stewardship Commission in 1913 was a Commission on Finance, which endeavored also to prepare and to recommend a denominational budget to General Conference for adoption.

What was heralded as the "most significant and advanced act" was the creation of the denominational Board of Administration in 1917.[41] It carried many of the obligations formerly borne by the Finance Commission, but there were others, among them the authority to act for General Conference in the interim between its quadrennial sessions. While the campaign for funds for the Ministerial Pension Plan was deferred, another involving the whole church in a four-year crusade to achieve financial and spiritual goals was approved by General Conference. Caught up in the exhilarating American mood during World War I, many denominations and interchurch organizations embarked upon campaigns for high goals. Under the Board of Administration, the United Brethren promoted the United Enlistment Movement seeking "advance in evangelism, education, missions and individual activities." The numerical goals specified were: 150,000 conversions, 100,000 accessions to the church, a twenty-five percent increase in Sunday school and Christian Endeavor enrollments, 2,000 more students in United Brethren colleges, 500 volunteers for full-time Christian service, and $2,000,000 for various church programs.[42] As these goals were not achieved by 1921, the movement was continued.

In addition to the multiplying activities, a distinctive development among United Brethren between 1889 and 1920 was the emergence of a new sense of coherence and unity. Earlier this was a church united largely by its Confession of Faith and constitution, around which numerous agencies clustered. But with experience and wisdom and through successive steps culminating in the Board of Administration, agencies and people were led to recognize themselves more clearly as related segments in one common enterprise endeavoring to make an effective Christian witness.

Ecumenical Relations

During most of the nineteenth century the United Brethren Church found its mission and its future in its distinctiveness and separateness from others. Its growth through most of these years was achieved in no small measure by winning people to these ideals, but as the century drew to its close the church became less suspicious of some of the cultural norms, less nervously anxious about its future and less narrowly sectarian. Though immersed in problems of its own, it discovered the joys and satisfactions of association and cooperation with other churches.

This change of stance may in part be attributed to the growing ecumenical spirit in Christendom whose manifestation has been called the great fact of our age. Even movements as diverse as liberal theology and the social gospel overleaped denominational lines and won advocates in many denominations becoming grounds for fraternization. Of quite another character and even more important in the expression of Christian unity were the Foreign Missions Conference of North America, the Home Missions Council, and the Federal Council of Churches but perhaps most significant of all, the International Missionary Conference in Edinburgh, 1910, from which stemmed the International Missionary Council and the conferences on Life and Work, and Faith and Order. A generation later these were joined in the World Council of Churches. All these were expressions of the ecumenical spirit, and United Brethren participated in them. The changed United Brethren stance cannot adequately be ascribed to the sociological process of maturation. Far more influential were the experiences of association with churchmen of other denominations, in America or abroad. Overseas missionaries were happily working coöperatively. From Japan one wrote: "In co-operating with the American Board we are doing what many more should do. There are too many fences among the Good Shepherd's sheep."[43]

This mood found further expression in 1901 when a Commission on Church Union was appointed. The commission's inactivity provoked twenty-two ministers and laymen to formally petition the bishops "to take such steps as are necessary to open negotiations with churches similar to ours in polity and doctrine, looking to their permanent union."[44] The churches similar included the Methodist Protestant, Evangelical Association, United Evangelical, Cumberland Presbyterian, and the Congregational Churches.

Negotiating conversations involving Methodist Protestants, Congregationalists, and United Brethren were initiated in 1903, and within a year the commissioners of these three were grappling with the gritty theological and political issues inherent in such

negotiations. Their "Church Union Syllabus" announcing principles and procedures was approved by the three denominations, by
the United Brethren with a vote of 253 to three.[45] Upon the proposals
for the faith and polity of the united church in 1906 the first
evidences of hesitancy became apparent. The six-paragraph creed
was acclaimed by some as the "first creed with an article on social
justice."[46] The creed was proposed not as obligatory for church
membership but as a testimony of faith. The Act of Union, specifying
the procedural steps to union, was rebuffed: by the Congregationalists in 1907, who failed to endorse it, and by the Methodist
Protestants in 1908, who turned away from it, preferring the
prospects of union with other Methodist churches. The United
Brethren in 1909 took no action on the Act of Union but in view of
what had occurred in the two other churches announced: "We regret
the halt in these efforts and stand as ready and anxious as we have
ever been to join these sister churches in the most complete
union."[47]

Many explanations have been offered for the collapse of this
venture. The faith articulated in the creed was alleged by some to be
too liberal, by others to be too conservative, by still others to be too
imprecise and confusing to be meaningful. Some attributed the
failure to the projected church polity, which dissatisfied people
whose previous patterns ranged from congregationalism to episcopacy. Still others attributed it to nontheological factors: the
numerical disparity and the widely divergent character of the three
negotiating churches. While no single or simple reason can wholly
explain it, this march toward merger was thwarted.[48]

Responding to an invitation from the United Brethren, in 1912
the Methodist Protestants entered consultative conversations, and at
a meeting of the commissions of the two churches, April 23, 1913, a
Syllabus of Union was issued containing a Declaration of Faith, a
constitution, and the proposed name "The United Protestant
Church." The Syllabus of Union was presented to the United
Brethren General Conference. While supported by some, it was
received with less than enthusiasm by the majority. Following a
spirited debate it was decided to submit the syllabus to a vote of the
Annual Conferences, and upon a three-fourths supportive vote to
submit it to the whole church in a general referendum after which
the next General Conference would make its decision.

While Methodist Protestants approved the syllabus, among the

United Brethren opposition to it intensified and became more vocal. The aggregate vote in the Annual Conferences approved the syllabus though by a narrow majority, and denominational leadership became apprehensive because of the stout opposition in the larger conferences. The syllabus was never voted upon by the whole church in a general referendum, allegedly because the bishops feared it would not receive the necessary three-fourths majority. General Conference, 1917, tersely concluded the matter with the recommendation that the matter of organic union be dropped and that "all our people press on in the even tenor of our way as a denomination."[49]

Inasmuch as United Brethren and Methodist Protestants had much in common by way of inheritance and faith and practice, the failure of this unitive endeavor cannot be attributed to matters of belief or polity. There was opposition to the proposed name, The United Protestant Church, there was disagreement as to whether a basis of union should precede union or issue thereafter, and there were allegations that only trivial and tardy efforts were made to keep the whole church informed on the union proceedings. Some church leaders were unsympathetic to the venture, and in the larger conferences there were determined pockets of opposition which led to the decision in 1917. However, this decision did not signify the retirement of United Brethren into isolation, for the same General Conference which terminated negotiations with the Methodist Protestants declared its readiness "to fraternize with other Christian bodies and co-operate with them in the larger work of the Kingdom."[50]

n 1921 the Church of the United Brethren in Christ with its 375,000 members stood on the threshold of an eventful quarter century. Its past was prized. The *Discipline* of 1925 carried an extended postscript informing the reader that the account of the beginning of the church was "substantially" what appeared first in 1815 to which were added "an account of the earlier conferences of 1789 and 1791 and the names of the members of the conference in 1800."[1] This was in the *Disciplines* without change until 1946.

The word "charge" entered the vocabulary of the church and was defined as a station or circuit with a number of congregations. The official board gained stature as an efficient administrative and promotional organization of the local congregation. At the same time, the class and the class leader, while continued in the *Discipline*, steadily lost significance and utility in the majority of churches. In 1945 a ritual for the dedication of infants appeared in the *Discipline* alongside the one for the baptism of infants.[2]

The basic ecclesiastical structure of conferences on three levels continued intact. The Quarterly Conference was the vital link between the local church and the Annual Conference. Its relationship to the official board was the occasion of much discussion and some confusion; nevertheless, constitutionally the official board was subordinated to the Quarterly Conference, which held singular powers such as the election of delegates to the Annual Conference.

UNITED BRETHREN: CHANGES IN A CHANGING WORLD, 1920–1946

The Annual Conference was the regional administrative and promotional agency of the denomination, and new circumstances evoked new regulations. For example, beginning in 1933 the pastor and lay delegate of a church which reported no accessions and was delinquent in its apportionment payments were cited to appear before a conference committee to make explanations. Among the actions of General Conferences was that in 1925 which specified July 1 as the date for the beginning of the fiscal year and that in 1941 whereby persons over seventy years of age were made ineligible for election to denominational offices and pension provisions for general officers were established.[3]

THE MINISTRY

Classification of ministers in 1929 was accorded in one of two categories: (1) licentiates with credentials from either Quarterly or Annual Conferences and (2) elders, sustaining active or retired connection with the Annual Conference. The rules for the licentiate were amended only slightly. In 1937 he was permitted to substitute one year's work in formal classes or correspondence study with the Board of Christian Education for a year in the study course. This was extended in 1941 when, if he were a college graduate, he was exempted from subjects in the study course which he had taken in college. While there was never any serious attempt to eliminate the Quarterly Conference preacher, the move to permit him to dispense the sacraments was disallowed.[4]

During this quarter century successive measures were taken to lift ministerial standards by establishing higher educational requirements for the Annual Conference license. It was reported in 1929 that among the active ministers of the church 569 were high school graduates, 300 were college graduates, and 149 had graduated from both college and seminary.[5] In 1933 it was ruled that by 1937 only college graduates would be eligible for license "except in extraordinary cases,"[6] but the rule and the prescriptions for handling emergency cases were ignored in some parts of the church. There were those who viewed these new measures apprehensively, seeing in them evidences of intellectualism and inordinate ecclesiastical authoritarianism which overrode the divine call. These notwithstanding, ministerial standards were raised, and as the church membership in increasing numbers gave support to such standards, in 1941 college and seminary graduation were required of applicants for license, exempting only those who because of age or special circumstances were unable to meet the rule.[7]

The study course for licentiates continued with bibliographical changes made with quadrennial regularity. In 1933, long after its usefulness had passed, work in the German language was discontinued. Then in 1941 the conference committee was instructed to solicit and file transcripts and the academic record of each candidate under its charge.

There was still a single order of ministry, the eldership, which was achieved by ordination. For several years there were attempts to reduce the time between licensing and ordination from two years to one, but the proposition failed to win majority support.

The church that was seeking to achieve a better educated ministry simultaneously was faced with another crucial issue—the need for more ministers. A committee on the Conservation and Recruiting of Ministers was appointed in 1925. Its report in 1929 declared that materialism, agnosticism, higher criticism, and modernist teachings discouraged commitment to full-time Christian service. Nevertheless, since the calling to the ministry could not be left exclusively to God, the church through pastors and parents bore responsibilities with Him in leading youth to vocational decisions.[8] Thereafter the Life Work Recruitment program was launched and brought good results.

Though the deaconess movement was accorded recognition in the *Discipline*, from the first it lacked significant enthusiasm and support. Such activity as there was, a few Annual Conferences promoted. Deaconess work attracted only a few volunteers, and its efforts were small, transitory and of no major significance.

MISSIONARY ENDEAVORS IN A TROUBLED TIME

Home Missions and Church Erection

The Home Missions Board under its secretary, P. M. Camp, set out to render its services to individual churches, Mission Conferences, and to "special missions." Through its education department, literature was devised and distributed over the denomination; slides, scripts, and moving pictures for promoting its cause were added in the 1940's. For the quadrennium ending in

1929, the Home Missions Board reported it was "managing seven annual conferences" and had aided 128 congregations in addition to its operations among Spanish-Americans in New Mexico. Additionally, the Church Erection Society had made loans to sixty-six congregations totaling $336,507. The latter, having made consulting architectural service available, expressed pleasure at the evidence of improved aesthetic tastes in the new churches which were more beautiful, churchly, and modern. For effective administration, loans were made to a congregation only when endorsed by its Annual Conference. Delinquency in meeting the obligation barred any other congregation in that conference from borrowing from the society.

Like all the agencies of the church, Home Missions and Church Erection suffered severely with the Great Depression that paralyzed American economic life after 1930. Its receipts from the denominational budget shrivelled from $67,000 in 1929 to $39,000 in 1932 while those of the Foreign Missionary Society declined from $194,229 to $147,418.[9] Drastic measures were taken to reduce operating expenses, but the church was shocked in 1933 to learn that missionary salaries for five months had not been paid. Before the depth of the Great Depression passed, missionaries' salaries were reduced by twenty-five percent and the number of missionaries sharply curtailed. As economic health revived, appropriate measures were undertaken. Church Erection set about refinancing its loans, reducing interest rates from five to four percent, and offering a five-year moratorium on interest payments if substantial payments were made on the principal of the loan.

Amid the painful and exasperating frustrations of these years, a new and thoughtful reflection was given to the mission of the church and published in study books, such as *Missions at Home and Abroad* in 1936, which was cordially received and widely used. In America there were teeming millions, among them many torn between the appeals of American culture and the desire to cling to cherished old world ideals, language, and religion. In America, too, there were problems, racial and urban, which the church was summoned to face both singly and in cooperation with other denominations.

By 1937 sixty-three churches had refinanced their obligations with Church Erection and another seventy-five had accepted the moratorium offered. Four years later Home Missions reported it was supporting 120 missionaries.[10] Facing the future, Home Missions proposed the establishment of fifty new missions in the next decade.

It would make appropriations, but only if together with local and conference funding there were sufficient money to assure an adequate salary for full-time leadership. Church Erection would give its aid only after approving the building site, the building plans, and the financing program, and upon the recommendation of the Annual Conference.

Within the United Brethren Church whose beginning and strength had been predominantly in rural areas, there was a strong, sentimental affection for rural mission. In 1937 a Rural Life Commission as created, and by 1941 sixteen Annual Conferences had set up similar commissions.[11] Dr. B. H. Cain's *The Church Ministering to Rural Life* generated enthusiasm, and the commission provided modest subsidies for pastors to attend rural life conferences and convocations. In 1941 it was proposed that the commission be awarded departmental status with a full-time director. The proposal was met by those who contended that urban centers were of first importance in an urban America and by those convinced that the budget could not afford a full-time director. General Conference postponed the decision to some future day.

Through this quarter century an increasing interest and support was attracted to two Home Mission enterprises among America's underprivileged people. Advocated first by the Women's Missionary Association in 1932, a mission was established at Barnett's Creek in south-central Kentucky. There in 1937 and 1941 respectively, a church and a community center were erected. With the construction of the Manntown and Normal chapels the operations expanded. In addition to evangelistic work, the mission developed handcraft projects and initiated family health and welfare programs with prenatal and postnatal clinics and elementary instruction in practical nursing.

But eclipsing the mountain mission in the hearts of most United Brethren was the one among Spanish-Americans in New Mexico, which in 1932 celebrated its twenty-fifth anniversary and was served by twenty missionary teachers and preachers. Its operations clustered around four centers: Santa Cruz, where there was a primary school and the Edith McCurdy High School; Alcalde and Velarde, where there were two lower-grade schools; and Vallecitos, where there was an elementary school. Evangelistic work was done in all four communities. By 1941 when there were 375 pupils in the schools, hopes were expressed that medical services would soon be initiated. A clinic was opened at Santa Cruz in 1945, but more exciting was the announcement that Frank Willard had donated twelve acres at Espanola and that Arthur N. Pack had offered to build and equip a hospital there. As architects drafted plans for a twenty-eight bed hospital, the recruitment of doctors and nurses began.

In 1943 another mission among Spanish-speaking Americans was launched as the Rev. Plutarcho Roa began his ministry in Ybor City on the fringe of Tampa, Florida. It met with an encouraging response, and in 1946 a congregation with thirty-three charter members was organized. Educational programs at kindergarten and primary school levels supplemented the conventional evangelistic efforts.

The Foreign Missionary Society

The Foreign Missionary Society supervised operations in Sierra Leone, China, Japan, the Philippines, Puerto Rico, Santo Domingo, and the West Indies. Serving these in 1929 were fifty-five American missionaries and 252 native workers in the 125 organized churches with their 10,824 communicant members. There were eighty-nine day and boarding schools with 3,888 pupils and eleven hospitals, dispensaries, and clinics.[12]

The United Brethren had previously shown their willingness to cooperate with others, and this was expanded with the growing ecumenical spirit in all of Christendom. By 1920 operations in the West Indies were cooperative. By 1928 the mission in China was affiliated with the United Church of Christ in China, and the same year the mission in the Philippines joined the United Evangelical Church in the Philippines.

The leadership of the church was alive and sensitive to the new moods and movements in the worldwide Christian enterprise. The whole church was called to restudy the character and scope of Christian mission in light of the proclamations of the Jerusalem Missionary Conference in 1928. The Laymen's Report in 1930 was received with far less cordiality. Many were dismayed, some were incensed at its sharp criticism of missionary evangelism and retorted with a sentence from the Jerusalem Conference: "Our concern is not to preach a religion, but to take a Person" to the non-Christian world.[13] The sterilizing influence of the negative criticisms was immeasurably compounded during the next years by the conflicts first between belligerent social ideologies and then by martial conflict around the world.

Sierra Leone

The West African Conference in Sierra Leone in 1929 was served by twenty-five American missionaries and one hundred Sierra Leonians who ministered in the churches to 1,823 members as well as in 1,563 preaching places. There were also five hospitals and dispensaries, and day and boarding schools with 2,146 students. An evangelistic missionary, a teacher, and a physician were sought for this thriving enterprise, and the prospect of new work in the upper Mendi country was presented as an exciting challenge.[14]

After a quadrennium the achievements among the Mendi were hailed with joy, but the depleted missionary treasury disallowed the fulfillment of pressing needs: a medical missionary, an agricultural missionary, and dollars for the Harford School for Girls where applicants exceeded the facilities of the school.[15]

When the missionary treasury began to warrant better things for Sierra Leone, World War II broke out, and transportation between New York and Freetown became difficult and precarious. In 1941 six missionaries were aboard the S.S. El Nil when it was torpedoed off Brazil, but fortunately they survived. During the war not only miles but a lack of communications separated the mission from the church; however, competent African leadership assisted the resident missionaries in those crucial years. When hostilities ceased, the number of missionaries was materially reduced, but the mission was energetically alert to the needs for an enlarged ministry in medicine, education, and evangelism.[16]

China

By 1929 Christian missions in China were encountering bitter anti-foreign and anti-Christian hostility. While affiliated with the United Church of Christ in China, the United Brethren operations numbered ten American missionaries, twenty-five Chinese workers, and 808 communicant members. There were eleven day and boarding schools with 651 scholars and four hospitals and dispensaries.[17] But all this lay under the ominous clouds of civil war and a belligerent communism. Nevertheless, a Five Year Movement was launched to strengthen the Christian enterprise, and a building was erected for the Union Normal School in Canton. When Japan began her invasion of China and Japanese soldiers descended upon Canton, the Normal School was transferred to Macao. Despite the military occupancy, most of the missionary personnel stayed on in Canton and reported their work was unexpectedly free from Japanese interference. However, following the disaster at Pearl Harbor and America's entrance into the war, circumstances changed radically. Three missionaries managed to escape to western Kwantung province, and two made their way to Hong Kong where they were interned until August 1942. The success of Mao's armies in continental China separated the United Brethren Church from whatever was left of more than fifty years of heroic missionary endeavor in China.

Japan

The mission in Japan continued to prosper after 1921, and in 1929 the Japan Conference reported a staff of four American missionaries assisted by thirty-five Japanese and ministering to 1,855 church members. Under its supervision also, were eight day and boarding schools where 359 pupils were enrolled. In the following years of more importance than the erection of chapels were the evangelistic achievements in the Chiba district. There and elsewhere Toyohiko Kagawa's Kingdom of God movement heartened and strengthened the whole Christian enterprise. Then as narrow, nationalistic patriotism engulfed the nation, Christian work became more difficult, but even so the conference anticipated further endeavors in Chiba and Ichikawa.

The American missionaries were aghast at the disrespect and dishonor paid Japan by America in the passage of the Japanese Exclusion Act in 1924, and they boldly expressed their sentiments. Today it is conceded that the Exclusion Act furthered the flames of violent military patriotism in Japan which were to engulf the nation and bring disaster and death to millions.

In April 1940 the swirling tides of this virulent nationalism swept the Religious Control Bill through the Japanese Diet and into law, a measure which among other things aimed at the careful scrutiny and control of missionary programs. The bill did not compel it, but the Christian response was the formation of the Church of Christ in Japan. The United Brethren participated in its organization. Before diplomatic relations between Japan and the United States were severed, the American missionaries in the conference had departed in order to ease the life of Japanese Christians who lived under the hostile eyes of an unfriendly Japanese military regime that was suspicious of Japanese who had American ties.[18]

Philippines

Though the Philippine mission was the youngest in the church, it had prospered so that in 1929 there were eleven American missionaries with seventy Filipinoes serving 4,856 church members. Two hospitals and dispensaries and twenty-seven day and boarding schools with 706 scholars were important elements of this enterprise. Under the United Evangelical Church, which the United Brethren joined in this work in the Philippines in 1928, they were given responsibility for evangelization in LaUnion and Mountain provinces, for the reopening of the Bible Training School, and for increased support for the hospital and for Union Theological Seminary in Manila. The result of tireless efforts is apparent in the accessions to the church which in 1937 exceeded those in any other overseas mission. When the Japanese armies swept across the islands, four United Brethren missionaries were subjected to the rigors of internment, and mission properties were vandalized or destroyed. When later under General Douglas MacArthur the Japanese were expelled, the United Brethren Church contributed generously for relief programs and for the rehabilitation of local churches, the printing plant in San Fernando, and Union Seminary in Manila.[19]

Puerto Rico and Santo Domingo

The United Brethren mission in Puerto Rico was small but virile. Its 1,482 communicant members in 1928 were served by five American missionaries and twenty-two native workers. A day school was in operation.[20] In 1933 this mission affiliated with the federation called the United Evangelical Church of Puerto Rico. United Brethren gave $14,400 toward the relocation of Union Theological Seminary at Rio Padres. Convinced of the necessity of meeting rural needs, the church established a rural center in 1945. In nearby Santo Domingo, United Brethren participated in an interchurch program which in 1929 set out to construct a hospital. While the ecumenical operation was inconspicuous in dimensions, its efforts and influence were fruitful and significant.

The years from 1921 to 1946 were trying ones for overseas missions, the missionaries, and the missionary administration. In the 1930's economic necessity required successive decisions to reduce missionary personnel, programs, and salaries. To further aggravate the situation there were the challenges from rising nationalism and communism, and then the dislocation and destruction attendant upon World War II. Nonetheless, through these years courageous Christian faith and hope persisted within dire limitations. Unquestionably the harsh facts of life influenced, but do not wholly account for, the emerging Christian consciousness of the oneness of the church and the Christian mission to the world, which led United Brethren into ecumenical enterprises in China, Japan, the Philippines, the Dominican Republic and Puerto Rico.

Women's Missionary Association

The constitutional structure of the Women's Missionary Association on the denominational, conference, and local levels was clearly drawn. With the emergence of new needs and new interests there were amendments. In 1929 a Department of Stewardship, with a secretary and in 1941 a director for children's work, was provided. Its educational program early was aligned with the Sunday schools and the Endeavor Societies, but later more closely related to the Board of Christian Education. The Women's Missionary Association became a constituent part of the Inter-Board Committee, created in 1945, along with the two missionary boards and the Board of Christian Education.

After 1930, like every denominational agency, the association suffered diminishing revenues and faced the stern necessity of retrenchments, but by 1940 both recovery and even advance were evident. In 1929 there were 1,837 local societies; in 1945, 1,424; and between these years the total membership decreased from 61,688 to 51,000.[21] Meanwhile the association's support of the Foreign and Home Missionary Societies increased from $584,784 to $987,184! Its services for the missionary cause were many and incalculable and obviously not the least of them was its financial support.

CHRISTIAN EDUCATION

Even in 1921 there were some advocating the consolidation of . the separate departments of Sunday schools, Christian Endeavor Societies, and Brotherhoods into a single unit, but they were a minority. They persisted, and in 1929 the consolidation was effected in the creation of a Board of Christian Education which also was awarded supervision of missionary education, evangelism, weekday and vacation schools, and the denominational colleges.[22] This was achieved but not without objectors. Some held this could work only to the disadvantage of Christian Endeavor; others held the proposal to create the new board was an unconsidered and impetuous one while others asserted it was in violation of disciplinary procedure. Objectors notwithstanding, the Board of Christian Education was established. To assist it, in each Annual Conference there was to be a similar board with a director and under it directors for adult, young people's, and children's work, and in the local church a Board of Christian Education which appointed directors for the three age-level groups. The unification of the denomination's educational program was an important one, following eight years of agitation. It came at a time when the number of Sunday schools and Endeavor Societies and their membership rolls were significantly declining.

Under the leadership of its general secretary, Dr. O. T. Deever, the Board of Christian Education set about its tasks. Standards were developed for all age-level groups so that an organization could appraise its work and take steps toward improvement. General conventions were promoted and also summer conferences, the latter chiefly for conference directors. In 1931 a United Advance was launched with specific goals: 500,000 in the Sunday schools, 60,000 "won to Christ," 100,000 in the Endeavor Societies, 30,000 in vacation schools, 20,000 in the Brotherhoods, and a leadership training school on every charge.[23] In July 1939 a National Youth Congress and Adult Convention met at Lakeside, Ohio, attracting 526 people. For use in the local church, Dr. J. G. Howard's *Catechism* for intermediates and his *Worship Pathways* were published.

After four years the advance was announced to be really just beginning. The fact is that while goals for vacation schools had been exceeded, less success had been achieved in other areas. Summer conventions and conferences attracted throngs, but Sunday schools and Endeavor Societies continued to diminish in enrollment and attendance, though the rate of decline had decreased. In these circumstances, Christian education leaders frequently expressed concern for evangelism.

Experience vindicated the decision made in 1929 to unify the several phases of the denominational educational program under a single board. Much energy was spent in establishing and amending procedures and developing new ones, always justified by the commendable quest for greater effectiveness. However, the basic insight that Christian education is the work of the whole church in and through all its auxiliaries and the endeavor to involve every churchman in this mission have been unreservedly approved.

BOARD OF EDUCATION: COLLEGES AND SEMINARY

The Board of Education was discontinued in 1929 when its responsibilities were given the Board of Christian Education. Also transferred to the new board were its funds: a Beneficiary Fund of $37,000 for the assistance of ministers in training, a Collegiate Scholarship fund of $14,000 for the aid of pre-ministerial students attending college, and a Permanent Fund of $38,350. In its final report the Board of Education noted with concern that the schools were receiving a diminishing percentage of the benevolence budget.

The Board of Christian Education assumed its responsibility to the schools seriously, in 1933 declaring they were doomed unless they received larger support from the church. Special offerings were introduced: one on Cash Day that went directly to the seminary and one on Education Day for the colleges with the sum credited to the local benevolence apportionment. Legislation in 1933 decreed that no school should be established, discontinued, relocated, or consolidated without the recommendation of the Board of Christian Education and the approval of General Conference.[24]

The Colleges

Several United Brethren schools were in a precarious plight in 1921. Philomath, in Philomath, Oregon, lacked in both students and funds. Unable to meet state requirements, Philomath closed its doors in 1929, the income from any remaining funds designated to assist any student in the northwest area desiring to attend a United Brethren college in the East. The trustees of Leander Clark College,

Toledo, Iowa, closed the school and transferred its resources to Coe College in Cedar Rapids. This action prompted repercussions for a decade. Attorneys for the Board of Christian Education endeavored to halt the transfer, but in two court cases their claims were denied. Kansas City University, where United Brethren had joined Methodist Protestants, was also mired in financial straits, but the situation became acute about 1929 when it lost accreditation and was given two years to meet state standards. All efforts to resolve the crisis proved futile. The school was closed, and United Brethren interests were transferred to York College.

By 1930 York College, York, Nebraska, was the sole United Brethren college west of the Mississippi River, and, amid difficulties, it was continuing with great determination. Its life during the Depression was fraught with great hardships, but supported by a devoted faculty, a courageous administration, and loyal donors, it survived and by 1937 boasted a balanced budget. Gratified by a $50,000 bequest and an enrollment of four hundred students in 1937, the school launched a financial campaign; this was vitiated, however, by the successive droughts which prostrated western agriculture. By 1945 sufficient funds had been accumulated to discharge the debts, and another $184,608 was in hand for endowment and an anticipated building program.

Indiana Central College in Indianapolis carried a heavy debt, but supporting it were people of indomitable spirit who deeply believed in the future of the school. A financial drive in supporting conferences met with gratifying results, and the college received its accreditation in 1941. In this episcopal district a campaign for $500,000 was undertaken, half for the college and half for the Ministerial Pension Fund. While the new president in 1945 enumerated the needs of Indiana Central College, there was understandable joy at his report that the mortgage debt of the college had been liquidated.

In 1930 the straitened circumstances of Shenandoah College and Conservatory of Music, Dayton, Virginia, began to intensify. In 1933 faculty salaries were slashed by fifty percent, and the indebtedness was $107,418. With the counsel of the Board of Christian Education, the conservatory of music was segregated from the college in 1937 and four years later won accreditation from the National Association of Schools of Music. Meanwhile the college managed to survive with a limited enrollment and much more limited resources.

Lebanon Valley College, Annville, Pennsylvania, and Otterbein College, Westerville, Ohio, were not without their anxieties, but being older and better endowed, and being situated where. the denomination was numerically stronger, they were not as acutely jeopardized during the Depression. Lebanon Valley in 1937 enrolled 393 students and reported a wholesome campus life. World War II sharply reduced the enrollment, and by 1944 it stood at 213, but anticipating a brighter future, it set out to raise $550,000 to liquidate debts, to erect a physical education building, and to augment the endowment fund.

Otterbein College survived the years of financial stringency somewhat diminished but vigorous and in 1937 set out on a four-fold program of advance, seeking an improved educational program, a stronger spiritual life, $200,000 to reimburse depleted funds, and improved public relations with the denomination. Progress was made in all four areas, and enrollment increased from 388 to 523. Inspired by a new president and the prospect of a centennial celebration in 1947, the college set out to raise $622,000. Within a year $438,666 was gathered, and the college dedicated itself "to develop a type of education which shall send out . . . young men and women whose attitude toward their fellow men shall be similar to the attitude of Christ toward human life."[25]

Bonebrake Theological Seminary

In 1923 Bonebrake Theological Seminary was moved from its original site to the beautiful campus in the Dayton view section of Dayton. The relocation had been considerately planned, and three buildings were built, but by 1925 the school was harrassed with a debt of $675,000. The plan to sell some of its Kansas land was scuttled as purchasers were unable to meet their purchase payments. To aid the school, congregations were asked to receive a Cash Day offering. The proposal in 1929 to sell part of the new campus was rejected lest it throttle the future life of the school. The recommendation to allot the seminary an extra $10,000 annually from the benevolence budget or to launch a churchwide financial campaign incurred opposition from other auxiliaries of the church who asserted their claims for funds. An abortive campaign, seeking

$100,000 for Bonebrake was launched in 1932, but with the Depression at its depth, little was achieved. Help for the desperate school came in 1933 when General Conference provided that $50,000 be given annually from the benevolence budget for debt liquidation. This continued yearly until 1945 when the last of the obligations was paid.

During these years filled with financial anxieties, the seminary was fulfilling its mission in preparing men for the ministry. In 1929 the curriculum was expanded and strengthened by additional courses in Bible, sociology, and psychology for students in both the degree and nondegree departments. The office of dean was established, and four years later a higher grade level was required for graduation. Measures such as these were the precedents for Bonebrake's reception into the membership of the American Association of Theological Schools in 1938.

As in American culture a college education came to be accepted as normal preparation for a profession, applicants for the Diploma Department declined in numbers until in 1942 it was eliminated. Between 1937 and 1941 enrollment increased from eighty-four to ninety-three. Various new measures were introduced to strengthen the program: day-long retreats were introduced to nurture the spiritual life of seminarians, a clinical program was established, limited scholarship aid was made available to deserving seminarians, and a sabbatical program for professors was initiated. In 1945 Bonebrake enrolled 155 students, its largest enrollment up to that time.

The seminary sought permission to launch a drive for $575,000 in 1945, but this was denied because of a previous understanding that the missionary cause would be the beneficiary of the next denominational campaign and also because of the impending union with the Evangelical Church.

THE PRINTING ESTABLISHMENT

Within a few months after the dedication of the United Brethren Building in 1924 in Dayton, the financial plight of the printing establishment became apparent. Much space in the new building was without tenants, and with the bankruptcy of the Louis Traxler Company there was much more. The total indebtedness was $1,399,589 and by 1929, $1,616,173.[26] At that juncture two separate corporations were created, one for printing operations and one for management of the real estate.

After 1930 the American economy sank to unprecedented depths. Between 1929 and 1933 revenues from printing operations dropped from $891,187 to $513,371, but the real estate corporation lay in grim desperation. In 1931 the major creditors demanded the appointment of Dr. J. Balmer Showers to the management of real estate affairs, promising him limited financial assistance. When he accepted the appointment, the debt stood at $1,988,228. Understandably he described his assignment as "the most perplexing, the most critical problem, the most thankless job in the denomination,"[27] but prompted by a deep sense of duty he accepted a task he neither relished nor coveted. Firmly rejecting the suggestions that the problem be solved legally through bankruptcy proceedings, he embarked upon a refinancing program which won the approval of all but a few obdurate note and bond holders. In 1934 Congress set up the National Administration Program which, under Section 77B, permitted reorganization of a troubled enterprise under the supervision of federal courts. Showers steered the refinancing plan through the required procedures, and in 1935 the court approved the plan of reorganization. By 1937 the debt was reduced to $1,117,500 and by 1941 to $700,000.[28]

The printing establishment became debt free in 1941, and in 1945 came the good news that all quarters in the United Brethren Building were rented and a debt of only $100,000 remained to be paid. It is understandable that at this report General Conference stood and sang the doxology, and that on a later day of the session Dr. J. Balmer Showers was elected to the episcopacy. The whole harrowing story beginning in 1921 is a compelling account of Christian integrity, not simply of one man or one board, but of an entire denomination. For many in the church there was a deep affection for the site and structure which symbolized so much of United Brethren sacrifice and service.

Between 1921 and 1946 numerous publications were issued by the Otterbein Press. The major periodicals in 1921 were The Religious Telescope, edited by J. M. Phillippi, and The Young People's Watchword, whose editor was H. F. Shupe. W. C. Fries edited the Sunday school literature. During this quarter century a number of denominational books were published, two of which merit mention. In 1924 A. W. Drury's History of the Church of the

United Brethren in Christ appeared and acquired status as the denominational history. In 1935 The Church Hymnal was published and accorded a hearty reception throughout the church.

Broadening Social Concerns

While the strength of the social gospel movement of the previous decades persisted, in 1921 United Brethren unflaggingly upheld by reaffirmation the norms of the nineteenth century for the Christian life. They heartily joined the body of Protestantism in the crusade which legislated the eighteenth amendment to the U.S. Constitution in 1919. When the widespread defiance of the law and the racketeering associated with it led to its repeal in 1933, this church was dismayed, but not defeated, and total abstinence continued to be required of church members.

This relentless struggle against the liquor traffic consumed much, but by no means all, the energies against social evils. Having experienced one war in this generation, United Brethren with prayers and resolutions supported successive efforts for international peace and justice—the League of Nations, the Locarno Conference and Kellogg peace formulas, and the Geneva Conference of 1932. However, the projections for a warless world withered as Nazi ambition and arrogance emerged, and with the German invasion of Poland, World War II enflamed the world. Before America became a belligerent, sentiment among United Brethren was rather evenly divided between those favoring and those opposing American protection on the open seas and the deployment of armed forces abroad. It was officially declared: "We as a church will not urge our men to arms nor will we urge them to take the position of the conscientious objector. We will include in our fellowship and respect each and all who are true to their convictions."[29] Only a few months after this declaration was issued the Japanese attacked Pearl Harbor, America declared war, and for four years national resources were concentrated upon the defeat of the enemy in Asia and in Europe. During those years the church ministered to its youth in all the national services through denominational and interdenominational channels.

The social and economic catastrophes in this country after 1930 prompted a deeper concern for the resolution of social issues than for Sabbath observance and temperance. In 1933, a focal year of concern for social issues, a new social creed was issued which, while very similar to the one of 1909, contained some significant singularities. The social gospel of the 1930's was freed from some assumptions of the earlier liberal theology and was clearly more evangelically oriented.

In the General Conference of 1933 pastors were exhorted to counsel with candidates for matrimony on "eugenic mating, home ideals, sex regulations, rearing of children and personal adjustments."[30] Later, churches were called upon to exercise their responsibilities toward the achievement of wholesome recreations and improved community and race relations.

To further this social witness, new structures and agencies were required. The efforts of the Commission on Social Advance until 1929 tended to be narrowly individualistic with a strong emphasis upon evangelism as the anodyne for social, economic, and international strife. In 1933 this commission was abandoned and a Social Service Commission created to study social life and lead the church forward in the advancement of social justice. From developments within the Social Service Commission a Rural Life Commission was created, which in 1941 became the Town and Country Commission. The Board of Christian Social Action superseded the Social Service Commission in 1945 and through many channels promoted economic equity, civic righteousness, racial brotherhood, and a just world order.[31]

In the recording of proclamations, exhortations, and actions, it is not presumed that the whole church concurred with all, or even with any. However, it may be concluded that for the great and silent majority the religious life was sensed not to consist of a single religious experience or weekly experiences in the sanctuary, but to be composed of a Christ-led attitude and relation in all of life.

HOMES

The solicitude to serve those in need expressed itself in benevolent institutions for children and the aged. The Baker Memorial Home remained small because residence was restricted to retired clergy. At the Quincy Home and Orphanage the staff was increased to permit offering vocational training for boys in baking, woodworking, printing, and farming and for girls in home economics—all of which won high commendation. In 1941 almost every organization which functions in a parish church was operative at Quincy for the participation and benefit of the 148 children and youth and the 52 elderly there.

In 1929 there were 121 children and 52 older people in the Otterbein Home and Orphanage. The ample acres supplied the table needs at Otterbein, with large quantities left over that could be marketed, but there was a heavy debt. A projected campaign to reduce the debt was sabotaged by the Depression. Through sales, by 1937 the farm land had been reduced to 1,600 acres and the debt to $238,167 but there remained many acres, a heavy debt, and an unfinished administration building on which construction had begun in 1926. However, with generous gifts, the sale of more acres, and with increased denominational support, by 1945 Otterbein Home was rendering Christian care to 411 children and 163 older people.

A movement was afoot in Kansas to establish a benevolent home there, and in 1945 General Conference gave its approval contingent upon the favorable vote of the Annual Conference participating in the venture.

MINISTERIAL PENSIONS

The ministerial Pension and Annuity Plan was adopted in 1921 with enthusiasm, and plans were laid to secure funds. These plans were successively thwarted in one quadrennium by the claims of the colleges and the seminary and in another in deference to the crucial needs of the seminary, the schools, and Otterbein Home. Plans to launch a financial campaign on July 1, 1930, were announced, but abruptly the campaign was canceled. The Depression, the plight of the printing establishment, the needs of the missionary societies, coupled with the crop failures in the Midwest were among the grounds cited to justify the wisdom of this action. Disenchanted, the field director of the pension plan resigned.

In 1933 when the economy was about the bleakest, the fortunes of the plan were about to change. After the bishops movingly bewailed the prostration of the Pension and Annuity Plan, a layman, H. H. Baish, who was the head of the Pennsylvania Teachers' Retirement Fund volunteered to serve as its manager without remuneration. The offer was accepted. None denied the grim fact "that we are paying our old, retired superannuated and disabled ministers $5 a month after they have rendered a lifetime of service to our denomination."[32] Amid the clamors from every church agency for more funds, the General Conference awarded it $35,000 annually from the benevolence budget. Under the leadership of its able manager, in 1937 approval was given for a churchwide campaign for funds and for the restructuring of the plan. After January 1, 1941, all ordained clergy were required to join the plan. Memberships were of two kinds, contributory, requiring annual premium payments and noncontributory; benefits were proportionately different.

The Ministerial Pension Plan campaign netted $299,310 by 1941 which enabled the plan to pay its contributory beneficiary who had thirty years of service to his credit $500 annually and a noncontributory beneficiary $400. The campaign continued until 1944 when the total collected was $1,394,227.

EVANGELISM

Before 1921 there were those advocating a specific agency for evangelism, but in that year a Department of Evangelism was created. During the preceding quadrennium evangelism had been one of the phases of the United Enlistment Movement and promoted by that churchwide crusade.

The new Department of Evangelism reminded the church that it had been born in a revival and that the successors of the founding fathers had continued evangelistic efforts in revivals and personal work. "The church should never have an empty penitential bench or pew."[33] The Department of Evangelism, with C. W. Brewbaker its secretary, was placed under supervision of the Board of Administration. Annual Conferences and local churches had their evangelism boards and committees.

The department, later the Bureau of Evangelism, and its secretary worked zealously. Through the Commission of Evangelism of the Federal Council of Churches, United Brethren joined other denominations in 1930 in the celebration of the nineteen-hundredth anniversary of the first Pentecost. The bureau gathered conference evangelists into an association and energetically promoted evangelism in Annual Conferences and local churches, but the results invariably were less than anticipated. The Depression induced no surging back-to-God movement. The final report of the bureau urged that more attention be paid to instructing candidates for church membership, to "social evangelism" (that is, the claims of Christian social justice), and to the winning of children and youth for Christ. In

1933, among the retrenchments necessitated by hard times, this bureau was a casualty, and evangelism was made the responsibility of the Board of Bishops, who initiated a practice of announcing evangelistic themes for the Easter-to-Pentecost season for each year of the quadrennium.

From 1933 to 1946 the bishops spoke for evangelism, but not alone, for in 1937 even the Committee on Program and Budget spoke its exhortations. The United Brethren participated in the preaching mission promoted by an agency of the Federal Council of Churches. The bishops in 1941 urged support for a program "scriptural in its basis . . . spiritual in its aim . . . born of the Holy Spirit . . . through prayer . . . personal in method . . . social in expression."[34] Four years later, at the same time the Board of Administration was directed "to prepare and promote an aggressive denominational program of evangelism in cooperation with the Board of Bishops,"[35] a Commission on Evangelism was created. During the preceding decade there had been many evangelistic experiments and many more exhortations to evangelistic activity. In some Annual Conferences clinics on evangelism were held. Throughout the church it was suggested that pastors conduct classes on evangelism during November and December, revival services in January and February, visitation evangelism during Lent, and church membership classes after Easter.

In all these proclamations and exhortations it is clear that evangelism was a sacrosanct word and cause which none challenged or denied. Equally clear is the continuing affection for the older measures of revivalism, even though in practice they were being abandoned. That generation confronted the same question faced by every generation: how shall men be led to Christian discipleship?

THE HISTORICAL SOCIETY

The Historical Society attracted slight interest and only intermittently gave evidence of vitality. Many said that Dr. A. W. Drury, professor at Bonebrake Theological Seminary, *was* the Historical Society. It was true that in 1933 the society and its collection was moved from quarters at the Otterbein Press to "Dr. Drury's recitation room in the seminary."[36] In 1937 its constitution was radically simplified in keeping with its operations, and the trustees of the seminary were made the trustees of the society. A new epoch opened for it when the seminary provided modest funds for its operation.

BOARD OF ADMINISTRATION

The Board of Administration, created in 1917, was the overall supervisory agency of the church in the interim between General Conferences, charged with numerous assignments ranging from coordinating the operations of the denomination to recommending changes in the *Discipline*.[37] The promotion of stewardship was added to the board's responsibilities. After 1930 there was an acute need for dollars and a quickened conscience on stewardship, brought about by urgent exigencies confronting a number of church agencies. To meet the somber situation, the board was increased in numbers to make it more representative of the whole church, and its powers were expanded so much that in a sense it was a new board. The production and distribution of stewardship literature and the promotion of stewardship programs intensified. Local churches were encouraged to pay apportionments in twelve regular monthly payments, and those who paid three or more percent above their apportionments were awarded distinction as Second Mile Churches. These and many more measures, coupled with the national economic recovery, produced obvious fruitage through the 1940's. Personal commitments to tithing increased thirty-eight percent between 1941 and 1945 and per capita giving increased from $12.24 in 1940 to $17.95 in 1944. Endeavoring to establish equity in the apportionments made to local churches, the board in 1945 named six determining factors: church membership, average Sunday school attendance, pastor's salary, total church expenses, payments to the benevolence budget, and the total benevolence support.[38]

Among the accomplishments of the Board of Administration over this quarter century, two are outstanding. Through its careful guidance, the church was led through the painful financial crisis of the 1930's and a deeper sense of Christian stewardship was nurtured. Perhaps of even greater importance was its role in bringing together the various agencies and thereupon effecting a comprehensive, unified denominational program.

UNITY AND CHURCH UNION

The United Brethren Church was a participant in the major interchurch agencies and movements—regional, national, and international—after 1921. It was a charter member of the International Council of Religious Education in 1922. It named two delegates for the Faith and Order Conference at Lausanne in 1927, and two attended the Oxford Conference on Life and Work at Oxford in 1937. In 1941 it signified its intention to join the World Council of Churches.

Church union activities were animated by leaders of the Reformed Church in the United States, more popularly known as the German Reformed Church, who envisioned a united church comprised of their own, the United Brethren Church, the Evangelical Synod of North America, and the Evangelical Church. The latter declined, explaining that continuing litigation with the dissenters to their union in 1922 made it unwise to initiate negotiations for another union. The three remaining communions had much in common. All were of German background, and while there were different manners and practices in each, there was a common pietistic tradition. They were of comparable numerical dimension so that the charge could not be raised that any one was absorbing any other, and there was a ready acknowledgment that with a united church a more effective Christian witness could be made. In the spring of 1928 a tentative draft of a Plan of Union was issued. Commissioners of the three denominations approved a plan, February 7, 1929, even though mindful of the difficulties still to be resolved. This plan proposed the creation of the United Church of America. Doctrinally, it presented a statement of faith which drew from the confessional statements of the three participating churches and from their common inheritance, the Heidelberg Confession. The polity proposed for the United Church provided at the apex a General Council composed of clergy and laity as the ultimate authority and, subordinate to it, annual and district conferences. Local congregations would continue their life without major alterations; ministers would be appointed by a stationing committee from nominees recommended by local churches.

United Brethren commissioners frankly admitted they entered the negotiations with a certain degree of hesitancy, but this was dispelled by the cordial spirit of those from the other denominations. Believing the effort was a result of a "distinct leading of the Holy Spirit," they announced to General Conference in 1929 their unanimous support of the plan and recommended the appointment of a committee of twenty to further study it and report in 1933. The suggestion received a unanimous and resounding approval. During 1930 circumstances changed quickly and drastically. While the Evangelical Synod endorsed the plan, balloting in the Reformed Church disclosed a large minority were either skeptical or openly opposed to it. At this, the United Brethren bishops did not present the plan for consideration of the Annual Conferences. They sought a meeting with the commissioners of the Reformed Church in February 1931, but the latter had arrived at the decision that it would be inexpedient to continue the negotiations. The meeting was not held, nor were the United Brethren involved in any thereafter.

Many people have alleged reasons for the collapse of this unitive venture.[39] For some it lay in the inability to reconcile theological issues. For some it lay in the inability to accommodate a church polity acceptable to everyone. For some it lay in the inability to arrive at satisfactory standards for church membership and the Christian life. Perhaps the most discerning and generous judgment is that the endeavor to unite distinctive traditions—Lutheran, Methodist, and Calvinist—was too idealistic and ambitious for that day. While this tripartite effort failed, subsequently the Reformed Church and the Evangelical Synod did merge to become the Evangelical and Reformed Church.

However, many hurdles inherent in the tripartite negotiations did not harrass the conversations between United Brethren and Evangelicals. Fraternal delegates had been exchanged between the two on frequent occasions. In 1911 when the commissioners of both Evangelical churches held their first meeting, United Brethren ambassadors came inquiring about the feasibility of their participation in the formation of a united church, but after consideration, Evangelicals responded negatively on the grounds that a third party would unduly compound their grievous difficulties.

Two years after the reunion of Evangelicals in 1922, at a meeting of the Federal Council of Churches, several Evangelicals and United Brethren met informally. In 1926, in response to United Brethren overtures, Evangelicals replied that certain affairs growing out of their union were still to be resolved in the courts but upon their settlement, negotiations would be welcomed. The fraternal delegate to the United Brethren in 1929, after citing the similarity in message and ministry of the two churches, went no further than to say: "With such an heritage these two churches should be able to render a great service in this time of great need and find it not difficult to unify their forces for an aggressive moral advance."[40] But at this time, the United Brethren were on the threshold of their tripartite negotiations.

In 1933, after the hopes for the trilateral union had evaporated, Bishop Matthew T. Maze, appearing before the United Brethren General Conference, declared the Evangelical Church "ready to enter into negotiations with the Church of the United Brethren in Christ for the fullest possible spiritual and organic union."[41] This notice was acted upon with alacrity, unanimity, and enthusiasm, and commissioners were appointed.

United Brethren and Evangelical commissioners met February 16, 1932, to undertake their arduous tasks. Both denominations had a common background and inheritance and many similarities, but in the course of a century each had developed singularities in church life and programs. For a decade commissioners grappled with issues, among them the matter of ministerial orders. Beyond these were engrossing problems related to institutions and the financial obligations of some church agencies. Subcommittees were named to consider: Confession of Faith, classification of ministers, conference organization, ministerial pensions, publishing interests, and educational institutions. By 1937 while negotiations were proceeding satisfactorily, "the greatest difficulty" appeared to be in drafting an equitable pension program for the united church. "Obstacles of a business nature," the bishops said, "have made it advisable to go slowly."[42] Nevertheless, approval was given to what had been accomplished, and encouragement was given to draft a Basis of Union.

The next four years were busy and decisive ones for the commissioners. In addition to the plenary meetings, the central committee met fifteen times, and the subcommittees met innumerable times. During these years the Evangelical Congregational Church and the Church of the United Brethren in Christ (Old Constitution) were invited to join this endeavor for church union. The former responded that among them there was "no crystallized sentiment" favoring their participation; the latter made no response.

By 1941 the United Brethren bishops enthusiastically said of the negotiating churches, "They belong together, and thank God, they are now not very far apart."[43] Bishop G. D. Batdorf described the proposed structure for the united church: a single ministerial order, the unification of home and foreign mission in one board, and a ministerial pension program. There remained but one hurdle—to find an agreeable plan for the publishing interests. When that was drafted, the Basis of Union would be ready for presentation.[44] Without a dissenting vote the General Conference approved the report of the commissioners.

The entire commission met for its final session February 24, 1942, to put the finishing touches on the Basis of Union. There, first in separate denominational groups and then together, the Basis of Union was approved and recommended to the two churches for approval. In achieving this basis for the new denomination, to be called the Evangelical United Brethren Church, each church made concessions, surrendering some manners and customs. Evangelicals abandoned the dual ministry of deacons and elders to accept the one ministry of elders, and the United Brethren gave up their two missionary societies—foreign and home—for one supervising both areas.

The Evangelical General Conference of 1942 by an overwhelming vote, 226 to 6, approved the Basis of Union. In 1945, following the report and recommendations of their commissioners, the United Brethren General Conference approved it, 224 to 2. Speaking to this Conference, the Evangelical fraternal delegate, Bishop John S. Stamm, spoke optimistically of the potentialities of the impending union, "There is a law in the universe that through union new qualities and new resources are revealed and released."[45] Following this conference the Basis of Union was submitted to the Annual Conferences. Twenty-eight conferences approved it unanimously, and the aggregate vote in all the conferences was 2,291 for and 134 against. It was then submitted to the vote in local churches where 80,777 members favored the proposed union and 13,032 did not. Upon these reports, a special session of the United Brethren General Conference was summoned to convene in Johnstown, Pennsylvania, in November 1946, in the same city and at the same time where the regular Evangelical General Conference was scheduled. There church union was consummated.

The success of this unitive endeavor has been attributed to the common inheritance and the general similarities of the two denominations. Beyond these, acknowledgment is due the majority in both churches who believed this church union was not only timely, but right, and to the unhurried progress through twelve years which allowed churchmen at every level to learn of the issues at stake and their resolution. "Negotiations were characterized by the desire for fairness to all concerned, a sincere quest for truth in doctrine and the best in church polity, organization and method."[46] In both denominations there was the will to achieve union which was declared to be inspired by the spirit of God and in accordance with his will. Judicious procedures contributed in large measure to the enviable and unprecedented achievement of this union in American Protestantism, for it was accomplished without the separation of any group of dissenters.

he contentiousness in the nation which was reflected in the United Brethren schism was far more virulently displayed in the division of the Evangelical Association. The latter was precipitated in 1887. In 1891 there were two General Conferences, each claiming to be the rightful one. There were no essential differences in doctrines, and there are grounds for believing that the differences in polity which were heralded stemmed from bitter personal antagonisms which were cultivated until the church was split with two-fifths of the constituency aligned with the minority. Without grace and often without truth, vindictive charges were raised by inflamed partisans. Locally, on occasion, rancor was expressed in incidents of manhandling. Some pastors found church doors locked or spiked to prevent their entrance; some were rudely evicted from their parsonages; some churches were despoiled of pews and chancel appointments. In one parish the raiders took everything but the "mourner's bench," which the reporter declared they needed most!

An epidemic of church trials began in Iowa in 1889. A year later in Ohio one bishop was found guilty of charges and suspended. His allies cited his episcopal rival for trial, but the latter's friends "tried" him and found him guiltless. Thereafter he ignored all citations on the grounds that he could not be tried twice for the same charges. Recourse to ecclesiastical courts was followed by appeals to civil courts. There were a few slander suits, but the bulk of litigation

THE EVANGELICAL ASSOCIATION AND THE UNITED EVANGELICAL CHURCH, 1891–1922

centered on the ownership of church properties. An early decision of a lower court in Illinois awarded local property to the majority in the local church, which in this instance was the minority in the denomination. Ultimately, suits were carried to supreme courts in Ohio, Nebraska, Iowa, Michigan, and Pennsylvania, where the denominational trust clause was upheld and properties were awarded the Evangelical Association. Unrecorded thousands of dollars were spent in litigation.

The turbulence in the Evangelical Association evoked concern outside the church. In 1891 Dr. H. K. Carrol, editor of *The New York Independent*, offered to arbitrate between the two belligerent parties. "There was never a division that had so poor an excuse," he wrote, but his peacemaking efforts met with contemptuous rebuff: "Compromise with wrong is wrong. All we ask of other denominations is non-interference. Compromise with sin, with wrong, with anarchy?"[1]

The courts having denied the minority any claims upon the name and the resources of the Evangelical Association, their delegates assembled in General Conference in Naperville, Illinois, November 30, 1894, where they adopted the name The United Evangelical Church and a *Book of Discipline* and elected the Revs. R. Dubs and W. M. Stanford their bishops. While this *Discipline* had much in common with that of the Evangelical Association, there were significant differences: the tenure and authority of bishops were limited, ownership of local properties was vested in the local church, and laymen were given membership in General Conference.

In 1894 in both Evangelical churches the class was the humblest organizational unit and was led by a class leader and served by stewards who received offerings and provided the bread and cup for the Lord's Supper.[2] The core structure of conferences—Quarterly, Annual, and General—was identical in the two churches. Experiences in the division led United Evangelicals immediately to grant laymen a larger role in the councils of the denomination. The initiative of the Layman's Society in the Illinois Conference and emulated in other conferences resulted in the election of the laymen who were members of the first United Evangelical General Conference. The inclusion of the laity was advanced on the grounds that they could contribute sound "business sense" and that their presence would discourage "ecclesiasticism" and "one man rule."[3] The United Evangelical *Discipline* authorized equal clerical and lay representation in General Conference. These were elected in Annual Conferences where in separate elections the clergy and laity selected their delegates. The same *Discipline* allowed the Quarterly Conference of each charge to elect a lay delegate to Annual Conference with full franchise except in matters pertaining to ministerial order. In 1895 Mrs. Hartman from the St. John's parish in Oregon was acclaimed as "the first female member of an annual conference."[4]

More cautiously the Evangelical Association was persuaded to accept lay delegation. In 1895 the proposal to seat laymen in General Conference was defeated, the objectors contending that the inclusion of laymen would unduly complicate the conference's procedures, their presence would be costly and expressive of "class legislation" (since only the wealthy could afford the time necessary to attend sessions), and that the church would reap no conceivable benefit. During eight years people changed their views, and in 1903 by a decisive majority laymen were awarded membership in General Conference, but by an equally decisive majority they were denied membership in the Annual Conference. What was denied in 1903 was approved in 1907, and thereafter each presiding elder district was entitled to four lay delegates in the Annual Conference.

The General Conference in both Evangelical churches was the ultimate authority but within specified limits. It could not alter the Articles of Faith. It could make changes in temporal economy by a three-fourths vote when such changes were either recommended or ratified by a two-thirds aggregate vote of the Annual Conferences.

For the care of local properties both denominations charged trustees for their maintenance. The Association exhorted the local building committee "to be careful that the structure be plain and cheap, nevertheless decent, durable and spacious."[5] Due to the painful experiences during the division,—although the Evangelical Association maintained the trust clause—United Evangelicals made local properties congregationally owned and gave detailed directions by which a local church might withdraw from the denomination.[6]

ARTICLES OF FAITH

While the Evangelical Association continued its nineteen Articles of Faith unchanged, United Evangelicals affirmed twenty-five. A few were essentially identical with those of the church before the schism while a larger number were rewritten but without change in substance. In addition there were new ones: Of the Witness of the Spirit, Of Apostacy, Of Immortality, Of the Ministry, Of Church Polity, and Of the Evangelization of the World. The positions affirmed in these new Articles were never issues during the days of division. The two churches continued with their respective Articles of Faith to the time of their union in 1922.

While the Evangelical Association never had an Article expounding entire sanctification and Christian perfection, its *Discipline* carried an explanation-homily on these subjects based on Matthew 5:48 and I Thessalonians 5:16-18 which testified to the Wesleyan influence upon this communion. The United Evangelical *Discipline* contained an exposition of the same subjects, distinguished by an extended quotation from John Wesley.[7] The exhortation to seek the grace of Christian perfection was commonly expressed in both churches until the early twentieth century.

Devastating perils were perceived in the new pronouncement of science about the origin and antiquity of the world and man and in the conjectures of human development through millenia. If one could make figurative the first chapters of Genesis, asked a bishop, where could this interpretative practice be halted, and what would become of biblical authority? When Henry Drummond espoused the principle of evolution, it was plaintively lamented that his "influence for God has been recklessly sacrificed" by his "apostasy," for such a scientific theory could only wither the gospel truth.[8] Scientific theories were abundant, extravagant, and transitory while scientific truth conformed with the Word of God.

With equal vigor biblical higher criticism was branded as "essentially destructive," and the faithful were warned against it. The conclusions of scholars like William R. Harper and Charles A. Briggs were dismissed as superficial and destructive, and with pride it was said that "this kind of biblical criticism has not invaded our church."[9] The speculations upholding the post-Mosaic authorship of Deuteronomy and the late dating of the Pentateuch were branded as preposterous because they undermined the authority of scripture. Critics were charged with presumptuous egotism, "relying too much on cold reason or logic without corresponding prayer."[10] While for most Evangelicals at this time the inerrancy of scripture was inseparable from its inspiration and authority, a few brave souls offered mild dissent. A college teacher observed that higher criticism testified to the developmental character of biblical literature from Genesis to Revelation. A seminary teacher recognized factual inaccuracies in the Bible, but judged them to be inconsequential in comparison to its purpose to reveal God's redemptive purposes They simply demonstrated the "fallibility of copyists and translators."[11]

Liberal theology, with its broad spirit and confidence in reason, offered little attraction for Evangelicals. It was accused of having no sense of sin, of repudiating divine retribution for sin, of shifting the center of redemption from the cross on Calvary to the manger at Bethlehem, and of minimizing the redemptive purpose of Christ's death.[12]

Few books by Evangelical authors were published. In 1890 the first of the two-volume *Geschichte der Evangelischen Gemeinschaft* by Reuben Yeakel was published. English translations were issued in 1894 and 1895. G. J. Kirn's *Religion, a Rational Demand* appeared in 1900 and R. Gulick's *Der Christliche Glaube* in 1904. The first volume of Bishop J. J. Esher's *Christliche Theologie* was issued in 1889, but it and the two following volumes were never translated into English, nor were they widely used in the church. In 1921 S. J. Gamertsfelder's *Systematic Theology* was published; for a decade it was the basic theological textbook for the seminarians of the denomination. Among these publications, Kirn's and Gamertsfelder's gave evidences of a considered confrontation with some of the newer critical, intellectual, and theological issues of the time.

THE MINISTRY

In both Evangelical churches there were local preachers whose services were restricted to visitation, preaching, and assisting the appointed pastors. In both, the route to ordination was substantially the same. Following the candidate's recommendation and examination by the Quarterly Conference, the Annual Conference, upon a two-thirds vote, granted him a license to preach and two years later after fulfillment of requirements, a deacon's ordination. Both denominations thereafter required two further years of guided study, probationary service, and a doctrinal examination to qualify for ordination as elder. The latter ordination qualified the candidate to serve a parish in all its pastoral and sacramental needs.

In the Evangelical Association pastors were appointed annually with the pastor's service on a parish initially limited to three consecutive years. In 1895 this was extended to four years, in 1907 to five, and in 1915 to seven years. For United Evangelicals there was a four-year time limit. Presiding elders were elected for a quadrennium by the Annual Conferences in both denominations. At first in the Association the presiding elder could not continue on the same district after reelection, but this restriction was removed in 1918. Among United Evangelicals, presiding elders after two terms of service were ineligible for reelection. In both churches bishops were elected by General Conference to a four-year term of office. They were eligible for reelection, but United Evangelicals limited episcopal tenure to eight consecutive years. For both churches bishops were "entrusted with certain prerogatives for a definite period of time: their functions are administrative and not priestly. They act for and by authority. . . . "[13]

MISSIONS

Institutionalism in the churches in the 1900's—and not wholly without some justification—was under strong attack. Nevertheless church institutions and organizations appear to be indispensable measures by which many people in one church family can make a corporate witness for Christ. Following the schism the Association continued its Missionary Society, and the United Evangelicals organized a Home and Foreign Missionary Society which in form, purpose, and structure was much like that of the Association. For many years the sole full-time officer in each society was the corresponding secretary. In 1917 in the Association he was displaced by an executive secretary, and a field secretary was added to the staff, the former charged with general administrative responsibilities and the latter with the dissemination of missionary information and the cultivation of mission enthusiasm.

Both societies were persistently compelled to cope with inadequate funds. Both began to promote "special days"—Children's Day and Foreign Day—each with its offering for missions. The corresponding secretaries were money raisers, and missionary offerings were regularly received at camp meetings and Annual Conference sessions. At the latter there was rivalry among the conferences: at its 1914 session the Canada Conference gave $7,000. This practice declined as most conferences followed the Indiana Conference in making "the apportionment to the fields sufficient to balance the amount usually raised on Sunday afternoon."[14] The emergency of the Commission on Finance and the adoption of budgets at all levels of church life altered the earlier and more elementary measures for mission support. From the first the Women's Societies were generous contributors to missions, and their example was followed by the youth organizations. While the Association inherited the missionary treasury of the undivided church, it inherited also the established operations. By 1895 its indebtedness was $170,178. It embarked upon an energetic program to reduce its expenditures and to raise money. Four years later it reported that $132,000 had been collected and that missionary contributions were $17 per member higher than during the preceding quadrennium.

Overseas Operations: Central Europe

The Germany Conference, which remained loyal to the Association when schism rent the American church, in 1900 was divided into two Annual Conferences, North Germany and South Germany.[15] The strong affection in the Association for its work in Germany is illustrated by the gift of $75,000 in 1903 for church construction in Berlin.

Die Evangelische Gemeinschaft, as it was known there, was confronted with restrictive laws in the German states, but on occasion these could be met with what some have called "episcopal subtlety." In 1892 Bishop J. J. Esher, standing before a gathering of the faithful, announced himself as a "law abiding citizen" and said that solicitation for the missionary enterprise would be a violation of existing laws. However, he added, if anyone "insisted on laying an offering upon the Redeemer's altar, we had no right to prohibit it."[16] Many "insisted," and six thousand marks were received!

Despite laws and local harrassments the work prospered, and in 1920 the Gemeinschaft was listed among the free churches in the civil directory of religious associations.

This enterprise in Germany first struck root in Württemberg and then spread into Baden, Alsace, and Prussia. The dedication of its first sanctuary in Berlin on October 16, 1904, was hailed with joy. Publishing interests centered in Stuttgart, and by 1902 an enlarged and better equipped printing plant was opened there. A school for prospective ministers was relocated in 1905 on a commanding height overlooking Reutlingen, Württemberg, where an impressive structure for the seminary was erected.

World War I confronted the *Gemeinschaft* with many grave problems. Within a month the seminary was closed. Clergy were impressed into military service, and by 1916 thirty-four congregations were pastorless. The rigorous blockade of Germany by the Allies made the plight of the German citizenry increasingly desperate, and though hostilities ceased in November 1918, it was June 1919 before the victors permitted aid to be sent the German people. That year church officials visited Germany to ascertain needs, and thereafter $107,506 was collected for relief.[17]

The Annual Conference in Switzerland was younger and smaller than the one in Germany, but it steadily grew and, like the Germany Conference, developed a healthy deaconess program. A Swiss joined the faculty of the seminary in Reutlingen in 1896, and there the prospective clergy for this conference received their preparation. In 1895 the Swiss petitioned for a book depository and in 1911 for a publishing house. Both requests were granted, and these operations were settled in Berne.

Before 1900 Evangelical missioners were in eastern Germany: in Posen, Bromberg, Vandsburg, and Danzig. With the redrafting of national boundaries by the Treaty of Versailles most of these cities fell within the newly created Poland. Since Poland was anti-Protestant and bitterly anti-German, after 1919 this missionary endeavor was severely restricted and reduced.

Responding to an appeal from an immigrant in Riga, Russia, the North German Conference began work among the Germans there, and two years later a congregation was organized. Inasmuch as this endeavor was exclusively for Germans, World War I brought it into grave difficulties. Officers of the Board of Missions visited Riga in 1920, now in the newly created Latvia, and thereafter a missionary was appointed and plans were drafted for new efforts, this time in the Lettish language.

Japan

In Japan, as in central Europe, the mission was little affected by the schism in the American church. The Japan Conference was formally organized in 1893, and later that year a denominational periodical, the *Fukuin no Taukai* was published. The Woman's

Missionary Society in America promoted the founding of the Bible Women's Training School in 1904. There followed other programs, all seeking to demonstrate Christian concern and win disciples. There were English-language schools, the first in 1909, Bible classes, and music classes. Kindergarten work was initiated in the Azabu Church, Tokyo, in May 1911. The Woman's Society established the Needy Girls' Home, Aisenryo, in 1918. After earlier efforts for a ministerial training school collapsed, Evangelicals joined Canadian and American Methodists in Aoyama Gakuin.

While the Evangelical mission began and centered in Tokyo, it was not confined there. In 1893 an enterprise earlier abandoned was begun again in Osaka, and a new mission was instituted in Koriyama, 150 miles north of Tokyo. The cultivation of Japanese leadership and the desirability of ecumenical relations expressed themselves in the passing years. Henry Tayama was elected presiding elder. From 1901 to 1903 Evangelicals and Methodists were in conversations in a Church Union Committee. General Conference listened to the pleas of the Japan Conference for closer cooperative measures but was unresponsive. As the treasury warranted, additional missionaries were sent to Japan, chief among them Paul S. Mayer, who arrived in 1909. Mayer spent almost half a century there, his mind and spirit serving and directing the mission in productive measures that were recognized by his church and the Japanese government.

China

The first United Evangelical General Conference announced that when $20,000 was collected for it, an overseas mission would be established; but the needs of the new denomination in America were crucial, and the fund for a foreign mission grew very slowly. Indeed, the goal had not been fully reached when in May 1899, Hunan, China, was named as the area for the mission's location. Before the end of the calendar year 1900, the Rev. and Mrs. C. Newton Dubs were in Shanghai, and in November 1901, despite the ominous threats of the Boxer Rebellion, they were settled in Changsha, Hunan. There a chapel was opened in 1902; within a year four additional missionaries arrived. From Changsha the mission expanded to Siangtan in 1903 and to Liling in 1904. These three cities became the center of the East Hunan Mission.

Besides evangelism, there were endeavors in educational and medical work. The first day-school was opened in Changsha in 1903, and by 1922 there were seventeen more in the mission. The arrival of an "educational missionary" in 1913 gave added impetus to the school programs. Bible classes began in 1904 and later "cross stitch" or embroidery classes. A Bible Women's School was opened in 1921. A Girls' Boarding School, established in 1910, by 1922 reported a faculty of eight and an enrollment of 120. A Boys' Boarding School, later named Albright Preparatory School, was founded in Liling in 1912; in 1920, 120 students were enrolled. The Workers' Training School, begun in 1915, was discontinued, but Evangelicals participated in the interchurch Hunan Union Theological School in Changsha. Upon the arrival of a doctor, the first dispensary was opened in Changsha, and in 1915 another was initiated in Liling which slowly evolved into a hospital. The latter was severely damaged by rioters in 1917 and closed for a year, but then enlarged and reopened. In 1917 the Emma Dubs Memorial Hospital was constructed in Yusein.

Overseas, inflexible denominational lines softened under the magisterial claims of Christ, and Evangelicals joined interchurch projects such as the Hunan Girls' High School in Changsha and the Yale Mission School. Not least significant was the declaration in 1913 that a "closer union" should be achieved between the East and West Hunan Missions, the enterprises of the United Evangelical Church and the Evangelical Association. "We feel we ought to be united," the superintendent of the latter wrote.[18]

In 1898 the Missions Board of the Evangelical Association was besieged with petitions to establish work in areas newly freed from Spain. Instead, the superintendent of the Japan Conference was directed to explore opportunities in China, and in 1899 it was determined that as soon as practicable a mission should be established there. Exasperating delays ensued, but in 1905 the first missionaries settled in Shen-chow-fu, later to be known as Yuanling, and the West Hunan Mission began its ministry. Upon the arrival of a doctor a dispensary was opened in Yuanling.

Despite interruptions due to the outbreak of violent civil disorders, a boys' school and a girls' school were inaugurated, and about 1914 a denominational periodical was published. The attempt to erect a hospital in Tungjen encountered stout local hostility, but in 1915 dispensary services were made available, and the next year the Evangelical Hospital, though still unfinished, began its ministry of healing. In 1919 a training school for nurses was inaugurated in connection with it. Tungjen gradually supplanted Yuanling as the center of the West Hunan Mission. About 1917 a girls' school was opened, and four years later the boys' school was transferred there.

The West Hunan Mission, like the East Hunan Mission, was repeatedly harrassed by the alternating tides of social and political unrest in China. Open rebellion broke out against the decrepit Manchu dynasty in 1910, and in the civil war in 1917 Hunan was a bitter battle ground between the northern and southern armies. A brief respite followed, but again in 1922 belligerent nationalistic movements proclaiming "China for the Chinese" wrought havoc to mission properties and programs and cast foreboding shadows over all Christian enterprises.

Africa

While the foreign mission work of United Evangelicals began in the Orient, there were church members deeply committed to work in Africa. Though their petitions were denied, they were not defeated. In 1906, a minister of this church, the Rev. C. W. Guinter, began his labors among the Wukari people in Nigeria under the recently formed Sudan United Mission, and some church members privately aided him with their gifts. The board in 1910 denied the request that he be designated as a denominational missionary but agreed to receive and forward contributions specified for him. In 1919 it was further agreed that the missionary treasury would pay any delinquency in his salary and then that the Woman's Society, which had requested it, might assume financial responsibility for Guinter.

Home Missions

The unparalleled immigration deluging the United States after 1890 with people from southern and eastern Europe, the rapid growth of American cities and their grave problems, the rapid industrialization of the nation, and the discovery of "forgotten Americans" impelled all churches to a new assessment of home missions and their responsibilities for Christian witness in the new circumstances. The Immigrant Mission of the Evangelicals in New York City declined as German immigration diminished until in the early 1900's, it was discontinued. Both Evangelical churches were almost wholly north of the Mason and Dixon line, meeting Negroes only in a few and isolated urban instances.

Several local churches and Annual Conferences undertook what were known as language missions. About 1900 the Adams Street Church in Chicago (United Evangelical) inaugurated a Sunday school for Chinese which continued for twenty years. In Cleveland there were several ventures. The Linden Street Church operated a mission for Jews until 1896, and the Rev. I. C. Imhof directed another which continued until 1950. The Madison Avenue Church in New York City promoted a mission for Hungarians in 1891 which lasted only briefly. The New York Conference (Association) established one for Poles; a congregation was organized, but it soon expired. The Association instituted a mission for Swedes in the Boston area which at its height reported three congregations before it declined and disappeared.

The most substantial Evangelical language mission was that for Italians. About 1900 the Evangelical Association in Wellsville, Ohio, initiated work among Italians and in 1904 employed Katherine Eyerick to serve it. Succeeding the local congregation, the Ohio Conference and then the Women's Board supervised this mission until it was discontinued. Louis Bucaletti from Wellsville enrolled in North Central College to prepare himself for the ministry. During weekends and vacation periods this collegian visited Italian communities in Chicago which issued in the opening of one mission in 1908 and another in 1913. Meanwhile an Italian mission was launched in Kansas City in 1908, another in Detroit in 1914, and still another in South Bethlehem, Pennsylvania. All these ventures were discontinued by 1917.

In the meantime in 1908 work among Italians was initiated in Milwaukee, and a year later a church was organized with twenty-two charter members. In 1911 a new chapel was dedicated. That year G. Busacca, a North Central College student, began a ministry among Italians in Racine where a chapel was erected in 1914. Under his leadership Italians in Kenosha were visited, a congregation was organized, and in 1921 a chapel was built. This work among Italians was at its zenith in 1922.[19]

Though a mountain mission had been suggested in 1913, it was 1921 before United Evangelicals acted to locate one on Red Bird Creek, Beverly, Kentucky. Before the end of the year three missionaries were in residence on the Red Bird, including the Rev. J. J. De Wall who was named superintendent.

Educational opportunities were sadly lacking in the area so from the first education as well as evangelism was promoted. A school was built in 1922 at Beverly, one at Jack's Creek and another at Beech Fork early the next year, and by fall the three reported an enrollment of 253. In February 1923 a three-story frame building, Knuckles Hall, was opened for boarding students at Beverly. With the arrival of a nurse, a community health program was begun. When a physician joined the staff, a small hospital was erected which was dedicated in 1928. While the Red Bird Mission centered at Beverly, where the Stull Memorial Chapel was built in 1927, Jack's Creek and Beech Fork became important substations. From these places missionaries extended the Christian testimony along the valleys and up the mountain sides so that within a decade evidences of improvements in moral and cultural patterns were reported.

As the twentieth century opened, the periodicals of both Evangelical churches sought to inform and arouse readers to missionary opportunities in the changing America where cities were growing twice as fast as the nation as a whole. Upon the premise that "density of population means the "intensity of sin" an editor asserted the city as "our greatest responsibility and also our greatest opportunity," and implored the church to discard its traditional fear and avoidance of the city and embark upon aggressive evangelistic endeavors.[20] This was imperative both for the good of God's Kingdom and the prosperity of the church.

In denominations that by birth and experience were primarily rural, this thrust toward cities was greeted with less than enthusiasm in some quarters. Given the same quality of preacher, the same salary and living conditions, the rural church would run way ahead of the urban church, someone wrote. Another pled: "If any church should apply itself to the problems of the rural church, we should. We must not lose our genius for rural evangelism."[21] This lively concern for the rural church contained a significantly broadened conception of ministry, reflected in the exhortations that rural pastors attend agricultural institutions and conferences to better understand rural life and how to cope with rural problems.

Offering its specific assistance, a Church Extension Society was formed in each church, legally independent but in practice integrally related to its Missionary Society. United Evangelicals created their society in 1898 to gather funds which could in turn be loaned to congregations to acquire real estate or to build or renovate sanctuaries. The Association formed its society in 1899 for the same purposes. Among the former by 1914 Church Extension had aided 181 congregations; among the latter, by 1922, 290 congregations had been helped by Church Extension.

Woman's Missionary Societies

In the midst of the sundering upheaval in the church, women who aligned with the minority met in 1891, elected leaders, and recommended that junior societies be organized and that a monthly magazine be published. During the following summer, conventions were held in several Annual Conferences, and in September there was a general convention where Mrs. Elizabeth Krecker was elected to leadership and where a fund was started "with a view to foreign mission work as God shall open the way."[22] With the creation of the United Evangelical Church this women's movement became the Woman's Home and Foreign Missionary Society. Meanwhile women loyal to the Evangelical Association gathered in Cleveland in 1892 for the perpetuation of their society and chose Mrs. E. M. Spreng president. The first efforts in both societies were in a time of anxiety and frustration, in part because of the enormous tasks to be done with meager resources, and in no small part because of the rancor that attended the feuding between the two Evangelical churches. To stimulate work in conference branches and local societies, organizers were appointed. Each society published a monthly magazine—*Missionary Messenger* by the Association and *Missionary Tidings* by United Evangelical, both heralding the work being done and seeking to inspire a contagious missionary enthusiasm. In one year, 1922, the Association's society raised $148,939. At that date the United Evangelical Society reported that over a twenty-five-year period it had collected $800,000 for missions.[23] The story of Evangelical mission cannot be told without a clear recognition of the unflagging devotion and generosity of the Woman's Missionary Societies.

These societies ardently worked within their respective denominations, but they also found values in interchurch associations. The Association's society had representation at the World Missionary Meeting in Chicago in 1893. Two delegates represented them at the Ecumenical Conference on Foreign Mission in New York in 1900. It had representation at the United Mission Study Conference and the Woman's Boards of Foreign Missions in 1905, and it contributed to the support of the work among migrants which was superintended by the Federal Council of Churches' Home Missions Council.[24]

DEACONESS SOCIETY

On the eve of the division of the church in America, the Germany Conference organized a Deaconess Society with headquarters in Elberfeld. Its objectives were to recruit and prepare young women for hospital service; this subsequently extended to include preparation for parish service. By 1901 there were more than three-hundred deaconesses in the ten branches of the society in German cities. Learning of these achievements in Germany, advocates of deaconess work in the American church became more numerous and vocal.[25]

Following initial steps in four Annual Conferences, the Association's General Conference in 1903 created a Deaconess Society. The next year a constitution was drafted and plans were laid for a home for deaconesses in Chicago. Proper garb was specified— black dresses for those in general service, blue-and-white striped dresses for those serving in hospitals. A preparatory course of study was drawn up, and before the end of the year ten deaconesses were enrolled. In 1905 a training school was opened, and on November 2 the Deaconess Home and Hospital was dedicated.[26] Construction had cost $30,466. The small hospital boasted a medical staff of fourteen physicians and surgeons. Hospitals were built in Bismarck, North Dakota, and St. Paul, Minnesota, and though these were initially local enterprises, they affiliated with the denominational society. "All live denominations of our day have deaconess societies and deaconesses. Any up-to-date church must have them," a bishop exclaimed.[27]

In fulfillment of Illinois statutes in 1912 a four-year course of study for deaconesses was introduced at the Chicago hospital which included instruction in nursing and religious education. The hospital received state accreditation in 1916. The next year two private hospitals, one in Monroe, Wisconsin, and one in Ortonville, Minnesota, affiliated with the general society. Triumphing over many obstacles not the least of which were financial, a new and larger home and hospital in Chicago was dedicated November 14, 1926.[28] Before this day Globe Hospital, Freeport, Illinois, and Allen Memorial Hospital, Waterloo, Iowa, were offered to and accepted by the Deaconess Society. In thirty years the deaconess movement in the Evangelical Association had achieved an impressive status and stature.

CHRISTIAN EDUCATION

Sunday Schools

In both Evangelical churches a Sunday school was expected in each local church. As the nineteenth century drew to a close, innovations appeared by the introduction of the Home Department for the benefit of those incapacitated and unable to attend the school on the Lord's Day. Then came the Cradle Roll Department about 1908, and about the same time the adult Bible Class movement found advocates. Adolescents were separated into age-level classes. The division of scholars into age-level groups led to the appeal for lesson materials suited to each grade, but this encountered resistance, and the Evangelical churches moved slowly and reluctantly toward the adoption of graded lessons.

Sunday schools observed "special days." Soon after the turn of the century with revivalism waning, Decision Day was introduced as the occasion to solicit youth to commit their lives to Christ. Rally Day became the time to summon all scholars to the work of the new school year. On Children's Day the activities of the Sunday school—its officers, teachers, and scholars—were presented before the congregation, and, not least important, an offering for missions was received.

It became apparent that an effective Sunday school required competent teachers. United Evangelicals in 1910 urged the formation of teacher training classes, and in 1918 Association pastors were exhorted to preach a sermon annually on the subject of teacher training and to form a class for it on each charge.

By 1920 religious education as a name and as a movement was coming into vogue. Its champions declared its purposes: to acquaint the student with the Scriptures, to relate religion to life, to nurture attitudes and ideals of service, and to cultivate a unique religious experience while allowing for a variety of religious experiences.[29] They did not repudiate the waning traditional revivalism, but they contended that educational evangelism promised to be more productive. Critics of religious education, on the other hand, declared it a "highly cultivated modernism" which presumed a child was not a sinful creature and could "grow up a Christian and never know himself as otherwise."[30]

Despite its objectors, religious education prospered and prevailed, and new measures were introduced. Among the first was the daily vacation Bible school. A Detroit church in 1921 gave a glowing report of its school, which inspired many more. The weekday school of religion appeared. While recommending it, its advocates cautioned against the perils of such interchurch endeavors. It should have the support of the leaders of the participating churches, it should avoid trespass on the American principles of the separation of church and state, and it should not be undertaken without careful and adequate preparatory planning.[31] Further, there were community schools of religion for adults.

Its curriculum and organization might change radically, but the Sunday school remained irreplaceable. In 1920 seventy percent of the accessions to the church came through the Sunday school. Through it scholars learned about and participated in Christian missions through their contributions. There was a growing conviction that the Sunday school deserved improved equipment and facilities. Zion church, Kitchener, Ontario, was the first to make a reality of this conviction when it erected a Sunday school unit with twenty-one classrooms.

Young People's Societies: YPA and KLCE

Inspired by Dr. Francis E. Clark's Christian Endeavor Society, youth societies began to appear in the Evangelical Association, but in some quarters they were viewed with suspicion: Would they be kept "spiritual"? Would they eventuate in a substitute for the church? Amid such suspicions Bishop J. J. Esher invited those interested to a meeting where a committee was named to draft regulations for a Young People's Alliance with provisions for the general church, conference branches, and local churches. General Conference gave approval in 1891, and the YPA won instant acclaim. "This movement is of God," one leader said, adding that it would do for youth what the Women's Missionary Society was doing for the distaff members of the church.[32]

The avowed purpose of the YPA was the promotion of "intellectual and religious culture." That it could be abused is illustrated in the only reported instance of its kind where a meeting was devoted to the reading of a court's decision against the minority in the church's civil war, after which the doxology was sung! Its literary, social, and religious activities received plaudits for filling the "dangerous gap between the Sunday school and the church," for while youth were not the "head" of the church, they were not the "foot" either![33] Cheered by its enthusiasm and high spirit, a church leader wrote, "We know of no institution whose growth has been so rapid as that of the Young People's Alliance."[34] After a busy quadrennium, the YPA had 22,000 members. It was decided that Junior YPA societies be organized for children six to fourteen years old and that a periodical be published. The *Evangelical Herald* appeared in 1896.

By 1890 among those who were to become United Evangelicals there was a similar zeal to form young people's societies which would provide "the keystone to the success of the church as well as the keystone in perfecting in each individual the Christian life," by promoting "faithfulness to the church, familiarity with God's word, a deepening of the spiritual life, and work for others."[35] In 1891 the Keystone League of Christian Endeavor was organized, placed under the supervision of a board, and affiliated with the Interdenominational Christian Endeavor Society. Its constitution provided for Junior societies for children. In 1896 the KLCE *Journal* was published.

The YPA and the KLCE were vigorous, supportive agencies of their respective churches. They grew numerically, and their conventions generated contagious enthusiasm. The weekly meetings became learning experiences in Bible study, in the understanding and practice of prayer, in social amenities, and in exploring the nature of the Christian life and Christian service. These agencies founded some missions and supported many more. Their dollars gave appreciated assistance to North Central College, Evangelical Theological Seminary, and the Superannuation Fund.

The initial constitutions for the Sunday schools and the youth societies were modified with almost quadrennial regularity as new circumstances warranted new measures. The Association created the office of a full-time secretary for the Sunday schools in 1907 and elected F. C. Berger to the new office. Three years later United Evangelicals elected Daniel A. Poling to a similar office.

Still another phase of Christian education, and one more frequently stressed in the Association, was catechetical instruction. The pastor was instructed to give this for six months each year, using the church's Smaller Catechism as the text. That this was more widely ignored than fulfilled is evident from the report in 1902 that catechetical classes were held in no more than forty percent of the churches and very rarely in churches using the English language.[36] Believing that the word catechism was repellent to many, religious education was proposed as a substitute, but this was not sustained. In 1922 the drafting of a "more teachable and practical" catechism was recommended.

ACADEMIC AGENCIES AND INSTITUTIONS

Within both Evangelical churches there were academic institutions over which the church exercised only the slightest supervision. The *Discipline* affirmed that in them only Christian believers and men of good religious and moral character should be employed as teachers and that the Scriptures were to be "read daily in the presence of the pupils and prayer offered with them."[37] Believing the schools deserved better support and supervision, United Evangelicals in 1914 and the Association in 1916 organized Boards of Education. To its board an institution could come presenting its needs and seeking counsel on matters of common concern to the church and the school.

At the schism, the Association had two schools in Pennsylvania: Central Pennsylvania College in New Berlin and Schuylkill Valley Seminary at Fredericksburg. After court decisions, United Evangelicals by negotiations acquired the former. Convinced the Fredricksburg school was unpropitiously located, in 1902 the Association transferred it to Reading. In the next decade, following campaigns to raise funds and lift academic standards, Schuylkill Valley Seminary became Schuylkill College.

At North Central College, Naperville, Illinois (Northwestern College until 1926), aggressive campaigns for funds made possible an increase in faculty and the construction of three buildings. Interesting, but of no great moment, was the trustees' decision in

1905 to discontinue intercollegiate football as "not compatible with the high standards of a Christian school."[38] The decision was short-lived! Indicative of the quality and character of the school was its acceptance into membership of the North Central Association of Colleges in 1914 and the report in 1909 that during two decades over thirty graduates had won appointments as foreign missionaries.

Union Biblical Institute, which in 1909 became Evangelical Theological Seminary, was the only theological school of the Evangelical Association. Previously domiciled in North Central's building, in 1913 its main building was erected. The seminary offered two basic, two-year courses: the one for the student lacking a college degree which led to a diploma of graduation, the other for the college graduate who received the degree, bachelor of divinity. The Association only cautiously advanced its educational standards for entrance into the ministry, but the seminary's enrollment of seventy-six in 1922 compared with the twenty-three in 1890 reflects the broadening acceptance of higher norms by the church.

United Evangelicals in 1894 were without any school but quickly took steps to enter the field of higher education. Through negotiations Central Pennsylvania College was acquired though at that time many were dissatisfied with its isolated location. At the Christmas recess, United Evangelical students left Schuylkill Valley Seminary and were settled in Myerstown, Pennsylvania, in what became Albright Collegiate Institute in 1896. To it in 1905 were brought the students and resources of Central Pennsylvania College; this consolidation became Albright College, which increased in enrollment, in faculty, and in physical facilities with the years.

In the Midwest at least three United Evangelical Annual Conferences attempted to found schools, but none was successful. However, in 1895 the Iowa Conference began its plans and in 1899 leased the facilities of a normal school in Le Mars. Despite a destructive fire, the school opened. The lease was supplanted by acquisition, and in 1901 with the erection of a new building Western Union College was on its way. Funds were imperative, but these came slowly. Nevertheless, three additional buildings were erected on the campus by 1921.

On the Pacific Coast on the eve of church division a school was launched at LaFayette, Oregon, which continued under United Evangelical patronage until about 1900. That year Dallas College was opened at Dallas, Oregon, only to expire in 1913.

For the preparation of its ministers, the United Evangelical Church first aspired to have two theological schools, one in the East and one in the West. But with every agency in the church clamoring for funds it was decided as less costly and more practicable that the colleges establish theological departments. Such a department, offering a two-year course, was announced to open in the fall of 1903 at Albright Collegiate Institute, which in the course of years developed into the Evangelical School of Theology. The theological department at Western Union College continued for about twenty years. Just when the United Evangelical Church entered its tenuous affiliation with White's Bible Teachers Training School in New York City has been inconclusively debated, but in 1919 it was announced as "the officially recognized and accepted training school for our ministers."[39] The number of the church's clergy who attended this school was not large. Indeed, in this church theological education was not among the priorities. In 1919 of its 519 ministers, 271 had no formal theological education.[40]

Several informal educational programs deserve mention, chief among them the Evangelical Correspondence Course in the Association. It offered "parts" or programs for ministers or laymen, all of which were intended to stimulate reading and study. The work was done by correspondence. In 1898 there were 2,075 enrolled in the several parts of the course. Far less significant was the Illinois Bible Institute of the United Evangelicals which about 1910 affiliated with the Chicago Training School. Still smaller and of brief duration was the American Training School for Young Women.

Evangelism

The overarching objective of the Evangelical churches had been and remained to proclaim Christ and lead people to surrender their lives to his mastery. Throughout the nineteenth century, camp meetings and revivals were the occasions where the lost were led to and through the conversion experience which was the doorway to church membership. Upon the perceptible decline in the effectiveness of revivalism, the Evangelical Association formed a Commission on Evangelism. Its purposes were to make preachers and people prayerful and expectant in evangelistic endeavors, to recruit candidates for full-time Christian service, to cultivate lay participation in the spiritual advancement of the church, and to promote city evangelism. A quadrennium later two bureaus were appointed, one for literature and one for social service. United Evangelicals established their Committee on Evangelism in 1914. In both churches it was assumed that in addition to the commission or committee, every denominational agency had its singular role in the promotion of evangelism.

Evangelistic concern found new methods of expression. As earlier prejudice against things "Romish" diminished, Passion Week and the Lenten season were observed for evangelistic purposes. Sunday schools yearly had their Decision Day, and colleges promoted an annual Week of Prayer as occasions to win personal commitments to Christ. The churchwide Forward Movements deepened spiritual life and led thousands to Christian discipleship. While revivalism had significantly declined, evangelistic proclamation and practices continued and with fruitful results.

Publications

Following the General Conference of 1887, on behalf of the minority a private publishing company was organized in Harrisburg. The *Evangelical*, edited by H. B. Hartzler, was published there beginning in November 1887 and in 1890 Sunday school materials also. The German-speaking sector of the minority were served first by the *Deutsche Allgemeine Zeitung* and then by the *Evangelische Zeitung*, which were published in Chicago. The first General Conference of United Evangelicals in 1894 created a Board of Publications, and by mid-June 1895 publications were consolidated in Harrisburg, where the private publishing company was purchased for $16,000.[41] In 1918 the printing plant was settled in new quarters at Third and Reily Streets. Precedent was broken in 1910 when a layman, J. J. Nungesser, was elected publisher, a post previously held by clergymen. Under his skills the publishing house prospered. Subscribers to *The Evangelical* consistently increased as those for the *Evangelische Zeitschrift* decreased, and in the midst of the anti-German hysteria in 1917 it was discontinued.

Aside from *Disciplines* and catechisms, the denominational books published were few. A German hymnbook, *Die Kleine Palme*, appeared in 1896 and *The Evangelical Hymnal* in 1897. There were two books by Ammon Stapleton: *Annals of the Evangelical*

Association of North America and *History of the United Evangelical Church* and in 1917 *A Wonderful Story of Old Time Evangelical Evangelism.* With the centenary of Evangelical beginnings the *Evangelical Centennial Celebration* was produced. *Evangelical Missions* by B. H. Niebel and Homer H. Dubs practically completes the roster of such publications to 1922.

Meanwhile with the division, the publishing house of the Association in Cleveland was faced with grave new problems. Subscriptions to the major publications dropped by 65,000 and receipts plummeted. Toward the costs of litigation as the church was dividing, the Board of Publication is alleged to have paid $194,165.[42] Several proposals to relocate the printing plant outside Ohio were considered but rejected since money needed for this and for the replacement of the older presses was not available. The major denominational periodicals were the *Evangelical Messenger* and the *Christliche Botschafter*, the latter surviving the anti-German fury during World War I and struggling on for another quarter century. In addition to these periodicals, Sunday school literature, youth and missionary publications, and promotional materials, a number of books were published. Bishop W. Horn's *Leben und Würkum von Bischof J. J. Esher* appeared in 1906. Bishop T. Bowman completed the catechism which Bishop J. J. Esher had initiated (1916). A brief *History of the Evangelical Association* (1913) was the work of Bishop S. P. Spreng, and in 1921 the *Evangelical Hymnal* was published.

EVANGELICAL STANDARDS

Evangelicals after 1890 continued to hold to the earlier prescriptive norms for the personal conduct of church members. The use of spiritous liquors was proscribed. That was clear enough, and the injunction to preserve the sanctity of the Sabbath was equally emphatic. The Sunday the World's Fair opened in Chicago was declared a "day of shame,"[43] a shame deepened because an entrance fee had to paid on Sunday. When a lone voice asked: "Why was it more wrong to pay an entrance fee to the Fair on Sunday than to pay one to a camp meeting?" there was no response.[44] Most Evangelicals then concurred with those who urged the avoidance of newspapers, museums, the purchase of commodities and even the patronage of public transportation and the mails on Sunday. And on any day the theater, card playing, social dancing, horse racing, and prize fighting were neither places nor activities worthy of the Christian's presence or participation. As for women's fashions, "When professed Christians . . . 'bang' their hair and frizz it all around. . . . heaven puts on robes of mourning and all hell holds a jubilee" wrote one.[45] But quaint and interesting as such contentions may be to a later generation, they may not be permitted to eclipse the far more significant positions taken by Evangelicals as they faced their world.

The increase of divorce was perceived as a dire threat to marriage and the home and as the result of a stubborn will to achieve personal freedom, to escape family responsibilities, and to attain "extravagant living."[46]

An Article of Faith affirmed that war was not consonant with the gospel or the spirit of Christ. Upon the outbreak of hostilities between America and Spain, Evangelicals for the first time since the Civil War faced war. Promptly there were Annual Conference denouncements of Spanish cruelty to innocent people, and the church periodicals sounded a clear reveille. "God is in this war. God has stirred up the American people to go to war with Spain . . . the American nation is God's minister of justice."[47]

Again, in August 1914 war exploded in Europe. This time the conflict was more distant, but this time many Evangelicals were tied to one of the belligerents by background, blood, and sentiment. By 1915 many Annual Conferences drafted resolutions urging the strictest American neutrality and decrying the shipment of war materials to any belligerent. Upon the sinking of the *Lusitania* an editor noted the circumstances: "An enemy's ship, laden with contraband of war, sailing into the war zone . . . in disregard of repeated warnings given by the German government," and readers were summoned to pray for peace.[48]

As America in 1916 took initial steps toward preparedness, most Evangelicals were unsympathetic, for to prepare was simply to invite war. However, the remorseless marauding of German submarines upon shipping became the grounds for America's declaration of war upon Germany in April 1917. Quickly new words and new positions issued from the church periodicals. No nation could allow itself to be insulted or its rights violated. What the German people would never have done "an Imperial Government, a mighty, terrible war machine . . . has done."[49]

With American involvement, Evangelicals were exhorted to

abstain from hatred, for that was unbecoming for Christians. They were called to be loyal to government and that on scriptural grounds. The church papers became ardently patriotic: America must win or her fate would be that of desolated Belgium. In 1917 the National Service Commission was organized to minister to Evangelicals in uniform in training camps and overseas. These soldiers were acclaimed as they departed and were the subjects of earnest prayers; local churches displayed service flags in their honor.

The war spirit became more unrestrained as the war progressed. Bishop S. C. Breyfogel declared: "He who is neutral in this country is a traitor: and he who is silent is disloyal."[50] A Pennsylvania church exulted that it was the first church in the city to eliminate German preaching. The Pittsburgh Conference execrated "the spirit of iniquity incarnate in the Beast of Berlin," and an editor with unrestrained vehemence wrote: "The answer of the Allies to the Kaiser's peace cry should not be an olive branch but a hangman's rope. . . . Men do not discuss peace terms with dogs and rattlesnakes."[51] Certainly there must have been joy in the realm of heaven as there was among men on earth when on November 11, 1918, armistice terms were signed and this war's hysteria and fury could subside. This is a grim episode in the story of the Evangelical churches. The descent into unbridled passion has found few to defend it, and it is cold comfort to learn that comparable behavior occurred in most denominations during those years. It can and should be added that after the armistice, Evangelicals gave immediately and generously to programs for the relief and rehabilitation of the defeated peoples in central Europe.

THE SOCIAL GOSPEL

Evangelicals in the nineteenth century were predominantly a rural people; the emerging industrial and urban problems lay outside their experience and concern. However, as the century drew to a close, they were compelled to face the realities of American life. Socialistic schemes in general they found to be unacceptable, in part because such schemes were deemed godless. Far preferable to socialism was Christianity, which upheld the dignity of labor and laborers, permitted the worthy to acquire wealth, exercise charity for those in need, and bolstered family relations.[52]

As crises increased in numbers and intensity, General Conferences chastized both contenders. Labor's resort to violence was intolerable, and its demands for unionization were indefensible;[53] capital's soullessness and greed were reprehensible.[54] For most Evangelicals the role of the church was to trumpet the call to righteousness, which meant preaching the gospel. But for a growing number of them, the older pietistic passivism was insufficient, and these arose to demand that the church "push into the thick of the battle for social and moral reforms,"[55] study the economic problems, and obtain a correct understanding of industrial conditions. The Rev. J. F. Dunlap wrote: "We cannot crowd the poor to the wall during the week and expect them to worship in fellowship with us on Sunday."[56]

By the end of the last century a new, virile emphasis was heard among Evangelicals for which there was no denominational precedent. Salvation, it held, was available for men individually and corporately. The gospel was pertinent to life and all of life—a perspective which emerged as more people became aware of gross inequities and injustices. The almost total silence of this generation to the wrongs suffered by Negroes, Chinese, and Indians have been cited by some; the accusation is true. However, no generation comprehends the full scope of the positions it affirms.

Sympathy for the victims of industrialization and urbanization was imperative, but it was not a cure for the ills which afflicted them; therefore Evangelicals were summoned to participate in public affairs. They should nurture competent and good men to enter politics as a vocation, but above all they should vote, for in America the ballot was the instrument for social reordering. In 1913 the episcopal message declared the success of Christianity was to be measured not by the number on the church rolls, but by its leavening influence in transforming society. Denominational periodicals heralded the Federal Council of Churches social creed. For a time the tensions between the individual and the social gospel persisted, but by 1920 this was subsiding with the recognition that the two were neither adversaries nor alternatives, but two aspects of the one gospel. Some few proposed the formation of a Department of Labor in the church, but twenty years were to elapse before something akin, Christian Social Action, was established.

Compassionate concern, freshly sensitized in these years, found expression in larger support for the Association's philanthropic agencies such as the Ebenezer Children's Home at Flat Rock, Ohio, the Ebenezer Old People's Home in New York, and the Philadelphia Manor in Pennsylvania. In addition to these older ones, there were more recent foundations: Western Old People's Home, Cedar Falls, Iowa, was opened in 1911, and the Haven Hubbard Home, New Carlisle, Indiana, was established in 1921. Among the United Evangelicals the new venture was the Lewisburg Home, Lewisburg, Pennsylvania, which was inaugurated in 1915.

MINISTERIAL PENSIONS

The more lively social sensitivity was partly responsible for the establishment of a soundly structured pension plan for the clergy. Until 1912 the Mutual Aid Society was operative, but its benefits were very meager; in 1911 the Superannuation Fund, championed by Bishop S. C. Breyfogel supplanted it. A financial campaign for the Superannuation Fund was launched in four years and $285,713 was collected. By 1921 its assets totalled $950,000. During its first decade the benefits to superannuates increased from nine dollars to twelve dollars per year of active ministerial service.

CHURCH REUNION

An immediate by-product of the Evangelical schism was the intensification of church loyalty in both the Evangelical Association and the United Evangelical Church. Rivalry and the will to survive nurtured this loyalty, frequently expressing itself vehemently in localities where the two denominations confronted one another. In circumstances other than this both churches participated in most of the major interchurch movements and agencies. Both had delegates at the Ecumenical Conferences on Mission in New York in 1900 and the National Federation of Churches and Christian Workers in 1905, and both were charter members of the Federal Council of Churches of Christ in America. The invitation from the Protestant Episcopal Church to participate in a Faith and Order Conference in 1916 was accepted by the Association. Bishop S. C. Breyfogel of this church served as an officer of the American Council of the Word Alliance for the Promotion of International Friendship through the Churches.[57] Despite some objections, in 1920 both churches aligned themselves with the Inter-Church World Movement.

The most gratifying and significant of all these irenic activities was the one that sought to heal the division that had separated them. The two had parted amid bitter invective and rancor, but with the passing years inflamed passions cooled and signs of a return to reasonableness and Christian charity appeared. At the death of Henry B. Esher, the grandson of the episcopal champion of the Association, the United Evangelical periodical published a note of Christian sympathy. That same year in Illinois several clergymen of the Association casually dropped in the Annual Conference of the United Evangelicals, and in Davis the congregations of both denominations cooperated in a revival meeting.[58]

Across both churches there were ministers and laity who remorsefully looked back on the dismal events of the schism and began to hope for reunion. In 1907 the leaders of the two denominational youth societies sat side by side in a Gypsy Smith revival in Chicago and were struck by the evangelist's word that the scope of urban sin made closer denominational cooperation imperative. Believing that this message had a singular meaning for them and their churches, they began projecting joint YPA and KLCE meetings which were later heralded as the beginning of the union movement. By 1910 the East and West Hunan missions in China were experiencing cordial fraternal relations.

The Association appointed its Commission on Fraternal Relations and Union in 1907, and later the United Evangelical Church its Commission on Federation and Union. A few optimistically held there were no serious obstacles to reunion, but time revealed there were thorny and frustrating ones. The forty commissioners from the two churches met first in the Adams Street Church, Chicago, in 1911 to initiate the procedures that eleven years later would consummate the union. In Chicago the commissioners appointed exploratory committees and exhorted the membership in both churches to prayer for the unitive endeavor.

In the months immediately following there were numberless fraternal meeting between local congregations in camp meetings and in the youth societies. A dramatic scene occurred at the UPA–KLCE rally in Chicago in 1913 when Bishops Thomas Bowman and Rudolph Dubs, who had not met on the same platform for twenty years, sat side by side. At the conclusion of Dubs' address "Bowman turned to Dr. Dubs and extended his hand of Christian brotherliness, and Dr. Dubs grasped it with the warmth of Christian love."[59] Between 1911 and 1914 the commissioners met six times, wrestling with knotty problems of church polity such as episcopal authority and the ownership of local church properties. Thereafter when these meetings became less frequent, at the grass roots it was rumored that the negotiators had reached an impasse.

The lull in negotiations terminated in 1918 when the commissioners hoped to ready a Basis for Union for presentation to the United Evangelical General Conference scheduled to meet in November. When that conference met in York, Pennsylvania, its session was drastically shortened by the public health authorities who were coping with a severe influenza epidemic. Under the pressure of time the conference appointed a committee to work with a similar one from the Association to draft a constitution and procedural steps to accomplish a union. The Association's General Conference in 1919 appointed its personnel for this joint committee.

The Basis of Union was submitted to the Annual Conferences in 1921. In the United Evangelical Church the delay and an alleged "campaign of silence" irked many who supported the merger. Opposition to union arose in the Annual Conferences. One eastern conference declined to vote on the Basis, and another postponed the vote for twelve months, though in six conferences the Basis was approved by the majority and in four unanimously. The aggregate vote in the Annual Conferences approved the Basis of Union by a decisive majority. From late 1921 through early 1922 the issues of union were debated by proponents and opponents in *The Evangelical*. Simultaneously, two Annual Conferences challenged the authority of the commission. Fully aware of the perils, United Evangelical leaders, supported by ten years of negotiations and the aggregate vote of the Annual Conferences, announced plans to proceed. At this, the bishops of the Association, where opposition to union was negligible, issued a call for a special General Conference to convene in the Mack Avenue Church, Detroit, in October 1922.

The United Evangelical General Conference convened in Barrington, Illinois, October 5, 1922, where the commission's report was adopted and the Basis of Union and the Enabling Act were approved. Fifteen delegates from the East Pennsylvania Conference protested these actions and abstained from voting. After concerted efforts to persuade the dissenters proved futile, it was voted to adjourn in Barrington and to reconvene in the Mack Avenue Church, Detroit, where the Association's General Conference was in session.

In Detroit United Evangelicals first met in separate session where again efforts were made to achieve unanimity, but when it became evident that the dissenters could not, or would not be persuaded, the Association was notified of their readiness to enter organic union. On October 12, 1922, by a unanimous vote (the dissenters abstaining) The Evangelical Church was created, the successor to the two preceding denominations, a church with 2,916 congregations, 2,431 ministers, and 259,417 members. Across the new denomination there were scores of meetings given to jubilation at the merger of the "sons of Albright." At Nescopek, Pennsylvania, the local church proudly reported its cornerstone was the first to bear the name, The Evangelical Church. Within months plans led to the merging of denominational agencies, conferences, and congregations. The ill consequences of the Evangelical division were history and irretrievable, but the wondrous work of God's grace in healing wounds and in restoring oneness was received with joy and thanksgiving.

The Evangelical Congregational Church

The joy at church union, however, was not unalloyed. The East Pennsylvania Conference, the center of dissent, announced its purpose to maintain the faith and polity of the United Evangelical Church.[60] A periodical, The United Evangelical, became the voice of this group which was augmented by the addition of a few scattered congregations in Ohio and Illinois. In several cases the ownership of local properties was contested, but in a crucial one the Supreme Court of Pennsylvania upheld the legality of the merger, and the plaintiffs were denied claims upon Albright College. Denied the right to the name The United Evangelical Church, they chose to be called The Evangelical Congregational Church.

This communion with about 20,000 members continued with the Articles of Faith of the United Evangelical Church. In polity it became more expressly congregational. It restricted the power of General and Annual Conferences; it provided that delegates to Annual Conferences vote in accordance with instructions from Quarterly Conferences; it required a congregational vote on issues pertaining to doctrine and church union.

In 1931 the churches in Ohio and Illinois were formed into a Western Conference. The customary denominational agencies were organized. Some overseas missionary operations were carried on through participation in faith missions. After a school for Negro girls in Atlanta was abandoned, a mountain school was opened in 1944 at Glen Eden, Kentucky, but when transportation made public education available, the building was used as a dispensary. The Burd and Rogers Home for the aged was established on a site adjacent to the Herndon camp meeting grounds in Pennsylvania. Five years later the Albright College campus at Myerstown was purchased. In 1932 one of the buildings became the center for publications; another became an old peoples' home and in 1953 one of the buildings housed the church's new school of theology.

The Evangelical Congregational Church has been wary of interdenominational involvements and was unresponsive to successive overtures for union coming from the Evangelical Church. It did affiliate with the International Christian Endeavor Society and the American Bible Society, and in 1947 its Western Conference joined the National Association of Evangelicals. In 1946 negotiations with the Primitive Methodist Church and the Church of the United Brethren in Christ (Old Constitution) were declined. It currently reports a constituency of 27,580.

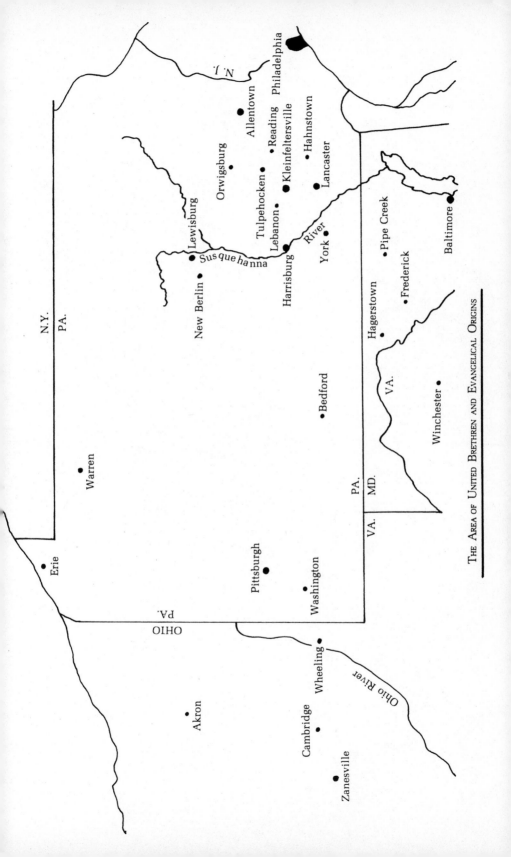

THE AREA OF UNITED BRETHREN AND EVANGELICAL ORIGINS

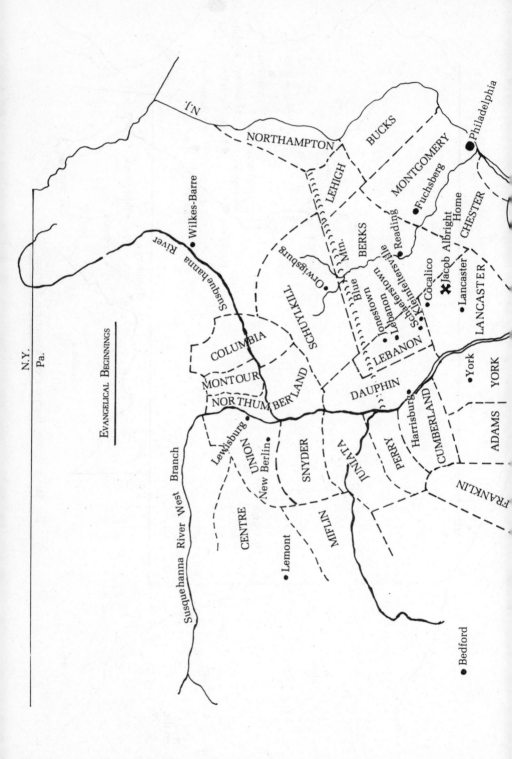

EVANGELICAL BEGINNINGS

GEOGRAPHIC EXTENSION OF THE UNITED BRETHREN CHURCH BY 1841, 1861, AND 1889

GEOGRAPHIC EXTENSION OF THE EVANGELICAL ASSOCIATION BY 1840, 1859, AND 1887

Martin Boehm

The Boehm Chapel near Willow Street, Pennsylvania

Otterbein's birthplace, Dillenburg, Germany

Philip William Otterbein

The Isaac Long Barn near Neffsville, Pennsylvania

The Old Otterbein Church, Baltimore, Maryland

Jacob Albright

Flickinger Church, Lancaster County, Pennsylvania, where Albright preached his
first formal sermon

Top: The Becker Homestead, Kleinfeltersville, Pennsylvania, site of the Evangelical Conference of 1807

Bottom: Albright Memorial Chapel, Kleinfeltersville, Pennsylvania

Top: The first Evangelical church and printing establishment, New Berlin, Pennsylvania, 1816

Center: Birthplace of Christian Newcomer, Bareville, Pennsylvania

Bottom: Bonnett School House, near Mount Pleasant, Pennsylvania, where the first United Brethren General Conference was held, 1815

Top: Preaching license issued by Bishop Newcomer to John Russel, 1819

Center: John Seybert

Bottom: Bishop Seybert's wagon

(Courtesy Garrett Evangelical Theological Seminary)

Plaque commemorating the merger of the Evangelical
Association and the United Evangelical Church, 1922
(Courtesy Garrett Evangelical Theological Seminary)

Red Bird Mission, Beverly, Kentucky

The United Brethren–Evangelical Uniting Conference, Johnstown, Pennsylvania, 1946

(Courtesy Garrett Evangelical Theological Seminary)

Bishops John S. Stamm and A. R. Clippinger symbolize the union of the Evangelical and United Brethren denominations, 1946

Board of Bishops of the Evangelical United Brethren Church, 1946. Front row: H. H. Fout, John S. Stamm, A. R. Clippinger, G. E. Epp, G. D. Batdorf; back row: V. O. Weidler, E. W. Praetorius, Ira D. Warner, Fred L. Dennis, C. H. Stauffacher, J. B. Showers

(Courtesy Garrett Evangelical Theological Seminary)

The Evangelical United Brethren Church Administrative Office Building, Dayton, Ohio

The Evangelical United Brethren Publishing House, Stuttgart, Germany

United Theological Seminary, Dayton, Ohio

Francis Asbury is consecrated as superintendent (bishop) of the
Methodist Episcopal Church, Baltimore, Maryland, 1784. Philip
William Otterbein assisted in this service at Asbury's request.

Ceremony of Union, The Methodist Church and the Evangelical United Brethren
Church, Dallas, Texas, 1968

espite modifying concessions made to achieve the union, the Evangelical Church in 1922 neither in theological positions nor in organization was substantially different from its predecessors. Its nineteen Articles of Faith affirmed positions which Evangelicals had affirmed for a century, and the chapter interpreting the doctrines of regeneration, sanctification, and Christian perfection was not new. The call of the church was to salvation and holy living.

Church members were admonished on matters of personal conduct. The Special Rules announced the Evangelical ethos on slavery, temperance, and marriage, and while the earlier counsel on dress was dropped, two new pronouncements appeared, one on divorce and the other on Bible study.[1]

The Evangelical Church continued the ecclesiastical structure of conferences: Quarterly, Annual, and General. The duties of the first remained essentially what they had been. The Annual Conference was composed of all ordained elders and the laymen elected by their respective Quarterly Conferences. The laymen exercised an unrestricted franchise except on matters relating to ministerial orders. The conference elected its secretary, and the bishop and presiding elders annually assigned preachers to their charges.[2] Ministerial service was limited to seven consecutive years on a parish.

For the General Conference, clergy and laity were elected in

EVANGELICALS FROM UNION TO UNION, 1922-1946

equal numbers by Annual Conferences on the basis of one of each per fourteen ministerial members of the Annual Conference. In the General Conference the secretary was elected, and Bishops held the right to speak but not to vote. Like its predecessors, General Conference was impotent to alter the Articles of Faith. It could make changes in the constitutional law, but to become effective, these required approval by a two-thirds majority of the aggregate vote of the Annual Conferences. Local church properties were held in trust for the denomination.

In the Evangelical Church there were two orders of ministers, deacons and elders. The process of achieving the two successive ordinations through licensing, probationary periods, study and examinations was not substantially different than it had been. The duties assigned the clergy in 1923 included little that was new, yet there was understandable satisfaction among many at the elimination of the previous restriction disallowing the marriage of probationers.

The Evangelical Church had a very adequate supply of ministers for its churches. Under the enthusiasm of the Forward Movement, 122 youths made vocational commitments for the ministry between 1922 and 1926. Then with the Depression many struggling churches were either consolidated or adjacent ones were placed under the supervision of one pastor to provide him a respectable livelihood. By this process the number of clergy needed was reduced.

The educational standards for entrance into the ministry were raised, but usually in the wake of independent regulations by those Annual Conferences most concerned to lift the standards. The first attempt to require college graduation for entrance into the ministry was unsuccessful. However, graduates of the theological schools were exempted from some assignments in the course of study, and under a broad interpretation of this provision a growing number of conferences began to accept seminary graduation as a substitute for most of the requirements of the course.

The new denomination inherited from its predecessors parallel and dynamic programs for the strengthening and expansion of church life. One especially served to promote unity in the merged church—the Forward Movement. A combination of idealism, will, and enthusiasm accompanied American entrance into the war to end wars and make the world safe for democracy, and the military victory in 1918 augmented this optimistic mood. In this roseate atmosphere the Inter-Church World Movement was born, dedicated to complete the evangelization of the world, to recreate society, and to collect millions of dollars. Infected by the glowing promises of this movement, numerous denominations began smaller but similar movements of their own. At the first of the United Evangelical Annual Conferences in 1919, the East Pennsylvania Conference proposed the denomination launch a crusade to deepen the spiritual life of the church and to raise $1,000,000.[3] Other conferences concurred, and because the next General Conference would not convene until 1922, the Commitee on Episcopal Activities took the initiative, setting a financial goal of $1,000,000 for what it called the Forward Campaign.[4]

The General Conference of the Evangelical Association in 1919 was challenged by the bishops to launch a Forward Movement with the slogan: "The whole church in a forward movement with Christ as leader." The proposal received an enthusiastic ratification. By January 1920 the organization of the Forward Movement was effected, able laymen playing important roles. Goals were specified: a family altar in every home, 100,000 conversions and 100,000 accessions to the church, 95,000 commitments to tithing, and 800 enlistments for full-time Christian service. A financial goal of $2,500,000 was set: $475,000 for home and foreign missions $200,000 for Church Extension, $100,000 for Ebenezer Orphans' Home and $100,000 for two other homes, $125,000 for Seminary Student Aid, $750,000 for Northwestern College, $250,000 for Albright College, $250,000 for Evangelical Theological Seminary, $50,000 for the Evangelical School of Theology, and $50,000 for the contingent fund.[5] Measures for the achievement of these goals were energetically undertaken.

The Forward Movement and the Forward Campaign were in mid-passage in 1922 when church union was effected so the two plans were fused and continued through 1926. At the end, 87.6 percent of the financial goal was attained, church membership was significantly increased, and the life of the church was quickened. Unquestionably, a sense of unity, which at the time was especially meaningful, was produced by this concerted effort, and the accomplishments of lay leadership did not pass unnoticed.

CHRISTIAN FAITH AND NEW CHALLENGES

In the 1920's the mood of the American people plunged from exuberant optimism to bleak despair as peace conferences and disarmament conferences ended in futility. Yet it was also the Jazz Age when the car, the radio, and the movies became common features in the American way of life. The next decade began under the spell of the nation's deepest depression, which evoked sobering reflections and new conclusions about social responsibilities. The sobriety was deepened by the growing feeling that international conflict waited in the wings. In times such as these, controversies were inevitable and passionate.

The conflict of science with religion climaxed with the Scopes trial in Tennessee in 1925 where a public school teacher was taken to court for teaching evolution in the public school, a trial in which national worthies, Clarence Darrow and William Jennings Bryan, were the contending lawyers. Some Evangelicals were decisive, asserting that evolution was an uncompromising alternative to Christianity. "The creation of man by a divine act as recorded in the Bible is the only consistent solution of human life."[6] A group of clergy charged that evolution was not only false, but stemmed from pernicious antecedents—"the teachings of the nihilism of Bakunin, Hertzel and the Bolshevism of more recent date, and Darrowism, and all avowed infidelism of most modernism."[7] The surprising thing is that when the Supreme Court of Tennessee freed Scopes from the charges against him, the subject of evolution was rarely discussed in the church paper. This could mean that the silent majority did not agree with those who previously declaimed against it; it could mean they did not understand the theory, or it could mean they were beginning to understand that scientific freedom was not destructive of faith.[8]

But there were issues that were not dispatched so summarily, such as those raised by modernism and biblical criticism. The alleged natural goodness of man was emphatically repudiated. Any casual observation of unredeemed human conduct in society and the world was sufficient to disprove the allegation. Beyond that, it was God's Word which testified that in Adam's fall, his posterity lost righteousness and holiness. The notion that if a child were kept in his pristine purity, he would naturally grow up into oneness with Christ was pronounced a "mischievous theory."[9]

Irrepressibly the issues centered in the character and authority of the Scriptures. No one wanted an "expurgated Bible," in fact none could be produced.[10] The inerrancy of the Bible was declared the foundation of Christianity; when this is denied, Christianity suffers irreparably. It was the authoritative, inerrant Bible that gave the incontrovertible testimony to those challenging the doctrine of the virgin birth. "The Virgin Birth of Jesus rests not upon theory but upon the unimpeachable record of Holy Writ," someone wrote.[11] And it was the Bible which spoke with clarity of the price paid for human redemption. Bishop S. P. Spreng was quoted as declaring, "Ours is emphatically a blood theology. The atonement through the sacrificial death of Jesus is the rock-ribbed center of our teaching."[12] Sheer sympathy without a genuine substitution could not effect redemption. Therefore a bloodless theology was not simply a faulty theology—it was a nontheology, for "God's Word teaches that the blood of Jesus is necessary to man's salvation."[13]

To spare the church from the dire effects of modernism with its proclamations of the natural goodness and competence of man and its loose interpretations of scripture, many suggestions were made. There must be a converted, sanctified, and divinely called ministry to cope with the threats to Christian faith and to instruct youth. Genuine conversion must become the carefully guarded door to church membership. College and seminary faculty must become more aware of their role as guardians of the treasury of faith.

That the foregoing expressions represent the theological slant of a sector of the Evangelical Church is not to be doubted, but that they are representative of the entire communion would not be true, for there were those with different convictions. One of these, confuting the expression that man was wholly depraved, held that while God's grace initiated salvation, the natural power inherent in man was needful to accomplish it. Another, more pragmatically motivated, was convinced that the church would fulfill its leavening mission in the world if churchmen became less concerned about precise definitions of Christ's person and more concerned to be mastered by him and live in his life. At the time when a militant fundamentalism was racking American Protestantism, another decried the proclamation of fundamentals that were not really fundamental but only served to divide God's people. If the Pharisees were fundamentalists and the Sadducees were modernists, Christ would wear neither tag. It was from this sector of the church that the admonition came to accept evolution for what it was—a theory—and confidently await more and further light on the subject.[14]

By the early 1930's this kind of theological controversy had run its course in the Evangelical Church. In part its subsidence may be attributed to sheer exhaustion. In part it may be due to the emergence of neo-orthodoxy which with biblical authority and more sophistication held that above human uncertainty, insecurity, and sinfulness there is a majestic, transcendent God. But perhaps most influential of all was the national economic debacle with its shattering dislocations and human agonies in which conscience and concern subordinated theological issues to the immediate ethical problems of social justice.

SHARING THE GOSPEL

The Missionary Society of the Evangelical Church in its overseas operations confronted a complicated and disintegrating world order. In Europe there were dictators with fearsome powers. Communism had spread to the far-flung quarters of the world. China was engulfed in a bloody civil war. There were wars and rumors of wars: the Japanese landing in Shanghai in 1932, the Italian invasion of Ethiopia in 1935, and finally the German invasion of Poland which led to World War II. Neither the League of Nations, nor the pacts between nations, nor disarmament conferences were able to halt the progress toward war. The worldwide moods of despair, cynicism, and disillusionment, the international economic crises, the aggressive ferocity of communism and nationalism, together with the strong isolationist sentiments in America made the work of the Missionary Society more necessary and more difficult.

In 1922 two general secretaries were elected for the Missionary Societies, the Revs. G. E. Epp and B. H. Niebel; four years later, in place of two general secretaries, an executive secretary and a field secretary were elected. After 1922, as before, the Church Extension Society was integrally related to the Missionary Society. Besides offering financial assistance, its Bureau of Church Architecture, when solicited, gave counsel. During the 1920's an unprecedented aesthetic interest appeared in the church, protesting against "deadly sins in architecture," "false acoustics," "false optics," poor ventilation, and garish organ pipes.[15] This new taste recommended a divided chancel with a centrally located pulpit and communion table for the sanctuary. Congregations were admonished to give heed to the external appearance of the church and its landscaping.[16]

In Europe

The needs in Germany, to which Evangelicals were particularly sensitive, were acute because of the desolation caused by the war and intensified by the postwar uncontrolled inflationary spiral. When Bishop Spreng arrived there in May 1923, the exchange was 80,000 marks for the dollar. When he left in July, it was 180,000 marks for the dollar. Before 1924 Evangelicals contributed $288,000 for European relief, $51,687 for the repair and construction of buildings, and despatched five tons of clothings and foodstuffs to their brethren in Germany.[17] To facilitate the distribution of funds and goods, Bishop G. Heinmiller was assigned there, and a Central Conference was created to superintend all operations in central Europe. In 1930 the North Germany Conference was divided into the East Germany and the West Germany Conferences,[18] and in 1939 all the conferences in Germany were brought together in the Reich's Conference.

Meanwhile a vigorous new political movement which held the seeds of disaster for Germany and anguish for the whole world began to raise its head. In 1933 Hitler became chancellor; the next year the Third Reich was proclaimed, and the churches were brought under stringent regulations to achieve national solidarity. The Reich's Conference was organized and, by German law, made independent of all authority outside Germany. Thus Evangelicals in Switzerland and elsewhere were divorced from their German brethren. But these events were dwarfed by the swift and terrible chain of secular events. In 1939 Nazi troops invaded Czechoslovakia; then the German-Russian accord was signed and on September 1, Hitler's soldiers invaded Poland, precipitating World War II.

The Deaconess Society in central Europe showed marked growth. Bethesda Hospital in Elberfeld, Germany, in 1930 was enlarged to care for 600 patients. In addition to this, the Deaconess Society had eight smaller hospitals and two clinics in major German cities and also several rest and vacation homes. In them 567 deaconesses were serving as well as another eighty-two parish programs,[19] but with the advent of a more inclement political climate in 1933, the number diminished. In Switzerland the work prospered. A new home and clinic were initiated in Basel in 1936, and one in Strassbourg, France, the next year. In 1938 there were 143 deaconesses in the various services. During World War II the

Strassbourg hospital was taken over by the French military and that in Elberfeld by the British who in 1946 still reserved it for their purposes.

The publishing house in Stuttgart was rebuilt after World War I and then faced the devastating havoc of inflation which diminished subscription lists. Some periodicals were discontinued. With improved economic conditions after 1930, the publishing house became more prosperous and by 1938 was employing 108.[20] This prospect was demolished by World War II. Paper and printing supplies became inaccessible, revenues plummeted, the work force was reduced by half, and then Allied bombing shattered the publishing house. After the cessation of hostilities, months elapsed before equipment and inventory could be repaired to enable another beginning for printing operations. In Berne, Switzerland, the publishing house faced French restrictions prohibiting the importation of German language publications into Alsace, and under duress a subsidiary operation in Colmar was closed. Despite a shrunken treasury, the Swiss in 1946 were drafting constructive plans for the future.

In Asia

The Japan Conference suffered the loss of two church buildings in the disastrous earthquake of 1923, but its American superintendent was far more deeply disturbed in 1924 when Congress enacted the Japanese Exclusion Act. Fearing a "vicious race problem" he set about to recast the role of the western missionary from that of an officer to that of a "spiritual guide."[21]

In accord with its intensified nationalistic program, the Japanese Diet in April 1940 enacted the Religious Organization Control Act which recognized the legal rights of Christianity but imposed new regulations on Christian programs. Administrative leadership must reside in Japanese hands, and the state was empowered to prohibit offensive religious practices. To meet the new circumstances, Christian leaders from twenty Protestant missions met and projected the creation of the Church of Christ in the ecumenical body of Protestant missions in Japan. By March 1941 a constitution for this church was adopted, and Evangelical missions became an integral part of the Kyodan.

In December 1941 the Japanese air force rained destruction upon the American navy in Pearl Harbor, and the two nations went to war. Concerned lest their presence bring embarrassment and hardship upon Japanese Christians, the great majority of western missionaries left Japan within several months. A few, and Evangelicals among them, chose internment. The Japanese church was very small, but its loyalty to Christ made it suspect when Shinto and emperor worship were the symbols of the fanatical patriotism. The Church of Christ in Japan survived the disastrous war, and after 1946 the Evangelical United Brethren Church supported it with funds, and as requested, with personnel.

Before the war, Evangelicals initiated numerous programs in addition to the conventional ones in evangelism. In 1922 Tokyo Bible School became the successor of the training school. A Deaf Oral School, established in 1920, prospered and in 1926 was moved to an improved site adjacent to the Setagaya chapel. Evangelicals joined Canadian and American Methodists in the support of Acyama Gakuin for theological education. Aisenryo, a girls' orphanage, was enlarged for greater service. A venture was launched in Osaka to serve boat workers and their families. In 1935 the Boshi Home was dedicated in Koriyama, offering child care to employed mothers.[22]

Civil war plagued China and almost annually grew more ominous and destructive. For a period Hunan was the bloody battle ground between the contending armies, and Evangelical missions suffered successive despoliation. At times every semblance of law and order collapsed and banditry ruled. At times when there was some semblance of authority, Chinese paraded the streets, shrieking their hatred of foreigners, the missionaries, and the missions. In 1934 the superintendent reported that for the first time since the evacuation of 1927 the mission had possession of all its buildings. Earlier there had been sixty-five Evangelical missionaries in Hunan; by 1928 there were eight, and for a short time in 1935 there was only one.

The conflict in China took on a new face in July 1937 when Japanese troops began their invasion to "chastise China," for then the warring communist and nationalist forces joined to battle the invader. Japan won successive battles in China but in 1945 lost the war; at once the conflict between communists and nationalists was resumed and continued until Chiang Kai-shek was expelled from continental China.

Upon the Japanese invasion of China, Chinese by the millions fled to central and western provinces. In Hunan the mission ministered to uncounted numbers of refugees. In 1937 Evangelicals organized a China Conference. Within a year the hospital at Yushein was reduced to rubble, and the one in Liling was so vandalized that it was useless. The latter was given to the China Public Health Service, and its staff was transferred to the hospital in Tungjen. Social dislocation reduced enrollments in the schools by half. One missionary and her class fled Hunan for the safety of Hong Kong. In spite of bleak prospects four new churches were dedicated in 1939 and four in 1940. In the next years the destruction of properties increased, the armies of General Mao marched irresistibly southward, and American missionaries were reappointed to service elsewhere. Thus the China Mission was in a state of prostration and dismay in 1946 when the Evangelical United Brethren Church was formed.

In Africa

The enterprise in Wurkumland, Nigeria, became an official denominational mission in 1926. The preceding year a church had been dedicated in Bambur, where a school was begun and the endeavor to provide a written language was undertaken. For a people who had no written language and whose oral language lacked many of the concepts of Christian virtues such as forgiveness, love, and mercy, this was an arduous task, but it was accomplished. Following the success of the primary school at Bambur, similar schools were begun at Pero, Kerum, Gewere and Bunyan. The mission entered the eastern section of Wurkumland in 1936 when work was initiated at Bambuka.

What role in the mission might be entrusted to Africans? That some converts who discarded their idols and fetishes lapsed into their traditional ways is not as significant as that some did not. Among the latter were those who aspired to be messengers of the gospel they had come to treasure. About 1930 the first of these dedicated native Africans commenced to speak their Christian testimonies. Four years later some were sent to the training school of the Sudan United Mission at Gindiri. With this elementary training, these devoted evangelists went among their own people sharing the gospel with a persuasiveness the American missionary could not match.

In Wurkumland Africans suffered from disease as well as from ignorance and evil. The first dispensary in the area was opened in

1932. By 1935 a few selected Africans had received sufficient paramedical training to be licensed. After British regulations required the missionary appointee to spend six months in elementary medical training, a dispensary was established on each mission station.

While Nigeria was far removed from the battle fields of World War II, the mission was affected by the war. Support from America was reduced, communication with the mission was difficult, and the transportation of missionaries to Africa was hazardous. However, the foundations had been well laid and the work grew. During these years emerged a new sense of fraternity with adjacent missions, and by 1942 exploratory steps were taken toward a United African Church, the Ekkleaya Chicken Sudan.

In America

In 1922 the Evangelical Church maintained a thriving mission among Italians with centers in Kenosha, Wauwatosa, Racine, and Milwaukee. In 1929 the joy at the erection of a new chapel in Milwaukee was tempered by the death of the superintendent, the Rev. A. Guliani.[23] At the start the ministry of this mission was carried on in the Italian language, but by 1920 while the older generation clung to the native language, their children were clamoring for the English language in public worship. By 1931 the complete transition to English was accomplished at Wauwatosa, and the other centers soon followed. With this acceptance of the English language the need for an Italian mission was open to question. In 1935 the superintendent of the Madison-Milwaukee district of the Wisconsin Conference was appointed superintendent of the Italian Mission. With the Americanization of the Italian immigrants and with less need for language and citizenship classes, it was just a matter of time until all the mission congregations were absorbed into the Wisconsin Conference.

The Red Bird Mission among the mountain people of Kentucky prospered. New preaching places were found. Enrollment in the schools increased from 235 in 1923 to 374 in 1935. In the latter year 113 applicants were denied enrollment because facilities were lacking. The high school at Beverly in 1957 reported with understandable pride that of its 103 alumni, eighty-one had continued their education in colleges or universities.

A trained nurse came to Red Bird in 1923, and upon the arrival of a physician in 1927, plans were projected for a new hospital. On August 31, 1928, a frame, two-story hospital near Beverly was dedicated. Its services expanded with the arrival of a second physician in 1931. The programs along the Red Bird Creek suffered limitations and restraints when the Depression compelled the Missionary Society to reduce support to all its enterprises.

The prevalence of drunkenness, lawlessness, and gun-feuding among the mountaineers provided ample evidence of the need for the gospel. From Beverly the evangelists went to adjacent communities establishing first preaching places and then churches at Jack's Creek, Beech Fork, Mill Creek, Spring Creek, and Greasy Creek. By 1942 there were 422 members in these churches.

Other factors were also at work altering the culture and eliminating the isolation of the area. With the advent of radio, the Red Bird country was only a flick of the switch away from the largest cities and cultural centers of the nation. In 1920 railroad construction began, connecting Hyden with the timberlands near Jack's Creek. Public highways were built making the wider world more accessible. However, none of these engineering achievements eliminated the need for educational, medical, and evangelistic services along the Red Bird.

The Evangelical Church in 1925 was rallied by its leadership to erect a church in the nation's capital. The church leadership felt that a denomination with operations in thirty states and overseas as well should be represented in Washington with an appropriate church. What more suitable memorial could be devised to honor the labors of Jacob Albright? A campaign for $110,000 was launched, and on April 4, 1927, the cornerstone of the first unit of the Albright Memorial Church was laid.[24] Too soon this project encountered the harsh realities of the Depression, and enthusiasm and dollars dwindled. By 1930 the glamor had departed, and there was apprehension that sociological change would engulf the area where the church was located. That fear became a fact.

The Missionary Society felt immediately and painfully the paralyzing economic collapse in 1930, and its woes increased with the next several years. By 1932 its deficit vaulted to $164,255, and the board made the anguished decision that expenditures must be limited to income. To do this, overseas missionaries retiring or withdrawing from service would not be replaced and salaries would be reduced by fifty percent. The effect of this decision was shattering but was borne by the missionaries with magnificent courage and faith.[25] Some anticipated programs were dropped and some indefinitely postponed. A few programs in operation were discontinued, and all received less support from the missionary treasury. A few simple efforts were made to augment income, but in hard times extra collections are not bountiful. However, upon the improvement of the financial climate of the nation, the plight of the Missionary Society was relieved. The Youth Societies and the Woman's Missionary Society were generous donors, the latter in 1941 contributing $147,426, or thirty-nine percent of the total income. Funds now being available, new missionaries were appointed, missionary salaries were restored, and new and old mission programs more adequately supported.

Christian Education

The upgrading of the educational work of the church received guidance and support from the International Council of Religious Education which was organized in 1922. Further support came as denominational colleges and seminaries offered courses in religious education which exposed church workers who were in training to progressive ideas.

While the number of scholars on the Sunday school rosters was unparalleled, there were sobering realities. Only forty percent of them became church members. Too many of them, adolescents and adults, remained aloof from the church's worship service.

Though there was stalwart resistance, Sunday school literature was improved, and graded lessons were introduced to give children of comparable age the materials best adapted to their stage of development. In 1931 a brochure promoting improved Sunday school architecture and facilities was issued, and the *Evangelical Church School Hymnal* was published. In response to the emphasis upon teacher training, by 1934 the Evangelical Church "stood first in the number of credits earned in the Standard Leadership Training Curriculum."[26] Despite these developments, in the late 1930's Sunday school enrollment and attendance declined. In 1942 a four-year Church School Advance program was launched. While statistically its results were not impressive, it did result in a closer relationship between religious education and other agencies of the church such as missions and evangelism.[27]

Conventions were held with some regularity, occasions generating enthusiasm and offering instruction. The one in 1936 with 1,253 registered delegates was the largest the church had known. By 1942 Annual Conferences were promoting summer camps for youth and for younger children. During the Christmas holiday 1940 the first Evangelical Student Conference was assembled, drawing several hundred college youth together for fellowship, inspiration, instructions, and the discussion of contemporary social and moral issues.

The inherited interest in catechetical instruction expressed itself in 1922 in the resolve to publish a junior catechism for children, a handbook of religion for adolescents, and a statement of beliefs for adults. Bishop Spreng's *What Evangelicals Believe* was the fulfillment of the last, but appeals for the catechism continued into the 1940's. This concern for catechetical materials was neither unanimous nor uniform.

The Evangelical League of Christian Endeavor became the denominational youth society of the church in 1922, its work directed toward four aspects of the Christian life: worship, instruction, service, and fellowship and recreation. Its services were pointed toward five age-level groups. In conventions held jointly with the Sunday schools and through conference "unions," its interests were promoted.[28]

In 1930 the Albright Brotherhood was organized to draw the men of the church together for fellowship and service; to lead them to a better understanding of scripture, the church, and evangelism; and to stimulate their interests and participation in ethical, community, national, and international issues. The Brotherhood was made a unit within the Board of Religious Education, but its beginning was without popular enthusiasm, and through 1946 it never developed a dynamic vitality.

Following a two-year study the Board of Religious Education was created to supersede the boards for the Sunday school and the KLCE. Its supervision was extensive, the list of sixteen areas beginning with the Sunday school and concluding with ushers in local churches.[29] Subsequently there were changes in the personnel of the board, and other agencies were brought under its supervision: the Brotherhood in 1930 and the Board of Education in 1934. In 1934 the Board of Religious Education was renamed the Board of Christian Education.

HIGHER EDUCATION

The concerns of the Evangelical Church for Christian higher education found expression in the Board of Education. By its authority Annual Conferences were discouraged from establishing schools without adequate preparation and finances, and established schools were encouraged to employ as teachers "persons of good religious and moral character . . . . who believe in the Christian religion" and to provide students with opportunities for religious education and inspiration.[30] Beyond these exhortations, this board was the agency to which the school administrator could come to confer on matters, financial or otherwise, involving the church and the school. It promoted Education Day, a Sunday on which the schools and their needs were presented in the churches. It upheld the claims of higher education at the formation of the denominational budget. In 1934 the Board of Education was discontinued, but its functions were given the Board of Christian Education.

The colleges of the church were scattered geographically from eastern Pennsylvania to western Iowa. Schuylkill College, now a four-year accredited school, was located in Reading, Pennsylvania. Plans for the merging of Albright College, Myerstown, with Schuylkill were retarded by the litigation of the Evangelical Congregational Church, but following the verdict of the court against them, the plans were effected quickly. In 1929 students, resources, and the school's name were brought to Reading, and the merged school became Albright College. During the Depression funds were in short supply and due to World War II enrollment declined, but in spite of these adversities Albright College emerged to develop a sound and strong academic program commanding respect and loyalty inside and outside the Evangelical Church.

Northwestern College, Naperville, Illinois, became North Central College in 1926. Enrollment diminished during the Depression and war years but in 1946 stood at an unprecedented high. In 1942 fifty-three percent of its students were from Evangelical homes and churches. The school recognized this denominational loyalty. The Depression necessitated stringent economizing measures, but in 1936 a modest seventy-fifth anniversary campaign was launched. The generosity of the Pfeiffer family, which over a decade brought $690,000 to North Central, was gratefully and publicly acknowledged. Over the quarter century ending in 1946 thirty acres of land was acquired, a field house, a dormitory, and an auditorium were erected, and a president's residence was given the college.

During the Depression the survival of Western Union College, Le Mars, Iowa, was precarious. The crisis was met by spartan measures to reduce expenditures and thus faculty salaries fell abruptly. To augment the treasury new measures were introduced to promote enrollment. Summer sessions were scheduled, and self-help programs for students were initiated—the manufacturing of venetian blinds and the canning of vegetables and fruits. Following the hardships of the Depression and World War II, there were evidences of fresh vitality. The college was awarded membership in the North Central Association of Colleges, and a physical education building was erected. By 1946 Western Union College had not simply survived its ordeals, but it had demonstrated a dedication to Christian learning that augured well for its future. In 1948 its name was changed to Westmar College.

There were two schools for ministerial education in the Evangelical Church in 1922. The Evangelical School of Theology was legally affiliated with Albright College. In 1941 inquiry was made into the possibility of making it an independent corporation, but the state's financial requirements were so high that the inquiry was halted. Enrollment in the school was small, but its academic program was sound. In 1934 the basic course leading to graduation was extended from two years to three.

At Evangelical Theological Seminary, Naperville, Illinois, from 1922 to 1927 there were summer sessions which were the threshold leading from the two-year course to the three-year course. As the latter was established, two additional teachers joined the faculty. After fifteen years of discussion the diploma course for students without a college degree was abandoned in 1947. The curriculum was strengthened by the addition of a field work program in 1929 and a clinical training program in 1936. The curricular developments were inspired in part by the endeavor to provide a more currently acceptable professional education, but also by the desire to achieve academic accreditation. In 1938 Evangelical Theological Seminary became an accredited member of the American Association of Theological Schools.

In the Evangelical Church where the seminaries were the agencies of associated Annual Conferences and not the agencies of

General Conference, it was the seminaries which took the initiative and bore much of the burden for advancing ministerial standards. Some conferences were more diffident and lethargic than others, yet despite them there was marked and significant improvement in the academic preparation for ministry in the church.

The Publishing House

In the Evangelical Church in 1922 there were two publishing houses, one in Cleveland and one in Harrisburg; there were two major denominational publications, the *Evangelical Messenger* and the *Christliche Botschafter*. Recommendations to relocate the Cleveland house to Madison, Wisconsin, or Kansas City, Missouri, were considered but rejected. Though the building in Cleveland on Woodland Avenue was old and in a deteriorating section of the city, it was kept until 1928 when a building at 1900 Superior Avenue was purchased. The frigid blasts of the Depression were felt most keenly at the Cleveland house which in addition to diminished revenues bore the heavy indebtedness from its relocation. In 1930 Roy H. Stettler was elected publisher for the Harrisburg and Cleveland houses. With the national economy still grim in 1934, General Conference after somber debate voted 158 to 70 to sell the property in Cleveland and to consolidate church publications in Harrisburg. The editorial offices were promptly moved to Harrisburg, but the Missionary and Christian Education offices remained as tenants in the Superior Avenue building until 1946.

The Harrisburg house emerged from the Depression bowed but not broken, and as the economy brightened, business increased. In 1938 the building was enlarged, and new equipment was purchased. That year too was hailed as "the first million dollar year" when the gross business amount to $1,276,169.[31] The debt on the Cleveland house was assumed at Harrisburg. Out of the profits in 1942 $60,000 was paid on that obligation, $44,500 was given the Superannuation Fund, and $60,000 was distributed among the Annual Conferences. For years the *Christliche Botschafter* had suffered a continuing loss of patronage. In 1947, after 110 years of distinguished services, it was discontinued. When it expired, it was the oldest Protestant, German-language religious periodical in the United States with an unbroken record of publication.

Developing Social Awareness

Evangelicals in 1922 lived in a nation in which moods of disillusionment, disappointment, hopefulness, and even anger were strangely commingled, but within a few years the prospects of fabulous economic prosperity were obliterated by the Depression.

This church perpetuated its traditional denunciation of slavery and intemperance, but beyond that its exhortations were at best only conventional. It cautioned against the social dance and degrading moving pictures. It invoked the "spirit of the Master" to dispell the grievous tensions between capital and labor, and it prayed that the specter of international war be dissolved.[32]

But there were churchmen convinced that the older pietistic, individualistic posture was inadequate for a new day in which the church must play a more muscular role in the social and political order. For them the popular American isolationism toward world affairs was both false and unchristian.[33] While some concurred that compulsory military training be enacted, many opposed it. Annual Conferences passed resolutions calling for the abolition of war as an instrument for settling international differences. General Conference in 1926 declared its opposition to military training in colleges. Petitions were circulated in camps and on college campuses in the early 1930's, committing signers to pacifism. Selective Service became a law in 1940, and the next year the surprise Japanese attack on Pearl Harbor made war an inescapable reality. With none of the exuberance so apparent in 1917, the Evangelical Church did what was held to be Christian duty—providing chaplains, distributing Bibles and religious literature, raising money for war service agencies, and endeavoring to keep in touch with its men in service. This church held that its conscientious objectors were entitled to the same exemptions from military service which were accorded members of the traditional peace churches. In 1942 there were thirty of these in camps, and the church contributed toward their maintenance.[34]

With the Depression the church was brought face to face with the grim domestic social realities of mass unemployment and its attendant agonies. Individual congregations, with episcopal blessings, began to study the unemployment situations in their own localities. In 1930 a new Board of Public Morals was formed for the denomination, but an appropriation for it was overlooked. There was quibbling about supervision and parliamentary procedures, and nothing happened for four years. But in 1934 its voice and that of General Conference were decisive: "Men must be converted not simply to a personal faith in Jesus Christ, but to the program of Jesus as a method of social reconstruction."[35] The bitter experience of recent years was held to be a judgment upon the American social order, and the church's support was declared for minimum wage laws, programs of profit sharing, old age pensions, and government ownership of natural resources. Whether such expressions would have won the concurrence of the whole church may be questioned, but those of this persuasion grew in numbers.

In 1938 the Board of Public Morals was supplanted by the Board of Christian Social Action. Convinced that the perception of injustice, exploitation, and economic deprivation carried with it the duty to struggle against them, this board promoted the discussion of economic and social issues at ministerial meetings, preaching on these issues, consideration of biblical light on these problems, cooperation with other denominations in facing them, and the support of legislation to resolve them. The board showered the church with literature. Upon America's declaration of war in 1941 it was the agency serving the church in ministry to Evangelicals in the armed forces and in conscientious objectors' camps. It participated in the National Study Conference on a Just and Durable Peace in 1942. In this year, also, an emerging issue was faced without equivocation: "A Christian society will oppose every discrimination against racial groups."[36]

By 1946 the Evangelical call to personal commitment to Christ remained unchanged, but the involvements of that commitment were described in broader social terms than ever before. There was none of the facile, idealistic optimism which had found expression in much of the liberal theology of the previous generation in projected plans to establish the Kingdom of God on earth. Out of the deep anguish of the Depression years had come a more profound understanding of the worth and dignity of every human being whose right to justice was God-given.

During these years the benevolent homes continued and expanded their ministry in relieving human needs. Ebenezer Orphans' Home, later renamed Flat Rock Orphans' Home, Flat Rock, Ohio, was the only one to minister to children and youth exclusively, though briefly in 1926 when Ebenezer Old People's

Home in New York was discontinued, there were a few of the aged at Flat Rock. The Pacific Old People's Home, Burbank, California, continued its services. The Philadelphia Manor was enmeshed in financial difficulties in the 1930's but by 1942 had surmounted them. The Lewisburg Home in Pennsylvania served both children and the aged. With careful administration it weathered the Depression years, though not without anxieties. Haven Hubbard Home, New Carlisle, Indiana, was launched in 1923 with a fine new building and a massive debt. Residents increased in number, but the indebtedness decreased far more slowly, remaining at $112,900 in 1942. Western Old People's Home, Cedar Falls, Iowa, was exempted from dire financial problems thanks to generous donors, particularly the Pfeiffer family, and its residents and facilities increased.

In Germany and Switzerland there were also benevolent institutions including: old peoples' homes, rest, and vacation homes. Economic necessity led to the disposal of some of these, but others, such as the ones in Honau, Germany, and Interlaken, Switzerland, outlived financial panics and the war years to continue their compassionate ministry.

The Deaconess Society in 1922 stood on the brink of unprecedented expansion. In 1923 in St. Paul, Minnesota, plans were under way for the West Side Hospital, and the next year a hospital was acquired in Brooklyn, New York.[37] In 1924 Globe Hospital, Freeport, Illinois, and Allen Memorial Hospital, Waterloo, Iowa, were received to join those already under the supervision of the society. Finding the hospital and home in Chicago too small and inadequate, the society launched a campaign in 1923 to gather $500,000 for new facilities. These were dedicated in 1927.

The Depression plunged the Deaconess Society into extreme financial straits. The Monroe Hospital in Wisconsin was transferred to the care of the local Evangelical church. The hospital in Waterloo, Iowa went into receivership, and initial steps were taken which led to the transfer of the one in Freeport, Illinois. The gravest situation centered in Chicago when the society failed to make interest payments to note and bond holders. The laments and ire of the latter, who were largely Evangelical people, were brought to General Conference in 1938 which recommended, as the only alternative to bankruptcy proceedings, a final settlement with the investors on the basis of twenty-five cents on the dollar.[38] If ninety-five percent of the bond holders agreed to this solution, general church treasuries would provide the money needed. Accompanied by much complaint, this agreement was reached, and in 1940 the hospital was closed.

No one has ever challenged the purposes, motivations, or services of the Deaconess Society, and its demise may be attributed to external factors as well as the injudicious internal operations of the society. The American cultural climate was not conducive to nurture the enlistment of many young women. Perhaps the Evangelical Church was neither of the right kind nor of the right size to warrant a deaconess program.

While the deaconess movement collapsed in the American church, in Germany and Switzerland it increased in numbers and services. By 1938 there were 647 deaconesses in Germany and another 159 in Switzerland. The Evangelical Church in Europe has never ceased to speak with prideful appreciation of the skillful, selfless services of this corps of women who in hospitals, on parishes, and in general social services demonstrated the kind of life that seeks to minister, rather than be ministered to.

THE SUPERANNUATION FUND

Upon the formation of the Evangelical Church in 1922 former United Evangelicals raised $125,000 for the Superannuation Fund after which the clergy, regardless of their antecedent affiliation, shared alike. The drive for $500,000 for the fund in 1926 was followed by the Depression years, but despite the hard times, in 1934 beneficiaries received ten dollars per year of active ministerial service. To aid the fund that year congregations were asked to receive an offering annually on Pioneer Day for it and to pay three percent of the minister's salary toward his pension. Upon improvement in the nation's economy, in 1936 a Jubilee Campaign was initiated to gather $100,000 for the fund.

After three years of study the pension program was substantially revised and thereafter administered through three departments or plans. The Superannuation Fund Plan continued the provisions of the previous program for clergy entering the itinerancy before January 1, 1943. The Ministers' Reserve Pension Plan was for clergy received into the itinerancy after January 1, 1943. In this, each minister made annual payments matched by those of his congregation, and upon his retirement at sixty-eight his benefits were determined by the payments made to his account during the years of his service. The Plan for Lay Employees was for the full-time, unordained employees of the church and its churches. In this, too, there were annual payments by employees and the employing agencies. In 1946 there were 2,712 members in the three pension plans. There were recommendations that the annual premiums be raised and the retirement age lowered, but in view of the prospect of union with the Church of the United Brethren in Christ these proposals were deferred.

AGENCIES AND ADMINISTRATION

Among Evangelicals, evangelism was a word that never failed to please though definitions and practices of evangelism ranged over a wide spectrum. It was important in the Forward Movement and the missionary programs, and increasingly its role in religious education was recognized. A proposal to elect a bishop specifically to oversee evangelism was not supported, but in 1926 a denominational Commission of Evangelism was created, and the Rev. B. R. Wiener was elected its secretary. Thereafter while a few conferences reported instances of "old time, evangelical evangelism," many more related the fruitfulness of newer measures such as visitation evangelism and "special meetings" held during the Lenten and Pentecostal seasons. In 1930 the Evangelical Church joined other denominations in the celebration of the nineteen-hundredth anniversary of the first Pentecost.

Upon the death of the secretary, while the Commission continued, its leadership devolved upon the bishops and remained there until 1942 when the secretaryships of evangelism and Christian education were combined. Beginning in 1934 quadrennial evangelistic themes were promoted and numerical goals for church membership and attendance were named.

Elected to the episcopal office in 1922 were Bishops S. C. Breyfogel, S. P. Spreng, L. H. Seager, M. T. Maze, J. F. Dunlap, and G. Heinmiller (for Europe). A bishop for Europe was dropped in 1934, and at this time the number of bishops of America was reduced to four. While the bishops served the entire church, an area system was adopted so that a particular bishop had supervision of a specified area—Eastern, Central, Northwestern, or Southwestern.

In 1922 the Comission on Finance prepared and recommended

a denominational budget, proposing appropriations to the twenty-one agencies and institutions of the church and apportionments for the Annual Conferences. With the Depression its work became more crucial as, for example, in 1932 when only thirty-two percent of the conference apportionments were paid. After a quadrennium of study, an Administrative Council was created in 1938 with appropriate subordinate councils for the Annual Conferences and the local churches. The General Administrative Council continued the work of the Commission on Finance and in addition was assigned the supervision of denominational life, the integration of programs, the promotion of stewardship, and the counseling of institutions and agencies. In the event of an "emergency" which could be declared by the bishop, the council was empowered to act for the General Conference.

Some changes in church life were interesting but of no great significance. For example, presiding elders became district superintendents in 1930. At the same time the rule limiting a pastor's service on the same parish to seven consecutive years was stricken.

The initiative of one Annual Conference in organizing a historical society led to a denominational society whose modest collection was granted a home in the publishing house in Harrisburg. In 1927 the collection was moved to Albright College where it remained until 1946. The most significant activity of the Historical Society was to recommend the preparation and publication of a denominational history, and in 1942 the *History of the Evangelical Church* by Raymond W. Albright was published.

ECUMENICITY AND CHURCH UNION

From its beginning the Evangelical Church participated in all the conventional interchurch agencies and movements promoting missions, religious education, evangelism, and a deeper understanding of Christian faith, order, life, and work. On the American scene in the 1930's cooperation and mutual understanding issued in a number of church unions—the American Lutheran Church in 1930, the Evangelical and Reformed Church in 1934, and the Methodist Church in 1939.

The merger of the Canada Conference with the United Church of Canada was taken under advisement, but no decision was made until after 1946. This deferral is attributed first to the pressing financial problems which demanded attention after 1930 and second, and more important, to the division of sentiment in the Canada Conference on the merger.

The United Brethren were no strangers to Evangelicals, for each had learned to know the other over many years and through many events ranging from the exchange of fraternal delegates at General Conferences to cooperation in common enterprises in local communities. The proposal by United Brethren Bishop William Bell in 1926 that the two denominations embark upon union conversations was received graciously and referred to the Commission on Church Federation and Union.[39] That nothing significant occurred in the quadrennium was not due to a lack of sympathetic diligence, but to the considered judgment that until the Evangelical Church was freed from the litigation by Evangelical Congregationalists it would not be judicious to enter any such negotiations. Evangelical Bishop John S. Stamm announced to the United Brethren General Conference in 1929 that the hindering obstacles had been removed. However, at that juncture the United Brethren were beginning negotiations with the German Reformed Church and the Evangelical Synod. These collapsed without accomplishments in 1931. The constructive consideration of union by Evangelicals and United Brethren was initiated after Evangelical Bishop Matthew T. Maze announced to United Brethren in 1933 the readiness of his church to embark upon union negotiations. The announcement won an immediate acceptance. The executive committee of the commissions of both churches met in February and July 1934, declaring their commitment to church union and to the resolution of problems thwarting it.

During the next four years commissions, committees, and subcommittees met on thirty-four occasions and painstakingly wrestled with many diverse subjects: faith, polity, ministry, pensions, programs, and institutions. In 1938 the Evanglical General Conference heard the recommendations of the commissioners that there be a pension fund which all itinerants must join, that some consolidation be effected among the colleges and that the number of seminaries be reduced to two, and that foreign and home missions be consolidated under a single society. While in Christian education there were no vital points of difference, in the publishing interests there were "serious barriers in the way of an immediate consolidation."[40] The commissioners expressed confidence that God's Spirit would lead to the successful consummation of the unitive efforts, and a Basis of Union was promised for presentation by 1942.

The Basis was readied for submission by February 1942. The name of the communion resulting from the merger would be the Evangelical United Brethren Church. For it the Confession of Faith (United Brethren) and the Articles of Faith (Evangelical) were continued intact, and a single order of ministry, the eldership, would serve it. Home and foreign missions would be united under a single missionary society. Local church properties would be held in trust for the denomination exempting such former United Evangelical churches which received no financial aid from denominational treasuries.

The Basis of Union was presented to the Evangelical General Conference in October 1942. Its advocates held: "The union will result in a greater spiritual power . . . effect a desirable economy . . . there will be an improved life for the church . . . there will be augmented influence . . . there will be larger resources."[41] General Conference overwhelmingly approved the Basis, 226 to 6. Subsequently twenty-one of the twenty-four Annual Conferences unanimously approved it. The aggregate vote in all these conferences was 2,174 for and 58 against. Thereafter further action was contingent upon United Brethren balloting in General Conference, Annual Conferences, and local churches. The next General Conference in the Evangelical church, and what was destined to be the last, met in November 1946 in Johnstown, Pennsylvania.

T he Evangelical United Brethren Church came into being November 16, 1946, in the First United Brethren Church in Johnstown, Pennsylvania. During the preceding three days the General Conferences of Evangelicals and United Brethren convened in separate sessions to put their houses in order for the more significant event which had drawn them to Johnstown.

At nine o'clock Saturday morning, November 16, the delegates of both churches gathered in the sanctuary. Infused with the high spirit of the occasion they sang with new commitment Ernest W. Shurtleff's hymn, "Lead On, O King Eternal" as the bishops processed to the chancel where Bishop J. S. Stamm introduced the presiding officer, Bishop A. R. Clippinger, who read the formal declaration of union creating the Evangelical United Brethren Church.[1] In confirmation of this the assemblage heartily sang "Blest Be the Tie That Binds." The first act of the new church was the celebration of Holy Communion. In these moments of pageantry and worship, following thirteen years of persistent prayers and patient efforts, church union was accomplished, and the Evangelical United Brethren Church with 4,702 organized churches and 705,102 members began its life. Extraordinary in the record of church unions in America, this one was achieved without the loss of a single congregation from either antecedent denomination.

THE EVANGELICAL UNITED BRETHREN CHURCH, 1946–1968

FAITH AND GENERAL ORGANIZATION

The creedal posture of the Evangelical United Brethren Church was expressed in the continuation, unamended, of the United Brethren Confession and the Evangelical Articles of Faith.[2] In 1958 the bishops were instructed to unify the two creedal documents. With care and the assistance of selected denominational theologians this was undertaken. The new Confession of Faith, consisting of sixteen articles, was submitted to General Conference in 1962 and unanimously adopted.[3] In substance it did not vary from its predecessors, but every endeavor was made to clarify and to find living language to match convictions.

The Evangelical United Brethren Church, like its antecedents, was a connectional church, that is, a cooperative endeavor in which elected leaders, pastors, conferences, and church members were bound together for common concerns under the *Discipline*.

The government of this church was vested in conferences on three levels, Quarterly, Annual, and General, a structure which Evangelicals and United Brethren had employed from their beginning. Councils of Administration were created for promotional and pragmatic purposes for the local churches, the conferences and the general church.

In 1946 the Revs. J. S. Stamm, J. B. Showers, G. E. Epp, A. R. Clippinger, E. W. Praetorius, F. L. Dennis, C. H. Stauffacher, V. O. Weidler, and I. D. Warner were elected to the episcopacy, and though each was a bishop of the whole church, each was assigned to one of the nine episcopal areas for immediate oversight. In this church, as in its predecessors, the episcopate was not a separate ministerial order but an administrative responsibility, quadrennially awarded to elders elected to the office. With the retirement of two in 1950, the number of bishops was reduced to seven, and the following episcopal areas were established: Eastern, East Central, Central, West Central, Northwestern, Southwestern, and Pacific. These areas were maintained to 1968.

In addition to their conventional pastoral and administrative responsibilities, with increasing frequency the bishops were called upon to express positions on numerous and various subjects such as faith healing, glossalalia, group ministry, moral rearmament, and intercommunion. They were called upon to clarify the use of certain rites. In the *Discipline* there was one ritual for infant baptism and next to it another for child dedication. In 1962 it was recommended that the latter be deleted because it was "not a part of the historical and theological heritage.⁴ The issue was remanded to the bishops who then advised the continuance of both rituals. On the subject of confirmation they counseled that the term be used prudently, not as an apostolic rite conveying spiritual virtue but as the occasion for personal dedication of faith in Jesus Christ.

After a four-year study, in 1962 the committee which had been appointed to appraise and streamline the episcopal office made its report. It described the bishop as a defender of the faith, an able and prophetic preacher, a chief pastor, and a man of four books—the *Bible,* the *Hymnal,* the *Discipline,* and Robert's *Rules of Order.* While advocating that episcopal membership be continued on all major boards, it urged that bishops be relieved of chairmanships on board subcommittees and institutional committees and that the bishops endeavor to work more closely with conference Councils of Administration and superintendents. Bishops were encouraged to arrange, at their convenience, a four-week vacation period annually.⁵ In actuality the report did little either to diminish or refine episcopal responsibilities.

Excepting the editorial offices for the *Telescope-Messenger* and *Builders*—the adult and youth periodicals—which were in the Harrisburg publishing house, the general offices of the church came to be located in the United Brethren Building in Dayton. In 1946 provision was made for associate secretaries in the major boards and associate editors for the church publications to achieve equitable representation from the two antecedent denominations, and in 1950 the future policy was announced "to discontinue the positions of . . . associate officers as death, retirement or disabilities occur."⁶ Optional retirement at sixty-eight with pension privileges after ten years of service was awarded general officers in 1954, and eight years later the retirement age was lowered to sixty-five.⁷ A new regulation in 1958 disqualified any elder from election to general office who became seventy-two years of age "within six months after the opening day of General Conference."⁸ The proposal four years earlier to establish the retirement age of bishops at sixty-eight was defeated.

THE MINISTRY AND ITS PREPARATION

Through its years the Evangelical United Brethren Church endeavored simultaneously to lift ministerial standards and to enlist an adequate ministerial supply. On occasion these goals conflicted. Its ministry was of a single order, that of elder, which was attained by ordination.

Among the prescribed ministerial duties were the ones instructing pastors that "children of believing parents are entitled to Christian baptism"[9] and that children nine or ten years of age were to receive instruction, be led into a personal acceptance of Jesus Christ, guided in Christian living, and recommended for church membership. Under specified circumstances, provisions were made for affiliate and nonresident church membership.

Despite expressed dissent, the office of Quarterly Conference preacher was not continued in the Evangelical United Brethren Church. Those who had been in this status were directed to choose whether to remain in it or to take the required steps to qualify for the conference license.

The qualifications for the candidate for the ministry were not substantially different from what they had been in the two churches before union.[10] Nor was there anything new in the procedure that followed: recommendation by the Quarterly Conference; examination and after an approving vote the issuance of license by the Annual Conference; one year of probationary service during which the course of study was pursued. Upon the fulfillment of the educational requirements, successfully passing a doctrinal examination, and an approving vote of two-thirds of the ministers of the Annual Conference, the probationer was qualified for ordination as an elder. The proposal in 1962 that the laity be permitted to vote on the candidacy for ordination was defeated.

Related to the consideration of the ministry are two matters that deserve mention. First, in this church as in its predecessors, the church membership of the minister was in the local church to which he had been appointed. Second, before church union United Brethren had ordained women, and while the united church made no specific provision for their licensing and ordination,[11] the status of those who had been ordained was not impaired. In the Evangelical United Brethren Church the ordination of women never became a controversial issue, but in 1950 it was referred to the General Council of Administration for study. The council passed the reference to the Board of Christian Education which in 1962 issued a murky conclusion: "Whereas the Discipline (Par. 354) may be interpreted to include women: therefore, be it resolved that we continue to accept the intent of Paragraph 354 . . . ."[12] The current discussion of the ordination of women in many denominations no doubt gave the motivation for the recommendation of this study. In several instances women were ordained in the Evangelical United Brethren Church, but these isolated instances neither provoked any recorded objections nor inspired any generally accepted practice.

In 1946 a General Commission on Ministerial Training was created to study the ministerial needs of the church, to prepare the course of study for the licentiates, and to give guidance to the Conference Commissions on Ministerial Training. The latter were charged with counseling with probationers enroute to ordination, soliciting from college offices reports on them and their record, and recruiting candidates for the ministry. Since some were unhappy at the requirement of two years of college study before ordination, it was ruled that "in rare instances exceptions" could be made to this academic requirement.[13]

Before 1950 a manual was produced for the guidance of conference commissions as well as explanatory pamphlets and enrollment forms for the candidates for the ministry. In this the helpfulness of the Federal Council of Churches Commission on the Ministry was freely acknowledged. Due to a growing anxiety at the inadequate ministerial supply, in 1950 conferences were authorized to issue temporary licenses to those district superintendents deemed useful in supplying parishes that otherwise would be pastorless, to license older persons who could not meet the academic requirements, and to ordain seminarians upon graduation without the year of probationary service. These measures reflected the crisis of those years: on the one hand the denomination strove for higher ministerial standards, on the other it needed pastors for its churches. At this time the General Commission on Ministerial Training operated under the supervision of the Board of Christian Education which appointed the commissioners, its associate secretary being one of them.

In 1946 there were three theological schools in the denomination: Evangelical School of Theology, constitutionally affiliated with Albright College in Reading, Bonebrake Theologial Seminary in Dayton, and Evangelical Theological Seminary in Naperville. Following a study initiated to examine the church's operations in its schools, the Board of Christian Education in 1950 recommended the consolidation of the three theological schools. The trustees of the seminary in Illinois did not concur with this recommendation, but in Pennsylvania where the circumstances and the prospects were very different, it was received favorably.

After 1946 Bonebrake Seminary gathered funds to increase the faculty and broaden and strengthen the academic program. The proposal to locate the consolidated schools at Dayton was seen as a "movement born of God,"[14] and in anticipation of its consummation a financial campaign was proposed. After a year of negotiations, in December 1952 committees from the schools in Reading and Dayton signed the contract of union, joining the Evangelical School of Theology and Bonebrake Theological Seminary on the Dayton campus, and the new school, United Theological Seminary, began its life July 1, 1954. Before that day a new library had been erected, and in 1959 the campaign was launched which came to its fruition in the dedication of the Breyfogel Chapel on this campus. Subsequently Roberts Hall, a dormitory, was built.

Meanwhile at Evangelical Seminary the academic program was strengthened and new facilities were built. In 1947 college graduation was made a requirement for enrollment, additions were made to the faculty, and the office of dean was inaugurated. In a joint venture with North Central College, the College and Seminary Library was erected in 1954. In 1958 a dormitory, Kimmel Hall, was built, and in 1967 the Academic Center was dedicated.

Enrollments at the denominational seminaries increased with almost annual regularity. A recommendation to abolish territorial lines for student solicitation was denied, and in 1954 specified conferences were allocated to each school with a joint territory of five conferences in the southwest which would be open to student solicitation by both schools. Concern for the improvement of professional and academic training found expression in both seminaries. At Dayton in 1958 matriculants with low college grades were admitted only on probation; faculty appointment was made contingent upon the completion of doctoral study, and in 1960 a Master's program was initiated. At Naperville the basic course was refined and intensified by the restructuring of the curriculum into four fields of study and the initiation of an intern program. The libraries of both seminaries were the beneficiaries of the Sealantic Fund, administered by the American Association of Theological Schools, enlarging the quantity and improving the quality of the book collections. Both seminaries entered cooperative educational programs with neighboring schools, and at both in 1966 the Master of Divinity degree supplanted the previous Bachelor of Divinity degree.

The Commission on Ministerial Training received new status in 1954 when it was granted representation on the Councils of Administration and in 1958 when the general commission became a board. But regardless of status, the inadequate ministerial supply continued to be a constant problem. Over the church in 1957 ninety-two parishes were left "to be supplied" because there were not sufficient ministers. In 1958 the loss in the ministerial ranks of the church was reported as 216, as over against the addition of 137 by ordination.[15] In these circumstances, renewed measures were undertaken to promote vocational enlistment. The modest results, small as they were, together with the increasing practice in the 1960's to "yoke" congregations somewhat diminished the anxiety about ministerial supply.

MISSIONARY DEVELOPMENT: IN THE WORLD

The year before the Evangelical United Brethren Church was created the armaments of World War II ceased their rain of terror and death. Technology had produced fleeter planes and deadlier bombs, and the devastation on both sides of battle lines was stupendous. The combined civilian and military death toll was placed at 22,060,000, and the direct military costs of the conflict were estimated to be $1,116,000,000,000. Victory celebrations in the conquering nations hailed the advent of peace, but too soon it became apparent that cessation of hostilities was not in itself peace. In the violence of war the world had become embittered and brutalized, and in the next years violent incidents periodically erupted. In 1945 the United Nations Organization was created to cope with international tensions. The United States in 1947 launched the Marshall Plan and in the following years dedicated thirteen billion dollars to reconstruction efforts. Our one world became the theater for the contention of two ideological partisans separated by curtains—sometimes of iron, sometimes of concrete, sometimes of bamboo—and a cold war ensued between them.

Ignorance, superstition, and want held a large part of the world in their thralldom while, at the same time in other parts of the world sophisticated technology and prosperity attained unprecedented heights. "Have not" people, believing themselves victimized by colonial powers and systems, became assertive, demanding, and ultimately politically independent. Not infrequently these new nations were ill prepared either by experience, training, or resources to fulfill the requirements of their new status. Ugly racism and provincial and tribal loyalties only added to the turbulence. In the Orient it was Indian versus Pakistani, in the Near East it was Jew versus Arab, and in Africa it was black versus white and even tribe versus tribe.

To oversee and promote the Christian testimony in a world so needy and anguished the Board of Missions operated through three divisions: the Department of World Missions, the Department of Home Missions and Church Extension, and the Department of Women's Service. The latter was the denominational Women's Society for World Service which while operating under its own constitution was an integral element of the board. It worked with and through conference branches and local societies. Locally in addition to the organization for adults, younger women were organized in Christian Service Guilds, younger girls in the Girls' Missionary Guilds, children in Mission Bands, and smaller children in the Little Heralds. In local churches wishing to unify the adult missionary society with other auxiliaries, a unified plan was offered. During twenty-two years through the publication and dissemination of missionary literature, through the promotion of the missionary cause, and not least important through the collection of money for missions the Women's Society for World Service rendered an uncalculated and incalculable ministry.

The Department of World Missions gave support or superintendence, or both, in diverse places overseas. In the Orient, West Indies, and South America, operations were carried on either through cooperation with other denominations or through national churches. Only in Sierra Leone, Germany, and Switzerland were there Evangelical United Brethren Annual Conferences.

The bomb dropped on Hiroshima destroyed the city and annihilated sixty percent of its people. There quickly followed the Japanese surrender on August 14, 1945. For a nation accustomed to a singular devotion to state and emperor the defeat was a shattering experience, but with prudent guidance a democratic constitution was adopted in 1947, and Japan proclaimed and demonstrated its friendship for the United States.

Evangelical and United Brethren activities had centered largely in the Tokyo and Kobe areas, but by 1946 all were integral parts of the United Church of Christ of Japan. At the invitation of the Japanese church, Dr. Paul S. Mayer returned to Tokyo, offering his counsel to help alleviate its crucial needs. Several other missionaries also returned for a short time. As the work of the Japanese church grew, new missionaries were solicited from the Evangelical United Brethren church, and by 1968 there were twelve of them in Japan, most engaged in educational enterprises such as kindergartens, middle schools, or specialized instruction.

During the quadrennium ending in December 1965 from general and restricted funds World Missions gave $629,288 toward the support of the Christian missionary enterprise in Japan.[16] Administrators have noted that following the changed ecclesiastical pattern in Japan and the departure of older career missionaries who had personalized missionary endeavors, there emerged in the American church a more detached and diffident interest in the Christian witness in Japan.

After the defeat of Japan in 1945, civil war broke out with fresh fury in China and, abetted with military supplies from communist allies, Mao Tse-tung's armies drove inexorably southward. The national government, surfeited with inefficiency, incompetence, and corruption, was defeated on the battle fields and ultimately abandoned the mainland for refuge on Taiwan. The conquests of Mao spelled first the isolation and then the disappearance of the promising Christian mission which had been nurtured through fifty years.

In China by 1946 Evangelical United Brethren operations were affiliated with the United Church of Christ, and twelve of its missionaries were there. With the continuing successes of the Red armies these were either retired to the United States or reassigned to service in Japan or the Philippines. As Chinese refugees poured into Hong Kong, a missionary was appointed to the staff of the True Light School in that British Crown Colony. In 1950, for the first time since 1900, this church had no missionaries in China. What has happened to the hospitals, the schools, the churches, and their members may only be surmised. After 1950 Evangelical United Brethren operations continued only in Hong Kong and there under the auspices of the United Church; in 1968 there were three American appointees ministering in that bustling, refugee-packed city.

In 1946 the Philippines acquired national independence, but independence brought neither domestic peace nor prosperity to the new nation. Open and brutal political tensions have periodically erupted with loud allegations of corruption and despotism; the needs of the masses remain unmet.

In 1948 the Evangelical United Brethren joined several other churches in reorganizing the former ecumenical structure to form the United Church of Christ in the Philippines. All the churches and schools and other agencies were transferred to the national church, · and increasingly mission administration and agencies were Filipinized. This church, in a traditionally and predominantly Roman Catholic nation, faced stern difficulties ranging from radical Protestant sectarianism to mass illiteracy, but it was consistently supported by the Evangelical United Brethren Church with dollars and personnel. In 1968 there were eight persons serving in various capacities in the national church.

When the door for mission operations in China was closed, Evangelical United Brethren responded to opportunity in the South Pacific. In 1954 a missionary couple was appointed for service in an interdenominational theological school in Makassar, Sulawesi (Indonesia), another to serve with the Karo-Batak Protestant Church in southern Sumatra, and another appointee to Sarawak to take part in an ecumenical literacy-literature venture.[17]

In Puerto Rico the Evangelical United Brethren enterprise was a part of the Evangelical Church of Puerto Rico. In 1954 General Conference granted status to it as a "special overseas conference" with the right to send a delegate to General Conference.[18] In 1960 several selected ministers were sent on a preaching mission that was graciously and enthusiastically received. Besides promoting evangelistic work, the preaching mission resulted in financial support for collegiate and theological education efforts of the Puerto Rican church.

About 1935 the Rev. A. W. Archibald, a minister of the Evangelical Church, went to central Brazil with a strong sense of urgency to begin an independent mission. Early endeavors to persuade the denomination to accept it were fruitless, but after further study it was received about 1948 and became part of a cooperative endeavor with the Evangelical Union of South America, a British society, and with "a small Brazilian church group."[19] By 1954 four missionary couples had been appointed who served in

Anapolis, Porto Alegra, and Santa Caterina, not far distant from Brazilia, the newly designated national capitol. The migration of many new settlers to the province of Goiaz presented challenging opportunities, and by 1968 there were five missionary couples in service there.

Soon after the church union in 1946, Evangelical United Brethren together with several other denominations embarked upon a venture in Ecuador. Until 1954 only money was invested in this United Andean Indian Mission, but that year a missionary couple was sent, and by July 1967 enough had been accomplished to warrant the organization of the United Evangelical Church of Ecuador.[20]

In Nigeria after church union in 1946 a hospital and medical center expanded the medical services at Bambur; thereafter new facilities for primary education were built at Bambur, Pero, and Sinna. The baptism of the first member of the Numuta tribe was heralded as another sign of the vitality of the mission. Despite negotiations, up to 1968 it had not been possible to achieve a united, ecumenical church in Nigeria; nevertheless there was significant interchurch cooperation, notably in the training school at Gindiri.

In Sierra Leone the West African Mission Conference aspired for status as an Annual Conference. In 1950 it was authorized to send one delegate to General Conference, and eight years later the Sierra Leone Conference was formed.[21] Meanwhile the mission was enhanced with new facilities: a hospital at Rotifunk, a science building at the Harford School, service buildings at Bo. The launching of a community development program at Taiama, larger school enrollments, marked improvement in school standards, and an increasing number of church members were further evidences of the vitality of this mission.

In Europe the Evangelical United Brethren Church was represented by four organized Annual Conferences: the East, West and South conferences in Germany and one in Switzerland. The conferences in Germany confronted grave problems. Sixty-four churches had been totally destroyed during the war while many others had been damaged by bombs and gunfire. By the extended national borders of Poland, the East Germany Conference lost half its territory and upon the westward flight of many Germans, half its members.[22] Undaunted, the conference took to the arduous task of rehabilitation and reconstruction, aided by generous financial support from the American church.

The supervision of European operations resided in the Central Conference, which met quadrennially, composed of delegates from the four European conferences, under the presidency of an American bishop. While the East Germany Conference was never relieved of the restrictions placed upon it by the German Democratic Republic, elsewhere the church operated more freely. In Reutlingen the seminary was reopened. In Germany and in Switzerland publications prospered, deaconess work continued to be held in high esteem, and conventional parish activities were resumed.

Amid the supervision of all these diverse enterprises, the Department of World Missions gave itself to reflecting and pondering on the nature and meaning of its task. The turbulence in the world, the rapid changes in it, and the interfusion of cultures, it was held, did not eliminate the need for the Christian mission or the missionary but did call for new perspectives and new measures unrecognized by earlier generations. Genuine satisfaction was expressed at the diminution of denominational authority over overseas programs as Christian nationals exercised creative and responsible leadership. Nationals, it was said, should have "freedom to adopt those forms of church life, worship and structure which they believe are best studied to their needs." Anything less would make the church a Western, alien community. A fine distinction was drawn between Christian mission and Christian missions, the former being the "task of evangelizing the members of the human family and establishing the Church of Christ" while Christian missions were simply "part of this task."[23] At a time when missionaries were receiving criticism for indiscriminate imposition of Western culture, church organization, architecture, theology, liturgy, and educational standards in overseas cultures, these expressions speak of the sensitivity of the denominational leadership to the newer moods of the day. Evangelical United Brethren by inheritance, by resolution, and by action were ecumenically minded. In 1962 the missions board was participating in sixty different ecumenical boards and agencies in promoting its overseas programs.[24]

MISSIONARY DEVELOPMENTS: IN THE UNITED STATES

The Division of North American Missions, as it came to be called, included church extension. Though the building of churches had virtually come to a halt during the war years, immediately thereafter its aid and counsel was sought for the location, design, and financing of churches. In the quadrennium following 1946, 163 churches were built in the denomination.[25]

The larger responsibilities of this division were with mission churches, conferences, and special missionary projects such as those in Kentucky, New Mexico, and Florida. At first the churches at the Barnetts Creek center were related to the Tennessee Conference, but later they were banded with those of the Red Bird Mission, and the Kentucky Missionary Conference was organized. The medical program, the educational programs with their ten schools and 1,200 pupils as well as the conference were under the supervision of the North American Division. The continuing evangelistic concern in Kentucky manifested in the new congregations that were organized and the eight chapels which were built. The New Mexican Mission among Spanish-Americans displayed an equally exciting vigor: new chapels were erected at Petaca and Alcalde. The schools enrolled 575 pupils; a health clinic was inaugurated at the McCurdy School, but overarching all was the dedication of the new hospital at Espanola in May 1948. The mission among Spanish-Americans at Ybor City, Florida, was modestly prospering in its evangelistic, kindergarten, and elementary education programs, but by 1966 the shifting population thrusts posed questions about its future.

Interest groups in the church promoted new undertakings by this division. In 1947 a director of rural life was appointed, and under this leadership literature was produced and distributed, a Rural Life Christian Fellowship was organized, and modest scholarship subsidies were offered pastors who enrolled for special studies of rural life. Then in 1950 the Urban Church Commission was created with auxiliary Rural and Urban (later called town and country) Commissions in the Annual Conferences.

The Division of North American Missions undertook many kinds of things. It was instrumental in producing a denominational road sign. It made an intensive study of 340 churches receiving missionary aid and posed knotty questions: What is mission? When is a mission not a mission? When ethnic issues were shaking American society, it issued timely literature such as *Ministry to People of Other Races*. It chastised congregations light-heartedly abandoning inner-city locations for the greener pastures of suburbia. It tried new forms of service: group ministries, inner-city programs, and those in Appalachia centering in Phillippi and South Charleston, West Virginia. In 1967 it formed a Department of Parish Development following an experiment in a high-rise apartment ministry in Washington, D. C.[26] The funds for world and home missions came from three major sources. First there were the earnings of capital funds and churchwide campaigns to increase those funds. The Kingdom Advance Program, launched in 1947, in three years collected $2,477,318.[27] The Mission Advance Program followed in 1960 with world missions receiving $892,500, home missions and church extension $127,500, and another $568,000 designated for reserve funds.[28] Second, the Women's Society for World Service, as well as promoting education and enthusiasm for missions, surpassed every other agency in providing dollars for missions. In 1962 thirty-two percent of the denominational missionary budget was contributed by this society. Between 1962 and 1966 it gathered $5,200,000 for missionary causes.[29] The third major source of support was the denominational budget. In 1962 fifteen percent of the missionary budget came from this source. Church members everywhere as they made their weekly contributions, through the apportionment system, were supporting the denominational missionary programs. Between 1950 and 1966 the budget support for missions and benevolences increased from $4,649,829 to $11,739,896. Evangelical United Brethren believed in missions and mission with their minds, hearts, and purses.

CHRISTIAN EDUCATION

The Board of Christian Education in 1946 was committed to supervising subsidiary educational agencies, developing well-rounded Christian character, preparing people of all ages for service, and promoting higher education.[30] In specified ways it was linked to the Boards of Missions, Publications, Evangelism, and Women's Society for World Service. In the latter instance the executive secretary of one board became ipso facto the associate secretary of the other. The initial pattern of directors for age-level groups was supplanted in 1958 by the appointment of a director for church school administration and leadership, camps and assemblies, another for Christian campus life, and assistant directors for adult and men's work and for youth education.[31] The structure of the board was revised in 1962, and thereafter there were three major divisions: Christian Higher Education, Christian Education, and Curriculum Development. Soon thereafter a director for the latter was named.

In 1946 "church school" became the official name for what had previously been the Sunday school. The decline in enrollment and attendance prompted a four-year long Strengthen the Church School crusade in 1930. This brought its benefits, but not the number of scholars which had been hoped for. In 1966 church school enrollment was 626,843, the lowest in twenty years, while the average attendance was 381,090, which was about what it had been in 1946. High on the list of grounds accounting for the plight of the church school were the inadequacies in curriculum and literature. A committee on curriculum development was appointed in 1950. The plans toward the development of a "total curriculum" were suspended in 1963 with the decision to join the cooperative curriculum project sponsored by the National Council of Churches.

In response to increasing requests from the church, a two-year course for catechetical or pastor's classes was developed. For the first year twenty-four lessons were devoted to the theme *Being a Christian* and supplemented with twelve lessons on *Foundations for Christian Youth.* For the second year there were twenty-four lessons on *The Christian Way,* supplemented with twelve more on *Foundations for Christian Youth.* Later, *Beliefs for Christian Youth* was substituted for *Foundations for Christian Youth.* Further modifications of this course were discouraged because of prospects of union with the Methodist Church.

The decline in the patronage of the church school cannot be appraised apart from the developments in other ministries to youth. The Youth Fellowship created in 1946 supplanted the two previous youth organizations, and with its attractive vitality its membership increased from 81,934 in 1950 to 167,663 in 1962. With the belief that a more effective service could be rendered by working with restricted age-level groups, in 1954 a fellowship organization was formed for young adults, and later on one for older adults. A Campus Christian Life program was initiated in 1959 which sought to provide a Christian ministry to students in selected public universities. This led to participation in the interchurch United Campus Christian Fellowship and later in the United Ministries in Higher Education.

The Brotherhood was formed in 1946 to promote organized men's work in the church, and after a few years it had a director. While it encouraged local organizations, promoted area congresses, and made financial contributions to missionary and educational projects, it evoked only a minimal response, and its accomplishments were likewise minimal. In 1954 the Brotherhood became Evangelical United Brethren Men.[32]

The Board of Christian Education promoted leadership training classes, weekday and vacation schools, and pastors' classes, and the enrollments in these substantially increased. It sponsored quadrennial conventions to bring information and inspiration. A student conference was held in 1953. In Estes Park, Colorado, a Youth Fellowship convention was held in 1962 which attracted 1,400 delegates. Conference camps grew in popularity, and in 1962 at 330 such camps 30,000 children, adolescents, youth, and adults participated. Together, the Boards of Christian Education and Evangelism announced the opportunity for selected youth to invest a year in supervised service as Youth Associates, or, as later called, Ambassadors.

For the promotions of its work the board made use of audio-visual materials, but far greater use was made of literature. *Builders* was the church's youth periodical. The board also issued a large number of pamphlets presenting the ideals of Christian education and offering helpful suggestions for local leaders. With the Board of Evangelism it distributed *Spotlight,* a bimonthly programmatic release for ministers.

In the supervision of the eight church colleges, the Board of Christian Education undertook many things, ranging from a study of the schools made by professional educators to the allocation of territory for the solicitation of students to each institution.

While the colleges pled for larger church support to meet increasing costs, only two of them were in dire financial straits. With the passing years, the curricula and faculties were significantly expanded. Financial campaigns increased endowment funds and real estate holdings, new buildings were erected and new equipment was acquired, attention was given to academic excellence, and self-studies were undertaken to ascertain what a church-related school was doing or what it might or ought to be doing. Not least gratifying was the substantial increase in enrollments. In 1966 the enrollments were: Albright, 1,050; Otterbein, 1,553; Lebanon Valley,

855; Indiana Central, 954; North Central, 845; Westmar, 940; and Shenandoah, 607.

Two of the colleges faced crises. At York, Nebraska, after fire destroyed a major building and the state supreme court denied permission to effect legal changes for the clearance of title, the trustees voted that York College be merged with Western Union College, Le Mars, Iowa. This consolidation was effected in 1955; soon thereafter the institution in Le Mars became Westmar College. Shenandoah College, Dayton, Virginia, was also in straitened circumstances, but its grim prospects were relieved when the city of Winchester, Virginia, offered thirty acres of land and $250,000 if the school were transferred there. Upon the approval of General Conference and after the construction of buildings this school began its new life in September 1960 in Winchester.

Two further educational projects claimed the attention of the board. The Northwest Canada Conference, affirming its singular need for it, initiated the Hillcrest Bible Institute, which in 1962 was relocated on an eight-acre campus at Medicine Hat, Alberta, and renamed Hillcrest Christian College, though at the time it consisted of little more than a high school and a Bible department. In 1965 a liberal arts curriculum was established and an arrangement was made with Cascade College, Portland, Oregon, by which a student, after two years at Hillcrest, could transfer and complete the degree course. Of the 106 students in Hillcrest in 1966, thirteen were in the liberal arts program. Responding to vigorous petitions, in 1954 the board affirmed its intention to "establish an Evangelical United Brethren college on the Pacific Coast in the foreseeable future."[33] Successive committees and successive negotiations met with discouraging frustrations, and in 1962 this project was decisively terminated by General Conference.[34]

THE CHURCH IN THE PRINTING BUSINESS

Two publishing houses, the Evangelical Press in Harrisburg and the Otterbein Press in Dayton, were prosperous agencies. The initial plan to consolidate them was superseded in 1950 by the decision that the Board of Publications supervise them through two departments, one for each house with each managed by its own board of trustees and publisher. Though it was reported in 1958 that the two establishments were growing "closer together," the proposal that a single publisher serve both was not supported. Nevertheless, following the decisive report of a professional management firm recommending it, in 1962 one publisher was elected for both houses.

To meet the increasing business opportunities in Harrisburg, additional real estate was purchased, buildings were enlarged, and new equipment was acquired. In Dayton the plans to relocate Otterbein Press on a site several miles removed from downtown Dayton were rejected when the city's renewal program made real estate available just across the street from its location. There in 1965 a Publications Center was built which provided quarters for publishing and editorial offices.

The *Telescope-Messenger* (edited by Dr. J. W. Krecker) and *Builders* (edited by Dr. R. M. Veh), the denominational adult and youth periodicals, were published in Harrisburg. Church school, youth, and missionary materials were edited and published in Dayton. To meet increasing costs and a declining subscription list, in 1959 the *Telescope-Messenger* was issued semimonthly instead of weekly. In 1962 it was superseded by *Church and Home*. To encourage a larger reception of this semimonthly, a four-color cover was added and the "family plan" was introduced by which in congregations making specified payments, each family received the periodical. The circulation reached over 200,000, an unusual achievement for a church with less than 750,000 members.

Likewise serving to fuse the two church traditions into the Evangelical United Brethren Church was the *Hymnal* which was published in 1957. In this book were 455 hymns expressive of many cultural, theological, and ecclesiastical traditions, a broad lectionary, and a modest collection of aids to worship. The *Hymnal* was greeted with unanticipated cordiality, and three editions, totaling 225,000 copies, were printed.

By the terms of union in 1946 the printing establishment of the Church of the United Brethren in Christ was continued, its almost sole responsibility being the management of the multi-story United Brethren Building in Dayton which was held as "a permanent foundation for the benefit of aged and retired ministers of the former Church of the United Brethren in Christ, their widows and orphans."[35] Most of the space in the building, apart from the denominational offices, was commercially occupied. After several fruitless negotiations, the building was sold in 1952 for $1,450,000.

The printing establishment became the beneficiary trust, supporting clerical retirees and their widows until 1966 when it transferred its funds, then amounting to $2,199,296 to the Board of Pensions and was dissolved.

In addition to those in Harrisburg and Dayton, the church had publishing houses in Stuttgart, Germany, and Berne, Switzerland, and a number of book stores. The house in Stuttgart was destroyed by bombs in 1944; eleven years passed before it was fully rebuilt. However, before this the presses were issuing denominational literature and an adult and a youth hymnbook were published. In Berne a hymnbook was printed for the Switzerland Conference. At both European houses, subscribers for the denominational periodicals decreased, a decline that continued without interruptions through 1966.

The Church in American Life

In 1946 began a period in American life marked by deep anxieties, strident partisanships, public religiosity, and economic prosperity. In 1960, sixty-nine percent of Americans were members of churches or synagogues, an all-time high, and a billion dollars were spent in the erection of new sanctuaries. Best sellers prescribed the paths to peace of mind, or soul, or positive thinking. Wages and dividends rose to new heights, and with new technology men began to explore space and ultimately reached the moon. More cars traveled improved roads than ever before, and the TV set became normal household equipment.

Still, there was a pervading disquietude, fed by grave international uncertainties, the cold war, the awful possibilities of nuclear fission, and the slow slide into moral morass in Vietnam. Compounding all this, the race issue led to disturbing crises of conscience. The Fair Deal, promoting civil rights, slum clearance, and low cost housing, the Supreme Court's outlawry of segregation in the public schools, and the termination of segregation in the buses in Montgomery, Alabama, reverberated through the nation. The harmonies of "We Shall Overcome" sung in nonviolent demonstrations were heard across the nations, but contentions were followed by confrontations, and in some of these the harmonies were obliterated by raw violence. The spreading loss of confidence in traditional codes, establishments, and leaders in some quarters evoked counter-cultures which declared open war on them.

Nor were Christian faith and the churches exempted from acrimony, and beginning in 1960 church attendance began to decline. A "new" theology proclaimed the "post-Christian age," the "death of God," and the need to "demythologize the message." Alongside the new theologies was a "new" morality, revolting against the hyprocrisies of moral codes and speaking freely on such themes as sex ethics, situational ethics, and the limits of loyalty to constituted authorities. Amid wrenching social and institutional dislocations, these were years of excitement, turbulence, anguish, and soul-searching.

The Evangelical United Brethren Church neither by tradition nor persuasion was prepared to subscribe to much that was heralded as new. It did call people to confront the crucial issues of life in the context of evangelical faith which centered in a living, loving God who had revealed himself in Jesus Christ. To accent this call in 1946 a Commission on Christian Social Action was authorized by General Conference and placed under the direction of a part-time secretary.[36] Auxiliary commissions were authorized for Annual Conferences and local churches. The meager funding for the general commission won instant criticism, but only slowly was its appropriation increased, and it was 1966 before it had a full-time director. With its limited funds it distributed literature for use in the churches, urging a more serious reflection upon the opportunities and obligations of Christian people in confronting social issues. It drafted position papers for presentation to General Conference. It related this church to the multiplying number of agencies and conventions, interdenominational and nondenominational, which sought to grapple with crucial social issues with Christian understanding, participating in twenty-eight such occasions in 1950. Its appointees attended the National Study Conference on Religion and Race in 1963, the Conference on Church and State in 1964, and two World Order Conferences. It promoted two denominational Study and Planning Conferences on Christian Social Action.

Its sensitivity to world and social issues was seconded in quadrennial episcopal messages when world order was held to be an objective for the church, and the United Nations Organization was extolled. Communism was denounced for its repudiation of the spiritual in the universe and in man. There was a summons to a new life style for man and society. "It is the duty of the church to be concerned about a just social order, but it is also the duty of the church to help men see that redemption implies more than the increase of things." "Our church cannot claim to preach a full gospel of the Kingdom unless we fulfill the prophetic mission as the herald and exemplar of social as well as individual righteousness."[37]

As in the past the summons to preserve the sanctity of the Sabbath and to avoid the use of spirits and tobacco were continued, but they were overshadowed by the more intense concerns for world order and social justice, freedom, human rights, and peace. It was assumed that the church should and must enliven and direct its dormant moral resources. The United Nations Organization was enthusiastically endorsed as the agency, par excellence, "to mobilize world opinion, provide for economic and social justice, and to work for the goal of universal disarmament."[38] In General Conference the resolution supporting the creation of an international atomic energy agency was unanimously supported. The resolution advocating "abolition of nuclear testing by all nations, including our own" was approved but not unanimously, as several delegates contended it was "not within the area of necessary and appropriate action by members of an ecclesiastical body."[39] There were no objectors to the resolution urging the American government to subscribe to the international conventions upholding human rights.

During these years, resolutions from the church's highest judicatories affirmed support for collective bargaining, labor's right to strike, a guaranteed annual wage, and profit sharing. Provisions for social security and adequate pensions in 1954 were declared a Christian duty.[40] Lowered protective tariffs and financial and commerical aid to underdeveloped nations were in 1958 supported as both morally virtuous and commercially healthful for the American economy. Though without significant black constituency, the Evangelical United Brethren Church acknowledged its shame at the discriminatory treatment accorded minority races[41] and gave its endorsement to the newly enacted fair employment practice legislation and the outlawry of poll taxes. Joy and gratitude were expressed at the United States Supreme Court's decision declaring segregation in the public schools unconstitutional. Guided by the counsels of scripture and the example of our Lord, church members were exhorted to "work for the establishing of equal opportunities for employment, education, housing, public accommodations and other privileges of citizenship and . . . co-operate with other organizations which seek these ends."[42]

New consideration was given to the family about 1950, and in the following years new positions were affirmed. The rule disallowing a clergyman to read the wedding service for a person who had been divorced was changed to permit it, provided that through counseling he had ascertained that "the divorced persons have sought and received forgiveness and are seeking a genuine Christian relationship not only in marriage, but with God."[43] New considerations were given to responsible marriage and parenthood, and the newly wedded were urged to the "planning at long range of the family they hope to establish." Further, it was affirmed "ethically and morally right to properly use methods and techniques medically approved for the purpose of achieving planned and responsible parenthood."[44]

National issues stimulated numerous affirmations. In 1954 one resolution supported the proposed amendment to the McCarren-Walter Immigration Act while another supported the objectors to the proposal to appoint an American ambassador to the Vatican. Peace time conscription and compulsory military training were decried. Capital punishment was declared a violation of Christian law, and neither remedial nor redemptive. In 1966 two resolutions won unanimous support. The first called for a "phased" withdrawal of all American troops from Vietnam; the second advocated a new national approach to China "in the spirit of understanding and good will."[45]

From these expressions toward various aspects of life, individual and social, it is clear that some traditional positions and norms were being modified and accorded a lesser role. To what extent these pronouncements were expressive of the convictions of the whole denomination is not at issue here. They were the expressions of the representatives of the whole church as they addressed themselves to the contemporary world and Christian responsibility in and toward it. In their concern these churchmen walked humbly, knowing that righteousness ever stands in jeopardy of stumbling over the brink into self-righteousness.

BENEVOLENT INSTITUTIONS

The Evangelical United Brethren Church supported eleven benevolent institutions of differing types, each dedicated to rendering a Christian service to its residents. This kind of Christian social action was not new, but changing mores and new public systems for the care of children, youth, and the aging brought new problems for them all.

By 1966 the ten cottages and five duplexes at the Baker Home (La Puenta, California) were occupied by thirty residents. The Pacific Home (Burbank, California) in 1950 was caring for forty-six people. In 1962 plans for its relocation were initiated, and in 1964 real estate was acquired in Santa Ana. Frustrations were soon encountered, yet by 1968 the goal was nearer realization. Flat Rock Home (Flat Rock, Ohio) was the only one in the church devoted exclusively to the care of children and youth, and in 1950 there were seventy-six residents. With decreasing applications for admission, temporarily consideration was given to the care of the aged. In 1966 Flat Rock celebrated its centenary, and to meet new public regulations, psychiatric and psychological services were instituted, supplementing the existing medical and dental ones. Western Home (Cedar Falls, Iowa), confronted with an increasing number of applicants, in 1958 began an expansion program which enlarged older buildings and constructed new ones. An infirmary was erected in 1963, and a dining hall was projected for 1957. In 1966 there were 224 residents in the home. Haven Hubbard (New Carlisle, Indiana) with eighty-two residents in 1950 had practically reached its capacity. An advanced nursing care program was introduced in 1962; the construction of a nursing center, and the enlargement of facilities increased the capacity of the home to 130.

Otterbein Home (Lebanon, Ohio) was serving 117 elderly persons and 110 children in 1950, but in the next years the number of children fell off sharply so that in 1954 those remaining were transferred to Flat Rock, and Otterbein became exclusively a home for the elderly. Calamities struck as two buildings were destroyed by fire and a third was condemned under the public fire code. This led to the renovation of the old buildings and the erection of a cluster of duplexes for residents.

Evangelical Home (Lewisburg, Pennsylvania) in 1950 cared for children and old people, but in 1967 those children in residence were transferred to Quincy. The quarters thus released were renovated for the aged, and by 1962 there were 112 residents in the home. In 1966 a hundred-bed nursing home was in prospect in a project sponsored jointly by Methodists and Evangelical United Brethren in Johnstown, Pennsylvania. Both elderly and children received care at the Quincy Home and Orphanage (Quincy, Pennsylvania) though the latter were more numerous. Believing that decentralized care would be wiser than continually increasing the size of existing facilities, the church began construction in 1965 on facilities in Lititz, Pennsylvania, for the elderly. This venture developed with such promise that studies were undertaken to ascertain the feasibilty of establishing additional units at York and Johnstown. Evangelical Manor (Philadelphia, Pennsylvania) in 1950 cared for seventy-five aged residents with this enrollment remaining constant over the next fifteen years.

Only two new ventures in benevolent institutions were approved by the Evangelical United Brethren. At the request of the Canada Conference in 1958 permission was granted that conference to join with the United Church of Canada in establishing a home for senior citizens. This home, Packwood Manor, is located in Waterloo, Ontario. In 1946 the Kansas Conference received approval to establish a home for the aged at Camp Webster, near Salina. Thereafter the Spangler Nursing Home in Newton was offered the conference, and following approval by the church and the transfer of the property, the institution was incorporated under the name Friendly Acres. Adjacent ground was purchased, and a building was erected to care for forty-eight additional residents.[46]

Broad supervision of the church's benevolent homes was exercised by the General Council of Administration which in 1959 appointed a special study commission to review the programs and conditions of all the homes, their financial circumstances and their prospects. The commission employed a professional social worker as consultant, and the report was decisive. Among its recommendations were that a denominational Commission on Health and Welfare be established, a social worker be added to the staff of each of the homes caring for children, and that staff members at all of the homes "be given more adequate training for their work."[47] General Conference in 1962 did create a Commission on Health and Welfare which four years later stamped its approval upon a cooperative venture by Methodists and Evangelical United Brethren in establishing a home for the elderly in Johnstown.

THE DEACONESS MOVEMENT

In the conferences in Germany and Switzerland it was the Deaconess Societies which supervised the same kind of services which in America were performed in the benevolent homes. In Germany in 1950 there were 670 enrolled deaconesses. Most of them served in hospitals, but many worked as pastors' assistants, in benevolent homes, as evangelists among refugees, and as kindergarten teachers. Grievous to the Deaconess Society was the military seizure by the British of the five hundred–bed hospital and mother-house in Elberfeld, Germany, in 1945 which was not released for a decade. Many of the eight smaller hospitals in other German cities had suffered war damage and had to be rebuilt. Of the forty deaconesses in the Swiss Society some were working in Switzerland, some in the hospital in Strassbourg, France, and a few in a center in Paris. The large hospital in Basel and the newer one in Zurich-Kussnacht needed deaconesses, but fewer were volunteering for this way of life. Even in Germany where hundreds served as deaconesses, their number was too limited to meet the calls for their services.

Although the deaconess movement in America collapsed, in central Europe it lived on, a small corp whose humble services rarely failed to impress the observing American visitor. Here was a company of women whose distinguishing significance was only that they had invested their lives in nothing more grandiose than performing simple services in the name of Christ for people who stood in need.

PENSION PLANS

The Board of Pensions of the Evangelical United Brethren Church in 1946 became the successor of the pension programs of the two merging denominations. It operated four departments, or plans: (1) the Ministerial and Annuity Plan, formerly United Brethren, (2) the Superannuation Plan, formerly Evangelical, (3) the Ministers Reserve Pension Plan, for clergy ordained after 1946, and (4) the Pension Plan for Lay Employees. The first two simply continued the programs in the two churches which were initiated before church union. The latter two plans were actuarially based. A fixed percentage of the cash salary paid constituted the annual premium and was paid by the minister and the salary paying unit. All ministers were obliged to the third plan unless they were ordained before 1947. Premiums, appropriations from the Christian Service Fund and the Board of Publications, and gifts flowed into the treasury, and from it the pensioner received benefits proportionate to his years of active service and the annual premiums which had been paid. In 1950 there were 827 clergy in Plan 1, 938 in Plan 2, and 468 in Plan 3.

After congressional legislation was enacted making the clergy eligible for Social Security, the small opposition in the church to it evaporated and by 1958 the majority of the ministers were enrolled. By this time hundreds of congregations were annually paying both the six percent congregational assessment and the three percent ministerial premium for the church pension. Plan 1 and Plan 2 were consolidated in 1962 and named the Senior Plan. Three years later death benefits were provided the family of the member of the Reserve Plan if under fifty years of age, $2,000, if over fifty, $1,000, and if superannuated, $500.

By 1967 there were 789 members in the Senior Plan, 2,004 in the Reserve Plan, and 191 in the Lay Employees Plan. The broadening acceptance of pensions as a "way of life" was reflected in the report that 78.6 percent of the congregations were annually paying the congregational and the ministerial assessments, totaling at that time twelve percent of the minister's cash salary. The assets of the Board of Pensions in 1966 were reported as $19,661,531.[48]

Evangelicals in 1920 established a Sustentation Fund for the benefit of retired clergymen in the European conferences, and a few years later the Bowman Memorial Fund for the benefit of children of deceased ministers. Both were reserve funds, both were small, and both were administered by the Board of Pensions, but in 1966 both, amounting to $50,086 and $9,913 respectively, were transferred to the European conferences.

CHANGING WAYS IN CHURCH LIFE

During the life of the Evangelical United Brethren Church there were changes in the personnel and procedures in its governing conferences—Quarterly, Annual and General—some of which were simply verbal, while some were substantial. Locally, its utility having passed, the class organization had long since disappeared. However, it was 1958 before the class leader was displaced with the lay leader. Many years had elapsed since the superintendent appeared four times a year to preside over the Quarterly Conference, which in 1950 was replaced by the Local Conference, the authoritative body on the charge to which all boards, committees, and agencies were amenable. Because of increasing complaints, the local Council of Administration which had been created in 1946 was eliminated in 1962, and the Program Council was established. The latter, amenable to the Local Conference, bore responsibility for developing a total, unified program for the local church functioning through adult, youth, and children's councils and through commission on worship and preaching, Christian education, evangelism and missions, and citizenship and fellowship.[49] This reorganization of the local church evoked some appeals for amendments in 1966, but with the bright prospects for union with the Methodist Church, no significant changes were made.

At the time of union in 1946 there were fifty-two Annual Conferences in North America, in most instances operating in the same geographical areas. The merging of conferences began almost immediately. Although the endeavors to merge the Missouri and Kansas Conferences and the Erie and New York Conferences were fruitless, by 1968 there were thirty-two Annual Conferences in the Evangelical United Brethren Church. The Kentucky Missionary Conference, the only new one organized by the denomination, was also the sole missionary conference. Overseas there were five conferences: Sierra Leone, Switzerland, and East, West, and South Germany.

The expanding operations of the conferences' Council of Administration led to the elimination of some committees just as the enlarging of the services of the Board of Ministerial Training narrowed the role of the Conference Relations Committee. Authority to elect the conference secretary quadrennially instead of annually was sought in 1950 but not granted until 1962. Petitions to eliminate the annual appointment of ministers met with no success in 1950 and 1954, but in 1962 General Conference authorized pastoral assignments "of indefinite tenure."[50] Then, too, a Program Council was added to the Annual Conference structure, amenable to the Council of Administration, serving to coordinate conference programs and as an intermediary between the denominational and local Program Councils.

Financial considerations led in 1958 to the reduction of Annual Conference representation, ministerial and lay, in the General Conference by about twenty-five percent and the rejection of the proposal that General Conference convene successively in each of the episcopal areas. For broader participation in the life of the church it became a rule that an individual should serve no more than twelve successive years on any major denominational board and on no more than two boards simultaneously. Following a four-year study of the church's denominational structure, in 1962 program councils at the three levels of church organization (the General Church, the Annual Conference, and the local congregation) were introduced to initiate, unify, and promote the work of the church.

The General Council of Administration was called upon to implement many of the actions of General Conference, and on occasion even to act on behalf of General Conference during the interim between its quadrennial sessions. To bring together in conversation and cooperation the multiplying operations of church agencies, it created the Inter-Board Program Committee, composed of representatives of major boards, to study church life and its needs and to make recommendations. The committee's study book, *The Christian Faith Encounters Communism* was well received and was followed by other publications. The need for candidates for the ministry and missionary service led the council to appoint a joint committee on recruiting in 1954, and for many years the council gave superintendence to the Board of Christian Social Action.

It became habitual for General Conference to refer items too important to be decided instantly to the General Council for study, recommendation, or even decision. Numerous and diverse were the items referred, for example: the ordination of women, the change in denominational name, the production of literature to assist laymen to serve more effectively in conference sessions, the reform of the factor basis in determining apportionments, changes in rituals, and the formation of a denominational lending agency.

A major responsibility of the General Council was the preparation of the denominational budget, which grew from $2,013,540 in 1946 to $3,243,300 in 1966. Recommendations were made both for appropriations to beneficiaries and for apportionments to Annual Conferences. Apportionments in 1946 were determined by five factors: church membership, average church-school attendance, net property values, total church expenses, and benevolent contributions. With quadrennial regularity the factor basis was reformed, each proposed change was met with vigorous debate as to what factors would be equitable in determining apportionments. By 1966 the factor computation reckoned only with membership, church attendance, per capita giving, and the average per capita income in the state as reported by the federal government.[51] Appropriations were recommended for general church administration, the general boards and agencies, for educational institutions, and for interdenominational activities. In 1962 nomenclature was changed, and what had been missions and benevolences became the Christian Service Fund. In 1964 the calendar year became the fiscal year.

Regional and churchwide campaigns for funds were launched. In 1946 four institutions were permitted drives in their areas which previous General Conferences had approved, and the Missionary Advance Program was authorized. In 1954 the churchwide United Crusade was sanctioned, which set out to collect $5,150,000 for educational institutions and church extension.[52] In the following quadrennium there was the Special Advance Campaign for Mission and Church Extension seeking $5,150,000: $1,750,000 for world missions, $1,400,000 for home missions, and $2,000,000 for conference interests.[53] This was the last of the churchwide campaigns.

After the sale of the United Brethren Building in Dayton, the General Council in 1958 purchased a site on Riverview Avenue, Dayton, and superintended the construction of a denominational office building which cost $781,249 and was dedicated in 1960.[54]

In 1946 a General Commission on Evangelism was established with provisions for commissions in the Annual Conferences and committees in local churches. Convinced of the mutual interests of evangelism and Christian education, the executive secretary of evangelism was, ipso facto, the associate secretary of the Board of Christian Education, and the executive secretary of Christian education was the associate secretary for evangelism.

In 1950 the commission became the Board of Evangelism, and a "Ten Win One" campaign was launched to win 75,000 to Christian discipleship and church membership. There followed the Bishops' Crusade and then Missions to Youth. In 1957 the youth evangelistic service was initiated in which four selected seminarians were invited to invest fifteen months in a supervised evangelistic enterprise. To promote a "worker witnessing movement," in 1958 a "mission to workers" was launched at a conference. All except two Annual Conferences responded to the invitation to send representatives to this gathering where "people to people" evangelism was stressed and alternative evangelistic methods were assessed. In conjunction with World Missions, a Mission to Missions venture selected clergy to visit Puerto Rico, and the Dominican Republic, and in later years the Philippines, Africa, and Japan. With imagination and vigor, new groupings with imaginative names were cultivated within local churches in America such as: Triple T (Two or Three Together) and FIRE (Finding Inner Renewal for Evangelism).

Preaching missions, at home and overseas, youth evangelistic services, and cooperative programs with other denominational agencies strove for church renewal, and still other measures were developed. In 1960 the first Four C Mission (Cooperative, Comprehensive, Christian, Confrontation) was held in York, Pennsylvania, followed by a dozen more in church centers. In 1964 Four C Missions were projected for every charge in one episcopal area. I K Groups (Koinonia), vocational clusters, and "mirror meetings" were encouraged for the creation of an intelligent understanding of evangelism and the cultivation of evangelistic spirit and work. Motivating all these efforts was the single conviction that the church must find ways to reach and tell people of God and his steadfast love for them. Pastors were cautioned against narrow and inflexible concepts of evangelism and also against the hasty acceptance into church membership of the uninstructed.[55]

After eight years the Youth Evangelistic Service (evangelism) was fused with the Youth Fellowship Associates (Christian education), and the Ambassadors program served the interests of both boards. In collaboration with home missions, an Inner City Pastors' Retreat was held in 1964, a Conference on the Church's Outreach in 1966, and there were endeavors in group ministry and in high-rise apartment ministry. With the Department of Stewardship, the Board of Evangelism sent a team of ministers to Sierra Leone on a preaching mission. In a Mission to North America it brought ten from overseas to tour the American church in 1966 on the premise that Christian people have values to give as well as to receive. With the General Program Council, the Board of Evangelism promoted the Undershepherd Plan in which the local congregation, gathered into small clusters, could fruitfully confront the meaning and responsibilities of the Christian faith.

Until the world and its inhabitants have been led into discipleship, this proclamation of God's redeeming love for the unloved and loveless, which is evangelism, remains the unfinished task of the people of God. The limitations of the many endeavors attempted over twenty years are readily confessed, even by their promoters; nevertheless, having heard the words of the Great Commissioner, the church responded.

A Department of Stewardship with a director was established in the General Council of Administration in 1958; its purpose was to develop a deeper understanding of and a wider practice of stewardship in the church. Workshops were held in most of the conferences, an Every Church Enlistment Program and an Eight Step Stewardship Plan were promoted with bounteous literature. The scope of the department was expanded to include family money management, stewardship of natural resources, stewardship of accumulated resources, as well as stewardship education and capital funds counseling. For the rendering of these services by 1966 an assistant director and a capital funds counselor were added to the staff of the department.

The church was tardy in its recognition and cautious in its support of the Historical Society. With its meager funds, the society quadrennially held councils for members of the conference historical boards. In 1953 it issued a *Manual for Conference Historians* and, for popular use, a pictorial history of the denomination with script, using color slides. Promotional activities and suggestions were reported in a *Bulletin*. As more materials were gathered for the denominational collection, cataloguing was initiated which continued at a more rapid pace after additional support allowed the appointment of a part-time curator. Under his direction a monthly newsletter was issued, a comprehensive program for microfilming materials of historical value was initiated, and the cataloguing of relevant materials not in the denominational collection was undertaken. With supplementary financial assistance in 1965 the Historical Society and its collection were established in commodious quarters in the new publications center in Dayton with a well disciplined archival program.

ECUMENICITY AND CHURCH UNION

During the life span of the Evangelical United Brethren Church there was an unparalleled sensitivity to the oneness of those in Christ, manifested in new and numerous forms of interdenominational associations and ultimately in church union. The church was a charter member of the World Council of Churches, and its delegates attended the successive assemblies in Amsterdam, Evanston, New Delhi, and Uppsala. When the Federal Council merged with other interdenominational agencies to form the National Council of Churches in 1950, the church promptly affiliated with the new organization and on two occasions, in the persons of Bishops S. Stamm and R. H. Mueller, provided it with presidential leadership. At state and local levels representatives of this church were invariably found in councils and federations, actively participating in programs of Christian education, evangelism, and social renewal. After 1962 as a participating member, the church had full membership and representation at the plenary meetings of the Conference on Church Union, an association seeking to realize a church "truly catholic, truly reformed, truly evangelical."

During these years denominational unions were consummated, sometimes uniting churches of diverse traditions and polities as in the instance of the United Church of Christ, formed by the merger of Congregational Christian Churches and the Evangelical and Reformed Church. More frequently, however, churches of like backgrounds and polities came together as in the mergers which formed the United Presbyterian Church in 1958, the American Lutheran Church in 1960, and the Lutheran Church in America in 1962.

The movement toward unitive ventures in the Evangelical United Brethren Church cannot be wholly explained in terms of what was happening in American Christendom, but it ought not be told without this reference. Evangelicals had experienced church unions in 1922 and 1946, the United Brethren in 1946, and out of these experiences they knew the satisfactions and rewards of judicious unitive efforts. So in 1950, just four years after the union of 1946, the Commission on Church Federation and Union was instructed "to explore carefully and sympathetically Christian union with other denominations of kindred spirit, and that we request the commission to report to the General Conference quadrennially."[56]

Evangelical United Brethren in Ontario had long and happy associations with their denomination, but they lived in a nation where a United Church, formed in 1925, became increasingly attractive. In 1946 authorization was given for a referendum in the Canada Conference on church union, but this was not implemented because conference leadership was apprehensive that the people were not sufficiently of one mind to produce a strong majority either for or against an affiliation with the United Church of Canada. Thereafter for a few years interest in the issue subsided.

When negotiations between the church in the United States and the Methodists took on serious proportions, the issue arose again, but this time in a new context. Now the question was not so much the matter of church union, but which of the alternatives was most judicious—union with an American denomination or with the United Church of Canada. Initiated in 1962 under the supervision of the Commission on Church Federation and Union, a plan of union with the United Church was drafted which was approved by General Conference and the Canada Conference in 1966. The final session of the Canada Conference convened in October 1967, and in January 1968 it became an integral part of the United Church of Canada.

The Northwest Canada Conference (Western provinces) voted to stay autonomous and formed The Evangelical Church of Canada.

During 150 years Evangelicals and United Brethren met with Methodists in a wide range of events, from the exchange of fraternal delegates at General Conferences to cooperation in camp meetings. A singular incident was the ballot at the 1871 Evangelical General Conference when by a majority of one vote union with the Methodists was approved. Lacking the necessary two-thirds majority, the issue was pursued no further.

Among the fraternal delegates from churches and interdenominational agencies appearing before the first Evangelical United Brethren General Conference in 1946 was Methodist Bishop G. Bromley Oxnam who, the record says, declared "he had been authorized by the Board of Bishops of the Methodist Church to state that if any time after we had come far enough in our own union that we would care to open negotiations with them, they would be pleased to receive such overtures."[57]

In 1958 the Commission on Church Federation reported that during the quadrennium it had had conversation with representatives of the Church of the Brethren, the Church of God in North

America, and The Methodist Church where issues were discussed. At this, General Conference instructed the commission to continue conversations with the Methodists "for the purpose of developing possible bases of consideration for union."[58] To this instruction a small minority registered its explicit and firm dissent. In 1962 the commission reported its meetings with commissions from several denominations were unproductive. During the same four years there had been eleven "formal consultations" with Methodists, in three of which the entire commissions of both churches were involved. These consultations dealt with the problems in merging two denominations of such unequal size, in each of which were prized traditions and ways of life. Toward the resolution of these problems eighteen subcommittees were appointed. In conclusion, the commission asked authorization to join the Methodist commission in drafting a Plan of Union, which was granted by a 310 to 94 vote of General Conference. Following this ballot a few requested their names be recorded as opposed to the decision of the majority.

Progress was temporarily retarded in 1964 by the reconstruction of the Methodist commission when only five of the previous members were continued. Nevertheless, the drafting of a Plan of Union proceeded studiously, steadily, and slowly. Among Evangelical United Brethren favorable to union much concern was expressed on positions in the church-to-be on such points as episcopal tenure, the manner of selecting superintendents, and race relations both within and outside the church. The pyramiding work of the commission led to the appointment of a full-time director, Dr. Paul A. Washburn, who assiduously traversed the church, explaining and interpreting the proposed union and distributing literature promoting it. During this quadrennium the commissions met together six times, the executive committee ten times, in addition to the scores of meetings of subcommittees involving 150 members who had been co-opted. Parts I, II, and III of the Plan and Basis of Union were published in April 1966 for presentation to the General Conferences in the fall.

The General Conference of the Evangelical United Brethren Church convened in regular session in the Conrad Hilton Hotel, Chicago, November 8, 1966, and a specially called General Conference of the Methodist Church in separate quarters met in the same place and at the same time, an arrangement that permitted instant conversations and adjudication on matters which had not been fully resolved. The union documents were scrutinized again, and suggestions were made to a mutual liaison committee. At length Parts I, II, and III were completed (consisting of the constitution, the affirmations of faith, and social principles) and were recommended for adoption by both conferences. Part IV, dealing with the ministry, the Board of Laity, and the local church, was recommended for adoption "in principle," a more definitive adoption delayed to a "uniting conference." Upon the decision in the Evangelical United Brethren conference that the vote be a standing vote, the roster of delegates was called by the secretary, each delegate singly and orally declaring his position. In this moment so radically affecting the denomination, by a vote of 325 to 88 union with the Methodists was approved with the adoption of Parts I, II, and III and the adoption of Part IV in principle.[59] Almost simultaneously and with a ninety-five percent majority the Methodist General Conference stamped its approval upon the uniting documents.

By church law such basic actions of a General Conference required the supportive votes of the Annual Conferences to become effective. By August 1967, this balloting was completed. The aggregate vote in the Evangelical United Brethren conference approved the union by 3,740 to 1,607[60] and in the Methodist Conferences by 29,627 to 4,192. Two small Evangelical United Brethren conferences in the northwest in 1966 staunchly opposed the impending union and petitioned that local churches of this mind be permitted to withdraw from the denomination. The petition was denied by General Conference, and a committee was appointed to attempt to dissuade the dissenters. At least twice the committee visited the two conferences, but without much success. Many but not all of the churches withdrew from the denomination. Observers noted the "basic incompatibility" of the majority of the clergy and laity there with the denomination in theology, social outlook, and ecumenical attitudes, an incompatibility which had a history beginning years before union with the Methodists was proposed.[61]

Following the decisions made by the General Conference and confirmed by the balloting in the Annual Conferences, an adjourned session of the Evangelical United Brethren General Conference was announced for April 22, 1968, in Dallas, Texas, where the Methodist General Conference was scheduled to convene. After separate sessions, both bodies would join in a uniting conference. Before that date, denominational and conference organizations met with their peers from the other church to lay plans for the future, and in numerous instances across the country local churches were "yoked" or merged. Before then, too, the commissions completed the draft of Part IV of the Plan and Basis of Union, which was later adopted in Dallas, and determined the legal and public acts which would consummate the creation of the United Methodist Church.

In the Memorial Auditorium, Dallas, April 23, 1968, amid expressions of rejoicing and flourishes of pageantry church union was brought to completion and celebrated. Delegates and thousands of visitors filled the capacious hall, and after prayer, confession, affirmation of faith, and song, heard the solemn declaration of union to which the congregation responded with a resounding and fervent "Amen." Concluding the service the assemblage united in a prayer that was simultaneously a commitment and a covenant on behalf of the United Methodist Church:

> We are no longer our own, but Thine. Put us to what Thou wilt, rank us with whom Thou wilt, put us to doing, put us to suffering: let us be employed for Thee or laid aside by Thee, exalted for Thee or brought low for Thee: let us be full, let us be empty: let us have all things, let us have nothing. We freely and heartily yield all things to Thy pleasure and disposal.
>
> And now, O glorious and blessed God, Father, Son and Holy Spirit, Thou art ours and we are Thine. So be it. And the covenant which we have made on earth, let it be ratified in heaven. Amen.[62]

EPILOGUE

The Evangelical United Brethren Church with origins in the early nineteenth century and corporate organization in 1946 came to its end in a uniting event that was singularly momentous and sentiment-packed for its people. No crucial plight or panic inexorably coerced church union. In 1968 in its 4,084 local churches in North America there were 768,099 members who that year contributed $59,819,189 or an average of $80 per member for diverse church purposes. Its educational and benevolent institutions were sound and expanding. Its world missions, with 145 missionaries under appointment, and its home missions programs were thriving. The Women's Society for World Service was flourishing, that year gathering $1,324,588 for missionary causes. All this was humbly recognized as evidence of God's grace. Of course there were problems too, for always where there is a lively sense of God's presence there are challenges and struggles.

Past experiences and current convictions readied Evangelical United Brethren to join the Methodists even though it meant the surrender of some treasured traditions and some of the more familial relations that are possible in a smaller denomination. In unions in 1922 and 1946 they had learned that mergers were not a betrayal or repudiation of the past but occasions for enrichment and new satisfactions. Even more impelling was the conviction that God's guidance, which in the early nineteenth century had led to separations, now led to union. The use of the German language which once had been a primary mark of their distinctiveness from Methodists had long since disappeared as a distinguishing barrier. Singular ways of administration had developed through the decades, but now it was believed that obedience to divine direction was more demanding than the perpetuation of the status quo, however convenient and comfortable the latter might be. God's people in scripture and subsequent history have been a pilgrim

395

people on faithful mission into the future with his living presence presiding over the trek.

The United Methodist Church is the inheritor of many, varied and rich traditions, Evangelical United Brethren and Methodist, but its high vocation is neither to its past nor to some self-serving prestige but to its Lord under whose leadership accomplishments, undreamed today, may be achieved. The challenges of the present call for sober consideration, but there is no reason for pessimism, for there is nothing wrong with the church that faith and faithful obedience cannot transcend. The United Methodist Church exists to call, encourage, and assist men and women to live in every phase of their lives under the mastery of Christ, nourished by his spirit and graces. For this demanding mission the church with flexible and strategic programs, moderation in expectations, and obedience to the Light as it is given, relies with confidence on the surprising and sustaining gifts of the living God.

N O T E S

NOTES FOR CHAPTER II

1. Henry G. Spayth, *History of the Church of the United Brethren in Christ* (Circleville, Ohio: Conference Office of the United Brethren in Christ, 1851), pt. I, p. 20.

2. For a comprehensive and penetrating study of the theological influences upon and the theological contributions of members of the Otterbein family see J. Steven O'Malley, *Pilgrimage of Faith: The Legacy of the Otterbeins* (Metuchen, N.J.: Scarecrow Press, 1973).

3. For a fuller discussion of the "Theology of the Covenants" in the Herborn Academy see A. C. Core, *Philip William Otterbein* (Dayton, Ohio: Board of Publication, Evangelical United Brethren Church, 1968), pp. 14 ff.

4. Otterbein's certificate of ordination is preserved in the United Methodist Archives, Junaluska, North Carolina.

5. H. Harbaugh and D. Y. Eiseler, *The Fathers of the German Reformed Church* (Lancaster, Pa.: J. W. Westhaeffer, 1857), II, 55, 56.

6. Core, *Phillip William Otterbein*, pp. 77-90.

7. W. S. Cramer, *History of the First Reformed Church, Lancaster, Pennsylvania, 1736–1904* (Lancaster, Pa.: Wickersham Printing Co., 1904), I, 24, 25.

8. W. J. Hinke, *Ministers of the German Reformed Congregations in Pennsylvania and Other Colonies of the Eighteenth Century*, ed. George W. Richards (Lancaster, Pa.: Historical Commission, Evangelical and Reformed Church, 1951), p. 74.

9. John Blair Linn, "Annals of Buffalo Valley, 1755-1855," in United Methodist Archives, pp. 9-11.

10. A. W. Drury, *History of the Church of the United Brethren in Christ* (Dayton, Ohio: Otterbein Press, 1924), p. 90.

11. *Ibid.*, p. 101

12. Phares Brubaker Gibble, *History of the East Pennsylvania Conference of the Church of the United Brethren in Christ* (Dayton, Ohio: Otterbein Press, 1951), p. 13.

13. John Lawrence, article in *Unity Magazine* (originally called *Unity with God*), February 1856.

14. Henry Boehm, *Reminiscences*, ed. Joseph B. Wakeley (New York: Carlton & Porter, 1865), p. 11.

15. Gibble, *History East Pennsylvania Conference*, pp. 12, 13. Boehm, *Reminiscences*, p. 13.

16. *Ibid.*, p. 28 n. 15.

17. Spayth, *History United Brethren*, pp. 28, 29.

18. Gibble, *History East Pennsylvania Conference*, p. 28 n. 15.

19. Spayth, *History United Brethren*, pp. 32-35.

20. *Ibid.*, p. 41.

21. Boehm, *Reminiscences*, p. 391.

22. John Funk, *The Mennonite Church and Her Accusers* (Elkhart, Ind.: Mennonite Publishing Co., 1878), pp. 42-56.

23. *Ibid.*, p. 56
24. *Ibid.*, pp. 43-45, 49.
25. Francis Asbury, *The Journal and Letters of Francis Asbury*, ed. Elmer T. Clark, J. Manning Potts, and Jacob S. Payton (Nashville: Abingdon Press, 1958), II, 610.
26. Boehm, *Reminiscences*, p. 31.
27. Asbury, *Journal and Letters*, p. 645.
28. Gibble, *History East Pennsylvania Conference*, p. 17.
29. Paul E. Holdcraft, "The Old Otterbein Story, " mimeographed (Baltimore, Md., 1959), in United Methodist Archives, p. 14.
30. *Ibid.*, pp. 14, 53; Drury, *History United Brethren*, p. 113 n.
31. Holdcraft, "*Otterbein Story*," p. 25.
32. Core, *Phillip William Otterbein*, pp. 109-14.
33. *Ibid.*, p. 100.
34. Drury, *History United Brethren*, chap. Xv.
35. *Ibid.*, p. 226.
36. Core, *Phillip William Otterbein*, pp. 115-19.
37. *Ibid.*, p. 115.
38. A. W. Drury, *Disciplines of the United Brethren in Christ, 1814–1841* (Dayton, Ohio: United Brethren Publishing House, 1895), p. 9.
39. *Ibid.*
40. *Ibid.*, p. 45.
41. C. S. Weyand and John H. Ness, Jr., typescript in United Methodist Archives.
42. Boehm, *Reminiscences*, p. 392.
43. Harbaugh and Eiseler, *Fathers of German Reformed Church*, III, 465.
44. Core, *Phillip William Otterbein*, pp. 124, 126.
45. Drury, *History United Brethren*, p. 311.
46. Christian Newcomer, *The Life and Journal of the Rev'd Christian Newcomer*, trans. and ed. John Hildt (Hagerstown, Md.: F. G. W. Kapp, 1834), p. 9.
47. *Ibid.*, p. 6.
48. *Ibid.*, p. 195.
49. *Ibid.*
50. *Hagerstown Mail*, March 19, 1830, in United Methodist Archives; "Death of Christian Newcomer;" *Religious Telescope*, September 21, 1836, p. 79.

Notes for Chapter III

1. R. B. Strassburger and W. J. Hinke, *Pennsylvania Pioneers* (Norristown, Pa.: Pennsylvania German Society, 1934), I, 71 ff.
2. Raymond W. Albright, *A History of the Evangelical Church* (Harrisburg, Pa.: Evangelical Press, 1956), p. 23.
3. Reuben Yeakel, *Jacob Albright and His Co-Laborers* (Cleveland, Ohio: Publishing House of the Evangelical Association, 1883), p. 19.
4. George Miller, *Jacob Albright: The First Biography of the Founder of the Evangelical Association*, trans. G. E. Epp (Dayton, Ohio: Historical Society, Evangelical United Brethren Church, 1959), p. 4.
5. Albright, *History Evangelical Church*, p. 35.
6. Miller, *Jacob Albright*, p. 7.
7. *Ibid.*, p. 8.
8. R. W. Albright, article in *Evangelical Messenger*, April 28, 1934.
9. R. W. Albright to Samuel S. Hough, May 5, 1931, in United Methodist Archives.

10. R. W. Albright to Samuel S. Hough, April 1930, in United Methodist Archives; Ammon Stapleton, *Annals of the Evangelical Association of North America and History of the United Evangelical Church* (Harrisburg, Pa.: Publishing House of the United Evangelical Church, 1896), p. 19; Reuben Yeakel, *History of the Evangelical Association* (Cleveland, Ohio: Thomas and Mattill, 1894), I, 50.

11. Ammon Stapleton, *A Wonderful Story of Old Time Evangelical Evangelism* (Harrisburg, Pa.: Board of Publication of the United Evangelical Church, 1917), p. 32.

12. Yeakle, *Jacob Albright*, pp. 65 ff.; Christian Newcomer, *The Life and Journal of the Rev'd Christian Newcomer*, trans. and ed. John Hildt (Hagerstown, Md.: F.G.W. Kapp, 1834), p. 32; Robert S. Wilson, *Jacob Albright, the Evangelical Pioneer* (Myerstown, Pa.: Church Center Press, 1940), p. 47; Stapleton, *Evangelical Annals*, pp. 515 ff.

13. Yeakel, *Jacob Albright*, p. 14.

14. In United Methodist Archives.

15. Yeakel, *History Evangelical Association*, I, 85 n.

16. Stapleton, *Evangelical Evangelism*, p. 111.

17. S. P. Spreng, memorial address at Albright's grave, September 11, 1932, in United Methodist Archives.

18. George Miller, manuscript General Conference Book, item in Conference Record, in United Methodist Archives.

19. Paul H. Eller, *These Evangelical United Brethren* (Dayton, Ohio: Otterbein Press, 1957), p. 46.

20. Stapleton, *Evangelical Evangelism*, pp. 60 ff.

21. Yeakel, *Jacob Albright*, pp. 174, 239-42.

22. Raymond W. Albright, article in *Berks County Review*, January 1944.

23. Yeakel, *History Evangelical Association*, I, 101.

24. Yeakel, *Jacob Albright*, p. 264.

25. *Ibid.*, p. 266.

26. S. C. Breyfogel, *Landmarks of the Evangelical Association* (Reading, Pa.: Eagle Book Print, 1888), p. 16.

27. W. W. Orwig, *History of the Evangelical Association* (Cleveland, Ohio: Charles Hammer, 1858), I, 33; Yeakel, *History Evangelical Association*, I, 82.

28. Yeakel, *History Evangelical Association*, I, 88 n., 96 n.

29. Yeakel, *Jacob Albright*, p. 238.

30. Miller, *Jacob Albright*, pp. 4, 6.

31. Yeakel, *Jacob Albright*, p. 116.

32. Stapleton, *Annals Evangelical Association*, p. 517.

33. Yeakel, *History Evangelical Association*, I, 96 n.

34. *Evangelical Messenger*, February 21, 1855, p. 28; Orwig, *History Evangelical Association*, pp. 56, 57; Yeakel, *History Evangelical Association*, I, 108, 109.

35. Orwig, *History Evangelical Association*, pp. 57-58.

36. Yeakel, *History Evangelical Association*, I, 120.

37. Breyfogel, *Landmarks*, p. 18; Yeakel, *History Evangelical Association*, I, 102 (in German edition: I, 97).

38. Breyfogel, *Landmarks*, p. 20.

39. John H. Ness, Jr., *One Hundred Fifty Years* (Dayton, Ohio: Board of Publication, Evangelical United Brethren Church, 1966), pp. 32, 33.

NOTES FOR CHAPTER IV

1. A. W. Drury, *Disciplines of the United Brethren in Christ, 1814–1841* (Dayton, Ohio: United Brethren Publishing House, 1895), p. 10.

2. Henry Boehm, "Manuscript of the Journal of Henry Boehm," microfilm, in United Methodist Archives, pp. 120-21.

3. A. W. Drury, *Minutes of the Annual and General Conferences of the Church of the United Brethren in Christ, 1800-1818* (Dayton, Ohio: Historical Society of the United Brethren in Christ, 1897), p. 71.

4. A. W. Drury, *History of the Church of the United Brethren in Christ* (Dayton, Ohio: United Brethren Publishing House, 1924), pp. 300-302.

5. Nathan Bangs, *A History of the Methodist Episcopal Church* (New York: T. Mason and G. Lane, Publishers, 1838-1841), II, 369-71.

6. Francis Asbury, *The Journal and Letters of Francis Asbury*, ed. E. T. Clark, J. Manning Potts, and Jacob S. Payton (Nashville: Abingdon Press, 1958), II, 753, 754.

7. W. W. Sweet, *The Story of Religion in America* (New York: Harpers, 1939), pp. 252-53; C. E. Olmstead, *History of Religion in the United States* (Englewood Cliffs, N. J.: Prentice Hall, 1960), p. 226.

8. Christian Newcomer, *The Life and Journal of the Rev'd Christian Newcomer*, trans. and ed. John Hildt (Hagerstown, Md.: F. G. W. Kapp, 1834), p. 105.

9. *Ibid.*, p. 175.

10. Drury, *History United Brethren*, pp. 808-20.

11. Newcomer, *Journal*, pp. 212, 213.

12. Drury, *Disciplines United Brethren*, pp. 3-6.

13. John H. Ness, Jr., *One Hundred Fifty Years* (Dayton, Ohio: Board of Publication, Evanglical United Brethren Church, 1966), pp. 244-46.

NOTES FOR CHAPTER V

1. A. W. Drury, *History of the Church of the United Brethren in Christ* (Dayton, Ohio: Otterbein Press, 1924), p. 341.

2. A. W. Drury, *Minutes of the Annual and General Conferences of the Church of the United Brethren in Christ, 1800-1818* (Dayton, Ohio: Historical Society of the United Brethren in Christ, 1897), p. 29 (1812, item 15).

3. Drury, *History United Brethren*, p. 803.

4. William Henry Nauman, "Theology in the Evangelical United Brethren Church" (Ph.D. diss., Yale, 1965), in United Methodist Archives.

5. *Religious Telescope*, August 18, 1841, p. 10.

6. John H. Ness, Jr., *One Hundred Fifty Years* (Dayton, Ohio: Board of Publication, Evangelical United Brethren Church, 1966), p. 254.

7. Drury, *History United Brethren*, p. 340

8. A. W. Drury, *Disciplines of the United Brethren in Christ, 1814-1841* (Dayton, Ohio: United Brethren Publishing House, 1895), p. 5

9. *Ibid.*, p. 159.

10. *Ibid.*, p. 5.

11. *Ibid.*, p. 159.

12. For comprehensive coverage of Evangelical, and Evangelical United Brethren, publishing see Ness, *One Hundred Fifty Years*.

13. D. H. Kendall, "Index Newcomer's Journal," typescript, 1964, in United Theological Seminary Library.

14. United Brethren General Conference Minutes, 1829.

15. Drury, *History United Brethren*, p. 345.

16. Dorothy Drain, "The United Brethren in Christ and the Slavery Issue," Unpublished paper, Department of History, University of Michigan, 1962. Microfilm in United Methodist Archives.

NOTES FOR CHAPTER VI

1. S. C. Breyfogel, *Landmarks of the Evangelical Association* (Reading, Pa.: Eagle Book Print, 1888), p. 19.

2. Reuben Yeakel, *History of the Evangelical Association* (Cleveland, Ohio: Thomas and Mattill, 1894), I, 153.

3. Ammon Stapleton, *Annals of the Evangelical Association of North America and History of the United Evangelical Church* (Harrisburg, Pa.: Publishing House of the United Evangelical Church, 1896), p. 528.

4. John Dreisbach, *Journal*, February 14, 1817.

5. Yeakel, *History Evangelical Association*, I, 145, 284.

6. R. B. Leedy, *The Evangelical Church in Ohio* (Harrisburg, Pa.: Ohio Conference of the Evangelical United Brethren Church, 1959), p. 68.

7. R. B. Leedy, trans., proceedings of the Evangelical Conferences, manuscript in United Methodist Archives.

8. Breyfogel, *Landmarks*, p. 28.

9. Yeakel, *History Evangelical Association*, I, 153.

10. *Ibid.*, p. 326.

11. Samuel P. Spreng, *The Life and Labors of John Seybert* (Cleveland, Ohio: Lauer and Matteli, 1888), p. 123.

12. Breyfogel, *Landmarks*, p. 68.

13. *Ibid.*, p. 34.

14. Spreng, *John Seybert*, pp. 131 ff.

15. Yeakel, *History Evangelical Association*, I, 244-45.

16. I Corinthians 1:12.

17. W. W. Orwig, *History of the Evangelical Association* (Cleveland, Ohio: Charles Hammer, 1858), I, 157.

18. *Ibid.*

19. *Ibid.*, p. 158.

20. *Ibid.*, p. 229.

21. R. W. Albright and Roy B. Leedy, *A Century's Progress: A Story of Religious Education in the Evangelical Church* (Cleveland, Ohio: Board of Education of the Evangelical Church, 1932), pp. 19 ff.

22. Breyfogel, *Landmarks*, p. 78.

23. *Ibid.*, p. 65.

24. Albright and Leedy, *Century's Progress*, p. 35.

25. Breyfogel, *Landmarks*, p. 107.

26. Stapleton, *Annals Evangelical Association*, pp. 174, 175.

27. See note 12 in chapter V.

28. Orwig, *History Evangelical Association*, p. 7.

29. Spreng, *John Seybert*, p. 162.

30. Breyfogel, *Landmarks*, p. 61.

31. *Ibid.*, p. 93.

32. Spreng, *John Seybert*, p. 300.

33. R. W. Albright, *A History of the Evangelical Church* (Harrisburg, Pa.: Evangelical Press, 1956), pp. 262, 263.

34. Ammon Stapleton, *Flashlights of Evangelical History* (York, Pa.: Ammon Stapleton, 1908), p. 58.

35. Spreng, *John Seybert*, pp. 429-33.

36. *Ibid.*, pp. 369, 370.

NOTES FOR CHAPTER VII

1. A. W. Drury, History of the Church of the United Brethren in Christ (Dayton, Ohio: United Brethren Publishing House, 1924), p. 803.
2. United Brethren General Conference Minutes, 1889, p. 7 (hereafter cited as UBGC Minutes).
3. Religious Telescope, April and May 1889.
4. UBGC Minutes, 1881, pp. 186-211.
5. UBGC Minutes, 1877, p. 169.
6. United Brethren Discipline, 1841, pp. 20, 21 (hereafter cited as UB Discipline).
7. UB Discipline, 1865, p. 27.
8. UBGC Minutes, 1849, pp. 109, 121, 122. All United Brethren General Conference Minutes from 1819 to 1861 are included in a one-volume English manuscript in the United Methodist Archives.
9. Miami Annual Conference Minutes, 1885, p. 18. In United Methodist Archives.
10. Scioto Annual Conference Minutes, 1841, manuscript, pp. 76-78, United Methodist Archives.
11. Scioto Annual Conference Minutes, 1843, p. 99.
12. UBGC Minutes, 1845, p. 96.
13. Drury, History United Brethren, pp. 425, 426.
14. UB Discipline, 1889, pp. 52, 53.
15. UBGC Minutes, 1861, p. 287.
16. UBGC Minutes, 1869, pp. 193-96.
17. UB Discipline, 1857, p. 20.
18. John Lawrence, History of the Church of the United Brethren in Christ (Dayton, Ohio: Vonneida and Sowers, 1860/61), II, 46.
19. Henry G. Spayth, History of the Church of the United Brethren in Christ (Circleville, Ohio: Conference Office of the United Brethren in Christ, 1851), p. 152.
20. UBGC Minutes, 1877, p. 161.
21. UBGC Minutes, 1881, pp. 184-85.
22. UBGC Minutes, 1877, p. 162.
23. UBGC Minutes, 1849, p. 127.
24. Religious Telescope, May 31, 1865, p. 158.
25. Religious Telescope, February 28, 1855, p. 99.
26. Religious Telescope, June 3, 1857, p. 158.
27. UBGC Minutes, 1889, pp. 270-74.
28. The discussion on missions is based almost entirely on Samuel G. Ziegler's typescript, "History of United Brethren Missions," which was used on loan from the author. From 1921 to 1946 Dr. Ziegler served as general secretary of the Foreign Missionary Society of the United Brethren Church.
29. For a fuller presentation of the Gomers and their work see Orlo Strunk, Jr., In Faith and Love (Nashville: Graded Press, 1968), chap. 7.
30. Robert W. Steele et al., History of Dayton, Ohio (Dayton: United Brethren Publishing House, 1889), p. 617.
31. UBGC Minutes, 1849, p. 119.
32. Religious Telescope, February 24, 1836, p. 18.
33. Religious Telescope, June 4, 1845, p. 181.
34. Henry Garst, History of Otterbein University (Dayton, Ohio: United Brethren Publishing House, 1907), p. 79.
35. Paul A. W. Wallace, Lebanon Valley College: A Centennial History (Annville, Pa.: Lebanon Valley College, 1966), p. 61.
36. Microfilmed minutes of the Russell Fund, Roll 26, United Methodist

Archives; Wallace, *Lebanon Valley College*, pp. 39, 40. Precise accuracy with respect to details about the Russell Biblical Chair is difficult to achieve inasmuch as source materials give varying accounts, as witnessed by the two sources here cited.
37. UBGC Minutes, 1869, p. 209.
38. *Religious Telescope*, December 31, 1843, p. 3.
39. John H. Ness, Jr., *One Hundred Fifty Years* (Dayton, Ohio: Board of Publication, Evangelical United Brethren Church, 1966), p. 381.
40. *Ibid.*, p. 374.
41. UB *Discipline*, 1889, p. 17.
42. *Ibid.*, p. 20.
43. *Ibid.*, p. 21.
44. UBGC Minutes, 1889, p. 173.
45. *Ibid.*, p. 196.

NOTES FOR CHAPTER VIII

1. Evangelical Association *Discipline*, 1844, p. 39 (hereafter cited as EA *Discipline*).
2. Evangelical General Conference Minutes, 1867, p. 88 (hereafter cited as EGC Minutes).
3. EA *Discipline*, 1868, p. 47.
4. Samuel P. Spreng, *The Life and Labors of John Seybert* (Cleveland, Ohio: Lauer and Matteli, 1888), p. 354.
5. EA *Discipline*, 1844, pp. 99, 100.
6. EGC Minutes, 1867, p. 77.
7. S. C. Breyfogel, *Landmarks of the Evangelical Association* (Reading, Pa.: Eagle Book Print, 1888), p. 69.
8. EGC Minutes, 1867, pp. 83, 84.
9. East Pennsylvania Annual Conference Minutes, 1880, p. 11.
10. Breyfogel, *Landmarks*, p. 106.
11. EA *Discipline*, 1889, pp. 74-79.
12. Ammon Stapleton, *Annals of the Evangelical Association of North America and History of the United Evangelical Church* (Harrisburg, Pa.: Publishing House of the United Evangelical Church, 1896), pp. 333, 334.
13. Reuben Yeakel, *History of the Evangelical Association* (Cleveland, Ohio: Thomas and Mattill, 1894), II, 108, 109; Stapleton, *Annals Evangelical Association*, p. 338.
14. EA *Discipline*, 1860 (English part), p. 50.
15. EGC Minutes, 1871, p. 26.
16. EA *Discipline*, 1860 (English part), Sections IV-V, pp. 57-76.
17. EA *Discipline*, 1872, pp. 36 ff.
18. Yeakel, *History Evangelical Association*, II, 14.
19. *Ibid.*, pp. 169, 195 ff., 203 ff.
20. EGC Minutes, 1863, p. 12.
21. EGC Minutes, 1867, p. 30.
22. *Ibid.*, pp. 72, 73.
23. Breyfogel, *Landmarks*, p. 107.
24. EGC Minutes, 1863, pp. 58-61.
25. EGC Minutes, 1883, pp. 52, 53.
26. W. E. Peffley, ed., *History of the Central Pennsylvania Conference of the Evangelical Church* (Harrisburg, Pa.: Evangelical Press, 1940), p. 76.
27. EGC Minutes, April 4, 1863, p. 53.
28. EGC Minutes, 1867, p. 33.

29. EA *Discipline*, 1860, Nineteenth Article of Faith, p. 18.
30. EGC Minutes, 1863, pp. 59, 60.
31. East Pennsylvania Annual Conference Minutes, 1879, p. 18.
32. EGC Minutes, 1867, p. 73.
33. East Pennsylvania Annual Conference Minutes, 1882, p. 13.
34. EGC Minutes, 1847, item 61.
35. EA *Discipline*, 1844, pp. 54-58.
36. Ralph Kendall Schwab, *The History of the Doctrine of Christian Perfection in the Evangelical Association* (Menasha, Wis.: Collegiate Press, 1922), p. 39.
37. *Ibid.*, p. 45.
38. These statements constitute a summary of several of Neitz's writings.
39. Yeakel, *History Evangelical Association*, II, 122.
40. EGC Minutes, 1867, p. 44.
41. Schwab, *Doctrine of Christian Perfection*, pp. 147-49.
42. *Ibid.*, p. 60.
43. *Ibid.*, chap. IV.
44. R. W. Albright and Roy B. Leedy, *A Century's Progress: A Story of Religious Education in the Evangelical Church* (Cleveland, Ohio: Board of Education of the Evangelical Church, 1932), p. 46.
45. *Ibid.*, p. 65.
46. EGC Minutes, 1847, items 66, 70.
47. EGC Minutes, 1867, p. 79.
48. *The Seminary Review* (Evangelical Theological Seminary), March 1946.
49. John G. Schwab and H. H. Thoren, *History of the Illinois Conference of the Evangelical Church, 1837-1937* (Harrisburg, Pa.: Evangelical Press, 1937), p. 293; Yeakel, *History Evangelical Association*, II, 223.
50. For a comprehensive study of the history of missions in the Evangelical Association see Paul H. Eller, *History of Evangelical Missions* (Harrisburg, Pa.: Evangelical Press, 1942).
51. Yeakel, *History Evangelical Association*, II, 19; Stapleton, *Annals Evangelical Association*, p. 458.
52. Eller, *History of Missions*, pp. 105ff.
53. Stapleton, *Annals Evangelical Association*, p. 434.
54. *Evangelical Messenger*, June 23, 1885, p. 393.
55. *Evangelical Messenger*, October 13, 1885, p. 650.
56. *Evangelical Messenger*, November 10, 1885, p. 714; April 21, 1885, p. 245.
57. *Evangelical Messenger*, April 21, 1885, p. 245; November 3, 1885, p. 698; November 18, 1885, p. 714.
58. EGC Minutes, 1863, p. 49.
59. Orphanage Catalog, 1912, p. 13.
60. EGC Minutes, 1879, p. 93.
61. EGC Minutes, 1887, p. 50.
62. EA *Discipline*, 1844, p. 100.

NOTES FOR CHAPTER IX

1. Howard Mumford Jones, *O Strange New World* (New York: Viking Press, 1964), p. 392.
2. W. E. Musgrave, *Church of the United Brethren in Christ* (Huntington, Ind.: Dept. of Christian Education, Church of the United Brethren in Christ, 1945), p. 8.
3. *Ibid.*, p. 60.
4. John H. Ness, Jr., *One Hundred Fifty Years* (Dayton, Ohio: Board of Publication, Evangelical United Brethren Church, 1966), p. 319, 409.

5. Musgrave, *Church of United Brethren*, pp. 54, 61. See also A. W. Drury, *History of the Church of the United Brethren in Christ* (Dayton, Ohio: United Brethren Publishing House, 1924), p. 516.
6. Musgrave, *Church of United Brethren*, p. 61.
7. United Brethren *Discipline*, 1893, p. 24 (full title is *Origin, Doctrine, Constitution, of the United Brethren in Christ*, hereafter cited as UB *Discipline*).
8. UB *Discipline*, 1913, p. 20.
9. UB *Discipine*, 1889, p. 34.
10. Drury, *History United Brethren*, p. 512.
11. UB *Discipline*, 1889, p. 7.
12. Drury, *History United Brethren*, p. 504.
13. UB *Discipline*, 1889, p. 54.
14. UB *Discipline*, 1913, p. 54.
15. UB *Discipline*, 1897, p. 67.
16. UB *Discipline*, 1901, pp. 66-68.
17. Drury, *History United Brethren*, p. 801.
18. UB *Discipline*, 1885, p. 109.
19. Drury, *History United Brethren*, p. 616.
20. *Ibid.*
21. UB *Discipline*, 1909, p. 124; Drury, *History United Brethren*, p. 614.
22. UB *Discipline*, 1909, pp. 123 ff.
23. United Brethren General Conference Minutes, 1946, pp. 167-74 (title is *Official Proceedings, Thirty-Fourth General Conference, 1946*, hereafter cited as UBGC Minutes). For this conference Dr. S. G. Ziegler reviewed the church's missionary operations in Sierra Leone, China, Japan, Puerto Rico, Santo Domingo, and the Philippines.
24. UB *Discipline*, 1913, pp. 138ff.
25. UB *Discipline*, 1905, p. 88.
26. UB *Discipline*, 1893, p. 123.
27. UB *Discipline*, 1909, pp. 98 ff.
28. Edwin H. Sponseller, *Crusade for Education* (Frederick, Md.: Edwin H. Sponseller, 1950), pp. 187 ff.; UB *Discipline*, 1913, p. 167.
29. UB *Discipline*, 1893, p. 155.
30. Sponseller, *Crusade for Education*, pp. 185 ff.
31. Ness, *One Hundred Fifty Years*, pp. 394-97.
32. United Brethren General Conference *Official Report*, 1893, p. 35 (title is *Official Report, XXI General Conference of the United Brethren in Christ* hereafter cited as UBGC *Official Report*).
33. UB *Discipline*, 1901, p. 79.
34. UBGC *Official Report*, 1909, p. 22.
35. *Ibid.*, p. 398.
36. *Ibid.*, p. 397-99.
37. UBGC *Official Report*, 1917, pp. 9 ff.
38. UBGC *Official Report*, 1897, p. 49.
39. UB *Discipline*, 1909, p. 11.
40. UB *Discipline*, 1913, p. 225.
41. UB *Discipline*, 1917, pp. 89 ff.
42. UB *Discipline*, 1917, p. 211; UBGC *Official Report*, 1917, p. 131.
43. A. T. Howard, "Christianity Better Understood," *The Search Light*, July 1902, p. 888.
44. *Religious Telescope*, August 27, 1902, p. 8.
45. Drury, *History United Brethren*, p. 530.
46. *Ibid.*, p. 531.

47. UBGC *Official Report*, 1909, p. 392.
48. K. James Stein, "Christian Unity Movements in the Church of the United Brethren in Christ Until 1946" (Ph.D. diss., Union Theological Seminary, 1946), pp. 112 ff.
49. UBGC *Official Report*, 1917, p. 658.
50. *Ibid.*

NOTES FOR CHAPTER X

1. United Brethren *Discipline*, 1925, p. 12 (title is *Discipline of the Church of the United Brethren in Christ*, hereafter cited as UB *Discipline*).
2. UB *Discipline*, 1945, p. 251.
3. UB *Discipline*, 1941, p. 47.
4. United Brethren General Conference Minutes, 1945, p. 202 (hereafter cited as UBGC Minutes).
5. United Brethren General Conference *Official Report*, 1929, p. 202 (hereafter cited as UBGC *Official Report*).
6. UB *Discipline*, 1937, p. 54.
7. UB *Discipline*, 1941, p. 80.
8. UBGC *Official Report*, 1929, p. 205.
9. UBGC Minutes, 1933, pp. 224, 235.
10. UBGC Minutes, 1941, p. 237.
11. *Ibid.*, p. 245.
12. UBGC *Official Report*, 1929, p. 150.
13. UBGC Minutes, 1933, pp. 33 ff.
14. UBGC Minutes, 1929, pp. 41, 150.
15. UBGC Minutes, 1933, p. 29; UBGC Minutes, 1937, pp. 29, 184; UBGC Minutes, 1941, p. 197.
16. UBGC Minutes, 1945, p. 509. Dr. Samuel G. Ziegler, who in 1958 retired after a distinguished career in missionary administration, provided helpful data.
17. UBGC *Official Report*, 1929, p. 150.
18. UBGC Minutes, 1933, pp. 29 ff.; UBGC Minutes, 1945, pp. 200, 507.
19. UBGC *Official Report*, 1929, p. 150; UBGC Minutes, 1937, p. 184; UBGC Minutes, 1945, p. 506.
20. UBGC Minutes, 1929, p. 150.
21. UBGC Minutes, 1945, p. 518.
22. UBGC Minutes, 1929, p. 186.
23. UBGC Minutes, 1937, pp. 123 ff.
24. UBGC Minutes, 1933, p. 471.
25. UBGC Minutes, 1945, p. 494.
26. John H. Ness, Jr., *One Hundred Fifty Years* (Dayton, Ohio: Board of Publication, Evangelical United Brethren Church, 1966), pp. 441 ff.
27. UBGC Minutes, 1933, p. 178; UBGC Minutes, 1937, p. 116.
28. Ness, *One Hundred Fifty Years*, p. 456.
29. UBGC Minutes, 1941, pp. 352, 443.
30. UBGC Minutes, 1933, pp. 24 ff.
31. UBGC Minutes, 1945, p. 96.
32. UBGC Minutes, 1933, pp. 31, 249.
33. UBGC *Official Report*, 1929, p. 35; A. W. Drury, *History of the Church of the United Brethren in Christ* (Dayton, Ohio: Otterbein Press, 1924), p. 669.
34. UBGC Minutes, 1941, p. 457.
35. UBGC Minutes, 1945, p. 52.
36. UBGC Minutes, 1933, pp. 201 ff.

37. Drury, History United Brethren, p. 668.
38. UBGC Minutes, 1945, p. 581.
39. K. James Stein, "Christian Unity Movements in the Church of the United Brethren in Christ Until 1946" (Ph.D. diss., Union Theological Seminary, 1946).
40. UBGC Official Report, 1929, pp. 419 ff.
41. UBGC Minutes, 1933, p. 66.
42. UBGC Minutes, 1937, p. 18.
43. UBGC Minutes, 1941, p. 26.
44. Ibid., p. 379.
45. UBGC Minutes, 1945, pp. 334 ff.
46. Ibid., p. 543.

NOTES FOR CHAPTER XI

1. For the offer of Dr. W. K. Carroll and its reception see The Evangelical, IV, 74, 109; Evangelical Messenger, XLVI, 185, 233, 312, 344, 664, 681, 760.
2. United Evangelical Discipline, 1894, pp. 39-42 (title is Doctrines and Discipline of the United Evangelical Church, hereafter cited as UE Discipline).
3. M. J. Ballantyne, "Benefits of Lay Representation, The Evangelical, VI (1893), 346.
4. W. M. Stanford, "Particulars from the Oregon Conference," The Evangelical, VI, no. 44 (1893), 346.
5. Evangelical Association Discipline, 1899, p. 140 (title is The Doctrines and Discipline of the Evangelical Association, hereafter cited as EA Discipline).
6. UE Discipline, 1894, pp. 151 ff.
7. Ibid., pp. 24-27.
8. J. B. Kanaga, "Drummond and Darwinism," Evangelical Messenger, XLVI (1893), 689.
9. J. B. Kanaga, "Present Status of Biblical Criticism," Evangelical Messenger, IL (1896), 609.
10. S. Hoy, "The Reason Why," Evangelical Messenger, L (1897), 113. See also Evangelical Messenger, XLV (1892), 292; W. A. Barr, "Higher Critics, the Troublers of Israel," The Evangelical, XIV (1901), 194.
11. S. J. Gamertsfelder, "The Inspiration of the Bible," Evangelical Messenger, LI (1898), 673.
12. A. Krecker, "Orthodoxy and the New Theology," Evangelical Messenger, LI (1898), 561; H. V. Summers, "Is the Soul of a Child Possessed of Adamic Purity?" The Evangelical, XVI (1903), 499.
13. J. B. Kanaga, "What Constitutes a Valid Episcopacy," Evangelical Messenger, IIL (1895), 226.
14. Evangelical Messenger, April 15, 1914, p. 35.
15. R. Kücklich, Die Evangelische Gemeinschaft in Europa (Stuttgart: Christliches Verlagshaus, G. M. b. H., 1925), pp. 33-75.
16. J. J. Esher, "More About My Trip and Our Work in Europe," Evangelical Messenger, XLVI (1892), 505.
17. For detail of Evangelical missionary operations in Europe, Africa, or the Orient see B. H. Niebel and C. N. Dubs, Evangelical Missions (Home and Foreign Missionary Society, Evangelical Association, 1919); Paul H. Eller, History of Evangelical Missions (Harrisburg, Pa.: Evangelical Press, 1942), pp. 146 ff.
18. Eller, History Missions, p. 243.
19. For further details on the language and mountain missions see R. W. Albright, A History of the Evangelical Church (Harrisburg, Pa.: Evangelical Press, 1942), p. 373; Eller, History Missions, p. 302.

20. *Evangelical Messenger*, LIII (1900), 584; *Evangelical Messenger*, LV (1902), 424; *The Evangelical*, LXIV, 53.

21. N. A. Barr, "Observations and Impressions," *The Evangelical*, XXX (1917), 9; C. H. Woodcock, "Trained Leadership for the Rural Church," *Evangelical Messenger*, LXXIII (1919), 6.

22. *The Evangelical*, V (1892), 317, 405; Mrs. S. J. Gamertsfelder and Sarah E. Snyder, *The Abiding Past* (Harrisburg, Pa.: Women's Missionary Society, 1936), p. 125.

23. Gamertsfelder and Snyder, *Abiding Past*, p. 183.

24. *Ibid.*, pp. 48, 63, 95.

25. *Evangelical Messenger*, LIV, no. 13 (1901), 2.

26. E. G. Fuessle, "Evangelical Deaconess Home," *Evangelical Messenger*, LIX (1905), 758.

27. *Evangelical Messenger*, June 14, 1911, p. 6.

28. *Evangelical Messenger*, November 27, 1926, p. 13.

29. D. W. Staffeld, "The Only Hope for a Better World," *Evangelical Messenger*, January 24, 1921, p. 5.

30. T. Bowman, "Religious Education," *Evangelical Messenger*, September 19, 1921, p. 5.

31. D. W. Staffeld, "How to Initiate a Community System of Week Day Religious Education," *Evangelical Messenger*, June 19, 1922, p. 5.

32. *Evangelical Messenger*, XLIV (1891), 520.

33. *Evangelical Messenger*, XLV (1892), 386.

34. *Ibid.*, p. 100.

35. W. H. Fouke, "A Keystone League," *The Evangelical*, IV (1891), 210.

36. J. C. Hornberger, "Why Is Catechism So Largely Neglected?" *Evangelical Messenger*, LVI (1902), 562.

37. EA *Discipline*, 1900. p. 151.

38. *Evangelical Messenger*, LIX (1905), 718.

39. *The Evangelical*, XXXII (1919), 3.

40. *The Evangelical*, December 31, 1919, p. 8.

41. John H. Ness, Jr., *One Hundred Fifty Years* (Dayton, Ohio: Board of Publication, Evangelical United Brethren Church, 1966), p. 187.

42. *Ibid.*, pp. 157-77.

43. *Evangelical Messenger*, XLVI (1893), 360, 372.

44. *Ibid.*, p. 453.

45. Charles Bickford, Romans 12:1, 2, *The Evangelical*, VIII (1895), 97.

46. R. B. Citizen, "Family Life with Reference to the Bible," *Evangelical Messenger*, LVI (1902), 722.

47. *Evangelical Messenger*, LI (1898), 200, 264, 360.

48. *The Evangelical*, XXVIII (1915), 7.

49. *The Evangelical*, XXX (1917), 6; *Evangelical Messenger*, LXXI (1917), 3; Samuel Batt, "Attitudes of the Evangelical Church Toward War" (thesis, Evangelical Theological Seminary, 1946).

50. *Evangelical Messenger*, June 19, 1918, p. 4.

51. *The Evangelical*, October 2, 1918, p. 16; *The Evangelical*, October 23, 1918, p. 2.

52. A. Halmhuber, "What Relation Do Christianity and Socialism Sustain to Each Other?" *Evangelical Messenger*, LIII (1900), 216, 402, 417.

53. *Evangelical Messenger*, XXX (1886), 216; *Evangelical Messenger*, XXXIX (1896), 520.

54. B. R. Schultze, "The Most Important Signs of Our Times," *The Evangelical*, VI (1893), 24; Albright, *History Evangelical Church*, p. 335.

55. A. Orth, "The Church and Reforms," *Evangelical Messenger*, XLIII (1890), 401.

56. *The Evangelical*, X (1897), 218.

57. *Evangelical Messenger*, August 9, 1916, p. 16.

58. *Evangelical Messenger*, XVI (1903), 172.

59. *Evangelical Messenger*, December 17, 1913, p. 22.

60. R. S. Wilson, *A Brief History of the Evangelical Congregational Church* (Myerstown, Pa.: Church Center Press, 1953), p. 28.

NOTES FOR CHAPTER XII

1. Evangelical Church *Discipline*, 1923, pp. 31-34 (title is *Doctrines and Discipline of the Evangelical Church*, hereafter cited as E *Discipline*).

2. *Ibid.*, pp. 45 ff.

3. *The Evangelical*, March 12, 1919, p. 11; *The Evangelical*, March 19, 1919, p. 9.

4. *The Evangelical*, June 4, 1919, p. 9.

5. *Evangelical Messenger*, LXXIV (January 21, 1920), 2.

6. W. H Bucks, "True Nobility of Man," *Evangelical Messenger*, LXXVIII (January 19, 1924), 9.

7. Resolution reported from Groveland Tabernacle meeting (Illinois) in *Evangelical Messenger*, LXXIX (November 28, 1925), 13.

8. J. A. Heck, "Evolution," *Evangelical Messenger*, LXXVII (September 29, 1923), 6.

9. C. S. Bergstresser, "Do Children Need Conversion?" *Evangelical Messenger*, LXXIII (October 4, 1924), 8; F. C. Berger, "Depravity," *Evangelical Messenger*, LXXX (February 6, 1926), 9.

10. *Evangelical Messenger*, LXXX (October 23, 1926), 2.

11. *Evangelical Messenger*, LXXIX (December 12, 1925), 2.

12. *Evangelical Messenger*, LXXX (March 13, 1926), 7.

13. C. S. Poling, "The Atonement," *Evangelical Messenger*, LXXX (March 20, 1926), 9.

14. For sundry expressions in this vein see *Evangelical Messenger*, LXXIX (March 14, 1925), 7; *Evangelical Messenger*, LXXVIII (January 26, 1924), 3; *Evangelical Messenger*, LXXVIII (November 1, 1924), 3.

15. E. W. Praetorius, "Deadly Sins in Architecture," *Evangelical Messenger*, LXXVIII (November 1, 1924), 3.

16. A. H. Nauman, "Horticulture-Landscaping," *Evangelical Messenger*, LXXX (April 24, 1926), 17; R. M. Veh, "Trends in Evangelical Church Architecture," *Evangelical Messenger*, LXXX (September 18, 1926), 9.

17. S. P. Spreng, "Evangelicals' Sufferings in Germany," *Evangelical Messenger*, LXXVII (December 29, 1923), 17.

18. *Missions of the Evangelical Church: Annual Report* (Cleveland, 1930), p. 22; R. W. Albright, *A History of the Evangelical Church* (Harrisburg, Pa: Evangelical Press, 1942), p. 431.

19. *Evangelical Messenger*, LXXXIV (June 7, 1930), 20.

20. Evangelical Church General Conference Minutes, 1938, p. 257 (title is *Proceedings of the General Conference of the Evangelical Church*, hereafter cited as EGC Minutes).

21. S. J. Umbreit, *Evangelical Messenger*, LXXVII (July 28, 1923), 11; *Evangelical Messenger*, LXXVIII (July 5, 1924), 17; S. J. Umbreit, *Zwanzig Jahre Missionar in Japan* (Stuttgart: Christliches Verlagshaus, G. m. b. H., 1929), *passim*.

22. For details on Evangelical missions in Japan, China, and Nigeria see Albright, *History Evangelical Church*, pp. 436-43; P. H. Eller, *History of Evangelical Missions* (Harrisburg, Pa.: Evangelical Press, 1942), pp. 193-285.

23. For further information on the Italian and Kentucky missions see Eller, *History Missions*, pp. 302 ff.

24. *Evangelical Messenger*, LXXXI (April 30, 1927), 10; *Evangelical Messenger*, LXXXII (April 14, 1928), 7.

25. EGC Minutes, 1934, p. 219.

26. *Ibid.*, p. 289.

27. EGC Minutes, 1944, p. 383.

28. R. W. Albright and Roy B. Leedy, *A Century's Progress: A Story of Religious Education in the Evangelical Church* (Cleveland, Ohio: Board of Education of the Evangelical Church, 1932), p. 82.

29. EGC Minutes, 1926, p. 264.

30. E *Discipline*, 1923, p. 190.

31. EGC Minutes, 1942, p. 326.

32. EGC Minutes, 1922, p. 792.

33. *Evangelical Messenger*, LXXVII (October 27, 1923), 3.

34. EGC Minutes, 1942, p. 413.

35. EGC Minutes, 1934, p. 160.

36. EGC Minutes, 1942, p. 173.

37. *Evangelical Messenger*, LXXVII (January 29, 1923), 10; *Evangelical Messenger*, LXXVIII (March 8, 1924), 1.

38. EGC Minutes, 1938, p. 180.

39. EGC Minutes, 1926, p. 295.

40. EGC Minutes, 1938, p. 280.

41. EGC Minutes, 1942, p. 181.

NOTES FOR CHAPTER XIII

1. Evangelical United Brethren General Conference Minutes, 1946, p. 15 (title is *Official Proceedings, General Conference of the Evangelical United Brethren Church*, hereafter cited as EUBGC Minutes).

2. Evangelical United Brethren *Discipline*, 1947, pp. 41-50 (title is *Discipline of the Evangelical United Brethren Church*, hereafter cited as EUB *Discipline*).

3. EUBGC Minutes, 1962, p. 513; EUB *Discipline*, 1963, p. 26.

4. EUBGC Minutes, 1962, p. 935.

5. *Ibid.*, p. 273.

6. EUBGC Minutes, 1950, p. 51.

7. EUBGC Minutes, 1954, p. 440; EUBGC Minutes, 1962, p. 935.

8. EUBGC Minutes, 1958, p. 253.

9. EUB *Discipline*, 1947, pp. 103 ff.

10. *Ibid.*, p. 115.

11. EUBGC Minutes, 1946, p. 269.

12. EUBGC Minutes, 1962, p. 663.

13. EUBGC Minutes, 1946, p. 301.

14. EUBGC Minutes, 1950, p. 382.

15. EUBGC Minutes, 1958, pp. 164, 277.

16. EUBGC Minutes, 1966, pp. 157 ff.

17. *Church and Home*, I (May 15, 1964), 6, 24; *Church and Home*, II (December 1, 1965), 22.

18. EUBGC Minutes, 1954, p. 44.

19. EUBGC Minutes, 1950, p. 220.

20. *Church and Home*, II (December 1, 1965), 22.

21. EUBGC Minutes, 1958, p. 575; EUBGC Minutes, 1966, p. 606; *Church and Home*, III (May 15, 1966), 29; *Church and Home*, IV, 25.

22. EUBGC Minutes, 1954, p. 429.

23. Positions expressed by executive secretaries in their reports to General Conferences, e. g., EUBGC Minutes, 1954, pp. 174 ff.; EUBGC Minutes, 1958, pp. 61 ff.; EUBGC Minutes, 1962, pp. 96 ff.

24. EUBGC Minutes, 1962, p. 99.

25. EUBGC Minutes, 1950, p. 224.

26. EUBGC Minutes, 1960, p. 140; Church and Home, IV (June 15, 1967), 24.

27. EUBGC Minutes, 1950, p.278.

28. EUBGC Minutes, 1962, p. 92.

29. EUBGC Minutes, 1966, p. 144.

30. EUB Discipline, 1947, p. 251.

31. EUB Discipline, 1959, p. 192.

32. EUBGC Minutes, 1954, p. 391.

33. EUBGC Minutes, 1962, pp. 207, 660.

34. Ibid., p. 664.

35. EUBGC Minutes, 1946, p. 349.

36. EUB Discipline, 1946, p. 401.

37. Episcopal message, EUBGC Minutes, 1950, pp. 103, 113; episcopal message, EUBGC Minutes, 1954, p. 107.

38. EUBGC Minutes, 1954, pp. 153. 409; EUBGC Minutes, 1958, p. 475.

39. EUBGC Minutes, 1954, p. 380.

40. EUBGC Minutes, 1954, p. 408.

41. EUBGC Minutes, 1958, p. 474.

42. EUBGC Minutes, 1962, p. 581.

43. Ibid., p. 673.

44. EUB Discipline, 1963, p. 174.

45. EUBGC Minutes, 1966, pp. 531 ff.

46. Ibid., p. 277.

47. EUBGC Minutes, 1962, pp. 277 ff.

48. EUBGC Minutes, 1966, pp. 166, 173, 623.

49. EUBGC Minutes, 1962, pp. 302 ff.

50. Ibid., p. 956.

51. EUBGC Minutes, 1966, p. 25.

52. EUBGC Minutes, 1954, p. 531.

53. EUBGC Minutes, 1958, p. 639.

54. EUBGC Minutes, 1962, pp. 11, 361, 85 ff.

55. Ibid., pp. 85 ff.

56. EUBGC Minutes, 1950, p. 61.

57. EUBGC Minutes, 1946, p. 292.

58. EUBGC Minutes, 1958, pp. 405, 481.

59. EUBGC Minutes, 1966, p. 372.

60. Church and Home, IV (August 1967), 37; Church and Home, IV (September 1967), 36.

61. Church and Home, V (February 1968), 28.

62. Litany for the uniting service, p. 13.

INDEX

Africa, 170-72, 293, 340-41
Albright, Jacob, 67-77, 78-80, 81-84,
Albright, Raymond W., 69, 353
Albright Church, 84, 197
Albright College, 210, 302, 313,
   333, 345, 372
Albright Memorial Church, 342
Albright Seminary, 197, 209
American Training School for
   Young Women, 303
Ammann, Jacob, 19
Amsterdam Classis, 24, 34, 37, 50
Anabaptists, 17
Antisecrecy rule, 183-84
Archibald, A. W., 366
Asbury, Francis, 46, 53, 54, 87-88,
   92, 104, 106
Aurand, Dietrich, 85

Baish, H. H., 273
Baker, Henry, 56
Baker Home, 249, 379
Baltimore Church (German Evan-
   gelical Reformed), 47-51
Baltimore Church Book of 1785,
   106
Baptism, 17, 19, 20-21, 40, 109, 148,
   162-63, 255, 360
Barnaby, N. Y. 227
Batdorf, G. D., 280
Becker, George, 79, 84
Becker, H. J., 227
Becker, Samuel, 81
Bel, William, 354
Benevolent institutions, 217, 249,
   272-73, 308-9, 349-50, 379-81
Berger, Daniel, 181, 245

Berger, F. C., 301
Betz, Matthias, 86, 132, 149
Bigler, Regina, 238
Bischoff, Christian, 173
Bisse, Charles, 81
Blairstown Seminary, 209
Boehm, Henry, 40, 44, 87, 98
Boehm, Martin, 39-45, 54, 56, 97,
   98, 101, 103-6
Boehm Revival, 40, 41, 42, 55
Boltzell, Isaiah, 181
Bonebrake Theological Seminary,
   234, 243-44, 268-69, 362
Bonnet, John, 108
Books of order, 48-51
Booth, B. F., 235
Bowman, Thomas, 206, 222-23,
   305, 310
Brazil, missions in, 366-67
Breidenbach, John, 138
Brewbaker, C. W., 274
Brewer, James, 140
Breyfogel, S. C., 168, 307, 309, 352
Briggs, Charles A., 226
Brown, William, 115
Bruer, James, 140
Bucaletti, Louis, 294
Busacca, G., 294
Byers, Daniel B., 206

Cain, B. H., 259
Camp, P. M., 257
Camp meetings, 30, 93, 120, 138,
   196, 207. See also Great meetings
Campbell College, 243
Carrell, J., 214
Carroll, H. K., 222, 284

Cassel, Homer D., 77
Catechism, 89, 142, 301, 344
Central College, 229
Central Pennsylvania College, 210, 301, 302
Children's Friend, 174
China, missions in, 238-39, 261-62, 291-93, 339-40, 365
Christian Conservator, 228
Christian Endeavor Societies, 208, 229, 241, 265-66, 300, 344
Church of the United Brethren in Christ (Old Constitution), 186-87, 227-30, 279
Circuit riders, 63-64, 76, 93, 150-51, 152, 194
Clark, Francis H., 241
Clewel, T. G., 206, 211
Clippinger, A. R., 358
Coe College, 243
Coetus. See Pennsylvania Coetus
Colleges. See under listings for each church and by name
Collegium pietatis, 20, 34, 35
Conner, T. J., 170
Contact, 229
Cowden, Robert, 175, 241-42
Crider, Martin, 56
Crouse, Isaac, 175
Crum, Christian, 56
Dallas College, 209, 302
Das Evangelische Magazin, 220
Das Geistliche Saitenspiel, 89
Dashields, George, 105-6
Davies, Isaac, 69, 70
Davis, Lewis, 176, 178-79
Deaconesses, 233, 234, 257, 297-98, 337, 350-51, 381
Deacons. See under listings for each church
Deever, O. J., 265
Dehoff, Moses, 138
Dennis, F. L., 358
Depravity controversy, 161-62
Der Christliche Botschafter, 141, 144-45, 202, 216, 219, 347
Der Christliche Kinderfreund, 220
Der Deutsche Telescop, 180
Der Froeliche Botschafter, 180, 245

Deutsche Allgemeine Zeitung, 304
De Wall, J. J., 295
Dickson, John, 185
Die Geschaeftige Martha, 127, 180
Die sogenannten Albrechts, 91
Die Vereinigten, 59
Discipline. See under listings for each church
Divorce, 165, 200, 246, 306, 378
Dreisbach, John, 81, 82, 83, 85-92, 132, 193, 201
Dreisbach, Martin, 80, 85, 94
Drury, A. W., 179, 275, 346
Drury, P. W., 239
Dubbs, J. H., 53
Dubs, C. Newton, 291
Dubs, Homer H., 305
Dubs, Rudolph, 218, 222-23, 284
Dunkers, 15, 16, 19-20
Dunlap, J. F., 352

Ebenezer Orphans' Home, 217, 333
Ecuador, missions in, 367
Edwards, David, 125, 156, 160
Epp, G. E., 336, 358
Erb, Jacob, 115, 156
Erb, John, 81, 91, 132
Ernst, John, 56
Esher, J. J., 134, 191, 205, 206, 210, 211, 214, 215-16, 221, 222-23, 287, 289, 299
Eternal security, doctrine of, 50
Ettinger, Adam, 142, 144
Europe, work in, 337-38, 367-68
Evangelical, 304, 311
Evangelical Association, 67-95, 131, 52, 189-223, 283-313
  Annual Conferences, 133-34, 189
  Articles of Faith, 78-79
  authority in the church, 190-92
  benevolent institutions, 217, 308-9
  bishops, 81-82, 132-33, 146, 190-91
  Charitable Society, 135-36
  Christian education, 142-43, 298-301
  Church Extension Society, 295-96

Evangelical Association, *cont.*
church schools. *See below*, Sunday schools
circuits, 76
colleges, 208-9, 301-2
Commission on Evangelism, 303-4
Conference of 1803, 75-76
"constitution of 1839," 147
Deaconess Society, 297-98
deacons, 91, 93, 131-33, 192
Discipline, 78-79, 82, 89, 145-48
districts, 92-93, 133, 134
doctrine, 140-41
ecumenical relations, 217-19, 309
and education, 207-12
elder, 132, 192. *See below*, presiding elder
General Conference. *See* General Conference, Evangelical Association
itinerancy, 193-94
jubilee, 197, 217
and language, 143, 197-98
lay representation, 195, 285
and liberal theology, 286-87
membership, 81, 134
the ministry, 131-33, 192-95, 287-88; dismissal of, 91, 136-37, 140; salaries of, 80, 91, 135-36; standards for, 136, 195
Missionary Society, 141-42
missions, 212-17, 288-97
moral standards, 136-37
name of, 91, 94, 191-92
pensions, 309
presiding elders, 85, 86, 92, 133
printing and publishing, 90, 144, 219-21
property, church, 191
publications, 89, 143-45, 208, 287, 305. *See also individual titles of periodicals*
schism, 221-23
seal of, 93
and social issues, 147-48, 198-201, 305-9
Sunday schools, 142-43, 207-8, 298-99
theology of, 201-7
union with the United Evangelical Church, 309-12
Women's Missionary Society, 216-17, 290-91, 296-97
worship practices of, 195-96
Young People's Alliance, 299-300
Evangelical Church, 331-55
Christian education, 343-44
Deaconess Society, 350-51
evangelism, 352
formation of, 312
higher education, 345-47
Historical Society, 353
men's organization, 344
the ministry, 332
missions, 336-43
pensions, 351-52
publishing house, 347
Superannuation Fund, 347, 351-52
union with the United Brethren, 277, 279-81, 354-55
Woman's Missionary Society, 343
youth organizations, 344
Evangelical Congregational Church, 279, 312-13
Evangelical Herald, 299
Evangelical Home, 379
Evangelical Manor, 380
Evangelical Messenger, 216, 219
Evangelical relations with Methodists, 87-88
Evangelical School of Theology, 303, 333, 346, 362
Evangelical Theological Seminary, 211-12, 302, 333, 346, 362
Evangelical United Brethren Church, 357-96
Annual Conferences, 383-84
apportionments, 384-85
benevolent institutions, 379-81
bishops, 358-59
Christian education, 370-73
church extension, 368-69

EUB Church, cont.
  colleges, 175-77, 372-73
  Confession of Faith, 358
  evangelistic endeavors, 385-86
  formation of, 277-81, 354-55, 357
  Historical Society, 387
  men's organizations, 372
  the ministry, 359-63
  missions, 363-70, 386
  organizational structure, 358, 383
  pension plans, 381-82
  publishing, 372, 373-75
  schools, 361-62, 372-73
  and social issues, 375-78
  stewardship, 387
  union with the Methodists, 389-92, 395-96
  Women's Society, 364, 370, 395
  youth groups, 371, 372, 386
Evangelische Zeitung, 304
Evans, J. A., 172
Evolution, 334
Eyerick, Katherine, 294

Faber, John Christopher, 45, 46
Faith and Order Conference, 309
Flat Rock Children's Home, 217, 379
Flickinger, D. K., 170-73
Floyd, H., 227
Focht, Daniel, 138
Footwashing, 20, 109, 120, 140, 163
Fortenbach, G., 56
Forward Movement, 304, 332-33
Free Masonry, 125-26, 129-30, 183
Friendly Acres, 380
Fries, W. C., 270
Fry, Jacob, 81, 82, 91-92
Fundamentalism, 335
Funkhouser, George A., 179

Gambling, 164-65
Gamertsfelder, S. J., 287
Garst, Henry, 178
Geeting, George Adam, 54, 56, 57-59, 85, 97, 110, 126
Gehr, Nicholes, 219
Gems of Cheer, 229
General Conference, Evangelical

Association, 146-47, 190-92
  of 1816, 94-95, 135
  of 1820, 134
  of 1830, 143, 146
  of 1836, 145, 146, 148
  of 1843, 192, 197-98, 209
  of 1847, 193, 201, 209
  of 1851, 220
  of 1859, 204, 207
  of 1863, 205, 214, 217
  of 1867, 190, 191, 197, 199, 205, 211
  of 1871, 191-92, 194, 200
  of 1875, 208
  of 1879, 192, 218
  of 1883, 208
  of 1887, 221-22
  of 1903, 297
  of 1922, 311
General Conference, United Brethren, 114, 129, 156-57, 231
  of 1815, 108-11, 119
  of 1817, 120
  of 1821, 124
  of 1825, 115, 183
  of 1829, 125-26, 128
  of 1837, 129
  of 1841, 125, 129, 169, 181
  of 1845, 115, 125, 159, 176
  of 1849, 167, 174
  of 1853, 158, 161, 163, 170
  of 1857, 161-62, 163, 168
  of 1861, 161, 163
  of 1865, 161, 166-67, 174
  of 1869, 161, 178
  of 1873, 168-69, 182
  of 1877, 164, 165, 182
  of 1881, 157, 164-65, 169
  of 1885, 173, 184-85
  of 1889, 160, 168, 186-87
  of 1893, 241
  of 1905, 237
  of 1909, 242
  of 1913, 244
  of 1917, 254
  of 1929, 278
  of 1933, 272
  of 1941, 280
  of 1945, 273, 280

General Conference, *cont.*
of 1946, 280
Germany, 173, 289-90, 337
Gibbon Collegiate Institute, 243
Glossbrenner, Jacob John, 156, 166-
67, 178
Gomer, Joseph, 171-72
Great Awakening, 26-27, 41
Great meetings, 38, 55, 58, 60, 85,
93, 104, 120. See *also* Camp
meetings
Greensburg Seminary, 209
Grosh, Christopher, 56, 107
Guinter, C. W., 293
Gulick, R., 287

Halmhuber, the Rev., 214-15
Hamilton, John, 140, 143
Hammer, Charles, 139
Hanby, William B., 121, 127-28,
158, 176
Hansing, C. F., 208
Hartzler, Henry B., 216, 221
Hartzler, Jacob, 215-16
Hautz, J., 56
Haven Hubbard Home, 309, 350,
379
Heinmiller, G., 352
Hendel, William, 53, 58
Hennig, Adam, 93
Henop, Frederick, 53
Herborn Academy, 32, 33, 38
Herre, Simon, 56
Hershey, Christian, 116
Hershey, John, 56
Hiestand, Samuel, 115
Hildt, John, 119-20, 126
Hillcrest Christian College, 373
Hoffman, Francis, 204
Hoffman, Joseph, 103, 114, 115
Hong Kong, missions in, 365
Horn, W., 305
Hott, J. W., 181
Hough, S. S., 236
Houtz, Anthony, 69
Howard, A. T., 237, 239
Hudson, Rachel, 214-15
Huffman, H. H., 239
Huntington College, 229

Hymnals, 61, 74, 89, 110, 144, 160,
181, 245, 271, 304, 305, 343, 374,
375

Illinois Bible Institute, 303
Imhof, I. C., 294
Indiana Central College, 243, 267,
373
Inerrancy of the Bible, 334-35
Iris, George, 239

Jameson, Alexander, 73, 80
Japan, missions in, 239, 262-63,
290-91, 338-39, 364-65
Journal, KLCE, 300

Kansas City University, 243, 267
Kemp, John, 178, 179
Kemp, Peter, 97, 123
Kendall, D. Homer, 126-27
Kephart, I. E., 245
Kiester, George, 179
Kimmel, George, 140
Kirn, G. J., 287
Kleinfelter, Adam, 93, 138
Kleinfelter, John, 93
Koch, Johann, 33
Krecker, Frederick, 214-15
Krecker, J. W., 374
Kreider, Michael, 102
Kumler, D. C., 170-71
Kumler, Henry, Sr., 95, 114, 115
Kurtz, J. D., 105
Kurtz, Sebastian, 213

La Fayette College, 209
Landis, Josiah P., 179
Lane University, 243
Lawrence, John, 181
Leander Clark College, 243, 266-67
Lebanon Valley College, 177, 243,
268, 372
Lehman, Adam, 56
Lewisburg Home, 309
Liberal theology, 286-87
Lick, J. H., 210
Liesser, Abraham, 73
Liesser, Samuel, 73, 75, 76, 82
Light, Felix, 139

Ling, Moy, 238
Link, John C., 213-14
Living Epistle, 220
Long, Joseph, 152, 204, 205-6, 207, 209
Lord's Supper, the, 20-21, 49, 109, 163
Lorenz, Edmund S., 181
Lorenz, Edward, 173
Lutherans, 16, 17, 19, 20, 22-24, 26

McCray, Robert, 88
Mack, Alexander, 20
Masonic Order, 125-26, 204. See also Free Masonry
Mayer, Paul S., 291, 365
Maze, Matthew T., 279, 352, 354
Mennonites, 15, 16, 17-19, 26
and Martin Boehm, 43-44
Methodist movement, differences from German movement, 55
Methodist Protestant Church, 128
Methodist relations with Evangelicals, 87-88
Metz, M., 91
Miller, George, 67, 75, 76-79, 80, 82, 85, 132
Miller, George (the printer), 144
Miller, Solomon, 81, 94, 144
Ministry, the. See under listings for each church
Missionary Messenger, 296
Missionary Monthly, 229
Missionary Tidings, 296
Missionary Visitor, 245
Missions. See under listings for each church
Mittendorf, William, 245
Modernism in theology, 334-35
Moeller, Henry, 72
Moravians, 15, 16, 21-22, 26
Mount Pleasant College, 176-77
Mueller, R. H., 388
Muhlenberg, Henry Melchior, 23-24, 25
Mullen, Mary, 229
Muller, M. J., 194

Nast, William, 218

Neidig, John, 56, 59
Neitz, Solomon, 203-6, 210, 214
Newcomer, Christian, 56, 61-66, 85, 95, 98-99, 100, 103, 106-7, 108-9, 114, 126
Nickolai, John 214
Niebel, B. H., 305, 336
Niebel, Henry, 86, 89, 92-94, 133
Nigeria, missions in, 367
North Central College, 210, 301-2, 345-46, 362, 373
Northwestern College, 210, 333
Nungesser, J. J., 304

Oath taking, 17, 20, 40, 123
Oberlin church, 59
Orwig, W. W., 138, 139, 141, 144-45, 152, 202-5, 210
Otterbein, William, 25, 31-39, 43-53, 56, 97-98, 101, 104-6
Otterbein College, 243, 268, 372
Otterbein Home, 249, 273, 379
Otterbein University, 176, 177
Our Bible Teacher, 175
Oxnam, G. Bromley, 389

Pacific Home, 379
Pacifism, 17, 20, 21, 40, 147, 167, 199, 271, 306, 348
Pack, Arthur N., 260
Packwood Manor, 380
Parker, Isaac, 152
Pennsylvania Coetus, 24, 34, 35, 37, 45-46, 58
"Pentecostal meetings," 73, 81, 83, 139, 148
Persecution of religious sects, 17, 19, 20-21, 37, 42
Petterson, Austia, 238
Pfrimmer, John George, 56, 60-61, 85, 121
Philadelphia Manor, 350
Philippines, 240, 263, 366
Philips, Jacob, 81
Phillippi, J. M., 270
Phillips, George, 73
Philomath College, 177, 266
Pietism, 19-20, 33, 118
Pipe Creek meetings, 53-54

Plainfield College, 210
Poling, Daniel A., 301
Pomp, Nicholas, 50
Praetorius, E. W., 358
Predestination, 49-50
Puerto Rico, 239, 263, 366

Quakers, 15, 16
Quincy Home, 249, 272-73, 380

Ranger, John, 53
Rawhouser, Jonathan, 85
Reformed Church, German, 16, 17,
    19, 20, 22-25, 26, 277-78
    classes of, 52-54
Religious Telescope, 121, 124-25,
    127, 245
Revival movements
    begun by John Seybert, 138-39
    Boehm Revival, 40, 41, 42, 55
    in eastern colleges, 30
    German, in USA, 31
    Great Awakening, 26-27
    Laymen's Revival, 154
    led by George Miller, 79
    Millersville revival, 80-81
    in Orwigsburg, PA, 134, 137-38
    Second Awakening, 29
    in 1797, 30
Rhinehart, William, 124-25, 127,
    129, 175-76
Richart, Samuel, 138
Riegel, Adam, 69, 71
Roa, Plutarcho, 260
Roman Catholic Church, 16, 17, 21,
    22, 145
Romer, Ignatius, 78, 100
Russell, John, 127, 175-78
Russell's Biblical Chair, 177-78
Ryland, William, 103, 104

Sanctification, 83, 95, 109, 138,
    201-3
Sanders, Benedict, 56
Santo Domingo, missions in, 263-
    64
Saylor, Jacob, 138
Saylor, Joseph, 138
Schaffer, Frederick, 56

Schell, W. E., 244
Schlatter, Michael, 24-25, 34
Schultz, David, 71
Schuylkill College, 301, 345
Schuylkill Valley Seminary, 210,
    301
Schwenckfelders, 15, 16, 20-21, 26
Schwope, Benedict, 45-46, 53, 55,
    56
Seager, L. H., 352
Searchlight, 245
Sects, German, 16-22
Seybert, John, 86, 133, 135, 138,
    141, 142, 148-52, 192
Shaffer, Frederick, 103
Shaffner, Lillian, 238
Shauer, Frederick, 93
Shenandoah College and Conserva-
    tory of Music 243, 267, 373
Showers, J. Balmer, 270, 358
Shuey, W. J., 168, 170-71, 181, 245
Shupe, H. F., 245
Sick, J., 173
Sickafoose, George, 238
Sierra Leone, 170-72, 174, 229,
    237-38, 261, 364, 367
Simons, Menno, 17
Slavery, 61, 65, 123-25, 146, 154,
    165-67, 198
Social Conference of 1817, 95
Social gospel, 247-48, 307-9
South Pacific, missions in, 366
Spangler, John, 56
Spayth, Henry G., 127
Spener, Philipp Jakob, 19-20
"Sporadisches," 206
Spreng, S. P., 305, 335, 352
Stamm, John S., 280, 358, 388
Stanford, W. M., 284
Stapleton, Ammon, 304-5
Statistics, 26, 117, 134, 186, 189,
    207, 212, 258
Stauffacher, C. H., 358
Stettler, Roy H., 347
Strickler, Daniel, 56
Sunday School Teacher, 208
Sunday schools, 61, 142-43, 207-8,
    241, 265-66, 298-99, 343
Switzerland, missions in, 290, 364

Tayama, Henry, 291
Temperance, 122-23, 163-64, 199, 246, 271
Thomas, John, 74
Tobacco, use of, 164, 200, 246
Troxel, Abraham, 56, 108
Two Covenants, doctrine of, 33
Union Biblical Institute, 211-12, 302
Union Biblical Seminary, 178-79, 243-44
Union, church, 22, 94-95, 106-7, 128, 217-19, 277-81, 309-12, 388-92
Union Messenger, 127
Union Seminary, 209-10
United Brethren, 228
United Brethren in Christ, Church of the, 29-66, 97-130, 153-87, 225-81
  Annual Conferences, 101-3, 113-14, 118, 155, 157-58, 256
  authority in the church, 110
  Benevolent Society, 122
  bishops, 97-98, 111, 114-15, 233; Board of, 182, 275; districts, 155-56; salaries of, 159
  Board of Administration, 251, 276
  Brotherhood, 242
  Church Erection Society, 236, 258-59
  colleges, 243, 244, 266-69
  Commission on Evangelism, 250, 275
  conferences, 113-14, 255-56
  Confession of Faith, 108, 109, 161-62, 183, 185
  constitution of, 128-30, 181-82, 184-86
  controversy and division, 181-87
  Council of Administration, 233
  course of study, 233-34
  Department of Evangelism, 274-75
  Discipline 100, 106-7, 108, 109, 120-21, 128-29
  districts, bishops', 155-56
  doctrine, 118-19, 246
  early leaders, 57-66
  Eastern Annual Conference, 108, 118
  ecclesiastical structure, 113-14, 230-31
  ecumenical relations, 128, 167-69, 251-54, 277-81
  and education, 121-22, 174-79, 243-45, 265-69
  elder, 116
  expulsion from, 119-20, 123, 126
  Foreign Missionary Society, 235, 236-37, 260-64
  General Conference. See General Conference, United Brethren
  German Annual Conferences, 121
  Historical Society, 250, 275-76
  homes, old people's and children's, 249, 272-73
  incorporation of, 230
  itinerant plan, 117
  and language, 257
  lay representation in conferences, 157-58, 182-83, 185
  life in the church, 118-22
  membership, 99, 117, 155
  Miami Annual Conference, 61, 108, 110
  the ministry, 114-17, 232-33, 256-57; dismissal of, 158-59, 186; qualifications for, 158; salaries of, 100, 116, 122, 159; women in, 159-60
  missions, 169-74, 235-40, 257-64
  music in worship, 161
  organizational structure, 97-101
  pensions, 249-50, 256, 273-74
  Permanent Fund, 266
  presiding elder, 100, 113, 116, 233
  printing establishment, 121, 127, 227-28, 245-46, 269-71, 374-75
  publications, 126-28, 245-46, 265, 270-71. See also individual titles of periodicals
  publishing interests, 180-81

United Brethren in Christ, *cont.*
Quarterly Conference, 113, 231, 255
Sabbath observance, 123, 246
schism, 181-87
schools, 121. *See above,* colleges
and secret societies, 125-26, 129-30, 183-84, 185
and social issues, 122-26, 163-67, 246-49, 271-72
stewardship, 250-51, 276
Sunday or Sabbath schools, 61, 174-75, 241
theological issues, 161-62
two-thirds rule, 181-82, 185
union with Evangelicals, 354-55
Women's Missionary Association, 173-74, 235, 236-37, 240-41, 259, 264
worship practices, 160-61
youth work, 241-42
United Brethren Magnet, 230
United Church of America, 277
United Church of Canada, 389
United Evangelical, 312
United Evangelical Church, 283-313
Articles of Faith, 285-86
Church Extension, 295-96
colleges, 302-3
Committee on Evangelism, 304
ecumenical relations, 309
formation of, 221-23
the ministry, 287-88
missions, 288-96
publications, 304-5
and social customs, 305-7
Sunday schools, 298-99
union with Evangelicals, 309-12
Woman's Home and Foreign Missionary Society, 296-97
youth society, 300-301
United Protestant Church, 253-54
United Theological Seminary, 362

Veh, R. M., 374
Virgin birth, 335
Voneida, Solomon, 181

Wagner, Daniel, 53

Wahl, Rudolph, 179
Walport, J. P., 214
Walter, John, 67, 73-75, 80, 82, 85, 94, 132
Walter, Peter, 73, 75, 76, 86
Warner, I. D., 358
Washburn, Paul A., 390
Weast, Conrad, 120
Weaver, Jonathan, 245
Weidler, V. O., 358
Weidner, Henry, 56
Weiker, George, 217
Weimer, Jacob, 53
Wesleyan Methodist Church, 167-68
Western Old People's Home, 309, 350, 379
Western Union College, 302, 303, 346, 373
Westmar College, 346, 373
Whitefield, George, 26, 41
White's Bible Teacher's Training School, 303
Whitney, E. F., 235
Widdoes, H. W., 240
Wiener, B. R., 352
Wilberforce, David Flickinger, 172
Willard, Frank, 260
Wolf, Christian, 88
Wolf, George, 90
Women in church affairs, 285
Women in church-related colleges, 176, 179
Women in ministry, 159-60, 360-61
Women's rights, 165
Wright, Milton, 181, 184, 185, 186-87, 227-28

Yeakel, Reuben, 139, 206, 211, 287
Yoniyama, U., 239
York College, 177, 243, 267, 373
Young People's Watchword, 242, 245, 270

Zeller, Andrew, 114, 115
Zentmoyer, Jacob, 71
Zinzendorf, Count von, 21, 22-23
Zion's Advocate, 127

Philosophy

	1600	1700	1800	1900

Descartes
Spinoza
French Sensationalism
Locke   Early British Empiricism
Comte
Biran
Later British Empiricism
James

Psychology

Weber/Fechner Galton
Wundt   APA
Brentano

Twentieth-Century Psychology: Major Representative Figures

1900	1910	1920	1930	1940	1950	1960	1970	1980	1990	2000

Binet
James Munsterberg Calkins Washburn Ladd-Franklin
Peirce   Hall   Cattell McDougall
                   Dewey Thorndike Carr
                        Wertheimer Koffka Köhler Lewin
                           Freud   Adler Jung
Spearman
Angell

Psychonomic Society   Soc. for Neuroscience   APS

Neuroscience
Cognitive Science

Sechenov Bekhterev Pavlov Watson
Weiss
Holt
Guthrie

Horney
Sullivan
Hunter
Tolman Hull
Brunswik

Fromm
Lashley Konorski
Luria   Skinner
Spence
Jaspers

Mowrer
Miller

Husserl
Camus Sartre
Heidegger
Merleau-Ponty Maslow
Buber Binswanger
Bühler Rogers
Chomsky
Eysenck

May

Piaget
Mead

Sperry

Seligman

History and Systems of Psychology

Sixth Edition

James F. Brennan
University of Louisville

Upper Saddle River, New Jersey 07458

Library of Congress Cataloging-in-Publication Data

Brennan, James F.
  History and systems of psychology / James F. Brennan.—6th ed.
    p.   cm.
  Includes bibliographical references and indexes.
  ISBN 0-13-048119-X
    1. Psychology—History. 2. Psychology—History—20th century. 3. Psychology—
  Philosophy. I. Title.
  BF81.B67 2002
  150′.9—dc21

                                                                                    2002022014

Editor-in-chief: Leah Jewell
Senior acquisition editor: Jayme Hefler
Editorial assistant: Kevin Doughton
Production liaison: Fran Russello
Production manager: P. M. Gordon Associates, Inc.
Prepress and manufacturing buyer: Tricia Kenny
Art director: Jayne Conte
Cover designer: Bruce Kenselaar
Director, image resource center: Melinda Lee Reo
Interior image specialist: Beth Boyd
Executive marketing manager: Sheryl Adams
Copy editor: Mary Miller

This book was set in 10/12 New Times Roman by TSI Graphics
and was printed and bound by RR Donnelly and Sons.
The cover was printed by Phoenix Color Corp.

 © 2003, 1998, 1994, 1990, 1986, 1982 by Pearson Education
Upper Saddle River, New Jersey 07458

Printed in the United States of America

10   9   8   7   6   5   4   3   2   1

ISBN   0-13-048119-X

PEARSON EDUCATION LTD., *London*
PEARSON EDUCATION AUSTRALIA PTY, LIMITED, *Sydney*
PEARSON EDUCATION SINGAPORE, PTE. LTD
PEARSON EDUCATION NORTH ASIA LTD, *Hong Kong*
PEARSON EDUCATION CANADA, LTD., *Toronto*
PEARSON EDUCACÍON DE MEXICO, S.A. DE C.V.
PEARSON EDUCATION–JAPAN, *Tokyo*
PEARSON EDUCATION MALAYSIA, PTE. LTD
PEARSON EDUCATION, *Upper Saddle River, New Jersey*

Para a minha mulher, Maria Cândida,
e para as minhas filhas, Tara e Mikala,
por todo o seu apoio.

Contents

Preface   ix

PSYCHOLOGY'S HISTORICAL FOUNDATION

1   Introduction: Past for Present   1
Approaches to Historical Investigation   2
Organization of the Book   3
Eastern Traditions in Psychology   4
A Note on Resources   12

2   Psychological Foundations in Ancient Greece   16
Early Explanations of Psychological Activity   17
The Crowning of Greek Philosophy   24
Chapter Summary   32

3   From Rome through the Middle Ages   34
Roman Philosophy   34
Christianity   39
The Dark Ages   43
The Crusades   49
Chapter Summary   50

4   The Reawakening of Intellectual Life   52
The Papacy and Church Power   52
The Universities   55
Some Eminent Thinkers   57
Scholasticism   60
The Italian Renaissance   65
The Challenge to Authority   67
Chapter Summary   70

5   The Emergence of Modern Science   72

Advances in Science   73
The Learned Societies   80
Advances in Philosophy   81
Chapter Summary   87

6   Sensationalism and Positivism: The French Tradition   89

Advances in Science   90
Advances in Philosophy   92
Chapter Summary   100

7   Mental Passivity: The British Tradition   102

Advances in Science   104
Advances in Philosophy   105
Chapter Summary   115

8   Mental Activity: The German Tradition   118

Advances in Science   119
Advances in Philosophy   122
Chapter Summary   130

9   Competing Models of Psychology   132

An Integration   132
Chapter Summary   139

10   Nineteenth-Century Bases of Psychology   140

Advances in Physiology   140
Psychophysics   146
Evolution   151
Chapter Summary   156

11   The Founding of Modern Psychology   159

Psychology as a Natural Science   161
Psychology as a Human Science   168
Chapter Summary   175

TWENTIETH-CENTURY SYSTEMS OF PSYCHOLOGY

12   American Functionalism   179

Background   180
Early American Psychology   183

Functional Psychology   193
Impact   200
Chapter Summary   200

13   The Gestalt Movement   205
Background in Germany   206
The Founding of Gestalt Psychology   208
Basic Principles of Gestalt Psychology   210
Implications of Gestalt Psychology   212
Chapter Summary   216

14   Psychoanalysis   218
Background   219
Sigmund Freud   221
The Disciples   228
Social Psychoanalysis   234
Contemporary Impact   235
Chapter Summary   236

15   Behaviorism   239
Immediate Background of Behaviorism   241
Watsonian Behaviorism   247
Broadening Behaviorism   252
The Role of Theory   263
Post-Theory Formulations   265
Chapter Summary   270

16   The Third Force Movement   278
European Philosophical Background   280
Existential–Phenomenological Psychology   288
The Third Force Movement in America   290
Chapter Summary   294

17   Contemporary Trends: Neofunctionalism   298
Postsystem Psychology   298
Learning, Motivation, and Memory   301
Perception   306
Developmental Psychology   307
Social Psychology   310
Personality   312
International Perspectives: Modern Asian Psychology   314
Chapter Summary   319

18   Epilogue   325
The Systems of Psychology: An Integration   326
The Problem of Science   332
Conclusions   334
Chapter Summary   336

Glossary   338

Name Index   351

Subject Index   356

Preface

❀

My prefatory remarks for this edition cover the same ground as in the prior editions—namely, that this text is written as an introduction to psychology's past, grounded firmly in the intellectual history of Western civilization. Psychology emerged as a scientific discipline within the context of the intellectual history of Western Europe. The progression of ideas that led to the post-Renaissance development of empirical science allowed psychology to assume its present diverse form. Accordingly, the scope of contemporary systems of psychology may be best understood in terms of the evolution of Western thought from the time of antiquity. This book contains a historical perspective on the intellectual development of Western civilization, which gradually focuses on the emergence of psychology as an independent, recognized scientific enterprise.

Chapters 1–11 introduce the major themes of psychological inquiry initially considered by early Greek scholars and subsequently modified by Christian and Islamic writers. As modern science grew out of the Renaissance, the place of psychological inquiry became a source of controversy that resulted in competing philosophical models of the nature of psychology. These models are organized along characteristic national trends of psychological views proposed by scholars in France, Britain, and Germany. The tremendous advances of the empirical disciplines, which culminated in the nineteenth century, led to the articulation of the formal study of psychology in the 1870s by Wundt and Brentano.

Chapters 12–16 deal with the major systems of psychology in the twentieth century and into the current century: the American functional movement, Gestalt psychology, psychoanalysis, behaviorism, and the third force movement. Chapter 17 concludes this survey of the systems with an outline of trends within the more contemporary, post-system period of psychology's development. In the 20 years of work on the five previous editions of this project, the database of psychology has seemed to grow exponentially. The disciplinary content of psychology has been diffused to various allied fields. Cognitive science and neuroscience have matured and brought psychology into intimate contact with research trends derived from other disciplines. This development is obviously difficult to capture in a book of this nature, yet justifies even more the need for understanding the historical background of psychology.

I would like to thank those who have taken the time with previous editions of this work to offer suggestions for improvement and clarification. I especially want to thank my colleague Dr. Michael Riccards, President of Fitchburg State College, for his continued support during the various iterations of this project. I must also thank the many students who, over the years, helped me to express my ideas and always ignited the spark that made teaching psychology so much fun.

I would like to acknowledge the helpful comments of the following people, who served as reviewers for the publisher: Mary Ballou, Northeastern College; Greg Bohemier, Culver-Stockton College; and Lori Van Wallendael, University of North Carolina at Charlotte.

For their ongoing help and support, I am grateful to my wife, Maria, and my family. My daughters, Tara and Mikala, and their respective husbands, Craig and Adam, have been and continue to be a source of consistent support and inspiration over the years devoted to this project and to other academic demands. Our grandsons, Sam and Luke, now add a note of respite and joy to our lives. My family is my life, and their patience with me and this project merits far more than a dedication.

James F. Brennan

Introduction:
Past for Present

Approaches to Historical Investigation
Organization of the Book
Eastern Traditions in Psychology
    The Crossroads: Persia and the Middle East
    India
        Hindu Science and Philosophy
        Buddhism
    China
        Early Philosophies
        Confucius
        Later Philosophies
A Note on Resources

A cursory glance at contemporary psychology reveals startling diversity. Psychology seems to mean many things to many people. In everyday life the word *psychology* has a variety of meanings with mentalistic, behavioristic, or abnormal implications. The popular media seem to reinforce this perception. For example, we often hear the words *psychological*, *psychiatric*, and *psychoanalytic* equated and used interchangeably. We often read or see research results on smoking or drug hazards conducted by psychologists but described as medical research. Or we see instances where a psychologist, using "armchair" methodology, responds with profound advice in a newspaper to a reader in distress. Nor does the college-level introductory course to psychology necessarily dispel the confusion. Those who have taken such courses may have dim, confused recollections of IQ tests, dogs salivating, hierarchies of anxiety, the Oedipus complex, figure-ground reversals, rats running through a maze, heart rate control, peer group influence, and so on. Similarly, listing the range of positions held by psychologists does not resolve the confusion. We find psychologists in hospitals and community mental health centers, in advertising and industry, in government and the military, and in universities.

    Whereas the diversity of modern psychology is a source of bewilderment, psychology's range of study is justifiably broad. As a formal, independent discipline studied and taught in universities, psychology has been in existence for only a century.

However, we should recognize that people have been "psychologizing" since they first began to wonder about themselves. The long history of theories and models of psychology slowly evolved, mostly within philosophy, until the nineteenth century, when the methodological spirit of science was applied to the study of psychology and the formal discipline of psychology appeared in Western intellectual institutions.

The emergence of psychology as a formal discipline takes us to the problem of science. Generally, *science* is defined as the systematic acquisition of knowledge. However, from a more narrow perspective, the acquisition of knowledge is limited to observations validated by our senses. That is, we must see, hear, touch, taste, or smell events to confirm their existence as scientific data. This type of science is called *empiricism*, and its most controlled application is called the *experimental method*, in which variables are manipulated and measured. Over a century ago this more narrow, empirical definition of science linked up with a nineteenth-century model of what psychology should study to form the discipline of psychology. Yet neither at that time nor during the last hundred years did that form of psychology win universal acceptance. Some scholars argued for a different model of psychology, a broader definition of science, or both. Thus, psychology's long past, coupled with more recent differences of opinion about the form that the discipline of psychology should take, resulted in the heterogeneous discipline we study today.

Although the variety of opinions about psychology can be confusing, it can also be a source of excitement. Psychology is a young, unsettled, and often unwieldy discipline that has a highly stimulating subject matter to investigate—human activity. The purpose of studying psychology's history is to help remove the confusion caused by the diversity of psychology. By using this diversity as a resource rather than a hindrance, our understanding of psychology's development makes contemporary psychology richer for us. There are other reasons to study the history of psychology. Knowledge of the past, per se, is certainly worthwhile and beneficial in providing perspectives. Furthermore, the study of psychology's history may help illuminate some of the questions that have concerned scholars through the ages. However, the most pressing reason to study the history of psychology may be to understand the basis of its present diversity.

APPROACHES TO HISTORICAL INVESTIGATION

In their examination of the past, historians have proposed structures, or models, within which events may be categorized, correlated, and explained. For example, the preeminent historian of psychology E. G. Boring (1950) contrasted the *great man* and *Zeitgeist* models as they applied to the history of psychology. Expressed succinctly, the *great man* view holds that historical progress occurs through the actions of great persons who are able to synthesize events and by their own efforts change the path of those events toward some innovation. The *Zeitgeist*, or "spirit of the times," model argues that events by themselves have a momentum that permits the right person at the right time to express an innovation. Accordingly, Martin Luther

(1483–1545), in nailing his theses condemning corruption in the Church to the church door at Wittenberg in 1517, may be viewed either as a formidable figure starting the Reformation or as the agent of Reformation forces already at work.

A variant of the *Zeitgeist* view for the history of science, proposed by Kuhn (1970), suggests that social and cultural forces develop paradigms, or models, of science at various stages and that scientific work is conducted within a given paradigm for a limited period until the paradigm is replaced. The change in paradigms is a by-product of both the cultural needs of the age and the inability of the old paradigm to accommodate new scientific findings. Accordingly, Kuhn presents scientific progress as a cyclic process. Within a given scientific paradigm that is accepted by a consensus of scientists, an anomaly arises that cannot be explained or accommodated by the paradigm. A crisis is generated, and new theories compete to replace the inadequate paradigm. Finally, a single view gains the commitment and allegiance of a group of scientists who implement a scientific revolution, and a new paradigm is accepted. When an anomaly again arises, the cycle is repeated. Thus, Kuhn proposed a relativity in the understanding of theories, facts, and observations that is sensitive to the implicit assumptions of scientists.

Watson (1971) has proposed another manner of structuring the historical progress of science. Watson offered prescriptions, or dimensions for classifying psychological issues, by examining and describing the relationship between scientific findings and the prevailing cultural forces of a given age. Essentially, Watson's strategy evaluated a number of possible underlying assumptions and consequent implications of theoretical positions (details of Watson's prescriptive dimensions are given in Chapter 9). This approach is useful as an evaluative tool to compare the issues and implications for various theoretical positions within psychology.

Interpretations and explanations of historical events certainly help us bring order to the history of psychology. As we examine psychology's past and its contemporary state, we shall refer to the various interpretations of scientific history to understand the meaning of specific intellectual movements. However, this book may be best described as eclectic in orientation. As its author, I am not a historian, but rather a psychologist writing of the historical antecedents of my discipline in the clearest way I can, without any commitment or allegiance to a particular interpretation of historical events.

ORGANIZATION OF THE BOOK

This work is divided into two parts. The first deals with the evolution of competing models of psychology from the classic Greek philosophers to the emergence of empirical psychology in the 1870s. Although the study of psychology is our main concern, such a study must be placed within the broad, rich context of western European intellectual thought. In so doing, we implicitly recognize that psychology is an integral part of the tradition of Western civilization. The first part of this book, then, present's psychology's history—a history that is intimately linked to the milestones of

Western civilization. In particular, the close association of psychology's history with Western traditions flows logically from basic philosophical premises about the nature of the person, which date back to the ancient Greeks. However, in order to keep an accurate perspective on psychology, it is critical to recognize that important statements about human activity were made within the rich traditions of non-Western thought. Thus, the next section summarizes some of those movements before we proceed to the main themes of psychology within Western intellectual history.

The second part of the book, starting with Chapter 12, considers the major movements that developed as psychology became more distinct from philosophy, physiology, and physics. It is difficult to conceive of twentieth-century systems of psychology without an understanding and appreciation of the events preceding the last hundred years. As will become apparent, few of the critical issues that have emerged during the last hundred years of psychology are really novel. Emphases have shifted, new technologies for study have been developed, and new jargon has been invented, but essentially we are stimulated and perplexed by the same issues that confronted our ancestors in their wonder about themselves.

At the end of the book is a glossary of terms. In the study of the history of psychology, we confront terminology derived from a variety of disciplines, a reflection of the diversity of psychology's antecedents. Jargon describing concepts and issues from such disciplines as philosophy, physics, and physiology fit into the development of psychology. Accordingly, the glossary offers ready definitions of some of the terms needed to understand the evolution of psychological thought.

EASTERN TRADITIONS IN PSYCHOLOGY

As noted previously, psychology, as it emerged as a formal discipline of study in nineteenth-century Europe, was the product of an intellectual tradition that viewed human experience through a particular set of assumptions. The very conceptualization of psychology as we know it today was formed, nurtured, structured, and argued over during the 2,500 years of turbulent intellectual progress that have elapsed since the flowering of classical Greek thought. Psychology's reliance on Western intellectual thought must be appreciated, and this relationship justifies limiting the focus of this book to Western traditions.

Whereas the long intellectual tie between contemporary empirical psychology and Western thought is apparent, it is also important to recognize that non-Western philosophies have given considerable attention to the nature of the person and the internal world of individual reflection. So, before proceeding with our story, it is appropriate to pause briefly to review some of the alternative approaches to the subject matter of psychology, articulated through a variety of intellectual works in religion and especially in Eastern philosophies. These non-Western sources of psychology's past often brought new achievements to Western intellectual progress or resulted in the rediscovery of ancient writings preserved by Eastern scholars. For example, algebra, usually attributed to ancient Indian philosophers, was first used in the West by ancient Greeks of the fourth century before Christ (B.C.), but was lost during the Middle Ages. Western Europe recovered it as a result of contacts with Islamic culture during the Crusades. Arab scholars had preserved algebra, and through them its methodology and very name were reintroduced to the West (*al-jbr* means "to reunite separate or broken parts").

As we begin the study of psychology's past, starting with ancient Greek thought in Chapter 2, keep in mind the broader perspective—namely, that intellectual achievements were occurring simultaneously in other cultures and traditions. For the most part, these events were parallel developments with little interaction, but in some cases these advances enriched Western traditions.

The Crossroads: Persia and the Middle East

The Crusades, which are described within their historical context in Chapter 3, produced many benefits to Western intellectual progress, especially in providing contacts beyond the intellectual limits of western European thought of that period. Indeed, it was the scholarship of Muslim and Jewish teachers in Islamic territories that had preserved the essential body of ancient Greek writings and extended their interpretations in philosophy, science, and medicine. Islamic scholars were able to extend earlier intellectual achievements because of their contacts with Eastern civilizations, so that Eastern thought was transmitted from its origins to centers of intellectual achievement in the Arab world, and consequently to western Europe.

In much the same way as her Arab neighbors, Persia served as a conduit between East and West. Occupying roughly the territory of present-day Iran and the immediately surrounding area, the ancient Persians were an Indo-European tribe that came into contact with India to the east, Russia and the Slavic tribes to the north, and Arabia and the Middle East to the west. Led by great kings such as Cyrus (reigned 550–529 B.C.) and Darius (reigned 521–486 B.C.), ancient Persia grew in territory and power. However, when Alexander the Great (356–323 B.C.) defeated Darius III (reigned 336–330 B.C.) at Arbela, resulting in the latter's death, Persia became a province of Macedonia. Wheras Persia lost its empire, ancient Greece increased its contacts with the East—to the ultimate benefit of Greek intellectual life.

The central religious philosophy of ancient Persia was named after the priest and prophet Zarathustra (reigned ca. 628–551 B.C.), also known by the Greek name Zoroaster. Legend has it that he was born of the spirit of the supreme god, Ahura-Mazda, the Lord of Life. Zarathustra personified goodness, love, wisdom, and beauty, but was severely tempted by the devil to do evil. As a reward for his virtue, God gave him the *Avesta*, a book of knowledge and wisdom, which formed the basis of Zarathustran teaching. The *Avesta*, or what survives of it, is a collection of prayers, legends, poetry, and laws that describes the struggle between the god of good and the devil. Earthly existence is a transition in this conflict between good and evil, and it will last for 12,000 years. The virtues of purity and honesty will lead to everlasting life. Because they are targets of evil in life, the bodies of the dead must not be burned or buried, but rather left to birds of prey or thrown to the dogs and returned rapidly to nature. The supreme god, Ahura-Mazda, created and ruled the world and was assisted by lesser gods; Zarathustra taught that Ahura-Mazda had seven aspects for people to emulate or strive for: light, good mind or wisdom, right, dominion, well-being, piety, and immortality.

As part of this earthly conflict, individuals were engaged in a struggle between good and evil, and had the free will to choose between them. This psychology led to a code of ethics and values that stressed honesty and piety. The major sin in this code was unbelief, which was dealt with swiftly. The moral code was enforced by the priests, called *magi* (from the Persian word for "sorcerer") because of their reputation for wisdom, who were also practitioners of Persian medicine. As in pre-Renaissance Europe, religion and medicine were mixed in their service to the masses by the priestly class.

The legacy of Zarathustran philosophy and religion was far-reaching. The conflict between good and evil found expression in the works of the ancient Greek philosophers. The emphasis on one god was paralleled in Judaism, and there may have been other Zarathustran influences on Hebrew thought. Even the Christmas visit of the Magi and the birth of the boy-god have precedents in Zarathustran tradition. Occupying the bridge between the Hindu society of India and the Arabic and Greek societies of the Middle East, Persia had an influential and rich position and imposed an imprint on the mix of ideas.

India

As the birthplace of Buddha, the historical home of the Hindus and the metaphysical *Upanishads*, the target of repeated Muslim invasion, and the object of colonial exploitation by several European powers, India is a storehouse of deep intellectual variation. As a subcontinent filled with polyglot tribes, often clashing yet more often living in mutual tolerance, India's material and human resources have attracted outsiders throughout history. Western interest in India goes back a considerable time in recent history. Marco Polo visited India in the thirteenth century, and was followed 200 years later by a Portuguese navigator, Vasco da Gama. Columbus was seeking India when he discovered the Americas in 1492. In succession, the Dutch, French, and British established power bases and colonial economies in India.

Hindu Science and Philosophy.   Much of the knowledge of ancient India comes from the *Vedas*, the *Book of Knowledge*. The *Vedas* are a collection of lessons, hymns, poetry, and prose that were compiled from oral recitations. The *Rig-veda* is perhaps most famous as a literary achievement, involving many hymns and poems praising various objects of worship, such as the sun, moon, wind, dawn, and fire. But the *Upanishads* are of interest to us because they represent the collected wisdom of Hindu scholars who thought about the person's relation to the world. An early expression of Hindu pantheistic philosophy, the *Upanishads* are a collection of over 1,000 discourses authored by various scholars. Written between 800 and 500 B.C., these teachings sought to describe individual relations to the universe. The *Upanishads* are important because several predominant themes in them reflect the unique character of Indian philosophy. Distrust of the intellect and sensory knowledge is a dominant theme, as is the search for self-control, unity, and universal knowledge. The process of attaining these goals involves shedding knowledge, participation, and even awareness of the particular and ephemeral. We are not body or mind or both; rather, we are an impersonal, neuter, and pervading reality. Within the lessons of the *Upanishads* are themes of special metaphysical knowledge that secure for us a release from the bonds of the particular and material. The *Upanishads* focus on methods of spiritual transcendence. Transmigration of a person's essence is viewed as punishment for evil living, and eventual release from successive reincarnations is the way in which we transcend these bonds. By eliminating individual desires through ascetic living, we can escape from our individualism and be reabsorbed into a whole unity of Being.

The goals expressed in the *Upanishads* lead to a psychology that is quite opposite to the basic philosophical tenets of Western psychology. Whereas the latter recognizes the individual asserting himself or herself as a process of successful development and adaptation—indeed, much of Western psychology actually describes and predicts ways to facilitate this individuation—the *Upanishads* propose the opposite. The mystical, impersonal, and unified themes of the *Upanishads* reveal a harmony that can be achieved by rejecting individual expression. These themes pervade Hindu and Buddhist thought and provide a striking contrast for understanding some of the basic differences between Indian and Western thought.

The Hindu philosophies have important implications for psychology. First, the individual is characteristically a part of a greater and more desirable unity. Individual growth, then, is away from individuality and toward an emergence into the bliss of universal knowledge. Second, the assertion of individuality is seen not as meaningful in itself, but rather as an activity to be minimized and avoided. Sensory and mental events are unreliable. Indeed, truth lies in transcending sensory and mental activities and voiding consciousness. Finally, the emphasis on humanism and the centrality of the individual self, expressed in some Western views of psychology, is out of synchrony with the major themes of Indian philosophy. According to the basic Hindu conceptualization, the integrity of the individual person is questionable, because the individual occupies an insignificant place relative to the entire, harmonious complexity that is the cosmos.

Buddhism. Although Buddhism spread to China, Japan, and Southeast Asia, it originated with the Indian philosopher and teacher Siddhartha Gautama (ca. 563–483 B.C.)—Buddha. Indeed, Buddhism served as a vehicle for exporting many Indian products besides philosophy. Buddhist missionaries introduced the decimal system to China, and the mathematical bases of Chinese astronomy came to China with Buddhism.

Like the Sophists of ancient Greece described in Chapter 2, Buddha traveled from town to town speaking to crowds of people who had heard of his reputation as "the enlightened one." His doctrine was assembled as threads (*sutras*) to jog a person's memory. Buddha taught a theology that bordered on the godless. He did not condemn the regular worship of the gods, but taught that some rituals were foolish. The pain and sorrow that pervade human experience overwhelmingly impressed Buddha. He found no order in the confusion of life, but rather some good and much evil, precluding any design by a knowing and personal deity. At best, Buddha taught a type of agnosticism, so that his religion became a prescription for virtuous living detailed by simple rules of deportment leading to a sense of subjective well-being.

Within this philosophy of religion, Buddha taught in a somewhat contradictory manner about the individual. In contrast to the Hindu traditions, but consistent with some expressions of modern Western psychology, Buddha dismissed the notion of a soul or mind as being merely a human invention needed to accommodate some unexplained aspects of experience. Sensory input is our only source of knowledge. The perceived unity of personality, according to Buddha, is caused by a succession of habits and memories. As individuals, we are not free to will our fate, but rather we are governed by the determinism of habit, heredity, and environmental events. The individual personality does not survive death.

Buddha's psychology sounds almost behavioristic and materialistic, similar to some twentieth-century expressions of psychology. Yet Buddha also accepted reincarnation and transmigration as unquestioned premises to his system. If there is no soul, what transmigrates? As far as we know, Buddha did not directly address this contradiction, but some resolution is provided in his belief in the goal of subjective well-being and the heritage of Hindu thought. A possible answer is that if we strive, through ascetic self-discipline and careful training, to attain the happiness of annihilating individual consciousness, then we begin to participate in the experience of the Spirit, which lies at our very essence. The spirit is that aspect of us that moves beyond individuality. Our separate beings are simply passing manifestations of little worth, and the study of psychological individualism is rather absurd, according to this view.

For psychology, as for other sciences, Indian achievement is not only significant, but also truly refreshing in the way that it conceptualizes human experience. The dominant theme of Hindu philosophy is to lose the individual, and this is the very antithesis of Western psychology. Even in Buddhism, where a psychological level is admitted, psychology is relegated to second-class status. Thus, Indian philosophy leaves little room for psychology in the Western sense of a discipline of scientific inquiry.

China

The Chinese have considered their country the "Middle Kingdom" between heaven and the rest of the earthly barbarians. Indeed, the emperor who first unified the nation, Shih Huang-ti (reigned 221–210 B.C.), started the Great Wall to keep out foreigners or barbarians. Within 10 years it extended 1,500 miles along China's borders. China's feudal age ended some 300 years before the birth of Christ, and literature, philosophy, and the arts flourished. Paper was manufactured as early as A.D. 100; books were commonly printed with block prints by the ninth century; A.D. 200 was the year of publication of the first Chinese encyclopedia. By 1041 the Chinese printer Pi Sheng made movable type of earthenware, and in 1611 the first known use of gunpowder in a war was recorded. When Marco Polo first arrived in China about 1270 to witness the absorption of yet another invading horde (this time those led by Kublai Khan), China's social and political system had operated on a national scale for almost 1,500 years. This brief list of ancient China's achievements provides a glimpse of the depth and wealth of Chinese civilization. Despite China's historical efforts to hoard and protect its achievements, Chinese culture became the dominant force in the Far East, spreading its influence throughout Asia. The West is a new-comer to culture and civilization when compared to China.

Early Philosophies.   One of the earliest recorded works in Chinese literature is the metaphysical *Book of Changes*, the *I-Ching*. Written around 1120 B.C. and tradi-tionally ascribed to Wen Wang, the book contains mystical trigrams that identify the laws and elements of nature. Each trigram consists of three lines. Some lines are continuous and represent the male principle of yang, indicating positive direction, activity, and productivity, and providing heavenly symbols of light, heat, and life. Other lines are broken and represent the female principle of yin, indicating negative direction and passivity, and providing earthly symbols of darkness, cold, and death. Wen Wang complicated the puzzling trigrams by doubling the strokes and increasing the yang and yin line combinations. Each arrangement signified some corresponding law. All history, wisdom, and reality lay in the combinations. Confucius placed it above all other writings. He is said to have wished for an additional 50 years to study the *I-Ching* further. This book is important because of the imprint that it left on sub-sequent Chinese philosophy. The "good life" taught in the *I-Ching* is a utopia, which is obtained through the keys to reality contained in the puzzles of the *I-Ching*. It un-derscores the uncertainty of theology and the relativity of morals. Thus, Chinese phi-losophy de-emphasized the search for absolute truth and universal principles and tended toward the practical.

Perhaps the greatest of the pre-Confucian philosophers was Lao-tze (604–531 B.C.), who wrote the *Book of the Ways and of Virtue*, *Tao-Te-Ching*, the most impor-tant work of Taoist philosophy. This system, literally meaning "the way" in the sense of a path to wise living, rejects intellectual enterprise in favor of a simple life that is close to nature. Lao-tze called for living in harmony with the laws and order of na-ture, and de-emphasized intellectual knowledge as a set of tricks or arguments de-signed to confuse people. The proper way of living is to find the laws of nature with which our lives must be harmonized. The person seeking Tao must begin the quest for wisdom with silence: "He who must speak about the way, does not know it." While denying the certitude of the intellect and stressing the relativity of knowledge, the Taoists did not offer an alternative, realistic prescription for the problems of liv-ing in society. A return to nature, if universally followed, would lead to the massive vulnerability of an entire people to forces that are part of nature—the aggression, poverty, and ignorance present in the "simple" life. Taoism and its idyllic versions throughout history have usually provoked a reaction, and in China the reaction came from one of the most influential philosophers in history—Confucius (551–479 B.C.).

Confucius.   Legend has clouded the circumstances of Confucius' birth, sug-gesting that he was an illegitimate descendant of the legendary emperor Huang Ti (2697–2597 B.C.). At age 22, Confucius began his teaching, attracting groups of students, who lived with him. A lover of music, he taught his students only three subjects: poetry, history, and rules of propriety of deportment. His reputation for wisdom and honesty spread widely. He was made a government leader and held several posts. He became famous for reforms and the honesty of his administration. However, jealous factions succeeded in getting Confucius dismissed when he disapproved of his royal superior's licentious behavior and argued that a ruler must be a model of proper behavior for his subjects. For the next 13 years, Confucius and his students wandered the countryside as homeless pilgrims living off meager donations. Finally, following a change in leadership, Confucius was exonerated and given a pension to live out his last 5 years in peace, surrounded only by his students.

Confucius' major thoughts were collected in nine volumes. The first five books deal with the laws of propriety, a commentary on the *I-Ching*, a book of odes describing the principles of morality, a history of his own state, and a legendary history of China. These pedagogical works are interesting for their selection of lessons from history to demonstrate principles of virtue, wisdom, and perfection. The last four books, mainly assembled by his students after Confucius' death, contain his philosophical treatises.

Although he did not deny the existence of God, Confucius can probably be described as an agnostic. Confucius' moral teachings are based upon the individual's commitment to sincerity, honesty, and personal harmony. From the person's desire for goodness, the family structure can be nurtured. For Confucius, the family is the critical social unit supporting the individual as well as the broader, more complex society. Thus, social constellations are formed by loyalties based upon respect from people who are, in turn, pledged to conform to rules of proper conduct.

Confucianism is not a comprehensive philosophy. Rather, it consists of a series of practical teachings directed toward morals and politics. The ideal person is trustworthy, loyal, sincere, and intellectually curious, but reserved and thoughtful. Confucianism is a rather conservative outlook intended to preserve the unity of life, which will easily slip into chaos without such cautions. The history of China has been marked by cycles of chaos and order, and Confucianism seems to respond to these cycles by providing rules for people to live together successfully.

The teachings of Confucius defined the future course of Chinese political and intellectual life. As a practical philosophy applied to the everyday problems of individual morality and social interaction, Confucian philosophy led to a conservatism that has supported Chinese society through periods of severe havoc. The emphasis on the family, characterized by loyalty within prescribed relationships, provided the basic framework for political, educational, military, and economic institutions. As in the moral codes coming from Christianity, Buddhism, and Islam, psychology was absorbed in the teachings of moral deportment, and deviations from the rules were considered abnormal.

Later Philosophies.   Following the death of Confucius, alternative philosophical systems were proposed, but in the end Confucianism triumphed. Examples of the various reactions to Confucius include Mo Ti (ca. 450 B.C.), known as a philosopher of universal love, who rejected Confucianism as impractical. Alternatively, he tried to develop a logical proof for the existence of spirits and ghosts. As the solution to social evil, Mo Ti advocated universal love, which would bring about a utopia, and his teachings became the basis for Chinese pacifism. In contrast to Mo Ti, the philosopher Yang Chu (ca. 390 B.C.) developed a theory based upon the denial of God and afterlife, leaving people helplessly subjected to natural fates. According to Yang Chu, in life the good suffer as well as the wicked, and the latter seem to have more fun. Complaining of the extreme positions of both Mo Ti and Yang Chu, Mencius (370–283 B.C.) presented a more moderate view and achieved a fame that was second only to that of Confucius. Mencius was interested in establishing a social order that allowed people to pursue the good life. In the practical vein of Confucius, he taught about benevolent leadership and individual goodness. These goals were to become social norms. Finally, another thinker, Chuang-tze (ca. 350 B.C.), came full circle to Lao-tze and the Tao by advocating a return to nature and a society without need for government. These reactions only underscored the primacy of the teachings of Confucius, who struck the proper chord of the applied and functional approach when he detailed his prescriptions for living.

Chinese history did not produce a scientific age like that of post-Renaissance Europe. Important scientific advances were made throughout Chinese civilization, yet science itself never became the dominant ideal for intellectual activity, as it did in nineteenth-century Europe. Rather, Chinese philosophy—especially Confucianism— seems to characterize better the major themes of Chinese thought and concerns. Issues of religion, morals, and politics were intermixed, and they influenced all intellectual concerns, including psychology. Superstition and skepticism, ancestor worship, social tolerance, goodness, and pantheism all provided dominant themes of Chinese thought and literature.

The place of psychology within this framework is certainly obscure. As a matter of practical consequence, psychology is limited to the extent of conformity or nonconformity with the moral code accepted by society. Fulfilling the prescribed codes of moral conduct became an important form of socialization. The codes themselves were imposed and accepted, with no further consideration given to individual expression or growth. On a more idealistic plane, psychological issues were integrated within the goals of such virtues as goodness and honesty. The themes of Chinese philosophy on the unity of the person as part of the family, society, the nation, and the cosmos all precluded the need for a psychology to study only one aspect of what the West considered a unified experience.

The remainder of the story in this book is told from a predominantly Western perspective in terms of psychology's emergence as an intellectual trend within the mosaic of Western civilization. The purpose of this brief and selected survey of the historical traditions of Asian psychology is to underscore the rich heritage from other civilizations for psychology as well as for any intellectual exercise seeking to understand human experience. Recognizing such recurring themes as unity, universal harmony, reflective knowledge, and virtuous living, we find psychology deeply embedded in the teachings of religion and moral philosophy. Thus, as we begin a more focused historical journey, we should be mindful of other rich traditions that readily accommodate the subject matter of psychology within alternative perspectives.

A NOTE ON RESOURCES

At the end of each chapter bibliographic materials are listed, usually under two categories: primary sources and studies. The primary sources include the writings of scholars discussed in the chapter. Citation references and dates are given for available publications. The studies list resource works or general commentaries on the period considered in the chapter. The research works cited reflect the exciting scholarly interest generated in the history of psychology in recent years. As a specialization, the study of the history and systems of psychology is a relatively recent development. Probably because of psychology's youth relative to other disciplines, the systematic study of its history was largely ignored before World War II. Several important and still interesting scholarly works, however, examined the history of psychology during the prewar period. The first was the erudite *History of Psychology* by G. S. Brett, published in three volumes between 1912 and 1921. Also in 1912, an anthology of excerpts of the psychological writings of scholars from Greek antiquity to the nineteenth century was published by B. Rand under the title *The Classical Psychologists*. In 1929, two Americans, W. B. Pillsbury and E. G. Boring, published books on the history of psychology. Of the two, Edwin Boring (1886–1968) became something of an institution and a spokesman for the history of psychology. His work *A History of Experimental Psychology*, published in 1929 and revised in 1950, became a classic reference for the study of the history of psychology.

Since World War II, the history and systems of psychology have evolved into a recognized field of specialized study. In 1966, the Graduate School at Loyola University Chicago awarded a PhD to Antos Rancurello, late professor of psychology at the University of Dayton, for the first discursive dissertation in psychology on a historical topic—a study of Franz Brentano. Subsequently, doctoral specialization in the history of psychology was offered in comprehensive programs at the University of New Hampshire and Carleton University. In 1966, the American Psychological Association established a division of the History of Psychology (Division 26); this was followed in 1969 by the formation of Cheiron: International Society for the History of the Behavioral and Social Sciences. The Archives of the History of American Psychology were started at the University of Akron in 1965. Most importantly, the *Journal of the History of the Behavioral Sciences* began publication in 1965 and continues to publish scholarly research of an interdisciplinary scope. All of these developments have stimulated research in the antecedents of modern psychology.

The bibliographic listings after each chapter are not intended to be exhaustive, but rather to represent the range of scholarship available to the reader who wishes to pursue the subject matter further. In addition, the bibliographic material following this first chapter presents some of the major classic and recent works in the history of psychology as general reference material.

BIBLIOGRAPHY

General Resources

BERRY, J., POORTINGA, Y., SEGALL, M., & DASEN, P. (1992). *Cross-cultural psychology: Research and applications*. Cambridge, UK: Cambridge University Press.

BORING, E. G. (1942). *Sensation and perception in the history of experimental psychology*. New York: Appleton-Century.

BORING, E. G. (1950). *A history of experimental psychology* (2nd ed.). Englewood Cliffs, NJ: Prentice Hall.

BORING, E. G., LANGFELD, H. S., WERNER, H., & YERKES, R. (Eds.) (1952). *A history of psychology in autobiography* (Vol. 4). Worcester, MA: Clark University Press.

BORING, E. G., & LINDZEY, G. (Eds.) (1967). *A history of psychology in autobiography* (Vol. 5). New York: Appleton-Century-Crofts.

COPLESTON, F. (1982). *Religion and the one: Philosophies East and West*. New York: Crossroad.

DENNIS, W. (1948). *Readings in the history of psychology*. New York: Appleton-Century-Crofts.

DIAMOND, S. (1974). *The roots of psychology*. New York: Basic Books.

DREVER, J. (1960). *Sourcebook in psychology*. New York: Philosophical Library.

DURANT, W. (1954). *Our Oriental heritage*. New York: Simon & Schuster.

GERGEN, K. J., GULERCE, A., LOCK, A., & MISRA, G. (1996). Psychological science in cultural context. *American Psychologist, 51*, 496–503.

HAYASHI, T. (1994). Indian mathematics. In I. Gratton-Guiness (Ed.), *Companion encyclopedia of the history and philosophy of mathematical sciences* (Vol. 1). London: Routledge, 118–130.

HEARNSHAW, L. S. (1987). *The shaping of modern psychology*. London: Routledge and Kegan Paul.

HEIDBREDER, E. (1963; orig. 1933). *Seven psychologies*. Englewood Cliffs, NJ: Prentice Hall.

HENLE, M., JAYNES, J., & SULLIVAN, J. (1973). *Historical conceptions of psychology*. New York: Springer.

HERRNSTEIN, R. J., & BORING, E. G. (1965). *A source book in the history of psychology*. Cambridge: Harvard University Press.

LINDZEY, G. (Ed.) (1974). *A history of psychology in autobiography* (Vol. 6). Englewood Cliffs, NJ: Prentice Hall.

MADSEN, K. B. (1988). *A history of psychology in metascientific perspective*. Amsterdam: Elsevier Science Publishing Co.

MARX, M. H., & CRONAN-HILLIX, W. A. (1987). *Systems and theories in psychology* (4th ed.). New York: McGraw-Hill.

MURCHISON, C. (Ed.) (1930–1936). *A history of psychology in autobiography* (Vols. 1, 2, 3). Worcester, MA: Clark University Press.

NAKAYAMA, S., & SIVIN, N. (Eds.) (1973). *Chinese science: Exploration of an ancient tradition.* Cambridge, MA: MIT Press.

NEEDHAM, J. (1970). *Clerks and craftsmen in China and the West.* Cambridge, UK: Cambridge University Press.

ORLEANS, L. A. (Ed.) (1980). *Science in contemporary China.* Stanford, CA: Stanford University Press.

PETERS, R. S. (Ed.) (1962). *Brett's history of psychology* (Rev. ed.). Cambridge, MA: MIT Press.

ROBACK, A. A. (1964; orig. 1952). *History of American psychology* (Rev. ed.). New York: Collier.

ROBINSON, D. N. (1981). *An intellectual history of psychology* (Rev. ed.). New York: Macmillan.

SAHAKIAN, W. S. (1968). *History of psychology: A source book in systematic psychology.* Itasca, IL: F. E. Peacock.

SINGER, C. J. (1959). *A short history of scientific ideas to 1900.* Oxford: Clarendon Press.

SPEARMAN, C. (1937). *Psychology down the ages* (2 vols.). New York: Macmillan.

WERTHEIMER, M. (1979). *A brief history of psychology* (Rev. ed.). New York: Holt, Rinehart, and Winston.

Approaches to the History of Psychology

BORING, E. G. (1955). Dual role of the *Zeitgeist* in scientific creativity. *Scientific Monthly, 80,* 101–106.

BROZEK, J. (1969). History of psychology: Diversity of approaches and uses. *Transactions of the New York Academy of Sciences, 31,* Serial II, 115–127.

BURGER, T. (1978). Droysen and the idea of Verstehen. *Journal of the History of the Behavioral Sciences, 14,* 6–19.

BUSS, A. R. (1977). In defense of a critical-presentist historiography: The fact-theory relationship and Marx's epistemology. *Journal of the History of the Behavioral Sciences, 13,* 252–260.

BUSS, A. R. (1978). The structure of psychological revolutions. *Journal of the History of the Behavioral Sciences, 14,* 57–64.

COAN, R. W. (1978). Toward a psychological interpretation of psychology. *Journal of the History of the Behavioral Sciences, 9,* 313–327.

FLANAGAN, O. J. (1981). Psychology, progress, and the problem of reflexology: A study in the epistemological foundations of psychology. *Journal of the History of the Behavioral Sciences, 17,* 375–386.

HELSON, H. (1972). What can we learn from the history of psychology? *Journal of the History of the Behavioral Sciences, 8,* 115–119.

HILGARD, E. R. (1982). Robert I. Watson and the founding of Division 26 of the American Psychological Association. *Journal of the History of the Behavioral Sciences, 18,* 308–311.

JAYNES, J. (1969). Edwin Garrigues Boring (1886–1968). *Journal of the History of the Behavioral Sciences, 5,* 99–112.

KANTOR, J. R. (1963, 1969). *The scientific evolution of psychology* (Vols. 1 & 2). Chicago: Principia Press.

KUHN, T. (1970). *The structure of scientific revolutions* (2nd ed.). Chicago: University of Chicago Press.

MACKENZIE, B. D., & MACKENZIE, S. L. (1974). The case for a revised systematic approach to the history of psychology. *Journal of the History of the Behavioral Sciences, 14,* 324–347.

MANICAS, P. T., & SECORD, P. F. (1983). Implications for psychology of the new philosophy of science. *American Psychologist, 38,* 399–413.

MAYR, E. (1994). The advance of science and scientific revolutions. *Journal of the History of the Behavioral Sciences, 30,* 328–334.

ROSS, B. (1982). Robert I. Watson and the founding of the *Journal of the History of the Behavioral Sciences. Journal of the History of the Behavioral Sciences, 18,* 312–316.

ROSS, D. (1969). The "Zeitgeist" and American psychology. *Journal of the History of the Behavioral Sciences, 5,* 256–262.

SHAPERE, D. (1976). Critique of the paradigm concept. In M. H. Marx & F. E. Goodson (Eds.), *Theories in contemporary psychology* (2nd ed.). New York: Macmillan.

STOCKING, G. W. (1965). On the limits of "presentism" and "historicism" in the historiography of the behavioral sciences. *Journal of the History of the Behavioral Sciences, 1,* 211–217.

TURNER, M. (1967). *Philosophy and the science of behavior.* New York: Appleton-Century-Crofts.

WATSON, R. I. (1971). Prescriptions as operative in the history of psychology. *Journal of the History of the Behavioral Sciences, 7,* 311–322.

WATSON, R. I. (1974). *Eminent contributors to psychology, Vol. I: A bibliography of primary references.* New York: Springer.

WATSON, R. I. (1976). *Eminent contributors to psychology,* Vol. II: *A bibliography of secondary references.* New York: Springer.

WETTERSEN, J. R. (1975). The historiography of scientific psychology. *Journal of the History of the Behavioral Sciences, 11,* 157–171.

❋ 2 ❋

Psychological Foundations in Ancient Greece

Early Explanations of Psychological Activity
    Naturalistic Orientation
    Biological Orientation
    Mathematical Orientation
    Eclectic Orientation
    Humanistic Orientation
The Crowning of Greek Philosophy
    Plato
    Aristotle
Chapter Summary

The common cliché holds that "history repeats itself." However, we may be closer to the truth if we assert that historical events are like snowflakes: Supposedly, no two snowflakes are exactly the same, although they may be similar. As we begin our sojourn through psychology's long past with the contribution of Greek thinkers, it may be appropriate to apply the analogy of snowflakes to historical events. We may be amazed at the similarities in the questions that human beings have asked about themselves—and at the similarities of their answers. However, we should also recognize that civilization has made some progress in the last 25 centuries; we will not have to close the book on psychology after simply reviewing Greek thought. Although both the formulations and the solutions of critical psychological issues in ancient and modern times are often strikingly similar, they are not identical.

Since the advent of human intelligence and understanding, people have thought about themselves with wonder. Why do we behave as we do? Why are we able to generate reasonable explanations of some actions but not of others? Why do we have moods? Why do we seem to know that we know? In the course of human experience, people have come up with answers for such questions, and usually their explanations have suggested some cause. For example, we run away because we are afraid. Or we cry because we are sad. The nature of these causal explanations has changed over time. The nineteenth-century French philosopher Auguste Comte characterized these causal explanations as a progression of intellectual stages. The most primitive level was labeled "theological," because people suggested that a god was the causal agent responsible for changes in themselves and in nature. Indeed, many ancient societies invented gods with tremendous power. The ancient Egyptians had a whole catalogue of gods ranging from the sun to house cats. Such spirits were used to explain human behavior, and people who wished to change themselves were best advised to pray or offer sacrifice to the relevant god. Moreover, changes in nature, such as volcanic eruptions or storms, were said to be a reflection of the displeasure of gods over some human activity. The theological stage confined people's explanations of themselves and their world to spiritual causes.

Comte's description of causal progression is discussed in a later chapter, but we should note here that he viewed the Greek thinkers as a transition between a theological stage and a later stage that focused on nature, or the environment, and the generalization of principles from natural laws. Prior to the flowering of Greek thought, the relationship between human beings and the environment was governed by a view that may be described as primitive animism; that is, early conceptualizations of life held that a spirit or ghostlike entity inhabits the body and makes the body alive and conscious. During sleep the ghost leaves temporarily, to return upon awakening, and at death the ghost permanently leaves the body. All psychological activities, including sensations, perceptions, thoughts, and emotions, are propelled by the ghost. A similar explanation was proposed for other aspects of nature that seemed to live or have movement, such as plants, animals, lightning, and rivers, so that the distinction between the animate and inanimate in nature was often blurred and ambiguous. Accordingly, a clear separation between the individual and the environment was not evident in the early study of human psychology.

EARLY EXPLANATIONS OF PSYCHOLOGICAL ACTIVITY

Many historians regard the birth of science in Western civilization as occurring when the Greeks became the first thinkers to shift the focus of causal explanations from god to nature, or to the environment. The early Greeks articulated their explanations of critical psychological issues along several categories, as diagrammed in Figure 2–1. Essentially, all five categories, or orientations, attempted to discover causal explanations of human activity by means of natural first principles, or at least analogies drawn from nature. The orientations differed in the emphasis they gave to various aspects of the environment, both internal and external to humans. Each orientation is presented in the following sections in rough chronology.

FIGURE 2–1   The major categories, or orientations, of early Greek explanations of human activity.

Orientations of Early Greek Explanations

Naturalistic   Biological   Mathematical   Eclectic   Humanistic

Naturalistic Orientation

All expressions of this interpretation looked to the physical environment, external to people, for causes of life-giving principles. The earliest, and perhaps clearest, expression of the naturalistic orientation is found in a group called the Ionian physicists, who lived in the sixth century B.C. The Ionian Federation of ancient Greece provided the setting for early advances in philosophy and science, which began predominantly in the city of Miletus.

These philosophers taught that life and physical matter are inseparable, so that people are intimately involved in the universe. Therefore, the determining physical principle from which all life flows had to be found in the universe.

Thales (ca. 640–546 B.C.) is widely recognized as an early sage of ancient Greece because of his introduction of mathematics and astronomy to Greek study. This pushed ancient Greek culture toward a commitment to science. According to Thales, water is the first element because it is intrinsic to all life. In reducing all of nature to water, Thales was stressing the unity of nature. Matter and life are inseparable because water is the origin of all nature as well as its final form. Thales expressed a monism that found the life-giving element water sufficient to explain all forms of nature, regardless of particular manifestations in time and place.

Another Ionian physicist, Anaximander (ca. 610–546 B.C.), advanced his teacher Thales's views of the universe by suggesting that the earth is a cylinder suspended in the center of the universe with the sun, moon, and stars revolving around it. Anaximander argued that it is the "boundless" space of the universe that contains the basic elements of nature. This boundless mass develops by its own amorphous forces the varied manifestations of nature. A student of Anaximander, Anaximenes (sixth century B.C.), speculated that the air around us, which he called *pneuma*, is this life-giving cause of nature. All three Ionian physicists represented a naturalistic orientation insofar as they searched for a first causal principle of life and found it in the physical world. Such a strategy was a radical departure from seeking explanations among the gods.

Another expression of the naturalistic orientation is derived from Democritus (ca. 460–362 B.C.), who traveled widely through the known world, supported by his father's generosity. For Democritus, our knowledge relies on our senses, which in turn receive "atoms" from objects in the world. Thus, the critical explanations of life are found in the atoms composing matter. Moreover, Democritus argued that the quantity of matter is always constant, leading to proposals for both the indestructibility of matter and its conservation. Atoms differ in size, weight, and configuration, but the relationships among atoms are completely governed by natural laws and not left to chance or spontaneity. Humans and animals consist of atoms that are the most sophisticated and mobile. Accordingly, Democritus saw in the materialism, or physical properties, of the world's atoms the basic explanatory principle of life.

Perhaps the most famous city of the Ionian Federation of ancient Greece was Ephesus, which developed into a rich center of trade and high culture. There Heraclitus (ca. 530–? B.C.) proposed a view of human activity consistent with the naturalistic orientation. Specifically, he searched for a single unifying principle or substance that could explain the nature of change and permanence in the world. His solution was fire, for both its physical properties and its symbolic value. Heraclitus felt that change is the most obvious fact of nature, and the physical properties of fire cause noticeable changes in other physical objects. Moreover, fire symbolizes the flux in nature. Thus in fire Heraclitus found a unifying substance in nature that serves as a basis for life.

The final representative of the naturalistic orientation, Parmenides of Elea (sixth century B.C.), attacked the problem of change using a rather different tactic than Heraclitus. Parmenides argued that changes in the world and all motion are superficial observations and distortions of our senses. Rather, the basic fact of nature is its permanence and immobility, which bring unity and form the basis of life. Accordingly, although Parmenides also based his solution to the question of the fundamental principle of life on matter, it was the unchanging character of matter that comprised the critical element.

Thus the naturalistic orientation viewed the environment as holding the key to the basis of life. Within this orientation, two clear trends are evident. First, there is an observational trend, represented by the Ionian physicists and Democritus, which proposed specific substances operating in our environment as the basis of life. Second, there is the view of Heraclitus and Parmenides, who hypothesized about the character of change and then deduced (to opposite conclusions) some implications about matter based on their hypotheses. Although the observational and the hypothetical deductive trends differ in their manner of dealing with the environment, both offered solutions to the character of life by examining the laws of nature and generalizing those laws to the causes of human activity.

Biological Orientation

As philosophers within the naturalistic orientation looked to the external environment in their search for the basis of life, philosophers with a biological orientation emphasized the internal state and physiology of humans as holding the clue to life.

Alcmaeon (fifth century B.C.) has been called the father of Greek medicine and is recorded as the first to use animal dissection and to discuss the optic nerve as well as the eustachian tubes. More germane to our purposes, he recognized the importance of the brain and clearly distinguished between sensory perceiving and thinking. He wrote that the causal determinants of human activity lie within the mechanisms of the body. The body seeks an equilibrium of its mechanisms, and this process explains the dynamics of human activity.

One of the more important advances in Greek philosophy and science was the separation of the practice of medicine from religion. This separation was personified in Hippocrates the physician (ca. 460–377 B.C.), who not only raised the level of medical investigation but also developed a code of ethics contained in the Hippocratic oath, followed by physicians to this day. Hippocrates, like Alcmaeon, emphasized the brain in psychological processes, and he approached the problems of medicine systematically, with what could be called a precursor of the scientific method. Relative to our concerns about psychological issues, Hippocrates contributed a theory of "humors" to account for the basis of human activity. He taught that the body contains four humors: blood, yellow bile, black bile, and phlegm. Borrowing the concept of equilibrium from his predecessors, Hippocrates argued that perfect health is a result of the proportionate mixture of these humors. The dominance of any of the humors results in characteristic indisposition. Interestingly, this theory outlasted Greek antiquity, even up to the nineteenth century, and our language still contains the phrase "bad humor" to describe someone who is not feeling well. Nevertheless, Hippocrates should be remembered for his positive efforts to free medicine from the superstitions that have historically plagued it.

The final representative of the biological orientation to consider is Empedocles (ca. 500–430 B.C.), a brilliant, eccentric, and eclectic physician whose interests and skills gained him fame as an orator, engineer, and poet. His psychology held that sensations are the product of particles from stimuli falling upon the "pores" of the sense organs. Thus, sensations have a time course, and their quality and intensity can be measured. He postulated that change develops from the conflicting forces of love and strife—that is, between attraction and repulsion. Moreover, human activity is intimately bound up in nature by means of an evolutionary process wherein change serves to differentiate aspects of the universe, followed by an amalgamation back to an indistinguishable mass. Thus, love and strife result in processes of development and decay. For human activity the focus of life is in the heart, which produces the dynamics of change.

The biological orientation tended to elevate the position of humans above the rest of nature by emphasizing the formulation of basic principles needed to account for human activity. In this sense, the biological orientation separated the uniqueness of human activity from the rest of natural relationships, in contrast to the naturalistic orientation, which emphasized human activity as a manifestation of the natural order. These early philosophers confined their explanations to primarily physiological means, and we will see how later developments made this solution inadequate.

Mathematical Orientation

Both the naturalistic and the biological approaches based their formulations of first principles firmly on the material of either the environment or the body. In contrast, the mathematical orientation attempted to extrapolate from the material level to a general principle for all life. By proposing a generalization not actually represented in the physical world but nevertheless used to explain physical reality, this orientation used the ordered beauty of mathematical structures to assert the unity of the world.

Perhaps the most famous mathematician of ancient Greece was Pythagoras (ca. 582–500 B.C.), who left a rich legacy to the modern world. After developing his mathematical system, familiar to us through Pythagorean theorems of geometry, Pythagoras examined the basis of life. He taught that we know the world through our sense impressions, but that this world is distorted and artificial. However, a second, more permanent reality exists in underlying relationships, essentially mathematical in nature, that are not available to the senses and must be discovered through intuitive reasoning. This second world of defined relationships explains all of reality by providing the essential unity of nature. Pythagoras further proposed the existence of an immortal entity as the life-giving principle. This life-giving element has functions of feeling, intuition, and reasoning, the first residing in the heart and the latter two in the brain. Both human and animal souls have feeling and intuition, but only humans have reasoning. Perhaps as the result of his exposure to Near Eastern mysticism in his wide travels, Pythagoras taught that at death the soul goes to Hades for cleansing and then returns to this life in a series of transmigrations that ends only at the completion of a life of definite goodness. Pythagoras founded a society of believers who continued adherence to his teaching for three centuries after his death. His influence as a mathematician and philosopher remains important to this day.

Although Pythagoras himself was by far the outstanding figure of this orientation, another person worth mentioning is Hippocrates the mathematician (ca. 500–450 B.C.). He wrote the first known book on geometry in 440 B.C., and Euclid was his most famous student. He is remembered as a systematist who reinforced the Pythagorean faith in the unity of numbers as the basis of life.

The mathematical orientation is interesting because it represents an approach to the problem of life's first principles that goes beyond the physical level. Although both the naturalistic and the biological orientations lent themselves to generalizations, they were firmly based in the physical world. The mathematical orientation tended to downgrade that world, and our knowledge of it, as untrustworthy. In its place it offered a different realm of mathematical relations, one we cannot know through our senses. However, by using our ability to reason we can arrive at some knowledge of this real but elusive world. Variations on this theme, stressing the unreliability of the senses and the need to extrapolate truth by our reasoning processes, will recur consistently throughout the history of psychology. Thus, the mathematical orientation gave us a de-emphasis on matter, or the material of the physical world, and an emphasis on a supposed overreaching form or structure of relationships.

Eclectic Orientation

Whereas the Pythagoreans built a system for explaining life based upon the ultimate nonphysical unity of mathematical relationships, a type of reaction occurred that was opposed even to the goal of trying to find any first principles. A group called the Sophists championed this approach, which we are calling eclectic because of its modest and practical directions. The Sophists of ancient Greece were learned men who went from place to place giving lectures and imparting wisdom to eager audiences able to afford it. In this sense, they constituted a mobile university of sorts by reaching larger groups than could be accommodated by the more traditional one-to-one arrangement of master and student. However, some Sophists became greedy and commercial in this enterprise, overcharging their constituents and causing the great philosopher Plato to ridicule them as pseudointellectuals. Plato's criticism has left the Sophists with a rather negative image that has masked some of the positive inheritance from this movement.

The best known of these wandering scholars, Protagoras (ca. 481–411 B.C.), admitted the value of sensory information as a guide to the pursuit of knowledge. However, he denied the value of making generalizations or extrapolating beyond the physical. The first principles of absolute generalization—that is, truth, goodness, and beauty—do not exist in themselves, and we only know of such concepts to the extent that they are embodied in people. This hypothesis has two far-reaching implications. First, the denial of first principles suggests that a search for the basis of life must be confined to the investigation of life as it operates in living beings. Such an operational attitude dictates that the study of living creatures is an end or goal in itself, and not simply a means to the end product of trying to find generalized, transcendent first principles. The second implication is that we must be constantly wary of assertions that generalize beyond what we observe. That is, we must be skeptical.

Another Sophist, Gorgias (ca. 485–380 B.C.), carried Protagoras's teaching further. His book *On Nature* stated the extreme position that nothing exists except what the senses perceive and that even if something did exist we could not know it or describe it to another person. Thus, Gorgias took Protagoras's assertion concerning the use of sense information from a *guide* to knowledge to the declaration that sense information is the *only* source of knowledge. Indeed, sense information and knowledge are synonymous descriptions of all we can know of life. This view was pursued further by Antiphon of Athens (ca. 480–411 B.C.), who elaborated on the value of sensory data and the limitations of knowledge.

The eclectic orientation was opposed to the pursuits of the naturalistic, biological, and mathematical strategies. According to the Sophists, a person's knowledge depends on that person's background of experience, thus precluding the possibility of objective truth. By denying first principles generalized from reality, they proposed a limited goal for seeking knowledge of life. Further, their reliance on sensory information stressed the importance of working on an operational level: If one wants to know about life, one should study life as it is presented to us by people living in the world. Coupled with the reinforcement of skepticism, this operational spirit resulted in a type of scientific method that cautioned against speculation beyond observable reality.

Humanistic Orientation

The choice of the description "humanistic" to label this orientation is meant to convey its goal of seeking out explanations of life by distinguishing people from the rest of life. In this sense, a humanistic approach places humanity on a higher plane than other life and emphasizes those characteristics that are considered to make humans unique, such as reason, language, and self-reflection.

The first person who explicitly held this orientation is Anaxagoras (488?–428 B.C.), who speculated on the origin and development of the world. He argued that the world was initially unordered chaos. Then a world-mind, or *nous*, brought order to the chaos and differentiated the world into four basic elements—fire, water, air, and earth. Like his Ionian predecessors, Anaxagoras taught that the world gradually evolved from these four elements. However, the addition of the knowing *nous* provides a new dimension. In postulating a mind to oversee the world's development, Anaxagoras attributed rationality and intentionality to this systematic agent of progress. Moreover, this nous permeates all life and forms a common basis that defines life itself. Anaxagoras attributed individual differences among people to biologically based variability. The essential nature of all people is commonly determined by the nous.

The great philosopher Socrates (470–399 B.C.) represents the full expression of the humanistic orientation and began a clear tradition that was developed further by Plato and Aristotle. Socrates derived inspiration from conflicting views of life. He held the conviction that a general conception of life is necessary. Moreover, it is the essential uniqueness of the individual that provides the key to understanding life. In opposition to the Sophists, he taught that without transcendent principles, morals would be debased and human progress would cease. Using what we now call the Socratic method, he first defined a critical issue at a general level, then ceaselessly questioned the adequacy of the definition, and finally moved logically to a clearer statement of the question to approach the resolution. Thus, he argued that the universality of knowledge allows a reasonable person to ascertain objective truth and make moral judgments. The philosophical substance of the teachings of Socrates is difficult to specify because he was not dogmatic and taught that his only certainty was his own ignorance. As a youth, Socrates studied the physical sciences, but he became increasingly skeptical, believing that resolving the facts and relations of the observable environment led only to new puzzles. He turned toward the individual, focusing at first on the psychological processes of sensation and perception. This led him to the conclusion that the acquisition of knowledge is the ultimate good. His turning from the physical level resulted in an emphasis on the role of the self and its relationship to reality. The uniqueness of the individual was expressed in his insistence on the immortality of the life-giving soul that defines a person's humanity. Socrates' teachings on politics and morals offended many Athenians, resulting in his forced suicide. However, he succeeded in establishing a clear direction for the pursuit of life's explanation. From Socrates we have a focus on people and their place in nature, a view that was articulated by his students and successors.

For Socrates and his successors, the study of human activity, whether through psychology or philosophy, must focus ultimately on ethics and politics. Moreover, logic must provide the method by which we gain knowledge of ourselves. Knowledge itself is inherently good because it leads to happiness, and ignorance is evil. Thus proper knowledge leads the individual to the proper action.

The outline of the five orientations provides us with a rich variety of strategies in the search for the basis of life. The naturalistic and biological views relied on physical explanations, whereas the Pythagoreans of the mathematical orientation asserted a basic unity to life from relationships that transcend physical expressions of life. Although the Sophists denied the possibility of this transcendence, their operational spirit and skepticism offered a methodological advance. However, it is

Socrates who culminated this development with a novel view, placing the humanity of people at the center of a system that holds general and absolute truth as a goal. This humanistic interpretation of life has profound implications for the study of people, and it is to the psychological views of Plato and Aristotle that we now turn to examine the elaboration of the concept of soul.

THE CROWNING OF GREEK PHILOSOPHY

Plato and Aristotle continued in the framework articulated by Socrates. Essentially, they tried to achieve a comprehensive framework of human knowledge designed to account for all of the following features found in human personality:

1. The intellectual abilities of unity, autonomy, consistency, and creativity
2. The behavioral manifestations of variability, contingency, and stereotypy
3. The purposeful or determined aspects of human activity

The teachings of Plato and Aristotle attained far-reaching influence throughout the ancient world. Through the military conquests of Alexander the Great, which are shown in Map 1, Greek philosophy and culture became part of many civilizations and formed an intellectual basis for subsequent philosophical developments.

Plato

Plato (427–347 B.C.) carried on the concept of his teacher, Socrates, by formulating the first clearly defined concept of immaterial existence. Plato's theory of Ideas, or Forms, held that the realm of immaterial, self-existent, and eternal entities comprises the perfect prototypes for all earthly, imperfect objects. The earthly objects are imperfect reflections of the perfect ideas or forms. Translating this theory to human activity, Plato asserted a psychophysical, mind–body dualism. In other words, human activity is composed of two entities: mind and body. Only the rational soul, or mind, can contemplate true knowledge, whereas the lesser part of the body is limited to the imperfect contributions of sensations.

Born into an old and established Athenian family and named Aristocles, Plato received his nickname from the Greek word *platon*, or "broad," which described his rugged athletic build. As a child and young man he excelled in mathematics, music, rhetoric, and poetry, and he fought in three battles, earning recognition for bravery. Around the age of 20 he came under the influence of Socrates, which led to a profound change in his life. Upon the death of his mentor, Plato traveled widely, studying mathematics and history at various centers of the ancient world. After his adventures he settled in Athens and opened his academy, which became the intellectual center of Greece.

The study of mathematics was central to Plato's teachings. Indeed, the portal of his academy contained the admonition, "Let no one without geometry enter here." Plato valued mathematics as the tool to develop logical thinking, and he worked on the systematization of mathematical knowledge. Moreover, he applied mathematics to the study of astronomy, leaving us a valuable methodological contribution.

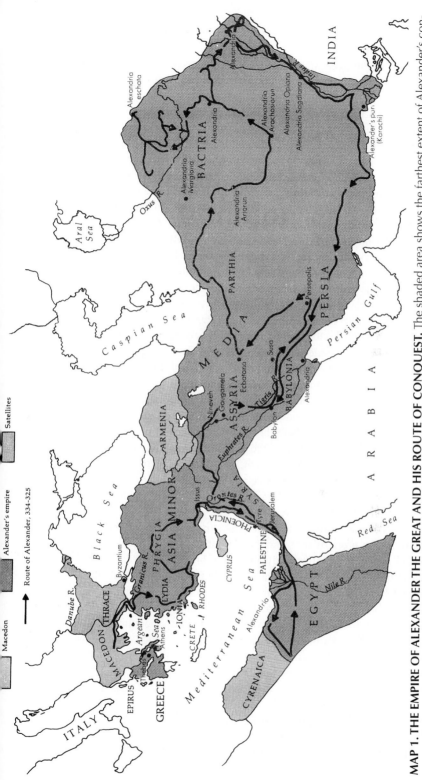

MAP 1. THE EMPIRE OF ALEXANDER THE GREAT AND HIS ROUTE OF CONQUEST. The shaded area shows the farthest extent of Alexander's conquests, from Macedonia to India. The major regions of ancient Greece—Thrace, Macedonia, Greece proper, and Ionia—are indicated, as are the important Greek cities. In addition, the Greek colonial settlements in Italy, Byzantium, and Egyptian Alexandria are shown, along with the ancient cultural centers of Babylon, Tyre, and Jerusalem.

Plato's teachings on psychological issues were far-reaching and elaborate. First, he viewed the interaction between people and their environment as a critical factor in understanding human activity. According to Plato, we deal with the environment through our senses, and this body-dependent type of knowledge forms one aspect of his mind–body dualism. However, this bodily level of sensory knowledge is primitive, distorted, and unreliable. Thus he rejected the Sophists' doctrine of the value of sense knowledge, arguing instead that the influx of sensory data gives us a percept, which he defined as a unit of information about the environment and subject to much flux. Percepts are inadequate in themselves for reliable and complete knowledge, but they give rise to "ideas." Ideas are stable generalizations based on percepts but not reliant on them. In Book VII of *The Republic*, Plato has his philosopher–hero Socrates tell the famous story of the cave in which prisoners are kept in darkness. Their only knowledge of the world is derived indirectly from the distorted images of physical events reflected off the wall of the cave by the flickering light of a fire. According to Plato, it is the philosopher's goal to go beyond the dark world of sense information to the clear brilliance of the sunlight of the outside world. Moreover, it is the philosopher's duty to go back to the cave in order to illuminate the minds of those imprisoned in the "darkness" of sensory knowledge.

The agent that forms and stores ideas is the soul. Plato described the soul as a spiritual substance consisting of reason and appetite. The soul has both rational and irrational parts, the former centered in the head and the latter in the body. The motivational principle of the soul is desire, which Plato described as the first condition of the soul. The activities of the soul are twofold: Pure intellect is the higher activity and provides intuitive knowledge and understanding; opinion is formed through bodily interactions with the environment, which give rise to belief and conjecture.

The study and content of science and philosophy consist of ideas, not specific concrete things or objects, according to Plato. Ideas are the sole reality, and all else that we experience through our senses are faint representations of ideas. The soul, or mind, is the mobilizing force in people, as it is part of the mobilizing force of all things, having the properties of vitality, immortality, and spirituality. Plato believed that the soul existed before the body and that it brings knowledge with it from previous incarnations, so that innate ideas of the mind are actually residual knowledge from the previous lives of individuals. The good life, according to Plato, is the appropriate mixture of reason and pleasure, and the supreme good is derived from pure knowledge of eternal forms of universal laws. Plato's contrast between sensory knowledge and rational knowledge reconciled the opposing conclusions of the naturalists Heraclitus and Parmenides regarding change in the world. Plato's view of sense knowledge accommodates Heraclitus' position on flux, whereas Parmenides' assertion about changeless unity also found support in Plato's notion of rational knowledge.

Several important implications for psychology may be drawn from Plato's description of soul and body. First, he relegated bodily functions to the negative state of unreliability and base functions. In this sense, the body is like a prison that interferes with the higher, more truly human functions of the soul. Second, Plato continued the tradition of Socrates with his view of the soul as containing all activities that separate humans from the rest of nature. Plato distinguished among a hierarchy of types of souls: nutritive, sensitive, and rational. At its highest level the processes of the human soul permit the formation of ideas in the intellect, leading to rational thought. Thus, the soul provides the order, symmetry, and beauty of human existence. Plato's conception of human beings presents a clear statement of mind–body dualism. At a physical level, there is motion in the world, eliciting sensations. Then, at an intellectual level, there is the formation of ideas that parallel, but go beyond, physical motion and allow abstractions from nature. Ideas do not rely on the physical level, and they become intellectually autonomous.

Plato applied his theory of the soul to politics and morals. Of interest to us is that these applications were marked by his basic distrust of human nature. Perhaps if people were pure souls, his predictions about government and society would have been more positive. However, he viewed the body as essentially evil, and believed that social structures must be built to protect people from themselves.

Aristotle

As a student of Plato for over 20 years, Aristotle (384–322 B.C.) fully appreciated Plato's mind–body dualism and his emphasis on the pure knowledge of the soul. Moreover, Aristotle brought to the study of Plato's teachings a recognition of the diversity and the dynamics of nature. Aristotle tried to understand the relationship between the abstract Idea, or Form, and the world of matter. His vast knowledge, especially of biology, facilitated his study, and the end product of Aristotle's search for knowledge was perhaps the most comprehensive and complete philosophy ever devised. Basic to Aristotle's view of life and the world was his belief that the world is ordered for some purpose or grand design and that all expressions of life are likewise propelled to develop according to some purpose.

Aristotle was born in Stagira, a small coastal settlement along the Aegean Sea in the region called Chalcidice bordering both Thrace and Macedonia. He journeyed to Athens, where he quickly established himself as a brilliant student of Plato. After Plato died, Aristotle went to Asia Minor and eventually served as the tutor of young Alexander the Great for 4 years. Probably with support from Alexander, Aristotle opened a school in Athens for the study of philosophy and rhetoric. Although he accepted the essential structure of Plato's system, Aristotle had vast knowledge of the physical world and attempted to incorporate that knowledge into the Platonic system. The end product of Aristotle's work was the categorization and systematization of all nature. In the process he dropped most of the pessimism of Plato's views on human nature.

Unfortunately, most of Aristotle's writings have come down to us in rather fragmentary form. He wrote approximately 27 dialogues, or books, but the original editions were destroyed in the repeated barbarian attacks and sacking of Rome, so that we have only dim reflections and notes on the original works and must rely on Arabic translations. The scope of Aristotle's treatises may be appreciated by categorizing his books under six general headings. The actual names of the books are those commonly titled in collected works or anthologies of Aristotle's writings:

1. Logic: *Categories, Interpretation, Prior Analytics, Posterior Analytics, Topics, Sophist Reasonings*
2. Science
   a. Natural Science: *Physics, Mechanics, Meteorology, On the Heavens*
   b. Biology: *History of Animals, Parts of Animals, Locomotion of Animals, Reproduction of Animals*
   c. Psychology: *De Anima (On the Soul), Little Essays on Nature*
3. *Metaphysics*
4. Esthetics: *Rhetoric, Poetics*
5. Ethics: *Nicomachean Ethics, Eudemian Ethics*
6. Politics: *Politics, The Constitution of Athens*

For our purposes in the history of psychology, it is appropriate to consider Aristotle's comprehensive system in terms of his views on logic and his books *Physics, Metaphysics,* and *De Anima.*

The core of Aristotle's methodological approach is found in his discourses on logic, which attempted to analyze the thought inherent in language. Aristotle's use of logic consisted of defining an object, constructing a proposition about the object, and then testing the proposition by an act of reasoning called a syllogism. This process may be seen in the following syllogism:

> White reflects light.
> Snow is white.
> Therefore, snow reflects light.

The two processes in logic are deductions and inductions. Deductions begin with a general proposition and proceed to a particular truth; inductions start with a particular and conclude with a general statement. Aristotle's use of logic provided a systematic, common structure to his goal of accumulating all knowledge, and logic has provided an essential criterion for valid methodologies in science ever since. Specifically, the essential procedure in empirical science involves both deductive and inductive elements. The process of sampling a particular group or individual that is representative of a population involves a deduction from general characteristics of the population to specific expressions of those characteristics in individual or group samples. After describing samples, the process of inferring the descriptions back to the population from which the samples were drawn constitutes an inductive process. Finally, generalizing the conclusions about populations to all members of the population again involves deduction. Aristotle's specification of the rules of deduction and induction remains the guideline for strategies of empirical science.

Probably as the result of what he learned from his physician father, as well as from his own extensive travels, Aristotle had a wide-ranging appreciation of the natural world. His *Physics* defined the science of nature, and he provided an intricate system for cataloguing and categorizing the physical world. In so doing, he established general principles that govern and characterize the animate and inanimate parts of our environment. The structure of botanical and zoological classifications into genus and species have essentially been retained in the form taught by Aristotle. His views on the physical world evolved only after meticulous observation, and because of the clarity of his methodology, many scholars have attributed the foundation of science to Aristotle. Indeed, it is difficult to overemphasize the legacy of Aristotle's organization of scientific knowledge. He set the stage for all further developments in scientific inquiry by specifying the premises and assumptions that defined disciplinary study, and his legacy has remained largely functional up to the present. Although his specific observations on the physical sciences and biology contained many errors, Aristotle consistently tried to find the purpose or the design of nature. He examined the behavioral functions of animal biology in terms of such activities as movement, sensation, reproduction, and defense to determine how these behaviors fit into the survival and propagation of the individual and the species.

Metaphysics, meaning literally "after the physics," is the branch of philosophy that seeks the first principles of nature. Metaphysics may be divided into the study of the origins and development of the world (cosmology), the study of being (ontology), and the study of knowing (epistemology). Aristotle gave metaphysics its fullest expression and devoted considerable energy to this enterprise, which began with the search for the first principles and causes of life by the Ionian physicists. In his metaphysics, Aristotle distinguished among four types of causality:

1. Material cause—that out of which something is made. For example, the material cause of a table might be wood or plastic.
2. Formal cause—that which distinguishes a thing from all other things. The formal cause of a table is that it usually has four legs and a top positioned in a certain relationship.
3. Efficient cause—that by whose action something is done or made. The efficient cause of a table is the carpenter who constructed it.
4. Final cause—that on account of which something is done or made. The final cause of the table is the desire of someone to have a piece of furniture on which to place objects.

Using the four types of causality, Aristotle investigated the nature of being to find explanations of reality. He taught that all beings have two basic entities: primary matter and substantial form. The former is the basic material that composes all objects in the world; it is the essence of all things. The latter gives primary matter its existence. Thus, in the world there are no accidents of creation, no mutations. The direction of development is determined by the form or structure of each object governed by the urges of causality. For example, during gestation the embryo is propelled toward growth in specific ways determined by the form of the species. In Aristotle, then, we have the culmination of the Greek search for the first principles, because Aristotle's metaphysical principles explain the physical world around us.

In addition to explaining the physical world, Aristotle's metaphysical teachings construct a picture of the nonphysical, spiritual part of the universe—the soul. Aristotle's treatise on the soul, *De Anima*, contains the major pronouncements of his psychology, which defined the subject matter of psychology until the Renaissance study of science. Like Plato, Aristotle postulated a dualism of body and soul. The body receives information at a primitive sensory level through touch, taste, smell, hearing, and vision. The body gives existence to the essence of each person—the soul. However, because the soul is the life-giving element of all living existence, Aristotle proposed a hierarchical gradation of souls—vegetative, animal, and rational. The vegetative soul is shared commonly with all forms of life and is nutritive in the sense of providing for self-nourishment and growth; the animal soul is shared by all animals and allows for sensation and simple forms of intelligence; the rational soul is shared among all people and is immortal. All intellectual powers are contained in the rational soul, and in addition, the rational soul has a will, or volition. All movement originates in the soul, producing imagination, reason, and creativity. Moreover, self-reflection and the will result in purposive activity for humans, determining the specific direction of individual human activity.

Aristotle's detailed views on psychology focused on the relationship between body and soul. He stated that the emotions of anger, courage, and desire, as well as the sensations, are functions of the soul, but they can act only through the body. By asserting the critical importance of the biological foundations of life to a true understanding of psychology, Aristotle justified a physiological psychology. Moreover, he viewed ideas as formed through a mechanism of association. Specifically, sensations elicit motion in the soul, and motion grows in strength with increasing repetition. Accordingly, reliable repetitions of sensations establish internal patterns of events, and memory is the recall of series of these patterns. Aristotle distinguished between memory and recollection in a manner that parallels the contemporary distinction between short- and long-term memory. He also related the properties of physical events to the structure of human knowing by postulating 10 categories that allow their classification, comparison, location, and judgment. Aristotle's 10 categories are basically derived from the rational powers of the soul to classify our knowledge of ourselves and the environment. The categories may be summarized briefly as follows:

1. *Substance* is the universal category that essentially distinguishes an object to be what it is—for example, a man, woman, cat, flower, chemical, mineral.

2. *Quantity* is the category of order of the parts of a substance and may be discrete or continuous. Discrete quantities are numerical, such as 5, 20, or 40; continuous quantities may be parts of a surface or a solid, such as line, square, or circle.

3. *Quality* is an important psychological category because it portrays the abilities or functions of a substance. Aristotle discussed habit and disposition as qualities of the mind. A habit is a firmly established mental disposition that may be positive—such as justice, virtue, or scientific knowledge—or negative—such as erroneous knowledge or the vice of dishonesty. Quality in the human substance also refers to the capacity to operate or function—such as thinking,

willing, or hearing—and may also describe an incapacity—such as mental re-
tardation, poor vision, or indecision. In addition, Aristotle used the category of
quality for sense qualities to describe colors, flavors, odors, and sounds.
Finally, he referred to the qualities of figure or shape, which may have degrees
of completion or perfection.

4. *Relation* is the category that gives the reference of one thing to another—
   motherhood, superiority, equality, or greatness, for example.
5. *Activity* is the category of action coming from one agent or substance to
   another—running, jumping, or fighting, for example.
6. *Passivity* is the category of receiving action from something else or being
   acted on, such as being hit, being kicked, or receiving warmth.
7. *When* is a category that places a substance in time—now, last week, or in the
   twenty-second century.
8. *Where* is a reference to place—in school, in the room, here or there.
9. *Position* refers to the assumption of a specific posture, such as sitting,
   sprawled out, or standing.
10. *Dress* is a uniquely human category because it refers to attire or garb, such as
    wearing a suit, wearing makeup, or being armed.

Aristotle's 10 categories are listed to illustrate the detail of his comprehensive
approach. The use of the categories is a psychological process, and Aristotle taught
that the powers of the rational soul to know and to understand constitute the highest
level of existence.

Although Aristotle is important because of his position as the culmination of
Greek thought, the structure of his system and his conceptualization of human activity cannot be overstressed. The dominance of Aristotelian thought and methodology
characterized the 1,500 years that followed. After dominating Greek and Roman
thought, Aristotle's works were lost to western Europe, but were carefully preserved
and nurtured by Islamic scholars, only to be rediscovered as western Europe shook
off the ignorance of the first part of the Middle Ages, often called the Dark Ages because of the characteristic intellectual stagnation of the period. His system was the
standard against which all other systems explaining human activity were compared.
Only with the Renaissance did any serious challenge to Aristotle emerge, and even
then, contrasting opinions were still dramatically influenced by his views. Aristotle
crowned the development of classical Greek thought by his attempt to represent the
world, in terms of physical, psychological, and moral knowledge, as a unitary system. He provided a philosophical synthesis that satisfied intellectual pursuit during
his own time and survived until the seventeenth century.

The philosophy of ancient Greece leaves us with a rich myriad of views on
the nature of life. The quest for the causes of life led to conflicting explanations of
the provocative issue of first principles. As we shall see, few really new orientations have been added to the array offered by the Greeks. Rather, both the context
and the methodology of each strategy were subsequently refined, and emphases
were changed during the historical development of psychology. Therefore, psychology emerged from the Greek period with the basic issues and solutions fairly

well defined. The classic Greek scholars successfully recognized the critical issues of psychology, and these scholars, especially Aristotle, tried to devise a systematic approach to investigate the issues. However, the emergence of science was slow, and alternative solutions to the nature of inquiry were offered before empirical science fully developed. The nonempirical, speculative approach to psychology constituted the major focus of psychological study until the use of empirical science emerged during the Renaissance.

CHAPTER SUMMARY

Ancient Greece provided the setting for the first detailed, recorded hypotheses about the causes of human activity in Western civilization. In the search for first principles of life, several systems of tentative explanations were offered. The naturalistic orientation, represented by the Ionian physicists Democritus, Heraclitus, and Parmenides, looked to some basic physical element in the world as this first principle. A biological orientation developed with Alcmaeon, Hippocrates, and Empedocles, which held that the physiology of the body contains the explanation of life. Pythagoras represented a mathematical orientation, postulating that the basis of life could be found in the essential coherence of mathematical relationships. The Sophists posited an eclectic orientation that denied the value of trying to seek out first principles. Rather, they advocated an operational attitude that relies on observations of life as it is lived. Finally, Anaxagoras and Socrates, rejecting the Sophists, proposed the existence of a soul that defines the humanity of people. This humanistic orientation developed the notion of the spiritual soul that possesses the unique human capabilities of the intellect and the will. The soul was elaborated as the central element in the interpretation of life offered by Plato and Aristotle. By the end of the Greek era the critical themes and issues of psychology as well as the methodological approaches were well identified and structured.

BIBLIOGRAPHY

Primary Sources

ARISTOTLE. (1941). *Basic works* (R. McKeon, Trans.). New York: Random House.
PLATO. (1956). *The works of Plato* (I. Edman, Ed.). New York: Modern Library.
RAND, B. (1912). *The classical psychologists*. New York: Houghton Mifflin.

Studies

BAUMRIN, J. M. (1976). Active power and causal flow in Aristotle's theory of vision. *Journal of the History of the Behavioral Sciences, 12*, 254–259.
JUHASZ, J. B. (1971). Greek theories of imagination. *Journal of the History of the Behavioral Sciences, 7*, 39–58.

LAVER, A. B. (1972). Precursors of psychology in ancient Egypt. *Journal of the History of the Behavioral Sciences, 8,* 181–195.

MANIOU-VAKALI, M. (1974). Some Aristotelian views on learning and memory. *Journal of the History of the Behavioral Sciences, 10,* 47–55.

ROYCE, J. E. (1970). Historical aspects of free choice. *Journal of the History of the Behavioral Sciences, 6,* 48–51.

SIMON, B. (1966). Models of mind and mental illness in ancient Greece: I. The Homeric model of mind. *Journal of the History of the Behavioral Sciences, 2,* 303–314.

SIMON, B. (1972). Models of mind and mental illness in ancient Greece: II. The Platonic model. *Journal of the History of the Behavioral Sciences, 8,* 389–404.

SIMON, B. (1973). Models of mind and mental illness in ancient Greece: II. The Platonic model, Section 2. *Journal of the History of the Behavioral Sciences, 9,* 3–17.

SMITH, N. W. (1971). Aristotle's dynamic approach to sensing and some current implications. *Journal of the History of the Behavioral Sciences, 7,* 375–377.

General Studies

BOURKE, V. J. (1964). *Will in Western thought.* New York: Sheed & Ward.

BURTT, E. A. (1955). *The metaphysical foundations of modern physical science.* New York: Doubleday.

COPLESTON, F. (1959) *A history of philosophy, Vol. 1, Parts I & II—Greece and Rome.* Garden City, NY: Image Books.

DURANT, W. (1939). *The life of Greece.* New York: Simon & Schuster.

KOREN, H. J. (1955). *An introduction to the science of metaphysics.* St. Louis: Herder.

MCKOEN, R. (1973). *Introduction to Aristotle.* Chicago: University of Chicago Press.

OESTERLE, J. A. (1963). *Logic: The art of defining and reasoning* (2nd ed.). Englewood Cliffs, NJ: Prentice Hall.

OWENS, J. (1959). *A history of ancient Western philosophy.* Englewood Cliffs, NJ: Prentice Hall.

ROBINSON, D. N. (1989). *Aristotle's psychology.* New York: Columbia University Press.

ROYCE, J. E. (1961). *Man and his nature.* New York: McGraw-Hill.

SAHAKIAN, W. S., & SAHAKIAN, M. L. (1977). *Plato.* Boston: Twayne.

SARTON, G. (1945–1948). *Introduction to the history of science.* Baltimore: Williams & Wilkins.

WATSON, R. I. (1971). *The great psychologists: From Aristotle to Freud* (3rd ed.). Philadelphia: J. B. Lippincott.

❈ 3 ❈

From Rome through the Middle Ages

Roman Philosophy
    Stoicism
    Epicureanism
    Neoplatonism
Christianity
    The Early Leaders
    The Church Fathers
        Church Defenders
        Saint Augustine
The Dark Ages
    The Eastern Empire
    Islamic Civilization
    The Feudal West
The Crusades
Chapter Summary

Rome existed as a republic for 500 years under a constitution that vested authority in a senate of wise men. The republic survived wars and internal dissent until the rise of Julius Caesar (100–44 B.C.). The republic ended with Caesar and his successors and was replaced by the empire, perhaps the most remarkable political institution in the history of Western civilization. At the height of its influence, the Roman Empire covered the entire Western world, from the Near East to the British Isles. The Roman civilization absorbed the cultural influences of the ancient societies of Mesopotamia, Egypt, Israel, and Greece. Moreover, the Romans assimilated new peoples into the mainstream of Western civilization. From the East, the Armenians and Assyrians were brought under Roman rule; in the West, the Romans conquered vast areas of North Africa, Spain, France, and Britain (Map 2). Along the frontiers of the empire, Roman culture touched German, Slavic, Nordic, and Celtic tribes. From the time of Augustus (63 B.C.–A.D. 14) until the barbarians began sacking the Western Empire around the year 400, the entire Mediterranean world enjoyed relative peace and orderly administration under the *Pax Romana*. Indeed, the eastern part of the empire lasted until 1453, when Constantinople (present-day Istanbul) was finally

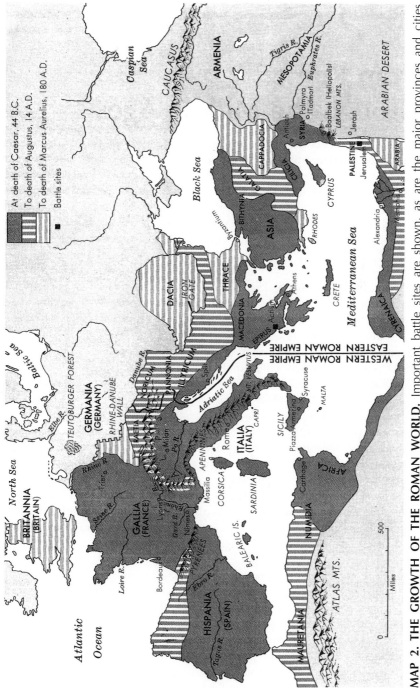

MAP 2. THE GROWTH OF THE ROMAN WORLD. Important battle sites are shown, as are the major provinces and cities of Roman commerce.

At death of Caesar, 44 B.C.
To death of Augustus, 14 A.D.
To death of Marcus Aurelius, 180 A.D.
Battle sites

Atlantic Ocean

North Sea

Baltic Sea

BRITANNIA
(BRITAIN)

GERMANIA
(GERMANY)

TEUTOBURGER FOREST

RHINE-DANUBE WALL

Elbe R.

Rhine R.

Trier

Loire R.

Seine R.

Bordeaux

GALLIA
(FRANCE)

Lyons

Nimes

Rhône R.

Gard B.

PYRENEES

Ebro R.

BALEARIC IS.

HISPANIA
(SPAIN)

Tagus R.

CORSICA

SARDINIA

Massilia

RAETIA

NORICUM

PANNONIA

Danube R.

ILLYRICUM

DACIA

IRON GATE

APENNINES

Milan

Po R.

Rome

ITALIA
(ITALY)

MT. VESUVIUS

CAPRI

Syracuse

SICILY

MALTA

Piazza Armerina

Adriatic Sea

WESTERN ROMAN EMPIRE

EASTERN ROMAN EMPIRE

EPIRUS

Actium

MACEDONIA

THRACE

Byzantium

Athens

CRETE

RHODES

Black Sea

BITHYNIA

GALATIA

ASIA

CAPPADOCIA

CILICIA

CYPRUS

Mediterranean Sea

ARMENIA

Caspian Sea

CAUCASUS

Tigris R.

MESOPOTAMIA

Euphrates R.

SYRIA

Antioch

Palmyra (Tadmor)

Baalbek (Heliopolis)

LEBANON MTS.

Jerash

PALESTINE

Jerusalem

ARABIA

ARABIAN DESERT

Alexandria

Memphis

CYRENAICA

AFRICA

Carthage

NUMIDIA

MAURETANIA

ATLAS MTS.

0   500
Miles

conquered by the Turks. During the period of their ascendancy, the Romans achieved successful rule by effective government. Through a system of laws and civil administration, the Romans were able to develop commerce and spread a common language and culture over diverse populations.

As administrators and builders, the Romans did not share the love of natural science that formed the basis of the philosophical systems of their Greek forebears. The Romans valued application and use over abstract studies. For example, the Romans did not dramatically advance the study of pure mathematics, but they used mathematical relationships in their architecture when they built the aqueducts. They used the abacus for calculations and teaching mathematics, and devised an accounting of time that produced the Julian calendar, which was universally accepted until Pope Gregory XIII introduced an improved version in 1582. Science prospered under the Romans to the extent that it benefited from the progress of technological advances. Throughout the history of the Roman Empire, centers of higher learning were established to educate the young and to serve the goal of supporting Roman rule and administration. Scholars and scribes were sent to Alexandria, the city in Egypt founded by the Greek conqueror and the site of a Hellenistic cultural revival in Roman times, to copy the texts of the ancient philosophers and scientists. Although the great library was eventually destroyed and even set on fire by Julius Caesar himself, the Romans generally recognized the value of Greek scholarship and sought to preserve rather than to destroy it.

The fostering of the practical side of science by the Romans resulted in advances and extensions of the earlier Greek advances. The philosopher Lucretius (99–55 B.C.) proposed a theory of natural order that recognized a hierarchy in nature from lower organisms to comparatively sophisticated mammals and human beings. The scholar and writer Varro (116–26 B.C.) developed an early version of an encyclopedia, dividing all knowledge into nine disciplinary studies: grammar, logical argumentation (or dialectics), rhetoric, geometry, arithmetic, astronomy, music, medicine, and architecture. The historian of Greek origin Polybius (ca. 204–122 B.C.) attempted a systematic description of the geography of the known world. One implication of the practice of applied science was the tendency for specialization. The Greek emphasis on the unity of knowledge had produced the universal philosophers. In contrast, the Roman appreciation of technical knowledge and detailed applications required specialists. Even the great teaching and scholarly centers of Alexandria agreed that human knowledge is best examined under three separate departments: science, ethics, and religion.

Although the Romans may have emphasized technical specialization at the expense of universal knowledge, their remarkable achievement of the *Pax Romana* contributed to the widespread dissemination of knowledge. The Roman system of government provided a means for the rapid spread of ideas. The tranquility and administration of Roman rule permitted the transfer of the essentials of Greek philosophy throughout the empire. Through the writings of such poets as Cicero (106–43 B.C.), Livy (59 B.C.–A.D. 17), and Virgil (70–19 B.C.), Latin literature flowered and successfully adapted the Greek heritage for a wider audience. Moreover, the empire provided the setting for the emergence of new institutions, most notably Christianity. Before considering the impact of early Christianity on the formulation of psychological thought, it is appropriate to examine briefly some advances in philosophy that the Romans developed as extensions of the Greek concept of the soul.

ROMAN PHILOSOPHY

The Stoic and Epicurean philosophies of Rome contributed to the development of psychology in ways that paralleled the fate of the natural sciences in Rome. Both philosophies were limited in scope and were expressed mainly in Roman religious practices. They did not follow the Greek attempts to devise a comprehensive system of human knowledge, for which the role of psychology was central. Rather, the Roman philosophies were specialized and limited to rather general attitudes toward life. The psychological implications of these views, in turn, were limited to guidelines of deportment and moral values. Likewise, the revival of Plato's teachings known as Neoplatonism enjoyed major influence in Roman intellectual spheres just as Christianity was expanding to include significant numbers of followers within the empire.

Stoicism

The Stoic period of Rome (roughly 500–200 B.C.) was characterized by a system of beliefs contained in the religion of ancient Rome, which greatly affected the moral and social values of Romans. The Stoics derived their views from the teachings of the Greek philosopher Zeno (ca. 336–264 B.C.), who believed in two basic types of matter—passive and active; that is, matter that is acted upon and matter that acts. The human soul's ability to act through intellectual capacities leads to the conclusion that human reason is intimately bound up in the universe of matter. Human freedom was simply described as the capability of cooperating with the causality of the universe. This latter view of freedom held the key to Stoic belief. It is the universe that determines life. Fate, derived from the laws of nature or whims of the gods, was the critical thesis of Stoicism. The Romans developed an elaborate religion to accommodate and cooperate with fate. Thus, in retreating from Aristotle's notion of the soul, the Stoics shifted the emphasis from inner determinism to universal determinism governed by the forces of fate. Within this perspective humans were once again viewed as a part of the environmental order.

Stoicism led to a personal resignation of the individual to the dictates of fate. In practice, this attitude advocated an abdication of personal responsibility and a surrender of individual initiative. Although the pessimistic overtones of Stoicism precluded individual behavior from degenerating to frivolity, Stoicism as a philosophy accepted the view that the individual is a reactive, not an active, organism. This theme of contrasting active and passive assumptions about the essential nature of human existence recurs consistently throughout the development of psychology. The Stoic solution left the person as part of the environment and subject to the governing pressures of environmental determinants.

Epicureanism

A somewhat later development (approximately 50 B.C.–A.D. 100) was the philosophy of the Epicureans. In dramatic contrast to the conservative Stoics, Roman followers of the Greek philosopher Epicurus (ca. 342–270 B.C.) held the sole principle that the end or goal of life is happiness. This value was reflected in the festivals and games of imperial Rome as well as in the religion that eventually asserted the deification of the emperor. The Epicureans denied the spiritual and immortal soul of the Stoics, suggesting instead that the soul is a material part of the body. The soul has knowledgeable functions of sensation and anticipation and an activity function of passion. However, the soul operates through the mechanical physiology of the body. The senses assumed a critical importance for Epicurean psychology, as thought processes are established through atoms of the environment striking the atoms of the soul. The concepts of reason and freedom, although acknowledged, exist only as individual expressions not connected to any universal, metaphysical principles. Rather, the guiding determination of human activity is the seeking of pleasure and avoidance of pain. Thus, we can see some similarities between the Roman Epicureans and Greek Sophists. The Epicureans reduced the concept of the soul to an emphasis on sensation. Moreover, this parsimonious explanation of life affirmed the view that the mechanisms of bodily functions were central to understanding life. The social and moral implications of this view are a rather mundane, self-seeking direction of individual behavior.

Both Stoicism and Epicureanism remained influential after the zenith of their respective teachings. Indeed, as Greek and Roman philosophical systems were absorbed into Christian theology, shades of these views were retained during the first centuries of the establishment of Christian belief and doctrine.

Neoplatonism

The last great pagan philosopher, Plotinus (ca. 203–270), was of Egyptian origin but spent most of his life in Rome, where he revived interest in the classic Greek philosophers, especially Plato. Plotinus argued that matter exists only as a formless potential to acquire form. Every form that matter assumes is made possible by the energy and direction of the soul. Nature itself is the total energy and universal soul, articulated into varying forms of life. Every form of life has a soul that determines the direction of growth. In human beings the vital principle within the soul molds individual progress toward maturity. The soul provides our knowledge of the environment through the generation of ideas, derived from sensations, perceptions, and thoughts. Ideas themselves transcend matter and provide the uniquely human experience of communication with the universal soul of nature. Reason is our ability to use ideas. It provides the highest form of life, allowing the individual ultimately to be conscious or aware of the creative direction of the soul.

Plotinus taught that the body is both the agent and the prison of the soul. The soul is capable of the highest form of activity—reason—which depends on sensory information but transcends the sensory level by the creative use of ideas. God is universal unity, reason, and soul. The human soul desires to seek God, but this attraction is the only certainty we have about God. Thus, life is a process whereby the soul seeks dominance over the body by rejecting the material world and finding universal truth in nature and God.

The importance of Roman Neoplatonism lies in its reception by Christianity. Greek philosophy entered Christianity in its Neoplatonist expression, so that Plato's teaching on body and soul were "Christianized" and dominated early Christian views on psychology. Christianity, in turn, dominated western Europe on the demise of the Roman order.

CHRISTIANITY

The life of Jesus, as interpreted by his followers, has offered an example and an invitation that have dramatically altered the lives of people. Beyond the religious significance of his claim to be the Messiah of the Hebrew prophesies, the story of Jesus has had a tremendous impact on the evolving importance of the soul in psychology's history. Specifically, his birth and life of poverty and his admonition to avoid worldly goods placed great emphasis on the spiritual. Moreover, his promise of love and salvation filled ordinary people with hope of deliverance from earthly problems of loneliness, poverty, and hunger. His death and bodily resurrection turned the natural order of the universe upside down, reinforcing the prominence of the spiritual life. The story of Jesus offered a message of universal appeal. The political tranquility of the *Pax Romana* provided an opportunity for that message to reach the millions of people under Roman rule.

It is difficult to distinguish the actual teachings of Jesus from the interpretations of his followers, who were intent on extending the message of Jesus beyond his Jewish context. However, like his immediate predecessor, John the Baptist, Jesus was preaching a renewal of religious commitment. Further, Jesus declared himself to be the fulfillment of the Hebrew prophesies of the Messiah. Some of his listeners perceived that the Messiah should offer the Jewish faithful a political deliverance from the occupation of Rome. However, Jesus made clear that he was not challenging Roman or any other secular authority. His kingdom was not of this world; rather, his domain consisted of the peace and love of the spiritual life in God. Whereas his teachings were consistent with the Jewish tradition, they were also amenable to the Greek concept of the body–soul dualism. Indeed, Jesus' message supported a dualistic view by enhancing the dignity and ultimate value of the spiritual, immaterial existence of the soul. Moreover, Jesus preached that human beings are distinct from the rest of nature because God has favored people by offering them the chance for immortality and salvation.

The apostles and their immediate followers took advantage of the communications network provided by Rome. If Christian teachings were to encompass more than a cult of Judaism, it would be necessary to appeal to cultural traditions beyond the Hebrew structure of the Torah. Such a movement was especially compelling in light of the loss of the Jewish foundation of Christianity after the destruction of Jerusalem in A.D. 70 by the Roman general Titus and subsequent dispersion of Jews from Palestine. Accordingly, during the first few centuries of Christianity, missionaries wandered clandestinely throughout the empire, and the center of Christian thought evolved to Rome, although important leaders of Christianity were also found elsewhere, principally in Antioch and Alexandria.

The Early Leaders

Saint Paul (ca. 10–64), the fervent missionary to the non-Jewish world, may be called the first Christian theologian. As a young Jew in his native Tarsus, he was forbidden to study classic Greek and Roman literature, but he picked up enough Greek to communicate in that language. In addition, his contact with Greeks and Romans of his time, as well as his possession of Roman citizenship, afforded a basis for his missionary activities. There is a definite Stoic influence in his writings on the strict morality of Christian society. Paul championed the separation of the new religion from Judaism and successfully fought against enforcing the practice of circumcision, a strict and basic requirement of Judaism. More importantly, his teaching identified the message of Jesus with the culture founded on Greek philosophy. Like the Stoics and Neoplatonists, Paul viewed the physical body as evil and inadequate and preached about the spiritual wisdom and perfection acquired through Jesus. He taught that Jesus is more than the Messiah fulfilling the Jewish prophecies. Rather, Jesus is God who came to the world to redeem all people, who had been condemned by the evil of original sin. As such, Jesus was the universal savior. By sacrificing himself, Jesus allowed all people to participate in the glory of perfect wisdom and knowledge. Thus, Paul radically transformed early Christianity by preaching the hopeful message of Jesus in a form that could be understood by the vast majority of the Roman Empire.

It was in the flourishing intellectual center of Alexandria that the relationship between Christianity and Greek philosophy became firmly established. Two Christian teachers, Clement (ca. 150–220) and Origen (185–254), both reconciled the Hebrew origins of Christianity with pagan Greek philosophy. The prolific Origen managed a Greek translation of the Hebrew Old Testament and provided comments and interpretations amenable to Greek understanding. The net result of his efforts was the assertion that the God of the Hebrews is the first cause or principle of life. The Hebrew doctrine of monotheism and the Greek tradition of polytheism were resolved by the concept of the Trinity. Employing the Aristotelian distinction between essence and existence, God was perceived as pure essence, capable of three expressions of existence: as the creative Father, the redeeming Son, and the Spirit that gives knowledge. Accordingly, the Trinity readily accommodates the essential tenet of Christianity that God sent his Son as the embodiment of supreme reason who organized and saved the world. Similarly, the view of the individual was Christianized within a basically dualistic context. Each person is composed of an essence, the soul, which takes on an existence through the body. The immortal soul passes through stages to eventual attachment with the body. After death, the soul continues in stages until it is eventually united in the perfect wisdom of God. All life and the sequence of the soul's development fall within the grand design of God. Thus, the Alexandrian teachers succeeded in giving Christianity a Greek foundation by incorporating the influences of Plato and Aristotle, and they added to that foundation the determinism of the Stoics.

The early theologians provided a basis for the greater appeal of Christianity, but Christianity had to cope with negative pressures from both within and outside. Internally, dissension among Christians spread through a variety of heresies. Perhaps the most important deviation from orthodox Christianity came from the Gnostics, whose mystical writings questioned basic beliefs on the resurrection and divinity of Jesus. Early Church councils settled such disputes, and gradually Church doctrine acquired form. Externally, Christians suffered waves of persecutions that did not end until the Emperor Constantine issued his Edict of Milan in 313, granting religious toleration throughout the empire.

A final problem resolved by early Christianity concerned the related issues of the gradual disintegration of the Western empire and authority from within the Church. Both issues paved the way for the emergence of papal supremacy, which had powerful implications for the European intellectual climate in succeeding centuries. The early Church had recognized the bishop of Rome as first among equals with respect to other bishops. Christianity in Rome took on many forms of Roman pagan worship in terms of liturgical dress and ritual. Indeed, the bishop of Rome assumed the title of Pontifex Maximus used by the pagan high priest. With the weakness of a series of emperors and eventual movement of the center of the empire to the East, the people of Rome began to call upon their bishop to assume the responsibilities of civil government. The evolution of papal authority was gradual and did not reach a culmination within the church until the split between Eastern and Western Christianity in 1054. Nevertheless, the centralization of authority and its identification with the pope had a tremendous impact, as we discuss later.

The Church Fathers

With the cessation of state persecution of Christianity by the Edict of Milan and the concurrent deterioration of civil authority in the Western empire, Western society began a restructuring of its values along Christian directions. A popular theology arose that contained many of the rituals of the earlier cults. The use of incense, candles, and processions as well as the veneration of saints were all adapted to Christian liturgy and served a need that was understood by the masses. As the cities declined and society assumed an increasingly agrarian character, the liturgical year was adapted to the agricultural cycle. Official Church policy tolerated some excesses that resulted in the rather primitive practice of Christianity because such customs and rites reinforced the moral teachings of the Church. In other words, the Church became the source of order and organization for both individual and social behavior. In the vacuum created by the breakdown of civil government, the Church assumed a position of the sole institution of social structure, but the Church was presiding over a decaying society with an eroding intellectual level. Accordingly, the customs and traditions of the practice of Christianity were used to preserve some semblance of moral order in the people.

Church Defenders.   A group of churchmen of the fourth and fifth centuries left Christianity with the basic formulations that prevail today. Saint Jerome (340–420) chastised the people and clergy of Rome for their worldliness, and then retired to the Palestinian desert to live a crusty existence writing nasty letters to other church leaders. However, he used his classical education in the monumental task of translating the Bible into Latin, the universally understood language. Saint Ambrose (340–397), as bishop of Milan, defended the basic doctrine of the Church and served as a model of charity to the poor. Saint Anthony (ca. 251–356) in Egypt and Saint Basil (330–379) in Palestine founded the monastic movement in the Eastern empire, which stressed the value of the hermit's solitude to achieve human perfection. When monasticism spread to the western areas of the empire, it gradually acquired more community organization and became an important movement to preserve learning in feudal Europe.

The teachings of the Church scholars were integrated with the scriptural sources of Christianity in a series of Church councils that standardized Christian teachings. The first Council of Nicea (325) produced a common creed accepted by all Christians, and deviation from the Nicene Creed was considered heretical. The bishops were charged with insuring that the practice of religion conformed to the defined doctrines, and increasingly the bishop of Rome assumed a precedence over the other bishops. Emperor Valentinian III issued an edict declaring that Pope Leo I (ca. 400–461) and his successors, as bishops of Rome, had authority over all Christian churches. Although the bishops of Constantinople, Alexandria, Jerusalem, and Antioch protested his edict, the papacy was increasingly recognized as the primary source of authority within Christian society.

Saint Augustine.   The writings of Saint Augustine (354–430) are critical to the history of psychology because of his reliance on Platonic thought. After receiving a sound background in classic Greek philosophy, he wandered from his native North Africa to Italy, taking various teaching posts. He led a rather Epicurean existence, reflected in his supposed injunction, "Lord, make me pure, but not right now!" While in Milan, he became infatuated with Neoplatonism and the writings of Plotinus. Finally, at age 33, he experienced a revelation from Christ and was baptized by Saint Ambrose. He returned to North Africa, founded a monastic group, and lived in poverty. In 396 he was elected bishop of the city of Hippo and remained there preaching and writing for the last 34 years of his life.

Two of Augustine's works are important to the historical evolution of psychology. His *Confessions*, written about 400, is perhaps the most famous autobiography in history. With keen introspection and masterly detail, he described how one person found peace through faith in God and resolved the conflict between the passions and reason. For Augustine, the mind is the receptor for divine wisdom and shares in the glory of God. Through it we can acquire a type of knowledge that is unknowable through the bodily senses. Moreover, this interior sense of the soul or mind allows us a level of consciousness that transcends, yet completely explains, physical reality. Thus, Augustine played down the rationality of the mind, which is dependent on unreliable sensory information. Rather, he proposed a more psychological view of the mind insofar as consciousness, or the self of the individual, endowed with the grace of divine wisdom, determines the direction of activity. According to Augustine, only by removing the faulty impressions of sensory knowledge can we reach this level of consciousness.

He wrote *City of God* in installments from 413 to 426 as a response to the outcry over the barbarian Alaric's sacking of Rome. Specifically, many people argued that this shocking event was the fault of Christianity, which had undermined the glories and power of imperial Rome. Augustine countered by asserting that Rome fell to invasion because of the inherent decay in the pagan society, which antedated the Christian era. Borrowing from Plato's notion of an ideal republic and Christian teachings on good and evil, Augustine suggested that humanity could be divided into two cities, or societies. The earthly city is concerned with worldliness and dominated by the evils of materialism. The city of God is everlasting with God and is identified for us by the Church. This city is spiritual and embodies goodness. Historically, people may vacillate between the cities and only at the last judgment will membership in each city be finally separated into those condemned to the sin and evil of Hell, and those who win happiness and perfection in God.

For our purposes in the study of the history of psychology, Augustine may be remembered for two great accomplishments. First, he completed the "Christianization" of Greek philosophy by affirming the Platonic relationship between body and soul. By relegating sensory information to a primitive level and positing a transcendent consciousness, Augustine taught the ideal of the mind reflecting upon itself as the key to ultimate beauty and love in God. This view dominated Christian thought until the end of the Middle Ages, so that all intellectual endeavors that studied life, including psychology, were done in a Platonic context. Second, he established a justification for a special relationship between the Church and the State. Augustine related the Church to the city of God. Worldly government would always be faulty and inferior to Church rule. Augustine was far more influential in the West than in the East. Because the Eastern empire was stronger there, the Church was subordinate to the State. However, in the West, with the deteriorating civil government of Rome, Augustine's arguments justified the Church's filling the void in civil as well as spiritual administration.

THE DARK AGES

A series of barbarian threats culminated in the sacking of Rome in 410, marking the first time in 800 years that the city fell to an enemy. From then until 476, when the succession of non-Roman Western emperors stopped and the Western empire came to an end, repeated invasions took their toll. Rome was reduced from a city of 1,500,000 to 300,000 people. The new tribes settled into various parts of the Western empire: The Germans moved into Italy, the Visigoths into Spain, the Franks changed Gaul to France, and the Angles and Saxons took Britain (Map 3). These tribes could not sustain the system of commercial centers in great cities, which had been managed from Rome. As a result, western Europe became rural. The strength of law given by Rome declined and was replaced by violence and individual aggression.

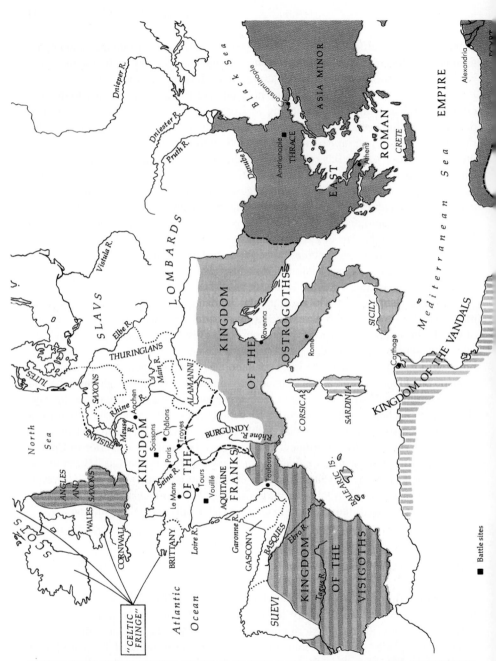

MAP 3. THE FRAGMENTED WEST AND THE EASTERN ROMAN, OR BYZANTINE, EMPIRE (ca. A.D. 500). In the west the kingdoms of the Angles and Saxons, the Franks, the Visigoths, the Suevi, the Vandals, the Ostrogoths, and Burgundy are shown. In addition, the less organized settlements of the Celts, the Frisians, the Jutes, the Thuringens, the Lombards, and the Slavs are indicated. In the east, the area governed by the emperor from Constantinople is darkly shaded, and the major cities of the Byzantine Empire are shown.

The Eastern Empire

The seat of civil government in the Roman Empire moved to the city of Constantinople, and the Byzantine Empire, with its own culture, gradually emerged while civilization in the West deteriorated. Under the leadership of Emperor Justinian (483–565), the Eastern empire flourished and a new code of law bearing the emperor's name clearly differentiated the culture and society of the East from the chaotic situation in the West. Great universities became centers of excellence at Constantinople, Alexandria, Athens, and Antioch, specializing, respectively, in literature, medicine, philosophy, and rhetoric.

Steadily, the Byzantine Empire acquired a character of its own. The Latin language gave way to Greek, and Christianity took on a Greek flavor in both ceremony and theology. The social chaos of western Europe and the increasing menace of Islamic tribes to the south made contact with the West difficult. The empire began to decline and became insulated and corrupt. However, the Byzantines supported a system of colonies in the Balkans and in the present-day Ukraine, introducing the Greek alphabet, culture, and religion. In 989 Vladimir (972–1015), grand duke of Kiev, became a Christian and brought his Ukrainian and Russian nations under the influence of the Byzantine culture. After the Byzantine Empire was finally obliterated with the fall of Constantinople to the Turks in 1453, Russia, then known as the duchy of Moscow, became the remaining repository of the Byzantine culture.

Islamic Civilization

The birth of Mohammed (570–632) in the poor desert region of Arabia marked one of the most extraordinary phenomena of the medieval period. Within a century, Mohammed's followers had conquered most of the Byzantine territories in Asia, all of Persia, Egypt, and North Africa, and were preparing to invade Spain. In 610 Mohammed experienced his first vision of the angel Gabriel, who informed him that he had been chosen as the messenger of God, or Allah, and began to reveal the sacred writings that eventually formed the holy book of Islam, the Koran. Mohammed gathered avid followers among the nomadic tribes of Arabia, and he soon conquered the holy cities of Mecca and Medina. By the time of his death Mohammed had established the essential doctrines of Islam, and his successors extended the theocratic state to an ever-expanding empire.

As the Muslim invaders occupied Christian territories once under the rule of the Byzantine Empire, they encountered the cultural heritage of Greek scholarship in philosophy and science. The Islamic intellectuals appreciated the Greek culture and borrowed freely in their formulations. Most importantly, they preserved the writings of the ancients at a time when scholarly works were being destroyed by the barbarian aggression in the West. During the rule of the Abbasid caliphs (750–1258), centered at Baghdad, the works of most classical Greek scholars as well as more recent commentaries were translated into Syrian. Islamic scholars, who in turn contributed to the development of arithmetic and algebra, also studied the mathematical treatises of the Greeks. Hospitals were established throughout the Islamic world, with the most famous in Damascus, which provided the setting for the education of physicians. Islamic physicians developed anesthesia and surgical procedures and published books on pharmacology.

One of the more famous scholars of Islam during the medieval period in the West was Abu ibn Sina, known as Avicenna (980–1037). He was a renowned physician who published a synopsis of medical treatments in his *Canon of Medicine*. As a philosopher, Avicenna was well acquainted with the writings of Aristotle. Avicenna's philosophy antedated by almost two centuries the revival in the West of interest in Aristotle, which was known as Scholasticism. Essentially, Avicenna accepted the metaphysics and psychology of Aristotle and attempted to reconcile them with his faith in Islam. He viewed the essence of the human soul as the extension of God's essence, and believed that through the rational powers of the soul we can share in the perfect knowledge of God. He treated the acquisition of sensory knowledge in some detail, concluding that the characteristic mind–body dualism of human beings reflects an interaction between sensory and rational knowledge. His synthesis of Aristotelian thought and Islamic faith was a remarkable tribute to Islamic scholarship.

Islam as a crusading, religious movement threatened the existence of Christianity. Its successes in the eastern Mediterranean virtually wiped out Christianity in that area (Map 4), and the possibility of Islamic forces overrunning western Europe was not completely eliminated until the seventeenth century. Nevertheless, in the attempt to preserve intellectual life from destruction, the Western Church scholars of later centuries were aided by the efforts of Islamic scholars who maintained the libraries of their vast empire, so that the classic authors of antiquity could be reintroduced to western Europe.

The Feudal West

The situation in western Europe after the capital of the empire moved from Rome to Constantinople steadily deteriorated. Plagued by wars, famine, and disease, Western social structures regressed, as did the general intellectual level, so that even the most elite of social classes were largely ignorant and illiterate. Because the invaders were eventually converted to Christianity, one institution that survived the devastation was the Church. The Church, left as the sole international institution in western Europe, sought to preserve a semblance of order and culture.

The Church institution most responsible for preserving the remnants of intellectual life in the West was monasticism. The founder of the monastic movement in the West was Saint Benedict (480–543), who in 529 opened the greatest monastery of the medieval period at Monte Casino in central Italy. In contrast to Eastern monasticism, which stressed the solitary existence of the hermit, Saint Benedict defined monasticism in terms of a group of men living in absolute poverty, chastity, and obedience. The famous Rule of Saint Benedict governed monastic life throughout western Europe, and variants of the rule are still followed today by contemplative religious orders of monks and nuns. A succession of monasteries composed of clerics living under the commune law of Saint Benedict spread throughout Europe and North

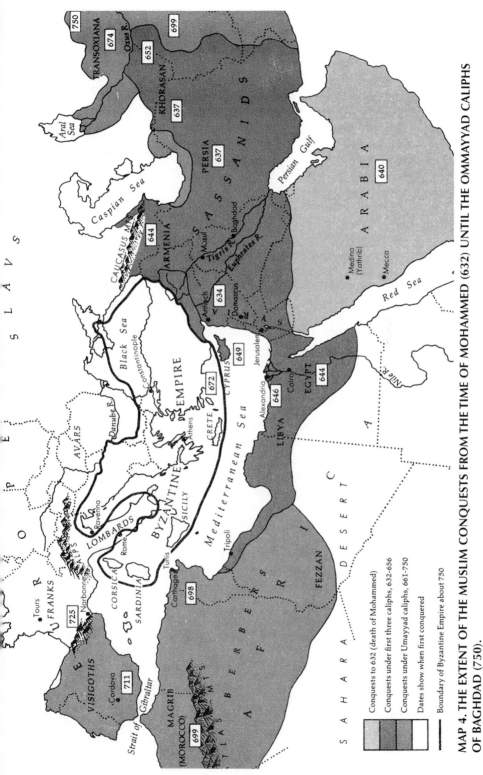

MAP 4. THE EXTENT OF THE MUSLIM CONQUESTS FROM THE TIME OF MOHAMMED (632) UNTIL THE OMMAYYAD CALIPHS OF BAGHDAD (750).

Conquests to 632 (death of Mohammed)

Conquests under first three caliphs, 632–656

Conquests under Umayyad caliphs, 661–750

Dates show when first conquered

Boundary of Byzantine Empire about 750

47

Africa. Indeed, it was the monks of faraway, but relatively tranquil, Ireland who kept Latin literature from the total destruction so widespread on the Continent. The monasteries, although not distinguished as intellectual centers, slowed the erosion of intellectual life and saved art, literature, and philosophy from complete eradication.

During the medieval period, the papacy gained enormous power. Pope Gregory the Great (540–604) was elected bishop of Rome in 590, a time when the city was decimated by a bubonic plague that had carried off his predecessor. He embarked on a reform movement that tightened discipline among the clergy and in the monasteries and improved the civil administration of the city. As a result a trend toward centralization within the Western Church was established, which led to increasing standardization in church practice and heightened the authority of the papacy. Papal authority was further enhanced in 756 when the Frank king, Pepin, donated the lands of central Italy to the Pope. These papal estates made the popes formal temporal rulers, which they continued to be until 1870. Finally, in 800, Pope Leo III crowned another Frank king, Charlemagne, as emperor of the Holy Roman Empire, a loose confederation of Christian princes, thus beginning the tradition of conferring legitimacy on the authority of Christian rulers.

The papacy continued to have both good and bad periods throughout the Middle Ages. There were cycles of abuses and reforms. Nevertheless, the spiritual and temporal authority of the popes grew steadily. Fulfilling the prophesy of Saint Augustine in *City of God*, the popes could bestow or withhold the legitimacy of social institutions. They confirmed the emperors and national monarchs, acted on the appointments of bishops, regulated the monasteries, and decided on correct beliefs for the people. Other members of the hierarchy gathered temporal power as well, but ultimately it was with the bishop of Rome that final and absolute authority rested.

One by-product of growing papal power was the schism between the Western and Eastern forms of Christianity. Theological disputes stemming from differences between Latin and Greek versions of scriptural and council documents, coupled with political rivalry over spheres of influence between Rome and Constantinople, led to increasing bitterness. Finally, in 1054, the patriarch of Constantinople and the pope excommunicated each other and each other's followers, so that the last remaining link between East and West was severed. In the meantime, the Holy Wars of Islam threatened all of Europe. In the West, Muslim invasion through Spain was finally stopped at Tours, France, in 732, but the Islamic armies were not completely driven out of Spain until 1492.

Feudal Europe was largely a loose collection of social hierarchies based on service and loyalty. At the bottom of the hierarchy were the peasants, who owed service to the landowner. The landowner, in turn, owed allegiance to a local or regional noble, who could be a vassal to a king, to the Holy Roman Emperor, or to the Pope himself. True national governments were yet to emerge, and issues of local concern mostly determined daily life. The Roman system of roads had been neglected, and communication over distances was very difficult. The papacy was the only source of authority that could possibly command the obedience of all levels of feudal society. The distinctions between Church and State, between ecclesiastical and civil law, and between religion and science were obscured.

By the year 1000, intellectual life in western Europe was isolated and losing ground. Most of the classic writings were lost, and the Church censored others because of their pagan authors. The cultural life of Europe was found largely in religious expressions of art and music. However, also by the year 1000, Europe was almost completely Christian. From Ireland in the west to Poland and Lithuania in the east, from Scandinavia in the north to the Mediterranean, people shared a common religion and a common allegiance to the papacy. Whereas feudal disputes among emerging nations would continue, sometimes with great severity, the era of greatest devastation was over, and intellectual activity slowly reemerged.

THE CRUSADES

In a sense, the Crusades represented the zenith of power for Christianity. They were a series of eight military or quasi-military campaigns from 1095 to 1291 to secure the Holy Lands of the Near East from Muslim control. Although unsuccessful in the long run, the Crusades reflected a fervent expression of Christianity. However, on another level, the Crusades may be viewed as the beginning of the reawakening of western Europe. They brought contact and commerce with other civilizations. Moreover, the Crusades produced stimulation from the intellectual life of Islam, where scholarship had fared much better than in Europe. Islamic scholars had preserved the Greek masters; mathematics, architecture, and medicine had flowered under Islamic rule. These new ideas were brought back to Europe, along with more complete copies of the ancient writers. The Crusades began to shake Europe out of its feudal provincialism. The political life of Europe and the rise of national states were facilitated by the Crusades, and this movement was at the expense of the papacy.

The Crusades were a product of a homogeneous Christianity that permeated all aspects of western European life. At the same time, however, the Crusades were symptomatic of great changes that were about to occur in western Europe. First, the papacy was powerful enough to decry the reports of persecution of Christians by the new Turkish rulers of Palestine, who had replaced the relatively tolerant Egyptian Fatimids. The First Crusade backed up papal indignation with impressive military force, but the popes lost control of the later campaigns, so that the net impact of the Crusades upon papal power and prestige was negative. Second, the Crusades filled a vacuum created by the weakness of the Byzantine Empire, which was no longer powerful enough to serve as an effective buffer between the Turks of the Middle East and the Christians of western Europe. After reaching its zenith of power and culture under Emperor Justinian, who contributed his name to the Byzantine revision and codification of Roman law, the Byzantine Empire sank into internal discord and strife, and its governing effectiveness diminished. Finally, the city-states of the Italian peninsula, such as Genoa and Venice, were developing as mercantile centers and needed extended markets. Thus, the Crusades served as a catalyst to move western Europe out of feudalism and intellectual lethargy.

As military enterprises and religious movements, the Crusades were failures. However, the Crusades did succeed in propelling western Europe into a more mature period of consolidation and organization. First, because the Crusades required the raising of large armies on an international scale, they fostered the restructuring of rivalries from a local level to a national identity. Second, because the Crusades opened the possibility for vast commercial markets, they facilitated the development of mercantile economics. Finally, the Crusades brought back the classical scholarship of antiquity. Fortunately, western Europe was ready to discard feudalism and begin the rebirth of intellectual life.

At the beginning of this chapter, we observed that the Romans inherited the Greek systems of philosophy and science and devised details of applications. However, with the fall of Roman rule in the West, scholarly pursuit, including the study of psychology, was halted and regressed. The theocratic character of feudal society mixed religion with psychology and science, so that psychology was reduced to the practice of Christianity. This loss of psychology to religion occurred on two levels. Psychology became part of the moral doctrines on behavior taught by the Church, and psychology became immersed in the mythology of Christian practice. On the first level, psychological explanations of any activity had to conform to the tenets of Christianity. For example, the directives of propagation within the exclusive bounds of marriage governed individual sexual activity, and any deviation was simply defined as wrong and abnormal. On the level of the practice of Christianity, psychology was confused with the superstitions of widely believed mythology. Mental illness and social deviancy were considered evil curses or demonic possession. The recognized cure for such maladies did not involve understanding or study, but rather prayer or exposure to relics. Medieval Europe was indeed an age of faith, and science, including psychology, was dormant.

CHAPTER SUMMARY

Roman culture adopted classic Greek philosophy but developed unique Roman perspectives, as illustrated by the Stoics and Epicureans. The Stoics held a conservative view of humanity, determined by the fates of nature. Human adjustment consisted of cooperating with universal designs. Conversely, for the Epicureans happiness consisted simply of the seeking of pleasure and avoidance of pain. The teachings of Plato were revived by Plotinus, and dominated Roman philosophy during the early years of Christianity. Both the missionary zeal of the Christian apostles and the tranquil efficiency of Roman administration contributed to the rapid spread of Christianity. The teachings of Jesus and interpretations of the Christian message evolved from a Hebrew basis to a foundation in Greek philosophy. In addition to the early fathers of the Church, Augustine successfully put a Platonic imprint on Christian theology. With the fall of the Western empire, intellectual life in Europe came to a virtual halt, and only the monastic movement preserved a rough semblance of Greek and Roman civilization. The papacy assumed a leading role not only in spiritual direction but also in civil administration, culminating in the call for the crusades. By the time of the crusades, however, Europe was relatively peaceful and intellectual life began to stir. Exposure to the cultural inheritance of Islam revived European interest in the masterpieces of ancient civilization, and a great intellectual awakening was about to shake Europe out of the intellectual nadir of feudalism.

BIBLIOGRAPHY

AUGUSTINE. (1948). *Basic writings of St. Augustine* (W. Oates, Ed.). New York: Random House.

AUGUSTINE. (1958). *City of God* (G. G. Walsh, D. B. Zema, G. Monahan, & D. H. Honan, Eds. and Trans.). New York: Image Books.

AUGUSTINE. (1955). *Confessions* (J. K. Ryan, Ed. and Trans.). New York: Image Books.

COPLESTON, F. (1961). *A history of philosophy, Vol. II, Medieval philosophy, Part I— Augustine to Bonaventure.* Garden City, NY: Image Books.

DURANT, W. (1944). *Caesar and Christ.* New York: Simon & Schuster.

DURANT, W. (1950). *The age of faith.* New York: Simon & Schuster.

MORA, G. (1978). Mind-body concepts in the middle ages: Part I. The classical background and the merging with the Judeo-Christian tradition in the early Middle Ages. *Journal of the History of the Behavioral Sciences, 14,* 344–361.

OATES, W. (Ed.). (1940). *The Stoic and Epicurean philosophers.* New York: Random House.

PAGELS, E. (1979). *The Gnostic Gospels.* New York: Random House.

WINTER, H. J. J. (1952). *Eastern science.* London: Murray.

✿ 4 ✿

The Reawakening of Intellectual Life

The Papacy and Church Power
The Universities
Some Eminent Thinkers
    Pierre Abélard
    Roger Bacon
    Albertus Magnus
Scholasticism
    Thomas Aquinas
    The Papacy and Authority
The Italian Renaissance
The Challenge to Authority
    Within the Church: The Reformation
    Within Science: The Copernican Revolution
Chapter Summary

During the period between 1000 and 1300, the map of Europe began to take its present form. The recovery in Europe led to the emergence of nation-states that consolidated civil administration under the political leadership of a monarch. In England the political power of the king relative to the rights of the landed barons and church authorities started to be defined through the Magna Carta, forced on the king in 1215. Similarly, the peoples of France, Spain, Portugal, and Denmark acquired national identities and cultures under the centralized order of powerful aristocracies. In the East, the monarchy of Poland merged that country initially with Hungary and later with Lithuania to form a powerful confederation that defended the Latin Christianity of western Europe from the Eastern Orthodoxy of Russia. Only in Germany, where direct and effective unification was stymied by the combined power of the landed barons and the papacy, and in Italy, which was directly under papal rule, were political consolidations under single monarchs delayed.

THE PAPACY AND CHURCH POWER

The papacy triumphed over this age. As indicated in Map 5, most of western Europe was under papal control. The institutional Church occupied a privileged role in society.

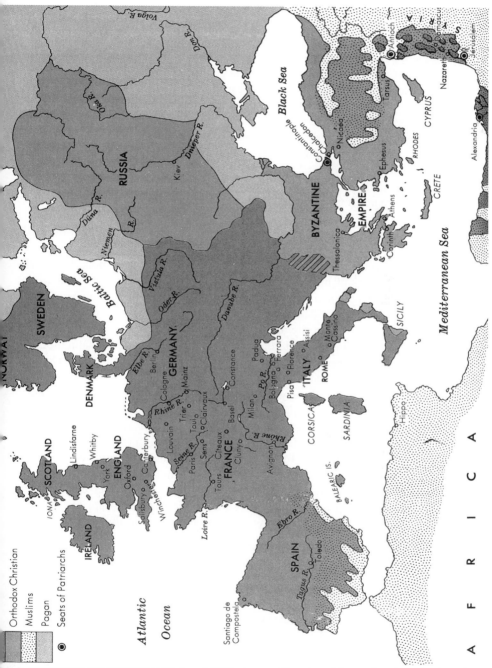

MAP 5. WESTERN CHRISTENDOM (ca. 1100). Areas of major cities and university locations ~western Europe are shown, as are the remnants of the Byzantine Empire and the advancing ~oman Turks, who finally captured Constantinople in 1453.

53

The papacy emerged from the early Middle Ages as the major source of authority over every aspect of religious, political, and cultural life. The essentially theocratic government from Rome dominated the feudal hierarchy. Moreover, because the pope confirmed the legitimacy of temporal rulers and was himself a temporal ruler over vast estates in central and northern Italy, the papacy assumed a political role unmatched by any other European political institution. The power of the papacy had political implications that led to disastrous events in the fourteenth century, when the popes left Rome for residency at Avignon in southern France (1309–1377). However, prior to the Avignon period, the pope was the most powerful person in Europe.

Several developments in the Church are of interest to us because of their effects on the emergence of intellectual life. First, a dramatic reform in the monastic movement led to the Church's having a more direct influence on intellectual formation. Saint Bernard of Clairvaux (1091–1153) founded monasteries under the most strict application of Benedictine rule. This order of clerics, called Cistercians, lived a life of work and prayer, avoiding all intellectual enterprises. Among Saint Bernard's followers, the monasteries—founded as self-sufficient units having no contact with society—reached their peak. However, in Italy a new reform in monasticism was taking place. Groups of men and women following the rules of clerical discipline lived among the people and attempted to serve their needs. Saint Francis of Assisi (1182–1226) was the spiritual father of several orders of men and women who sought to live a life of humility and to sacrifice their material goods for the poor. Francis himself led an ascetic life of absolute poverty, rejoicing in natural beauty, harmony, and love of people and the world. Meanwhile, in Spain, Saint Dominic Guzman (1170–1221) founded the Order of Preachers, whose members used their intellectual abilities to fight heresy. These men, popularly called Dominicans, spread throughout Europe and eventually formed an intellectual elite within the Church. As the universities emerged in western Europe, the Dominicans and Franciscans occupied positions in the theology faculties and in turn exerted powerful influences on the entire university structure. Together, the new religious orders fostered a movement away from the isolation of the monasteries to a mission of service among the people. In so doing, the members of the new religious orders presented the people with a contrast to their parish priests, whose typical level of intellectual preparation was notoriously inadequate. Accordingly, the very presence of the Dominicans and Franciscans produced a general uplifting of the intellectual caliber of the Church.

A second Church development at this time concerned the attempt to keep the belief of the people free from error, as defined by the Church. It was the Dominicans who undertook this effort, and its most visible expression was the infamous Inquisition, which investigated people accused of heresy or deviation from official Church doctrine. However, this development encompassed a more widespread system of censorship, which had a tremendous impact on the intellectual reawakening of Europe. Specifically, all intellectual activity, from the writing of books to teaching, had to be scrutinized for possible errors. In those institutions most directly controlled by the Church, such as the universities, this censorship was sometimes heavy-handed, stifling imaginative inquiry. The system produced an Index of Books, forbidden for the faithful to read, and the censors had power to condemn individuals to either death or imprisonment. The censorship system was applied unevenly from country to country, depending on the extent of papal power and of cooperation from civil authorities. However, the system was generally effective, and it gave the Church direct control of intellectual inquiry. Out of fear—or perhaps simply to avoid potential problems—many scholars were forced to work in secret or at least outside those institutions under Church control.

The Inquisition lasted several centuries in a checkered history of cyclic intensity. In addition to finding heretics, the Inquisition extended its authority to investigating demonic possession, witches, and others with deviant behavior. Unfortunately, many persons who would today be judged mentally ill, retarded, or socially incompetent were caught up in the Inquisition and suffered tortures and death because of their nonconformity. As late as 1487, the Dominican friars Jacob Sprenger and Heinrich Kraemer published *Malleus Maleficarum* (*The Hammer of Witches*), an encyclopedia of demonology and witchcraft with suggested remedies and tortures. This sordid chapter in the treatment of the mentally ill extended to the seventeenth and eighteenth centuries, as evidenced by such colorful characters as Cotton Mather and by the Salem witch trials of colonial America.

The cruel and abusive nature of the Inquisition was a means of social control in the name of Christian orthodoxy. The Inquisition was an invention of a society that subordinated all human activity to the doctrines of the Church. In turn, the Church defended its authority as based on God's will, and the people accepted Church authority on faith. Accordingly, psychology was identified with Christianity, and an understanding of individual behavior and mental activity required an appreciation of the person's desire to achieve eternal salvation. In this age of unquestioned Church supremacy, there was simply no room for other considerations. Those who questioned the authority of the Church or deviated from the social teachings of the Church, for whatever reason, were considered abnormal. Indeed, any deviation from Church teaching was contrary to what was perceived as the natural order, and therefore some abnormal and powerful agent, such as the devil, was assumed to be responsible. Thus the policing function of the Inquisition, although a sad episode in Western history, was not an unreasonable reflection of this age.

THE UNIVERSITIES

One of the characteristics of the breakdown in communication and commerce during the early Middle Ages was the loss of Latin as a universally understood language. What began as dialects of Latin after the fall of Rome emerged by 1000 as the distinct Romance languages of French, Spanish, and Portuguese. Italian evolved more slowly, but by 1300 Dante chose to write *The Divine Comedy* in the Italian dialect of Tuscany. Similarly, the Old German of the northern European tribes evolved into a family of language forms, including a forerunner of English. The French influence contributed to the development of the hybrid of modern English after the

Norman invasion of England in 1066, and the Middle English of Chaucer's four-teenth-century *Canterbury Tales* still reflected a heavy French influence. By 1300, varieties of local languages were established in spoken communication at the expense of Latin. The painstaking process of hand-copying books was still predominantly done in Latin, but that, too, was soon to change.

Education in medieval times was largely limited to moral instruction that took place in schools related to cathedrals, monasteries, and convents. The Church supported fundamental education, and the Fourth Lateran Council of Rome (1215) instructed bishops to establish in every cathedral teaching positions in grammar, philosophy, and church law. However, the cathedral schools soon proved insufficient to cope with growing numbers of clerics and nonclerics interested in learning and scholarship. A revival of interest in Roman law led to the founding of Europe's oldest university in Bologna in 1088. Soon the two schools of law—church and civil—were described as a *universitas scholarium* in Bologna, and the university was recognized by a papal decree as a place where one could engage in *studium generale*. Under the auspices of wealthy princes and Church leaders, universities shortly spread throughout Italy: Modena (1175), Vicenza (1204), Padua (1222), Naples (1224), Siena (1246), Rome (1303), Pisa (1343), Florence (1349), and Ferrara (1391). Although strong in law and medicine, these centers of learning provided Italy with the push toward the renaissance of intellectual activity in all areas of inquiry that flowered in the fourteenth and fifteenth centuries.

The University of Paris, perhaps the greatest center of philosophy and theology during medieval times, was started in 1160 and enrolled as many as 5,000 to 7,000 students. The curriculum began with the study of the seven "arts" of grammar, logic, rhetoric, arithmetic, geometry, music, and astronomy. Students then went on to study philosophy and, finally, theology. By the fourteenth century, the University of Paris consisted of 40 colleges, or residencies, of which the Sorbonne remains the most famous. As France emerged from the medieval period to the Renaissance, the sense of national identity grew faster than in other parts of Europe. Moreover, France became the most populous country in Europe, which gave the French monarchs large armies to support their political ambitions. As the leading university in the leading European country, the University of Paris acquired great prestige throughout Europe, and the opinions of the Paris scholars were considered definitive statements throughout the Continent. In particular, the faculty of theology at the University of Paris, consisting mostly of Dominican priests, embodied the culmination of intellectual activity at that time. Noblemen, kings, emperors, and even the pope deferred to the theological interpretations emanating from Paris.

Elsewhere in continental Europe the spread of universities as centers of learning continued. In Portugal, the king founded a university in Lisbon in 1290, which was later moved to the old Roman town of Coimbra, where it still prospers. Great university centers were founded in the Spanish-speaking cities of Salamanca (1227), Valladolid (1250), and Seville (1254). In German-speaking nations, universities were founded in Vienna (1365), Heidelberg (1386), and Cologne (1388). The oldest university of central Europe is in Prague, founded in 1348 by King Charles IV, who had studied at the University of Paris. The Jagellonian University, founded in the Polish capital of Krakow in 1364, gained a reputation in humanistic studies and in astronomy. It was here that Copernicus received his education.

In England, groups of students gathered at Oxford as early as 1167, and by 1190 a university had developed. As a result of disturbances in the town of Oxford in 1209, when the townsfolk killed several students, some scholars and students journeyed to Cambridge, and by 1281 another university was functioning there. Four faculties of arts, Church law, medicine, and theology were organized in both English universities. By 1300 Oxford rivaled the University of Paris for prestige and scholarly productivity.

The organization of the universities was a critical stage in the reawakening of European intellectual thought. Not since the Greek and Roman academies had centers of scholarship existed in western Europe. However, we must not forget that the Church, with its system of censorship, pervaded medieval societies, including the universities. Theology was recognized as the most sophisticated discipline, and the theology faculty dominated other faculties of the universities. The medieval universities had their shortcomings. Internally, the dominance of theology often restricted independent study that relied on methods of reason rather than faith. As institutions of the Church, the universities required conformity to Church discipline, so that intellectual pursuit was qualified. Both the Church and the national monarchs exerted external pressure through their control of financial support. Often those pressures were political and clearly violated the integrity and independence of the universities. Nevertheless, the early universities filled an invaluable role in the rebirth of intellectual life in western European culture. With their libraries and learned teachers, the universities attracted people to the common pursuit of intellectual activity.

SOME EMINENT THINKERS

The accomplishments of a few of the outstanding university scholars of awakening Europe attest to the significant level of learning in the medieval university. Moreover, these scholars reflected the steady questioning of Church authority by those who demonstrated the benefits of pursuing knowledge through means other than those based on faith. This movement allowed for the eventual emergence of science and the triumph of reason over faith in scholarly inquiry.

Pierre Abélard

Pierre Abélard (1079–1142) was a brilliant philosopher and one of the pioneers of the University of Paris. Born in Brittany, he eventually wandered to Paris, where he studied under the Platonic philosopher William of Champeaux (1070–1121) at the cathedral of Notre Dame. At that time a philosophical controversy raged concerning the metaphysical problem of universal beings. Plato had argued, from the presence of constant change in physical appearances, that the universal is more lasting, permanent, and therefore real, compared to particular events based upon sensory information. In other words, people change, but not humanity. Conversely, Aristotle argued that the universal is a mental idea to represent a classification for particular physical manifestations; that is, we use the concept of humanity to classify people as separate from other animals. The Church had some vested interest in the dispute because it considered itself to be a spiritual universal, greater than the sum of individual believers; that is, the Church was not simply a mental abstraction. William of Champeaux took the extreme Platonic view that universals are the only reality and individuals are only incidental manifestations of that universal. Abélard used his excellent rhetorical and logical skills to show rationally the absurdity of William's extreme position—that is, the relegation of individual persons simply to instances of a universal defies our observed order of reality in nature. Soon Abélard was teaching at the Notre Dame School as a canon of the cathedral.

However, before proceeding with his brilliant teachings, Abélard's career was interrupted by one of the most famous romantic tragedies of medieval Europe. He fell in love with the intelligent and beautiful Héloïse, niece of the head canon of the cathedral. As nature took its course, Héloïse became pregnant, prompting Abélard secretly to take her to his sister's home in Brittany, where she gave birth to their son. Héloïse refused to marry Abélard because such a formal union would preclude his ordination as a priest and a promising career as a high Church official. Rather, she preferred to remain his mistress. However, after leaving the child in Brittany, they were secretly married in Paris, although they continued to live separately. After continued fights with her uncle, Héloïse again fled—this time to a convent. Thinking that Abélard had forced Héloïse to become a nun to cover his own transgression, the uncle and some aides pounced on Abélard and, to paraphrase Abélard, severed that part of his anatomy that had done the harm. Thus, Abélard became a monk and Héloïse became a nun, limiting their future intercourse to a romantic and somewhat spicy written correspondence.

Abélard then resumed with intensity his study and teaching. He tried to place Christian thought on a rational plane and deal with the critical relationship between faith and reason. His method, based upon the ancient teaching technique of Socrates and adopted by later writers, was to exhaust all sides of an issue by outlining in question-and-answer form the logical consequences of philosophical and theological assumptions. He taught that if truth is given from God, then both faith and reason will, through parallel directions, reach the same conclusion. Abélard's efforts were an important contribution to the development of science because he relied on arguments that appealed to reason.

Abélard's writings were confined to logical discourses on the manner of knowing God and nature, and the weight of his conclusions gave legitimacy to the place of reason in the pursuit of knowledge. He did not discard faith as a source of knowledge, but his success in securing at least the acceptance of reason as coequal with faith in intellectual inquiry was a major accomplishment. Both his views and his caustic manner of presentation led Abélard to trouble with his superiors, and in 1140 he was condemned to cease teaching and writing by Pope Innocent II. Soon after, he died a lonely and bitter man. However, he introduced to medieval philosophy a systematic method that rested firmly on reason, independent of theology. Others followed who explored the implications of Abélard's teachings to their fullest.

Roger Bacon

Called by many scholars the greatest medieval scientist, Roger Bacon (ca. 1214–1292) was born in Somerset in southwestern England and spent most of his student and teaching years at Oxford University. Exposed to ancient Hebrew teaching by Jews in England, he went to the University of Paris and was further educated in ancient and modern languages. However, he was not impressed with the metaphysical and logical methods in the approach to natural philosophy or science while in Paris. After joining the Franciscan order, Bacon returned to England to teach natural philosophy at Oxford. Bacon emphasized the importance of study through systematic observation and a reliance on mathematics, his first love, to describe careful observations.

Bacon wrote extensively on philosophical and moral issues, but he was clearly at his best on scientific matters. His substantial contributions to science are rather minor and limited to some discourses on optics and on the reform of the Julian calendar. Nevertheless, his position in the emergence of scientific activity is well deserved. First, he revived interest in the ancient authors, especially mathematicians such as Euclid. Second, and more important, he stressed that empirical demonstration, based upon the deliberate observation of the physical world, will gain more than logical arguments. In other words, the validation of truth by sensory agreement among observers, aided by mathematics, holds the key to science. Thus, empiricism was reintroduced to science. Bacon's emphasis on an inductive approach in science was in contrast to the prevailing interpretation of Aristotle, which stressed definition and classification in the study of the physical world. Medieval knowledge of Aristotle's writings had emphasized logical reasoning as the primary method of demonstration—at the expense of Aristotle's views on the importance of observation. There is an underlying truth to the anecdote describing medieval monks standing in the monastery courtyard, arguing endlessly over the number of teeth of the horse, until finally, a brash young novice walked over to a horse, opened its mouth, and counted the number of teeth. Bacon's major accomplishment reinforced Aristotle's traditional teachings on the importance of observation. Thus, it was established that knowledge can be gained by both logical deduction, based on reason, and inductive empiricism, based on careful and controlled observations through the senses.

Albertus Magnus

Albertus Magnus (ca. 1193–1280) was a Dominican scholar who worked in schools and monasteries in Germany and also spent two periods of time at the University of Paris. He was one of the first western European scholars to review completely all of the known works of Aristotle, a daring accomplishment for a

Christian intellectual at a time when Aristotle's writings were considered heretical by the Church. Albertus Magnus wrote extensively on Aristotelian logic as the basis of correct reasoning and proposed six principles of logical inquiry. The metaphysical treatises of Albertus included an evaluation of the interpretation of Aristotle's views offered by the Muslim scholar Averroës (1126–1198), who taught in Spain and Morocco about the relationship between Aristotle's philosophy and the tenets of Islam. In addition, Albertus produced books on ethics, politics, and theology. Interestingly, Albertus' writings on psychology were rather comprehensive, dealing with such topics as sensation, intelligence, and memory. Although Albertus did not add much original work on psychology, his reliance on Aristotle as an authority was a significant step in itself. Moreover, he took Aristotle's mind–body dualism and related the potential of the soul to the Christian ethic of seeking eternal salvation. The end result of this merger, contained in his treatise *De Potentiis Animae* (*On the Powers of the Soul*), was a proposal for a dynamic psychology of human striving for goodness and intellectual fulfillment in the knowledge of God. Albertus' views on psychology were innovative because he elevated human rational powers as a source of salvation in addition to faith.

Albertus Magnus was a brilliant and prolific scholar who successfully ignored the intimidating censorship of the Church and drew inspiration from non-Christian resources of scholarship. He championed exact observation and his detailed studies of plant life contributed to the science of botany. He visited areas in Europe or corresponded with other observers to classify and describe varieties of fauna. As a naturalist, he reinforced Bacon's teachings on the importance and efficacy of careful empirical observation. Moreover, as one of the first Christian scholars to rely on the work of the pagan Aristotle, Albertus provided a refreshing source of intellectual stimulation that was to have a tremendous impact on the awakening of scholarly pursuit.

SCHOLASTICISM

One of Abélard's students, Peter Lombard, used the question-and-answer method in an influential book, *Sententiarum Libri IV* (*Four Volumes of Opinion*), written around 1150. His book attempted to reconcile the Bible with human reason. This work advanced the use of reasoning in addition to faith as a source in the pursuit of knowledge and became a classic of Christian theology. At the same time, Aristotle's works, translated from the Arabic, reached wider audiences in the universities, especially the University of Paris. Albertus Magnus had set the stage by liberally using Aristotle's teachings to explain nature and human psychology. However, it was a Christian age, and faith was dominant. Somehow, Aristotle's teachings on metaphysics and on the soul had to be systematically reconciled with Christian theology. This task was accomplished by Thomas Aquinas. The results are known as Scholasticism, which opened the door for the life of the mind by admitting human reason, along with faith, as a tool for seeking the truth. Indeed, it may be argued that the very admittance of reason spelled the end of the dominance of faith as the source of human knowledge.

Thomas Aquinas

Saint Thomas Aquinas (1225–1274) was born of a German father and a Sicilian mother descended from Norman invaders, in his father's castle near the town of Aquino, which lies within sight of the great Benedictine abbey of Monte Casino, where he received his early schooling. He grew to such robust proportions and exhibited such quiet studiousness that he was dubbed the "dumb ox of Sicily." No appellation could be further from the truth. In 1882, Pope Leo XIII commissioned a group of Dominican priests to assemble a compendium of Aquinas' writings. After well over a century of continuous effort and many changes in personnel, the group is still working and is far from finished. Aquinas joined the Dominicans in 1244, and by the following year he was studying with Albertus Magnus in Paris. He spent most of his remaining years teaching in Paris and occasionally in Italy. During all of this time he consistently defended reason against those arguing for faith alone as the source of truth. To prove his thesis he attempted to reconcile Aristotelian philosophy with Christian thought, a goal similar to Augustine's reconciliation of Plato with Christianity 800 years earlier. In 1272, the ruler of Naples, Charles of Anjou, asked Aquinas to reorganize the university there. Shortly after beginning this effort, Aquinas reportedly received a vision showing the completeness of divine knowledge, causing his own comprehensive work to have only minimum value, and he ceased writing. He was known throughout Europe as a learned man, yet he had great humility and gentleness, and he continually asserted his own inadequacies. The scope and depth of Aquinas' scholarship mark him as one of the outstanding intellectuals of Western culture.

His greatest work, the *Summa Theologica* (*A Summary of Theology*), represents the embodiment of Christian thought in its most detailed and comprehensive presentation. Underlying his system is Aristotelian logic. Thomas used the logic of the question-and-answer method to arrive at the essential truth of God. He took

THOMAS AQUINAS (1225–1274). (Courtesy, New York Public Library.)

Aristotle's metaphysical principles of matter and form and described a dynamic relationship between the body and the soul, Christianizing the system in the process. A diagrammatic presentation of Aquinas' relationship of body and soul is shown in Figure 4–1, which expresses the basic features of Aristotelian dualism. In this description, the person is defined in terms of essence and existence. The essence of a person is the universal that classifies the nature of all people. It is composed of the physical world, from which the body is derived, and the soul, which is immortal and has primary functions of intellect and will. From the potential to the principle of actualization, a person's existence defines her or his individuality. Thus, the person consists of necessary bodily and spiritual constituents, whose dynamic interaction results in the sharing of humanity, expressed individually.

According to Aquinas, the human person is not simply a physical machine propelled by external stimuli or environmental pressures. Neither is the person a soul imprisoned within a body, as Plato and Augustine taught. Rather, the person is a dynamic entity, motivated internally by the soul. The human soul possesses five faculties, or powers:

1. Vegetative: concerns the functions of physical growth and reproduction. To accomplish growth, the organism seeks food and nourishment.
2. Sensitive: concerns the ability of the soul to accept information about the external world through the five senses.
3. Appetitive: concerns the desires and goals of the organism and the ability to will.
4. Locomotive: describes the capacity to initiate motion toward desirable goals or away from repulsive environmental objects.
5. Intellectual: relates to the power of thinking, or cognition.

Aquinas' psychology, then, contained two key elements of human learning. First, there is an environmental dependency, in that our knowledge is based on input through the senses. However, the sensory input does not enter an empty, passive intellect. Rather, sensory knowing is acted on by the second element, *sensus communis*, or the center of common sense, which actively organizes, mediates, and coordinates the sensory input. Thus, Aquinas argued for two types of knowledge. Sensory knowledge, shared with other animals, provides information about physical reality, whereas human reason provides abstractions of universal principles. The

FIGURE 4–1   A diagrammatic representation of Aquinas' concept of the dualistic relationship between body and soul, constituting the nature of the human person.

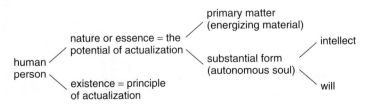

soul, then, accomplishes the highest and most powerful form of human activity through the rational intellect. It is the capacity to reason that makes humanity unique and also joins humanity to God. Moreover, although freedom motivates the will, human freedom lies in the intellect. Freedom increases with increased rationality, wisdom, and knowledge. The pursuit of wisdom is the highest calling of people, and the act of understanding characterizes the proper human state.

The motivational factor in Aquinas' psychology is the will, comprising the critical force of growth and movement. The intellect is subordinated to the will because the will determines the direction of the intellect. The proper end, or goal, of the will is to seek goodness. Although God is the ultimate good, according to Aquinas, the will seeks intermediary goodness in the form of earthly beauty, harmony, and organized proportion, which are pleasing to the soul. The autonomous soul, composed of intellect and will, is a unified, active entity that is dependent on sensory input while serving as the supreme arbitrator of sensory knowledge.

Aquinas made a significant step toward the emergence of modern science when he spelled out how we can know ourselves, our environment, and even God. He dismissed the ideas of those philosophers influenced by Plato, such as Augustine, who stressed the unreliability of sensory information. Rather, knowledge is a natural product of the bodily senses. Limited as it is to the constraints of natural laws, sensory knowledge is nevertheless trustworthy. Further, by our own powers of reason, we may derive supersensory knowledge, such as the existence of an impersonal First Cause or a Prime Mover, through analogy based on sensory knowledge.

It is beyond our scope in this book to present a complete overview of all of the Thomistic contributions to Scholasticism; we must be content with some conclusions. Thomas Aquinas and the Scholastic movement represent a transition to the emergence of science. Prior to the Scholastics, Aristotle was viewed as suspect, if not outright heretical. After Aquinas, Aristotle's teachings were mandatory in Christian universities. Using that criterion, Aquinas was successful in reconciling Aristotle with Christianity. More important, he completed the intellectual justification that elevated reason to a level with faith as a source of truth and knowledge. This contribution was critical to the emergence of science. By accepting Aquinas' defense of reason, the Church also accepted a new set of rules for evaluating intellectual activity. In a very real sense, Aquinas' strategy of studying theology inadvertently left the Church vulnerable to scrutiny under a new standard, which is reason. Before the triumph of Scholasticism, the Church held its authority on faith, based on Scripture and the revelation of Christian tradition. After the work of Aquinas was accepted, the Church was required to respond to rational arguments.

The Papacy and Authority

At this point, it is important to summarize briefly the position of the Church and the papacy in the late medieval period. Superficially, the power and authority of the Church were at their zenith, present in every facet of life. However, two forces were operating that eventually undermined the power of the Church and led to the questioning of papal authority. The first was Scholasticism itself, which destroyed the effectiveness of Church dictates based on faith alone. The medieval scholars, culminating in the work of Aquinas, had secured the place of reason and demonstration in the seeking of truth and knowledge. After the admission of Scholastic thought to Church teaching, the papacy could not successfully revert to the demands of obedience justified by faith alone. The acceptance of rational argument imposed a serious restriction on the basis of traditional papal authority. Subsequent intellectual progress in science made the foundation of papal authority on faith increasingly untenable, and papal authority steadily eroded during the following 500 years. Finally, in 1870, the First Vatican Council declared that, as part of Roman Catholic doctrine, the pope is infallible when teaching on matters of faith and morals. Although contemporary political events contributed to the reactionary clerical forces that devised the 1870 statement (see Chapter 11), it is important to recognize that papal infallibility is a formal policy based on faith. Interestingly, the very need for the Church to make such a pronouncement in 1870 stemmed from a process that began in the thirteenth and fourteenth centuries: Admitting reason as a source of truth precluded exclusive reliance on faith.

The second force eroding papal authority was political. The rising nation-states of western Europe competed with the papacy and other Church institutions for revenues. When temporal authority was centralized in the monarchy in France, money was needed for government and military operations. After exhausting available resources, the monarchy began taxing the wealth of the Church in France. This issue led to a church–state confrontation. Philip IV (Philip the Fair) of France seized Pope Boniface VIII in retaliation for the pope's dictum against Philip's taxation of Church property. Boniface died shortly after his abduction, and Philip succeeded in getting a French bishop elected pope as Clement V. Fearing the reprisals of pro-Boniface forces in Rome, Clement settled in 1309 at Avignon, a Church-owned town in France, near the Italian border. There the next six popes, all French, remained until 1377. The period of the Avignon papacy was marked by the depths of corruption. To support the sumptuous papal court, anything could be bought, from bishoprics to dispensations from Church law to indulgences. Moreover, the return to Rome after the Avignon papacy was accompanied by a schism within the Church, caused by rival popes, with each claimant having the support of competing political factions. England, Flanders, most of the German states, Poland, Hungary, Bohemia, and Portugal followed the Roman pope, Urban VI; France, Naples, Spain, and Scotland declared for the Avignon pope, Clement VII. In an attempt to resolve the conflict, a Church council held at Pisa elected a compromise pope. However, when the Roman and Avignon popes refused to yield their claims, there were three rival popes. The confusion was finally settled by the Council of Constance (1414–1418), and after 39 years of schism the Church was once again unified under a single pope in Rome— Martin V—who was accepted by all Western countries. However, during the schism the papacy had become a political ploy, and political corruption was rampant. Although the Church was reunited, the papacy never completely recovered its prestige and authority.

THE ITALIAN RENAISSANCE

From the end of the fourteenth century to the beginning of the sixteenth century, a remarkable event of profound cultural significance occurred in Italy (Map 6). This rebirth, or Renaissance, of European culture was characterized by a turn toward humanism in art, literature, and music. It marked a change in emphasis from the dominance of traditional Christian themes to a glorification of humanity, often reverting to styles of painting and sculpture reminiscent of Epicurean Rome.

Beginning in Florence under the beneficial patronage of the Medici family, the rulers of that city, a new wave of artistic accomplishment spread throughout Italy. Florence itself was beautified by the architectural achievements of Brunelleschi and Verrocchio, and civic buildings, churches, and palaces were filled with the sculpture of Ghiberti and Donatello. Paintings of humanistic and religious subjects by Fra Angelico, Ghirlandaio, and Botticelli attracted students from all over Europe. Under the enlightened rule of Lorenzo de Medici, the Magnificent (1449–1492), Florence became the focus of the Italian Renaissance in art, music, and literature.

The genius Leonardo da Vinci (1452–1519) typified the "Renaissance person" by the depth of his abilities as painter, inventor, and scientist. Beginning in Milan, where his Last Supper may still be admired, the Renaissance traveled with da Vinci through Florence and finally to Rome. It was da Vinci, the scientist and engineer, who translated the humanistic spirit to anatomical drawings and machine designs. His genius captured the imagination of Europe, elevating the physical reality of the body in the world to new visions of capabilities. Equally competent as an inventor, da Vinci's curiosity led him to develop such diverse inventions as a machine gun, a machine for cutting screws, and an adjustable monkey wrench. His fascination with physics drew him to studies of motion and weight, and he devised sophisticated experiments in magnetism and acoustics. In his study of anatomy, he made systematic comparisons between the structure and mechanics of human and animal limbs. Da Vinci's genius has been called one of the most remarkable of all time. His imagination and compulsion for perfection blended well with the spirit of the Renaissance, and he demonstrated the vast potential for the free exercise of human intelligence, which subsequently served as a model and an inspiration.

Throughout Italy, in Mantua, Ferrara, Naples, and Venice, the entire peninsula was infused with the excitement of the Renaissance. In Rome, supported by the patronage of powerful popes such as Julius II (reigned 1503–1513) and Leo X (reigned 1513–1521), the classical art of the ancient world was recovered and imported to adorn buildings and avenues. To insure a return to the glories of old, new construction was undertaken, most notably Saint Peter's Basilica and the palaces of the Vatican. The immense dome of Michelangelo Buonarroti (1475–1564) crowned the physical glory of the capital of Christendom, and his *Pietà* remains to adorn its entrance. Moreover, in his *Last Judgment*, painted over the walls and ceiling of the Sistine Chapel in a palace adjoining the basilica, the full magnificence of the Renaissance shines forth. These 200 years produced an awesome statement confirming that Europe had indeed emerged from the Middle

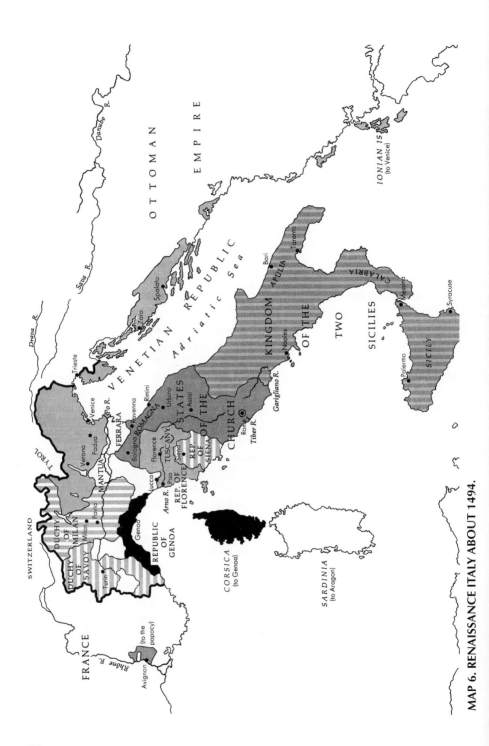

MAP 6. RENAISSANCE ITALY ABOUT 1494.

66

Ages and that a new age of enlightenment had arrived. Italy still capitalizes on the glory of this era of cultural achievement as tourists annually flock to gaze in wonder at the creations of men.

The Italian Renaissance spread throughout Europe. As far away as Krakow in Poland, there are splendid tombs in the Wawel Cathedral, designed and executed by Italian artisans, reflecting specific characteristics of the Florentine Renaissance. The spread of Renaissance ideas was facilitated by improvements in printing. By the early fifteenth century, Venetian printers were producing books of superb quality. In the German city of Mainz, Johann Gutenberg (1400–1468) perfected movable type, a process used for centuries by the Chinese, ending the age when access to written resources was limited to a select few. The spread of reborn cultural influences served to complement the rational spirit developed by Scholasticism. Together, these movements set the stage for a new strategy in the pursuit of human knowledge and values, a strategy that involved the emergence of science. However, the authority of the Church remained a challenge that had yet to be finally resolved.

THE CHALLENGE TO AUTHORITY

The combined developments of the elevation of reason by the Scholastics, the political divisions of the papal schisms, and, most notably, the Renaissance were radically changing European society. These forces had a negative effect on the authority of the Church and, in particular, on the power of the papacy. The direct challenge to Church authority occurred in two parallel spheres—from within the Church itself and from external intellectual progress. The former consisted of the Protestant Reformation, which questioned the structure of the Church and threatened the very survival of the Roman institution. The latter hurled a direct challenge against Church teachings, pitting knowledge based on reason against knowledge based on faith. Both developments seriously undermined the strength of Church authority in European society.

Within the Church: The Reformation

The causes of the Protestant revolt against papal authority, leading to doctrinal disputes, have been extensively argued by historians. Certainly we are not able to add much to their analyses, but a few observations are appropriate. First, the political scene contributed greatly to strife between the papacy and national states, especially in Germany and England. The popes, who so generously supported the Italian Renaissance, were true temporal leaders, controlling vast stretches of estates in central Italy and maintaining large armies. This temporal power, coupled with the medieval prerogatives of the Church in all Christian nations, created a perception of the papacy as threatening to the emerging national identity and the monarchical consolidation proceeding quite steadily in individual European nations. Accordingly, the political climate encouraged any dissension within Christendom that would work to the detriment of papal authority.

A second contribution to the Reformation concerned the revived intellectual atmosphere of Europe. One by-product of the rise of the universities, the elevation of reason by the Scholastics, and the cultural innovations of the Renaissance was the creation of an intelligentsia that had access to, and understanding of, ancient pagan and early Christian documents. These scholars focused on the abuses of Church authority, such as the selling of indulgences to underwrite the construction of Saint Peter's Basilica. The errors of such practices—departing as they did from early Christian teachings of antimaterialism—became more evident to early reformers. This conclusion occurred to Martin Luther and formed the basis of his indictment of the Church. Luther certainly did not seek an alternative in the study of reasoning processes; rather he reverted to a greater reliance on faith. Nevertheless, it was the intellectual spirit and freedom of the times that permitted him to follow his convictions.

A third force supporting the Reformation was the interest in humanism, so beautifully articulated in the artistic productivity of the Italian Renaissance. Of interest to us is the humanistic attitude in philosophy expressed most clearly by Desiderius Erasmus (1469–1536). He was born in Rotterdam, and his early inclination toward the scholarly life led him to take vows as an Augustinian priest in 1492. As a scholar and teacher, his career took him all over western Europe and put him in touch with the major figures of his time. He studied at Paris, Oxford, and Louvain University in Belgium. He was a great friend of Thomas More, a future chancellor of England, and he tutored the sons of Henry VII while they visited Bologna. His satirical *The Praise of Folly* mocked the hypocrisy of contemporary moral life, and he lectured the monarchs of Europe in his *Education of a Christian Prince*. Although his greatest contribution may lie in his revision and translation of the New Testament from Greek and Latin, it was his notes compiled while pursuing this work that proved to be a popular resource of his views as a humanist. Despite some errors contained in the work, Erasmus presented a critical study of the basis of faith from Scripture in light of rational scholarly scrutiny. As such, Erasmus revealed the context of the writers and the pitfalls of subsequent interpretations. Although the Church reforms of the Council of Trent (1545–1563) condemned this translation and critique, Erasmus' work showed that even the most sacred resource of faith could be better understood in terms of the human context of its authors.

The leaders of the Reformation on the Continent, Martin Luther (1483–1546), John Calvin (1509–1564), and Ulrich Zwingli (1484–1531), were motivated by a sincere desire to correct the abuses of Church authority. In the process, they and their followers questioned the tenets of Roman teachings. From that point, European Christianity became fragmented, and society was divided along religious lines. Similarly, in England, political dissension between King Henry VIII and Pope Clement VII led to England's separation from Roman direction, although it still retained the basic doctrine of Catholicism. The Church attempted to minimize losses through internal reform, and the Council of Trent (1545–1563) succeeded in restoring discipline in the clergy and an evangelical spirit in the Church itself, which was represented by the newly founded Society of Jesus, or Jesuits, in 1540. Nevertheless, the Reformation marked the definitive end to the medieval society that fell under the authority of the pope.

Within Science: The Copernican Revolution

Aside from the internal dissension of the Church, the times were ripe for a direct challenge to the authority of the Church through the acceptable strategy of reasoned arguments. Since ancient times, the problem of motion in the universe had baffled scholars. The resolution that prevailed up to the Renaissance was the Ptolemaic, or geocentric, explanation, which placed the earth at the center of the universe. Such a view fit well into certain religious and theological considerations, including Christianity, because an earth-centered universe placed humanity in a unique position as the special creation of God.

Nicholas Copernicus (1473–1543) was born in the merchant town of Torún in northwestern Poland and sent to Jagellonian University in Krakow to study for a clerical career. Not satisfied with Scholasticism, he began to pursue mathematics and astronomy. Some of his notes and primitive instruments are still preserved in the museum of that university. He eventually journeyed to Bologna, where he studied law and medicine, and around 1512 he settled as a cathedral canon in northern Poland near the Baltic Sea. There, he practiced medicine and advised the Polish monarchy on matters of currency reform. All this while, he was studying the question of planetary motion, using data reported by the ancients. His findings led him to conclude

NICHOLAS COPERNICUS (1473–1543). (Courtesy, New York Public Library.)

that a heliocentric, or sun-centered, universe provided a simpler, more parsimonious explanation of planetary motion. He tested his ideas in correspondence with various scholars throughout Europe. His major findings, contained in *De Revolutionibus Orbium Coelestium* (*On the Revolutions of Celestial Planets*), were not published until the year of his death.

It should be remembered that Copernicus did not present convincing new evidence. Indeed, it was left to later scholars with better instrumentation, such as Kepler, Galileo, and Newton, to provide empirical observations to support the heliocentric theory. Rather, Copernicus used the basic tools of logic, through mathematical demonstration, to provide his simpler explanation of planetary motions—tools sanctioned by the Church after the success of Scholasticism.

Although Copernicus was encouraged by certain Church authorities, such as Leo X, and he dedicated *De Revolutionibus* to Pope Paul III, Church leaders soon recognized the danger inherent in his work. *De Revolutionibus* was placed on the Index of Forbidden Books in 1616. The theological implication of this work meant that humanity was a part of a small planet in a vast universe. This realization had a far-reaching effect on Church history, requiring a reappraisal of the position of humanity in relation to the rest of the universe and to God. Indeed, the conclusion of Copernicus was truly a revolution in thinking that continued through the rise of modern science, culminating in the writings of Darwin, who firmly placed humanity in the natural order, subject to the same constraints and determinants as other species of life. Copernicus challenged the authority of the Church, which had supported the Ptolemaic theory. The opposition between faith in the Ptolemaic view and rational justification of the heliocentric theory was ultimately resolved in favor of the latter. Thus, the Copernican revolution may be interpreted as the beginning of the drift away from an emphasis on God and the hereafter to an examination of humanity existing in the environment of the present.

CHAPTER SUMMARY

The five centuries from 1000 to 1500 saw the consolidation and then the fractionation of Christianity and the decline of the papacy. The authority of the Church faced serious challenges. On a political level, the rising nation-states of Europe successfully competed with the papacy and undermined both the temporal and the spiritual powers of the Church. On an intellectual level, the teachings of Pierre Abélard, Roger Bacon, and Albertus Magnus led to a revival of interest in the ancient writers with their emphasis on rational thought to secure human knowledge. It was Thomas Aquinas who reconciled Aristotle's rationalism and Christian theology, which resulted in the Church's accepting both reason and faith as sources of human knowledge. On a cultural level, the Italian Renaissance lifted Europe into a new era of humanism that glorified humanity and shifted attention to the present needs and desires of people. Erasmus translated this humanistic attitude into scholarly pursuits that revealed the frailties and needs of the human authors of Scripture. All of these forces eroded the authority of the Church, leading to dramatic confrontation, both from inside and outside the Church. The Protestant Reformation took advantage of the rift between Christian monarchs and the papacy, successfully fragmenting the unity of Western Christendom. However, it was Copernicus who used the strategy and tools of reasoned arguments to arrive at his heliocentric theory of planetary motion. This bold assertion successfully demonstrated a truth arrived at through reason that differed from the conclusion supported by the authority of the Church. As a result, reason triumphed over faith, and the age of science began.

BIBLIOGRAPHY

Primary Sources

ERASMUS. (1941). *The praise of folly*. Princeton, NJ: University Press.

MCKEON, R. (Ed.) (1929). *Selections from medieval philosophers*. New York: Scribner's.

AQUINAS, T. (1945). *Summa Theologica* (A. Pegis, Trans.). In *Basic writings of Thomas Aquinas*. New York: Random House.

Studies

CROMBIE, A. G. (1959). *Augustine to Galileo*. New York: Anchor.

DIETHELM, O. (1970). The medical teaching of demonology in the 17th and 18th centuries. *Journal of the History of the Behavioral Sciences, 6,* 3–15.

DURANT, W. (1953). *The Renaissance*. New York: Simon & Schuster.

DURANT, W. (1957). *The Reformation*. New York: Simon & Schuster.

JACKSON, W. T. H. (1962). *The literature of the Middle Ages*. New York: Columbia University Press.

KIRSCH, I. (1978). Demonology and the use of science: An example of the misperception of historical data. *Journal of the History of the Behavioral Sciences, 14,* 149–157.

KUHN, T. S. (1959). *The Copernican Revolution: Planetary astronomy in the development of Western thought*. New York: Modern Library.

TUCHMAN, B. W. (1978). *A distant mirror: The calamitous 14th century*. New York: Ballantine Books.

❈ 5 ❈

The Emergence
of Modern Science

Advances in Science
    Francis Bacon
    Galileo Galilei
    Johann Kepler
    Isaac Newton
    Other Scientists
The Learned Societies
Advances in Philosophy
    Baruch Spinoza
    René Descartes
Chapter Summary

Psychology was recognized as an independent science by the end of the nineteenth century. During the preceding two centuries, models were developed of what psychology should study and how such study should be conducted. Specifically, during the seventeenth and eighteenth centuries, competing models of psychology vied with each other for dominance. We deal with this very important period, under the structure of national movements advancing philosophy and science, in Chapters 6 through 9. The present chapter sets the intellectual background, especially in the physical sciences, for the articulation of models of psychological inquiry. In approaching the intellectual background of science, we first consider particular themes and issues to pursue, then backtrack to follow through on another theme. This approach is necessary to deal with the volume of material, but it is also somewhat artificial; therefore, we must remember the simultaneity of events, despite their successive presentations.

The sixteenth and seventeenth centuries witnessed the successful demonstration of the value of empirical science. The empirical disciplines triumphed at the expense of speculative approaches, particularly metaphysics. Recalling Comte's hypothesis from Chapter 2 concerning the stages of intellectual progress, we may consider the sixteenth and seventeenth centuries as the transitional phase of the post-Renaissance development of empiricism. Somewhat paradoxically, it may be argued that the downfall of Aristotelian metaphysics, resulting from the rise of empiricism, was initiated by the Scholastic reliance on reason as a source of knowledge, which in turn was based on Aristotelian teachings. In other words, the Scholastic elevation of reason as a source of knowledge made possible the efficacy of observation, which is the basis of empiricism. Accordingly, Aristotelian philosophy, supported by the Scholastic affirmation, was a comprehensive system that accommodated both metaphysical and empirical approaches.

ADVANCES IN SCIENCE

Post-Copernican advances in science and mathematics were crucial to the eventual success of science. With the downfall of Church authority based upon faith, the age of reason began; the human intellect was valued and used to generate knowledge. Accordingly, a trend started that witnessed the triumph of science. In a very real sense, science, based on reason, was viewed as a replacement for religious doctrine, based on faith. Science and scientific methods were valued as the best approach to any area of investigation. This trend culminated in the nineteenth century, when physics was seen as the queen of the sciences, and the more closely any discipline emulated physics, the greater the value placed on that disciplinary inquiry. Thus, whereas Niccolo Machiavelli (1469–1527) in *The Prince* used common sense and compelling logic to analyze the principles of effective leadership, Marx and Engels, writing in the nineteenth century, were able to look to their "age of the proletariat" as a utopia of economic and political life derived scientifically. Machiavelli is viewed as an artist; Marx and Engels are called political scientists. A similar movement occurred within psychological inquiry, as we shall see, so that one of the models of psychology in the nineteenth century was almost bound to emulate physics. At any rate, we shall now review some of the major people and events that formed the foundation of assumptions and methods common to all approaches that we call scientific.

Francis Bacon

One of the most influential, colorful, and brilliant men of Elizabethan England, Francis Bacon (1561–1626), was born in London to the Lord Keeper of the Great Seal for Queen Elizabeth I. Prone to the solitary life of a scholar but finding that he was left with little wealth at his father's death, Bacon had to rely on his own resources for support. With his birth and lineage, as well as his superb education in law, literature, and diplomacy, Bacon yearned for a secure political appointment, but that eluded him until James I, who ascended to the throne in 1603, appointed Bacon Solicitor General in 1613. His political career accelerated, and by 1618 he was Chancellor of England. However, Bacon was caught in the crossfire of a movement to discredit the king, and his position was threatened in 1621, when he was impeached for corruption and abuse of his offices. Pardoned from prison and a heavy fine, Bacon retired a wealthy man to pursue his interests in philosophy and science.

FRANCIS BACON (1561–1626).
(Courtesy, New York Public
Library.)

In his writings, Bacon's essential goal was to reorganize the approach to scientific study. Although Aristotle and the Scholastics recognized both deductive and inductive logical reasoning, Bacon noted that the deductive was stressed at the expense of the inductive. In other words, the traditional approach to science created a rigid mental set that limited investigation of the person in the environment to a relatively sterile procedure filled with a priori assumptions. From the assumed nature of humanity (that is, the relationship between body and soul), particulars of human life or the physical world were deduced. Bacon believed that the validity of this approach was limited to the extent that the underlying assumptions were correct or relevant.

In his work *Novum Organum* (*A New Instrument;* 1620), Bacon called for better situations to study the world directly—more laboratories, botanical gardens, libraries, and museums. By eliminating any preconceived notions of the world, the scientist could then study people and the environment using detailed and controlled observation. On the basis of such observations, best expressed quantitatively, cautious generalizations could be made. Thus, Bacon emphasized an approach to science that stressed practical observation as the primary setting for scientific inquiry.

Bacon held that the method of science must be predominantly inductive, proceeding from particular to general. Moreover, he qualified this position by building in several critical elements for scientific inquiry. First, the scientist's study of particulars must be done through observation. Sense validation of quantitative observations becomes an important source of agreement among scientists. In other words, if one scientist describes a particular event by observing its measurement, a second scientist could repeat the observation and support the first scientist. Presumably, if enough scientists agree about a certain observation, this agreement itself represents a compelling argument for the validity of a finding. A second implication of Bacon's method was that scientists must rid their inquiry of any influences not derived from observation. Thus, the scientist must be skeptical and not accept formulations that cannot be tested through observation. Rather, the scientist must take a critical view of the world and proceed carefully with the study of observables. Bacon, then, presented a strong statement of empiricism as the basis of science. Scientists must experience particular events through their ability to observe them via sensory processes. Moreover, Bacon indicated that observations have no value if made casually and carelessly. Rather, he advocated the goal of controlled observations. Thus, Bacon's empiricism was expressed in terms of a systematic inductive method.

As a scientist, Bacon was concerned about the process of discovery and the demonstration of discovery in the generation of new knowledge. Empirical science for Bacon was a new, refreshing approach to the ageless puzzles of the universe. Bacon's views on scientific methods required a dependence on sense information about environmental events. This perspective in British science became a prevailing theme and formed the basis of the subsequent British empirical tradition of psychology, which is presented in Chapter 7.

Galileo Galilei

Advances in astronomy and mathematics provided the quantitative foundation for Bacon's methodological innovation. It was Galileo Galilei (1564–1642) who asserted that science is necessarily synonymous with measurement. Born in Pisa, Galileo received a sound education in the classic languages and mathematics from his Florentine father. While at the University of Pisa, he was introduced to the mathematics of Euclid, which opened a new world for him. At age 25, he was appointed to the professorship of mathematics at Pisa. In 1592, he left for a teaching position at the University of Padua, where he set up a laboratory for experiments in physics. His findings on the velocity of moving objects were later confirmed and elaborated by Newton.

In 1609, Galileo built his first telescope, then constantly improved the magnification. He made accurate observations of stellar constellations, the moon's surface, and sunspots. His colleagues at Padua would not accept Galileo's discoveries, and he left the university for a secure stipend provided by the grand duke of Florence. In his writings and lectures, Galileo asserted that only the heliocentric explanation could account for his astronomical data, and he accepted the Copernican system as fact. This assertion brought him to the attention of the Jesuits, the newly founded society of militant scholars determined to defend papal authority. Convicted by the Inquisition, Galileo was forced to recant publicly his belief in the Copernican system, and he was allowed to retire to Florence. However, he continued to study and made significant contributions to mechanics and astronomy.

Although Galileo had the misfortune to work in a place under the jurisdiction of the Inquisition, his trial and conviction enhanced his popularity in Protestant northern Europe. His works were widely read and acclaimed, and he secured acceptance of the

Copernican teachings. Galileo's synthesis of science and mathematics extended beyond the limits of Copernican astronomy. Galileo's studies led him to the view of a mechanical world inhabited by mechanical people. His telescope was essentially a mechanical extension of the senses. This interpretation of human activity had enormous implications for psychology. First, it implied that human activity itself is ultimately subject to mechanical laws. Second, the emphasis on mathematical relationships in the universe suggested that it is profitable to examine external, environmental forces as the source of human activity, rather than limiting examination to internally generated sources, such as the Scholastic interpretation of the will as the motivational principle of human existence. Galileo distinguished the world in terms of primary qualities, which are unchangeable and quantitative, and secondary qualities, which are fluctuating, unstable characteristics knowable through the senses. Primary qualities, such as motion, position, and extension, are subject to mathematical relations and descriptions, whereas secondary qualities, such as colors, sounds, and tastes, are elusive and reside in the consciousness of the perceiving person. Ultimately, he thought scientific discovery might allow secondary qualities to be expressed in terms of the mathematical relationships of primary qualities. Galileo's work drew a sharp dichotomy between science and religion, reinforcing separate and rival interpretations of life.

Johann Kepler

Johann Kepler (1571–1630) was another scientist whose experiments supported the Copernican view. Born in Germany, Kepler spent his most productive years in Prague. He had a brilliant mind and constantly wondered about the universe, generating a myriad of hypotheses. His major findings included the proof of elliptical planetary orbits, rather than the circular orbits proposed by Copernicus. His discovery that planets closer to the sun have a more rapid orbit than those further away anticipated Newton's findings of gravitation and magnetism. Kepler consistently wrote of the harmony and order of the universe that impressed him so much. Moreover, he provided the detailed mathematical proof required by the Copernican system, thus winning its further acceptance.

Like Galileo, Kepler believed in the fundamental mathematical basis of the universe. His empirically derived mathematical laws of planetary motion convinced him that the mathematical basis of the physical world must have parallel expression in other levels of reality, such as the psychological world of the person. Kepler also studied vision and made important contributions to our understanding of binocular vision and visual accommodation. He proposed critical hypotheses that were tested eventually in the nineteenth-century psychophysics movement that served as an immediate precursor of modern psychology. Finally, Kepler provided strong evidence to support the distinction between primary and secondary qualities in the world—the former being absolute, immutable, and objective; the latter, relative, fluctuating, and subjective. This distinction was a source of controversy in the subsequent development of models of psychological inquiry.

Isaac Newton

A mathematical genius who formulated the basics of modern physics, Isaac Newton (1642–1727) represents the climax of the scientific development started by Copernicus. Born in the midlands of England, Newton entered Trinity College of Cambridge University in 1661 and began his studies of mathematics, astronomy, and optics. In 1669 he was appointed professor of mathematics at Cambridge and remained in that post for 34 years. Following in the spirit of Francis Bacon, Newton devised a methodological strategy that attempted to remain true to the level of observations without going beyond what they could directly support. Accordingly, he approached a problem by thinking of every possible solution, and then tested the mathematical and experimental implications of each hypothesis.

Newton is credited with devising calculus, independently of the German philosopher Leibniz, whom we consider later. As a physicist, Newton used his mathematical tools to investigate light. In 1666, viewing light projected through a prism, he discovered that white light is actually a compound of the color spectrum. However, Newton's most significant contributions are contained in his *Principia Mathematica (Principles of Mathematics)* (1687), a classic in the history of science. His views of the mechanics of the world were spelled out in the three laws of motion:

1. Every object remains in a state of rest or steady motion unless acted on by external forces.
2. The change of motion is proportional to the external impressing force and is made in the direction of the straight line in which that force is impressed.
3. To every action there is an equal and opposite reaction.

Newton then developed the principle of gravitation and applied it to the planetary system, greatly elaborating on Kepler's work and proposing a mechanical model of the universe. Thus the Copernican system was completed.

ISAAC NEWTON (1642–1727).
(Courtesy, New York Public Library.)

Newton's mechanical conceptualization of the universe embodied the revolutionary conclusion of complete determinism. He provided evidence and derived formulations that described the orderly nature of matter. His physics of matter offered a framework for examining its transformation, leading to the study of gases and the chemical elements. The conservation of matter formed a basis for the investigation of the relationships of mass and weight and eventually led to the development of molecular theory and the study of the transformation of forces. The success of Newton's research supported the physical basis of biology and ultimately reinforced views focusing on the mechanical laws that govern living organisms.

Newton's method, firmly based on observation, embodied three rules of reasoning to guide empirical investigations:

1. Causal explanations of observed events are confined to the observed events and nothing more.
2. The same causes are responsible for the same observations.
3. The guiding logic of empirical investigation is inductive, which provides explanations that may be accepted until new observations call for modifications of explanations or new hypotheses.

Accordingly, Newton advocated a close adherence to observation and careful induction. Casual generalizations and all speculations are to be avoided. The first stage of scientific inquiry is skepticism, and subsequent stages are guided by observations.

Newton's views were not universally accepted. Many religious leaders attacked his predominantly mechanical view of the universe, which left little room for God. Indeed, their perceptions were valid, and Newtonian science provided new criteria for evaluating the products of intellectual scholarship. Newton did, however, enjoy wide prestige, and in his old age he was praised as the greatest living scientist. From our perspective in the history of psychology, Newton's work had a powerful implication. By careful observation and sophisticated quantification, Newton examined the most immense problem in all of the physical world—namely, the relationships among heavenly bodies—and he showed that they all follow the same rules. If the universe is so orderly, many scholars thought that surely mental activities must be governed by some system of laws.

Other Scientists

The sixteenth and seventeenth centuries were exciting times, in that exploration of the world revealed almost unlimited horizons of adventure and discovery. The Portuguese and Spanish dominated the sixteenth century, but the English gained supremacy of the sea in the seventeenth century and began their empire of expansion beyond their small island. In 1600 a physician to Queen Elizabeth I, William Gilbert, published a work describing the magnetic compass, a device well known to Arab scholars, which facilitated British navigation. With discoveries of previously unknown societies and unknown species of plants and animals, European science received an impetus for expansion.

In medicine and physiology, great advances were made in the understanding of bodily processes. William Harvey, a physician, studied his patients, animals, and cadavers and, in 1628, published a work explaining circulation of the blood. In 1662, Robert Boyle published his finding that the pressure of any gas varies inversely with its volume. With a colleague, Robert Hooke, Boyle related his law to bodily heat and posited a reasonable explanation of respiration. By 1690 Anton van Leeuwenhoek had developed the microscope, and a new world was opened for investigation. In Bologna, Marcello Malpighi, while investigating the lungs of frogs in 1661, discovered how the blood passes from arteries to veins; he called these tiny fibers capillaries. By the end of the seventeenth century, the results of careful empirical investigation were finally beginning to erode much of the superstition surrounding the mechanisms of the human body.

Not all advances of science were automatically accompanied by a complete reliance on reason and rejection of faith. For example, the brilliant French scholar and writer Blaise Pascal (1623–1662) studied the effects of atmospheric pressure on a column of mercury and devised the first barometer. His mathematical studies led him to the development of probability distributions, most notably "Pascal's triangle" of probabilities, and the formulation of the binomial theorem. However, during the period of his most productive investigations, Pascal became involved with religious issues. In particular, Pascal and his sister Jacqueline were followers of the Jansenist movement of seventeenth-century French Catholicism. The Jansenists advocated a complete commitment to faith and were eventually condemned by the Vatican for holding essentially Lutheran and Calvinistic beliefs. Despite Pascal's scientific achievements, his religious convictions led him to downplay science as an inaccurate effort because it is based on reason and the senses, which Pascal asserted were faulty. Rather, Pascal accepted the existence of the mysteries surrounding God and individuals and believed that only religion can deal with this level of knowledge. Pascal was an exception to the personal belief in science held by most scientists. Nevertheless, his life demonstrates that an acceptance of reason did not necessarily lead to a rejection of faith. Most scholars tried to accommodate both perspectives, and the triumph of reason and science was a gradual process.

The theories and scientific strategies proposed by Bacon, Kepler, Galileo, and Newton, along with specific scientific discoveries of practical usefulness, clearly demonstrated the value of empirical science. Indeed, the emergence of the natural sciences of biology, chemistry, and physics, all grounded in observational methods relating scientific findings to mathematics, provided a tested model for successful inquiry. In addition, the definition of the planetary system was characterized by the order of matter and motion. A mechanical model that described the physical basis of matter provided an attractive direction for psychological study as psychology made the transition from speculative to empirical inquiry.

THE LEARNED SOCIETIES

Scientific progress in the seventeenth century developed an organizational structure of its own in the form of societies of men dedicated to the advancement of disciplinary study. The form and power of these societies varied from country to country. In southern Europe they tended to be secret so as to avoid conflict with Church authorities. Elsewhere, they were recognized and sometimes supported by the government. The societies all shared two traits. First, they attempted to be independent associations devoted to advancing scientific knowledge and divorced from official Church or governmental control. Second, they were formed to compensate for the lag in scientific progress within the universities. As mentioned earlier, the universities came under the control of the government and the Church, and science could not truly flower under such bureaucratic control. Moreover, the theology faculties within the universities were still dominant and slow to yield to scientific inquiry. This is not to say that science was absent from the universities. As we have seen, many eminent scientists were in fact university professors. However, academic freedom is a twentieth-century concept, and whether opposition arose from the hostility of the theologians or from the petty jealousies that have always plagued academia, scientific study was a new enterprise that ran against university conservatism. Accordingly, the learned societies filled an important role not fully met by the universities.

The first societies in Italy were secret, permitting scientific communication while protecting scientists. The Accademia Secretorum Natural was founded in Naples in 1560, and the Accademia dei Lencei began in Rome in 1603. Galileo's experimental work provided the inspiration for the Accademia del Cimento, founded in Florence in 1657. In northern Europe, scientific societies were started in Berlin (1700), in Uppsala, Sweden (1710), and in St. Petersburg (1724). The Académie des Sciences in Paris was founded by Jean Baptiste Colbert (1618–1683), the financial wizard under Louis XIV, and received a royal charter in 1666. However, the Académie was closely tied to the king, and in turn to the Church, so that some of its activity was at times inhibited. It was disbanded by the Revolution in 1793 but managed to revive and continues to this day, still with vast government support. Perhaps the strongest learned society was the Royal Society, officially called the "Royal Society of London for Improving Natural Knowledge" when chartered by Charles II in 1662. The Royal Society was always privately endowed and managed to be independent. As time went on, membership in the Royal Society became an honor bestowed on distinguished scientists, and projects sponsored or certified by the Society were valued.

The tradition of learned societies has continued to this day. In some nations, such as Russia and some eastern European countries, they became official agents of governments that determine scientific policy; in others, such as the United States, they are essentially private foundations with limited government support. During the last century, many disciplinary societies (e.g., the American Psychological Association, the American Psychological Society, and the Psychonomic Society) as well as interdisciplinary societies (such as the Society for Neuroscience and the

Society of the Sigma XI) have appeared. Such organizations serve vital functions as advocates of scientific study and as conduits of communication among scientists. At their inception in the seventeenth century, the learned societies played a critical role in advancing science. They were organizations of scientists set up to direct, sponsor, certify, and evaluate scientific enterprise under the criteria established by a community of scholars. For the most part, the scientific societies succeeded, remaining aloof from the political and religious pressures of the State and the Church.

ADVANCES IN PHILOSOPHY

The scientific progress of the sixteenth and seventeenth centuries provided methodological advancements in the approaches to scientific issues and established the importance of quantification. In addition, a coherent body of knowledge of the physical world began to emerge from the empirical efforts of this period. Despite these advances, psychology was far from ready to pursue the scientific study of human activity. The major obstacle remained the problem of defining the nature of the person. How the scientist pursues the study of psychology depends completely on how human activity is initially viewed. Should psychology study mental activity? Behavior? Consciousness? Furthermore, precisely how should these terms be defined so that various empirical approaches can be applied? These questions are basically philosophical, and the answers are necessarily based on preconceptions about the nature of the individual. Two parallel trends emerged during these centuries that would eventually lead to the formulation of psychology. The first, consistent with the steady reliance on empiricism, was methodological; it developed as the natural and physical sciences made dramatic advances in the accumulation of findings. The second intellectual trend was more philosophically oriented; it consisted of arguments exploring the relationship between body and mind (or soul) and the functions of each constituent in what we may call human activity.

Baruch Spinoza

The philosophical system of Baruch Spinoza (1632–1677) offered an alternative to the theistic morality of the Scholastic philosophers by commenting on the individual, society, and government from a naturalistic perspective. Born in Amsterdam of emigré Portuguese Jews and educated in the Jewish tradition at a synagogue school, Spinoza supported himself by grinding and polishing lenses for eyeglasses and microscopes after his father died in 1654. His Hebrew first name, for "blessed," was translated into the rough equivalent in Latin, so that he is generally known as Benedict Spinoza. He secured a position as a tutor in a progressive Latin school, gaining exposure to the Scholastic philosophers. In 1670, Spinoza published *Tractatus theologico-politicus* (*Treatise on theology and politics*). In this work, he set forth his conception of God as not being the personalistic patriarch who, according to traditional Judeo-Christian teachings, guides the world. Rather, he postulated that God is the underlying principle that brings unity to matter and mind; God is synonymous with nature. By this definition of God as nature, Spinoza identified himself as a pantheist. Spinoza taught that, despite the absence of evaluative and determining judgments by a personal God, people must still seek to live an ethical existence by striving for virtue based on natural laws. Nature itself has both the power of motion, seen in the movement of all objects in nature, and the powers of generation, growth, and feeling in all living organisms. Thus, Spinoza sought to reconcile the conflict between science and religion by redefining the deity in terms of the universe, revealed initially by Copernicus.

Spinoza viewed the mind and the body as different aspects of the same substance. The mind is the internal manifestation and the body the external manifestation of the individual's unity. Spinoza, then, was one of the first post-Renaissance philosophers to offer an alternative to the Aristotelian notion of mind–body dualism. Rather, Spinoza's stress on the integrity and unity of human existence interpreted the mind and body as different ways that scholars have found to describe different functions of common human experience. From a psychological perspective, Spinoza described the mental functions of feelings, memories, and sensations as mechanical processes mediated by the physical senses and originating through the stimulation of physical objects. This conclusion about the relationship among the physical environmental stimuli, sensory processes, and mental activity places all three elements of experience on a single continuum, underscoring the unity achieved by input from all three sources. Higher mental processes of perception and reason, as well as what Spinoza called intuitive knowledge, are derived not from the external world but from the mind acting on itself. The mind, then, is not an entity or agent, but rather an abstraction: The mind and the activities of the mind are identical. Spinoza wrote that the essential state of the person is to act. Action ultimately motivated by self-preservation is guided by desire. According to Spinoza, the wise person can resolve the conflicts of desires, but for most of us conflicting desires give rise to emotions. Absolute freedom does not exist for the individual, and people are governed by the desires that eventually secure self-preservation.

Spinoza's notion of self-preservation, because it contains the major motivational elements of human activity, is critical to his psychological views. Survival, for Spinoza, was a biological predisposition, a hypothesis that anticipated the evidence of Darwin in the nineteenth century. The individual struggle for survival was seen as the source of all motives and desires, although a person may not be always conscious or aware of the ongoing struggle. Echoing an Epicurean theme, Spinoza asserted that all desires ultimately involve the seeking of pleasure and avoidance of pain. Desires give rise to emotions that, in turn, have both physiological and mental aspects, again reiterating the emphasis on the unity of experience. Indeed, Spinoza's description of the physiological and mental relationship during emotional states was remarkably similar to the theory of emotions offered by William James and Carl Lange in the nineteenth century (see Chapter 12). Ultimately, however, reason must prevail over the emotions if we are to achieve the relative freedom to act.

These highlights of Spinoza's views allow us to draw a few conclusions. First, Spinoza offered a dynamic, action-oriented conception of the mind–body relationship. Mind and body are the same, and personal harmony may be achieved in the mediation of conflicting desires through the highest intellectual powers of reason. Second, Spinoza's system was deterministic, derived not from the providence of God but through natural laws. In his emphasis on natural laws, Spinoza offered a philosophical view of determinism paralleling the advances in science that were to culminate in the mechanical determinism of Newtonian physics. Thus, although he did not deny the existence of God, Spinoza relegated God to a role far removed from human activity and placed humanity securely in the natural world under the same constraints of natural laws as other forms of life. Third, according to Spinoza, the particular dynamics of human activity nevertheless make humanity unique in its intellectual abilities. Specifically, Spinoza acknowledged the central role of rational activity in modulating emotional states. Harkening back to Plato's negative evaluation of the emotions, Spinoza argued that the emotions are a necessary part of human experience, arising from the desires of self-preservation. However, reason must control the emotions, and rational acts constitute the uniquely human ability of individuals to direct their own lives properly in accordance with natural laws.

Spinoza's views were unpopular and distorted in England, and his influence in France was minimal, as Descartes dominated French philosophy. However, as we shall see in Chapter 8, Spinoza's teachings were attractive to German philosophers, who accepted his views and developed the concept of the essential dynamic action of the mind.

René Descartes

We are considering René Descartes (1596–1650) last, and out of chronological order, because his views represented a stepping-off point for philosophical developments up to the nineteenth century. His philosophy was the first comprehensive system since the contribution of the Scholastics, and he is labeled the first modern philosopher. He was born in La Haye, in central France, the son of a prosperous lawyer, who left him an annual income for life. After receiving an early education from the Jesuits, he went on to earn degrees in civil and church law at the University of Poitiers. His insatiable interest in mathematics led him to pursue the examination of philosophical issues by the methods of mathematical reasoning. From 1628 on, he lived in Holland, with only occasional visits to France. Although he affirmed his Christian belief throughout his life, he was nevertheless controversial, and perhaps felt that a quiet life of scholarship in Holland, away from the intellectual control of France, would give him greater personal freedom.

His *Discours de la méthode,* published in 1637, described the evolution of his thinking. Starting with complete doubt and skepticism, Descartes went on to the first principle of certainty and validity: "I think, therefore I am" *(Cogito, ergo sum; Je pense, donc je suis).* This famous statement asserts Descartes' affirmation of the realization of experience. He is stating that the only sure fact about which we have

RENÉ DESCARTES (1596–1650).
(Courtesy, New York Public Library.)

absolute certainty is our own experience and our awareness of the knowledge of ourselves. By defining the self in terms of the subjective knowledge of the experienced idea as the first principle, Descartes radically departed from previous views, which had always begun with the external world and then concluded to the mind as necessary for knowing this external world. Reversing the traditional views, Descartes asserted that our knowledge of ourselves is the most certain principle, and the reality of the external world may be questionable.

However, to deal with the external world, Descartes used the concept of God—that is, because we know the idea of perfection, some entity must possess complete perfection, and this entity is God. Rejecting Platonism, Descartes asserted that the perfect God would not create people with unreliable senses; therefore, sense information is an accurate depiction of the environment, ordered again by the perfection that is God. The critical factor in Descartes' thinking is his reliance on self-awareness of our ideas, which then permit us to know God and eventually our external surroundings. Thus, for Descartes, the ideas of the self, God, and the dimensions of space, time, and motion are all innate to the soul, or mind; that is, they are not derived from experience but from the essential rationality of the mind.

Descartes developed his views on the relationships between mind and body and among the individual, the environment, and God in his subsequent works: *Meditationes de prima philosophia* (*The meditations on first philosophy;* 1641), *Principia philosophiae* (*Principles of philosophy;* 1644); *Traité des passions de l'âme* (*Treatise on the passions of the soul;* 1650), and *Traité de l'homme* (*Treatise on man;* 1662). Descartes' system recognized the advances in the natural sciences, which conceptualized the physical world as governed by mechanical laws. With the exception of God and the human rational soul, all reality is physical and can be explained through mechanical relations. Descartes believed that as science progressed and revealed the intricacies of the activities of life, the operations of human existence would fall within the same guiding principles as all life, and only the human capacity to reason would lie beyond these mechanical principles. Accordingly, Descartes' system held two levels of activity in the universe: the physical world of matter following the order of mechanical laws, and the spiritual world represented solely in human reasoning.

The famous Cartesian dualism, then, is an application to human activity of Descartes' general distinction between mechanical and spiritual levels of the universe. In Descartes' psychology, the mind is a spiritual, immaterial entity, different from the body and easier to know than the body because of the first principle of self-reflection. The body is the physical entity that, in common with all animals, responds to the external world through the mechanics of physiology. The emotions are rooted in the body and represent movement or reflexes to the stimulation of sensory impulses by environmental sources. The relationship between the mind and the body is truly a psychophysical interaction. The human body with its mechanical operations is distinguished from other animals only because it is acted upon by the mind. The exact manner of this interaction is left unclear, although Descartes suggested that the site of the mind–body interaction may be the pineal gland of the midbrain because this organ is singular and situated between the hemispheres of the brain. Although Descartes' hypothesis about the pineal gland reflected the relatively primitive state of physiology, it is nevertheless important to recognize that Descartes consistently pointed to the role of the brain as the transitional agent between the spiritual energies of the mind and the physical forces of bodily mechanics. Descartes taught that the study of bodily processes was the province of physiology and the study of the mind belonged to psychology; thus the first modern philosopher firmly defined psychology's subject matter as the mind.

Descartes was dedicated to empirical observations, and his interest in laboratory study seemed to increase as he grew older. His dissections led him to speculate about a nervous system of hollow tubes through which flow animal spirits that account for voluntary movement. In analyzing vision, he studied the lens of the eye and also described the mechanisms that underlie ocular reflexes. In mathematics, he developed analytic geometry and made studies toward a primitive calculus. The consensus of these wide-ranging investigations confirmed his belief that mechanical laws govern the entire universe, except for God and the human soul. According to Descartes, if our knowledge were sufficient, we would be able to reduce all sciences—astronomy, chemistry, and physics—and all bodily operations—respiration, digestion, and sensation—to mechanical explanations. The single exception to this conclusion, directly from our own experience, is human reasoning.

Toward the end of his life, Descartes' system became widely known, gaining him both praise and condemnation. The Calvinist theologians were especially vehement against Descartes' support of free will as contrary to their rigid beliefs on predestination. However, the great and noble of Europe protected Descartes from harm by either Protestant or Catholic clerical authorities. Descartes agreed to the request of Queen Christina of Sweden to journey to Stockholm to tutor her in philosophy. Unfortunately, the chilly climate took its toll and he died a good Catholic on

February 11, 1650. Consigned to the same fate as Galileo's efforts, Descartes' works were placed on the Index of Forbidden Books by the Church in 1663, again ensuring their author at least notoriety, if not further success. Descartes' views on the supremacy of rationalism and on the derivation of all knowledge from the self won widespread acceptance throughout Europe, challenging the dominance of Scholasticism.

Three trends in psychology may be traced to Descartes. First, psychology as an introspective science investigating human consciousness finds support in the validity of the first principle of the mind espoused by Descartes. Second, psychology as a purely behavioral study is reinforced, although somewhat indirectly, by Cartesian dualism; that is, the interaction between mind and body indicates that overt, observable behavior is meaningful. Such activity reflects the mind, as the mind acts on the body, producing behavior. Finally, psychology as a physiological science is supported by Descartes' assertion that all human activities except thinking and feeling are related to bodily physiology and may be understood as truly psychophysiological. The successors to Descartes were able to find some support for differing orientations by selectively emphasizing certain aspects of Cartesian thought in their search for models of psychological inquiry. Thus, Descartes' importance lies in his directly stimulating the movement toward the founding of psychology.

In concluding this chapter, we can say that the sixteenth and seventeenth centuries witnessed several trends important to the eventual emergence of an empirical scientific psychology. The first concerned the products of scientific advancement, which clearly demonstrated the value of empirical inquiry. From their studies of the physical universe, scientists not only completed the Copernican revolution by providing empirical support for the theory of planetary motion, but also showed the impressive extent to which the physical world operates under specific lawful relationships. The orderliness of nature suggests that all of reality, including the operations of life, may conform to lawful relations revealed through scientific study.

The second trend, represented in the philosophical views of Spinoza and Descartes, offered an alternative to the Scholastic commitment to Christian morality. Both philosophers focused on the primacy of reason. Spinoza's philosophy was the more radical, in that it departed from belief in the guidance of a personal God and the advocacy of a monistic mind–body relationship. Spinoza's description of the unity of mind and body resulted in his emphasis on the uniquely human capacity of reasoning. Others followed Spinoza, taking his monistic concept, but they shifted the emphasis to either the materialism of the body or the spiritualism of the mind. Descartes was clearly a dualist in his interpretation of the mind–body interaction. However, his impressive discourses on the mechanics of bodily action opened the way for successive philosophers to reduce the mental aspect of experience to the physical mechanics of the body. Both Spinoza and Descartes provided a philosophical transition from Scholasticism and proposed a variety of assumptions about the nature of human experience, which later philosophers used as a basis for models of psychology.

CHAPTER SUMMARY

Two parallel trends prepared scholars for the investigation of the mind–body relationship so that a model of psychological inquiry could evolve. The first trend was methodological, characterized by the triumph of empiricism. Scientific innovations by Francis Bacon, Galileo, Kepler, and Newton were firmly based on careful observations and quantification of observables. Using inductive methods, moving from observed particulars to cautious generalization, empiricism stood in contrast to the deductive methods of the Scholastic philosophers. The second trend occurred in the attempt to develop conceptions on the nature of humanity and was more a philosophical enterprise. Spinoza taught that mind and body are manifestations of the same unity of the person. Human activity, although unique because of humanity's higher intellectual powers, is determined by the laws of nature. Descartes stated that the first principle of life is self-awareness of the idea, and all else that we know proceeds from self-reflection. His dualism of the interaction between mind and body distinguishes psychology from physiology. Descartes' views were developed in the French and British philosophical traditions; Spinoza influenced the German efforts to develop a model of psychology.

BIBLIOGRAPHY

Primary Sources

BACON, F. (1878). *Novum Organum*. In *The works of Francis Bacon* (Vol. 1). Cambridge, MA: Hurd & Houghton.

DESCARTES, R. (1955). *The philosophical works of Descartes* (E. Haldane & G. R. T. Moss, Trans.). New York: Dover.

NEWTON, I. (1953). *Newton's philosophy of nature* (H. S. Thayer, Ed.). New York: Hafner.

SPINOZA, B. (1955). *The chief works of Benedict de Spinoza* (R. H. M. Eleves, Trans.). New York: Dover.

Resources

BUTTERFIELD, H. (1959). *The origins of modern science: 1300–1800*. New York: Macmillan.

HALL, A. R. (1963). *From Galileo to Newton: 1630–1720*. London: Collins.

SARTON, G. (1957). *Six wings: Men of science in the Renaissance*. Bloomington: Indiana University Press.

Studies

BALZ, A. G. A. (1952). *Descartes and the modern mind*. New Haven: Yale University Press.

BERNARD, W. (1972). Spinoza's influence on the rise of scientific psychology. *Journal of the History of the Behavioral Sciences, 8*, 208–215.

ORNSTEIN, M. (1928). *The role of scientific societies in the 17th century.* Chicago: University of Chicago Press.

PIRENNE, M. H. (1950). Descartes and the body-mind problem in physiology. *British Journal of the Philosophy of Science, 1,* 43–59.

TIBBITTS, P. (1975). An historical note on Descartes' psychophysical dualism. *Journal of the History of the Behavioral Sciences, 9,* 162–165.

WATSON, R. I. (1971). A prescriptive analysis of Descartes' psychological views. *Journal of the History of Behavioral Sciences, 7,* 223–248.

Sensationalism and Positivism: The French Tradition

Advances in Science
Advances in Philosophy
    Sensationalism
        Étienne Bonnot de Condillac
        Charles Bonnet
        Julien Offroy de La Mettrie
        Claude Adrien Helvétius
        Pierre Cabanis
    The Psychology of Maine de Biran
    The Advent of French Positivism: Auguste Comte
Chapter Summary

This chapter and the three that follow examine advances in science and philosophy during the seventeenth, eighteenth, and nineteenth centuries, advances that provide background for the emergence of modern psychology. The chapters are organized around respective developments in France, Britain, and Germany, because the structure of national movements in science and philosophy provided differing models for the building of psychology. Although these traditions overlapped, the teachings of Descartes and Spinoza were interpreted along characteristic national lines. In France, the mind–body dualism of Descartes was reduced to a materialism that focused on the mechanics of sensory processes to explain all psychological activity. The British tradition, while retaining the notion of the mind, stressed environmental input to explain the contents of the mind. The German tradition, following Spinoza more than Descartes, emphasized the self-initiating, dynamic qualities of mental activity that transcend both environmental stimuli and the mechanics of sensory physiology.

After the death of Descartes in 1650, France entered a golden era of political and cultural ascendancy under the long rule of two absolute monarchs, Louis XIV (reigned 1643–1715) and Louis XV (reigned 1715–1774). Although this was not a period of complete political tranquility, an intellectual enlightenment prevailed, and led to a flowering of literary, scientific, and philosophical achievements. France became the leading nation of continental Europe during this time (Map 7). Especially significant were the works of the dramatists Jean Baptiste Poquelin, better known as Molière (1622–1673), and Jean Baptiste Racine (1639–1699), as well as the writings of Pierre Corneille (1606–1684) and Jean de La Fontaine (1621–1695). Collectively, they made French the language of literary society.

The view of education as the responsibility of society became increasingly prevalent. The rational ideal of the age, reflecting belief in the limitless horizons of human knowledge, resulted in educational opportunities no longer being limited to the nobility. The acquisition of knowledge through education was viewed as the key to success and class mobility. The Church continued to provide early educational opportunities for most people, and the great philosophers of France, such as Denis Diderot (1713–1784) and Jean Jacques Rousseau (1712–1778), established the intellectual basis for universal education. It was François Marie Arouet, better known as Voltaire (1694–1778), who personified this Age of Reason. Voltaire's prolific writings on every aspect of life provided the foundation for transforming the conception of Western government from aristocratic obligation to modern social responsibility.

ADVANCES IN SCIENCE

Scientific inquiry developed rapidly during the seventeenth and eighteenth centuries, aided by advances in both mathematical and empirical disciplines. These developments are important for the history of psychology because they contributed to the supremacy of nineteenth-century science, upon which psychology was modeled. In France, as well as in England and Germany, mathematics and the physical sciences began to assume modern forms.

The French mathematician Joseph Louis Lagrange (1736–1813) was born of French parents living in Turin, Italy. After his preliminary education in Italy, he went to Berlin to study calculus under the mathematician Euler. During his 20 years in Berlin, Lagrange formulated his work *Mécanique Analytique (Mechanical Analysis)*, which gave physics a series of formulations for mechanical relationships based on algebraic proof and calculus. After the death of his benefactor Frederick the Great in 1786, he accepted an invitation to join the Académie des Sciences. His prestige allowed him to escape the excesses of the French Revolution. He was instrumental in rebuilding French educational institutions and played a leading role in devising and introducing the metric system. Through his long life of research and teaching, Lagrange produced a group of distinguished students who contributed to nineteenth-century mathematics, physics, and engineering. A contemporary of Lagrange, Jean Le Rond d'Alembert (1717–1783), published classic works on such problems of applied mathematics as the refraction of light and fluid mechanics.

The discovery of oxygen is an example of the growth of a true international scientific community. A Swedish scientist, Karl Wilhelm Schule (1742–1786), is credited with the pioneering research that anticipated the discovery of oxygen, and the English investigator Joseph Priestley (1733–1804) effectively claimed the discovery in a publication of

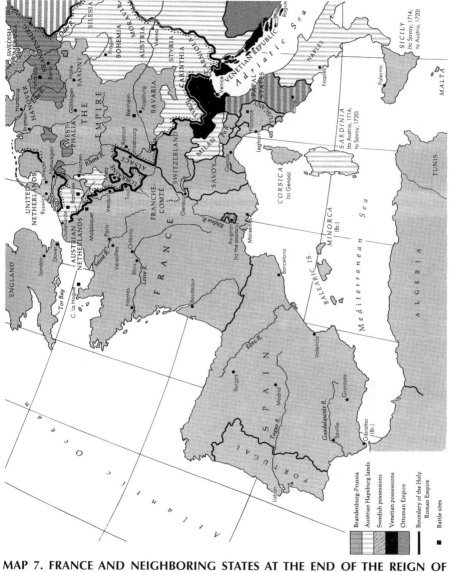

MAP 7. FRANCE AND NEIGHBORING STATES AT THE END OF THE REIGN OF LOUIS XIV, 1715.

1775. However, it was a group of French researchers, headed by Antoine Lavoisier (1743–1794), who actually named the element and went on to establish the scientific methodology of modern chemistry. Like many others, Priestley believed that a substance is given off during combustion, joining with atmospheric constituents to form "phlogisticated air." Lavoisier was able to divorce himself from this dated conception to argue that oxygen is absorbed during the process of combustion. In papers delivered to the French academy, Lavoisier related the combustion process to animal respiration and began a radical change by viewing physiology in chemical terms. He and his colleagues were able to isolate 32 "simple substances" that formed the basis of the modern periodic table of chemical elements. Unfortunately, Lavoisier's politics and his identification with the Académie des Sciences led to his condemnation for supposed counterrevolutionary ideas, and he was guillotined during the French Reign of Terror.

Astronomy also made great advances in France, centered around the empirical work of the Paris Observatory, founded in 1671. Between 1799 and 1825, the mathematician Pierre Simon Laplace (1749–1827) published his multivolume *Mécanique Céleste (Mechanics of the Heavens)*, which summarized the advances in astronomical observations and theories. He believed that scientific discoveries of the essential order of the universe suggest that all explanations of life may eventually be found through scientific investigation. Laplace formulated classic equations to determine the intensity of energy and velocity of motion. He is remembered for his contributions to the theory of probability, establishing the basis of modern statistics.

Clearly the natural sciences were prospering in France. Through a solid basis in mathematics, sophisticated methods of observation provided a systematic approach to the physical world. Although severely disrupted by the Revolution, French science proved resilient enough to respond with further achievements throughout the nineteenth century.

ADVANCES IN PHILOSOPHY

In the France of Louis XIV and Louis XV, prior to the Revolution, the government maintained a vast censorship. Books were examined for religious agreement, support of public order, and moral righteousness to secure the "permission and privilege of the King" necessary for publication. Although 76 official censors were employed by 1741, censorship was relatively loose during the first half of the eighteenth century and informal permission was granted even for publication of some controversial materials. This toleration ended in 1757 when an unsuccessful assassination attempt on the life of Louis XV prompted severe restrictions of literature criticizing state or church. This repression succeeded in uniting all writers holding anti-Church or anti-state views. They were collectively called the *philosophes,* and they cooperated in clandestine publication within France and collaborated to have works printed outside of France to smuggle into the country. The net result was a widespread distribution system of censored works, which, aided by the learned academies, guaranteed the dissemination and success of the writings of the philosophes.

As individuals, the philosophes held wide-ranging views, agreeing only in their opposition to government repression. Through their antigovernment writings, the philosophes influenced some of the leaders of the American Revolution and contributed to the growing concerns that led to the French Revolution. The anti-Church writings of the philosophes had an important impact on psychology, most notably by developing a view that tried to purge the Christian (that is, the Scholastic) notion of soul from consideration in psychology.

Sensationalism

After Descartes, French thought on psychological issues concentrated on the sensory aspects of human experience. Specifically, a coherent theme of French thought involved the study of human nature based on sensations and perceptions. Accordingly, a group of philosophes examined the mechanisms of sensation, and in so doing gradually reduced mental activity to sensory mechanisms. Thus, the mind–body distinction, so carefully made by Descartes, became obscured in French thought.

Étienne Bonnot de Condillac.   The first major figure in this trend of sensationalism, Étienne Bonnot de Condillac (1715–1780), was born in Grenoble and educated at a Jesuit seminary in Paris. Soon after his ordination to the Roman Catholic priesthood, he found his way into the literary and philosophical salons of Paris and steadily lost interest in his religious career. Condillac's early publications illustrated his appreciation of antecedent philosophical views on psychology, especially those of Descartes and the English philosopher John Locke, whom we consider in the next chapter. In his most famous work, *Traité des sensations* (*Treatise on Sensation;* 1754), Condillac radically departed from his predecessors and offered an interpretation of psychological activity based on sensory experience alone.

Condillac began by denying Descartes' notion that the mind is born with certain innate ideas. Rather, he argued that the entire complexity of the mind can be derived from a single sense capacity. To illustrate his argument, Condillac proposed the analogy of a statue, endowed as human beings are with an internal organization and a mind, empty of any ideas. The statue has the single sense of smell, and it is capable of realizing the difference between pleasure and pain. Condillac then attempted to demonstrate how complete psychological activity may be derived from this relatively simple statue as it gradually develops additional sensory capacities. With the first sense alone, attention is acquired by the compelling stimulation of sensory input. When a second sense is developed, judgment is acquired because the statue can now compare the input of two sensory modalities. Memory is a past sensation that is retrieved because of the stimulus of a present sensation, and imagination is an enhanced memory or a new combination of past sensations. Approach and avoidance behaviors are the active recall of pleasant or unpleasant sensations, and the will is a desire based on an exaggerated approach tendency toward an attainable object. Condillac stated that the capacity for self-reflection occurs as the result of alternations between memories and the objects of the will. Aspects of personality, such as

**ÉTIENNE BONNOT DE CONDILLAC
(1715–1780).** (Courtesy, New York
Public Library.)

the concept of the self, develop only gradually with the accumulation of experiences through memories and desires. Thus, Condillac formulated psychological functions from a single sense by adding the four other senses. The mind, then, is reduced to the roles of a receptor for sensory experience and a receptacle for memories. Moreover, the mind is shorn of any initiating functions.

The simplicity of Condillac's view was appealing. He also caused quite a furor in French intellectual circles. He was criticized for his deductive approach and lack of any inductive support from empirical evidence. However, in contrast to philosophers such as Descartes who postulated an active mind that required some kind of spiritual, or at least nonphysical, entity, Condillac relied solely on the physiologically based senses. In addition, Condillac introduced the notion of materialism to modern psychological thought. If the contents of the mind are reduced to their sensory bases, one does not have to go much further to equate the mind and the senses. Thus, the concept of a "mind" itself becomes superfluous. Indeed, Condillac's materialistic psychology was adopted in the school system reforms instituted by the French Revolution and was discarded only with the advent of Napoleon and the accompanying reaction against materialism.

Charles Bonnet.   Born in Geneva, the most prominent French-speaking city of Switzerland, Charles Bonnet (1720–1793) studied plants and insects intensively and presented several experiments to the Académie des Sciences beginning in the 1740s. He studied reproduction in tree lice and reported that the female can reproduce fertile offspring without the male of the species, and suggested that sex may be not only for reproduction, but also for enriching offspring with the diverse characteristics of two parents. He was one of the first scientists of the eighteenth century to use the term *evolution,* although he meant by it the chain of life from simple atoms to human beings. His investigations of plants led him to conclude that plants are endowed with sensation, discrimination, and even judgment, which Bonnet viewed as evidence of intelligence. Accordingly, Bonnet's interpretation of the living world focused on the unity of living beings based upon the mediation of mechanical agents.

Bonnet extended Condillac's views by examining the physiological mechanisms of sensory processes. To continue with Condillac's statue analogy, Bonnet gave the statue a nervous system to accomplish sensation. He argued that the tracing of nerve fibers would explain not only sensory processes but also the psychological functions of attention, memory, and recognition. In so doing, Bonnet was one of the first scholars to mention specific nerve energies, wherein a given function is accommodated by a certain system of neural fibers. He viewed higher mental processes in terms of the association of sensations or memories through the commonality of some dimension, such as time, place, or meaning. For example, sensory event A may be linked to sensory event B by their simultaneous occurrence. Thus, Bonnet added to Condillac's view by establishing a more reasonable basis for psychological materialism through the nervous system, and the necessity of a special mental agency was further diminished.

Julien Offroy de La Mettrie. Julien Offroy de La Mettrie's (1709–1751) most famous work, *L'Homme Machine* (*Man, a Machine;* 1748), shook intellectual Europe because of its simple and clear statement of materialism. La Mettrie was the son of a wealthy merchant, who gave his precocious son a superb education. After receiving his doctorate in medicine, La Mettrie studied anatomy in Leiden, the Netherlands, and published several works that emphasized the role of the brain in human pathology. He eventually became a surgeon in the French army but continued his studies and writings.

La Mettrie's materialism held that matter has an active element, which is motion. He based this conclusion on sensory feelings found in the lowest animals and plants. This observation led him to propose a type of evolutionary hierarchy in the motion of matter. Thus, in the higher animals, the motion of matter allows the heart to beat and the brain to think. La Mettrie argued that psychology is ultimately physiology, and the dualism of Descartes was completely forsaken for the animal machine.

La Mettrie's views created problems for him with his military superiors, and he had to flee to Leiden for safety, but eventually, in 1748, he received an invitation from Frederick the Great to join the Berlin Academy of Sciences with a stipend. There La Mettrie developed his psychology further by asserting a motivational principle for human activity. This principle was hedonistic in that the seeking of pleasure was the ultimate force that propels the individual. In three publications he opposed Christian teachings and argued the importance of sensual pleasure. He established an ethic that judged the actions of people as determined by their desire for sensual gratification. Although La Mettrie's views were received with considerable scorn, he placed French psychology under the direction of the mechanistic laws of physiology. In his short, frantic life, La Mettrie succeeded in arguing against the need for a separate discipline of psychology. Faith in materialistic science was pushing psychology out of consideration only 100 years after Descartes first defined psychology by distinguishing it from physiology.

Claude Adrien Helvétius.   Retreating from the extreme materialistic position of the French tradition, Claude Adrien Helvétius (1715–1771) retained some use for the concept of mind. The son of the queen's physician, he was born in Paris and educated by the Jesuits. As a tax collector, he became wealthy, married a beautiful countess, and retired to the countryside to live a contented life as a gentleman philosopher. The charm of his estate drew many of Europe's finest thinkers, and in 1758 Helvétius published his memorable work, *De l'Esprit (On Intelligence).*

In this work Helvétius added a critical, complementary dimension to the French sensationalistic tradition. He concentrated on the environmental determinants of the individual. Although agreeing with La Mettrie on the basis of desire in pleasure seeking, he related this motivational principle to environmental influences. According to Helvétius, all people are born with equal capacities, but the environment acts differently on individuals, strengthening attention and widening perception in some people but not in others. This difference in capacity to deal with the environment is what Helvétius defined as intelligence. Believing that the key to success in the environment is the opportunity for enriching experiences, Helvétius argued for better educational benefits and more open social structures. Thus, although he did not disagree with the French sensationalists, Helvétius' emphasis on the environment reserved a place for psychology: Physiology may explain the mechanisms of psychological functions, but the mechanisms are still dependent on environmental context.

Pierre Cabanis.   A final figure in the French sensationalistic tradition is Pierre Cabanis (1757–1808). Like Helvétius, Cabanis modified the extreme views of Condillac, Bonnet, and La Mettrie. A distinguished physician, he met the great thinkers who gathered in the literary salons of Paris. Although accepting the materialism of mechanical sensations, Cabanis nevertheless argued against the complete reductionism of his predecessors. Their view equated mental operations with their sensory input, logically leading to the discarding of the mind as unnecessary. Cabanis drew back from this position and proposed a central ego of the brain that acts as the integrator and synthesizer of sensory input. Cabanis' view, then, preserves the need for the concept of mind, even if described in terms of the physical brain. Moreover, he recognized levels of consciousness, including unconscious and semi-conscious processes. According to Cabanis, sensations do not exist as pure forms; rather, sensations are part of an entire system, mediated by the central ego, or self, and sensations are known only through the integration of the entire system.

Cabanis' additions to Condillac's psychology rescued the mind, but tied it firmly to brain physiology. Unlike the British thinkers (considered in the next chapter), Cabanis disagreed with the view of the mind as passive and reactive, filled up by the accumulation of experiences. In contrast to German philosophers, especially Kant (see Chapter 8), Cabanis did not consider the mind as an entity having an integrity and independent processes divorced from physiology. Without necessarily attempting a compromise, Cabanis articulated a view that retained the need for the mind, recognized by the British and German scholars. Loyal to the French tradition, however, he embedded mental processes in the materialism of the nervous system.

To summarize briefly, although the major figures of the French sensationalistic tradition held differing views, they limited the concept of psychological processes to the level of sensory input. Emphasizing the critical role of sensory experience, they de-emphasized the need for the initiating central construct of the mind. Thus, their selectivity within Cartesian psychology tended to be one-sided, neglecting Descartes' defined province of psychology—the mind.

The Psychology of Maine de Biran

The renowned American philosopher and psychologist of the late nineteenth century, William James, referred to Maine de Biran (1766–1824) as the greatest psychologist of the eighteenth century. Biran began his writing committed to the French sensationalist tradition, but steadily moved beyond such restrictions to advocate a more complete, dynamic psychology. Although his writings reflect the interest of the sensationalists, he cannot be categorized in that group, as he personified the full gamut of eighteenth-century psychological views.

Biran was a soldier of the Garde du Corps of Louis XVI and witnessed the women's march on Versailles in 1789. During the Revolution he wisely retired to his country estate, reemerging to oppose the rule of Napoleon. He ended his political career as treasurer of the Chamber of Deputies after the restoration of Louis XVIII. During this politically tense time he continued his writings, which went through four rather distinct phases of intellectual evolution.

During the first phase, 1790–1800, Biran belonged to a group called the Ideologists, which had been founded by Cabanis to promote the teachings of Condillac. At this stage of Biran's thinking, he agreed that human understanding comprised the sum of the associations of the brain, caused by the stimulation of nerve fibers from motion in the environment. Accordingly, Biran believed in a physiological psychology explained by sensory processes. He broke with the Ideologists in 1805 and published *Mémoire sur la décomposition de la pensée (Essay on the decomposition of thought)*. In this work he argued against the "fiber" psychology of the Ideologists that relegated human activity to the mechanistic atomism of sensory elements. Biran wrote that thought is a whole entity composed of distinct processes, but that it is not simply an aggregate of those processes. He focused on the will as an intentional activity that defines the essential character of the self. Thus, the will makes the individual more than the passive receptacle of sensations; it defines a spiritual force that explains life itself.

By 1810 Biran had moved into a third phase, and his conception of psychology took final form in *Essai sur les fondements de la psychologie (Essay on the fundamentals of psychology; 1812)*. He concluded that psychology is the science of the immediate data of consciousness. To Descartes' "I think, therefore I am," Biran responded, "I will, therefore I am." Psychology's province is to study the intentionality of the self represented in consciousness. In terms of methodology, Biran insisted on the objective observation of the self through individual experience. Thus, the active self or ego is the central fact of psychology, so that the individual is intelligent to the extent that he or she is free. In his fourth phase, beginning in 1820, Biran turned to religious experience and attempted to integrate religious aspirations in life to his total concept of psychology.

Biran has been criticized for his changing views of psychology, ranging from physiological to mystical interpretations. However, the range of his opinions is fascinating. Indeed, Biran seems to have expanded his conception as he became dissatisfied with the limitations of fundamental explanations based on sensory physiology. His emphasis on the uniqueness of the individual dictated his intellectual evolution. Biran was impressed not with the commonality of physiological makeup or even psychological processes. Rather, his interest steadily centered on those aspects of human nature that result in creative, unpredictable activities fully expressive of the individual person. This same trend toward expanding psychology into a more comprehensive discipline aimed at explaining individual diversity is common to several figures in the history of psychology. Although Biran died at the comparatively early age of 58, he was able to accommodate an entire evolution in his thinking. Others who lived longer, such as Wundt, whom we shall consider in a later chapter, did not succeed in completing the cycle, although they were well on their way to the same goal that Biran achieved. Nevertheless, we can well understand James' appreciation of Biran for the breadth of his vision of psychology as well as for his anticipation of the variety of models that may be applied to psychology.

The Advent of French Positivism: Auguste Comte

By considering Auguste Comte (1798–1857) at this point, we are jumping ahead somewhat and leaving the historical sequence of psychology in a strict sense. Indeed, Comte's place in history is clouded by ambiguity. He expressed the scientific spirit that psychology adopted as it emerged as a formal discipline. At the same time, Comte's application of his own views resulted in an attempted utopia that proved embarrassing to those who tried to take him seriously.

The controversial life of Auguste Comte began at Montpellier, where he received his early education under Catholic auspices. He then studied at the École Polytechnique in Paris under some of the leading scientists of France. Expelled because of his republican sympathies, Comte remained in Paris and continued to study with the Ideologists. He secured a position as secretary to the social philosopher Saint-Simon (1760–1825), who advocated a reorganization of society under the guidance of emerging social science. Comte incorporated many of Saint-Simon's ideas into his own views. After a bitter quarrel, he parted with Saint-Simon and supported himself mainly by tutoring and giving lectures through private subscriptions. The lectures formed the basis of his most famous work, *Cours de Philosophie Positive (Course on Positive Philosophy),* published in six volumes between 1830 and 1842. This monumental and revolutionary work took on the ambitious task of completely reorganizing intellectual conceptions of knowledge and applying this theory to the eventual reformation of social structures.

AUGUSTE COMTE (1798–1857).
(Courtesy, New York Public Library.)

Although Comte never gained a professorship, he did gather loyal and devoted students, and his views spread widely. The British philosopher-feminist Harriet Martineau (1802–1876) translated the *Cours* into English in 1858, and Comte carried on an extensive correspondence with the foremost spokesman of British psychology, John Stuart Mill. His precarious livelihood and seemingly reckless ventures soured many of his earlier admirers, including Mill. By the late 1840s, Comte's application of his theory took the form of a religion of humanity. The structure of his proposed society was remarkably similar to the hierarchical organization of the Roman Catholic Church, with humanity substituted for God and Comte substituted for the pope. This fanciful utopia based on reformulated social relationships tainted Comte's entire systematic thought.

However, Comte's earlier writings contained in the *Cours* are important, both for their consistency with the model of sensationalism in French thought and for their attempt to instill an objective method of science for psychology. We have already touched on Comte's notion of historical progress in Chapter 2. Briefly, he argued that explanations of life shift in focus from a theological to a metaphysical basis as human intellectual progress continues. A final shift from a metaphysical to a positivist basis defined the maturity of science for Comte. Whereas the metaphysical stage seeks causal explanations in nonphysical abstractions or universals, the positivist stage seeks to coordinate observable facts and find descriptive laws of natural events. By emphasizing description, Comte did not preclude causal relations in positivism, but he did argue against the preoccupation with the search for causality, which concerned so many previous philosophers. According to Comte, such a preoccupation led to artificiality because philosophers were susceptible to a preconceived notion of universals at the expense of observables, the true level of scientific enterprise.

Various sciences progress at different rates through these stages of intellectual development. Accordingly, science for Comte is relative knowledge, for positivism permits only a limited and changing view of nature. Comte listed six basic sciences: mathematics, astronomy, physics, chemistry, physiology or biology, and social physics or sociology. Interestingly, he omitted psychology, and placed the study of the individual under physiology, thereby agreeing with the sensory–physiological view of psychology advocated by Condillac and La Mettrie. The individual behaving in a group context is the subject matter of sociology for Comte. Elaborating on this "social psychology," Comte later added the science of ethics, which he meant not as the study of morals but rather as the study of observable social behavior aimed at finding laws of prediction for social planning.

It may be argued that Comte, writing before the advent of psychology's formal emergence, could not foresee the later coherence of psychology as a discipline. However, it appears that he recognized the trend of French sensationalism and saw disparity rather than unity. Accordingly, he was consistent with the French trend and simply carried to its logical conclusion the reduction of psychology, defined as sensation, to physiology. Comte's conclusions about psychology did not directly help the push toward its recognition as a discipline. However, his positivism indirectly helped identify a methodological strategy that helped psychology emerge as a recognized, separate discipline within the sciences. The emphasis on objective observation was clearer among British writers, whom we shall consider next. Moreover, Comte's positivism was resurrected in an updated form during the early part of the twentieth century and succeeded in establishing behaviorism as a dominant model in contemporary psychology.

This survey of two centuries of French thought identifies several influences on psychology. First, the benefits of a natural science were articulated, and they created an ideal model for psychology to emulate. Second, Descartes' dualistic conception of mind–body interaction was seriously challenged. Emphasizing materialism at the expense of mentalism, the main theme of French thought opted to restrict mental operations to sensory mechanisms, leading to the questioning of psychology's place by both Biran and Comte.

CHAPTER SUMMARY

The seventeenth and eighteenth centuries marked the ascendancy of French political power, literary success, and scientific achievement. In the natural sciences, such investigators as Lagrange, Laplace, and Lavoisier gave mathematical and empirical support to the modern basis of chemistry, physics, and biology. In a parallel movement, philosophical discourses on psychology led to a reinterpretation of Descartes' formulation so as to focus on sensation. Condillac, Bonnet, and La Mettrie progressively argued for the equation of mental operations with sensory input and worked to articulate the physiological mechanisms of sensation. In so doing, they logically reduced psychology to sensation. Helvétius and Cabanis attempted to back off from such extremism by asserting the mediating role of a central ego, although both remained committed to sensory physiology. Biran and Comte recognized the consequences of reducing psychology to mere sensory physiology, but each worked out separate solutions. Biran rejected sensationalism as completely inadequate, suggesting a total view of individuality based on the immediate data of consciousness expressing the dynamics of the will. In contrast,

Comte ultimately accepted the conclusions of sensationalism and dismissed psychology. Human activity of the individual should properly be studied by physiology; the individual behaving in a group is the province of sociology. Comte, however, advocated a spirit of objective observation that was eventually useful to psychology. Thus, the successors to Descartes in France left psychology in a somewhat tenuous position, removed from recognition as a formal discipline.

BIBLIOGRAPHY

Primary Sources

COMTE, A. (1858). *Cours de philosophie positive (1830–1842) [The positive philosophy of Auguste Comte]* (H. Martineau, Trans.). New York: Calvin Blanchard.

LA METTRIE, J. O. DE. (1912). *L'homme machine [Man, a machine]* (M. W. Calkins, Trans.). New York: Open Court.

MILL, J. S. (1965). *Auguste Comte and positivism.* Ann Arbor: University of Michigan Press.

RAND, B. (1912). *The classical psychologists.* New York: Houghton Mifflin.

General References

COPLESTON, F. (1960). *A history of philosophy, Vol. 4, Modern philosophy—Descartes to Leibniz.* Garden City, NY: Image Books.

COPLESTON, F. (1964). *A history of philosophy, Vol. 6, Modern philosophy, Part I—The French enlightenment to Kant.* Garden City, NY: Image Books.

COPLESTON, F. (1977). *A history of philosophy, Vol. 9—Maine de Biran to Sartre.* Garden City, NY: Image Books.

DURANT, W., & DURANT, A. (1965). *The age of Voltaire.* New York: Simon & Schuster.

DURANT, W., & DURANT, A. (1965). *Rousseau and revolution.* New York: Simon & Schuster.

DURANT, W., & DURANT, A. (1975). *The age of Napoleon.* New York: Simon & Schuster.

Studies

CHARLTON, D. G. (1959). *Positivist thought in France during the second empire.* Oxford: Clarendon Press.

DIAMOND, S. (1969). Seventeenth century French "connectionism": La Forge, Dilly, and Regis. *Journal of the History of the Behavioral Sciences, 5,* 3–9.

LEWISOHN, D. (1972). Mill and Comte on the method of social sciences. *Journal of the History of Ideas, 33,* 315–324.

MCMAHON, C. E. (1975). Harvey on the soul: A unique episode in the history of psychophysiological thought. *Journal of the History of the Behavioral Sciences, 11,* 276–283.

MOORE, F. C. (1970). *The psychology of Maine de Biran.* London: Oxford University Press.

STAUM, M. S. (1974). Cabanis and the science of man. *Journal of the History of the Behavioral Sciences, 10,* 135–143.

WOLF, A. (1939). *A history of science, technology, and philosophy in the eighteenth century.* New York: Macmillan.

Mental Passivity:
The British Tradition

Advances in Science
Advances in Philosophy
    The Early Empiricists
        Thomas Hobbes
        John Locke
        George Berkeley
        David Hume
        David Hartley
    Scottish Common Sense
        Thomas Reid
        Thomas Brown
    The Later Empiricists
        James Mill
        John Stuart Mill
        Alexander Bain
Chapter Summary

The strong affinity between American and British intellectual thought has been forged through four centuries, beginning with the colonial period and continuing through decades of sharing a common language and cultural inheritance. The British influence, more than any other European movement, was a primary determinant in the development of psychology in the United States. This influence is readily apparent when we consider both the content and the methodology during the dynamic growth of twentieth-century American psychology. For this reason, the earliest expressions of modern psychological inquiry in Britain are of special significance.

Britain of the seventeenth and eighteenth centuries was an exciting place of political and economic progress as the nation moved steadily toward its position as the dominant power of the nineteenth century. The seventeenth century witnessed the consolidation of national interests in the British Isles (Map 8) under the monarchy and the established Church of England, both controlled by Parliament. The eighteenth century saw the extension of British influence throughout the

MAP 8. THE UNITED KINGDOM OF ENGLAND, WALES, IRELAND, AND SCOTLAND AT THE ACCESSION OF WILLIAM AND MARY, 1689. The shaded area shows lands controlled by the English rulers as early as the twelfth century. Also shown are the major cities and university towns (circles) and historical battle sites (squares).

world, with the American Revolution the only setback in colonial expansion. The writings of the epic poet John Milton (1608–1674) successfully challenged the British licensing regulations for censorship, which were abolished in 1694 by William III, and freedom of the press became a reality in Britain. English literature then entered a period of achievement through the writings of John Dryden (1631–1700), Daniel Defoe (1659–1731), and Jonathan Swift (1667–1745). The cause of science was also advanced by the intellectual freedom of Britain, and even the restored Stuart monarch Charles II (reigned 1660–1685) favored scientists with approval and support. As we have already seen in the brief biography of Isaac Newton, the policy of the British government and society rewarded scientific achievement and encouraged such efforts, seeing them as national assets.

ADVANCES IN SCIENCE

In mathematics, the spirit of Newton continued in England with the full development of calculus. The British also made great strides in the application of mathematics in physics. Joseph Black (1728–1799), working at the University of Glasgow, did pioneer experiments in oxidation and discovered the exchange of heat in substances changing from liquid to gas and gas to liquid. A later scientist, James Watt (1736–1819), applied this principle in his improvement of the steam engine.

Although the frictional properties of electricity had been known since ancient Greek times, a British scientist, Stephen Gray (1666?–1736), did the precise experimental work on the conduction of electricity. The American scientist and statesman Benjamin Franklin (1706–1790) described the identity between electric sparks and lightning in a letter he sent to the Royal Society in 1750. Franklin's famous experiment harnessing electric power using a kite during an electric storm earned him membership and an award from the Royal Society in 1754.

The astronomers of Britain contributed to the country's developing naval superiority. Edmund Halley (1656–1742) published his first paper on planetary orbits at the age of 20 and was instrumental in building the observatory at Greenwich, which in turn established the definitive methods of calculating longitudes to aid British shipping. Halley is perhaps best remembered for his successful prediction of the comet that bears his name. James Bradley (1693–1762) succeeded Halley as the royal astronomer at Greenwich and studied the annual parallax of the stars. Bradley also influenced the adoption of the Gregorian calendar in 1750, after 170 years of British resistance to the papal reform. British astronomy reached a peak with William Herschel (1738–1822), who not only discovered the planet Uranus but also developed models of the motion of the solar system through space.

Of interest in the field of biology during this period is Erasmus Darwin (1731–1802), grandfather of the advocate of nineteenth-century evolutionary theory, Charles Darwin. Educated as a physician at Cambridge and the University of Edinburgh, Erasmus settled into the practice of medicine and joined the Lunar Society in Birmingham. This group of scientists, which included Priestley, provided a forum for Erasmus Darwin's thoughts on biology. He proposed a theory of plant and animal evolution based on the needs of the organism. His grandson took this concept and introduced the principle of natural selection, greatly changing the shape of the scholarly examination of species diversification.

British medicine made slow advances. The anatomical teachings of William Hunter (1718–1783) and the animal experimentation of his brother John Hunter (1728–1793) improved the quality of medical education. Epidemics of infectious diseases periodically resulted in cries to clean up the filth of the cities, and pioneering work in immunization helped control outbreaks. Smallpox inoculations were tried in England by Charles Martland in 1718 and in Boston by Zabdiel Boylston in 1721. However, quackery was still prevalent and bloodletting was the standard cure for varieties of illnesses. Nowhere were superstition and intolerance

THE ROYAL OBSERVATORY AT GREENWICH, OUTSIDE LONDON.
(Courtesy, New York Public Library.)

greater than in the treatment of the mentally ill. For a small fee, visitors could enter Bethlehem (Bedlam) Hospital for Lunatics in London to stare at the antics of the inmates chained with ankle and collar restraints. Patients were "treated" with bloodletting, enemas, or mustard plasters on the head. The first attempts to treat the mentally ill humanely and to recognize their maladies as a disease were accomplished by the Quakers of Pennsylvania, who founded asylums to care for such individuals.

ADVANCES IN PHILOSOPHY

The major theme of psychology pursued by British philosophers centered on a faith in empiricism. Empiricism has been generally defined as the view that experience is the only source of knowledge. Accordingly, the theme that prevailed throughout the British tradition emphasized the development of the individual psychological framework through the accumulation of experiences. As a major implication of this stand, British psychological inquiry studied the relationship between the sensory input of experience and the operations of the mind.

The Early Empiricists

The initial formulation of British psychological opinion derived from issues originally proposed by Descartes. As Cartesian dualism stimulated French thought and evolved into sensationalism, so too we may find in Descartes' writings the basic position that promoted the empirical basis of British thought.

Thomas Hobbes.   Recognized as the most brilliant philosopher of his age, Thomas Hobbes (1588–1679) published on wide-ranging subjects that collectively advocated the submission of society and the Church to the orderly rule attained only under absolute monarchy. His views on psychology were likewise radical and started the British empiricist tradition.

A rich uncle provided Hobbes with an Oxford education, and he secured employment with an aristocratic family, allowing him some protection for his anti-parliamentary and anti-Church views as well as offering him some financial security. He became acquainted with the great scholars of his time, including Galileo and Descartes, and served briefly as secretary to Francis Bacon. During Cromwell's protectorate he lived in exile in France, tutoring the children of the aristocracy, including the future Charles II, but soon alienated the devout Anglicans among his fellow expatriates by insisting that the Church should be subordinate to the monarch. Upon the restoration of Charles II in 1660, Hobbes received an annual pension. He spent the remaining days of his long life defending his views.

His most famous work, *The Leviathan, or Matter, Form, and Power of a Commonwealth, Ecclesiastical and Civil* (1651), was primarily intended as a political treatise, but Hobbes also expounded his essential views on psychology. His first principle of psychology asserted that all knowledge is derived through sensations. Moreover, he went on to suggest that nothing exists, internal or external to us, except matter and motion, thus grounding his psychology firmly in materialism. Sensations, then, are reduced to motion in the form of change. For example, we know the sensory qualities of light and dark by their contrast; we could know neither alone or absolutely. Hobbes did not agree with Bacon's faith in induction, but rather believed that deduction from experience constitutes the only valid method of knowing.

By proposing that the motion of physical objects in the environment gives rise to sensations, Hobbes used the rules of mechanical association to derive ideas and memory. For Hobbes and his successors in the British tradition, the mind acquires knowledge through associations. Associations are organized into general principles that are usually mechanical in nature and that describe how the relationships between sensations are formed into ideas. For Hobbes, the contiguity in time or place of events provided the association of sensations to form the idea unit, which is then stored by the mind in memory. It is the association mechanism that determines the sequence of ideas, defined as thought. The motivational principle in Hobbes' psychology was desire, ultimately a physiological process governed by seeking pleasure and avoiding pain. Thought sequences, according to Hobbes, are directed by desire and based on external sensation. Hobbes argued that dreams are thought sequences unregulated by sensations. The determinants of associative mechanisms built into thought sequences precluded the notion of free will for Hobbes. Rather, he viewed the will as a convenient label for the alternating desire and aversion confronting the individual with respect to a given object in the environment.

Hobbes described the universe as an environmental machine of matter in motion. His psychology portrayed the individual as a machine operating in this mechanized world. Sensations arise from motion and result in ideas, following the laws of association. The nervous system accomplishes the transference of sensory motion to muscular motion, so that the mind is a physical process centered in the brain. The major inconsistency in Hobbes' view lies in consciousness. His sequence of thought implies an awareness of a cognitive content, but he was unclear on the manner of movement from physically based sensations to nonphysical thought. Despite this problem, Hobbes established the importance of associations in understanding the accumulation of experiences. His successors in the British tradition amplified the empiricist position.

John Locke. In addition to being the major leader of the British empiricist tradition, John Locke (1632–1704) was one of the most influential political philosophers of post-Renaissance Europe. Born near Bristol, England, Locke was educated in classics and medicine at Oxford. He remained at Oxford as a don, studying the writings of Descartes and assisting Robert Boyle in his laboratory experiments. In 1667 he became physician to the Earl of Shaftesbury and, through him, began close contact with the political turmoil of the 1680s. Because of his identification with Shaftesbury, he eventually had to flee to the Netherlands, where he remained until the revolution that deposed James II and brought William and Mary to the throne by the invitation of Parliament in 1688. Locke's political views asserted that individual abilities are determined not by heredity but by environment or experience and that the sole appropriate government is by authorization of the governed. These views justified the parliamentary invitation of new monarchs. Locke's political views also influenced some of the founding fathers of the American republic, such as Thomas Jefferson, John Adams, and James Madison.

JOHN LOCKE (1632–1704). (Courtesy, New York Public Library.)

Locke's psychological views were expressed in his *Essay Concerning Human Understanding* (1690). Extending Hobbes' first principle, Locke stated, "*Nihil est in intellectu nisi quod prius fuerit in sensu*—There is nothing in the mind that was not first in the senses." This principle was affirmed in Locke's description of the mind at birth in terms of a *tabula rasa*, or blank slate, upon which the accumulation of life's experiences are gradually impressed to constitute the entire contents of the mind. Locke rejected other sources of knowledge, innately endowed through God or otherwise built into our mental structure at birth. Rather, all knowledge, including our ideas of God or morality, is derived from experience. He distinguished between sensations, which are physical, and perceptions, which are the reflected products of sensations. The units of the mind, called ideas, are derived from sensations through self-reflection. Further, he affirmed that physical objects have inherent primary and perceived secondary qualities. The primary qualities are the properties of the objects as they exist—their volume, length, number, motion. The secondary qualities, however, are produced by us and attributed to the objects in the process of perceiving—sounds, colors, odors, tastes. This distinction led Locke into the dilemma of whether objects exist in themselves as substances. Locke concluded that there are two kinds of substances. Material substances exist in the physical world, but we know them only through their primary qualities. Mind substances exist as mental elements and are our perceptions of objects.

In contrast to the French sensationalists, who eliminated the need for the mind by equating it with sensations, Locke's empiricism has definite need for the concept of a mind. However, we can characterize this mind construct as predominantly passive; the denial of innate ideas coupled with the dependency on sensory ideas limits the mind's role to reacting to the environment. Locke, however, did reserve two important operations for the mind. The first was association. Although less associationistic than Hobbes, Locke believed that the mind links together sensations to form perceptions by the principles of logical position or chance. His notion of logical position was broader than Hobbes' contiguity principle; it meant that the contiguity, the contingent relationship, or the meaning of two or more events would result in the association of those events. Associations by chance are spontaneous linkages without an apparent logical position. They constitute what we today call superstitious reinforcement. The second type of mental operation was reflection. Through reflection the operations of the mind in themselves produce a new or compound idea based on the simple ideas derived from sensation. Locke's view is at odds with Hobbes' position because Locke believed that reflection may be viewed as an activity of the mind, only remotely related to the sensory level.

As we have already seen and will explore further below, Locke's views were highly influential. His psychology may be described as rational empiricism, as he succeeded in retaining the need for the mind construct while discarding the theological implications of the soul. Others such as Condillac, however, were able to take the basic teachings of Locke and, by dropping the reflective operations of the mind, use them to question the need for the mind construct. Nevertheless, Locke's environmental determinacy provided the staging for the remainder of the British empiricist movement.

George Berkeley.   George Berkeley (1685–1753) was a fascinating character because his interest in Locke's notion of mental perception led him to deny reality. Berkeley was born in County Kilkenny, Ireland, and entered Trinity College,
Dublin, at age 15. By age 29 he had completed three significant works, including
An Essay Towards a New Theory of Vision (1709), which contained his important
psychological views. Berkeley became an Anglican clergyman and in 1728 set
out for the New World to establish a college for the spread of the Gospel among
the "American savages." He reached Newport, Rhode Island, and spent 3 years
among the leading New England intellectuals, including Jonathan Edwards.
Whitehall, his home near Newport, is now a museum containing artifacts of
Berkeley's stay in colonial America. However, the funds for his college never arrived from England, and he had to return to Britain. In 1734 he was appointed
Bishop of Cloyne in Ireland.

According to Berkeley's view, if all knowledge is derived from the senses, reality exists only to the extent that the mind perceives it. Locke had tried to salvage
reality by his notion of primary qualities possessed by objects themselves. However,
Berkeley asserted that we have no way of proving the existence of primary qualities
independent of the senses (that is, through secondary qualities), so he dismissed the
notion and asserted that sensation and perception are the only reality about which we
can be certain. Berkeley used the principles of associations to explain the accumulation of knowledge. Simple ideas of sensory origin are compounded or constructed to
form complex ideas. This mechanical coupling adds nothing in the association
process, so that complex ideas are directly reducible to simple elements. Berkeley's
association principle, active during perceptual processes, allows us to acquire knowledge of the environment. Berkeley explained depth perception through associations.
That is, two-dimensional perception is readily accommodated by the physiology of
the retina. However, the third dimension of depth results from our experiences with
objects of various distances and our movements toward or away from them. An association is formed between the ocular sensation and our experience, producing the
perception of depth.

Berkeley's solution to the problem of reality was that God, not matter, is the
source of our sensations, and God provides the necessary order to our sensations.
Some critics saw Berkeley's position as absurd. The question of the existence of
physical objects, independent of a perceiving mind, has sometimes been proposed in
the form of the situation of a tree falling in a forest: Does the tree make any noise?
Berkeley would state that the tree could not make any sound without a mind to hear
it. Indeed, for Berkeley there would be neither falling tree nor forest without a mind.
Nevertheless, Berkeley's views represent a progression from Descartes that fortified
the empiricist position against dismissing the mind as the sensationalists had done.
As Descartes asserted *"Cogito ergo sum,"* Berkeley held that *"Esse est percipi*—To
be is to be perceived." To paraphrase Boring's (1950, p. 184) summary of the progressive relationship among Descartes, Locke, and Berkeley: Berkeley saw the problem not as how the mind is related to matter (Descartes), nor how matter generates
the mind (Locke), but how the mind generates matter.

David Hume.   Although agreeing with Berkeley's conclusion that matter, independent of perception, cannot be demonstrated, David Hume (1711–1776) applied the same strategy to mind and denied its existence. He was born in Edinburgh of a moderately affluent family and reared in the Calvinistic tenets of Scottish Presbyterianism. He entered the University of Edinburgh at an early age but left after 3 years to devote himself completely to philosophy at the expense of his childhood religion. He took various positions as secretary and tutor to supplement his inherited income. His initial writings on psychology, politics, and religion gained him little attention, but gradually his attacks on established Christian beliefs earned him a controversial reputation as an atheistic political theorist. Finally, in 1752, he was elected librarian of the law faculty at Edinburgh. With access to a vast literary collection, he wrote his *History of England* (1754–1761) and secured praise for his admirable scholarship.

Hume's psychological works were contained in *A Treatise of Human Nature* (1739), later elaborated in *An Enquiry Concerning the Human Understanding* (1748). He accepted the basic empirical premise that all ideas are ultimately derived from sensation, and acknowledged the distinction between primary and secondary qualities proposed by Locke. However, he defined mind solely in terms of the sensations, perceptions, ideas, emotions, or desires of a person at any given point. In so doing, like Berkeley, he denied matter because we know our mental world only. Moreover, by confining "mind" to only ongoing sensory and perceptual processes, any additional spiritual characteristics of the mind are unnecessary. Accordingly, "mind" for Hume was the transitory collection of impressions. The mental operations of reflection suggested by Locke were dismissed. Associations are recognized as compelling links of sensations, links that are formed by the contiguity and similarity of events. Hume's skeptical account adopted a very passive view of association processes, far removed from Locke's notion of reflection. Even such basic relationships as cause and effect were illusory for Hume. As an example, Hume cited the perception of a flame followed by the perception of heat. Although we may attribute the heat to the causal agency of the flame, Hume insisted that all we have observed is a succession of events, and we have simply imposed the cause–effect relationship as derived from custom. Thus, Hume extended Berkeley's skepticism of matter to a denial of the traditional Cartesian notion of the mind. In its place he promoted the role of ideas to account for mental activity.

Personal freedom was also an illusion for Hume. Because we are determined by the momentary influx of sensory events, any subjective freedom is simply some idealistic concept again taught to us by custom or religion. The primary motivational construct for Hume was based on emotion or passion governed by the seeking of pleasure and avoidance of pain. Indeed for Hume it is the antagonism or tension between emotions that results in their control, or ethical constraint, not the pretense that reason, as a higher mental process, should control emotions. Hume believed that reason is slave to the emotions. The motivational states derived from emotional interplay are integrated and mediated by physiological mechanisms.

Thus Hume succumbed to reductionism. Following Berkeley's inadvertent conclusion about matter, Hume taught a most passive view of empirical psychology.

He viewed human activity as reactive and having little initiative or control of the environmental events impinging on the organism. By identifying mind solely with its functions and nothing else, Hume questioned the need for a mind construct.

David Hartley.   David Hartley (1705–1757) was originally trained as a member of the clergy, but found biology more to his liking and became a physician. After spending considerable time collecting data, he published *Observations on Man* (1749), containing his views on psychology. Essentially, Hartley established a physiological basis for Hume's brand of empiricist psychology. Extending Hobbes' and Locke's principles of associations as responsible for the formation of ideas and storage in memory, Hartley advocated the explanation of all human activity, including emotion and reason, through the mechanism of association. For Hartley, associations were formed by the contiguity of events and strengthened by repetition. Further, he stated that fiber connections of the brain comprise the correlates of all mental operations. He believed that the vibrations of brain fibers form the basis of ideas. Hartley viewed nerves as solid tubes that are set in motion by external stimuli, causing vibrations that transmit the stimulation to various parts of the body. The neural vibrations in turn stimulate smaller vibrations in the brain, which Hartley argued were the physiological basis of ideas, thus proposing a physical mechanism that underlies a so-called mental operation.

Hartley's importance in the British empiricist movement was in his role as a synthesizer. He defined his psychology in the empirical mold suggested by Hobbes and fully elaborated by Locke. Accepting the material skepticism of Berkeley and the mental skepticism of Hume, Hartley took the latter's reliance on the association of ideas and built for it a physiological basis. According to Hartley, every mental activity has a concomitant physiological activity; the association of ideas is the mental aspect of the sensory association of events occurring together in time and place. Hartley's physiological psychology brought together trends that resembled the psychology of Condillac and his followers in France. However, Hartley made a significant distinction in retaining the need for some notion of mental activity.

To summarize briefly at this point, the early British empiricists presented a psychology resting firmly on experience. Sensory input constituted the first state of the mind. The critical mechanism relating the sensory level to higher mental processes was associations. Thus, what we might call learning occupied a critical position in early British psychology. The tendency to reduce such mental operations to simpler ideas or sensations was readily seen by Hume and Hartley. Such reductionism, as in French thought, is a problem for psychology because the logical implications of reduction eliminate the very need for psychology. The successors to the early tradition attempted to remedy the situation by qualifying radical empiricism.

Scottish Common Sense

The eighteenth century in Scotland was a period of intellectual activity centered around the universities in Edinburgh and Glasgow. We have already seen in Hume a major figure in the development of empiricism. However, Hume was rather atypical of the Scottish Enlightenment because he fits more appropriately into the British tradition. Most of the philosophers and literary contributors to the Scottish Enlightenment were more independent of British thought, perhaps as a reaction to British political domination or as a reflection of the traditional link between Scotland and France. At any rate, for psychology, the Scottish writers succeeded in shaking the foundations of British empiricism by highlighting the absurdity of skeptically denying the existence of matter and mind.

Thomas Reid.   While teaching at Glasgow, Thomas Reid (1710–1796) wrote his *Inquiry into the Human Mind on the Principles of Common Sense* (1764), which became the cornerstone of his successors in Scotland. Reid took issue with the skepticism that had led Berkeley and Hume to extreme doubt and reductionism. Rather, acknowledging Locke's distinction between the primary and secondary qualities of physical objects, Reid argued that the primary qualities justify belief in the reality of physical objects. That is, he believed that we perceive objects directly; we do not perceive sensations arising from objects. He viewed secondary qualities not as projections of the mind but as mental judgments stimulated by the objects. Thus secondary qualities make sensations the product of a true interaction between physical objects and mental operations.

Reid proposed that these principles of common sense are instinctive parts of a person's constitution, taken for granted in daily life and their value continually confirmed. In contrast, he viewed the metaphysical discourses of Berkeley and Hume as intellectual games. Not only are objects present in reality, but ideas need a mind contained in the self. Thus Reid used his common sense to save empiricism from the sterile path that Hume had followed.

Thomas Brown.   Another figure of importance from the Scottish Enlightenment was Thomas Brown (1778–1820), a student of Reid. Essentially, Brown emphasized the role of associations in mental operations and restored the importance of associative processes in empiricism. However, his views on associationistic processes were less mechanical than those of Hartley and Hume. Arguing that associations may be suggestions, he used associations to propose an explanation for mental consciousness. He introduced the notion of mental chemistry as a contrast to the reductionistic notion of mental compounding suggested by the early empiricists. Brown described two kinds of suggestion: simple and relative. Simple suggestion produces complete ideas; for example, the title of a musical work can evoke an entire thought sequence of melodies. Relative suggestion involves nonsensory input, resulting in exclusively mental operations. For example, multidimensional mathematics is studied in topology and is not represented through sensory experience. Thus Brown attempted to broaden the basis of associations by utilizing suggestion to explain the complexity of mental operations.

Scottish common sense was like a breath of fresh air for the empirical movement. By absorbing both the spirit and the content of the Scottish writers, the later British empiricists were able to broaden the scope of their consideration of the mind and to lay the foundation of modern psychology. Without the contributions of common sense psychology, empiricism might have stagnated and withered in the sterility of skepticism.

The Later Empiricists

The major focus of the later empiricists concerned principles of association. Recognizing the environmental determinacy of the early empiricists and bolstered by the common sense of Reid and Brown, they viewed the contents of the mind in terms of the acquisition of experiences by the individual. Association was the mechanism of acquisition, and an emphasis on learning and memory evolved in British psychology.

James Mill. A throwback to the earlier empiricists, James Mill (1773–1836) was educated at the University of Edinburgh and became a journalist in London. He began writing his *History of British India* in 1806 and completed it in 1818, providing an indictment against British colonial management. In 1808 Mill met Jeremy Bentham (1748–1832), the spokesman for the movement called utilitarianism in British political philosophy. Bentham's utilitarian views had a major impact on Mill's psychology. Briefly, Bentham dismissed the theological and metaphysical assumptions behind social institutions, such as divine law, natural law, and the "rights" of people. Rather, he held that the usefulness of an act for the individual determines its morality and lawfulness. Thus, the ultimate test for any action or law is whether it adds to the benefit and happiness of people. Bentham defined happiness in terms of the individual's seeking pleasure and avoiding pain. Although his work had its greatest impact on British legal and social institutions and led to many reforms, James Mill was sufficiently captivated to become the champion of Bentham's views in psychology.

Mill's major contributions to psychology were contained in his *Analysis of the Phenomena of the Human Mind* (1829). He held the extreme associationist position that ideas are the residual of sensations when the physical stimulating object is removed in the environment. His view of association postulated complete mental passivity; he saw contiguity between events as giving rise to associations. Mill argued that thought sequences are trains of successive or synchronous ideas, and they mimic the order of sensations. Moreover, complex ideas are simply aggregates of simpler ideas and reducible to them. Thus, Mill gets into the absurdity of reducing complex psychological constructs such as the self to constituent, additive components. Accordingly, his system leaves little room for any dynamic synthesis; rather, it sees the mind as only reacting to sensation.

Mill's background was humanistic, and his lack of appreciation of the physiological basis of sensory processes probably hindered his conceptualization of the possibilities of sensory mechanisms that could have admitted some flexibility into his psychology. Thus his views on the additivity of mental processes led him to reduce psychology to absurdity. Nevertheless, Mill saw the utility of associations as a means of explaining environmental determinacy. His son, John Stuart Mill, succeeded in moderating the extreme view of associations as mental combinations.

John Stuart Mill. Subjected to a severe regimen of education as a child, John Stuart Mill (1806–1873) lived timidly under his father's eye for 30 years, and then burst forth with independent opinions after the latter's death. We have already

JOHN STUART MILL (1806–1873).
(Courtesy, New York Public Library.)

noted that John Stuart Mill's empiricism found common points of agreement with Comte's positivism, and indeed much of that commonality stemmed from the influence of Bentham. Mill's major writings in psychology were contained in his *System of Logic* (1843), which was immediately popular and went through eight editions before Mill died. This work served as the standard scientific reference for many years.

Mill's empirical psychology was firmly based on induction. He argued that human thought, feelings, and actions are the province of psychology. The goal of psychology is to try to find underlying causality in human cognitive and emotional activity. Rather than viewing associations as mental combinations—as his father did—John Stuart Mill saw associations as governed by three principles:

1. Every experience has a corresponding idea.
2. Contiguity and similarity produce associations.
3. The intensity of an association is determined by the frequency of its presentation.

Moreover, in his views on habit formation, Mill recognized the subjective perception of relationships between events and agreed with the notion of mental suggestion offered by Brown. Thus Mill acknowledged the mind as generating the complex out of the simple.

Mill also noted contemporary advances in the neurophysiology of the brain, but was not prepared to settle into the materialistic basis of thought proposed by Hartley and, to some extent, his father. He argued that psychology, by virtue of the changing social context of humanity and concomitant individual differences, would not evolve laws to predict human activity. Rather, he was content to advocate the search for "empirical laws," which were expressions of systematic variation. We shall see in Chapter 10 that others, such as Galton, pursued empirical laws to develop the statistical techniques of systematic covariation, or correlation.

Alexander Bain.   Educated at the University of Aberdeen, Alexander Bain (1818–1903) was impressed with the essential compatibility between philosophy and the natural sciences. Although his views on psychology, initially formed by 1855, were empiricist in approach and inductive in method, he later modified his system to conform with the evolutionary theory of Darwin. We shall consider the tremendous impact of Darwin at a later point; however, natural selection confirmed Bain's stress on the importance of the physiological correlates of psychological events. He argued for the concept of psychophysical parallelism, which holds that any given event has both a psychological side and a physical side. Bain believed that the body responds to the physical limitations of cause-and-effect relationships and conforms to quantitative laws of movement, or reflexology. The mind is not quantifiable, according to Bain, but possesses innate abilities or aptitudes.

Bain's major works in psychology were *The Senses and the Intellect* (1855) and *The Emotions and the Will* (1859), and he founded the philosophical journal *Mind*, which dealt almost exclusively with psychological issues. Bain's empiricist views of the mind relied on the association principles derived from contiguity, similarity, and agreement among environmental events. This last point was derived from the recognition that present experience is based on past events. Bain was quite aware of nineteenth-century advances in neurophysiology, and incorporated such findings into his work by asserting the possibility of spontaneous action of the nervous system. Thus, because of the biological makeup of the individual, Bain allowed for psychological activity independent of experience. Accordingly, he moved away from the sterile materialism of Hartley and James Mill, allowing British empiricism to finish the nineteenth century in a flexible position.

The entire course of British empiricism encompassed a variety of interpretations and emphases in describing the mind. However, all of the empiricists accepted the view that the mind is determined by individual experience. Further, they agreed that the predominant activity of the mind is associating sensations and ideas. Psychology as a form of scientific inquiry was seen as a legitimate and acceptable intellectual endeavor of British philosophy.

CHAPTER SUMMARY

The relative freedom and political stability of seventeenth- and eighteenth-century Britain produced an intellectual milieu amenable to advances in the natural sciences and philosophy. The major theme of British psychological thought was empiricistic, emphasizing knowledge acquired through sensation. The mechanism of this acquisition process was association. Founded by Hobbes but fully articulated by Locke, British empiricism retained the necessity of the mind construct while underlining the importance of sensations. Berkeley, Hume, and Hartley evolved skeptical positions concerning the reality of matter and mind that could have left the British movement in the same sterile position as French sensationalism. In addition, James Mill, although he was somewhat salvaged by the utilitarian influence, reduced associations to mental compounding. However, the Scottish common sense writers succeeded in restoring empiricism to a more flexible and open-ended position that recognized complex and integrative psychological phenomena. Thus, the later empiricism of John Stuart Mill, while adhering to scientific inductive methods, adopted a broadly based model of psychology that viewed mental operations and physiological processes as complementary and necessary dimensions of psychological inquiry. By the nineteenth century British philosophy was providing strong support for the study of psychology.

BIBLIOGRAPHY

Primary Sources

BERKELEY, G. (1963). An essay towards a new theory of vision. In C. M. Turbayne (Ed.), *Works on vision*. Indianapolis: Bobbs-Merrill.

HUME, D. (1957). *An enquiry concerning the human understanding* (L. A. Selby-Bigge, Ed.). Oxford: Clarendon Press.

LOCKE, J. (1956). *An essay concerning human understanding*. Chicago: Henry Regnery.

MILL, J. S. (1909). *Autobiography*. New York: P. F. Collier.

MILL, J. S. (1973). *Collected works*. Toronto: University of Toronto Press.

RAND, B. (1912). *The classical psychologists*. New York: Houghton Mifflin.

General References

BORING, E. G. (1950). *A history of experimental psychology*, 2nd ed. Englewood Cliffs, NJ: Prentice Hall.

COPLESTON, F. (1964). *A history of philosophy, Vol. 5, Modern philosophy: The British philosophers, Part I—Hobbes to Paley*. Garden City, NY: Image Books.

COPLESTON, F. (1964). *A history of philosophy, Vol. 5, Modern philosophy: The British philosophers, Part II—Berkeley to Hume*. Garden City, NY: Image Books.

DURANT, W., & DURANT, A. (1965). *The age of Voltaire*. New York: Simon & Schuster.

DURANT, W., & DURANT, A. (1967). *Rousseau and revolution*. New York: Simon & Schuster.

DURANT, W., & DURANT, A. (1975). *The age of Napoleon*. New York: Simon & Schuster.

MAZLISH, B. (1975). *James and John Stuart Mill: Father and son in the nineteenth century*. New York: Basic Books.

Studies

ALBRECHT, F. M. (1970). A reappraisal of faculty psychology. *Journal of the History of the Behavioral Sciences, 6,* 36–40.

ARMSTRONG, R. L. (1969). Cambridge Platonists and Locke on innate ideas. *Journal of the History of Ideas, 30,* 187–202.

BALL, T. (1982). Platonism and penology: James Mill's attempted synthesis. *Journal of the History of the Behavioral Sciences, 18,* 222–230.

BRICKE, J. (1974). Hume's associationistic psychology. *Journal of the History of the Behavioral Sciences, 10,* 397–409.

BROOKS, G. P. (1976). The faculty psychology of Thomas Reid. *Journal of the History of the Behavioral Sciences, 12,* 65–77.

DREUER, J. (1965). The historical background for national trends in psychology: On the nonexistence of British empiricism. *Journal of the History of the Behavioral Sciences, 1,* 126–127.

GREENWAY, A. P. (1973). The incorporation of action into associationism: The psychology of Alexander Bain. *Journal of the History of the Behavioral Sciences, 9,* 42–52.

HEYD, T. (1989). Mill and Comte on psychology. *Journal of the History of the Behavioral Sciences, 25,* 125–138.

JAMES, R. A. (1970). Comte and Spencer: A priority dispute in social science. *Journal of the History of the Behavioral Sciences, 6,* 241–254.

MILLER, E. F. (1971). Hume's contribution to behavioral science. *Journal of the History of the Behavioral Sciences, 7,* 154–168.

MOORE-RUSSELL, M. E. (1978). The philosopher and society: John Locke and the English Revolution. *Journal of the History of the Behavioral Sciences, 14,* 65–73.

MUELLER, I. W. (1956). *John Stuart Mill and French thought.* Freeport, NY: Books for Libraries Press.

PETRYSZAK, N. G. (1981). Tabula rasa—Its origins and implications. *Journal of the History of the Behavioral Sciences, 17,* 15–27.

ROBINSON, D. N. (1989). Thomas Reid and the Aberdeen years: Common sense at the wise club. *Journal of the History of the Behavioral Sciences, 25,* 154–162.

ROBSON, J. M. (1971). "Joint authorship" again: The evidence in the third edition of Mill's Logic. *Mill's News Letter, 6,* 15–20.

SHEARER, N. A. (1974). Alexander Bain and the classification of knowledge. *Journal of the History of the Behavioral Sciences, 10,* 56–73.

SMITH, C. U. (1987). David Hartley's Newtonian neuropsychology. *Journal of the History of the Behavioral Sciences, 23,* 123–136.

WEBB, M. E. (1988). A new history of Hartley's Observations on Man. *Journal of the History of the Behavioral Sciences, 24,* 202–211.

❊ 8 ❊

Mental Activity: The German Tradition

Advances in Science
Advances in Philosophy
    The Founders
        Gottfried Wilhelm von Leibniz
        Christian von Wolff
        Immanuel Kant
    The Psychology of the Self-Conscious
        Johann Friedrich Herbart
        Friedrich Eduard Beneke
        Rudolf Hermann Lotze
        Arthur Schopenhauer
        Eduard von Hartmann
Chapter Summary

The German philosophical basis of psychology took greater inspiration from Spinoza than from Descartes. The mind–body dualism of the latter gave rise to the distinction between physiological and psychological levels of study, which provided a conceptual framework contrasting the two realms of investigation. The French sensationalists blurred the distinction through reductionism; the British retained the distinction but allowed some mentalistic functions, such as associations, with a physiological basis. Spinoza conceived of physiological and psychological processes as descriptions of the same entity, which resulted in an emphasis on continuity in the activity of human functioning. Thus, rather than viewing physiology and psychology as contrasting areas of investigation, he viewed them as integrative aspects of human activity. The German model of psychology was not confounded by the contrast between sensations and ideas, as both were seen as aspects of the same active process. Before examining the specifics of the German model, we briefly consider the diverse intellectual climate of Germany.

German history has been characterized by political fragmentation. Surviving the Middle Ages and the Renaissance as a loose confederation of small kingdoms, principalities, and bishoprics, Germany entered the modern era under the nominal leadership of the Holy Roman Emperor, one of the last vestiges of the feudal political structure. Moreover, Germany was sharply divided by the Reformation and by the attempt of the Roman Catholic Church to regain ground lost during the Counter Reformation. The disastrous Thirty Years' War (1618–1648) was fought over the religious allegiance of the Protestant North and Catholic South of Germany.

Amid this political and religious confusion, the German state of Prussia developed in the northeastern portion of Germany. Modern Prussia evolved through the combination of the estates of the Teutonic Knights and the Brandenburg lands. In 1411, Frederick of Hohenzollern became ruler of Brandenburg, with headquarters in Berlin. His successors continued a steady policy of small acquisitions, so that by 1619 the Hohenzollerns ruled over Brandenburg as well as East Prussia. In the nineteenth century, the family presided over the unification of all German lands under their chancellor Otto von Bismarck (1815–1898) and the German Empire (Map 9) lasted until the last Hohenzollern emperor abdicated in 1918.

In the seventeenth and eighteenth centuries Prussia took the lead in German cultural activities, which reached a zenith under the versatile Frederick the Great (reigned 1740–1786). Under his leadership Prussia grew in wealth and power, and the population prospered as education spread and religious tolerance prevailed. Frederick ran an efficient government that was merciless in stamping out bureaucratic corruption. He fostered scientific societies, invited scholars from throughout Europe to Berlin, and even pursued a learned correspondence with Voltaire. University professors were appointed and paid by the government, and German replaced Latin as the language of instruction. German literature flowered and reached its fullest expression in the writings of Johann Wolfgang von Goethe (1749–1832). German music enjoyed a period of creativity unrivaled in history with the contributions of the family of Johann Sebastian Bach (1685–1750) and culminating in the genius of Austrian Wolfgang Amadeus Mozart (1756–1791) and Ludwig van Beethoven (1770–1827).

ADVANCES IN SCIENCE

As in France and Britain, seventeenth-century advances in science saw the triumph of mathematics and physics in Germany. Otto von Guericke (1602–1686) developed the barometer and invented an air pump that examined the physics of the vacuum. Gabriel Fahrenheit (1686–1736) proposed a system of temperature measurement with a column of mercury, leaving his name attached to the resulting scale. Ehrenfried von Tschirnhaus (1651–1708), who explored the basis of radiation from the sun, studied heat absorption.

Perhaps the greatest mathematician of the eighteenth century was Leonhard Euler (1707–1783), who was born in Basel and at the age of 26 became director of mathematics for the St. Petersburg Academy of Sciences. Later, he took a similar post in Berlin, but eventually returned to Russia. He applied calculus to light vibrations and determined the systematic relationship between density and elasticity. Moreover, he contributed much to establishing the modern forms of geometry,

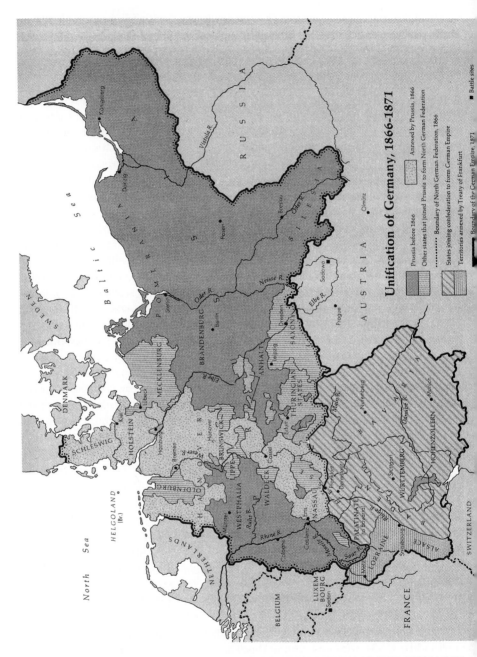

MAP 9. THE GERMAN STATES AT THE TIME OF UNIFICATION UNDER BISMARCK.
At the end of the eighteenth century, Poland was occupied by Prussia, Russia, and
Austria, and ceased to exist as an independent state.

trigonometry, and algebra. His work charting the planets and lunar positions gave a basis to determining longitude. Euler's genius, and his extensive travels, produced many students who spread his teachings throughout Europe.

Advances in electrical theories also occured. George Bose presented a paper to the Berlin Academy in 1742 arguing that the aurora borealis is of electrical origin, and then went on to show how electricity can be used in explosives. In 1745, E. G. von Kleist developed a battery capable of sustaining an electric charge for several hours, leading Daniel Gralath of Leiden to develop stores of potent electrical charges in 1746 by using jars placed in series.

Following in the tradition of the spokesman of modern botany, Swedish scientist Carolus Linnaeus (1707–1778), Philip Miller in 1721 wrote of plant fertilization by bees. In 1760, Josef Krölreuter reported extensive experiments in the physiochemistry of pollination. In 1793, Konrad Sprengel investigated cross-fertilization and postulated the basis of plant anatomy, and in 1791 Josef Gärtner finished an encyclopedic study of the fruit and seeds of plants, which became a classic work of nineteenth-century botany.

Turning to medicine, it is perhaps unfair to include the most famous quack of the eighteenth century, Franz Anton Mesmer (1734–1815), in a chapter on German culture. He was German only by virtue of his birth and education in German speaking Vienna, and spent his lucrative years catering to the idle rich in Paris before being forced to flee the Revolution to exile in Switzerland. However, we shall momentarily consider an active model of mental processing, and Mesmer's teachings are in clearer agreement with the dynamics of mental activity than are the passive views discussed earlier.

Mesmer's thesis for a doctorate at the University of Vienna revived speculation in astrological influences on personality, which he conceived as apparent in the form of magnetic waves. After opening an office for faith healing, he was exposed as a charlatan by the police, who gave him 2 days to leave Vienna. Arriving in Paris, he published *Mémoire sur la découverte du magnetisme animal (A statement on the discovery of animal magnetism;* 1779). Affluent patients soon arrived to be "mesmerized," a process wherein he touched them with a wand or stared in their eyes to the point of making them immobile and susceptible to suggestion. He even provided magnetic tubes filled with a hydrogen sulfide solution to effect his cures. After Mesmer's demise, others used similar curative techniques throughout the Continent and in Britain. Essentially, these quacks struck a responsive chord among a population serviced by primitive medicine and barbaric methods of treating behavioral abnormalities. It was not until late in the nineteenth century that more sophisticated scholars in France gave hypnotism an aura of respectability, prompting the young Sigmund Freud to study under them.

With the exception of Mesmer's work, science in Germany enjoyed success similar to that in France and Britain. Moreover, the Prussian government's efficiency and support of scientific enterprises provided a climate for the ascendancy of the German university system in the nineteenth century, and within that system psychology formally emerged.

ADVANCES IN PHILOSOPHY

The psychology that emerged within German philosophy differed from the sensationalism of France and the empiricism of Britain. Common to this German school was the essential activity of the mind. Whereas the other schools of thought looked to the environmental input of the mind, these German figures initially looked to the preexisting dynamics of the mind to order the environment.

The Founders

Descartes' writings were known and were influential in German philosophical circles. Unlike the French and British scholars, German philosophers emphasized Descartes' views on the activity of the mind, especially innate ideas. However, more than Descartes, it was Spinoza who served as the intellectual forebear of German philosophy. Spinoza's attempt to realign philosophical inquiry away from theological determinacy while retaining the dynamic activity of the mind found loyal followers among German thinkers.

Gottfried Wilhelm von Leibniz.   As a statesman, mathematician, and philosopher, Gottfried Wilhelm von Leibniz (1646–1716) lived a full life that tended to minimize discord and exemplify optimism, to the point of his simultaneous profession of Catholicism and Protestantism. His father was a professor of moral philosophy at the University of Leipzig, which Gottfried entered at age 15. Later denied a doctoral degree because he was only 20 years old, he went to Nuremberg, and his thesis so impressed the faculty that he was offered a professorship. Rejecting the offer for more exciting prospects, he secured a diplomatic post as counselor to the Archbishop of Mainz, a position that allowed him to travel throughout France and Germany and brought him into contact with contemporary intellectual leaders. Working independently, he published his works on differential calculus (1684) and integral calculus (1686) before Newton, although Newton had completed his formulations by 1666.

Leibniz's views on psychology were initially undertaken as part of a commentary on the publication of Locke's *Essay Concerning Human Understanding*. He expanded the commentary to a discourse in dialogue form, *Nouveaux Essais sur l'Entendement Humain* (*New Essays on Human Understanding*), which was completed by the year of Locke's death in 1704, but not published until 1765. Leibniz viewed the mind not as a passive receptor of experiences, but rather as a complex entity that transforms the input of sensations by both its structure and its functions. Leibniz edited the empirical dictum to say: *Nihil est in intellectu quod non fuerit in sensu, nisi ipse intellectus*—Nothing is in the intellect that has not been in the senses, except the intellect itself. Acknowledging Locke's mental operation of reflection, Leibniz argued that the ultimate dependency of reflection on sense data is unsatisfactory. He stated that the mind itself possesses certain principles or categories, such as unity, substance, being, cause, identity, reason, and perception. These categories are keys to understanding and are innate to the mind; they are not in the senses nor in physical objects. Without these categories, we would be aware only of a succession of motions or sensations, so that for Leibniz all ideas were innate. Leibniz also added the notion of continuity in describing the activity of the mind. Thus, *thinking* was viewed as an incessant activity, and the thinking process allowed for both conscious and unconscious dimensions.

To this point, Leibniz elaborated on Spinoza's views in response to Locke's passivity of the mind. Leibniz's original contribution to psychology was in his agent of activity, the monad. Perhaps borrowing the term from its prevalent use to describe small seeds created by God from which all matter and life grow, Leibniz employed "monadology" to describe the essential activity of the mind. Considering the diversification of life expressed in plants and animals, the problem of defining life itself leads to absurd division. A field of grain is composed of living entities—individual plants that in turn have growing stalks with living seeds. The seeds themselves may be individually divided into the living structures of embryo, endosperm, and seed coat. With the aid of a microscope, we can conceivably divide these seed structures into components, and so the endless divisibility continues. As Democritus taught, life may be found in the smallest of atoms, but if we confine our view of life to the extension of matter, we are left with the puzzle of the continuing divisibility of the components of life. Leibniz dismissed the definition of life as infinite divisibility in the search for basic atoms. Instead he offered the concept of monads, which he defined as unextended units of force or energy. Each monad is a separate, independent force asserting its uniqueness against all other centers of force. All living beings are composed of monads that define individuality and reflect the universe. The monad of an individual human being is mind, to the extent that it has sensitivity and responsivity. The monad grows and develops throughout life; change occurs because of internal, individual striving. The elements of life in the individual are the result of a collection of various monads, each with a specific purpose and direction and with varying degrees of consciousness. This aggregate becomes the living harmonious organism of the person under the organizational direction of the dominating monad of the soul. Whereas Descartes advocated psychic and physical interaction in the person, and Spinoza denied this interaction because the physical and the psychic are two aspects of the same entity, Leibniz denied the interaction and yet asserted independent physical and mental processes. In place of the interaction, the harmony of personality is achieved by the purpose and direction of individual monads orchestrated by the organization of God.

A number of important themes may be extrapolated from Leibniz's psychological views. First, the individual is not at the mercy of environmental determinants. Rather, a person's mind is structured to act on the environment. Second, the concept of monadology, although perhaps vague and abstruse, does offer an explanation for the dynamics of mental activity. Processes such as attention, selective memory, and the unconscious are easily accommodated in ways not permitted in empiricist or sensationalist frameworks. With Leibniz, German psychology was committed to the mind construct and capable of fully exploring the implications of mental energy.

Christian von Wolff.   The son of a tanner who rose to be a professor at the University of Halle, Christian von Wolff (1679–1754) published a total of 67 books in an attempt to scrutinize all knowledge under the guiding principle of reason. Consistent with Leibniz and the major theme of German thought, Wolff rejected Locke's assertion of knowledge as dependent upon sensory input, but drew back from some of the difficulties of Leibniz's alternative, monadology. Wolff served as a transition figure between Leibniz and Kant by emphasizing mental activity and bodily activity as two separate, noninteracting processes. Wolff was one of the most praised scholars of his time and was decorated by both French and Prussian academies. Exiled from Prussia out of fear that his writings might encourage rebellion, he was invited to return as chancellor of the University of Halle upon the accession of Frederick the Great.

His major works on psychology were *Psychologia Empirica* (1732) and *Psychologia Rationalis* (1734). As suggested by the separate titles, he elaborated two approaches to psychology. The first was the more limited and dealt with the sensory process, not unlike what we have seen in the British tradition. However, in his *Rational Psychology*, he argued for a full elaboration of mental activity within the framework of Leibniz; that is, he asserted the active role of the mind in the formation of ideas. Like Leibniz, Wolff taught that body and mind are known by action and idea, respectively. Action and idea are parallel and independent processes. The body and sensory level operate mechanically under purposive design. The mind is governed by the determinacy of cause and effect, and it controls the environment by its categories. In so arguing, Wolff's rational psychology may also be described as "faculty psychology" in which the capacities, or faculties, of mental activity form the proper area for study of human understanding. Psychology, then, is defined as the study of mental faculties, and the uniqueness of the human mind transcends all forms of life.

Immanuel Kant.   German psychology received its permanent imprint in rationalism from the writings of Immanuel Kant (1724–1804), one of the most influential philosophers of post-Renaissance Europe. He never journeyed from his birthplace in the capital of East Prussia, Königsberg (since 1945 known as the Soviet, now Russian, city of Kalingrad). In 1740, he began his studies at the University of Königsberg, where he was introduced to the writings of Wolff, although he concentrated on the natural sciences. From 1755, when he received his doctorate, until 1770, when he finally received a professorship in logic and metaphysics after two earlier rejections, Kant supported himself through meager fees as a tutor or as a *privatdozent*, a lowly private teacher whose pay was determined by the students.

As was the tradition at this time, all new professors gave an inaugural address in Latin before the university community. Kant chose to describe the sensible world and intelligible world. The sensible world for Kant meant sense information or the world of appearances, whereas the intelligible world was conceived by the intellect or reason. To this distinction Kant added the basic position that the

IMMANUEL KANT (1724–1804).
(Courtesy, New York Public Library.)

dimensions of time and space are not properties of the objective environment, but rather perceptual forms innate in the mind. Thus the mind is not the passive agent produced by sensations, as the empiricists suggested. The mind is an active entity governed by innate laws and structures, and it translates sensations into ideas. Kant's position implied a psychology of mental operations that is not solely dependent on sensory experience.

After 12 years of contemplation, Kant formalized his psychological views with his monumental *Kritik der Reinen Vernunft* (*Critique of Pure Reason*; 1781). By pure reason, Kant meant knowledge requiring no experiential proof, which he called a priori knowledge. Kant admitted that he was prompted to this undertaking after reading Hume, who had written that all reasoning is based on the notion of cause and effect, which in turn is actually an observation of sequences but has no reality; such relationships are intellectual artifacts. Kant wanted to rescue causation by showing it to be independent of experience and a priori knowledge, and inherent to the structure of the mind. He began by dividing all knowledge into empirical knowledge, which depends on sense experience, and transcendental knowledge, independent of experience. Kant accepted that all knowledge begins with sensations insofar as they provide stimulation to activate the operations of the mind. However, once that stimulation has occurred, the experience is then molded by the mind's inherent forms of perception and conception. The perceptual forms then transform the experience as the external sense of space and the internal sense of time. Reminiscent of

Aristotle's teachings on mental categories, the forms of conceptualization for Kant are independent of experience and mold an experience through mental categories, summarized as follows:

Categories of quality: limitation, negation, and reality

Categories of quantity: plurality, totality, and unity

Categories of relation: substance and quality, cause and effect, activity and passivity

Categories of modality: possibility and impossibility, existence and nonexistence, necessity and contingency

Each perception falls into at least one of these categories, so that perceptions are sensations interpreted by the inherent forms of time and space. Knowledge, then, is perception molded into an idea of judgment. The subjective experience of the individual is not the passive processing of sense impressions but the product of the mind operating on sensation.

In 1788, Kant finished another work of importance to German psychology, *Kritik per Praktischen Vernunft* (*Critique of Practical Reason*). Kant wanted to extend the earlier work to a consideration of morality to show that values are not a posteriori social traditions, but a priori conditions of the mind. To do this, he had to examine the will. Kant asserted that every person has a moral consciousness that is determined not by experience but by the structure of the mind. This consciousness is absolute and basically follows the Golden Rule. According to Kant, in our subjective world of perceptions and ideas—the only world we know—we are free to make judgments that conform to our moral consciousness. It was Kant's intention to give society social responsibility, relying on something more than human reason without resorting to theological arguments. By linking a priori moral consciousness with the will, he elevated the notion of volition to a level of great psychological importance.

Kant's system held that the objective world is unknowable and that sense data are ordered by the mind. Thus, all knowledge exists in the form of ideas. The materialism that dominated French thought and influenced British empiricism was impossible for Kant. At the same time, in contrast to Hume, Kant did not dismiss the objective world, because its existence is confirmed by the stimulating and initiating functions of sense data in the formation of ideas. Accordingly, Kant included both empiricism and rationalism, although his major impact on psychology rests in the latter. Finally, Kant's emphasis on the primacy of the will, along with his rationalism, provided a dominant theme for the future of German psychology and added a critical dimension to the definition of mental activity.

To summarize briefly at this point, the founders of the German psychological tradition presented a new perspective relative to the French and British views. They opted for a model of the mind that was clearly active and dynamic. Mental activity was not a new hypothesis. However, the German movement, crowned by Kant, was developed in full light of and in response to other, alternative models. Thus this particular outline of mental activity formed a powerful argument for preconceived notions of the nature of people. This movement determined the immediate course of psychology in Germany. Moreover, the German model established a standard of mental operations with which all psychological models from that point had to deal.

The Psychology of the Self-Conscious

After Kant, the German tradition of mental activity elaborated and modified details of Kantian psychology, but retained the essential activity of the system. Thus, by the nineteenth century, psychological discussion within German philosophy was confined to the assumption of mental activity, just as psychological issues within British philosophy assumed mental passivity.

Johann Friedrich Herbart.   The title of Johann Friedrich Herbart's (1776–1841) major work in psychology may hold the record for the most encompassing scope: *Psychology as a Science Newly Founded upon Experience, Metaphysics and Mathematics* (1824–1825). Born in Oldenburg, Herbart received his doctorate at the University of Göttingen and taught there in philosophy and education. Although in his doctoral thesis he was at odds with Kant in certain details, he nevertheless falls into the dynamic tradition of mental activity started by Leibniz. In 1809, Herbart was appointed to the chair of philosophy previously occupied by Kant at Königsberg. He remained there until 1833, when he returned to Göttingen to take a similar position.

For Herbart, psychology was a science based on observation. In contrast to Kant's, Herbart's psychology was empirically based in experience. However, psychology was not an experimental science, like physics, and the central province of psychology, the mind, was not subject to analysis. Reminiscent of Pythagoras,

JOHANN FRIEDRICH HERBART (1776–1841). (Courtesy, New York Public Library.)

Herbart asserted that psychology should use mathematics to move beyond simple description and expound the relations of mental operations. The basic units of the mind are ideas, which have characteristics of time, intensity, and quality. Ideas are active in terms of a tendency toward self-preservation against opposing ideas. Accordingly, the dynamics of self-preservation and opposition explain the flow between the conscious and the unconscious presence of ideas. Herbart viewed those dynamics as a type of mental mechanics, analogous to physical mechanics.

Herbart dismissed from psychology physiological considerations and the use of the experimental method. Moreover, his metaphysics of mental operations leading to a system of mental mechanics appears inconsistent with his objection to analysis. Nevertheless, Herbart successfully moved German thought away from the pure rationalism of Kant toward a better appreciation of empiricism. In addition, he must be credited with attempting to establish a psychology that was independent of philosophy and physiology.

Friedrich Eduard Beneke. Friedrich Eduard Beneke (1798–1854) was a contemporary opponent of Herbart. His major work, *Psychological Sketches* (1825–1827), was condensed and subsequently published as *Psychology as a Natural Science* (1833). Beneke's choice of the latter title was startling by German philosophical traditions, and would be considered somewhat misleading by a contemporary interpretation of natural science methodology. In contrast to Herbart, Beneke envisioned a psychology that included physiological data. Moreover, he held that psychology is not derived from philosophy, but rather is the basis of philosophy and all other disciplines. For Beneke, the mind was essentially active, and the psychological processes of knowing, feeling, and willing were mediated by both acquired and native mental dispositions.

Beneke was influenced by the association hypotheses of the British empiricists, and in opposition to Herbart's mathematical approach, Beneke favored the introspective methods of the British philosophers. Although he took exception to Kant's faculties of the mind, he did assert that mental dispositions exist and accomplish approximately the same functions. However, his importance lies in his recognition of physiological components of the experiential input to mental operations.

Rudolf Hermann Lotze. The son of an army physician, Rudolf Hermann Lotze (1817–1881) received his university education at Leipzig. He was a medical student and received scientific training from Weber and Fechner of the psychophysics movement (we shall consider this movement in Chapter 10), but he was drawn toward philosophy as a student. After briefly trying to practice medicine, he decided on an academic career and returned to Leipzig in a teaching post. In 1844, he succeeded Herbart at Göttingen, and remained there for 37 years. Lotze was not the founder of a novel and influential movement in psychology but rather, by virtue of his teaching and writing, succeeded in influencing a generation of German scholars active in the founding of the new discipline.

Lotze's contribution in psychology was titled, *Medical Psychology*, or *Physiology of the Soul* (1852). In it he attempted to blend the mechanical and the ideal through a synthesis of science and metaphysics, although he seems to have ended up firmly emphasizing the latter. He provided a multitude of data from physiology to determine empirically how the physical becomes psychic. He argued that objective, environmental events stimulate inner senses that are conducted by nerve fibers to the central agent. The soul, a term he retained, is affected unconsciously; a conscious reaction can occur, but the degree of the reaction is dependent on attention factors. To Lotze, then, the nervous system was simply a mechanical conductor of motion. Sensations themselves were experiences mediated by the central agency of the soul. In describing mental operations, Lotze rejected Herbart's mathematical speculation. Rather, he posited that the elements of experience are qualitative and require a qualitative, not a quantitative, methodology. Lotze, for example, viewed space perception as a process initiated by raw data entering the person via neural conduction and having intensity and qualitative dimensions only. Perceived space is inferred from conscious data through past experiences by means of a mental capacity. The entire process was labeled "the empiricistic intuition of space."

Lotze opposed materialism and entirely mechanical explanations. His inclusion of physiological data was limited to a portion of the total process of mental activity, and he was not proposing any reduction of mental processes to the initial physiological stage. For Lotze, the central agency of the soul provided mental processes and activity with an essential unity that preserved the integrity of the self in psychology.

The Kantian views on the will and the unconscious were elaborated by two additional figures of the German tradition, who in turn provide a direct link between Kant and Freud.

Arthur Schopenhauer.   Arthur Schopenhauer (1788–1860), known for his philosophical position of decided pessimism, pursued the concept of the will, which he described as the functionally autonomous will-in-itself. Reacting against the idealism surrounding Kant's description, Schopenhauer noted that many forms of activity are not intellectual but still achieve rational results. Below the animal level, expressions of activity are clearly not intellectual. Accordingly, Schopenhauer depicted the will as an irrational striving to live, with its own force removed from intellectual understanding or even awareness. The will, then, is a fundamental impulse. Consequently, psychology must extend its subject matter beyond the purely rational level to encompass the full underlying motivation of human activity in the will.

Eduard von Hartmann.   Eduard von Hartmann (1842–1906) postulated the unconscious as the fundamental universal principle, creatively synthesizing intellect and will. The unconscious is defined as instinct in action with purpose, although without knowledge of the result. In this sense, von Hartmann viewed the unconscious as teleological, or as the determining motivational principle of the self. Von Hartmann suggested three unconscious levels. The first is the physiological level, exemplified by such actions as reflexes. The second level is psychic and includes mental events not within the awareness of the individual. The third level he described as absolute; it represents the underlying principal force for all life. Thus von Hartmann was able to express one side of a paradox that suggests that the individual does not act through conscious reason but rather constructs reasons to explain her or his acts. The implications of this view were fully developed by Freud through his dynamic theory of unconscious determinacy in personality.

As might be expected, the assertion of mental activity, as opposed to passivity, opened the way for a variety of interpretations. Specifically, these interpretations of human activity produced models of psychology that focused on the uniqueness of human life, as exemplified by the issue of personal freedom, levels of consciousness, or moral attitudes. Moreover, these interpretations of human activity rejected the mechanical and reducible aspects of mental passivity, and adherents of such models had to search for methodological approaches outside the physical sciences. It is the wealth of this German tradition that provided much of the antecedent views of twentieth-century psychology.

CHAPTER SUMMARY

German science and culture of the seventeenth and eighteenth centuries benefited from the enlightened patronage of the Prussian King Frederick the Great. Moreover, the universities of Germany prospered and became centers of excellence in the West, especially in science. Advances in psychology by German philosophers focused primarily on mental activity. Discarding the environmental determinacy of British empiricism, Leibniz defended the active agency of the mind in molding sensory data to provide experience. The active principle of his monadology lent itself to a dynamic view of harmony between independent physical and psychic processes. The rationalism of Wolff was fully elaborated by Kant, who described pure reason as the formation of perceptions innately through time and space, and asserted an elaborate structure of the mind in terms of categories that order the environment. From these formulations, German psychology received a variety of models suggested by Herbart, Beneke, and Lotze. Further, the Kantian notions of the strivings of the will and the unconscious were explored more fully by Schopenhauer and von Hartmann. Collectively, the German tradition is diverse but united by the belief in the activity of the mind and its control of environmental influences.

BIBLIOGRAPHY

Primary Sources

KANT, I. (1965). *Critique of pure reason* (N. K. Smith, Trans.). New York: St. Martin's.

RAND, B. (1912). *The classical psychologists.* New York: Houghton Mifflin.

General References

COPLESTON, F. (1964). *A history of philosophy, Vol. 6, Modern philosophy, Part II—Kant.* Garden City, NY: Image Books.

COPLESTON, F. (1965). *A history of philosophy, Vol. 7, Modern philosophy, Part II—Schopenhauer to Nietzsche.* Garden City, NY: Image Books.

DURANT, W., & DURANT, A. (1965). *The age of Voltaire*. New York: Simon & Schuster.

DURANT, W., & DURANT, A. (1967). *Rousseau and revolution*. New York: Simon & Schuster.

Studies

BUCHNER, E. F. (1897). A study of Kant's psychology. *Psychological Review, 1* (monograph suppl. 4).

DOBSON, V., & BRUCE, D. (1972). The German university and the development of experimental psychology. *Journal of the History of the Behavioral Sciences, 8,* 204–207.

GOUAUX, C. (1972). Kant's view on the nature of empirical psychology. *Journal of the History of the Behavioral Sciences, 8,* 237–242.

LEARY, D. E. (1978). The philosophical development of the conception of psychology in Germany, 1780–1858. *Journal of the History of the Behavioral Sciences, 14,* 113–121.

9

Competing Models of Psychology

An Integration
Chapter Summary

To appreciate the emergence of psychology as an independent scientific discipline, it is critical to understand its philosophical precursors. Western European philosophers inherited from the Greeks various approaches to psychological inquiry. These were refined, passed on to Christian thinkers, and later combined or otherwise modified throughout the Renaissance. Finally, the native intellectual movements in France, Britain, and Germany combined philosophical advances with an essential faith in science to set the stage for the nineteenth century.

The philosophical developments that immediately preceded the nineteenth century have an importance that exceeds mere historical interest. They directly affect all students of psychology, because before undertaking any psychological study, one must assume a basic belief in the specific nature of life, which is a philosophical exercise. For example, if one believes that people are governed entirely by the mechanics of neural action and the "mind" is a superfluous pseudoconstruct, then the major data of psychological significance are necessarily confined to observations of overt organismic behavior. In contrast, if one holds that dynamic mental processes determine psychological activity, then observable behavior may have meaning both of itself and for its symbolic value. Each model dictates a different approach to psychological inquiry. Obviously, we are aided in our trust in a given model by our understanding of current psychological research that may either support or refute the assumptions behind a model. However, given psychology's contemporary diversity, there is no easy way to avoid making some choice from among competing models.

AN INTEGRATION

The philosophical positions surveyed in Chapters 6 through 8 take on essential significance for the foundations of modern psychology. Further organization and articulation of those diverse views may be informative as we now consider nineteenth- and twentieth-century psychology. The task of examining the relationships among the various philosophers may be facilitated by isolating certain themes prevalent in their views. Such an approach can generate dimensions along which philosophers may be evaluated relative to each other. This technique has been proposed by Watson (1967), who listed 18 dimensions, described in terms of contrasting labels, and used them as prescriptions of psychology's evolution as a discipline.

Prescriptive Dimensions of Psychology

1. *Conscious mentalism/Unconscious mentalism*: awareness of mental operations or activity versus unawareness of them
2. *Contentual objectivism/Contentual subjectivism*: psychological activity viewed as observable (e.g., behavior) versus nonobservable mental activity
3. *Determinism/Indeterminism*: psychological activity explained by antecedent events versus not explained by such events
4. *Empiricism/Rationalism*: emphasis on experience as the source of knowledge versus reason as the source of knowledge
5. *Functionalism/Structuralism*: psychological events described as activities versus such events described as contents
6. *Inductive/Deductive*: method of approach from particular to general versus general to particular
7. *Mechanism/Vitalism*: psychological events explained as physiologically based versus other than physiologically based
8. *Methodological objectivism/Methodological subjectivism*: methods repeated and verified by another scientist versus not able to be replicated by another
9. *Molecularism/Molarism*: psychological data described in terms of relatively small units versus relatively large units
10. *Monism/Dualism*: basic principle of life of one kind (e.g., materialism) versus two kinds (e.g., matter and mind)
11. *Naturalism/Supernaturalism*: psychological events explained solely in terms of the resources of the organism versus the need for some other active power (e.g., God)
12. *Nomotheticism/Idiographicism*: emphasis on finding general principles versus individual events
13. *Peripheralism/Centralism*: emphasis on psychological events occurring away from the presumed center of the organism (e.g., sensory processes) versus at the center (e.g., thinking)
14. *Purism/Utilitarianism*: emphasis on knowledge for its own sake versus emphasis on the usefulness of knowledge
15. *Quantitativism/Qualitativism*: data of psychology in measurable form versus differing in kind or type
16. *Rationalism/Irrationalism*: emphasis on intellectual or common sense determinants versus emotional or nonintellectual dominance
17. *Staticism/Developmentalism*: cross-sectional view versus changes with time
18. *Staticism/Dynamism*: nonchanging versus changing factors emphasized

(Based on Watson, R. I. [1967]. Psychology: A prescriptive science. *American Psychologist, 22*, 436–437. Copyright 1967 by the American Psychological Association. Reprinted by permission.)

These dimensions are somewhat redundant and their use may be artificial as identifying a single dimension for evaluation distorts the totality of any given model. Nevertheless, they can be of assistance in ordering the diversity of models in psychology. For example, Marx and Cronan-Hillix (1987) asked subjects to rate twentieth-century systems of psychology (associationism, structuralism, functionalism, behaviorism, Gestalt theory, and psychoanalysis) along Watson's 18 dimensions. They reported fairly reasonable discriminations among the systems, and the variability of ratings was quite low, justifying the value of this technique.

In another approach, Coan (1968) asked 232 psychologists to rate 54 figures influencing the development of psychology on 34 characteristics. Six factors, or dimensions, emerged that accounted for most of the variability in the responses:

1. Subjectivism versus Objectivism
2. Holistic versus Elementaristic
3. Transpersonal versus Personal
4. Quantitative versus Qualitative
5. Dynamic versus Static
6. Synthetic versus Analytic

The use of dimensions such as those of Watson and Coan seems to offer an effective way to discriminate some of the major figures and movements in psychology. Such an evaluative approach along several dimensions may be applied to the philosophers of the national movements surveyed in Chapters 6 through 8. In so doing, schematic arrangements of philosophical positions may be generated. Such arrangements are not quantitatively meaningful, but serve a useful purpose in organizing the philosophical positions in qualitative relationships. For example, the most pronounced differences in the national intellectual traditions relate to the concept of the mind. At one extreme, the mind is viewed as essentially active; at the opposite pole, the mind is a superfluous concept. In between is the position that the mind concept is needed, but its role is confined to a passive receptor of ideas and memories.

Figure 9–1 illustrates how the various philosophers might be arranged along this dimension. At the extreme active position on this dimension are the views of Leibniz, Wolff, Schopenhauer, and von Hartmann, a position reflecting their commitment to inner, determining mental activity. Kant and Biran are placed slightly away from the extreme because of their recognition of the stimulating role of sensation. At the opposite pole, La Mettrie's complete materialism places his views at the extreme, and the somewhat moderating positions of Condillac, Bonnet, Helvétius, and Cabanis reflect their allowance for minimal mental activity. Comte's positivism results in his position in the materialist cluster. Hobbes' initial statement of empiricism places him in the center of the dimension, along with James Mill, because of his additive association view. Locke's notion of self-reflection moves him slightly toward the active pole; Berkeley's dependency on creative associations places him even closer to the mental activity pole.

We find that views on the mind coming from separate models converge. The more dynamic empiricism of the Scottish philosophers Reid and Brown, along with

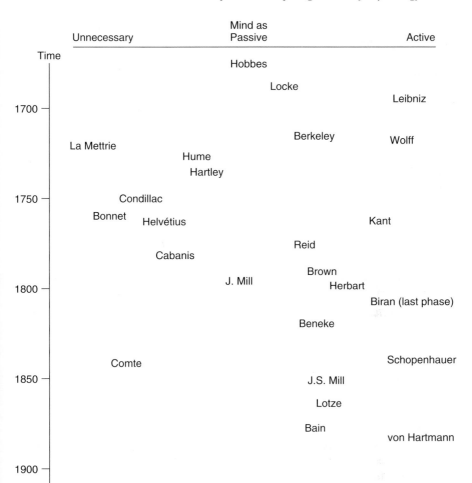

FIGURE 9–1 **Psychological views of seventeenth-, eighteenth-, and nineteenth-century French, British, and German philosophers along the dimension of mental activity.**

that of John Stuart Mill and Bain, is basically consistent with the views on mental activity tempered with a sensory basis offered by Herbart, Beneke, and Lotze. Thus, along this dimension of mental activity, the organizational scheme shows relatively clear distinctions among earlier expressions of the native intellectual movements. However, by the beginning of the nineteenth century, elements of the British and the German schools found common areas of agreement on mental activity.

Similarly, a dimension contrasting sources of knowledge as empirically or rationally based is illustrated in Figure 9–2. At the extreme pole, reflecting complete reliance on rational knowledge, are the Germans—Wolff, Schopenhauer, and von Hartmann. Biran joins them because of his emphasis on the will during his last phase.

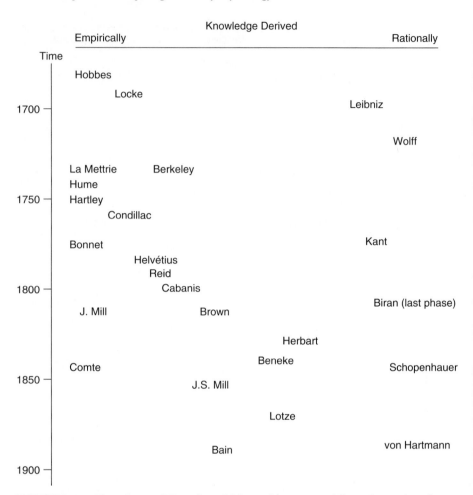

FIGURE 9–2 **The views of French, British, and German philosophers placed on a dimension showing sources of human knowledge.**

Leibniz and Kant are slightly removed from this extreme because of their acceptance of limited sensory input. At the other extreme, the empiricists relying exclusively on sensory knowledge include both British and French views. Locke's admittance of self-reflection pushes his views away from the extreme, as do the views of Berkeley, who, although mostly empirical, posited more generative activity in the mind. Condillac is also placed away from the extreme, but only because he did not carry his views to the conclusion reached by Bonnet and La Mettrie. Both the "common sense" of Reid and the moderating views of Helvétius and Cabanis recognized some nonsensory, rationalistic functions of the mind. Brown's notion of suggestion in his views on associations moves him still further away from extreme empiricism. Again, there is a nineteenth-century merger between British and German traditions. Thus the organization of this figure shows the early contrast between the isolated position of German rationalism and the united positions of British empiricism and French sensationalism. Following the Scottish influence on empiricism, however, the British view of the mental chemistry of associations approaches the modified rationalist tradition of those German figures who evolved to a position that recognized the significance of sensory physiology.

Another recurring theme concerned the opposing views of monism, which asserted a single materialistic foundation of psychology, and dualism, which retained the mind–body distinction. As arranged in Figure 9–3, both the British empiricistic and German rationalistic traditions retained the need for a mind construct, although for different purposes. In contrast, extreme French sensationalism reduced psychology to materialism. The conclusions of the additive associationistic interpretation in

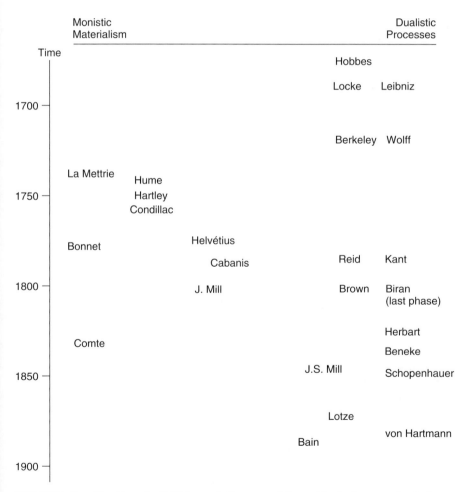

FIGURE 9–3   The French, British, and German philosophical views evaluated on a dimension of belief in monism versus dualism.

empiricism led to a denial of the need for a mind construct, firmly expressed by Hume and Hartley and, to a lesser extent, by James Mill. The moderation of sensationalism offered by Helvétius and Cabanis allowed some functions not adequately explained by sensory physiology only.

The method of acquiring knowledge may be placed on a dimension contrasting sensory associations with dynamic mental activity shown in Figure 9–4. The monadology of Leibniz, the extreme rationalism of Wolff, and the emphasis on the will of Biran, Schopenhauer, and von Hartmann all fit at the extreme mentalistic pole of this dimension. Again, Kant is removed from that extreme position because of his acceptance of the initiating role of sensory stimulation for the operations of the mind. At the other extreme pole of sensory-based associations, French materialism

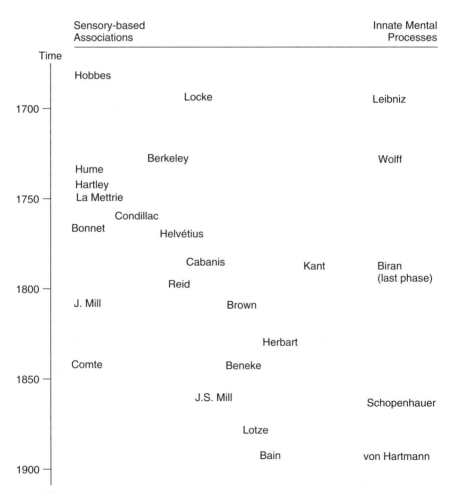

FIGURE 9–4 The views of French, British, and German philosophers on a dimension describing the formation of ideas.

and British empiricism merge, because both relied on the additive properties of associations in the formation of ideas. Locke's position admitted nonsensory associations in his notion of self-reflection, whereas Berkeley's antimaterialistic view of the mind removes him from the extreme pole. The mental chemistry of Reid, John Stuart Mill, and Bain, and Brown's notion of suggestion, allow their views to approach the recognition of sensory elements proposed by Herbart and Beneke.

These schematic organizational arrangements, and others that may easily be constructed, have value only to the extent of the qualitative, relative positioning of the major figures of the philosophical movements. As quantitative statements, they need further validation. Nevertheless, within such limitations, this technique provides insight into the flow of ideas that preceded the emergence of psychology. All four representations affirm the static position of French materialism; that is, with the moderating exceptions of Helvétius and Cabanis, the reduction of psychological processes to sensory elements left the French tradition with little room for a psychology separate from physiology. However, the clear differences between the German and British traditions allowed some eventual accommodation based on their mutual acceptance of dualism. It is important to qualify this statement, however, because the apparent agreement on single-dimensional illustrations of later German and British thought may mask very real differences. The German and British figures of the nineteenth century approached the common ground of agreement from very different positions. Mental chemistry and sensory-based mentalistic activity may serve similar functions, but they are modifications of different perspectives on psychology. Accordingly, although we may acknowledge the fluid character of British and German positions relative to the French, we must cautiously avoid interpreting areas of agreement as points of equality.

CHAPTER SUMMARY

The 25 figures selected to describe the place of psychology within the British, French, and German philosophical movements reflect important subtleties. Watson's prescriptive dimensions, Coan's factors, and the schemes diagrammed in Figures 9–1 through 9–4 are all useful in the organization of these diverse views. As psychology emerged in the nineteenth century, various forms of the new discipline reflected the underlying philosophical models developed over three centuries of post-Renaissance thought. To a great extent, the assumptions of those models are still relevant to the contemporary study of psychology.

BIBLIOGRAPHY

Coan, R. W. (1968). Dimensions of psychological theory. *American Psychologist, 23,* 715–722.

Marx, M. H., & Cronan-Hillix, W. A. (1987). *Systems and theories in psychology* (4th ed.). New York: McGraw-Hill.

Watson, R. I. (1967). Psychology: A prescriptive science. *American Psychologist, 22,* 435–443.

10

Nineteenth-Century Bases of Psychology

Advances in Physiology
    General Physiology of the Nervous System
    Physiology of the Brain
    Physiology of Sensations
Psychophysics
    Ernst Heinrich Weber
    Gustav Theodor Fechner
    Hermann von Helmholtz
Evolution
    Charles Darwin
    Herbert Spencer
    Francis Galton
Chapter Summary

This chapter considers three nineteenth-century scientific movements that had a direct impact on both the founding of psychology and its subsequent expression in the twentieth century. First, in physiology, research on nervous activity provided an empirical basis for many human functions that were previously considered functions of the mind. Second, a German development called psychophysics attempted to find the quantitative basis for the mind–body relationship, but it went beyond Herbart's psychological writings by employing an empirical approach. Finally, the writings of Charles Darwin in Britain affirmed a theory of evolution based on the empirical evidence of natural selection. All three movements directly helped to establish the formal study of psychology.

ADVANCES IN PHYSIOLOGY

Empirical research in physiology made important strides in the nineteenth century. The study of nervous activity, sensations, and brain physiology confirmed the benefits of careful systematic empirical strategies. For psychology, these benefits pointed to the possibility of elucidating the physiological basis of mental operations.

General Physiology of the Nervous System

The distinction between sensory and motor nerves was independently demonstrated by the experimental work of Charles Bell (1774–1842) and François Magendie (1783–1855). Bell was born in Edinburgh and achieved fame as an anatomist in London; Magendie was a widely esteemed professor and member of the French Academy. Their collective work, encapsulated in the Bell–Magendie Law, was based on their discovery that the posterior roots of the spinal cord contain sensory fibers only, whereas the anterior roots contain motor fibers. Thus, neural fibers were no longer considered either "hollow tubes" transmitting "spirits" of activity or all-encompassing fibers communicating both sensory and motor functions through "vibrations" arising from sensory stimulation. Rather, neural fibers were specific in function, and neural conduction seemed to occur predominantly in one direction.

The work of Bell and Magendie received systematic elaboration in the writings of Johannes Müller (1801–1858), who set the tone for nineteenth-century physiology. His exhaustive *Handbuch der Physiologie des Menschen* (*Handbook of Human Physiology*; 1833–1840) became the classic compilation of contemporary physiology. After receiving his doctorate from the University of Bonn in 1822, Müller served there as a professor until 1833, when he was called to be professor of physiology at Berlin. Many of the foremost European physiologists of the nineteenth century were his pupils, and still more were certainly influenced by the *Handbuch*. Based on the work of Bell and Magendie, Müller fully articulated the so-called doctrine of specific nerve energies. He described the specific qualities of neural transmission, formulating them under ten laws. The major implication of Müller's doctrine is the explicit statement that our awareness is not of objects, but rather of our nerves themselves. Accordingly, the nervous system serves as the intermediary between sensed objects and the mind. Müller asserted that five kinds of nerves each impose their own quality on the mind. As a physiological parallel of Kant's philosophical notion of categories of the mind, Müller's work stimulated the study of localization of functions in the brain, which is considered in the following sections.

The understanding of sensory physiology took a major step when neural conduction was discovered to be basically an electrical process, putting to final rest the traditional view of nerve fibers containing "animal spirits." We already noted in Chapter 8 that Gralath of Leiden was able to store electrical charges in a series of jars. An Italian physiologist, Luigi Galvani (1737–1798), used Leiden jars as an electrical source to do the classic experiment eliciting reflex action in the leg of a frog with a partially intact spinal cord. Galvani correctly concluded that nerves are capable of conducting electricity, although in attempting to fit his discovery into existing views, he thought he had isolated a unique substance—"animal electricity"—which is transported via a fluid from the nerve to the muscles. It was a student of Johannes Müller, Emil Du Bois–Reymond (1818–1896), who broke away from the traditional view of "animal spirits" and established the modern basis of neural transmission by describing the electrical properties of the neural impulse.

The speed of a nerve impulse was measured by another of Müller's students, Hermann von Helmholtz (1821–1894), whom we consider later in this chapter. In his

Handbuch, Müller had acknowledged, although somewhat skeptically, one of the major implications of the "animal spirits" view of neural transmission—namely, the speed of a nerve impulse is too rapid to be observed and studied empirically. However, Helmholtz devised a method of measuring temporal duration between the application of an electrical stimulus to a frog's nerve and the twitch of the muscle. In the frog he found reaction times of 0.0014 second and 0.0020 second for 60 millimeters and 50 millimeters of nerve fiber, respectively, yielding limits of 42.9 and 25.0 meters per second. Using the same method to measure reaction time in humans, Helmholtz stimulated a subject on the toe and thigh and calculated differences in reaction times. He found that the rate of transmission for sensory impulses is between 50 and 100 meters per second. Although others, such as Du Bois–Reymond, would later report more accurate calculations, Helmholtz had succeeded in empirically demonstrating neural transmission, increasing faith in the efficacy of empirical science. Moreover, because Helmholtz reliably measured the effects of stimulation through the overt behavioral responses (that is, the reaction time) of subjects, the reaction time experiment served as a prototype of empirical psychology.

Physiology of the Brain

Perhaps the most dramatic reflection of the major advances in brain physiology during the nineteenth century occurred in 1906 with the joint award of a Nobel Prize to an Italian neurologist, Camillo Golgi (1844–1926), and a Spanish anatomist, Santiago Ramón y Cajal (1852–1934). In 1873, Golgi published a paper reporting his use of silver nitrate to stain nerve cells, revealing under a microscope the structural details of nerves. Ramón y Cajal, a professor of neuroanatomy at the University of Madrid, later used this staining technique to make his discovery of the neuron, the basic unit of the nervous system. Their work, concluding a century that began with the prevailing view that the workings of the nervous system were analogous to those of the circulatory system, demonstrated the value of empirical strategies in the study of nervous activity.

At the beginning of the nineteenth century, the dominant interpretation of brain functions was contained in the doctrine of phrenology, expressed by Franz Joseph Gall (1758–1828) and his student J. G. Spurzheim (1776–1832). To a large extent, phrenology and similar movements in brain physiology were a logical consequence of the mentalistic model embodied in the "faculty" psychology championed by Wolff and Kant. Specifically, phrenology attempted to find a physiological localization of mental faculties. Gall began as a lecturer in Vienna, but in 1800 was pressured into leaving by the Austrian government and spent his remaining years in Paris. Gall and Spurzheim suggested that there are 37 mental powers corresponding to the same number of brain organs, and the development of these organs causes characteristic enlargements of the skull. Accordingly, they developed a pseudoscience that claimed extreme localization of brain functions. Phrenology held that the degree of a mental faculty or trait possessed by an individual is determined by the size of the brain area controlling that function and that this can be evaluated by measuring the overlying skull area.

Gall's phrenology forced the question of brain localization into the forefront of physiological investigation. One scientist whose work led him to reject phrenology and substitute better evidence of brain localization was Luigi Rolando (1773–1831). In 1809, Rolando published his research efforts in Italy, and in 1822 they were reviewed in French. Using pathological observations, Rolando argued that the cerebral hemispheres are the primary mediators of sleep, dementia, melancholia, and mania. Sensory functions are localized in the medulla oblongata. Although Rolando's experiments were primitive, he found that electrical stimulation elicited more violent muscle contractions as the stimulation point was moved to higher brain centers. Similarly, Pierre-Paul Broca (1824–1880), a French scientist, performed a postmortem examination of a man who had speech aphasia. Broca found damage in a specific area of the frontal cortex (now called Broca's area), which he interpreted in support of the thesis of localization of function by describing the area as the physiological basis of expressive language.

The study of brain physiology took on definitive form from both the precise methodology and the coherent interpretations offered by Pierre Flourens (1794–1867). After studying sensory physiology in Paris, Flourens secured a professorship in comparative anatomy and was elected to the French Academy for his clear and concise refutation of phrenology, summarized in *Examen de la Phrénologie (An Examination of Phrenology*; 1824).

Rather than relying on pathological clinical evidence observed during postmortem examinations, Flourens perfected the more controlled method of extirpation. Essentially, in this procedure an area of the brain of a living animal is isolated, then removed surgically or destroyed without damaging the remainder of the brain. After recuperation, the animal is observed for loss of function and recovery of function. Flourens assumed that six separate areas exist in the brain and, using his surgical skills, was able to identify the important functions of each area:

1. *Cerebral hemispheres*: willing, judging, memory, seeing, and hearing
2. *Cerebellum*: motor coordination
3. *Medulla oblongata*: mediation of sensory and motor functions
4. *Corpora quadrigemina* (containing inferior and superior colliculi): vision
5. *Spinal cord*: conduction
6. *Nerves*: excitation

Flourens noted the essential unity of the nervous system by stressing the common action of the various parts in addition to their specific functions. Although his anatomical approach reflected the localization stressed by the phrenologists, his emphasis on the common unity of the entire system represented a move away from the extremism of Gall. Moreover, his methodological innovations resulted in data that clearly anticipated the future of neurophysiological research.

The culmination of nineteenth-century advances in brain physiology, which formed the basis of modern neurophysiology and allied approaches in electrophysiology and histology, was reached by Charles S. Sherrington (1857–1952). His long career may be viewed in two parts. In the earlier phase, lasting until 1906, Sherrington carried to its conclusion the nineteenth-century work of such scientists as Müller, Bell, Magendie, and Flourens, which led to modern neurophysiology. This work established the neuroanatomical basis of reflexology—that is, the physiological causality underlying overt behavioral responses to environmental stimuli. Sherrington's research, summarized in his classic work *The Integrative Action of the Nervous System* (1906), paved the way for the behavioristic psychology of the twentieth century, initiated by the Russian physiologist Pavlov and the American psychologist J. B. Watson. During the second half of his career, crowned by his award of the Nobel Prize in 1932, Sherrington continued his prolific experiments and educated a future generation of neurophysiologists at Oxford University. Thus, he not only established the foundations of neurophysiology, but also continued to build on those foundations, which resulted in tremendous strides in the understanding of the physiological basis of psychological events.

Sherrington's early research into reflexes was dominated by his analysis of spinal-level activity and the reciprocal action of antagonistic muscles. To describe his findings, he developed a terminology that is now basic to the neurosciences. Such terms as *nociceptive, proprioceptive, fractionation, recruitment, occlusion, myotatic, neuron pool,* and *motoneuron* were coined by him to describe his observations. His neuroanatomical contributions, published in the 1890s, consisted of mapping motor pathways, identifying sensory nerves in muscles, and tracing the cutaneous distribution of the posterior spinal roots. These studies revealed the dynamics of nervous coordination, which he described as the "compounding" of reflexes constructed by the interacting of reflex arcs around common pathways. Sherrington concluded that underlying this reflex activity are the critical processes of inhibitory and excitatory actions at the regions between nerve cells; he labeled these junctions *synapses.*

Sherrington used the method of extirpation in his studies, and his 1906 work fully explored the potential for neurophysiology based on the integrative properties of the nervous system. In this work, complex reflexes were described in terms of the synaptic chain of converging pathways. It is difficult to overemphasize the impact of Sherrington's work and its significance for contemporary psychology. Sherrington's concept of excitatory and inhibitory processes forms a central place in our understanding of brain–behavior relationships and comprises the cornerstone of conditioning theory. His views have been greatly expanded, but essentially confirmed, during the intervening time, most notably by his brilliant students, especially John C. Eccles (1903–1997), who opened the possibility of entirely new interpretations in psychology.

Physiology of Sensations

A related nineteenth-century movement attempted to study sensations from the perspectives of physics and anatomy. The anatomical properties of the organ of reception (for example, the eye) were examined in terms of the physical properties of the stimulus (light), and the resulting psychological experience—sensation—was analyzed in terms of the combined physical and physiological processes.

This approach had been used by the English scientist Thomas Young (1773–1829), who is also known as one of the first translators of Egyptian hieroglyphics. Young attempted to extend Newton's work in optics, and successfully developed a theory of color vision. In papers published in 1801 and 1807, Young argued that there are three primary colors—red, yellow, and blue—that have characteristic wavelengths and differentially stimulate specific areas of the retina. This trichromatic theory was later bolstered with better evidence by the German psychophysicist Helmholtz (who shall be considered later) and is now known as the Young–Helmholtz theory of color vision. The physiologist Müller also contributed to sensory physiology by his description of direct subjective experience of neural action, not description of the environment, which we can know only indirectly. In addition, Müller attempted, less successfully, to develop a theory of hearing.

Perhaps the most interesting researcher of nineteenth-century sensory physiology was the Czech scientist Jan Purkinje (1787–1869). His varied investigations made him famous as a physiologist. He permitted subjective experience in his methodological approach relating the physical and physiological components to sensation. As a child, he was intended by his parents for the priesthood, but his own advanced study of contemporary philosophers led him to reject this direction. Instead, he supported himself by tutoring and eventually received a scientific education at Prague. From 1823 to 1850 he was a professor of physiology at the University of Breslau (now the Polish city of Wrocław), where he founded the first institute of physiology in any European university. In 1850, he returned to Prague, where he succeeded in having Czech accepted as a language of instruction along with German. During his last years he was active in the revival of Czech political life and the general uplifting of Slavic culture.

In his early research on sensory physiology Purkinje used himself as a subject because of lack of funds. In studying his visual reactions through meticulous self-observations, he was impressed that certain events, such as perceptual errors, discrepancies between stimulus intensity and perceptual strength, and uncaused sensory experiences, were not random. Rather, they were governed by the systematic relationship between the structure of the eye and the neural connection to the brain. In 1825, he published his observation, known as the Purkinje effect, that the relative luminosity of colors in faint light differs from that in full light. This difference between scotopic and photopic vision was later explained by the separate mediation of rods and cones of the retina. Purkinje also noted the inability to differentiate colors in the periphery of the retina.

Others, such as the celebrated German Romantic poet and dramatist Johann Wolfgang von Goethe, had made similar self-observations of perceptual illusions. As a scientist, Purkinje saw these phenomena in terms of their physiological value. He proposed a corresponding objective, physiological basis for all subjective sensory phenomena, and showed how these subjective phenomena may be used as an appropriate tool to explore the objective bases. Thus, Purkinje admitted a method of self-observation or self-description as a valid investigative approach. Moreover, he suggested several procedures for its utilization. Purkinje's substantial contributions, as well as his methodological approach, were recognized by later psychophysicists and incorporated into one of the first formal models of psychology.

Purkinje also worked extensively in neurophysiology, as reflected by his identification of certain cells of the cerebrum (Purkinje cells) and in the structure of the heart (Purkinje fibers). His recognition of the need for experimentation and self-observation in physiological research made a great impact on the methodological direction of psychology; he allowed for the study of subjective experience in addition to more objective physical and physiological components in the understanding of sensory processes. We now consider the movement called psychophysics, an immediate precursor of modern psychology, which owed a debt to Purkinje.

PSYCHOPHYSICS

The label *psychophysics* is given to a type of sensory physiology that emphasized subjective experience in the study of the relationship between physical stimuli and sensations. As a group, psychophysicists examined sensations from several perspectives. They considered sensations as a reflection of the mind–body problem, rather than as a situation for anatomical and physical study alone. At the same time, however, these psychophysicists were not psychologists, because they did not seek a new and comprehensive discipline. Rather, they remained inside the traditional disciplines of their training—physiology, physics, or natural philosophy. Indeed, only with the hindsight knowledge of the subsequent emergence of psychology does psychophysics take on coherence as a movement. Nevertheless, psychophysics served as a critical transition between the study of the physiological and physical components of sensation and the emergence of psychology itself. Thus, the scholars of the psychophysical movement were the immediate precursors of modern psychology.

Ernst Heinrich Weber

Ernst Heinrich Weber (1795–1878), the first person who may be categorized as a psychophysicist, was professor of anatomy and physiology at Leipzig from 1818 until his death. The University of Leipzig became the dominant institution for both the psychophysical movement and the emergence of a psychology modeled after the natural sciences. Weber's contributions included an exhaustive investigation of the sense of touch. He established a methodological orientation that seemed to demonstrate the possibility of quantifying mental or psychological operations.

His major work in psychology, *De Tactu: Annotationes Anatomicae et Physiologiae* (*On Touch: Anatomical and Physiological Notes*), was published in 1834 and contained extensive experimental work. He distinguished three manifestations of the sense of touch: temperature, pressure, and locality sensations. Temperature was dichotomized into positive and negative sensations of cold and warm, which Weber felt were analogous to the light and dark sensations of vision. In his investigations of pressure, Weber developed a methodological innovation known as the two-point threshold. Briefly, he used a compass with two points and attempted to measure cutaneous sensitivity by the smallest detectable distance between the two points that could be sensed by a subject. Weber found that this threshold of detectable difference between the two points varied with the places of stimulation, a variation he explained by postulating differential densities of nerve fibers underlying the skin's surface. This method led him to a study of weight discrimination and eventually to the formulation of "Weber's Law," named for him by his colleague Gustav Fechner, who is considered in the following discussion. Weber found that the smallest detectable difference between two weights can be expressed by the ratio of the difference between the weights relative to the absolute value of the weights, and that this ratio is independent of the absolute values of the weights. He extended his research to other senses and found general validity for the ratio of the smallest detectable difference between two stimuli. The last touch sensation, locality, was viewed by Weber to be more than a sensory dimension. Rather, he believed locality was more dependent on perception, which he interpreted as mental activity.

Weber succeeded in using a quantified approach to sensations, an approach that was adopted by his successors. However, in his interpretation of mental action on these sensations, he relied on the prevailing philosophical system of Germany— namely, Kant's views of the mind. In other words, Weber viewed perceptions as governed by mental categories of time and space, and did not speculate further.

Gustav Theodor Fechner

Gustav Theodor Fechner (1801–1887), the major proponent of psychophysics, attempted to explore more fully the relationships between sensations and perceptions. He labeled this movement through his *Elemente der Psychophysik* (*Elements of Psychophysics*; 1860), which was designed to be an exact science of the functional relations between the body and the mind. Moreover, Fechner's psychophysics was constructed as an attack on materialism. This goal is of interest because of the implied assumptions behind his psychophysics. Specifically, he did not believe that the notions of science and the mind are necessarily mutually exclusive; there is no compelling reason to reduce the mind to materialism (as in physiology) in order to study mental operations scientifically. Rather, in the tradition of German philosophy, he acknowledged the essential activity of the mind and proposed an empirical science of the mind that allows the relative increase of bodily, sensory stimulation to serve as the measure of the mental intensity of experiences.

Fechner was born in a small village in southeastern Germany, the son of the local church pastor. At age 16, he began to study medicine at the University of Leipzig and received his degree in 1822. Fechner's interest shifted to physics, and he remained in Leipzig to study, supporting himself by translating, tutoring, and giving occasional lectures. In 1831, he published a paper on the measurement of direct current, using the relationships published by Georg Ohm in 1826. Fechner was appointed professor of physics at Leipzig in 1834, and his future seemed secure. His interests began to move toward problems of sensations, and by 1840 he had published research on color vision and subjective afterimages. At about this time Fechner had what might be called today a nervous breakdown. He had overworked, exhausting himself, and he also damaged his eyes by gazing at the sun during his research on afterimages. Fechner's collapse seemed total, and he resigned his position at the university to live in seclusion for 3 years.

Fechner recovered, but his illness and confinement had a profound effect on him. He emerged from his crisis committed to the spiritual aspects of life, and renewed his religious convictions. He was convinced of the existence of both mind and matter, and believed that the materialism of science, exemplified by prevailing sensory physiology, is a distortion. For the rest of his life, he published on wide-ranging topics. In addition to psychophysics, he attempted to formulate an experimental esthetics, and even proposed a solution to the problem of determining the shape of angels.

His contributions to psychophysics are his most important works. After publishing two short papers on the subject, his *Elemente* appeared in 1860. This work was not widely recognized at first, but did attract the attention of two important leaders in German psychology—Helmholtz and Wundt. Any overview of Fechner's psychophysics must begin with the concept of *limen*, or threshold, which originated with Herbart and was developed by Weber. The notion of threshold is a quantitative expression that has two applications. The first usage refers to the minimal amount of physical energy needed in a stimulus for it to be detected by the observing subject, which was termed the *absolute threshold*. The second usage refers to the minimal amount of change in physical energy required for sensory detection.

Fechner began with the relationship expressed in Weber's Law:

$$\frac{\Delta R}{R} = K$$

Here, using the German symbols ($R = Reiz = $ stimulus), Fechner expressed Weber's findings that the ratio of the change in stimulus value (ΔR) to the absolute value of the stimulus (R) is equal to a constant. This constant is a measure of the second usage of threshold, which Fechner called the *just noticeable difference* (jnd.) in stimulus intensity detected by the subject. Fechner then related the magnitude of an experienced sensation (S) to the magnitude of the stimulus using the jnd., or k, by the following relationship:

$$S = k \log R$$

Quadrant B of Figure 10–1 shows Fechner's empirically derived function for the relationship between the magnitude of the stimulus value (ordinate axis) and the strength of the sensation (abscissa). It is possible to extend Fechner's reasoning beyond his empirical demonstration, and quadrants A, C, and D of Figure 10–1 attempt to represent some of the hypothetical relationships within Fechner's approach. For example, the relationship between stimulus intensity and sensation that could occur in quadrant A would describe the nondetection of stimuli present, which relates to the subthreshold of attention. Quadrant C depicts possible sensory experiences in the absence of physical stimulation, and quadrant D describes nonsensory experiences of nonstimuli. The former (C) might define hallucinations; the latter (D) could be a definition of dreams. Although this interpretation may be pushing Fechner's conceptualization beyond his intention, it is fascinating that his views of the relationship between sensations and stimuli include a complete framework within the active model of the mind prevalent in German philosophy. Indeed, Fechner was very much a part of the intellectual climate of his contemporary Germany.

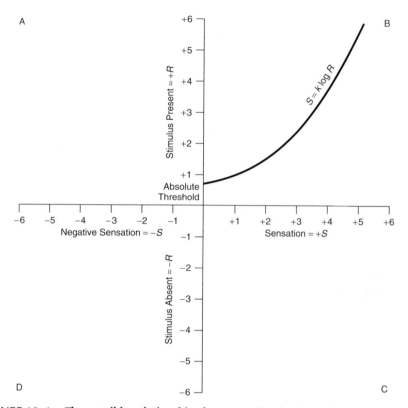

FIGURE 10–1   The possible relationships between stimulus intensity and the magnitude of sensation. The abscissa and ordinate axes are ordered in arbitrary units. Quadrant B shows the empirically derived relationship between the intensity of a stimulus and the magnitude of the sensation described by the function $S = k \log R$. In quadrant A, the nondetection (negative sensation) of a stimulus value would appear. Quadrant C describes a sensation in the absence of a stimulus. Quadrant D shows the nondetection of a nonstimulus.

Fechner proposed three fundamental methods to determine thresholds. The first was called the *method of just noticeable differences*, wherein the subject is asked to detect or respond to minimal change in stimulus values. The second was called the *method of right and wrong cases*, or the *method of constant stimuli*, in which the subject has to judge repeatedly which of two stimuli is the more intense. The third, the *method of average error*, requires subjects to adjust stimuli until they are equal. These techniques effectively estimate the major variables in psychophysical studies, and similar procedures are still employed in psychological investigations.

To judge by Fechner's stated goals of antimaterialism, he probably would not be very pleased with his own contributions to psychology, which have been largely methodological. However, without trying to begin a new disciplinary study, he established a systematic area of investigation that no longer fitted neatly into sensory physiology or physics. Others who did intend to define a new scientific discipline of psychology recognized the significance of Fechner's psychophysics and readily adopted it.

Hermann von Helmholtz

Hermann von Helmholtz (1821–1894) was one of the most distinguished scientists of the nineteenth century, achieving remarkable findings in physiology and physics as well as in psychology. We have already noted his measurement of the speed of a nerve impulse and his studies in optics which, through careful experimentation, affirmed Young's trichromatic theory of color vision. Helmholtz was born outside of Berlin, the son of a Prussian army officer, and was destined for a military career himself. From 1838 to 1842 he attended a medical institute in Berlin, where tuition was free for those who entered the army as surgeons. He served in this capacity until 1849, but during that time became involved with intellectual leaders of the University of Berlin, most notably Johannes Müller. In 1849, Helmholtz received an offer to be professor of physiology and pathology at the University of Königsberg. Later, he served at universities in Bonn, Heidelberg, and finally Berlin, where he remained for the last 23 years of his life. In addition to his celebrated scientific work, he became known as a superb lecturer, attracting students from all over Europe and America.

Helmholtz's most famous work of psychological significance was his *Handbuch der Physiologischen Optik* (*Handbook of the Physiology of Optics*), published between 1856 and 1866. In addition, he published his *Tonempfindungen* (*Tonal Sensations*; 1863), containing his resonance theory of hearing, which proposed that the transverse fibers of the basilar membrane act as a tonal analyzer and selectively respond to varying tonal frequencies. In contrast to Fechner, Helmholtz placed greater reliance on environmental or physical determinants of sensory activity. To some extent his approach to sensory physiology was closer to the British philosophical tradition than to the German—that is, Helmholtz agreed that experiences explain perceptions and not vice versa. Although not denying innate knowledge, and indeed recognizing the existence of instincts, he argued that the development of perceptions can be adequately explained from experiences.

Helmholtz postulated a perceptual doctrine of unconscious inference that may seem inconsistent with his empirical outlook. However, he proposed it as a perceptual response based on accumulated experiences. Helmholtz recognized that certain perceptual experiences are not readily accounted for by available elements in an actual stimulus presentation. For example, the age-old problem of depth perception cannot be completely explained by sensory stimulation alone. Helmholtz argued that we infer perceptual characteristics as a result of repeated experiences over time; the inferences are unconscious to the extent that we make them instantaneously, without conscious calculation or solution. He described unconscious inferences as "irresistible" because, once formed, they cannot be consciously modified. Moreover, he described this process as inductive, as the brain is unconsciously capable of generalizing an inference, once acquired, to other similar stimuli in the environment.

HERMANN VON HELMHOLTZ (1821–1894). (Courtesy, New York Public Library.)

Methodologically, Helmholtz stressed the importance of observing sensations as opposed to objects sensed—that is, the critical level of observation is the experiencing person, not characteristics of the stimulating object. Accordingly, he had high regard for the work of Purkinje, who obtained interesting data from his innovative observational techniques. Helmholtz's overview of perceptual processes clearly emphasized the dependency of sensory patterns on central functions such as unconscious inference and imagination. Thus, he advanced the study of psychophysics because he used an empiricist methodological approach to define perception as being more than sensory physiology.

This brief description of the major psychophysicists reveals quite different orientations. On the one hand, Fechner studied sensory and perceptual events from the perspective of the underlying mental activity characteristic of the German tradition. On the other, Helmholtz studied the same phenomena and developed interpretations consistent with an empirical orientation, related more to the British tradition. However, both scientists succeeded in pointing to an area of investigation not easily accommodated in physics, physiology, or natural philosophy alone, and that was the emerging subject matter of psychology.

EVOLUTION

The publication of Charles Darwin's *On the Origin of Species* (1859) represented for science a triumph of advances that began with Copernicus. The questioning of theologically based authority started with Copernicus and continued as various other thinkers chipped away at the province of theology throughout post-Renaissance development. The sciences of physics, physiology, and chemistry and early empiricist psychology provided reliable answers to the perplexing issues of life without reverting to explanations involving divine mediation. Darwin's theory of evolution, although not a complete innovation, provided convincing evidence that shocked theologians. First, if humans and apes derive from common ancestry, then the traditional privileged position of humanity, created in God's image, is unwarranted. Second, if all life evolved by the principle of natural selection, the role of God as the final cause of creation is unnecessary. For psychology, Darwin's theory of evolution represented the third movement of the nineteenth century (the other two being the sophistication of physiological research and the development of psychophysics) that not only allowed the formal study of psychology to emerge as a discipline but, indeed, made its establishment unavoidable and compelling.

Charles Darwin

We have already seen that Erasmus Darwin suggested an evolutionary concept in eighteenth-century England. His grandson Charles Darwin (1809–1882) was the fifth child of Robert Darwin, a successful physician in Shrewsbury in western England. In 1825, Charles was sent to the University of Edinburgh to study medicine, but the practicalities of clinical medicine were not to his liking. However, during his stay at Edinburgh, Darwin was exposed to the evolutionary teachings proposed by the French naturalist Jean Baptiste Pierre Lamarck (1744–1829). Briefly, Lamarck argued that changes in animals occur through the efforts of the species to adapt to its environment; that is, giraffes adapt to better food sources by developing longer necks. Thus, the acquired characteristics of environmental adaptation are passed from generation to generation. While at Edinburgh, Darwin was also introduced to the methodology of naturalistic biology and geology.

In an effort to find a new career for him, Darwin's father sent him to Cambridge University to prepare for the Anglican clergy. Darwin received his degree in 1831, and through his Cambridge contacts secured an invitation to join an expedition sponsored by the British Admiralty. He was to serve as an unpaid naturalist in a survey of the coasts of Patagonia, Tierra del Fuego, Chile, Peru, and some of the Pacific islands. After overriding objections from his family, Darwin set sail on December 27, 1831, aboard the H.M.S. *Beagle*, under the command of Robert Fitzroy.

The 5 years of the voyage of the *Beagle* had profound effects on Darwin, and he used the observations and evidence collected during those years as the basis for his subsequent writings. The places visited by the *Beagle*—from the Cape Verde Islands off the west coast of Africa to the isolated Galápagos Islands in the Pacific Ocean off South America—provided not only a living laboratory for Darwin but also a preserved history of tremendous significance. He was able to journey on land and observe primitive forms of human life and innumerable species of animal life. His work during these 5 years provided convincing botanical, geological, and anatomical evidence to support the theory of natural selection.

CHARLES DARWIN (1809–1882).
(Courtesy, New York Public Library.)

Darwin's theory of evolution differed from Lamarck's on several important points. Darwin proposed that, first, species variation over time results from chance and not by the adaptive effort of animals. Second, natural selection is an inherent struggle for species survival, a view Darwin found consistent with the economic views of the British philosopher Thomas Malthus (1766–1834). Darwin's argument for evolution by natural selection relied on several compatible lines of evidence. He postulated that the numbers of members of species are relatively constant, but also noted the overproduction of pollen, seeds, eggs, and larvae, leading him to conclude that there is a high mortality rate in nature. In addition, he gathered ample evidence to prove that all members of a given species are not identical but, rather, show variability along anatomical, behavioral, and physiological dimensions. He concluded that in the same species some members are better able to adapt than others, and they will tend to have more offspring, who will in turn reproduce. Finally, he pointed to the resemblance between parents and their offspring, concluding that subsequent generations will not only maintain but also improve their adaptability to environmental conditions. As environmental conditions vary, the criteria of natural selection differ, and over time, divergent generations gradually arise from common ancestry. For Darwin, the missing piece of his evolutionary theory was the exact nature of hereditary transmission, which he could not supply. A rather obscure Czech monk, Gregor Johann Mendel (1822–1884), completed Darwin's theory through his botanical experiments showing the inheritance of particular characteristics, and thus founded the study of genetics.

The implications of evolution by natural selection for psychology were addressed in two later works of Darwin, *The Descent of Man* (1871) and *The Expression of the Emotions in Man and Animals* (1872). Darwin argued that the essential difference between humans and the highest primates is one of gradation, not quality. He pointed to the full gamut of activities, ranging from self-preservation to cognition to emotions, shared by all animals, including humans. Moreover, Darwin included the evolution of moral attitudes in his framework, pointing out the survival value of moral development. An admirer of Darwin, George Romanes (1848–1894), pursued the comparative value of cross-species study in his work *Animal Intelligence* (1882). Romanes presented evidence to establish common dimensions of evolution between human and infrahuman activity and offered a primitive form of comparative psychology. The methodology of Romanes' work was somewhat loose and anecdotal in nature, leading to the criticism that his conclusions were anthropomorphic. Another early comparative psychologist, Lloyd Morgan (1852–1936), attempted to counteract the anthropomorphism of Romanes by urging a parsimonious convention, known as "Lloyd Morgan's Canon," in comparative studies: If a particular animal behavior could be explained by any one of several functions, the simpler, and presumably phylogenetically lower, explanation should be chosen. The validity of a comparative approach to psychological study was firmly established in Britain as a direct by-product of Darwin's teachings.

Herbert Spencer

A more comprehensive view of psychological studies with social implications derived from evolutionary theory was contained in the writings of Herbert Spencer (1820–1903). Spencer has been described as an "evolutionary associationist." His writings on the association of ideas, advocating associations as the principal mediating experiences, place him clearly in the British empirical tradition. Moreover, Spencer's writings come almost full circle to the Ionian physicists of ancient Greece, who were searching in nature for the basic substance of life that accounts for change. In a similar manner, Spencer used evolution as the basic principle and applied this interpretation of change in life to the individual in society.

Spencer stressed that the relations between feelings are based on the association principle of similarity. His evolutionary perspective led him to suggest that associations made repeatedly are passed along through heredity. Accordingly, Spencer's view of the inheritance of acquired associations led him to conclude that instincts become an inherent part of our ethnic and racial heritage. Indeed, it was Spencer, in applying evolution on the human social level, who coined the phrase "survival of the fittest," which not only distorts Darwin's theory but ultimately falls into redundancy. Spencer's evolutionary associationism, for all the empirical aura embodied in the concept of associationism from the British tradition, clearly supports a perspective more akin to the German philosophical position because of its proposal for inherited dispositions.

Francis Galton

A final figure in the nineteenth-century evolutionary context of Britain was Francis Galton (1822–1911). Both Darwin and Galton were grandsons of Erasmus Darwin, the former through Erasmus' first wife and the latter through his second wife. Galton's primary interest was human evolution and the inheritance of specific traits. Surely, his own family offered a ready example of the inheritance of intelligence. His two major works of psychological significance were *Hereditary Genius* (1869) and *Inquiries into Human Faculty and Its Development* (1883). Both works examined the inheritance of mental abilities with the goal of racial improvement. Indeed, the latter book took on an intense fervor as Galton argued the benefits of a belief in the attainment of human progress through evolutionary theory at the expense of religious approaches to human betterment.

Galton was a person of many talents, and his time spent in psychological inquiry was so significant that many psychologists point to him as the founder of experimental psychology in Britain. Perhaps because of the way in which nineteenth-century British philosophy accommodated psychological inquiry, the founding of modern psychology as a discipline separate from philosophy is looked upon as a German event. Another reason for attributing the separation of psychology from philosophy to the Germans is that psychology needed visible champions in the "hostile" climate of German philosophy. In this context, Galton's role as an early advocate of psychology tends to be overlooked. However, his methodological rigor and his emphasis on long-term adaptation in terms of species improvement had an impact on early American functional psychology. This is described in Chapter 12.

To assess human abilities, Galton developed a methodological strategy that rested on the statistical analyses of mental tests. Galton's tests were designed to measure individual achievement on mental exercises; they were brief to permit a wide sampling of subjects. Accordingly, Galton placed great emphasis on the measurement of individual differences, and attempted to study systematically varieties of mental activities ranging from motor behavior to mental imagery. Later, he devised a variety of apparatus to measure such characteristics as olfactory discrimination and space perception. He opened a laboratory where people could pay a small fee and receive a battery of tests, enabling him to sample over 9,000 people along many dimensions of intellectual and motor performance.

Galton started a movement in psychology that emphasized the value of testing and an associated statistical approach to defining population trends. This movement gained momentum during the beginning of the twentieth century, when psychologists, most notably in France and America, began to use mental testing on an increasingly wide scale. Moreover, Galton demonstrated the practicality or utility of translating Darwin's views on evolution from a biological abstraction into a mechanism for bettering society.

In summary, three nineteenth-century developments—neurophysiology, psychophysics, and evolutionary theory—formed an intellectual climate that demanded the founding of the new discipline of psychology. These movements were the immediate precursors of psychology and overlapped with the early development of modern psychology. We next turn to Germany, where the volatile intellectual climate of the nineteenth century produced the foundation of modern psychology, presented to the world in the context of two opposing models of psychological inquiry.

CHAPTER SUMMARY

Three movements in the nineteenth century formed the intellectual background from which psychology emerged as a discipline separate from the natural sciences and philosophy. In physiology, great advances were made in the understanding of the nervous system. The specific functions of nerve fibers were described by Bell and Magendie. Müller's systematic analysis of neural conduction led researchers such as Du Bois–Reymond and Helmholtz to describe the nature of the nerve impulse. As a reaction against Gall's phrenology, the localization of brain functions was studied through neuroanatomy and histology, reaching a culmination in the works of Flourens and Sherrington. The strides in physiological investigations were combined with advances in knowledge of physics to examine sensations, and Young, Helmholtz, and Müller all contributed theories of sensory processing. The methodological integrity of subjective sensory experience was justified by Purkinje.

The second nineteenth-century intellectual backdrop to modern psychology was psychophysics. This movement differed from sensory physiology by proposing that the integrity of sensory experience is not completely reducible to physics and physiology. Although Weber contributed both methodologically and substantively to psychophysics, its clearest expression is found in the work of Fechner. The quantitative analysis of sensory and perceptual experiences marked the need for a disciplinary approach not accommodated by the natural sciences. This view received strong support from the experiments of Helmholtz, especially in his doctrine of unconscious inference in perception—clearly a mental construct.

The final movement centered around Darwin's theory of evolution by natural selection. Darwin's writings completed the Copernican revolution in science and established the primacy of scientific empiricism in our quest for knowledge. Spencer applied Darwin's writings to evolutionary associationism, and Galton, also influenced by Darwin, made an intensive examination of individual differences through mental testing. All three movements aptly demonstrate the supreme position of empirical science in the nineteenth century. The scientific ideal represented the appropriate framework for the pursuit of psychological inquiry.

BIBLIOGRAPHY

Primary Sources

DARWIN, C. G. (1868, 1875). *The expression of the emotions in man and animals*. London: Murray.

DARWIN, C. G. (1871). *The descent of man, and selection in relation to sex*. New York: Appleton.

DARWIN, C. G. (1964). *On the origin of species by means of natural selection, or The preservation of favoured races in the struggle for life* (1859). Cambridge: Harvard University Press.

DENNIS, W. (Ed.). (1948). *Readings in the history of psychology*. New York: Appleton-Century-Crofts.

FECHNER, G. (1966). *Elements of psychophysics* (H. Adler, Trans.). New York: Holt, Rinehart & Winston.

GALTON, F. (1869). *Hereditary genius*. London: Macmillan.

RAND, B. (1912). *The classical psychologists*. New York: Houghton Mifflin.

ROMANES, G. J. (1883). *Animal intelligence*. London: Kegan Paul.

SHERRINGTON, C. S. (1906). *The integrative action of the nervous system*. New Haven: Yale University Press.

Studies

BOAKES, R. A. (1984). *From Darwin to behaviourism*. London: Cambridge University Press.

BUSS, A. R. (1976). Galton and the birth of differential psychology and eugenics: Social and political forces. *Journal of the History of the Behavioral Sciences, 12,* 47–58.

BUSS, A. R. (1976). Galton and sex differences: An historical note. *Journal of the History of the Behavioral Sciences, 12,* 283–285.

DE BEER, G. (1964). Mendel, Darwin and Fechner. *Notes and Records of the Royal Society, 19,* 192–226.

DENNY-BROWN, D. (1957). The Sherrington school of physiology. *Journal of Neurophysiology, 20,* 543–548.

DEWSBURY, D. A. (1979). Retrospective review: An introduction to the comparative psychology of C. Lloyd Morgan. *Contemporary Psychology, 24,* 677–680.

ERICKSON, R. P. (1984). On the neural bases of behavior. *American Scientists, 72,* 233–241.

FACTOR, R. A., & TURNER, S. P. (1982). Weber's influence in Weimar Germany. *Journal of the History of the Behavioral Sciences, 18,* 147–156.

FULTON, J. F. (1952). Sir Charles Scott Sherrington, O. M. *Journal of Neurophysiology, 15,* 167–190.

FROGGATI, P., & NEVIN, N. C. (1971). Galton's law of ancestral heredity: Its influence on the early development of human genetics. *History of Science, 10,* 1–27.

GILLISPIE, C. C. (1959). Lamarck and Darwin in the history of science. In B. Glaco, O. Temkin, and W. L. Straus (Eds.), *Forerunners of Darwin, 1745–1859*. Baltimore: Johns Hopkins University Press, 265–291.

GILMAN, S. L. (1979). Darwin sees the insane. *Journal of the History of the Behavioral Sciences, 15,* 253–262.

GREENBLATT, S. H. (1984). The multiple roles of Broca's discovery in the development of the modern neurosciences. *Brain and Cognition, 3,* 249–258.

GREENE, J. C. (1959). *The death of Adam. Evolution and its impact on Western thought*. Ames: University of Iowa Press.

GRUBER, H. E. (1983). History and creative work: From the most ordinary to the most exalted. *Journal of the History of the Behavioral Sciences, 19,* 4–14.

HURVICH, L. M., & JAMESON, D. (1979). Helmholtz's vision: Looking backward. *Contemporary Psychology, 24,* 901–904.

KRUTA, V. (1969). *J. E. Purkyne (1787–1869) Physiologist: A short account of his contributions to the progress of physiology with a bibliography of his works*. Prague: Czechoslovak Academy of Sciences.

MACKENZIE, B. (1976). Darwinism and positivism as methodological influences on the development of psychology. *Journal of the History of the Behavioral Sciences, 12,* 330–337.

MACLEOD, R. B. (1970). Newtonian and Darwinian conceptions of man, and some alternatives. *Journal of the History of the Behavioral Sciences, 6,* 207–218.

MOIRE, J. R. (1979). *The post-Darwinian controversies: A study of the Protestant struggle to come to terms with Darwin in Great Britain and America, 1870–1900.* Cambridge: Cambridge University Press.

PASTORE, N. (1973). Helmholtz's "popular lecture on vision." *Journal of the History of the Behavioral Sciences, 9,* 190–202.

RICHARDS, R. J. (1977). Lloyd Morgan's theory of instinct: From Darwinism to neo-Darwinism. *Journal of the History of the Behavioral Sciences, 13,* 12–32.

SOHN, D. (1976). Two concepts of adaptation: Darwin's and psychology's. *Journal of the History of the Behavioral Sciences, 12,* 367–375.

STROMBERG, W. J. (1989). Helmholtz and Zoellner: Nineteenth-century empiricism, spiritism, and the theory of space perception. *Journal of the History of the Behavioral Sciences, 25,* 371–383.

TURNER, R. S. (1977). Hermann von Helmholtz and the empiricist vision. *Journal of the History of the Behavioral Sciences, 13,* 48–58.

WARREN, R. M., & WARREN, R. P. (1968). *Helmholtz on perception: Its physiology and development.* New York: Wiley.

WASSERMAN, G. S. (1978). *Color vision: An historical introduction.* New York: Wiley.

WOODWARD, W. R. (1972). Fechner's panpsychism: A scientific solution to the mind-body problem. *Journal of the History of the Behavioral Sciences, 8,* 367–386.

ZUPAN, M. L. (1976). The conceptual development of quantification in experimental psychology. *Journal of the History of the Behavioral Sciences, 12,* 145–158.

The Founding of Modern Psychology

Psychology as a Natural Science
    Structural, or Content Psychology
        Wilhelm Wundt
        Edward Bradford Titchener
        Structuralism
    Other Expressions of the Natural Science Model
        Ewald Hering
        Georg Elias Müller
        Hermann Ebbinghaus
        Ernst Mach and Richard Avenarius
Psychology as a Human Science
    Act Psychology
        Franz Brentano
        Karl Stumpf
        Christian von Ehrenfels
    Alternative Scientific Approaches
        Wilhelm Dilthey
        Henri Bergson
    The Würzburg School
Chapter Summary

By the last quarter of the nineteenth century, European science had achieved widely recognized prestige as the optimal form of intellectual activity. The inductive method, successfully employed by Copernicus and subsequently nurtured through three centuries of philosophical endeavors, acquired a sense of reliability that evoked a faith in the scientific approach throughout the nineteenth century. Indeed, the dramatic advances in biology, chemistry, and physics, with their demonstrated implications for the betterment of society, provided ready justification for trust in scientific methods.

As psychology began to break away from the provinces of religion and speculative philosophy, the prevailing dominance of nineteenth-century scientific inquiry had profound importance. Specifically, if psychology was to embody a collection of knowledge derived from authoritative sources other than religious belief, science offered the most promising direction of pursuit. The findings of British natural philosophers and German psychophysicists had already demonstrated the viability of scientific methodology for certain psychological issues. Thus, by the end of the nineteenth century, the *Zeitgeist* ("spirit of the times") in the intellectual climate of Europe showed a readiness to accept the formalized study of psychology. The immediate problem was the specific scientific model for psychology to emulate. As had occurred since the time of early Greek philosophy, several models of scientific inquiry, derived from varying underlying assumptions about the nature of people and their concomitant psychological processes, competed to express the definition and form of modern psychology.

This chapter concentrates on the emergence of psychology in Germany. In a sense, it is curious that psychology first emerged as a formal discipline in Germany, as the intellectual climate of Britain was actually more amenable to its acceptance. As we have seen, the relatively homogeneous model of empiricism was widely accepted in Britain, and natural philosophers there investigated mental associations as the mediational agent of cognitive and emotional processes. Moreover, Darwin's evolutionary theory by natural selection had an impact that resulted in further acceptance of the possibility for psychology's studying the full range of animal activity. However, it was precisely this tolerant atmosphere that prevented the emergence of psychology from natural philosophy; there simply was no need for a separate discipline. In other words, the philosophical traditions of Britain were quite open to the study of psychological issues and ably accommodated new questions and methodological approaches. In contrast, the intellectual climate in Germany was varied; German philosophy reflected this diversity and was uncommitted to a single model of psychological inquiry. As seen earlier, the predominant underlying commonality of German philosophical views on psychology was the essential activity of the mind. Mental activity was expressed in the logical and metaphysical systems of rationalism proposed by Kant and Wolff, in the unconsciously motivated strivings inherent in the views of Schopenhauer and von Hartmann, and in the mechanical model of Herbart. Such diversity precluded the ready acceptance of scientific psychology within the province of German philosophy. Indeed, the preliminary attempt to study sensory and perceptual processes scientifically in psychophysics came about through the work of physiologists and physicists, not philosophers.

Accordingly, it was Germany that provided the setting for the emergence of psychology. The diverse intellectual climate of Germany was perhaps the most exciting in Europe. The nation had been recently united under the Hohenzollern dynasty, and the strong tradition of Prussian support for universities was extended throughout Germany. In all fields of science, philosophy, and literature, the German intelligentsia achieved international recognition. In psychology two separate models emerged. Although neither was successful in establishing the definitive framework of the new science, both gave psychology its push into science and served as anchor points for the discipline's progress.

PSYCHOLOGY AS A NATURAL SCIENCE

The label *natural science* as applied to psychology is meant to describe a framework of psychology that emulates the methodology and analytic goals common to biology, chemistry, and physics. It implies that psychology should be studied by defining psychological events in terms of variables and submitting such variables to the analytic scrutiny of the experimental method. Accordingly, this model of psychology was a radical departure from the German philosophical establishment of metaphysical psychology. This natural science conceptualization, in its attempt to set psychology off from the prevailing philosophical systems of Germany, limited both the scope and methodology of psychology to a level that confined its growth and led to its eventual rejection.

Structural, or Content Psychology

Psychology as defined in this system is the analytic study of the generalized adult human mind through the method of introspection. This approach originated with Wilhelm Wundt and was championed in the United States by his student Edward Bradford Titchener. Their conclusions about psychology were highly compatible, and our overview will consist of a synopsis of their collective writings. Because psychology was to study the contents of the mind, this system is sometimes called *content psychology*. In addition, Titchener, writing in 1898, emphasized mental structures and named this system *structural psychology*. The system, whatever the name given it, had as its goal the analysis of the human mind through the careful application of the experimental method of introspection carried out by trained scientists. By analogy, this system aimed to develop the "chemistry of consciousness."

In the following description of structural psychology, it is important to put into proper perspective the relative contributions of Wundt and Titchener. It should be emphasized that structural psychology was Wundt's invention. Titchener was only one of his many students, and probably a minor student at that, in comparison to some of the major figures in European and American psychology who trained with Wundt. But it was Titchener who strove to bring his own inflexible sense of Wundt's psychology to the American audience. Unlike other followers of Wundt in America, the British-born Titchener remained impervious to the influences that caused schools of psychological thought to develop uniquely American styles. Perhaps one reason for Titchener's unique place in the history of American psychology was that most of Wundt's other students in America were native Americans, or at least quite adapted to American life. Nevertheless, structural psychology for the most part reached American scholars through Titchener's teaching and writing, and this may have placed Titchener in an artificially preeminent position. We should give Wundt his rightful credit as the founder, but we must recognize Titchener's role as the prime spokesperson for structural psychology in the United States.

Wilhelm Wundt.   Wilhelm Wundt (1832–1920) was born in the southwestern German province of Baden, the son of a Lutheran pastor. During his childhood and adolescence, he was allowed only a strict regimen of learning, with little time for

WILHELM WUNDT (1832–1920).
(Courtesy, The Granger Collection.)

play or idleness. This upbringing produced a rather dour person, totally committed to intellectual endeavors of a systematic type, and a prolific nature. Wundt eventually studied at the University of Heidelberg, intending to become a physiologist, but turned to medicine because of the practicalities of earning his own support. After 4 years of study, he recognized that he was definitely not interested in being a physician. In 1856, he went to Berlin to study in Johannes Müller's institute of physiology, where he also worked with Du Bois–Reymond. After this brief but stimulating experience, Wundt returned to Heidelberg, finished his doctorate in medicine, and took a minor teaching post in physiology. In 1858, Helmholtz came to Heidelberg, and for the next 13 years he and Wundt worked in the same physiological laboratory. When Helmholtz left Heidelberg for Berlin in 1871, Wundt was passed over as his successor. Wundt left Heidelberg in 1874 for a year as professor of inductive philosophy at Zurich, and then in 1875 accepted a professorship of philosophy at Leipzig, where he remained for the rest of his long career.

Wundt was attracted to psychological study after having acquired a firm basis in physiology. As a result, he transferred his appreciation for science—and especially for the experimental method—to his developing interests. In 1873 and 1874 he published in two parts his systematic call for a new discipline of psychology, *Grundzüge der Physiologischen Psychologie* (*Principles of Physiological Psychology*). This work, which went through six editions in Wundt's lifetime, attempted to establish the paradigm, or framework, of psychology as an experimental science of the mind, to be studied through its processes. In addition, Wundt envisioned a type of ethnic psychology in which the scientific study of human nature could reveal higher mental processes through an anthropological approach, relating to areas of child psychology and animal psychology.

Wundt started a laboratory at Leipzig in 1879, which may be viewed as the first laboratory dedicated exclusively to psychological research. In 1881, he founded *Philosophische Studien* (*Philosophical Studies*), a journal to report the experimental studies of his laboratory. The list of Wundt's students includes the names of many of the founders of psychological systems in Germany, throughout Europe, and in America. The vast majority of his students deviated from Wundt's conception of psychology to varying extents.

Edward Bradford Titchener. Edward Bradford Titchener (1867–1927) was one of Wundt's students who carried away from his studies a fixed view of Wundt's system, which he imported to America. Although Titchener studied with Wundt for only 2 years, that brief period made an indelible impression on him, and he adhered strictly to his interpretation of Wundt's system during his career at Cornell University in New York.

Titchener was born in southern England to a family of old lineage but little money. He entered Oxford University in 1885 on a scholarship to study philosophy, and became interested in Wundt's writings, translating the third edition of the *Principles of Physiological Psychology*. However, the new psychology of Wundt was not enthusiastically received at Oxford, so Titchener resolved to go to Leipzig and work directly under Wundt. There he took his doctorate after completing a dissertation in 1892 on binocular effects of monocular stimulation. After unsuccessfully searching for a position in England, Titchener accepted a professorship at Cornell, which had opened up when Frank Angell, another American student of Wundt, went to the newly founded Stanford University. For 35 years Titchener presided over psychology at Cornell, where he was a formidable institution unto himself, advocating a rigid version of structural psychology and tolerating no dissent.

Titchener's views are appropriately considered here with the founding of psychology in Germany because he never joined the mainstream of early American psychology, which is considered in the next chapter. Titchener's major works include *Outline of Psychology* (1896), *A Primer of Psychology* (1898), *Experimental Psychology* (1901–1905), *Psychology of Feeling and Attention* (1908), *Experimental Psychology of the Thought Processes* (1909), and *A Text-Book of Psychology* (1909–1910). These works are scholarly and systematic, almost encyclopedic in their scope. However, because Titchener would not admit applied aspects of psychology, he removed himself from the major theme of American psychology, which was the study of such topics as child psychology, abnormal psychology, and animal psychology. Titchener was solely concerned with the experimental analysis of the normal adult human mind, not with individual differences. In addition, he quarreled often with his American colleagues and founded his own organization to rival the fledgling American Psychological Association because of a dispute with members of the latter group. Although Titchener supervised a large number of students in early twentieth-century American psychology, his system (and therefore Wundt's) died with him in 1927.

Structuralism. The structural psychology of Wundt and Titchener had a threefold aim: to describe the components of consciousness in terms of basic elements, to describe the combinations of basic elements, and to explain the connections of the elements of consciousness to the nervous system. Consciousness was defined as immediate experience—that is, experience as it is being experienced. Mediate experience, in contrast, is flavored by contents already in the mind, such as previous associations and the emotional and motivational states of a person. Thus, immediate experience was presumed to be unprejudiced by mediated experience. Structural psychology attempted to defend the integrity of psychology by contrasting it with physics: Physics studies the physical, or material world, without reference to the person, through observational methods of carefully controlled inspection. Psychology studies the world, with reference to the experiencing person, through the observational method of controlled introspections of the contents of consciousness. The proper subject of structural psychology is the process of consciousness, free of associations. As such, Wundt and Titchener argued, psychology must be kept free of the forces of metaphysics, common sense, and utilitarian or applied interests, which would destroy its integrity.

The experimental method proposed to secure appropriate analysis of mental contents was introspection. This technique of self-report is the ageless approach to describing self-experience. We have seen earlier that Augustine employed it with remarkable clarity in his *Confessions*. An introspective approach in nineteenth-century German science was endorsed through the elegant work of Purkinje, described in the previous chapter. However, introspection as defined by Wundt and Titchener was far more rigorous and controlled. Moreover, the credibility of structural psychology rested on the proper use of introspection—that is, the emphasis on immediate experience (rather than mediate experience) as the subject matter of psychology dictated a reliance on the method of assessing such pure experiences. Accordingly, introspection was considered valid only if done by exceptionally well-trained scientists, not naive observers. Introspection depends on the nature of consciousness observed, the purpose of the experiment, and the instructions given by the experimenters. The most common error made by untrained introspectionists was labeled the "stimulus error"—describing the object observed rather than the conscious content. Stimulus errors, according to Titchener, result not in psychological data but in physical descriptions. Not surprisingly, making introspection the only acceptable method of psychological investigation was seriously questioned because no facts or principles could be derived from the introspective method. Unfortunately, there was no group agreement among trained introspectionists on the properties of sensory experiences.

Most of the major findings of this system were seriously challenged. In terms of higher mental processes, Titchener called "thought" a mental element that is probably an unanalyzed complex of kinesthetic sensations and images. Moreover, he perceived what we call the "will" as an element composed of a complex of images that form ideas in advance of action. As a result, thought and will are linked through mental images. According to this analysis, thought must be accompanied by images. This imperative gave rise to the "imageless thought controversy," in which others, most notably Külpe, Binet, and Woodworth (who are discussed later), argued the possibility of thought processes without discrete mental images. Such an interpretation was unacceptable to Titchener because it contradicted his analytic view of thought, which required description of elements consisting of images. Instead, it substituted a more holistic or phenomenal view of thought processes, unanalyzed into constituent elements.

In the 1890s Wundt developed a three-dimensional theory of feeling. Essentially, Wundt thought that feelings vary along three dimensions. Titchener agreed with only one:

Wundt	*Titchener*
Pleasant–unpleasant	Yes
Strain–relaxation	No
Excitement–calm	No

Titchener's acceptance of only the first dimension led him to relegate emotions to organic visceral reactions. Wundt's wider interpretation led him beyond the unconscious inference of Helmholtz to posit apperception as the creative process of the components making up total perception. That is, apperception is the focus of attention within the field of consciousness at a given point in time. As such, apperception was a cognitive activity that recognized the logical bond between mental contents; feelings were viewed as the product of apperception of sensory contents. Thus, Wundt's theory of feeling as a reflection of mental apperception approached a phenomenologic interpretation of higher mental processing. Titchener did not accept this more holistic direction in Wundt's thought but instead adhered to a more reductionistic view. Titchener did propose a theory of meaning suggesting that the context in which a sensation occurs in consciousness determines its meaning. Accordingly, a simple sensation has no meaning by itself, but acquires meaning by association with other sensations or images. Thus, Titchener described the mind in terms of formal elements with attributes of their own, connected and combined by the mechanism of associations. Wundt believed that associative combinations occur by fusion, as in tonal melodies; by assimilation, as in the integrating contrast and similarity of optical illusions; or by complication, defined as the bond formed by sensations of several modalities.

Structural psychology, in its attempt to adhere strictly to a natural science model, tended to overlook psychological processes and activities that did not easily fit into its methodological framework. In addition, the overreliance on the questionable, strict methodology of introspection led structural psychology into a dead end. In a sense, structuralism was caught between the empiricism of the British tradition and the nativism of the German tradition. In other words, Wundt and Titchener articulated a view of the mind as determined by the elements of sensation; at the same time they recognized mental activity and attempted to deal with activity through such constructs as apperception. Besides the inadequacies of introspection, structuralism failed to accommodate conflicting philosophical assumptions about the nature of the mind. Accordingly, the contributions of structural psychology are somewhat mixed. First and most important, this system gave psychology a push into science. Despite all its shortcomings, Wundt did proclaim a formal discipline of psychology based upon scientific formulations, and psychology was recognized as a science. Second, structural psychology put introspection as a method to the test, which it rather dismally failed. Finally, structuralism served as an anchor of opposition to subsequent developments within psychology. Boring (1950), who was a student of

Titchener, conceded that the Wundtian influence was most apparent as a negative force, motivating scientists to discredit both the substance and the methodology of this system. Perhaps this reaction to structural psychology in America was the product of a misunderstanding of Wundt's writings or of a reliance on Titchener's version of Wundt. Nevertheless, by 1930, just three years after Titchener's death, structural psychology had ceased to be a viable force in psychology.

Other Expressions of the Natural Science Model

Structural psychology holds a unique place in the German development of the natural science model for psychology. Specifically, the writings of Wundt and Titchener constitute a systematic attempt to start a coherent science encompassing all that they considered to be psychological. As such, structural psychology was a system of psychology. However, other scientists in Germany, contemporary with Wundt, responded to the same *Zeitgeist* and wrote on psychology. They wrote as individuals, though, not as system builders, and within the limits of a natural science approach to psychology, they all rejected the extremism of Wundt and Titchener, in terms of both the substance and the methodology of structuralism. These scientists were experimentalist in the sense that they were guided in their progress not by the framework of a preconceived system, as were Wundt and Titchener, but rather by the results and implications of their laboratory studies.

Ewald Hering. Ewald Hering (1834–1918), who succeeded Purkinje as professor of physiology at Prague in 1870, did extensive work in vision and touch. He proposed a three–substance, six-color theory of color vision, involving the dichotomous contrast of red–green, yellow–blue, and white–black receptors, which produce substances of differential retinal sensitivity. In addition, he opposed the empirical views of Helmholtz on visual space perception and cited evidence to support a more nativistic interpretation consistent with Kant's philosophy. Both at Prague and, after 1895, at Leipzig, Hering refrained from grand theorizing or systematic development of a complete psychology.

Georg Elias Müller. A similar approach may be seen in the long career of Georg Elias Müller (1850–1934). Born near Leipzig and educated in history, his lifelong interest, Müller's service in the Franco–Prussian War (1870–1871) convinced him of the narrow perspective of traditional historical study, and he returned to Leipzig to study the natural sciences. In 1872, he went to Göttingen to study under Lotze, whose antimechanical, metaphysical views of psychology exerted a consistent influence on Müller. Müller succeeded Lotze as professor of philosophy at Göttingen when Lotze went to Berlin in 1881. Müller's 40 years of research at Göttingen were marked by consistent experimentation, mostly in psychophysics, and many students from both Europe and America came to study in his laboratory. He became a leader in German psychology because of his commitment to data gathering at the expense of a determining overview, and he left not a system but rather an accumulation of experimental results. Such a true experimental attitude led to some unexpected directions; for example, Müller's student David

Katz published a paper in 1909 that attempted to describe color perception without the prevailing analytical sensory approach and anticipated several major tenets of Gestalt psychology.

Hermann Ebbinghaus. Another formidable figure of German psychology known for his individual experimentation rather than for system building was Hermann Ebbinghaus (1850–1909). Educated at the University of Bonn, Ebbinghaus wrote his doctoral dissertation on von Hartmann's views of the unconscious. After receiving his degree, Ebbinghaus spent 7 years in England and France, tutoring to support himself. While in Paris he came across a copy of Fechner's *Elemente der Psychophysik*, which became an intellectual stimulant for him. Essentially, he started to study memory in the same manner as Fechner had studied sensations. Having become acquainted with the classic associationistic philosophers of Britain, Ebbinghaus viewed the law of repetition as the key to the quantification of memory. He used the nonsense syllable as a means to measure the formation of associations. Basically, he presented the subject with a series of three-letter syllables, typically a vowel separating two consonants. He deliberately chose ones without meaning that might confound memorization (for example, MEV, LUS, PAQ). He used this method on himself to measure time to mastery and retention savings over time. His work *Ueber das Gedächtnis* (translated into English as *Memory*), published in 1885, described his methodology and findings, including the famous retention curve showing forgetting over time from initial acquisition. This work was widely acclaimed, not only because of its range of topics, completeness of data, and clarity of writing, but also because Ebbinghaus documented a full experimental attack on higher mental processes that was precluded by Wundt's system.

Ebbinghaus held professorships at Berlin, Wrocław (Breslau), and Halle, and attracted many students. He started a psychological journal with a national audience, *Zeitschrift für Psychologie und Physiologie der Sinnesorgane* (*New Writing for the Psychology and Physiology of Sense Organs*; 1890) that surpassed the provincial character of Wundt's journal. From the study of memory he moved on to study color vision, and also developed early versions of intelligence tests, anticipating by several years the work of the French psychologist Binet.

His reputation was enhanced with publication of his text of general psychology, *Grundzüge der Psychologie* (*Foundations of Psychology*; 1897–1902), which became the standard text in German universities, much as William James's *Principles of Psychology* (1890) was in American universities. Although noted for his work on memory, Ebbinghaus should be best remembered as an exponent of careful experimentation in psychology. Like the others whose work is described in this section, Ebbinghaus did not leave a "school" but rather contributed to the intellectual atmosphere that established psychology as a scientific enterprise.

Ernst Mach and Richard Avenarius.   A final movement within the German natural science model for psychology contributed a philosophical justification for the scientific bases of psychology. The major figures were Ernst Mach (1838–1916) and Richard Avenarius (1843–1896). Their writings have been labeled radical empiricism or, more simply, Machian positivism. We have already seen positivism in Comte's attempt to explain intellectual progress through a reliance on observable events, undercutting metaphysical explanations that go beyond such direct observations, and we will again discuss positivism when behaviorism is presented. Behaviorism includes a modern expression of "logical positivism," a scientific attitude that defines scientific events in terms of the operations that produce them. The positivism of Mach and Avenarius was consistent with the skepticism of Hume, which held that causality is only the observed covariation of events and is valid only to that extent. Moreover, all events are reducible to the psychological and physical components of observations, defined as the process of sensation. Thus sensations and sensory data form the critical essence of science, so that the introspection of the scientist forms the basis of all methodology.

Mach, who was a professor of physics in Prague during his most productive years, published his most important work for psychology in 1886, *Analyse der Empfindungen* (*Analysis of Sensations*). In asserting that sensations are the data of all science, Mach pushed psychology further from metaphysics and established a standard of scientific criteria for psychology to emulate. According to Mach, the only certain reality is our own experience. His analysis of space and time viewed these processes as sensory and not the mental categories suggested by Kant. Avenarius, a professor of philosophy at Zurich, essentially agreed with Mach's conclusions, although his writing did not have the clarity and compelling justification of Mach's.

Both Mach and Avenarius presented complex views on science in general and psychology in particular. Their importance lies in their positive views on the sensory basis of science, which gave psychology a position alongside physics, adding greatly to its integrity as an independent discipline. Mach moved to Vienna in 1895 and influenced a new generation of philosophers of science. They in turn reformulated positivism at a time when behaviorism was being proposed as the revised definition of psychology, a view we consider later.

To summarize briefly, psychology emerged as a recognized discipline within a natural science model. The most coherent and systematic expression of psychology was by Wundt, although others contributed to the credibility of psychology as a natural science. Whereas this "founding" was somewhat of a false beginning, these German psychologists did succeed in establishing a scientific ideal for psychology. We now turn to a competing model of psychology, which, while not as well known as the natural science model, provided an alternative for a broad-based science of psychology.

PSYCHOLOGY AS A HUMAN SCIENCE

At the time of psychology's modern founding in the 1870s, science was largely equated with the study of physical events in the natural sciences of biology, chemistry, and physics. Structural psychology emerged from the joining of sensory physiology and the British empirical assumptions about the mind, methodologically combined by the psychophysicists and finally expressed systematically by Wundt. However, the strict definition of the scientific method in terms of experimental study confined the scope of psychology.

As it turned out, certain contemporaries of Wundt, including those who immediately and critically reacted to his views, did not agree with the restrictions that Wundt and Titchener imposed on psychology. This group of psychologists did not present a common alternative or a coherent rival school to structural psychology. Rather, they differed as individuals with both the scope and methodology of Wundt's formulations. However, they agreed that psychology should not be bound to a single method of science, and that science itself encompasses more than just the experimental method. Moreover, their conclusions on psychology fit the German philosophical assumption of mental activity better than Wundt's psychology, and subsequently more systematic expressions of psychology were derived from their teachings.

Act Psychology

Although varying interpretations of act psychology may be found in both historical and contemporary expressions of psychology, the defining character of this movement centers around the inseparable interaction of the individual and the environment. As such, psychological events are often defined as *phenomena*; that is, events that cannot be reduced to component elements without losing their identity. The form of act psychology we now examine was a contrast to the elementarism of structural psychology. However, contemporary forms of act psychology currently exist in contrast to the atomistic reductionism of stimulus-response behaviorism.

Franz Brentano.   The person who came closest to Wundt, both in influence and in temporal contiguity in late nineteenth-century Germany, was Franz Brentano (1838–1917). Whereas Wundt's long career was characterized by systematic scholarship in a stable intellectual environment, Brentano's career was marked by controversy and upheaval. However, his relatively few works were significant and represented a viable alternative to Wundt's dominating conception of psychology. Indeed, Titchener, writing in 1925, named Brentano's act psychology as one of the major threats to psychology's integrity, inadvertently giving Brentano's views enhanced stature.

Brentano, the grandson of an Italian merchant who immigrated to Germany, was born in Marienberg near the Rhine. The family was known for literary achievements. Brentano's aunt and uncle were writers in the German romantic tradition, and his brother Lujo won the Nobel Prize in 1927 for his work in intellectual history. At age 17, Franz began studying for the Catholic priesthood in Germany.

He joined the same order of priests, the Dominicans, as did the great Scholastic Saint Thomas Aquinas, and his study of Scholasticism may have influenced his choice of a dissertation topic—*On the Manifold Meaning of Being According to Aristotle*—for which he was awarded a doctorate in philosophy from the University of Tübingen in 1862. During the next 2 years he finished his studies in

FRANZ BRENTANO (1838–1917). (Courtesy, The Granger Collection.)

theology and was ordained a priest at Würzburg. There he continued his work in philosophy, and in 1866 he became a docent at Würzburg in recognition of his study on the psychology of Aristotle, a work acclaimed as the most scholarly presented to the philosophy faculty since the turn of the nineteenth century. While at Würzburg, Brentano became known as an effective teacher because of the clarity of his presentations in philosophy and mathematics as well as because of his love of research. However, Brentano's revision of scholastic logic, his appreciation of British empiricism, and his favorable study of Comte published in 1869 earned him the sharp criticism of the Catholic establishment. Nevertheless, on the strong recommendation of Lotze and over the objections of the Austrian emperor and the archbishop of Vienna, Brentano was appointed professor of philosophy at Vienna in 1874. There he remained as a popular but controversial teacher until 1894, and enjoyed his most productive period. His many students included Karl Stumpf; Edmund Husserl, the founder of modern phenomenology; and Sigmund Freud, who took his only nonmedical courses from Brentano at the University of Vienna between 1874 and 1876.

The controversy that surrounded Brentano from 1870 onward revolved around his criticism of the Church. During this period the Church felt threatened by the forces of intellectual liberalism and political nationalism in Italy. Viewing these developments from Würzburg and Vienna, Brentano became increasingly disturbed by the anti-intellectualism of the Church. Finally, in April 1873, he left the priesthood and openly attacked the reactionary attitudes of the Church hierarchy and the doctrine of papal infallibility, which had been declared in 1870 by the First Vatican Council. In 1880, wishing to marry and being prohibited from doing so by Austrian law, he resigned his professorship and his Austrian citizenship so that he could marry legally in Savoy. He returned to Vienna in the lesser post of docent, which meant he could not direct doctoral students. However, the more conservative forces of the theology faculty continued to exert pressure against him and he severed all relations with the university in 1894, eventually finding a home in Florence. As a pacifist, he protested Italy's entrance into World War I by moving to Zurich, where he died in 1917.

Brentano's most important work in psychology, *Psychologie vom empirischen Standpunkt* (*Psychology from an Empirical Standpoint*), appeared in 1874 and was intended as the first of a multivolume explication of psychology's scope and methodologies. He never finished the later volumes, so we have only an outline of his views on psychology. Nevertheless, Brentano's proposals for psychology's progress stand in sharp contrast to Wundt's. Brentano defined psychology as the science of psychic phenomena expressed as acts and processes. This definition contrasts with psychology viewed in terms of physical reductionism, consciousness, or associationism. Brentano viewed consciousness in terms of a unity expressed by acts. Thus, structuralism's inherent goal of finding the elements of consciousness was meaningless for Brentano because such study destroys the essential unity of consciousness, and such elements, if they exist, do not have psychological meaning. Rather, according to Brentano, only the product of consciousness—the acts and processes—are truly psychological. Brentano subscribed to a physiological or biological substrate of psychological acts, which supplies information about, but is not identical with, psychological acts. Moreover, Brentano recognized two levels of psychological study: pure and applied. Pure psychology studies physiological considerations, individual differences, personality, and social levels. Applied psychology consists of the value of psychology for other sciences. Thus, to Brentano, psychology is the pinnacle of science and is differentiated from other sciences by its study of intentionality, or the ability of people to reach for some object–goal beyond themselves. The psychological act is directed; it is intentional, and this characteristic is unique and purposive.

Brentano argued for hierarchical levels of classes of psychic phenomena. At the representational level is mere awareness; it corresponds to the nonmediated experiences that Wundt saw as psychology's entire subject matter. However, Brentano taught that beyond the representational level is a cognitive class, which he described as a level of judgment. Finally, there is a level of personalization of psychic phenomena, a type of assimilation that individualizes experience, which he labeled the class of interest. As an empirical science, psychology is studied through observation, but it is not reduced to elementary components. Rather, Brentano allowed for various empirical methods that are adaptable to the subject matter of psychology. Perhaps most important was the method of inner perception of ongoing acts. This method was not introspection in the Wundtian sense, but rather the naive reporting of evident psychic phenomena. Other methods described by Brentano were the objective observation of past psychic acts in memory, the observation of the overt behavior of people, and the observation of antecedent and physiological processes concomitant to psychological acts. Accordingly, Brentano's empiricism was open-ended but firmly based on observation.

Brentano's later views did not benefit from the intellectual stimulation and interaction of a stable academic environment. Nevertheless, he moved toward the development of a phenomenological method for psychology. Specifically, he argued that phenomenology is a descriptive method that is explanatory and leads to understanding. This method is based partly on the a priori science that examines the ways we come to knowing and partly on empiricism. By using a personalistic orientation with the self as the point of reference, Brentano hoped for a psychological method that allows psychological acts to be described in terms of the subjective, experiencing person. Accordingly, objects in the environment may be described as part of the process of perceiving. For example, the physical light stimulus, the visual sensory mechanisms, and perceptual levels are interrelated in a psychological mode, best termed "seeing." It was left to Brentano's students, most notably Husserl, to develop this methodology further.

Brentano's psychology did not have the recognized impact of structural psychology. Indeed, the relatively scant outline of his views leaves the reader somewhat confused, because his works contain a framework that, although interesting, is rather vague. Various parts of Brentano's teachings were influential in psychology's subsequent developments. The Gestalt movement, the third force movement of phenomenological psychology, and even the eclectic orientation of American functionalism all owe a debt to Brentano.

Karl Stumpf.   Karl Stumpf (1848–1936) was a major figure in German psychology and led the way to the acceptance of psychology by the European academic establishment. Moreover, he engaged Wundt in a dispute over the introspection of music that drew sharp distinctions between their views. However, Stumpf was not an originator of psychological views. Rather, his importance lies in his expression of the tremendous personal influence of Brentano, as well as in the achievements of his many students.

Stumpf was born in Bavaria, in southwestern Germany, the son of a court physician. Through his grandfather, he received a superb early education in the classics and the natural sciences. He also showed an early talent for music, and began composing at age 10. By the time he was an adult, he had mastered five musical instruments. In 1865, Stumpf entered the university at Würzburg, where he met Brentano and was captivated by the vitality of his teaching and his love of scholarship. Brentano sent him to Lotze at Göttingen to complete his degree, and there he studied physiology, physics, and mathematics. Stumpf's first psychological work, published while he was a docent at Göttingen, was a nativistic theory of space perception. This work won him a professorship at Würzburg. For the next 20 years, he moved among various universities in Germany and Prague, until he was appointed to the prestigious professorship at Berlin in 1894. During the time preceding this appointment, Stumpf published his *Tonpsychologie* (*Psychology of Tones*; 1883, 1890), in which he was able to blend his love of music and science. Also at this time, Wundt and Stumpf conducted a public argument over the proper description of melodies: through introspection or through the trained ear of the musician. Stumpf obviously favored the latter, but the importance of his argument rested on his emphasis on the essential unity of musical experience. In other words, whereas the introspectionist claimed a melody is reducible to its constituent sensory elements—that is, the individual notes—Stumpf held that the melody is a unity itself, noting that a key transformation, which would actually change the individual notes, would not change the perception of the melody. This interpretation is consistent with a phenomenological view, both reflecting Brentano's influence and anticipating Husserl's development after he finished his degree with Stumpf.

In bringing phenomenology into psychology, Stumpf followed the classification of levels of experience articulated by Brentano. The first level concerns the phenomena of sensory and imaginal data of experience. The second classification involves the psychic functions of perceiving, desiring, and willing, equivalent to Brentano's acts. Finally, there is the level of relations, a cognitive classification somewhat akin to Brentano's interests. Stumpf passed along his version of act psychology and his phenomenology to a generation of students. Köhler and Koffka, two of the three founders of the Gestalt movement in psychology, received their degrees under Stumpf at Berlin. Accordingly, Stumpf accomplished what Brentano was unable to do. He offered an alternative to Wundt's structural psychology, and as psychology progressed in Germany, it was Stumpf's students who came to dominate.

Christian von Ehrenfels.   A student of Brentano, Christian von Ehrenfels (1859–1932) held views that actually represented a bridge between the natural and the human science models. He took Mach's notion of form in space and time and suggested that form is more than the sum of the parts. In a paper published in 1890, Ehrenfels introduced the concept of form quality, *Gestaltqualität*, as a new identity that appears when elements are brought together. Further, Ehrenfels distinguished between temporal and nontemporal form qualities. The former include sensations that are time related, such as a musical melody. Nontemporal form qualities are usually spatial and include the perception of movement. Following Brentano's lead, Ehrenfels pursued an empirical (but not necessarily an experimental) demonstration of form qualities. For example, as evidence of the presence of form qualities, he cited the reports of subjects indicating the persistence of form despite changes in the elements of the stimuli evoking the sensation.

Although dissatisfied with Wundt's system, Ehrenfels nevertheless retained an emphasis on the elements of perception. It was left to the Würzburg school to extend the progression from Mach to Ehrenfels and to pave the way for Gestalt psychology, which successfully challenged Wundt's system in Europe.

Alternative Scientific Approaches

Before continuing with the next expression of psychology as a human science, it is appropriate to mention briefly some issues for psychology in the philosophy of science. The human science model for psychology basically questions the equating of the methods of the natural sciences with the notion of science itself. Whereas the developing phenomenology of Brentano and Stumpf proposed methodological alternatives within psychology, other writers were also questioning the natural science model from a more general perspective.

Wilhelm Dilthey.   A German philosopher, Wilhelm Dilthey (1833–1911) objected to the dominance of the natural science approach and proposed a view that emphasizes the person perceived in terms of historical contingency and change. In seeking understanding of the human situation, Dilthey argued that understanding is a matter of finding meaning—a mental operation just as perception and reasoning are mental operations. He actually used the term "human science" to propose an appropriate criterion for evaluating human understanding that is not distorted by artificially trying to conform to natural science criteria. Thus he viewed historical evaluation as a humanistic enterprise based on the meaning of a person's place in time. Natural science techniques, whether in experiments or through introspection, are far too narrow to assess the meaning of humanity adequately (see also Chapter 16).

Henri Bergson.   Henri Bergson's (1859–1941) work is somewhat similar to Dilthey's. Bergson, a major figure in French philosophical thought, wrote an exhaustive treatment of the metaphysical problems of knowledge and time. He argued that the methodology of the natural sciences distorts time, motion, and change by interpreting them as static concepts. According to Bergson, the progress of life should be evaluated by appropriate criteria, and such criteria are not represented in natural science methodology. He defined "true empiricism" as finding the dynamics of becoming through participating in it. By using a method of intuition, metaphysics can provide the appropriate perspective to secure the meaning of life. Bergson concluded that the key to understanding life is found by viewing life as a process of creative evolution through the subjective consciousness arising in each individual.

This brief outline of the views of Dilthey and Bergson does not begin to touch on their depth and complexity. However, both philosophers questioned the prevailing scientific methodologies. As we shall see when we come to twentieth-century psychology, shades of these varying interpretations of science are found in the works of others. At this point it is important to note that the dominance of natural scientific methodology was beginning to erode, and in many respects, Brentano and Stumpf were furthering that process.

The Würzburg School

A final expression of a human science model for psychology came from the Würzburg school, associated with Oswald Külpe (1862–1915). Essentially, the Würzburg school investigated two areas, with dramatic results. Its first major finding was that thoughts do not necessarily have accompanying images, giving rise to a confrontation with the basic tenets of structural psychology. Second, it contended that thinking cannot be fully accounted for by associationism. The Würzburg school's short-lived productivity seriously challenged structural psychology on its own grounds. The Würzburg psychologists were not nearly as radical as Brentano, and accepted many of the proposals of Wundt's structural psychology. However, using the same framework as Wundt, they succeeded in doing far greater damage to belief in the validity of structural psychology.

Külpe was born in Latvia of German ancestry and received his early education there before journeying to Leipzig to study history. His contact with Wundt left him undecided about continuing to study history or changing to psychology. After studying both disciplines at several universities, he returned to Wundt and took his doctoral degree in 1887. He largely adhered to Wundtian psychology until he was appointed professor at Würzburg and his interests led him to investigate thought processes. In 1901, two of Külpe's students published a paper on associations, using empirical methods that went beyond introspection, accepting self-reports on thought processes. For the next 10 years Külpe and his associates produced data questioning the interpretation of thought processes inherent in structural psychology. They did not resolve the problem of imageless thought, but the very existence of the problem was enough to suggest that there are contents other than sensory elements in consciousness. Moreover, the Würzburg workers published data on thought processes, suggesting that such activities as judgment and willing are not the orderly and logical sequences that association theory proposed. Rather, spontaneous and extraneous patterns are present in thought processing, seriously undermining assumptions about the structures of the mind.

When Külpe left Würzburg for a new position at Bonn in 1909, the Würzburg school ceased. At Bonn, Külpe turned to the relationship between psychology and medicine. The burst of activity at Würzburg was an incomplete movement. Although the school's experiments seriously challenged the legitimacy of structural psychology on its own terms, the Würzburg school did not break out to provide an alternative system for German psychology. Rather, the break with the past was left to another movement—Gestalt psychology, to be considered later.

In summary, neither dominant figure of each model of psychology, Wundt or Brentano, succeeded in establishing contemporary psychology in a definitive way. With the hindsight of history, we may conclude that Brentano was the more successful, despite his lower profile, because his views were transmitted intact and not completely repudiated. However, in a very real sense, psychology was forced to go through sequences of being reestablished in the twentieth century.

CHAPTER SUMMARY

Psychology emerged in Germany during the 1870s as a recognized scientific discipline. The recurrent theme in German philosophy of the essential activity of the mind provided the exciting intellectual setting that made a compelling case for psychology's founding, and also gave rise to competing models of the proposed substance and methodology of psychology. One model, an outgrowth of studies of sensory physiology and psychophysics, has been labeled structural, or content, psychology, and Wundt and Titchener were its major spokesmen. Under this natural science approach, psychology was defined as the experimental study of the data of immediate experience through the method of trained introspection. The goal of psychology was to reduce the contents of consciousness to constituent elements of sensory origin. Both its restricted subject matter and ambiguous methodology led to structural psychology's being seriously challenged as the definitive framework for the new science. Nevertheless, structural psychology secured recognition of psychology as a new science, and others, such as Müller, Hering, and Ebbinghaus, attempted to modify structural psychology to accommodate more sophisticated psychological issues. Moreover, philosophers such as Mach and Avenarius bolstered the justification for the natural science approach to psychology.

An alternative, described as a human science model, proposed more open methodologies empirically based on observation but not necessarily experimental. Within this context, Brentano's act psychology defined its subject matter as processes of psychological events inseparable from the environment and consciousness. This phenomenological view offered a greater scope and several accepted methodologies for psychology. The works of Stumpf and Külpe, supported by the philosophical critiques of the natural science methods proposed by Dilthey and Bergson, fall into the human science model. However, these men's individual views did not offer a coherent or systematic theory able to compete successfully with structural psychology. Nevertheless, subsequent developments in psychology established viable alternatives. In many respects, the "founding" of modern psychology was a false beginning. Neither dominant model, as expressed by Wundt and Brentano, was successful in establishing a lasting framework for psychology. It was left to the immediate successors of these German psychologists to rethink the formulation of psychology's scope and method.

BIBLIOGRAPHY

Primary Sources

BERGSON, H. L. (1910). *Time and free will: An essay on the immediate data of consciousness* (F. L. Podgsen, Trans.). New York: Macmillan.

BRENTANO, F. (1973). *Psychology from an empirical standpoint (1874)* (O. Krauss, A. C. Rancurello, D. B. Terrell, & L. L. McAlister, Trans.). Atlantic Highlands, NJ: Humanities Press.

EBBINGHAUS, H. (1948). Memory. In W. Dennis (Ed.), *Readings in the history of psychology.* New York: Appleton-Century-Crofts, 304–313.

TITCHENER, E. B. (1898). A psychological laboratory. *Mind, 7,* 311–331.

TITCHENER, E. B. (1898). Postulates of a structural psychology. *Philosophical Review, 7,* 449–465.

TITCHENER, E. B. (1899). Structural and functional psychology. *Philosophical Review, 8,* 290–299.

TITCHENER, E. B. (1910). *A textbook of psychology.* New York: Macmillan.

TITCHENER, E. B. (1925). Experimental psychology: A retrospect. *American Journal of Psychology, 36,* 313–323.

WUNDT, W. (1907). *Principles of physiological psychology (I)* (E. B. Titchener, Trans.). New York: Macmillan.

WUNDT, W. (1912). *An introduction to psychology.* London: George Allen.

WUNDT, W. (1916). *Elements of folk psychology.* London: Allen & Unwin.

WUNDT, W. (1969). *Outlines of psychology.* Leipzig: Englemann, 1897; reprinted: St. Clair Shores, MI: Scholarly Press.

WUNDT, W. (1973). *The language of gestures.* The Hague: Mouton.

Studies

ANDERSON, R. J. (1975). The untranslated content of Wundt's *Grundzüge der Physiologischen Psychologie. Journal of the History of the Behavioral Sciences, 10,* 381–386.

BLUMENTHAL, A. L. (1975). A reappraisal of Wilhelm Wundt. *American Psychologist, 30,* 1081–1088.

BLUMENTHAL, A. (1979). Retrospective review: Wilhelm Wundt—the founding father we never knew. *Contemporary Psychology, 24,* 547–550.

BORING, E. G. (1927). Edward Bradford Titchener. *American Journal of Psychology, 38,* 489–506.

BORING, E. G. (1950). *A history of experimental psychology,* 2nd ed. Englewood Cliffs, NJ: Prentice Hall.

BRINGMANN, W. G., BALANCE, W. D. G., & EVANS, R. B. (1975). Wilhelm Wundt 1832–1920: A brief biographical sketch. *Journal of the History of the Behavioral Sciences, 11,* 287–297.

BROZEK, J. (1970). Wayward history: F. C. Donders (1818–1889) and the timing of mental operations. *Psychological Reports, 26,* 563–569.

COPLESTON, F. (1974). *A history of philosophy, Vol. 9, Maine de Biran to Sartre, Part I—The revolution to Henri Bergson.* Garden City, NY: Image Books.

DANZIGER, K. (1979). The positivist repudiation of Wundt. *Journal of the History of the Behavioral Sciences, 15,* 205–230.

EVANS, R. B. (1972). E. B. Titchener and his lost system. *Journal of the History of the Behavioral Sciences, 8,* 168–180.

EVANS, R. B. (1975). The origins of Titchener's doctrine of meaning. *Journal of the History of the Behavioral Sciences, 11,* 334–341.

FANCHER, R. E. (1977). Brentano's psychology from an empirical standpoint and Freud's early metapsychology. *Journal of the History of the Behavioral Sciences, 13,* 207–227.

HENLE, M. (1971). Did Titchener commit the stimulus error? The problem of meaning in structural psychology. *Journal of the History of the Behavioral Sciences, 7,* 279–282.

HENLE, M. (1974). E. B. Titchener and the case of the missing element. *Journal of the History of the Behavioral Sciences, 10,* 227–237.

HINDELAND, M. J. (1971). Edward Bradford Titchener: A pioneer in perception. *Journal of the History of the Behavioral Sciences, 7,* 23–28.

LEAHEY, T. H. (1979). Something old, something new: Attention in Wundt and modern cognitive psychology. *Journal of the History of the Behavioral Sciences, 15,* 242–252.

LEARY, D. E. (1979). Wundt and after: Psychology's shifting relations with the natural sciences, social sciences, and philosophy. *Journal of the History of the Behavioral Sciences, 15,* 231–241.

LINDENFELD, D. (1978). Oswald Külpe and the Würzburg school. *Journal of the History of the Behavioral Sciences, 14,* 132–141.

PILLSBURY, W. B. (1928). The psychology of Edward Bradford Titchener. *Philosophical Review, 37,* 104–131.

POSTMAN, L. (1968). Hermann Ebbinghaus. *American Psychologist, 23,* 149–157.

RANCURELLO, A. C. (1968). *A study of Franz Brentano.* New York: Academic Press.

ROSS, B. (1979). Psychology's centennial year. *Journal of the History of the Behavioral Sciences, 15,* 203–204.

SABAT, S. R. (1979). Wundt's physiological psychology in retrospect. *American Psychologist, 34,* 635–638.

SHAKOW, D. (1930). Hermann Ebbinghaus. *American Journal of Psychology, 43,* 505– 518.

STAGNER, R. (1979). Wundt and applied psychology. *American Psychologist, 34,* 638– 639.

SULLIVAN, J. J. (1968). Franz Brentano and the problems of intentionality. In B. Wolman (Ed.), *Historical roots of contemporary psychology.* New York: Harper & Row, 248–274.

TINKER, M. A. (1932). Wundt's doctorate students and their theses, 1875–1920. *American Journal of Psychology, 44,* 630–637.

WOODWORTH, R. S. (1906). Imageless thought. *The Journal of Philosophy, Psychology and Scientific Methods, 3,* 701–708.

❋ 12 ❋

American Functionalism

Background
    The Legacy of Nineteenth-Century British Thought
    The American Character
Early American Psychology
    Moral Philosophy and Medicine
    American Pragmatism
        William James
        Charles Sanders Peirce
    Transitional Figures
        Hugo Münsterberg
        William McDougall
        G. Stanley Hall
Functional Psychology
    Chicago Functionalism
        John Dewey
        James Angell
        Harvey Carr
    Columbia Functionalism
        James McKeen Cattell
        Edward Lee Thorndike
        Robert S. Woodworth
    Women in Early American Psychology
        Mary Whiton Calkins
        Christine Ladd-Franklin
        Margaret Floy Washburn
Impact
Chapter Summary

When the new German psychology of Wundt was introduced to the United States, it immediately took on a particular American character. With the exception of Titchener, who remained a strict adherent to Wundt's formulations, the American psychologists who had been trained in Germany imposed a functional interpretation on structural psychology when they returned to America. Briefly, functionalism was an orientation in psychology that emphasized mental processes rather than mental content and that valued the usefulness of psychology. Ironically, it was Titchener who in 1898 coined the term *functional psychology*, to distinguish such views from his own "true" structural psychology.

Functional psychology was not a formal system of psychology in the way represented by structural psychology or later systems of Gestalt psychology, behaviorism, or psychoanalysis. Functional psychology did not provide a comprehensive view of psychological activity with underlying philosophical assumptions and prescribed research strategies and goals. Rather, it differed from structural psychology in a spirit or an attitude that emphasized the applications and usefulness of psychology. As Boring (1950) suggested, it was not so much that the functional psychologists did different experiments than the structural psychologists. Rather, it was their reason for doing an experiment that distinguished them from the structuralists. The functionalists wanted to know how the mind works and what uses the mind has, not simply what contents and structures are involved in mental processes.

Functional psychology changed the new German science by adding influences historically absent from the German intellectual milieu. Specifically, while accepting the underlying Lockean assumptions of the mind inherent in Wundt's formulation, the Americans retained a general commitment to other prevailing aspects of British thought. Most notable was the strong influence of Darwin's theory of evolution. Functional psychology valued the importance of adaptation of both the species and the individual to environmental influences. Adaptation as a survival mechanism was amenable to the American national experience as a pioneering enterprise that saw itself as having transplanted the best of European civilization and left behind the shortcomings of European society in the attempt to tame a wild continent.

American functionalism was a relatively short-lived movement. It introduced to America Wundt's attempt to identify a new science, but in the process of importing structuralism, the functionalists discarded the rigidity of Wundt's system. As a movement within psychology, functionalism prepared the way for the eventual redefinition of psychology in terms of a behavioristic approach that rapidly came to dominate American psychology. On the one hand, functionalism may be viewed as a transitional stage in America between structuralism and behaviorism. On the other, psychology was firmly entrenched in America through the concerted efforts of the functionalists, who successfully conveyed its value for academic as well as applied purposes. Thus, it may be argued that the functionalists were progressives who gave psychology an American imprint that the discipline retains to this day.

BACKGROUND

The Legacy of Nineteenth-Century British Thought

The common language uniting Britain and the United States has forged deep-rooted ties in economic, political, and social spheres throughout the last four centuries. This relationship is reflected in the philosophical bases of science, and for psychology this relationship has implied a reliance on empiricism and the Lockean model of mental process. In a general way, the Lockean model, so central to the development of empirical psychology, also played a significant role in the nurturing of eighteenth-century political thought and had a profound effect on the emergence of the American nation. The social implications of the Lockean model were recognized in the founding ideals of the United States. Jefferson's *Declaration of Independence* justified the actions of the American colonies against Britain by asserting that society is an organic unit that is propelled toward its own betterment. Society itself, according to Jefferson, is composed of men born equal—the *tabula rasa* state proposed by Locke.

As outlined in Chapter 10, the flowering of British science in the nineteenth century confirmed the justification of empiricism. The impact of Darwin's theory, evolution by natural selection, may be best appreciated within the context of the Lockean model: Darwin provided empirical support for the improvement of species through successful adaptation to the environment. Darwin's theory found ready acceptance in the United States because his findings offered a mechanism that explained American progress. The United States was emerging from the nineteenth century as a nation of boundless potential, welcoming Europe's oppressed masses to participate in its opportunities. Thus, America was proving Spencer's interpretations of evolutionary improvement on a vast social scale.

The impact of evolutionary theory was felt far beyond the scope of biology. Galton's study of mental inheritance was one of the initial applications of Darwinism that eventually led to the development of testing as a valuable tool of psychologists. This movement received its initial impetus from British scholars, but the testing movement reached full expansion in the United States and eventually became an important part of functional psychology.

Following Galton's analysis of the inheritance of mental traits and his development of the basis for regression and correlation (see Chapter 10), Karl Pearson (1857–1936) provided the mathematical support for the assessment of the covariation of multiple traits. Pearson started a statistical laboratory at University College in London and, with Galton, founded *Biometrika* in 1901 to publish statistical papers dealing with biological and psychological variables. Also in 1901, Pearson published a theoretical paper on the mathematical possibility of predicting aptitude on the basis of many tests of various mental traits. The statistical implications of Pearson's views were applied to intelligence testing by Charles Spearman (1863–1945), who wrote a paper in 1904 suggesting that intelligence consists of a single general factor and a number of specific factors or traits. Spearman's two-factor theory of mental ability described a common factor of intelligence and a group of specific factors that were related to individual tests. Later workers in Britain, such as Godfrey Thomson and Cyril Burt, became dissatisfied with Spearman's two-factor theory and proposed alternative models, at the same time improving the statistical techniques to provide support for tests of multiple abilities. Finally, an American at the University of Chicago, L. L. Thurstone (1887–1955), used factor analysis as an invaluable aid in interpreting multiple tests, because it provided a means of weighing factors according to the extent that they account for total variability. Factor analysis made possible the development of a composite prediction method for individual abilities.

While Pearson and his followers were examining statistical techniques to predict mental abilities better, Alfred Binet (1857–1911) in France developed the first widely used standardized intelligence test. Asked by the minister of education to devise a method of assessing the intellectual aptitude of schoolchildren, Binet and his coworkers invented specific test items to measure various kinds of intellectual processes. From these efforts came the concept of mental age, an individual index of a child's ability compared to a reference group. A German psychologist, William Stern (1871–1938), later suggested dividing the mental age by the chronological age to calculate an individual's intelligence quotient (IQ). In 1916, a group at Stanford University revised and restandardized the Binet test for American use. In 1917, intelligence testing received significant reinforcement in America when the army adapted it as a selection device for young men drafted for World War I.

The American Character

Before reviewing the development of functional psychology, it is appropriate to describe briefly the American scene at the turn of the twentieth century. The United States entered the twentieth century as a nation just beginning to tap its vast resources and exert its strength in the international community. Nineteenth-century America had been divided by the Civil War, and glaring social inequities based on race and ethnicity were prevalent. However, the United States had remained relatively aloof from the European turmoil of the nineteenth century. By 1900, the United States was a colonial power, having ousted Spain from the Western Hemisphere. Yet even colonial rule was justified as being a missionary effort to bring the benefits of American life to the masses who had been exploited by European imperialism in the former Spanish possessions. Accordingly, there was an exciting and idealistic sense of purpose and righteousness in America, and Americans had an overwhelming faith and confidence in themselves.

That spirit of moral and economic superiority was present in American academia as well. Although American universities existed from the seventeenth century, they were mostly small institutions intended for training clergy and physicians. Until late in the nineteenth century, most Americans in search of quality education went to European institutions. However, American universities began to change their character, moving away from denominational control and toward more liberal studies. President Charles Eliot of Harvard began a radical upgrading of medical education in 1870. Professional and graduate centers of education were established at such institutions as Johns Hopkins University in 1876 and the Columbia School of Political Science in 1880, making it possible for Americans to study at the doctoral level in their own country.

Public support of universities increased dramatically as a result of the Morrill Act of 1862, which provided federal land and support to start state agricultural schools. In those areas of the country without the tradition of private universities, especially in the Midwest, these land grant schools expanded to include comprehensive education in liberal arts and sciences, at both undergraduate and graduate levels.

Psychology was introduced to America at a time coinciding with expansion and revitalization of both the universities and the nation at large. Whereas the new science was received with some skepticism by the conservative academicians of Europe, the American universities reacted with greater acceptance simply because psychology was new. Psychology as an independent discipline benefited from the American atmosphere and gained an identity and a stability that were unmatched in Europe.

EARLY AMERICAN PSYCHOLOGY

Even after American universities improved to the point of competing with European institutions, the character of intellectual pursuit in America was still marked by the earlier emphasis on the applied aspects of human knowledge. American values tended to play down questions of abstract science while glorifying technology. In philosophy, the problems of essence and being, studied in metaphysics, yielded to ethical questions of the concrete standards for human deportment. Issues relating to psychology were considered in such applied fields as medicine and ethics.

Moral Philosophy and Medicine

In colonial America moral values and psychological activity were intertwined with theology. Periodic movements of intense evangelical Christianity have occurred from time to time in American history, one of which was sparked in 1734 when Jonathan Edwards (1703–1758) preached revivalist sermons in Northampton, Massachusetts. Edwards was America's first native philosopher of note, and he inspired a fundamentalist crusade to bring people back to the beauty and purity of God and nature. Edwards had read Locke while he was a student at Yale and chose to study the relationship between God and man through a revision of the deterministic theology of John Calvin. Preaching predestination and faith in God, Edwards urged people to return to the absolute rule of God, who gave everything to humanity, born with nothing. In a similar vein, the New Jersey Quaker John Woolman (1720–1772) tempered his recognition of God's will with humanitarian gestures in proposing the ideal standards of deportment.

Perhaps the American who came closest to being an all-around scholar was Benjamin Franklin (1706–1790), whose appreciation of learning complemented his inventive genius for technological advances. His interest in practical science, reflected in his observations on electricity (see Chapter 7), was not at the expense of theoretical learning. In 1744, he was instrumental in founding the American

Philosophical Society, the first learned society in America. As a scientist, philosopher, and inventor, and later as a statesman, Franklin embodied the American ideals of the eclectic and the useful.

Most colonial physicians gained their knowledge through experience as working practitioners, and the first American medical school—at the University of Pennsylvania—was not started until 1765. A professor there and the most famous physician in revolutionary America was Benjamin Rush (1745–1813). Rush received his medical degree in Edinburgh and carried back to America some of the views of the commonsense Scottish empiricists. However, he is better known as the chief physician of the Revolutionary Army, urging better sanitation and diet to counteract rampant disease among the soldiers. After the war, he made pioneering observations on psychosomatic disorders and psychiatric treatment. He was also a strong proponent of abstinence from alcohol and organized efforts that led to the formation of temperance societies in several regions of the country.

Science and research with no immediate practical application were generally ignored. A tenth of the population of Philadelphia died from an epidemic of yellow fever in 1793, despite Rush's suggestion that the epidemic might have been spreading through vapors given off by decomposing matter. Nobody followed through to investigate Rush's hypothesis until after that plague. The primitive state of medicine may inadvertently have led to the death of George Washington: He was treated for a throat infection by bleedings and purgings, reducing his bodily resistance. Gradually, however, scientific inquiry gained support. In 1780, the American Academy of Arts and Sciences was founded in Boston to promote learning and advance the interest and betterment of society. There was enthusiastic support for applied science and technology, in contrast to basic science. Indeed, the American success story is filled with creative inventions, architectural wonders, and engineering feats. The steamboat, cotton gin, and Erie Canal are only a few of the many accomplishments of Americans who were able to win business and government support for projects with immediate practical applications.

American Pragmatism

Pragmatism is a native American philosophical system. The word *pragmatism* is derived from a Greek root meaning an act or a deed. As a philosophy, pragmatism emphasizes results rather than method. A pragmatic view of science accepts various methodological approaches to knowledge. In ethics, pragmatism stresses the way that the individual makes compromises between desires and reason. Pragmatic philosophy, then, does not contain a comprehensive collection of doctrines or beliefs, but rather consists of a characteristic manner of philosophizing. As the immediate precedent of functional psychology, early pragmatic philosophy created an intellectual atmosphere that studied not so much what a person does as how the person goes about doing it.

William James.   As the first person associated with the new empirical science of psychology in America, William James (1842–1910) actually deserves the title of advocate rather than practitioner. Although he introduced experimental psychol-

WILLIAM JAMES (1842–1910).
(Courtesy, New York Public Library.)

ogy to American academia and imported one of Wundt's students specifically to start a laboratory at Harvard University, he remained a philosopher. He appreciated the efforts of others to establish an empirical science of psychology, but was not an empiricist. He excited the interest of his many students in psychology, but James himself did not become committed to the narrow focus of experimental work. His genius was not contained within psychology, and he followed a wide range of interests throughout his long career.

James was born into an eminent and wealthy family that had the resources and motivation to foster scholarly pursuit. His brother, Henry, gained literary fame as a novelist, and William and his four siblings received superb educations in Europe and America. At first, William showed an interest in painting, but his talent was not convincing, so he enrolled at Harvard. While studying biology and medicine there, he was influenced by Louis Agassiz (1807–1873), the Swiss-born naturalist and zoologist. His studies were interrupted by a period of illness, described as a nervous and emotional crisis, and he traveled to Europe to recuperate. While in Germany and France, James read widely in philosophy and psychology, and attended the lectures of some of the eminent continental thinkers. Upon his return to America, he completed his medical degree at Harvard but decided to pursue philosophy. During his long career at Harvard, he became a legend, admired and respected by both students and colleagues. He carried on a voluminous correspondence with such contemporaries as Oliver Wendell Holmes, Henri Bergson, and G. Stanley Hall. Among his prolific writings, his major contributions to psychology were contained in *The Principles of Psychology* (1890), published in two volumes. This work is a comprehensive treatment of psychology and was used as an introductory textbook for many years. It remains a classic work of American psychology.

The pragmatism of William James was based on a firm appreciation of empiricism and can be summarized by the following points:

1. The consequences of theoretical positions form the major criteria for judging differences among the positions. Different philosophical theories may state disparate views, but only their consequences can truly differentiate them. Thus, James accepted empirical tests of the validity of a theory.

2. If a theory asserts a useful, satisfying effect in organizing experience, then the theory should win at least tentative acceptance. This point allows a subjective, utilitarian perspective on individual experience. For example, if a person holds a religious belief that is critical and reassuring for the individual, then the belief is "true" for that person.

3. Experience itself is not reduced to either the elements of consciousness or the mechanical laws of matter. In contrast to Wundt, James argued that experience is not a succession of discrete sensations bound together by associations. Rather, experience is a continuous flow of subjective events.

James believed that mind and body, subjective and objective aspects of experience, are not two different interacting subsystems. Rather, reminiscent of the earlier views of Spinoza, he proposed that mental and physical experiences are different aspects of the same experience. For example, we may read from a book or use the book as a paperweight. We do not have two experiences of the book, but only one experience that is described in two different ways. Thus, James blurred the distinction between mind and body because he believed the distinction was an intellectual artifact used to describe how we experience. Experience itself is a singular entity.

By defining psychology as the "science of mental life" and proposing that experience is a continuous stream of consciousness, James accepted an enlarged scope of psychology compared to the Wundtian model. Because experience must be described in both physical and mental terms, James emphasized a truly physiological psychology that stressed brain functions in accounting for mental experience, or consciousness. In addition, the mind for James was a process that was personal, changing, continuous, and selective. Accordingly, he advocated an empirical approach to the study of experience that focused on the mind in terms of its functions, so that the psychologist must observe the mind in use.

One part of James' psychology, illustrative of his belief that consciousness should be appropriately described in terms of both physical and mental dimensions, concerned his theory of emotions. First formulated by James in 1884, this theory has come down to us as the James–Lange theory of emotions, because a Danish psychologist, Carl Lange (1834–1900), developed a similar interpretation in 1885. James noted that the body responds with certain automatic reflex actions when confronted by emotional stimuli, and these reactions are usually confined to skeletal and visceral levels. When we become aware of these reactions, we then experience the emotion, according to James. For example, if a speeding car races toward you and narrowly misses hitting you, your autonomic nervous system responds automatically and immediately with increased heart rate, rapid breathing, and perspiration, all in preparation for a motor response of fleeing or freezing, if either becomes necessary. Experiencing that sequence of reactions, James asserted, is the emotion of fright. Thus, James argued that we first become aware of the physiological aspects of the experience, and then the psychological aspect comes into focus. Emotions, then, are the result of a sequence of autonomic reactions, not the cause. Of interest in James' view on emotions are the emphases on the two dimensions of the total experience, physical and psychological, and the description of emotions in terms of observable functions of activity.

Boring (1950) suggested three reasons for James' prominent place in the development of American psychology. First, his dynamic personality, clear writing, and effective teaching excited students about psychology. He created an atmosphere that facilitated the growth of psychology in American academia. Second, James offered an alternative to the Wundtian formulation of the new science, represented in America by Titchener. James based his definition of psychology on experience, described as a stream of consciousness and not a collection of sensory elements. Finally, James proposed a distinctive American psychology that was functional in character. Functional psychology was open to practical applications and admitted the data of observable behavior.

Charles Sanders Peirce.   About as opposite in temperament to James as one could be, Charles Sanders Peirce (1839–1914) was an important figure in pragmatism because he integrated elements of diverse philosophies to produce an eclectic theory of consciousness. Although he had considerably less influence on functional psychology than James, Peirce's pragmatism nevertheless forms an intellectual basis of note for American psychology, which was recognized by James.

Peirce was the son of a Harvard mathematician and received sound training in mathematics and biology while pursuing his own reading in history and philosophy. After graduating from Harvard, he worked as a scientist for the United States Coast and Geodetic Society until 1879, when he received an appointment as an instructor of logic at Johns Hopkins University. He was unsuccessful as a teacher and left Hopkins after 4 years. Despite the efforts of James to secure a position for him at Harvard, Peirce never again had regular employment. He lived a poor existence supported by occasional jobs reviewing papers, and became increasingly alone and cantankerous. Most of his works were published after his death.

Peirce was influenced by the writings of Kant and Bain, who came from different philosophical traditions. Peirce agreed with Kant that the mind contributes to the organization of experience by relating and unifying sensory information through a priori categories. At the same time, adhering to an empirical position, Peirce believed that only questions able to be subjected to empirical scrutiny have scientific validity. From Bain, Peirce expanded his empiricist assumptions by accepting the basic tenets of British associationism and a definition of individual belief in terms of habits of activity confirmed by the satisfaction of needs.

Like James, Peirce viewed consciousness and mental processes in terms of their practical consequences. Moreover, he defined the higher mental process of judgment in terms of the person seeking the meaning of the consequences of ideas. Any meaningful idea has three mental categories: quality, essence, and its relationship to other ideas. In contrast to James, however, Peirce stressed the logical rather than the psychological consequences of ideas. In so doing, Peirce reflected his belief that the mind is intimately tied to the organizational structure that it imposes on sensory information.

Both James and Peirce contributed to the intellectual atmosphere that readily accepted new formulations of psychology. Elements of their pragmatic views anticipated later systems of American thought. James's empiricism, for example, favored an acceptance of observable behavior as psychological data; Peirce's emphasis on mental organization was consistent with the subsequent development of Gestalt psychology. Pragmatism as a philosophical movement defined the immediate character of American psychology, and functional psychology, in turn, provided the needed transition from the rigid model of Wundt to the varied systems of psychology that began to blossom in America during the 1930s.

Transitional Figures

As mentioned earlier, functional psychology was a diffuse system of psychology, characterized more by an attitude toward psychological study than by coherent theory. Nevertheless, centers of functional psychology did emerge, and these are considered in the next section. First, however, the views of several psychologists should be surveyed. These psychologists were functionalists to the extent that they contributed to the formation of the American approach to psychology. Moreover, they were individualists who expressed rather personalized views of psychology; they did not fit neatly with the more formal expositions of functional psychology.

Hugo Münsterberg.   A student of Wundt, Hugo Münsterberg (1863–1916) was recruited from Germany by William James to expand and manage the psychology laboratory at Harvard University. He fulfilled that task, but Münsterberg also possessed a wide vision of psychology's potential for becoming a valuable applied discipline. He gained popular fame for his varied writings on the applications of psychology to social, commercial, and educational issues. On an abstract level, he remained nominally a structural psychologist. However, he generally ignored theory and became part of the American functional spirit.

Münsterberg's life was marked by views that earned him prestige and admiration followed by scorn and ridicule. He was born in the East Prussian port city of Danzig (now Gdańsk, Poland) to a cultured and intellectually oriented family. He received his PhD under Wundt at Leipzig in 1885 and a year later was awarded a medical degree. Wundt had earlier rejected some of his initial research on the will, but Münsterberg continued this work independently and later expanded the rejected paper to a small book, further alienating Wundt when he published it in 1888. Münsterberg was appointed to the faculty of the University of Freiburg in 1887, where he started a laboratory and began to publish papers on time perception, attentional processes, and learning and memory. These papers attracted the attention of psychologists in Germany and America, and William James cited several of them in his *Principles of Psychology*. James met Münsterberg in Paris at the First International Congress of Psychology in 1889. Following that meeting, the two corresponded, and James sent one of his students to Freiburg to work with Münsterberg. In 1892, James secured an offer from Harvard for Münsterberg to become director of the psychology laboratories for 3 years. In addition to expanding the laboratories and directing students, Münsterberg learned English and prepared a German textbook. He returned to Freiburg in 1895 to think over the offer of a permanent professorship at Harvard. In 1897, he returned to Harvard and remained in America for the rest of his life, with the exception of brief visits to Europe and a year as an exchange professor at Berlin.

In addition to his prolific publications in psychology, Münsterberg became a spokesperson for German–American relations. He never sought American citizenship and maintained a fierce nationalism toward Germany. He published a popular book on the American character, culture, and social structures for Germans. In the first years of this century, he was honored by political leaders in both countries, and advocated increased contact between American and German scholars. However, the political winds changed and the good will began to evaporate in the years prior to World War I, when Germany's image among the American public deteriorated. Münsterberg was caught in the middle of the American public outrage over German political and military aggression. In particular, he became a symbol of German arrogance in the American newspapers that earlier liked to quote him on the benefits of German–American cooperation. This vilification no doubt created considerable pressure for Münsterberg and probably contributed to his fatal stroke in 1916, a year before the United States' entry into the war against Germany.

Münsterberg, like James and most psychologists of his era, considered himself a philosopher. Interestingly, Münsterberg condemned pragmatism as a mere updating of the Greek Sophist tradition. He believed psychology would be constraining itself by alignment with pragmatism, which he thought was ultimately too limiting and operational in scope. Rather, he adhered to the idealistic basis of the German model of mental activity and posited a distinction between causal and purposive psychology: Causal psychology is empirically based and examines the relationship between mental events and psychological processes; purposive psychology is the study of the pursuit of goals by activities of the will. Although Münsterberg initially stated that purposive psychology belongs in the metaphysical province of philosophy, he later placed it in psychology proper. Münsterberg's purposive psychology influenced one of his students, Edwin Holt, in his conceptualization of behaviorism (see Chapter 15), and, in turn, Holt influenced Edward Tolman's later expansion of the behavioristic model of psychology.

Almost from its inception, Münsterberg's laboratory at Harvard expanded its research to subject matter beyond the restrictions of the introspective psychology of Wundt and Titchener. He organized divisions of human and infrahuman investigations, and his laboratory soon became one of the more productive centers of experimental psychology. His views of psychological research were broad and eclectic, combining the German tradition of Wundt's structural psychology and Brentano's act psychology, an integration permitted by Münsterberg's conceptualization of causal and purposive psychology.

Münsterberg's applications of psychology may be clearly seen in his writings on a variety of subjects. From his background as a psychologist and a physician, he was interested in psychotherapy and published a review of the area in 1903. He disagreed with Freud on the nature of unconscious motivations, but he valued the interest in psychopathology generated by Freud's emerging theory. His book *On the Witness Stand* (1908) was an initial effort in forensic psychology, and he developed a precursor of the "lie detector" polygraph in his laboratory. His book *Psychology and the Teacher* (1909) paid particular attention to individual differences in learning arising from variability in inherited dispositions, and he suggested several tests to measure student aptitude. In two books, *Vocation and Learning* (1912) and *Psychology and Industrial Efficiency* (1913), Münsterberg described studies of personnel selection and labor management. He even wrote an analysis of film technique in *The Photoplay: A Psychological Study* (1916).

Münsterberg was a remarkable person whose wide intellectual capacity joined easily with the American utilitarian ethic. Although he rejected pragmatism in the abstract, he contributed to the making of functional psychology in practice. Münsterberg's place in the history of American psychology has not been given the emphasis it deserves, probably because of the anti-German attacks on him and his own shortcomings at an interpersonal level. Nevertheless, as William James is credited with popularizing the new science of psychology within academia, Hugo Münsterberg should be credited with popularizing psychology among the masses of people by demonstrating its practical worth.

William McDougall.   Freud and William McDougall (1871–1938) have often been compared because of their reliance on inherited instinctual patterns of psychological activity. McDougall also has sometimes been classified as a behaviorist because he emphasized overt, observable behavior as a reflection of psychological activity. However, McDougall was an individualist pursuing his own directions in psychology, which for the most part moved against the grain of the American psychology of his time. More recently, McDougall's psychology has received favorable review for his eclectic combination of instinct and purpose in the analysis of comparative behavior. He formulated most of his important views in his native Britain, but they were better tolerated within the functional spirit of early American psychology.

McDougall received a strong background in the humanities and in medicine at Cambridge and Oxford Universities, followed by a year of physiological study at Göttingen in Germany. After 4 years as an intern at St. Thomas Hospital in England, he joined the Cambridge Anthropological Expedition to New Guinea and Borneo. His studies of primitive societies, published in several volumes, reflected McDougall's early research inclination as a master of detailed observation. He taught briefly at University College in London and then for 16 years at Oxford University. During World War I, he worked as a physician for the British army and studied cases of psychoneurosis, which were to form the basis of his later views on abnormal psychology.

In 1920, he accepted the professorship at Harvard that became vacant when Münsterberg died in 1916. He stayed at Harvard for only 7 years and left for Duke University. His dissatisfaction with Harvard probably resulted from his perception that his views did not receive the admiration and followers that they deserved. Also, he believed that the more moderate climate of North Carolina might benefit his increasing deafness. While at Duke, he chaired the psychology department and fostered an atmosphere of intellectual tolerance for diverse expressions of psychology, including studies of parapsychology.

McDougall's scientific background was in the same nineteenth-century tradition that produced Darwin. Philosophically, he was attuned to the Scottish empiricists as well as the open-ended association views of John Stuart Mill. McDougall was also influenced by James's psychology and dedicated a book to his memory.

McDougall called his psychology *hormic*, a word derived from the same Greek root as hormone and which means "an impulse." By choosing this label, he stressed that psychological activity has a purpose, or goal, that prods the individual to action, although the person may not have any real understanding or knowledge of the goal itself. The dynamism or propelling force of activity was termed an *instinct* or *urge*. Psychological activity, as opposed to physiological activity, was defined as behavior, and it had seven critical characteristics:

1. Spontaneity of movement
2. Persistence of activity beyond the action of some initiating stimulus
3. Variation in the direction of movement
4. Termination upon the perception of a change in the situation
5. Preparation for new situations
6. The capacity to improve with practice
7. The reflection of the totality of organismic reactions

This restricted definition of behavior excluded reflexive actions, which McDougall believed were physiological responses. McDougall's behavioral views were overshadowed by the wider, less rigorous definition offered by Watson. Nevertheless, for McDougall, behavior arising from inherited instincts provided a mechanism of action that can be modified by experiences, especially in higher animals.

McDougall's formulations stressed the importance of inherited characteristics and of behavior that can be learned and modified by environmental influences. He asserted personal freedom in the variabilities of behaviors in seeking goals, so his psychology was not deterministic. McDougall's views stand in contrast to Watson's complete reliance on environmental determination of behavior. The mind for McDougall has organization and interacts with bodily processes. The individual, then, is portrayed as free to determine her or his own purpose or pathways to personal goals.

One of McDougall's major contributions was his recognition of the social context of human and animal behavior. He emphasized critical social variables that influence interactions within species and how such behaviors are instinctually based and inherited. His *Introduction to Social Psychology* (1908) remained a definitive resource for many years.

McDougall's psychology was somewhat apart from the mainstream of American psychology of his time. Although functional in character, his views did not inspire the imaginations of American psychologists in the way that Watson's were able to do. However, as ethology has gained wider recognition in recent years, it may be argued that McDougall's "behaviorism" had a sounder conceptualization than Watson's. Certainly, the cogent research efforts of ethologists such as Konrad Lorenz and Niko Tinbergen are more consistent with McDougall's views than with any of the other versions of early behaviorism in America.

G. Stanley Hall.   Perhaps the most independent of the early American psychologists, Stanley Hall (1844–1924) was instrumental in firmly establishing psychology in the United States through both substantive and practical activities. In addition to his contributions to child psychology and educational issues, he succeeded in securing recognition of psychology as a profession.

Hall's biography may be described as a series of "firsts." His was the first PhD granted from Harvard's philosophy department (1878), and he became the first American to work in Wundt's psychology laboratory in Leipzig (1879). He started the first legitimate psychology research laboratory in America (1883) at Johns Hopkins University. In 1887, he founded the first English language journal devoted exclusively to psychology, *The American Journal of Psychology*. The following year he became the first president of Clark University in Worcester, Massachusetts, and in 1892 organized the American Psychological Association, becoming its first president. He was involved in the founding of other journals: *Pedagogical Seminary* (1891), after 1927 known as the *Journal of Genetic Psychology*; the *Journal of Religious Psychology* (1904–1914); the *Journal of Race Development* (1910), later known as the *Journal of International Relations* and still later known as *Foreign Affairs*; and the *Journal of Applied Psychology*, in which Hall ended up investing $8,000 of his own money.

Hall was born on a farm near Boston and received his bachelor's degree in 1867 from Williams College in western Massachusetts. He then went to Union Theological Seminary in New York City to prepare for a career as a clergyman. Boring (1950) recounted the story of Hall's preaching a trial sermon before a critic on the faculty. At the end of the sermon the faculty member, forsaking any criticism, simply began to pray for the salvation of Hall's soul. Probably taking a hint, Hall went to Germany for 3 years, where he studied philosophy and also attended Du Bois–Reymond's lectures on physiology. Returning to New York in 1871, he completed his divinity degree and served briefly at a country church. He then secured a position at Antioch College near Dayton, Ohio, and taught a variety of courses. Impressed by Wundt's *Physiological Psychology*, Hall set out again for Germany to learn from Wundt. However, President Eliot of Harvard offered him a minor teaching post in English, which also allowed him to work with William James. He received his doctorate in 1878 for a dissertation on muscular perception. From then to 1880 Hall lived in Germany, where he worked for Wundt during the first year of the Leipzig laboratory.

In 1881, Hall joined the newly founded Johns Hopkins University, devoted to graduate education, where he worked with young people who later went on to positions of note within psychology, among them John Dewey, James McKeen Cattell, and

Edmund Clark Sanford. In 1888, Hall was named to the presidency of Clark University. He brought along Sanford to start the psychology laboratory while he began a department of educational psychology. Clark's psychology department soon gained a fine reputation and in 1909 was the site of Freud's lectures at Hall's invitation. In the year of his death, Hall was elected to a second term as president of the American Psychological Association; the only other person to be so honored was William James.

Hall's many accomplishments secured a firm foundation for psychology in America. However, like James, Hall did not have the temperament for laboratory work. Rather, he created an intellectual atmosphere to support those who were more empirically inclined. Nevertheless, Hall did contribute to the emerging body of psychological knowledge. Specifically, he was convinced of the importance of genetics and evolution for psychology, which was reflected in his writings and his support of the study of developmental psychology. In addition, Hall pioneered survey techniques, which have remained a fixture of social science research.

These three early psychologists, Münsterberg, McDougall, and Hall, were independent thinkers. They did not start systems of psychology, nor develop coherent theoretical frameworks, nor leave behind loyal followers. However, they made psychology functional and left it firmly entrenched in America.

FUNCTIONAL PSYCHOLOGY

We now come to the more formal statements of functional psychology. As stated earlier, functional psychology was more an attitude toward the results of psychological investigation than a comprehensive system. However, centers of functional psychology developed at the University of Chicago and at Columbia University. No substantial difference discriminated these two centers of functionalism. Indeed, the great American philosopher–psychologist John Dewey was associated with both universities. Rather, both Chicago and Columbia served as focal places for the spread of the new science in America, and both imposed a functional identification on psychology.

Chicago Functionalism

At Chicago, psychology was easily related to other disciplines. Applied directions in education were especially paramount, and research on issues of psychological and biological importance served as a precursor to the subsequent emergence of behavioral psychology.

John Dewey. John Dewey (1859–1952) initiated functionalism at the University of Chicago, and his long career was characterized by a commitment to social change. He fully appreciated the democratic implications of Darwin's theory, and saw education as the key to individual improvement and the betterment of society. Accordingly, rather than dedicating himself to enhancing the field of psychology per se, Dewey used psychology as a means to his social vision.

After receiving his degree in 1884 at Hopkins for a dissertation on Kant's psychology, Dewey spent the next 20 years in the Midwest, first at Michigan and then at Chicago, before moving on to Columbia University in 1904. Still a young man, Dewey published the first textbook, *Psychology* (1886), on the new science in America. Although this work defined psychology in functional terms, Dewey was very much the philosopher, describing sensation, for example, as elementary consciousness arising as a response of the soul. Dewey's major contribution to psychology was contained in a famous paper published while he was at Chicago, "The Reflex Arc Concept in Psychology" (1896). Anticipating the later Gestalt interpretation of behavioral activities, Dewey argued against an elementaristic analysis of reflexive responses, in contrast to the reflexology that shortly developed through Pavlovian and Watsonian behaviorism. Dewey emphasized the totality of movement, contending that coordination is more than the sum of reflexes. Dewey rejected the view that reflexes are discrete series of stimulus actions followed by responses and separated by intervening sensations. Reflexes are smooth and orderly sequences of coordinated movements that are indivisible.

By the time Dewey moved to Columbia, his views had increasingly evolved toward education and social philosophy. His major contribution, from his time at Chicago, consisted of leading a group of young scholars convinced of the utility of psychology and advocating the position that American psychology and functional psychology are synonymous.

James Angell.   The organizer of Chicago functionalism, James Angell (1869–1949) went to Chicago in 1894 and stayed until 1920. Born in Vermont, Angell was the grandson of a president of Brown University and the son of the president of the University of Vermont and later the University of Michigan; he himself became the president of Yale in 1921. He did his undergraduate work at Michigan while Dewey was there, and received a master's degree at Harvard under William James in 1892. He went to Halle, Germany, for doctoral work and completed all requirements, but left before revising his dissertation to accept a job offer from the University of Minnesota. Thus, he never received his doctorate, but his new position allowed him to get married, and he effectively compensated for the lack of a doctorate by collecting more than 20 honorary degrees during his long and distinguished career.

His presidential address to the American Psychological Association in 1906, published the following year in the *Psychological Review*, was titled "The Province of Functional Psychology," and it contained a very clear statement of the agenda of functional psychology. Essentially, Angell defined the core of functional psychology as the acceptance of a biological approach to determine how the mind works in adjustments of the psychophysical person to the environment. This definition placed functional psychology in line with British natural science and Darwinism. In contrast to Wundt, Angell stated that consciousness progressively improves the adaptive activities of a person, and that attentional processes are the center of consciousness. Elaborating, Angell described three areas included in functional psychology. First, functional psychology studies mental operations, as opposed to the mental elements of a structural psychology. Second, functional psychology's emphasis on the adaptive activities of the mind means that the mind is viewed in a mediational role between the person's needs and the environment. Because consciousness habituates to environmental events after successful accommodation, according to Angell, novel stimuli elicit attentional fluctuations in consciousness and assume a critical role. Third, functional psychology assumes a psychophysical, mind–body interaction; hence, traditional psychophysics would continue to occupy an important place in research.

Under Angell's leadership, functional psychology at Chicago flourished and research papers on human as well as infrahuman levels were widely published. Perhaps Angell's most famous student was the founder of American behaviorism, John B. Watson, whose dissertation was titled *Animal Education: The Psychical Development of the White Rat* (1903). Although Angell subsequently rejected Watson's behaviorism as philosophically absurd and psychologically pernicious, Watson's views were nevertheless a logical consequence of some of the basic goals of functional psychology.

Harvey Carr.   The major spokesperson of Chicago functionalism after Angell, Harvey Carr (1873–1954) received his doctorate there in 1905. He became department chair in 1919 and during the next 19 years presided over the awarding of 150 doctorates. By the time Carr wrote his influential textbook, *Psychology*, in 1925, the development of functional psychology was essentially complete. Moreover, the major reason for functional psychology—its attack on Wundt and Titchener and their structural psychology—no longer existed as a viable force in psychology. Although functional psychology continued as a nominal system, it was steadily absorbed into American behaviorism during Carr's tenure at Chicago.

Carr defined psychology as the science of mental processes, and emphasized motor responses, adaptive activities, and motivation. Carr recognized both subjective, introspective methods and objective measures in psychology. However, with his background in animal psychology, he tended toward the objective at the expense of the subjective methods of research. In the experiments done at Chicago, the widespread use of objective measurements of psychological activities paved the way for the subsequent research approach that emphasized overt, observable behavior as the primary source of psychological data. Accordingly, Carr's place in functional psychology was to summarize the basic principles commonly shared in this movement: First, mental processes are adaptive and have purpose. Second, mental activity is elicited by environmental stimuli. Third, motivation always affects mental processes and modifies stimulus influences. Fourth, behavioral responses have consequences. Finally, all mental activity is continuous and coordinated.

Columbia Functionalism

Psychology at Columbia University had a broadly based functional character with varied applications. The three psychologists who will be considered illustrate the diversity of approaches to functional psychology at Columbia.

James McKeen Cattell.   James McKeen Cattell (1860–1944) was probably second only to Hall in his efforts to establish a sense of professionalism among psychologists. Cattell received his undergraduate education at Lafayette College in Easton, Pennsylvania, and then went to Germany, where he studied under Lotze and Wundt. After returning to America for a year of study at Hopkins, Cattell acquired a definite commitment to psychology. He went back to Germany, boldly told Wundt that he needed an assistant—namely, himself—and worked productively for 3 years, receiving his doctorate in 1886. While in Wundt's laboratory, Cattell became fascinated with reaction time experiments, and studied individual differences in reaction times, an unusual topic for one of Wundt's students. After a year of teaching in the United States, Cattell spent 1888 lecturing at Cambridge University. While in England, he met Sir Francis Galton, with whom he shared an interest in individual variability. From 1888 to 1891, Cattell was a professor of psychology at the University of Pennsylvania, and from 1891 to 1917, he held a similar position at Columbia. He started psychology laboratories at both institutions. Cattell, along with many prominent Americans, including Secretary of State William Jennings Bryan, was ardently opposed to America's entry into World War I. Cattell was fired from Columbia University for his pacifistic position, and devoted the remainder of his life to his interests in psychological testing and his many editorial duties. In 1894, he cofounded the *Psychological Review* with James Baldwin (1861–1934), and in 1900 started *Popular Science* (later *Scientific Monthly*). Cattell edited *American Men of Science* for 32 years and served at various times as editor of *Science, School and Society* and *American Naturalist*.

By the 1890s, Cattell's interest in individual differences led him to promote mental testing. In 1892, he published a monograph, *On the Perception of Small Differences*, in which he introduced detailed statistical analyses of errors in judgments made by subjects in traditional psychophysical experiments. That study was followed by research along the direction taken by Galton. In 1896, Cattell published a report of the physical and mental measures of students at Columbia, followed by an evaluative survey of eminent scientists. He started his own company, The Psychological Corporation, to market psychological expertise and measurement instruments to the public.

Cattell's lifelong interest in individual differences was functional in both theoretical terms and applications. He was concerned with the measurement of human capacity, which he viewed in an evolutionary sense, as did Galton. As a leading American psychologist, Cattell influenced many students. His advocacy of the use of statistics and testing bolstered an entire applied specialization within psychology.

Edward Lee Thorndike.   A biographical sketch of Edward Lee Thorndike (1874–1949) is given in Chapter 15 as a predecessor of American behaviorism. Indeed, Thorndike's earlier work on animal learning reflects his appropriate classification in the behaviorist tradition that grew out of the functional spirit of American psychology. He received his doctorate under Cattell in 1898, and his subsequent association with Columbia Teacher's College influenced his later interest in human intelligence and testing.

Thorndike published two works outlining applications of learning and testing principles: *Educational Psychology* (1903) and *Introduction to the Theory of Mental and Social Measurement* (1904). Both texts became necessary reading for a generation of students of psychology and the social sciences. Thorndike described intelligence through a somewhat elementaristic approach by stressing that intelligence is composed of a number of abilities. Although Thorndike's views on association processes, presented in Chapter 15, earned him greater fame in behavioristic psychology, his capacity to use his research reflected an applied direction, entirely consistent with American functionalism.

Robert S. Woodworth.   After receiving his doctorate under Cattell in 1899, Robert S. Woodworth (1869–1962) remained at Columbia for his entire career, with the exception of a postdoctoral year studying with the British neurophysiologist Charles Sherrington. Woodworth's first major work, *Dynamic Psychology* (1918), was an eclectic combination of prevailing views on psychology. Among his other works, *Contemporary Schools of Psychology* (1931) and *Dynamics of Behavior* (1958) offer careful functional perspectives on psychology. His *Experimental Psychology* (1938), revised in 1954 with Harold Schlosberg, was for many years the dominant textbook in university-level laboratory courses in psychology.

Woodworth's "dynamic" psychology focused on motivation. His views were not dynamic in terms of any essential deviation from the Lockean model of empiricism. Rather, Woodworth followed a fairly accepted interpretation of psychological processes, consistent with Chicago functionalism and Thorndike's views, but stressed individual motivation and underlying physiological correlates as central to adaptation. He used the term *mechanism* to describe the psychological act of adaptation, similar to the position of Carr. Mechanisms are elicited by drives, both internal and external in origin. For Woodworth, the entire repertoire of psychological activity gains a coherence and unity because of the individual's sense of purpose.

Women in Early American Psychology

An additional topic in this chapter on the history of early American psychology that deserves special mention concerns the role of women. Although women have contributed to psychology throughout its long history, because of psychology's particular success in the United States it is appropriate to underscore the role of women in the founding of American psychology. At the same time, it is important to note that psychology has not been immune to the biases and prejudices that have historically plagued all disciplines and have resulted in limited opportunities for women at all levels of intellectual endeavor. Although many women were barred from making contributions to the study of psychology, it may be argued that psychology has a record of access for women when compared to other sciences. Perhaps this relative openness reflected psychology's newness as a discipline emerging in the twentieth century at a time when women were making significant strides toward participation in the universities, the political arena, and the marketplace. Nevertheless, success for women in all fields, including psychology, often meant great personal sacrifices that included leaving the security of home and family to obtain a competitive education, remaining unmarried, becoming financially self-supporting, and continually proving themselves under male-dominated review.

The three women briefly described here were successful early American psychologists. Each reflected the particular American spirit in psychology, which is functional; each provided significant research in fostering the development of psychology; and each influenced many students.

Mary Whiton Calkins. After graduating from Smith College and touring Europe for a year during which she studied at the University of Leipzig, Mary Whiton Calkins (1863–1930) started a 40-year affiliation with Wellesley College, where she began as a tutor of ancient Greek. Recognizing her intelligence and interest in the new science, Wellesley officials asked her to develop a course in experimental psychology and urged her to pursue her own education in psychology. She finished the doctoral degree requirements at Harvard under William James and Hugo Münsterberg, but was not awarded the degree because Harvard University itself was not at that time coeducational, and Radcliffe, the women's college of Harvard, did not grant doctoral degrees. Thus, despite the awarding of the degree from the Department of Philosophy and Psychology, the Harvard Corporation would not confer the PhD. In 1896 Calkins published a paper in *Psychological Review*, in which she reported a method for presenting pairs of verbal items having no existing meaningful relation. She used this technique to vary the influence of the major determinants of memory—primacy, frequency, recency, and vividness. In extending the research of Ebbinghaus, Calkins also provided data supporting the secondary laws of association, originally proposed by the Scottish philosopher Thomas Reid.

Calkins was a faculty member of Wellesley College for most of her career, and established a laboratory there in 1891. In 1909 she published an influential introductory psychology textbook, *A First Book in Psychology*. In 1905 she was elected the first woman president of the American Psychological Association and in 1918 was the first woman to serve as president of the American Philosophical Society.

After about 10 years of amazing laboratory-based productivity, Calkins' attention shifted to more theoretical and philosophical concerns. She is remembered chiefly for her contributions toward a psychology of the self. Calkins' self-psychology emphasized the essential unity and coherence of consciousness, very dependent on both interpersonal and environmental interactions. This perspective is very interesting because for the remainder of her career she consistently provided an alternative to the emergence and eventual domination of behaviorism. In a very real sense Calkins reflected the wide definition of psychology from two of her Harvard mentors, Hugo Münsterberg and William James, that psychology can accommodate investigations that are at several levels, from mental elements to the unity of conscious experience. Her career represents the full gamut of eclectic concerns reflecting the functional spirit of American psychology.

Christine Ladd-Franklin. Born and raised in New England, Christine Ladd (1847–1930) graduated from Vassar in 1869 with a strong background in physics and mathematics. She taught in secondary schools in several locations and began to submit solutions and papers to various popular and scholarly journals. When Johns Hopkins University opened in 1876, Ladd applied and, after overcoming resistance because of her sex, was admitted in 1878, where she worked at first with the mathematician, James J. Sylvester. In 1879, as she began working with Charles Sanders Peirce and was teaching part-time at Hopkins, Ladd's interest turned to symbolic logic and experimental psychology. After completing all of the requirements for a doctorate at Hopkins, she married a fellow graduate student and instructor, Fabian Franklin. Because Hopkins did not grant degrees to women, it was not until 1926 that the university granted her the PhD. In 1891–92, Franklin's sabbatical leave from Hopkins permitted a trip to Europe, where Ladd-Franklin studied at Göttingen and Berlin universities. In 1895, Franklin left Hopkins to embark on an editorial career, first in Baltimore, then in New York. After her move to New York, Ladd-Franklin maintained a type of unpaid courtesy appointment at Columbia University as an academic base for her many publications.

Best remembered for her theory of color vision, Ladd-Franklin attempted to reconcile the trichromatic theory of Helmholtz with the tetrachromatic theory of Hering and Georg Elias Müller. Her solution, building on the finding that yellow–blue cones develop before red–green sensitivity, proposed that from white (gray) sensitivity, blue and yellow emerge, and from yellow sensitivity, green and red emerge. Color vision, then, is a product of these stages, which she also related to other visual processes, such as afterimages, as well as to pathology, such as color blindness.

Ladd-Franklin was recognized as an important psychologist in her lifetime. She received an honorary LLD from Vassar in 1887, and she consistently advocated women's rights. She was active in women's organizations, including a forerunner of the American Association of University Women.

Margaret Floy Washburn.   Like Ladd-Franklin, Margaret Floy Washburn (1871–1939) was also a graduate of Vassar and became the first woman to receive a doctorate in psychology in the United States. She completed her training with Titchener at Cornell University in 1894, and Titchener sent her thesis results to Wundt for publication in *Philosophische Studien* in 1895. She also translated some of Wundt's writings into English. In 1903, she joined the faculty of Vassar College, where she remained until her death. A pioneer in animal psychology, she wrote *The Animal Mind* in 1908, which attempted to look at conscious states reflected in observable behavior. She returned to this theme in her 1916 work *Movement and Mental Imagery*, which proposed a reconciliation between behaviorism and introspection.

Widely recognized during her lifetime for her contributions as a scholar and academic, in 1921 she was elected president of the American Psychological Association. She was the first woman psychologist and second woman scientist to be elected to the National Academy of Sciences (1932).

These psychologists offered significant contributions to the development of American psychology and provided admirable role models for future generations of women psychologists.

IMPACT

Because of the unsystematic nature of functional psychology, it is difficult to appreciate this movement without concentrating on individual functionalists. The psychologists surveyed are representative, but brief mention of other leaders of the movement is also appropriate. George Trumbull Ladd (1842–1921) stressed the adaptive value of the mind and argued for the necessity of an active self-concept. Edward Wheeler Scripture (1864–1945) was a detailed methodologist who studied speech patterns and phonetics. We have already mentioned James Baldwin in connection with the start of the *Psychological Review*; he also did much to integrate Darwinism and functional psychology, and he founded Princeton's psychology laboratories. Joseph Jastrow (1863–1944), a student of Peirce, went on to work in psychophysical research and became a popular writer on psychology. Edmund Clark Sanford (1859–1924) founded the psychology laboratory at Clark University and wrote an early textbook on experimental psychology. Finally, Edmund Burke Delabarre (1863–1945), a student of James and Münsterberg, chaired the psychology department at Brown University and investigated visual perception. He took over the Harvard laboratories during Münsterberg's occasional trips to Europe. Collectively, their views were varied, but they were people of talent who valued psychology and placed the discipline on a firm foundation in America.

This diversity of functional psychology, reflected by the lack of systematic substance, dictated functionalism's disintegration. The functionalists were arguing against structural psychology, represented in America by Titchener, just as the Gestaltists were arguing with Wundt in Germany. This context should be recalled, because in many respects functional psychology was defined in terms of structural psychology; that is, Wundt's system served as the reference, albeit negative, for functional psychology. In contrast to the Gestalt development, however, functional psychology did not grow to the point of offering a comprehensive alternative model of psychology. As structural psychology began to wither, so, too, did functional psychology. It served its purpose by providing a transition from structural psychology to behaviorism.

CHAPTER SUMMARY

Functional psychology was less a system than an attitude that valued the utility of psychological inquiry. Assuming a philosophical underpinning from the pragmatism of William James and Charles Sanders Peirce, functional psychology fit well into the pioneering spirit of America. From its beginning, functional psychology had a clear emphasis on applying psychology to individual and social improvement, as was evident from the works of Münsterberg, McDougall, and Hall. The tradition of British natural science and evolutionary theory was integrated into psychology in the views on adaptation championed by the Chicago functionalists, such as Dewey, Angell, and Carr. Mental testing and the study of human capacity constituted important areas of investigation among the Columbia functionalists, represented by Cattell, Thorndike, and Woodworth. Although its reaction to structural psychology kept functional psychology from developing a systematic alternative model of psychological inquiry, this phase of American psychology resulted in two critical benefits. First, functionalism firmly entrenched the new science of psychology in America and imposed on it a particular American orientation toward applied psychology. Second, functional psychology provided a necessary transition from the restricted context of structural psychology to more viable models of psychology, permitting the science to progress.

BIBLIOGRAPHY

Primary Sources

ANGELL, J. R. (1907). The province of functional psychology. *Psychological Review, 14,* 61–91.

CALKINS, M. W. (1896). Association. *Psychological Review, 3,* 32–49.

CALKINS, M. W. (1900). Psychology as science of selves. *Philosophical Review, 9,* 490–501.

CALKINS, M. W. (1909, 1914). *A first book in psychology.* New York: Macmillan.

CALKINS, M. W. (1961). Mary Whiton Calkins. In C. Murchison (Ed.), *A history of psychology in autobiography,* Vol. 1. New York: Russell & Russell, 31–62.

CARR, H. (1925). *Psychology.* New York: Longmans Green.

CARR, H. (1930). Functionalism. In C. Murchison (Ed.), *Psychologies of 1930.* Worcester, MA: Clark University Press.

CATTELL, J. McK. (1904). The conceptions and methods of psychology. *Popular Science Monthly, 46,* 176–186.

CATTELL, J. McK. (1943). The founding of the association and of the Hopkins and Clark laboratories. *Psychological Review, 50,* 61–64.

DEWEY, J. (1886). *Psychology.* New York: Harper.

DEWEY, J. (1896). The reflex arc concept in psychology. *Psychological Review, 3,* 357–370.

GALTON, F. (1889). *Natural inheritance.* London: Macmillan.

HALL, G. S. (1917). *The life and confessions of a psychologist.* Garden City, NY: Doubleday.

JAMES, W. (1890). *The principles of psychology.* New York: Holt.

JAMES, W. (1902). *Varieties of religious experience.* New York: Longmans Green.

JAMES, W. (1907). *Pragmatism.* New York: Longmans Green.

JAMES, W. (1985). Habit (1892). *Occupational Therapy in Mental Health, 5,* 55–67.

LADD-FRANKLIN, C. (1911, 1924). The nature of the colour sensation: A new chapter on the subject. In H. Helmholtz (Ed.), *Physiological optics,* 3rd ed. Rochester, NY: Optical Society of America, 455–468.

LADD-FRANKLIN, C. (1929). *Colour and colour theories.* New York: Harcourt Brace Jovanovich.

McDOUGALL, W. (1908). *Introduction to social psychology.* London: Methuen.

MÜNSTERBERG, H. (1903). *Psychotherapy.* New York: Moffat Yard.

MÜNSTERBERG, H. (1904). *The Americans* (E. B. Holt, Trans.). New York: McClure Philips.

MÜNSTERBERG, H. (1908). *On the witness stand.* New York: Doubleday.

MÜNSTERBERG, H. (1909). *Psychology and the teacher.* New York: Appleton.

MÜNSTERBERG, H. (1912). *Vocation and learning.* St. Louis: The People's University.

MÜNSTERBERG, H. (1913). *Psychology and industrial efficiency.* Boston: Houghton Mifflin.

MÜNSTERBERG, H. (1916). *Psychology, general and applied.* New York: Appleton.

MÜNSTERBERG, H. (1916). *The photoplay: A psychological study.* New York: Appleton.

PEARSON, K. (1901). On lines and planes of closest fit to systems of points in space. *Philosophical Magazine, 6,* 559–572.

PEIRCE, C. S. (1962). *The collected papers of Charles Sanders Peirce* (C. Hartshorne, P. Weiss, & A. Burks, Eds.). Cambridge: Harvard University Press.

SPEARMAN, C. (1904). General intelligence, objectively determined and measured. *American Journal of Psychology, 15,* 201–293.

THORNDIKE, E. L. (1931). *Human learning.* New York: Appleton.

THURSTONE, L. L. (1935). *Vectors of the mind.* Chicago: University of Chicago Press.

WASHBURN, M. F. (1908). *The animal mind.* New York: Macmillan.

WASHBURN, M. F. (1961). Margaret Floy Washburn. In C. Murchison (Ed.), *A history of psychology in autobiography,* Vol. II. New York: Russell & Russell, 333–358.

WOODWORTH, R. S. (1918). *Dynamic psychology.* New York: Columbia University Press.

WOODWORTH, R. S. (1931, 1948). *Contemporary schools of psychology* (Rev. ed.). New York: Ronald Press.

WOODWORTH, R. S., & SCHLOSBERG, H. (1954). *Experimental psychology* (Rev. ed.). New York: Holt, Rinehart & Winston.

Studies

BENDY, M. (1974). Psychiatric antecedents of psychological testing (before Binet). *Journal of the History of the Behavioral Sciences, 10,* 180–194.

BORING, E. G. (1950). *A history of experimental psychology,* 2nd ed. Englewood Cliffs, NJ: Prentice Hall.

BRENNAN, J. F. (1975). Edmund Burke Delabarre and the petroglyphs of Southeastern New England. *Journal of the History of the Behavioral Sciences, 11,* 107–122.

BURNHAM, W. H. (1925). The man, G. Stanley Hall. *Psychological Review, 32,* 89–102.

CADWALLADER, T. C. (1974). Charles S. Peirce (1839–1914): The first American experimental psychologist. *Journal of the History of the Behavioral Sciences, 10,* 291–298.

CADWALLADER, T. C., & CADWALLADER, J. V. (1990). Christine Ladd-Franklin (1847–1930). In A. N. O'Connell and N. F. Russo (Eds.), *Women in psychology: A biobibliographic sourcebook.* New York: Greenwood Press, 220–229.

CAMFIELD, T. M. (1973). The professionalization of American psychology, 1870–1917. *Journal of the History of the Behavioral Sciences, 9,* 66–75.

CARLSON, E. T., & SIMPSON, M. M. (1970). Perkinism vs. mesmerism. *Journal of the History of the Behavioral Sciences, 6,* 16–24.

FISHER, S. C. (1925). The psychological and educational work of Granville Stanley Hall. *American Journal of Psychology, 36,* 1–52.

FULCHER, J. R. (1973). Puritans and the passions: The faculty psychology in American puritanism. *Journal of the History of the Behavioral Sciences, 9,* 123–139.

FURUMOTO, L. (1979). Mary Whiton Calkins (1863–1930). Fourteenth President of the American Psychological Association. *Journal of the History of the Behavioral Sciences, 15,* 346–356.

FURUMOTO, L. (1990). Mary Whiton Calkins (1863–1930). In A. N. O'Connell and N. F. Russo (Eds.), *Women in psychology: a bio-bibliographic sourcebook.* New York: Greenwood Press, 57–65.

GILLHAM, N. W. (2001). *A life of Sir Francis Galton from African exploration to the birth of eugenics.* New York: Oxford University Press.

GUBER, C. (1972). Academic freedom at Columbia University, 1917–1918: The case of James McKeen Cattell. *American Association of University Professors Bulletin, 58,* 297–305.

HARRISON, F. (1963). Functionalism and its historical significance. *Genetic Psychology Monographs, 68,* 387–423.

HENLE, M., & SULLIVAN, J. (1974). Seven psychologies revisited. *Journal of the History of the Behavioral Sciences, 10,* 40–46.

HEIDBREDER, E. (1972). Mary Whiton Calkins: A discussion. *Journal of the History of the Behavioral Sciences, 8,* 56–68.

JONCICH, G. (1968). *The sane positivist: A biography of Edward L. Thorndike.* Middletown, CT: Wesleyan University Press.

KLOPPER, W. G. (1973). The short history of projective techniques. *Journal of the History of the Behavioral Sciences, 9,* 60–65.

KRANTZ, D. L., HALL, R., & ALLEN, D. (1969). William McDougall and the problems of purpose. *Journal of the History of the Behavioral Sciences, 5,* 25–38.

MCCURDY, H. C. (1968). William McDougall. In B. Wolman (Ed.), *Historical roots of contemporary psychology.* New York: Harper & Row, 4–47.

MCKINNEY, F. (1978). Functionalism at Chicago—Memories of a graduate student: 1929–1931. *Journal of the History of the Behavioral Sciences, 14,* 142–148.

MILLS, E. S. (1974). George Trumbull Ladd: The great textbook writer. *Journal of the History of the Behavioral Sciences, 10,* 299–303.

MOSKOWITZ, M. J. (1977). Hugo Münsterberg: A study in the history of applied psychology. *American Psychologist, 32,* 824–842.

MUELLER, R. H. (1976). A chapter in the history of the relationship between psychology and sociology in America: James Mark Baldwin. *Journal of the History of the Behavioral Sciences, 12,* 240–253.

MURPHY, G. (1971). William James and the will. *Journal of the History of the Behavioral Sciences, 7,* 249–260.

NANCE, R. D. (1970). G. Stanley Hall and John B. Watson as child psychologists. *Journal of the History of the Behavioral Sciences, 6,* 303–316.

NOEL, P. S., & CARLSON, E. T. (1973). The faculty psychology of Benjamin Rush. *Journal of the History of the Behavioral Sciences, 9,* 369–377.

PASTORE, N. (1977). William James: A contradiction. *Journal of the History of the Behavioral Sciences, 13,* 126–130.

RAPHELSEN, A. C. (1973). The pre-Chicago association of early functionalists. *Journal of the History of the Behavioral Sciences, 9,* 115–122.

ROBACK, A. (1964). *A history of American psychology* (Rev. ed.). New York: Collier.

RUCKMICK, C. (1912). The history and status of psychology in America. *American Journal of Psychology, 23,* 517–531.

RYAN, T. A. (1982). Psychology at Cornell after Titchener: Madison Bentley to Robert MacLeod, 1928–1948. *Journal of the History of the Behavioral Sciences, 18,* 347–369.

SAMELSON, F. (1977). World War I intelligence testing and the development of psychology. *Journal of the History of the Behavioral Sciences, 13,* 274–282.

SCARBOROUGH, E. Margaret Floy Washburn (1871–1939). In A. N. O'Connell and N. F. Russo (Eds.), *Women in psychology: A bio-bibliographic sourcebook.* New York: Greenwood Press, 342–349.

SCHNEIDER, W. H. (1992). After Binet: French intelligence testing, 1900–1950. *Journal of the History of the Behavioral Sciences, 28,* 111–132.

SOKAL, M. M. (1981). The origins of the Psychological Corporation. *Journal of the History of the Behavioral Sciences, 17,* 54–67.

SOKAL, M. M. (1990). G. Stanley Hall and the institutional character of psychology at Clark University (1889–1920). *Journal of the History of the Behavioral Sciences, 26,* 114–124.

WALLIN, J. E. (1968). A tribute to G. Stanley Hall. *Journal of Genetic Psychology, 113,* 149–153.

❄ 13 ❄

The Gestalt Movement

Background in Germany
    The Würzburg Legacy
    German Phenomenology
The Founding of Gestalt Psychology
    Max Wertheimer
    Wolfgang Köhler
    Kurt Koffka
Basic Principles of Gestalt Psychology
Implications of Gestalt Psychology
    As a European Movement
    As an American Movement
    Field Theory
Chapter Summary

The German word *Gestalt* cannot be rendered into a single English word. It describes a configuration or form that is unified. A Gestalt may refer to a figure or object that is different from the sum of its parts. Any attempt to explain the figure by analyzing its parts results in the loss of the figure's Gestalt. For example, a square has a unity and an identity that cannot be fully appreciated by its description as four straight lines connected by right angles. Accordingly, Gestalt expresses the fundamental premise of a system of psychology that conceptualizes psychological events as organized, unified, and coherent phenomena. This view stresses the integrity of a clear psychological level of human activity, which loses its identity if analyzed into preconceived components. Gestalt psychology is characteristically antireductionistic. For example, if learning is considered as a psychological activity, then according to Gestalt psychologists, it cannot be reduced to the physiological mechanisms of conditioning. Gestaltists argue that the very attempt to reduce the psychological event to its physiological components results in the loss of the psychological event. The Gestalt is removed, so that the psychological event of learning is not explained, and only a physiological mechanism is described.

Gestalt psychology was a German movement that directly challenged Wundt's structural psychology. The Gestaltists inherited the tradition of the act psychology of Brentano and Stumpf, as well as the Würzburg school, which attempted to devise an alternative to the model of psychology proposed by the reductionistic and analytic natural science model of Wundt. The Gestalt movement was more consistent than Wundt's system with the major theme of mental activity in German philosophy, following in the tradition of Kant; that is, underlying Gestalt psychology was the nativistic proposition that the organization of mental activity predisposes the individual to interact with the environment in characteristic ways. Accordingly, the goals of Gestalt psychology were to investigate the organization of mental activity and to determine the exact nature of person–environmental interactions.

By 1930, the Gestalt movement had largely succeeded in replacing the Wundtian model in German psychology. However, the movement's success was short-lived because of the advent of Hitlerism, with its accompanying intellectual sterility and physical barbarism. The leaders of the movement fled to America, but there Gestalt psychology never enjoyed the dominance it had achieved in Germany. Essentially, the initial views of Gestalt psychology were contrasted with Wundt's psychology. Those arguments were out of touch with American psychology because Wundt's system was largely irrelevant by the 1930s. American psychology had evolved through the functional period and by the 1930s was dominated by behaviorism. Accordingly, the framework of Gestalt psychology was not in step with American developments. Nevertheless, the attractiveness of Gestalt psychology influenced many behaviorists, as reviewed in Chapter 15, and the movement played an important role in the expansion of the behavioristic model of psychology in America.

BACKGROUND IN GERMANY

Before the specific views of the Gestalt psychologists are examined, two immediate precedents should be reviewed. Both contributed to the intellectual climate of German psychology as well as to the acceptance and success of Gestalt psychology.

The Würzburg Legacy

As discussed in Chapter 11, the German intellectual atmosphere may be broadly described as containing two schools of psychology. One was the Wundtian natural science model of psychology, which revolved around the study of immediate experience through controlled introspection. By virtue of his strong personality and tremendous productivity, Wundt introduced a unified system of structural psychology that restricted the new science to a view of mental contents as wholly dependent on sensory input. The other school consisted of a loose collection of writers who, although they held various views, shared a dissatisfaction with Wundt's model. Brentano and Stumpf, as we have seen, were dominant figures in the attempt to remove psychology from the limitations of Wundt's rigid formulation.

As a development of the anti-Wundt movement in Germany, the Würzburg school under Külpe attempted to define mental activity in terms of nonsensory consciousness. The "imageless thought" controversy served as a catalytic agent for various trends that were moving toward a viewpoint involving more self-initiated activity in mental processes. Indeed, Külpe viewed the mind as predisposed to the ordering of environmental events along dimensions of quality, intensity, time, and space, restoring to German psychology the mental categories of Kant. These predispositions, together with the recognition of the existence of mental contents having nonsensory origin, radically challenged the assumptions underlying mental processes, such as those of Wundt's psychology. The Würzburg psychologists asserted that the mind has characteristic sets, or determining tendencies, that result in patterns of perception. Depending on the organism's set at a given time, associations may change from one pattern or sequence to another. This type of mental activity, then, is dependent on the mind's organization.

As noted in Chapter 11, the Würzburg school enjoyed a relatively brief period of productivity but did not devise a comprehensive, alternative model of psychology to compete with the formulations of Wundt. Nevertheless, their careful observations, leading to their advocacy of nonsensory consciousness, presented a serious challenge to Wundt's model. It was the Gestaltists who followed the conclusions of the Würzburg school to a systematic position in opposition to Wundt.

German Phenomenology

As the word indicates, phenomenology is the study of phenomena. A phenomenon is literally that which appears. However, in the context of phenomenology, phenomena are taken as events studied for themselves, without concern for underlying causality or inferences. For psychology, a phenomenological approach characteristically emphasizes experiences as perceived by an individual. It stands in sharp contrast to any form of analysis that breaks a psychological event into elements or reduces an event to other levels of explanations.

We have already seen examples of phenomenological approaches. The empirical strategies of many eighteenth- and nineteenth-century physiologists typically contained keen observations, as opposed to tight experimental controls. The sensory investigations of Purkinje stand out as a clear example of this type of phenomenological study in physiology. Certainly, the act psychology of Brentano and Stumpf was more amenable to the observational foundation of phenomenology than to an experimental method of controls imposed over psychological variables. Moreover, the scientific positions of Dilthey and Bergson were more conducive to the descriptive data of phenomenology than to the causal inferences of experimentation. Accordingly, phenomenology is a traditional method of empiricism, but its variations have differed according to the particular assumptions attached to the subject matter under investigation, especially in psychology.

The modern expression of phenomenology came from a student of Brentano, Edmund Husserl (1859–1938). Husserl's application of phenomenology to psychological issues called for a pure science of consciousness; he advocated detailed and sophisticated description of experienced mental activity. Husserl developed a method of observation that elaborated all levels of the modes by which phenomena could appear in consciousness. Yet Husserl's method was not analytical and was opposed to reduction. Thus Husserl's phenomenology left a purely psychological level of investigation intact. Husserl and the Gestalt psychologists had different views of the content of psychology. It was left to later thinkers to explore fully Husserl's brand of phenomenology for psychology, which is examined in Chapter 16. However, Husserl's phenomenology and the Gestalt movement were both products of the same intellectual forces in Germany at the beginning of the twentieth century. While pursuing different implications, both the Gestalt psychologists and Husserl were dubious of the analytical character of the controlled laboratory method, and they searched for alternative formulations of psychology that recognized the inherent organization and activity of the mind.

THE FOUNDING OF GESTALT PSYCHOLOGY

As stated earlier, Gestalt psychologists emphasized the organization and unity of their data, defined in terms of phenomena. The wholeness and unity of experiences were examined in terms of forms. In contrast to the study of immediate experience of Wundtian psychology, the Gestaltists' study of phenomena was purposefully defined as mediated experience. Gestalt psychology included the investigation of objects and their meaning; it valued mediated perceived thoughts over sensory events. The individual was viewed as actively interacting with the environment, within a dynamic field or system of interactions. Whereas not completely rejecting analytic methodologies as the pure phenomenologists did, the Gestalt psychologists asserted the freedom to use varieties of methodologies that did not interfere with the integrity of phenomena.

Gestalt psychology was originated and nurtured by the writings of three persons: Max Wertheimer, Wolfgang Köhler, and Kurt Koffka. All were educated in the exciting intellectual atmosphere of early twentieth-century Germany, and all later fled Nazi persecution and immigrated to America.

Max Wertheimer

Born in Prague and educated at Charles University there, Max Wertheimer (1880–1943) studied with Stumpf in Berlin for several years before joining Külpe at Würzburg, where he received his doctorate in 1904. While traveling on a summer holiday in 1910, Wertheimer came upon an idea for an experiment on apparent movement. According to the story recounted by Boring (1950, p. 595), Wertheimer left the train at Frankfurt am Main and bought a toy stroboscope, a primitive device for showing moving pictures, to try to determine the optimal conditions for the phenomena to occur. We encounter this type of illusion daily in motion pictures or through special lighting effects that simulate motion through the appropriate, successive presentation of static stimuli. Wertheimer stayed on to become associated with the Psychological Institute of Frankfurt and gained access to a tachistoscope at the university to investigate the illusion more thoroughly. There he met Koffka and Köhler, who served as subjects for his experiments. He named this illusion the "phi phenomenon," and in 1912 he published "Experimental Studies of the Perception of Movement." His findings marked the formal beginnings of Gestalt psychology. The major implication of Wertheimer's research was that the phi phenomenon cannot be reduced to the stimulus elements presented to the subjects, as Wundt's system would predict. The subjective experience of motion is the result of a dynamic interaction between an observer and the stimuli.

Wertheimer was the scholarly guiding force among the early founders of Gestalt psychology. After working in military research during World War I, he lectured at various universities before accepting a professorship at Frankfurt in 1929. In 1933, he fled Germany for the United States and joined the faculty of the New School for Social Research (now the New School University) in New York City, where he stayed until his death. Through his teaching and personal meetings with American psychologists, he attempted to extend the scope of Gestalt principles beyond perceptual problems to thought processes. His final ideas on cognitive psychology within a Gestalt perspective were contained in *Productive Thinking*, published posthumously in 1945. In it he suggested guidelines to facilitate the development of creative strategies in problem solving. Despite the difficulties of moving to a new country and having to master a foreign language, he served as an inspirational force to the Gestalt movement in the United States.

Wolfgang Köhler

Perhaps the most systematic of the early Gestaltists, Wolfgang Köhler's (1887–1967) many publications gave Gestalt psychology definitive form. Born in Reval near the Baltic Sea area of East Prussia, Köhler attended various universities before receiving his doctorate under Stumpf's direction at Berlin in 1909. After working with Wertheimer in Frankfurt, Köhler went to the Canary Islands in 1913 to study chimpanzees. As a German national caught on the other side of Allied lines at the outbreak of World War I, he remained there until the end of the hostilities. In 1917, he published his *Intellegenzprüfungen an Menschenaffen*, based on his work during internment; it was translated into English in 1925 as *The Mentality of Apes*. After his experiences with Wertheimer and Koffka at Frankfurt, Köhler was able to offer an innovative approach to his studies of discrimination learning and problem solving. He applied a Gestalt interpretation to the acquisition of relationships between stimuli, as opposed to learning the absolute value of stimulus dimensions. Further, he found that the chimps used insightful strategies in solving puzzles rather than relying only on trial-and-error learning. Köhler's most intelligent subject, Sultan, was able to master various tasks to secure food reward, easily switching among problem-solving strategies. The rapidity of solutions impressed Köhler as evidence of insightful learning. Köhler's book is important in the history of the movement because he demonstrated specific instances of many of the principles of mental organization underlying Gestalt psychology.

Köhler returned to Germany in 1920 and taught at Göttingen for a year before being named to succeed Stumpf at Berlin in 1922. This prestigious appointment was largely the result of a scholarly and erudite work published in 1920, *Die Physischen Gestalten in Ruhe und im stationärem Zustand* (*Static and Stationary Physical Gestalts*). From 1934 to 1935, Köhler lectured at Harvard, and in 1935 finally left

Germany to join the faculty of Swarthmore College, where he stayed until his retirement. He adapted to America better than did Wertheimer, becoming the major spokesman for the Gestalt movement, and continued to edit the primary Gestalt journal, *Psychologische Forschung (Psychological Research)*. This journal, started in Germany by the founders of the Gestalt movement, published 22 volumes before it was suspended in 1938. Finally, in 1959, Köhler was elected president of the American Psychological Association, a fitting testimonial to his life of creative research and scholarly writing.

Kurt Koffka

Like Köhler, Kurt Koffka (1886–1941) received his doctorate from Stumpf in 1909 at the university in Berlin, the city of Koffka's birth. After working with Wertheimer and Köhler in Frankfurt, Koffka joined the University of Giessen, near Frankfurt, where he remained until 1924. He traveled in the United States while a visiting professor at several American universities, and secured a faculty position at Smith College in 1927, remaining there until his death.

It was Koffka who introduced Gestalt psychology to wide American audiences through his publication in 1922 of "Perception: An Introduction to the Gestalt-Theorie" in the *Psychological Bulletin*. In addition, Koffka published a book on developmental child psychology, *The Growth of the Mind* (1921), which was widely acclaimed in America as well as in Germany. However, his major aim—to write the definitive work on the Gestalt movement—was not fulfilled by his *Principles of Gestalt Psychology* (1935), which is now remembered chiefly as a very difficult book. Koffka was perhaps the most prolific writer of the three founders, yet lacked the inspirational quality of Wertheimer and the thoughtful, systematic capacity of Köhler. However, he did succeed in bringing the teachings of the Gestalt movement to a great number of psychologists, especially in the United States.

BASIC PRINCIPLES OF GESTALT PSYCHOLOGY

Consistent with the original work of Wertheimer on the phi phenomenon, the principles of Gestalt psychology grew out of research on sensory and perceptual processes. Much of the terminology and many of the examples illustrating Gestalt principles were derived from such studies. Only later were these principles extended to other psychological activities. This extension was especially appropriate in the applications of Gestalt principles to learning processes, when the focus of the Gestalt movement shifted to America. The Gestalt movement provided an alternative to Thorndike's trial-and-error learning as the behavioristic model was expanded.

In Gestalt psychology the focus of person–environment interactions is termed the *perceptual field*. The major characteristic of any perceptual field is organization, which has a natural tendency to be structured in terms of figure and ground. Thus, seeing the salient features of shapes and forms on a background within a perceptual field is a spontaneous innate activity and not an acquired skill; we are predisposed

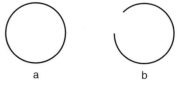

FIGURE 13–1   Circle *a* is complete and shows good Gestalt; line *b* is incomplete but is perceived as a circle because of closure.

to perceive in such a manner. A good figure is complete, tending toward symmetry, balance, and proportion. For example, a circle has a perfect Gestalt in terms of completeness. Incomplete figures tend to be perceived as complete, and this organizational characteristic is called closure; for example, a curved line with ends not quite touching will still be perceived as a circle because of the compelling tendency for closure. The two drawings in Figure 13–1 compare a complete Gestalt with a form illustrating closure. Similarly, in Figure 13–2 the importance of the relative saliency of context is illustrated; center circles in both illustrations are of equal size, but the surrounding circles make them appear to be of different sizes.

Organization leading to meaning, then, is the key to our perceptual structure, according to the Gestaltists. Other principles of organization in addition to closure include proximity and similarity. Organized figures are stable and tend to retain their stability as structural wholes despite changes in the stimulus characteristics; the Gestaltists called this *object constancy.* For example, an actor viewed on a television program is still perceived as a man, although the figure itself may be only a few inches tall.

The critical dimension in comparisons among figures or objects in the environment, according to the Gestaltists, is the relationships between parts of a figure, not the characteristics of the parts. If particular aspects of stimuli change, but not the relationships, the perception remains the same. Accordingly, the Gestaltists were able to accommodate Stumpf's argument with Wundt that the transposition of a

FIGURE 13–2   Because of the relationship of contexts, the center circle in *a* is perceived as larger than the center circle in *b*. Both center circles are the same size.

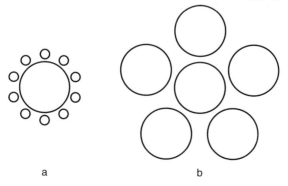

melody from one key to another retains the melody although the elements (the notes) have changed. This relativity as the basis for acquiring discriminations was demonstrated in varieties of learning situations. For example, rats trained to respond to the brighter and larger of two stimulus objects continued to select the brighter and larger of two new stimuli. The recognition of the salient relationships and the transfer of that knowledge from one learning situation to another was called *transposition*, and it was repeatedly demonstrated with varying species tested under many stimulus parameters.

Perhaps the weakest, and certainly the most elusive, part of Gestalt theory concerns the explanation of underlying brain activity mediating perceptual processes, which Gestaltists called *isomorphism*. The Soviet physiologist Ivan Pavlov, discussed in Chapter 15, criticized the Gestalt movement in a 1935 paper in which he pointed to the idealistic basis of Gestalt psychology as being mentalistic and without a mechanical, physiological foundation. The Gestalt attempt to define the physiological basis of perceptual processes was a deliberate attempt to get away from the mechanical notion of cortical excitation corresponding to stimulus action and associated sensory processing. Rather, the Gestaltists argued for what they called "brain experience," which involved the assertion that a perceptual field has an underlying excitatory brain field that corresponds to the perceptual field in order, but not necessarily in exact form. Hence, their choice of the term *isomorphic*, derived from Greek *iso* (similar) and *morphic* (shape). Isomorphic representation is defined as parallel processes between perceptual and physiological levels. The perceptual experience and the brain experience do not correspond on a one-to-one basis, but rather correspond in terms of relations. Accordingly, as Köhler described isomorphism, this principle relates the perceptual field to the brain field. The former is elicited by stimulus activity, whereas the latter consists of electrochemical activity. When Gestalt principles were formulated, isomorphism ran contrary to the prevailing concepts contained in Pavlovian and Sherringtonian neurophysiology. However, although the Gestalt notion of isomorphism remained rather vague, subsequent developments viewing cortical activity as a cybernetic system have made the hypothesis of isomorphism somewhat more tenable, at least as an analog, as we shall see in Chapter 15.

IMPLICATIONS OF GESTALT PSYCHOLOGY

As a European Movement

In its short-lived success as the dominant model of German psychology, the Gestalt movement replaced the Wundtian formulation of structural psychology. Indeed, it is in this context, as a reaction against structural psychology, that the Gestalt arguments make the most sense. The Gestaltists sharply criticized any model of psychology based on associationism and the elements of sensation. They expanded psychological inquiry from the limited sphere of immediate experience to include the mediated experience of consciousness, both sensory and nonsensory. In this sense, Gestalt psychology was an act psychology in the tradition of Brentano and Stumpf. In contrast to Wundt, Gestalt psychology studied the *how* of mental processing, not the *what*.

By admitting phenomenology as a methodological approach, the Gestalt movement expanded the empirical basis of psychology. Its practitioners demonstrated how a psychology defined in terms of the higher mental processes of mediated experience could nevertheless retain a scientific, empirical framework. In moving beyond their initial investigations of perceptual processes to a comprehensive psychology, the Gestaltists emphasized that consciousness and behavior should not be viewed separately but must be considered together. Thus the Gestalt movement in Europe showed every promise of integrating the positive developments of European psychology to consider all of the complexities of human activity.

Unfortunately, that promise was not fulfilled, as European intellectual life disintegrated. What remained of the Gestalt movement in Germany after its leaders fled to America quickly became distorted in the propaganda of Hitlerism. When European intellectual life revived after World War II, too much time had elapsed and other models of psychology appeared. During the interim, the Gestalt movement had been absorbed into American neobehaviorism and was no longer recognizable as a separate system of psychology.

As an American Movement

When the chief Gestaltists left Germany and came to America, the prevailing system in the United States was not structural psychology but behaviorism. Moreover, American behaviorism had evolved out of the functional period of early American psychology with its characteristic utilitarian flavor, in contrast to the European orientation of defining the mind per se and caring less about its functions. Accordingly, the Gestalt movement was not in tune with ongoing developments on the American psychological scene.

Although unable to compete with behaviorism, the Gestalt movement played a major role in redefining behaviorism. A major behaviorist who showed an early inclination toward Gestalt theory was Edward C. Tolman, whose work is considered in more detail in Chapter 15. A few of the research areas Tolman investigated were provoked by Gestalt thoughts. Tolman did important experiments on latent learning and showed that learned responses can be acquired without apparent manifestation in observed performance. This learning versus performance distinction is not readily explained by stimulus–response (S–R) reductionistic theory but is predicted from the Gestalt view of organized fields of behavior or, as referred to by Tolman, cognitive learning. Similarly, transpositional learning in the acquisition of successive discrimination problems has been found in various species and could not be easily accommodated by initial S–R formulations.

Perhaps the most important Gestalt studies of learning processes come from those investigations, beginning with Köhler's reports on higher learning processes in chimpanzees, dealing with problem solving and insight. The traditional S–R models of learning were based on logical deductions (for example, refinement of responses through trial-and-error elimination of choices) or associations (such as principles of conditioning). The Gestaltists' demonstrations of insight, rapid solutions, and creativity opened the consideration of learning processes in psychology to a broader spectrum of possibilities. Entire areas of research were proposed, ranging from remote retrieval of memory traces to the study of understanding. As mentioned earlier, Wertheimer's *Productive Thinking* offered a refreshing perspective on the facilitation of potential strategies of problem solving.

Field Theory

One application derived from Gestalt theory involved a view of social activities and personality dynamics, termed *field theory*, which received articulate expression in the work of Kurt Lewin (1890–1947). Lewin's views were a product of the active model of the mind prevalent in German philosophy, and in some respects certain parallels can be seen between Freud and Lewin in their formulations within the German tradition. However, Lewin was most directly influenced by the specific principles of the Gestalt movement, and although much of his work was done independently, he contributed heavily to applications of Gestalt principles that are prevalent to this day.

Lewin received his doctorate at Berlin in 1914, where he studied mathematics and physics as well as psychology. After military service during World War I, he returned to Berlin and became involved with the Gestalt group led by Köhler. He quickly gained international fame and spent several years as a visiting professor at Stanford and Cornell. He immigrated to the United States permanently in 1935 and spent the next 9 years at the University of Iowa, where he made innovative studies of childhood socialization. In 1944, he went to the Massachusetts Institute of Technology to lead a research center devoted to group dynamics, which continued working after his death.

In the Gestalt tradition, Lewin argued that personality should be viewed in the context of a dynamic field of individual–environmental interactions. Lewin taught that the restriction of psychological description to group averages or statistical summaries loses sight of the individual. If all of the general laws of behavior were known, the psychologist would still need to appreciate the specific individual's interactions with the environment to make any meaningful predictions. Lewin's model of the interactive field of an individual was based on his notion of hodological space, which was defined as a geometric system emphasizing (1) movement along psychologically directed pathways, (2) the dynamics of person–environment interactions, and (3) the person's behavior at environmental obstacles or barriers. Moreover, the person was viewed in terms of an individual life space, containing not only the predominance of the present hodological space with psychologically directed pathways of movement, but also representations of past experiences and future expectations.

The dynamics of the life space are governed by motivational constructs consisting of several components. Individual needs may arise through physiological conditions, a desired environmental object, or an internalized goal. Such needs produce tensions, or emotional states, that must be reduced. Objects in the environment related to needs have values of attraction or repulsion, and these values are termed *valences*. For example, an apple may have a positive valence for a hungry child, but if the child has just finished eating ten green apples, the apple may assume a negative valence. The directed action toward or away from an object is termed a *vector*; two opposing vectors define a *conflict*. Finally, there are barriers in the environment that may come from other objects, people, or a moral code, and thwart activity. Putting these constructs together as diagrammed in Figure 13–3, let us suppose that C represents a hungry child who wants an apple (A) available in the environment, but the child is told by a parent not to eat before dinner, imposing a barrier. The apple has a positive valence, and the barrier has a negative valence and prevents movement. The hodological space produces a vector of action (arrow) toward the apple until the barrier is confronted and conflict arises. The conflict will be resolved only when the positive or negative valence of one object exceeds the other and results in motion either further toward or away from the apple. Thus, Lewin's model is a motivational system seeking an equilibrium of forces within the life space.

This survey of parts of Lewin's field theory reflects an interesting application of Gestalt theory to personality and social behaviors. Lewin's views fascinated many psychologists because of the complex types of behavior that can be considered in the context of life space. As the behavioristic model of psychology expanded to include cognitive variables, Lewin's teachings were readily adopted to develop a comprehensive theory of behaviorism.

FIGURE 13–3   Diagrammatic representation of the life space of a child (C) attracted to an apple (A) having a positive valence. Prohibitions by the parent set up a barrier with a negative valence, which thwarts the vector of approaching movement.

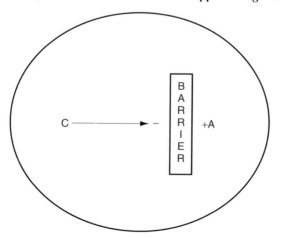

CHAPTER SUMMARY

Gestalt psychology originated as a German intellectual movement heavily influenced by the precedents of the Würzburg school and phenomenological approaches to science. The early Gestaltists directly challenged Wundt's structural psychology and were largely successful in pursuing the traditions of Brentano and Stumpf. Originating in Wertheimer's research on apparent movement, or the phi phenomenon, the Gestalt principles were founded on the assumption of the inherent organization of person–environment interactions. The writings of Köhler and Koffka expanded the perceptual basis to formulate a comprehensive system of psychology especially amenable to higher thought processes of insight, understanding, and productive thinking. When the movement was threatened with destruction by the intellectual sterility of Nazi tyranny, the leaders fled to America. Unfortunately, the Gestalt movement was out of tune with the prevailing behavioristic character of American psychology. However, the Gestaltists assumed an important role in broadening the basis of behaviorism to foster a complete view of learning processes. One application of Gestalt views, contained in Lewin's field theory, met with success in providing an empirical model of personality and social activities. The Gestalt movement, although it did not retain a separate identity, contributed greatly to the reformulation of psychology.

BIBLIOGRAPHY

Primary Sources

HELSON, H. (1925, 1927). The psychology of Gestalt. *American Journal of Psychology, 36,* 342–370, 494–526; *27, 25*–62, 189–223.

HENLE, M. (1961). *Documents of Gestalt psychology.* Berkeley: University of California Press.

KOFFKA, K. (1922). Perception: An introduction to the Gestalt-theorie. *Psychological Bulletin, 19,* 531–585.

KOFFKA, K. (1935). *Principles of Gestalt psychology.* New York: Harcourt Brace Jovanovich.

KÖHLER, W. (1938). *The mentality of apes.* New York: Liveright.

KÖHLER, W. (1947). *Gestalt psychology.* New York: Mentes.

KÖHLER, W. (1971). *The selected papers of Wolfgang Köhler.* New York: Liveright.

KÖHLER, W., & WALLACH, H. (1944). Figural after-effects. *Proceedings of the American Philosophical Society, 88,* 269–357.

LEWIN, K. (1936). *Principles of topological psychology.* New York: McGraw-Hill.

LEWIN, K. (1951). *Field theory in social science* (D. Cartwright, Ed.). New York: Harper & Row.

LEWIN, K., LIPPITT, R., & WHITE, R. (1939). Patterns of aggressive behavior in experimentally created social climates. *Journal of Social Psychology, 10,* 271–299.

WERTHEIMER, M. (1950). Gestalt theory. In W. D. Ellis (Ed.), *A source book of Gestalt psychology*. London: Routledge and Kegan Paul.

WERTHEIMER, M. (1959). *Productive thinking* (Enlarged ed.). New York: Harper & Row.

ZEIGARNIK, B. (1927). Uber das Behalten von erledigten und unerledigten Handlungen. *Psychologische Forschung, 9,* 1–85.

Studies

BORING, E. G. (1950). *A history of experimental psychology*, 2nd ed. Englewood Cliffs, NJ: Prentice Hall.

DOLEZAL, H. (1975). Psychological phenomenology face to face with the persistent problems of psychology. *Journal of the History of the Behavioral Sciences, 11,* 223–234.

GIBSON, J. J. (1971). The legacies of Koffka's Principles. *Journal of the History of the Behavioral Sciences, 7,* 3–9.

HARROWER-ERICKSEN, M. (1942). Kurt Koffka: 1886–1941. *American Journal of Psychology, 55,* 278–281.

HEIDER, F. (1970). Gestalt theory: Early history and reminiscences. *Journal of the History of the Behavioral Sciences, 6,* 131–139.

HENLE, M. (1978). Gestalt psychology and Gestalt therapy. *Journal of the History of the Behavioral Sciences, 14,* 23–32.

HENLE, M. (1978). Kurt Lewin as metatheorist. *Journal of the History of the Behavioral Sciences, 14,* 233–237.

HENLE, M. (1984). Robert M. Ogden and Gestalt psychology in America. *Journal of the History of the Behavioral Sciences, 20,* 9–19.

HOCHBERG, J. (1974). Organization and the Gestalt tradition. In E. Carterette and M. Friedman (Eds.), *Handbook of perception, Vol. 1: Historical and philosophical roots of perception.* New York: Academic Press.

LINDENFIELD, D. (1978). Oswald Külpe and the Würzburg school. *Journal of the History of the Behavioral Sciences, 14,* 132–141.

MACLEOD, R. B. (1964). Phenomenology: A challenge to experimental psychology. In T. Wann (Ed.), *Behaviorism and phenomenology: Contrasting bases for modern psychology.* Chicago: University of Chicago Press, 47–78.

MORROW, A. (1969). *Kurt Lewin.* New York: Basic Books.

WERTHEIMER, M., KING, D. B., PECKLER, M. A., RANEY, S., & SCHAEF, R. W. (1992). Carl Jung and Max Wertheimer on a priority issue. *Journal of the History of the Behavioral Sciences, 28,* 45–56.

14

Psychoanalysis

Background
- The Active Mind
- The Treatment of Mental Illness

Sigmund Freud
- Biography
- An Overview of Freud's System
- Freud's Legacy

The Disciples
- Alfred Adler
- Carl Jung
- Karen Horney

Social Psychoanalysis
- Harry Stack Sullivan
- Erich Fromm

Contemporary Impact
Chapter Summary

The psychoanalytic movement's place in contemporary psychology is both unique and paradoxical. On the one hand, psychoanalysis is probably the most widely known, although perhaps not universally understood, of the systems of psychology. Its founder, Sigmund Freud, is certainly one of the most famous persons of the last century. On the other hand, the psychoanalytic movement has little in common with the other expressions of psychology. Psychoanalysis is most clearly aligned with the German tradition of the mind as an active, dynamic, and self-generating entity. Freud was trained in science, yet his system shows little appreciation for systematic empiricism. As a physician, Freud used his keen powers of observation to build his system within a medical framework, basing his theory on individual case studies. He did not depart from his understanding of nineteenth-century science in the effort to organize his observations. He did not attempt to test his hypotheses rigorously by independent verification. As he himself testified, he *was* psychoanalysis, and he did not tolerate dissension from his orthodox views. Nevertheless, Freud had a tremendous impact on twentieth-century psychology. Perhaps more importantly, the influence of psychoanalysis on Western thought, as reflected in literature, philosophy, and art, significantly exceeds the impact of any other system of psychology.

BACKGROUND

The Active Mind

In our consideration of the philosophical precedents of modern psychology in Germany during the seventeenth, eighteenth, and nineteenth centuries, we saw that the tradition of Leibniz and Kant clearly emphasized mental activity. In contrast to British empiricism, which viewed the mind as passive, or the French sensationalistic view of the mind as an unnecessary construct, the German tradition held that the mind itself generates and structures human experience in characteristic ways. Whether through Leibniz's monadology or Kant's categories, the psychology of the individual could be understood only by examining the dynamic, inherent activity of the mind.

As psychology emerged as an independent discipline in the latter part of the nineteenth century under Wundt's tutelage, the British model of mental passivity served as the guiding force. Wundt's empiricistic formulation was at odds with German philosophical precedents, recognized by both Stumpf and Brentano. Act psychology and the psychology of nonsensory consciousness represented by the Würzburg School were closer to the German philosophical assumptions of mental activity than to Wundt's structural psychology. The Gestalt movement encompassed these alternatives to Wundt's psychology in Germany. Eventually Wundt's system was replaced by Gestalt psychology, making the dominant psychology in Germany prior to World War II one based on a model of the mind that admitted inherent organizational activity.

However, the assumptions underlying mental activity in Gestalt psychology were highly qualified. The Gestalt construct for mind involved the organization of perception, based on the principle of isomorphism, which resulted in a predisposition toward patterns of person–environmental interactions. The emphasis on organization meant that the manner of mental processes, not their content, was inherently structured. In other words, people were not born with specific ideas, energies, or other content in the mind; rather, they inherited the organizational structure to acquire mental contents in characteristic ways. Accordingly, the Gestalt movement, while rejecting the rigidity of Wundt's empiricistic views, did not reject empiricism as such. Instead, the Gestaltists advocated a compromise between the empiricist basis of British philosophy and the German model of activity. They opened psychological investigation to the study of complex problem solving and perceptual processes.

Consistent with the Gestalt position, psychoanalysis was firmly grounded in an active model of mental processes, but it shared little of the Gestalt commitment to empiricism. Freud's views on personality were consistent not only with the activities of mental processing suggested by Leibniz and Kant, but also with the nineteenth-century belief in conscious and unconscious levels of mental activity. In accepting the teachings of such philosophers as von Hartmann and Schopenhauer, Freud developed motivational principles that depended on energy forces beyond the level of self-awareness. Moreover, for Freud, the development of personality was determined by individual, unconscious adaptation to these forces. The details of personality development as formulated by Freud are outlined below; however, it is also important to recognize the context of Freud's thinking. Psychoanalysis carried the implication of mental activity further than any other system of psychology. As the major representative of an extreme reliance on mental activity to account for personality, psychoanalysis is set apart from other movements in contemporary psychology. In addition, psychoanalysis did not emerge from academic research, as did the other systems; rather, it was a product of the applied consequences of clinical practice.

The Treatment of Mental Illness

Apart from his fame as the founder of the psychoanalytic movement in modern psychology, Freud is also remembered for his pioneering efforts in upgrading the treatment of mental and behavioral abnormalities. He was instrumental in psychiatry's being recognized as a branch of medicine that specifically deals with psychopathology. Before Freud's attempt to devise effective methods of treating the mentally ill, people who deviated from socially acceptable norms were usually treated as if they were criminals or demonically possessed. Although shocking scandals in the contemporary treatment of mental deviancy appear occasionally, not so long ago such abuses were often the rule rather than the exception.

The treatment of the mentally ill is not a pleasant chapter in Western civilization. It has already been pointed out that abnormal behavior has often been mixed up with criminal behavior as well as with heresy and treason. Even during the enlightened period of the European Renaissance, the tortures and cruelties of the Inquisition were readily adapted to treat what we now consider mental illness. Witchcraft continued to offer a reasonable explanation of such behavior until relatively recent times. Prisons were established to house criminals, paupers, and the insane without differentiation. Mental illness was viewed as governed by obscure or evil forces, and the mentally ill were looked upon as crazed by such bizarre influences as moon rays. Lunatics, or "moonstruck" persons, were appropriately kept in lunatic asylums. As recently as the latter part of the nineteenth century and the beginning of the twentieth century, the institution for the insane in Utica, New York, which was progressive by the standards of the time, was called the Utica Lunatic Asylum. The name reflected the prevailing attitude toward mental illness.

Reforms in the treatment of the institutionalized insane were slowly introduced during the nineteenth century. In 1794, Philippe Pinel (1745–1826) was appointed the chief of hospitals for the insane in Paris, and managed to improve both the attitude toward and the treatment of the institutionalized insane. In the United States, Dorothea Dix (1802–1887) accomplished the most noticeable reforms in the treatment of the mentally ill. Beginning in 1841, Dix led a campaign to improve the condition of indigent, mentally ill persons kept in jails and in poorhouses. However, these reforms succeeded in improving only the physical surroundings and maintenance conditions of the mentally ill; legitimate treatment was minimal. Efforts to develop comprehensive treatment were plagued by various quacks. A pseudoscience developed by Mesmer dealt with the "animal spirits" underlying mental illness. Similarly, the phrenology of Gall and Spurzheim advocated a physical explanation based on skull contours and localization of brain functions.

Gradually attempts were made to develop legitimate and effective techniques to treat emotional and behavioral abnormalities. One of the more productive investigations involved hypnotism and was pioneered by a French physician, Jean Martin Charcot (1825–1893). He gained widespread fame in Europe, and Freud studied under him, as did many other physicians and physiologists. Charcot treated hysterical patients with symptoms ranging from hyperemotionality to physical conversions of underlying emotional disturbances. He used hypnotism as a tool to explore underlying emotional problems that the patient could not confront when conscious. Another French physician in Nancy, Hippolyte Bernheim (1837–1919), developed a sophisticated analysis of hypnotism as a form of treatment, using underlying suggestibility to modify the intentions of the patient. Finally, Pierre Janet (1859–1947), a student of Charcot, used hypnotism to resolve the forces of emotional conflict, which he believed were basic to hysterical symptoms. However, it was Freud who went beyond the techniques of hypnotism to develop a comprehensive theory of psychopathology, from which systematic treatments evolved.

SIGMUND FREUD

Biography

Because psychoanalysis is identified to such a great extent with Freud himself, it is worthwhile to outline the major points in Freud's distinguished life. Sigmund Freud (1856–1939) was born May 6, 1856, in Freiberg, Moravia, at that time a northern province of the Austro-Hungarian Empire and today part of the Czech Republic.

SIGMUND FREUD (1856–1939).
(Courtesy, The Bettmann Archive, Inc.)

Freud was the eldest of eight children, and his father was a relatively poor and not very successful wool merchant. When his business failed, Freud's father moved with his wife and children first to Leipzig and then to Vienna when Sigmund was 4 years old. Freud remained in Vienna for most of the rest of his life. His precocious genius was recognized by his family, and he was allowed many concessions and favors not permitted his siblings. For example, young Freud was provided with better lighting to read in the evening, and when he was studying, noise in the house was kept to a minimum so he would not be disturbed.

Freud's interests were varied and intense, and he showed an early inclination and aptitude for various intellectual pursuits. Unfortunately, Freud was a victim of nineteenth-century anti-Semitism, which was obvious and severe in central and Eastern Europe. Specifically, his Jewish birth precluded certain career opportunities, most notably an academic career in university research. Indeed, medicine and law were the only professions open to Vienna Jews. Freud's early reading of Darwin intrigued and impressed him to the point that a career in science was most appealing. However, the closest path that he could follow for training as a researcher was an education in medicine. Freud entered the University of Vienna in 1873 at age 17. Because of his interests in a variety of fields and specific research projects, it took him 8 years to complete the medical coursework that normally required 6 years. In 1881, he received his doctorate in medicine. While at the university, Freud was part of an investigation of the precise structure of the testes of eels, which involved his dissecting over 400 eels. He later moved on to physiology and neuroanatomy and conducted experiments examining the spinal cord of fish. While at Vienna, Freud also took courses with Franz Brentano, which formed his only formal introduction to nineteenth-century psychology.

After a 4-year engagement, Freud married Martha Bernays in 1886. Recognizing that a scientific career would not provide adequate support, because anti-Semitism worked against the advancement of Jews in academia, Freud reluctantly decided to begin a private practice. Although he and his wife were very poor in the early years of their marriage, he was able to support her and his growing family, which eventually included six children. Freud's early years in private practice were very difficult, requiring long hours for a meager financial reward at work that basically did not challenge him.

During his hospital training, Freud had worked with patients with anatomical and organic problems of the nervous system. Shortly after starting private practice, he became friendly with Josef Breuer (1842–1925), a general practitioner who had acquired some local fame for his respiration studies. Breuer's friendship provided needed stimulation for Freud, and they began to collaborate on several patients with nervous disorders, most notably the famous case of Anna O., an intelligent young woman with severe, diffuse hysterical symptoms. In using hypnosis to treat Anna O., Breuer noticed that certain specific experiences emerged under hypnosis that the patient could not recall while conscious. Her symptoms seemed to be relieved after talking about these experiences under hypnosis. Breuer treated Anna O. daily for over a year, and became convinced that the "talking cure," or "catharsis," involving discussion of unpleasant and repulsive memories revealed under hypnosis, was an effective means of alleviating her symptoms. Unfortunately, Breuer's wife became jealous of the relationship; what would later be called the positive transference of emotional feelings to the therapist at characteristic stages of therapy looked suspicious to her. As a result, Breuer terminated his treatment of Anna O.

In 1885, Freud received a modest grant that allowed him to go to Paris to study with Charcot for 4 and a half months. During that time he not only observed Charcot's method of hypnosis but also attended his lectures, learning of Charcot's views on the importance of unresolved sexual problems in the underlying causality of hysteria. When he returned to Vienna, Freud gave a report of his work with Charcot to the medical society, but its cool reception left Freud with resentment that affected his future interactions with the entrenched medical establishment.

Freud continued his work with Breuer on hypnosis and catharsis, but gradually abandoned the former in favor of the latter. Specifically, he rejected hypnosis as a treatment with general applicability for three reasons. First, not everyone can be hypnotized; hence, its usefulness is limited to a select group. Second, some patients refused to believe what they revealed under hypnosis, prompting Freud to conclude that the patient must be aware during the step-by-step process of discovering memories hidden from accessible consciousness. Third, when one set of symptoms was alleviated under hypnotic suggestibility, new symptoms often emerged. Freud and Breuer were moving in separate directions, and Freud's increasing emphasis on the primacy of sexuality as the key to psychoneurosis contributed to their break. Nevertheless, in 1895 they published *Studies on Hysteria*, often cited as the first work of the psychoanalytic movement, although it sold only 626 copies during the following 13 years.

Freud came to rely on catharsis as a form of treatment. Catharsis involves encouraging patients to speak of anything that comes to mind, regardless of how discomforting or embarrassing it might be. This "free association" took place in a relaxed atmosphere, usually achieved by having the patient recline on a couch. Freud reasoned that free association, like hypnosis, would allow hidden thoughts and memories to be manifested in consciousness. However, in contrast to hypnosis, the patient would be aware of these emerging recollections. Also ongoing during the course of free association is the process of transference, involving emotionally laden experiences that allow the patient to relive earlier, repressed episodes. Because the psychoanalyst is part of the transference process and is often the object of the emotions, Freud recognized transference as a powerful tool to assist the patient in resolving sources of anxiety.

In 1897, Freud began a self-analysis of his dreams, which evolved into another technique important to the psychoanalytic movement. In the analysis of dreams, Freud distinguished between the manifest content (the actual depictions of a dream) and the latent content, which represented the symbolic world of the patient. In 1900, he published his first major work, *The Interpretation of Dreams*. Although it sold only 600 copies in 8 years, it later went through eight editions in his lifetime. In 1901, he published *The Psychopathology of Everyday Life*, the book in which his theory began to take shape. Freud argued that the psychology of all people, not just those with neurotic symptoms, could be understood in terms of unconscious forces in need of resolution.

When his writings began to win him a reputation as a pioneer in psychiatry, Freud attracted admiring followers, among them Alfred Adler and Carl Jung. In 1909, G. Stanley Hall, president of Clark University, invited him to the United States to give a lecture series as part of that institution's twentieth anniversary. The lectures were published in the *American Journal of Psychology* and later in book form, serving as an appropriate introduction to psychoanalytic thought for American audiences.

Because psychoanalysis was perceived as radical by the medical establishment, early believers formed their own associations and founded journals to disseminate their views. However, Freud's demand for strict loyalty to his interpretation of psychoanalysis led to discord within the movement. Adler broke away in 1911, followed by Jung in 1914, so that by the following year, three rival groups existed within the psychoanalytic movement. Nevertheless, Freud's views continued to evolve. Impressed by the devastation and tragedy of World War I, Freud came to view aggression, along with sexuality, as a primal instinctual motivation. During the 1920s Freud expanded psychoanalysis from a method of treatment for mentally ill or emotionally disturbed persons to a systematic framework for all human motivation and personality.

In 1923, Freud developed cancer of the jaw and experienced almost constant pain for the remaining 16 years of his life. He underwent 33 operations and had to wear a prosthetic device. Throughout this ordeal he continued to write and see patients, although he shunned public appearances. With the rise of Hitler and the anti-Semitic campaign of the Nazis, Freud's works were singled out, and his books were burned throughout Germany. However, Freud resisted fleeing from Vienna. When Germany and Austria were politically united in 1938, the Gestapo began harassing Freud and his family. President Roosevelt indirectly relayed to the German government that Freud must be protected. Nevertheless, in March of 1938 some Nazi thugs invaded Freud's home. Finally, through the efforts of friends, Freud was granted permission to leave Austria, but only after promising to send for his unsold books in Swiss storage so that they could be destroyed. After he signed a statement saying that he had received good treatment from the police, the German government allowed him to leave for England, where he died shortly after, on September 23, 1939.

An Overview of Freud's System

Freud's views evolved continually throughout his long career. The collective result of his extensive writings is an elaborate system of personality development. Freud described personality in terms of an energy system that seeks an equilibrium of forces. This homeostatic model of human personality was determined by the constant attempt to identify appropriate ways to discharge instinctual energies, which originate in the depths of the unconscious. The structure of personality, according to Freud, consists of a dynamic interchange of activities energized by forces that are present in the person at birth. Freud's homeostatic model was consistent with the prevailing view of nineteenth-century science, which saw the mechanical relations of physical events studied by physics as the epitome of scientific inquiry. Freud's model for psychoanalysis translated physical stimuli to psychic energies or forces and retained an essentially mechanical description of how such forces interact.

Freud posited three specific structures of personality—the id, ego, and superego—which he believed were essentially formed by age 7. These structures may be diagrammatically represented in terms of their accessibility to a person's awareness or extent of consciousness, as in Figure 14–1. The id is the most primitive and least accessible structure of personality. As originally described by Freud, the id is pure libido, or psychic energy of an irrational nature and sexual character, which instinctually determines unconscious processes. The id is not in contact with the environment, but rather relates to the other structures of personality that in turn must mediate between the id's instincts and the external world. Immune from reality and social conventions, the id is guided by the pleasure principle, seeking to gratify instinctual libidinal needs either directly, through a sexual experience, or indirectly, by dreaming or fantasizing. The latter, indirect gratification was called the primary process. The exact object of direct gratification in the pleasure principle is determined by the psychosexual stage of the individual's development, outlined below.

FIGURE 14–1 Diagrammatic representation of the structures of personality according to Freud's formulation. The horizontal line marks the boundary between conscious and unconscious processes, which is penetrated only in dreams, under hypnosis, or during free association.

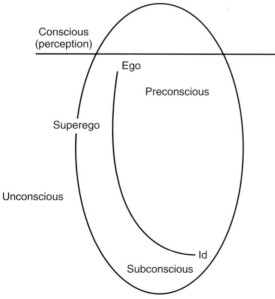

The division or structure of personality that is first differentiated from the id is the ego, often called the "executive" of personality because of its role in channeling id energies into socially acceptable outlets. The development of the ego occurs between the ages of 1 and 2, when the child initially confronts the environment. The ego is governed by the reality principle; it is aware of environmental demands and adjusts behavior so that the instinctual pressures of the id are satisfied in acceptable ways. The attainment of specific objects to reduce libidinal energy in socially appropriate ways was called the secondary process.

The final differentiation of the structures of personality, called the superego, appears by age 5. In contrast to the id and ego, which are internal developments of personality, the superego is an external imposition. That is, the superego is the incorporation of moral standards perceived by the ego from some agent of authority in the environment, usually an assimilation of the parents' views. Both positive and negative aspects of these standards of behavior are represented in the superego. The positive moral code is the ego ideal, a representation of perfect behavior for the individual to emulate. The conscience embodies the negative aspect of the superego, and determines which activities are to be taboo. Conduct that violates the dictates of the conscience produces guilt. The superego and id are in direct conflict, leaving the ego to mediate. Thus the superego imposes a pattern of conduct that results in some degree of self-control through an internalized system of rewards and punishments.

The major motivational construct of Freud's theory of personality was derived from instincts, defined as biological forces that release mental energy. The goal of personality is to reduce the energy drive through some activity acceptable to the constraints of the superego. Freud classed inborn instincts into life (*eros*) and death (*thanatos*) drives. Life instincts involve self-preservation and include hunger, sex, and thirst. The libido is that specific form of energy through which the life instincts arise in the id. The death instincts may be directed inward, as in suicide or masochism, or outward, as in hate and aggression.

With the imperative that personality equilibrium must be maintained by discharging energy in acceptable ways, anxiety plays a central role. Essentially, Freud viewed anxiety as a diffuse fear in anticipation of unmet desires and future evils. Given the primitive character of id instincts, it is unlikely that primary goals are ever an acceptable means of drive reduction; rather they are apt to give rise to continual anxiety in personality. Freud described three general forms of anxiety. Reality, or objective, anxiety is a fear of a real environmental danger with an obvious cause; such fear is appropriate and has survival value for the organism. Neurotic anxiety comes about from the fear of potential punishment inherent in the goal of instinctual gratification. It is a fear of punishment for expressing impulsive desires. Finally, Freud posited moral anxiety as the fear of the conscience through guilt or shame. In order to cope with anxiety, the ego develops defense mechanisms, which are elaborate, largely unconscious processes that allow a person to avoid unpleasantness and anxiety-provoking events. For example, a person may avoid confronting anxiety by self-denial, conversion, or projection, or may repress thoughts that are a source of anxiety to the unconscious. Many defense mechanisms are described in the psychoanalytic literature, which generally agrees that although defense mechanisms are typical ways of handling anxiety, they must be recognized and controlled by the individual for psychological health.

Freud placed great emphasis on the development of the child because he was convinced that neurotic disturbances manifested by his adult patients had origins in childhood experiences. He described psychosexual stages that are characterized by different sources of primary gratification determined by the pleasure principle. Freud wrote that a child is essentially autoerotic. The child derives sexual pleasure from the stimulation of various erogenous zones of the body or by having the mother provide stimulation. Each stage of psychosexual development tends to localize the primary source of gratification to a specific erogenous area. In the oral stage the child seeks primary gratification through sucking, biting, and swallowing. Unsatisfied needs at this stage result in excessive mouth habits, and Freud believed that optimism, sarcasm, and cynicism are all adult behaviors attributable to incidents at this stage. From oral gratification the child progresses to a stage where anal gratification, associated with processes of elimination, is primary. Freud talked about neat, overly clean, and compulsive adults as not having successfully resolved their anal needs. The anal stage is succeeded by the phallic stage of infantile sexuality (ages 3 to 7) where the primary source of gratification is attached to the penis for boys, and for girls, according to Freud, whatever symbolically represents a penis. Following the phallic stage the child enters into an asexual latent period that lasts until the onset of puberty. However, during these psychosexual stages the child is also moving through the Oedipal cycle to eventual adult (that is, what Freud considered appropriate) sexual behavior. At the initial phases of the Oedipal cycle, the young boy has strong sexual desires for his mother. Gradually, this desire is suppressed as the child comes to fear the father and experiences the neurotic anxiety of castration if the father knew of the boy's desires. The boy then identifies with the father as he moves through the latent period and into the pubertal genital stage with a masculine identification. An unresolved Oedipal cycle results in an Oedipus complex—a maladaptive sexual outlook. Thus Freud viewed homosexual behavior as immature sexuality reflecting unresolved Oedipal urges. Later writers attempted a similar description for girls, termed an Electra complex. Corresponding complex psychosexual development in young girls, according to Freud, was complicated by penis envy—the repressed wish to possess masculinity.

This overview of Freud's detailed and complicated theory reflects many of the difficulties with Freud's evolving system. He had few qualms about modifying his views (as long as he did the changing), but often did not change the language, so that the same terminology was frequently used in several ways. Nevertheless, the sheer complexity and uniqueness of his system formed a remarkable achievement. Indeed, he often had to invent new terminology to express his thoughts, and these terms have become an accepted part of our vocabulary.

Freud's Legacy

Relative to the rather single-minded development of psychology as an empirical discipline, whether studied rigorously using an experimental method or less rigorously but still systematically, as in the phenomenological method, Freud's system is most vulnerable. Quite simply, Freud was not a methodologist. His data collection was unsystematic and uncontrolled, consisting primarily of what Freud remembered his patients telling him. He made no independent attempt to confirm the accuracy of his patients' reports. Freud offers only his conclusions; he never discloses how his inferences and conclusions were derived. His variables and constructs are unclear. They are only loosely defined and not quantifiable. His theory emphasizes childhood to the point of asserting that personality is essentially formed by age 7. Yet the only record of Freud's having studied a child concerned a young boy with a phobia, and then Freud worked indirectly through the boy's father. Freud's emphasis on childhood appears to be a deduction from his observations of adults.

Perhaps more seriously, Freud's theory has little predictive value. We examine the role of theory in Chapter 15, but at this point it is important to acknowledge that predictions from a theory permit modification of ongoing events. For example, the theory that cigarette smoking causes cancer allows us confidently to advise younger people not to smoke cigarettes. The person for Freud is over determined. Since a need may be satisfied through any one of many goals, it is difficult to predict adult adjustment by observing the behavior of a child. We just have to wait and see. This criticism is perhaps especially pertinent to Freud, since he advocated both a theory of personality and a treatment for personality disturbances.

As mentioned earlier in this chapter, psychoanalysis has a unique position in the history of psychology. Freud did not develop a theory that generated testable hypotheses or other empirical implications. Yet, on another level, Freud accomplished what few other theorists have: He revolutionized attitudes and created a new set for thinking about personality. It may be said of Freud that his powers of observation allowed him to be right for the wrong reasons. The findings of other more empiricistic theories of personality disturbance have often confirmed many of Freud's observations. If his views do not meet the criteria of empiricistic study, they nevertheless mark a person of genius and insight, whose influence pervades people's thinking about themselves in ways that few others have achieved.

THE DISCIPLES

The psychoanalytic movement was largely the invention of Freud, and his influence far exceeds that of his early followers who subsequently tried to modify psychoanalysis. The major principles of psychoanalysis were redefined and reinterpreted until, by 1930, the movement was fragmented into competing views. Nevertheless, those writers who departed from Freud's speculation retained the basic model of psychoanalysis that conceived of personality in terms of an energy reduction system.

Alfred Adler

Alfred Adler (1870–1937) was born into a wealthy Viennese family but had an unhappy childhood. He was often sick and his accomplishments, compared to those of his oldest brother, failed to fulfill his parents' expectations. He received his doctorate in medicine in 1895, and by 1902 was regularly attending Freud's weekly meetings. He was one of Freud's earliest followers and accompanied him to America in 1909. Gradually, however, Adler began to criticize Freud openly, especially for Freud's emphasis on and literal interpretations of sexuality. By 1911 their split was final, and Adler formed his own circle of followers. Adler was brilliant and a superb speaker who attracted many students with his dynamic and charismatic personality. He lectured widely and in 1934 became a permanent resident in the United States, teaching at Long Island College of Medicine. He continued his extensive lecture trips, and died while on a speaking tour in Europe, in Aberdeen, Scotland, in 1937.

Adler rejected the rigidity of Freud's system. Adler argued, for example, that penis envy in females should not be taken literally, but should rather be viewed as symbolic jealousy of male dominance in society. Indeed, Adler believed that a denial of femininity would be necessarily neurotic. Gradually, Adler developed an alternative to Freud's views, but remained within the psychoanalytic model. His "individual psychology" was not as detailed as the exposition of Freud's theory. Rather, Adler offered a general view of human activity that acknowledged the inferior state of the individual at birth, resulting in the person's continually striving for positive feelings and perfection. By defining a personalistic psychology of the individual, Adler's holistic view of personality emphasized the individual's need for self-unity, perfection, and specifically designed goals. Motivation, in Adler's theory, was not the negative "push" of drive reduction, as Freud had stated, but the positive "pull" of individual striving for self-improvement and superiority. Adler's orientation is similar to the outline of

ALFRED ADLER (1870–1937).
(Courtesy, New York Public Library.)

personality offered by Brentano. The unity of personality is the product of the individual's efforts, so that all psychic phenomena truly originate in the unique creative forces of the individual. The mind itself exhibits definite tendencies to strive for superiority and to attain perfection. Thus, Adler's motivational principle is not reduced to biological instincts, but rather described in psychic, almost spiritual terms of the mind. The striving for superiority, in turn, is a direct reaction to childhood feelings of inferiority, imperfection, and incompleteness. For Adler, a person's present state is guided by his or her future expectations of perfection. These expectations, described as a "finalism" by Adler, are fictional because they are not attainable, but they serve as the collective expression of lifelong goals. Thus, a person's existence is reflected in individual living within a social context and seeking personal harmony in efforts to reach a sense of superiority.

Adler offered case studies of appropriate individual lifestyles that illustrate compensations for inferiority in striving for superiority. However, he was most specific and detailed in his teachings about child rearing. He believed that birth order and the family constellation dramatically affect the development of the individual's lifestyle and creative self. Adler viewed the family as the primary agent of individual socialization, in that subsequent critical patterns of behavior depend on successful upbringing.

Adler introduced an emphasis on the social and creative aspects of human experience into psychoanalysis, and moved away from Freud's rigid emphasis on energy reduction. Adler influenced other important theorists in the psychoanalytic movement, most notably Horney and Fromm. However, the same criticism leveled at Freud—a lack of empiricistic referents and the questionable predictive values of the theory—applies to Adler as well. Moreover, Adler's vagueness, frequent inconsistencies, and lack of a detailed theory of development contribute to an elusiveness that makes him perhaps further removed from an empirical approach than is Freud. Nevertheless, Adler added to psychoanalysis a commonsense approach that made Freud's psychodynamic model more attractive while keeping the model itself intact.

Carl Jung

One of the most fascinating and complicated scholars of this century, Carl Jung (1875–1961) was born to a poor family in a northern Swiss village. He managed to gain entrance to the University of Basel and received a doctorate in medicine in 1900. Jung spent most of the rest of his life in Zurich, teaching, writing, and working with patients. After reading *The Interpretation of Dreams* in 1900, Jung began corresponding with Freud and finally met him in 1907. With Adler, Jung accompanied Freud to America in 1909, where he also lectured and introduced his own work to American audiences. However, Jung began to apply psychoanalytic insights to ancient myths and legends in a search for the key to the nature of the human psyche. Such independent thinking did not meet with Freud's approval, and there is also some speculation that Jung made a critical analysis of Freud's personal life that may have contributed to tensions between them. Freud secured the post of the first president of the International

Psychoanalytic Association for Jung in 1911, but by this time their rift was beyond healing. Finally, in 1914, Jung withdrew from the association and severed all interactions with Freud. Jung continued his own interpretations of psychoanalysis and made several expeditions to study primitive societies in the western United States, Africa, Australia, and Central America. His prolific writings on subjects ranging from anthropology to religion provided novel insights to age-old problems of human existence from a psychoanalytic perspective.

Jung's "analytic psychology" redefined many Freudian concepts; however, Jung retained Freud's terminology, and as a result the same terms often carry different meanings. Jung, like Freud, believed that the central purpose of personality is to achieve a balance between conscious and unconscious forces within the personality. However, Jung described two sources of unconscious forces. One is the personal unconscious, consisting of repressed or forgotten experiences and similar to Freud's preconscious level. The contents of the personal unconscious are accessible to full consciousness. Jung's personal unconscious held complexes, which were groups of feelings with a defined theme that give rise to distorted behavioral responses. For example, a boy who repressed negative emotions about his mother could become an adult with a mother complex, experiencing intense feelings and anxieties when images or stimuli associated with motherhood are encountered. The second source of unconscious forces, unique to Jung's theory, is the collective unconscious, a more powerful source of energy that contains inherited contents shared with other members of an ethnic or racial group. As the personal unconscious has complexes, the collective unconscious has archetypes, defined as primordial images evolved from a primitive tribal ancestry of specific experiences and attitudes passed on over centuries. Jung listed such archetypes as birth, death, unity, power, God, the devil, magic, the old sage, and the earth mother. The notion of a collective unconscious in personality that provides the individual with patterns of behavior, especially at times of life crises, fits well with Jung's preoccupation with myths and symbols. Jung believed that the adequacies of a society's symbols to express archetypal images are an index of the progress of civilization.

Jung focused on the middle years of life, when the pressures of sexual drives supposedly give way to anxiety about the more profound philosophical and religious issues of the meaning of life and death. By reinstating the notion of the spiritual soul, Jung argued that the healthy personality has realized the fullness of human potential to achieve self-unity and complete integration. According to Jung, this realization occurs only after the person has mastered obstacles during the development of personality from infancy to middle age. Failure to grow in this sense results in the disintegration of personality. Accordingly, the person must individualize experiences to achieve a "transcendent function" by which differentiated personality structures are unified to form a fully aware *self*.

Jung redefined libidinal energy as the opposition of introversion–extraversion in personality, bypassing Freud's sexual emphasis. Extraversion forces are directed externally at other people and the environment, and they nurture self-confidence. Introversion leads the person to an inner direction of contemplation, introspection, and stability. The opposing energies must be balanced for the proper psychological functioning of sensation, thinking, feeling, and intuition. An imbalance between extraversion and introversion is partly compensated for in dreams. Indeed, for Jung dreams have important adaptive value in helping the person maintain equilibrium.

As Jung grew older, his writings increasingly came to emphasize mysticism and religious experiences, domains usually ignored by mainstream psychology. Of all the early founders of psychoanalysis, Jung held views in sharpest contrast to those of empiricism. However, he offered a unique treatment of critical human issues that had not been systematically studied by psychologists and still remain in the realm of speculative philosophy. Perhaps Jung was more of a philosopher than a psychologist, and he provoked and confronted issues not readily accommodated in other systems of psychology.

Karen Horney

Born in the German city of Hamburg, Karen Horney (1885–1952) received a medical degree from the University of Berlin in 1913. She was associated with the Berlin Psychoanalytic Institute from 1918 to 1932, and followed the traditional interpretations of Freudian psychoanalysis, having herself been analyzed by Karl Abraham and Hanns Sachs, renowned in Europe for training Freudian psychoanalysts. In 1932, she was named associate director of the Chicago Psychoanalytic Institute and, while there, began to develop a more independent position within the psychoanalytic movement. Two years later she moved to New York City, where she maintained a private practice and taught at the New School for Social Research (New School University). After a few years she was accused of departing radically from orthodox psychoanalysis and was ejected from the New York Psychoanalytic Society. She then founded the American Institute for Psychoanalysis, which she headed until her death.

Horney made significant contributions to the development of a psychology of women. As is clear from the overview of Freud's theory, he reflected his times by giving prime consideration to the goal of attaining an equilibrium of sexual and aggressive energies in human development. Horney, like Adler, rejected such constructs as penis envy as being social standards. Moreover, she offered important insights into the rapidly changing role of women in industrialized society, recognizing that women who had historically been subjected to the repressive burdens of traditional peasant society were undergoing radical changes in the urban work environment.

Horney's views were not acceptable to the entrenched psychoanalytic organization dominated by Freudians. However, despite Horney's expulsion from the psychoanalytic establishment, her revision of Freud's theory remained within the psychoanalytic model. She agreed that human activity is caused by unconscious motivations, and she recognized the primacy of emotional drives. She also saw the value of Freud's description of the defense mechanisms, and shared the Freudian emphasis on transference, free association, and dream analysis in therapy. Although she perceived herself as more of a therapist than a theorist, she asserted important differences with Freud in the structure of personality. She denied the strict distinction and compartmentalization represented by Freud's idea of the id, ego, and superego. If the Oedipus complex exists, according to Horney, it is not a sexual and aggressive interaction between the child and parent, but rather an emotional interplay of anxiety resulting from feelings of insecurity in the child because of rejection, hurt, and overprotection. Horney described libidinal energy in terms of emotional drives rather than the primarily sexual and aggressive energy proposed by Freud. Sexual problems, for Horney, were an effect, not a cause, of emotional distortions.

Horney stressed basic anxiety arising from childhood insecurities that continue throughout life. She argued that humanity has lost the security of medieval society, and neurosis is the natural product of industrialization. Accordingly, psychology is intimately linked with cultural and social values. The total experience that an individual accumulates in life is termed the "character structure," the product of continual development. Horney believed the individual has a great capacity for inner directedness, which may be fully explored through self-analysis, which in turn yields self-knowledge, the prerequisite for psychological growth. The process of proper self-analysis results in the emergence of a strong self-concept, a construct somewhat similar to Freud's idea of the ego ideal. The well-integrated self-concept can effectively combat overreliance on the defense mechanisms that mitigate against self-knowledge by alienating people from themselves. When this alienation does occur, people need the assistance of professional analysis to regain judgment and spontaneity.

Horney described human activity in terms of three modes that are essentially protective and defensive. "Moving toward" is characteristic of infantile behavior and helplessness. For example, if another person is perceived as loving me, then that person will not hurt me. Characteristic activity in adolescence is "moving against"; it is hostile and attempts to control. For example, if I have power, no one will hurt me. Finally, "moving away" is characteristic of isolated adult behavior—if I withdraw, no one can hurt me. These modes of activity are used in pursuing ten neurotic needs described by Horney:

Neurotic Need	*Mode of Activity*
1. Affection and approval	Moving toward
2. A dominant partner in life	Moving toward
3. Seeking a narrowly confined life	Moving away
4. Self-sufficiency and independence	Moving away
5. Perfection	Moving away
6. Power	Moving against
7. Exploiting others	Moving against
8. Prestige	Moving against
9. Ambition	Moving against
10. Personal admiration	Moving against

These neurotic needs can only be overcome by self-analysis. Accordingly, Horney viewed therapy in marked contrast to Freud, who regarded the goal of therapy as the restoration of equilibrium in personality. Rather, Horney believed that the aim of therapy ultimately supports psychological health defined in terms of the continuing process of seeking self-knowledge.

Horney criticized Freud for limiting his observations to children and hysterical women, yet she confined her own perspective to an urban environment. This emphasis leaves her theory without an acceptable concept of normality. According to Horney, personal conflicts do not arise internally but are the product of cultural determinants from industrialization. This weakness, however, is also a strength of her version of psychoanalysis. She recognized the radically changing nature of the social environment and emphasized its great impact on the psychology of the individual. Accordingly, her views are not static but are adjusted to meet the changing demands of society on the roles of both men and women.

SOCIAL PSYCHOANALYSIS

The modifications of Freudian psychoanalysis proposed by Adler and Horney led to a distinct trend in psychoanalysis toward an examination of the social setting of human experience. Two particular theorists, Sullivan and Fromm, are especially representative of this development.

Harry Stack Sullivan

Born in rural New York State, Harry Stack Sullivan (1892–1949) received his medical degree in 1917 from the Chicago College of Medicine and Surgery. Beginning in 1922, he worked in several hospitals conducting research on schizophrenia. In 1933, he became director of a psychiatric foundation, and from 1936 until his death headed its training institute, the Washington School of Psychiatry. He published only one book, *Conceptions of Modern Psychiatry* (1947), but kept extensive notebooks on his work, which were edited and published by his former students after his death. These works form the sources of Sullivan's interpersonal theory of psychiatry.

Sullivan viewed personality, or the self, as an open system interacting with the environment, so that at any given time the individual is defined as the sum of these interacting experiences. Although reminiscent of field theory such as that of Lewin, Sullivan's formulations nevertheless fit into the psychoanalytic movement because he accepted a homeostatic model of anxiety reduction. Tensions emerge from needs and anxieties and require reduction. In his views on development, Sullivan defined several stages that are marked by the nature of social interactions. He suggested various "dynamisms," or propelling social relationships, used as the individual matures to appropriate socialization in adulthood and develops self-esteem.

Sullivan's interpersonal psychology was firmly based on detailed observation, and his views gained wide acceptance because of their specificity as well as their applicability to clinical settings. In many respects Sullivan extended the work of Adler, making a more complete study of the social potential of psychoanalytic theory.

Erich Fromm

Erich Fromm's (1900–1980) idealistic theory is an interesting combination of the psychoanalytic model with existential overtones. He was born in Frankfurt am Main and received his PhD from the University of Heidelberg in 1922, after which he studied at the Psychoanalytic Institute in Berlin. In 1934, he went to America, and taught at several universities in the United States and Mexico.

Fromm consistently stressed the existential view of modern persons as lonely and alienated from themselves and from society (existential influences in psychology are reviewed in Chapter 16). Consistent with Horney's view of the individual searching for security, Fromm viewed the modern world as leaving the individual in a state of loneliness and helplessness. In order to deal with this condition, a person may attempt escape. The methods of escape, analogous to Freud's defense mechanisms, are not satisfactory. Rather, Fromm believed that the essential human freedom of the individual is the key to fulfilling personal needs. Fromm argued that human progress has resulted in five basic needs that go beyond the biological needs of hunger, sex, and thirst.

1. We have a need for relatedness, to establish interpersonal relationships through love and understanding.
2. We have a need for transcendence, to develop the uniquely human capacity of rational and creative thinking.
3. We have a need for rootedness, to belong and become a part of the environment.
4. We have a need for personal identity, to distinguish ourselves from our surroundings.
5. We have a need for a consistent orientation that allows us to understand ourselves and our environment.

Fromm taught that neither capitalism nor communism has succeeded in providing the appropriate social structure for truly human development. He offered his own ideas on a utopia that could facilitate individual growth to meet the five needs. As Fromm continued to develop his views, he moved beyond the traditional role of a psychologist to that of a social philosopher. However, he did try to adjust the psychoanalytic model to respond better to the fluid nature of social change and to recognize the individual dilemma of the modern person attempting to live in a hostile environment.

CONTEMPORARY IMPACT

As mentioned at the beginning of this chapter, psychoanalysis is a unique movement in psychology. It grew out of the same German model of mental activity that produced act psychology and the Gestalt movement. However, psychoanalysis received its immediate expression through the needs of the mentally ill. It was a clinical, not an academic, development. For this reason, psychoanalysis, especially as proposed by writers after Freud, gives the impression of an ad hoc movement that develops as particular problems arise and not a coherent system. Psychoanalysis did not adhere to the commitment to methodology expressed in those systems generated by academic research. Accordingly, there was and is little interaction between psychoanalysis and those systems with comprehensive methods, either empirical or phenomenological. Stated quite simply, psychoanalysis and the other expressions of psychological models do not speak the same language.

The selection of post-Freudian contributors to the psychoanalytic movement presented in this chapter was not intended to be comprehensive, only representative. However, this myriad of psychoanalytic views also reflects the problem of unsystematic methodology. Psychoanalysis has never formulated systematic criteria against which new interpretations may be compared. In a very real sense, there are as many psychoanalytic theories as there are psychoanalysts. This problem plagued the movement in Freud's time and continues to do so. Contemporary psychoanalysis is severely fragmented.

Although not accepted by mainstream psychology, psychoanalysis did assume a dominant role in psychiatry. This is understandable in light of the origins of psychoanalysis as a response to clinical problems. Indeed, psychoanalytic writings enjoyed an almost exclusive position in psychiatry and clinical psychology until the 1960s, when behavior modification began to compete as an alternate model of therapy.

Psychoanalysis also continued to exert a marked influence on art, literature, and philosophy. This influence reflects the major contribution of Freud: his comprehensive analysis of the unconscious. Accordingly, literary and artistic expressions are interpreted in light of the unconscious activities of the artist as well as the unconscious impressions of the perceiver. Psychologists may choose to ignore unconscious motivations or simply to refer to subliminal or subthreshold activities. However, any truly comprehensive theory of psychological activity can no longer be limited to conscious aspects of behavior. Although psychologists may disagree with Freud's interpretation, he did identify some dynamic processes that influence the activity of the individual, processes that psychology cannot ignore.

CHAPTER SUMMARY

The psychoanalytic movement introduced the study of unconscious processes that influence human activity. The movement was fully consistent with the German model of mental activity, going back to the writings of Leibniz and Kant. Although act psychology and the Gestalt movement were also modern expressions of the German model, psychoanalysis emphasized the goal of a homeostatic balance of unconscious energies within personality. Its founder, Sigmund Freud, used his keen powers of observation to devise much-needed therapeutic approaches, and later expanded his formulations to a psychodynamic theory of personality growth dependent on tension reduction. Other theorists modified Freud's model to include cultural influences (Jung) and social needs (Adler and Horney). In addition, scholars have integrated the psychoanalytic model with a field approach (Sullivan) and existential assumptions (Fromm).

As a contemporary movement, psychoanalysis still exerts considerable influence in psychiatry and clinical psychology, although the movement is fragmented owing to a lack of methodological agreement. In addition, Freud's statements on the unconscious have led to new interpretations of artistic expression. However, as a viable model for psychology, psychoanalysis has departed from the empiricistic foundations of psychology and shares little with other systems of psychology that rely on that methodological approach.

BIBLIOGRAPHY

Primary Sources

ADLER, A. (1927). Individual psychology. *Journal of Abnormal and Social Psychology, 22,* 116–122.

ADLER, A. (1956). *The individual psychology of Alfred Adler.* H. L. Ansbacher & R. R. Ansbacher (Eds.). New York: Basic Books.

ADLER, A. (1958). *What life should mean to you.* New York: Capricorn Books.

FREUD, S. (1920). *The psychopathology of everyday life.* New York: Mentor.

FREUD, S. (1938). The history of the psychoanalytic movement. In A. A. Brill (Ed. and Trans.), *The basic writing of Sigmund Freud.* New York: Random House.

FREUD, S. (1955). *The interpretation of dreams.* In J. Strachey (Ed.), *The standard edition of the complete works of Sigmund Freud* (Vols. IV and V). London: Hogarth.

FREUD, S. (1965). *New introductory lectures on psychoanalysis.* New York: W. W. Norton.

FROMM, E. (1941). *Escape from freedom.* New York: Holt, Rinehart & Winston.

FROMM, E. (1947). *Man for himself.* New York: Holt, Rinehart & Winston.

FROMM, E. (1947). *The sane society.* New York: Holt, Rinehart & Winston.

HORNEY, K. (1939). *New ways in psychoanalysis.* New York: W. W. Norton.

JUNG, C. G. (1933). *Modern man in search of a soul.* New York: Harcourt Brace.

JUNG, C. G. (1953). *Psychological reflections* (J. Jacobi, Ed.). New York: Harper & Row.

JUNG, C. G. (1959). *The basic writings of C. G. Jung.* New York: Random House.

SANDLER, J. (Ed.) (1994). *The Harvard lectures of Anna Freud.* Madison, CT: International Universities Press.

SULLIVAN, H. S. (1947). *Conceptions of modern psychiatry.* Washington: W. A. White Foundation.

SULLIVAN, H. S. (1953). *The interpersonal theory of psychiatry.* New York: W. W. Norton.

Studies

ANSBACHER, H. L. (1970). Alfred Adler—A historical perspective. *American Journal of Psychiatry, 127,* 777–782.

ANSBACHER, H. L. (1971). Alfred Adler and G. Stanley Hall: Correspondence and general relationship. *Journal of the History of the Behavioral Sciences, 7,* 337–352.

CAPPS, D. (1970). Hartmann's relationship to Freud: A reappraisal. *Journal of the History of the Behavioral Sciences, 6,* 162–175.

ELLENBERGER, H. F. (1970). *The discovery of the unconscious*. New York: Basic Books.

FORDHAM, F. (1953). *An introduction to Jung's psychology*. London: Penguin.

GAY, P. (1988). *Freud: A life for our time*. New York: Norton.

GRAVITZ, M. A., & GERTON, M. I. (1981). Freud and hypnosis: Report of post-rejection use. *Journal of the History of the Behavioral Sciences, 17,* 68–74.

HALE, N. G. (1971). *Freud and the Americans*. New York: Oxford University Press.

HALL, C. S., & LINDZEY, G. (1970). *Theories of personality* (Rev. ed.). New York: Wiley.

JONES, E. (1955). *The life and work of Sigmund Freud*. New York: Basic Books.

KAINER, R. G. (1984). Art and the canvas of the self: Otto Rank and creative transcendence. *American Imago, 14,* 359–372.

KELMAN, H. (1967). Karen Horney on feminine psychology. *American Journal of Psychoanalysis, 27,* 163–183.

MACMILLAN, M. (1985). Souvenir de la Salpêtrière: M. le Dr. Freud à Paris, 1885. *New Zealand Journal of Psychology, 14,* 41–57.

ORGLER, H. (1963). *Alfred Adler: The man and his works*. New York: Liveright.

RENDON, M. (1984). Karen Horney's biocultural dialectic. *American Journal of Psychoanalysis, 44,* 267–279.

RUBINS, J. L. (1978). *Karen Horney: Gentle rebel of psychoanalysis*. New York: Dial.

SAMUELS, A. (1994). The professionalization of Carl G. Jung's analytical psychology clubs. *Journal of the History of the Behavioral Sciences, 30,* 138–147.

SCHICK, A. (1968–1969). The Vienna of Sigmund Freud. *Psychoanalytic Review, 55,* 529–551.

SIRKIN, M., & Fleming, M. (1982). Freud's "project" and its relationship to psychoanalytic theory. *Journal of the History of the Behavioral Sciences, 18,* 230–241.

STEPANSKY, P. E. (1976). The empiricist as rebel: Jung, Freud, and the burdens of discipleship. *Journal of the History of the Behavioral Sciences, 12,* 216–239.

15

Behaviorism

Immediate Background of Behaviorism
    Russian Reflexology and Its Dominance in the Soviet Union
        Ivan Mikhailovich Sechenov
        Vladimir Mikhailovich Bekhterev
        Ivan Petrovich Pavlov
    American Connectionism: Thorndike
Watsonian Behaviorism
    Other Early American Behaviorists
        Edwin B. Holt
        Albert P. Weiss
        Walter S. Hunter
        Karl S. Lashley
    Operational Positivism
Broadening Behaviorism
    Reflexology Expanded
    The American Behaviorists
        Guthrie's Contiguity Theory
        Hull's Hypotheticodeductive Theory
        Tolman's Cognitive Behaviorism
        Skinner's Radical Positivism
The Role of Theory
Post-Theory Formulations
    Neobehavioristic Models
        Information-Processing and Mathematical Models
        The Neo-Hullians
        Cognitive Models
        Operant Models
    Applications
Chapter Summary

The system that defines psychology as the study of behavior received firm support in a twentieth-century development that occurred largely in the United States. Observable and quantifiable behavior was assumed to have meaning in itself, rather than simply serving as a manifestation of underlying mental events. This movement was formally initiated by an American psychologist, John Broadus Watson (1878–1958), in a famous paper, "Psychology as the Behaviorist Views It," published in 1913. Watson proposed a radical departure from existing formulations of psychology by asserting that the proper direction for psychology's development is not the study of "inner" consciousness. In fact, he dismissed the entire notion of some nonphysical mental state of consciousness as a pseudoproblem for science. In its place Watson advocated overt, observable behavior as the sole legitimate subject matter for a true science of psychology.

Watson was largely successful in initiating a redirection of the development of psychology. Later in this chapter we examine the various intellectual forces that converged in Watson's time and fostered the acceptance of his views. Although Watson may have been the spokesman for a revolutionary movement defining the scope of psychology, it should be recognized that the subsequent success of the behavioristic movement in psychology is best characterized as evolutionary rather than revolutionary. Behaviorism, especially in the United States, has gradually changed from Watson's initial definition to one that encompasses a wide range of human and infrahuman activity, studied under varieties of empirical methodologies.

The historical trend that led to Watsonian behaviorism may be traced from antiquity to the nineteenth century. The pre-Socratic philosophers, such as the Ionian physicists and Hippocrates (Chapter 2), attempted to explain human activity as mechanical reactions reducible to biological or physical causes. Much later, the French sensationalist tradition, rejecting Descartes' unextended substance in favor of a mechanical system responding to environmental stimuli, served as an important predecessor of twentieth-century behaviorism. Both the sensory reductionism of Condillac and the mechanical physiology of La Mettrie led to the position that mental events are determined completely by sensory input and that the critical level of psychological inquiry concerns sensory processes. Perhaps the British philosophers provided behaviorism with its clearest intellectual foundation. Locke's notion of mental passivity meant that the mind is dependent on the environment for its contents, and the two dominant themes of the British philosophers, empiricism and associationism, contained the major tenets of behaviorism. Behavioristic psychology emerged in the twentieth century as an empirical discipline that studied behavior in terms of adaptation to environmental stimuli. The essential core of behaviorism is that an organism learns behavioral adaptation, and its learning is governed by the principles of association.

A fundamental empirical approach to the examination of associations in behavioristic psychology, although in general agreement with the British philosophers, may be found in the work of a group of predominantly Russian physiologists studying reflexology. Indeed, although important research on the acquisition of reflexes was done prior to Watson's writings, the Russian group had a major impact on behaviorism after Watson's publications and served as a force to expand his original formulation.

IMMEDIATE BACKGROUND OF BEHAVIORISM

Russian Reflexology and Its Dominance in the Soviet Union

We already mentioned in Chapter 10 the advances in the physiology of the brain, most notably in the neurophysiology of Sherrington. In somewhat parallel work during the first years of the twentieth century, a group of Russian physiologists was investigating the physiological basis of behavioral processes. Although Sherrington's work was probably more significant—and indeed it was left for later scientists to examine the full implications of his neurophysiology for behavioristic psychology— the research of the Russian physiologists had a practical direction that was easily adopted into behaviorism as the basic mechanism of learning. However, the Russian researchers were physiologists, not psychologists, and the reduction of psychological processes to physiological mechanisms was inherent in their work. They were not philosophers seeking to articulate a new science of psychology. Rather, they wanted to expand existing knowledge of physiology to include processes that had been labeled psychological. Accordingly, they had little use for a new science of psychology. This tradition continues to this day in Russia and Eastern Europe, where investigations of such processes as learning, sensation, and perception are often included in the study of neurobiology rather than in psychology.

Ivan Mikhailovich Sechenov.   Considered the founder of modern Russian physiology, Ivan Mikhailovich Sechenov (1829–1905) received a doctorate in physiology from the University of St. Petersburg. Beginning in 1856, he spent 7 years visiting Western Europe, coming into contact with such eminent physiologists as Hermann von Helmholtz, Johannes Müller, and Dimitri Mendeleyev (1834–1907), the émigré Russian chemist working at Heidelberg. Sechenov held professorships in physiology at universities in St. Petersburg and Odessa; he finished his career in Moscow.

In 1863, Sechenov published *Reflexes of the Brain*, containing his hypothesis that all activities, including the seemingly complex processes of thinking and language, are reducible to reflexes. Moreover, he stressed the excitatory and inhibitory mediational role of the cerebral cortex as the central locus of reflex actions. Sechenov believed that the cause of all intellectual activity, as well as motor activity, involves external stimulation. Thus the entire repertoire of behavior is the result of responses to environmental stimuli, mediated at the cortical level. In a later paper published in 1870, Sechenov dismissed contemporary views of psychology as a collection of surplus concepts that reflected the current state of ignorance of physiology. With further investigation, Sechenov argued, the constructs of psychology would disappear, having been reduced to their proper physiological level of explanation.

Sechenov reduced both psychic and physiological responses to reflexes, so that ideas became associations of reflexes mediated by the central nervous system. Thus, the founder of modern Russian physiology defined *reflexology* as a monistic interpretation of human activity, which equated psychological processes with essential neural processes. Sechenov began an experimental tradition to seek validation of his view of reflexology, which was not very different from that of the successors of Descartes within the French sensationalistic tradition. Interestingly, Sechenov's writings were censored by the imperial government because of their heavy emphasis on materialistic explanations of mental activities. Sechenov did not live to see the advent of Lenin, who established a government based on dialectical materialism, which was more amenable to the reflexology of Sechenov and his successors.

Vladimir Mikhailovich Bekhterev.   One of Sechenov's most famous students, Vladimir Mikhailovich Bekhterev (1857–1927), coined the term *reflexology* to describe his work. After studying in St. Petersburg, Bekhterev left Russia to work under Wundt, Du Bois–Reymond, and Jean Martin Charcot, the French neurologist who pioneered the modern use of hypnotism. Bekhterev's interest led him to apply the objective reflexology of Sechenov to psychiatric problems, and in 1907 he founded the St. Petersburg Psychoneurological Institute.

In 1910, Bekhterev published his *Objective Psychology*, which called for discarding mentalistic concepts from the description of psychological events. Although Bekhterev did some innovative experiments on punishment, his major contribution was his extensive writings, which brought greater knowledge and acceptance of reflexology to a wider audience. Moreover, his applications of reflexology to abnormal behavior demonstrated the utility of objective psychology.

Bekhterev was a contemporary and often a rival of Pavlov. Because he was acquainted with Wundt's psychology, he was more sensitive to the issues of concern to psychologists than was Pavlov. Accordingly, his general writings on reflexology earned faster acceptance among psychologists than did the more systematic work of Pavlov.

Rejecting introspection as an acceptable method because it assumes that psychological activity is somehow different from other human activities, Bekhterev stressed the unity of reflexology. Psychological and physiological processes involve the same neural energy, and the observable reflexes, whether inherited or acquired, are governed by lawful relations with internal and external stimulation. The goal of objective psychology is to discover the underlying laws mediating the occurrence of reflexes.

Ivan Petrovich Pavlov.   The most comprehensive system of Russian reflexology was offered by Ivan Petrovich Pavlov (1849–1936), whose long productive career was never seriously disrupted despite the upheavals of revolutionary Russia. Pavlov was born in a small town in central Russia, the son of a village orthodox priest. He originally intended to follow his father's vocation, but decided otherwise and went to the university at St. Petersburg in 1870. After several years of tutoring, which provided only a bare subsistence, Pavlov secured a fellowship to the university in 1879 and completed his medical degree in 1883. From 1884 to 1886 he studied in Leipzig and in Breslau (now Wrocław), where he joined a group of scientists investigating pancreatic secretion. In 1890, he became professor of pharmacology at the Military Medical Academy of St. Petersburg, and 5 years later was named professor of physiology. Also in that year, Pavlov helped to start the Imperial Institute of Experimental Medicine and served as its director as well as head of its physiology

**IVAN PETROVICH PAVLOV
(1849–1936).** (Courtesy, New York
Public Library.)

department. Along with Marceli Nencki (1849–1901), a pioneering biochemist of Polish origin who had left the University of Berne to lead the biochemistry department of the Institute, Pavlov established a research center of international reputation, moving in the 1930s to new facilities just outside St. Petersburg (renamed Leningrad in 1924 and reverted to St. Petersburg in 1990). Pavlov presided over a vastly expanded institute, and the Pavlovian Institute of Physiology of the Russian Academy of Sciences remains a prestigious center of physiological research on reflexology.

Pavlov was a stern and scholarly person with severe self-discipline. He imposed both his discipline and his rigid expectations on the multitude of students who worked under him during his many productive years. He was a systematic methodologist, for whom data gathering was a serious enterprise. The new laboratory built for Pavlov by Stalin's government was termed the "tower of silence," reflecting both its soundproof construction and the demeanor of the laboratory workers.

Pavlov received the Nobel Prize in 1904 for his work on the neural and glandular bases of digestion. In connection with this research, Pavlov discovered the essential principles of associative conditioning for which he is remembered today. Pavlov had developed a device that he implanted in the cheek of his dog subjects that collected saliva as a measure of digestive processes under investigation. During his careful experimentation, Pavlov noted that the subject reliably salivated in anticipation of receiving food, which was signaled by the approach of an experimenter or the presentation of a food dish. This astute observation launched Pavlov on a program of research that led to the development of conditioning reflexology. He found that he could take a neutral stimulus, such as a metronome beat, a tone, or a light, and after successively pairing it with a primary reward, such as food, a motivated (that is, hungry) dog would respond with salivation to the neutral stimulus presented without the food. He termed the neutral stimulus that acquired the eliciting properties of the primary reward the *conditional stimulus*. In an early translation, *conditional* was rendered as *conditioned*, and so *conditioned stimulus* became the standard terminology. However, the word *conditional* captures Pavlov's meaning better, because he regarded the acquisition of response-eliciting properties as a learned association. To fulfill the criteria of learning, the bond between the conditioned stimulus and the response must be temporary—that is, the bond must be capable of dissipating, resulting in the conditional stimulus losing its response-eliciting properties. Pavlov defined *extinction* as the repeated presentation of the conditioned stimulus in the absence of primary reward, so that the capacity of the conditioned stimulus to elicit the response is diminished. Pavlov specified four experimental events in the acquisition and extinction processes:

1. *Unconditioned Stimulus (US):* an environmental event (such as food) that, by its inherent properties, can elicit an organismic reflex.
2. *Conditioned Stimulus (CS):* an environmental event (such as a tone) that is neutral with respect to the response prior to pairings with the US.
3. *Unconditioned Response (UR):* the natural reflex (such as salivation) elicited autonomically, or involuntarily, by the US.
4. *Conditioned Response (CR):* the acquired reflex (such as salivation) elicited by the CS after association with the US.

Note that the UR and CR are the same response; they differ in their eliciting stimulus and usually in subtle indices of their strength. Pavlov found that different temporal relationships between the CS and the US produced varying rates of acquisition and extinction of CRs. The optimal relationship, making use of the anticipatory response, involves the presentation of the CS just prior to the US and is called *delayed conditioning*:

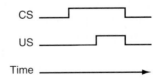

Other temporal relationships also produce conditioning, although at less optimal rates:

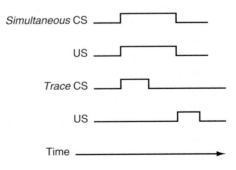

From this basic paradigm, Pavlov drew several principles. First, conditioning procedures represent the quantification and objectification of the acquisition and forgetting of associations. Pavlov had examined under experimental scrutiny the accepted concepts of association theory, discussed by such philosophers as Hume and the Mills, and established what he argued was a complete explanation of the formation of associations on the basis of the materialism of physiological reflexology. In Pavlov's conditioning theory, there was no need for any mental constructs. Rather, the nervous system, and especially the cortex, provided the mechanisms of reflexology. Second, the highly controlled experimental paradigm of conditioning offered the possibility of investigating all of higher nervous activity. Pavlov considered his procedures, involving careful experimenter control of environmental stimuli to produce response changes, to be ideally suited to investigating all types of behavior. Although he later modified his views, Pavlov initially thought that the formation of all associations ultimately involves variants of his basic paradigm. Third, Pavlov was firmly convinced that the temporal relationship, or contiguity, was the basic principle of the acquisition of associations. Again, this view was modified by later theorists, but Pavlov remained adamant that he had discovered the basic form of associations and that all learning reduces to the contiguous relationship between environmental stimuli and the mediational role of the cortex.

Pavlov regularly held laboratory meetings each Wednesday afternoon, presenting coherent overviews of his empirical work. A series of those lectures was published in English in 1927, translated by a former student, G. V. Anrep, under the title *Conditioned Reflexes: An Investigation of the Physiological Activity of the Cerebral Cortex*. In these lectures, representing the first systematic presentation of his views to Western scientists, Pavlov elaborated on his methodological approach to investigating behavioral processes mediated by the cortex. He described the spread of cortical excitation, termed *irradiation*, that results in behavioral generalization among similar environmental stimuli. With his notion of cortical inhibition, Pavlov was able to accommodate discriminative behavior. He discussed such now-common experimental findings as postextinction response elicitation (spontaneous recovery), internal inhibition, and modulation of postasymptotic response levels. In addition, Pavlov described his inducement of "experimental neurosis" in dogs, and devoted five lectures to investigations of cortical pathology.

Pavlov's other works were gradually translated and they, along with the writings of his students, gained him unprecedented eminence in psychology. His reputation remains largely intact to this day. If we rightly acknowledge Pavlov's fundamental position in modern psychology, we pay his memory a paradoxical tribute, for he had little use for psychology. Further, in comparing Pavlov with the founder of American behaviorism, Watson, it is readily obvious that Pavlov's data and interpretations have met the test of time far better. Pavlov, although a physiologist of impeccable competence, was first an experimentalist. He recognized the experimental method as the sole means of finding truth in science. To the extent that behavioristic psychology emulates an experimental approach, Pavlov's objective reflexology remains an honored and unmatched precedent.

American Connectionism: Thorndike

The major American researcher relevant to the precursors of Watsonian behaviorism is Edward Lee Thorndike (1874–1949), although Thorndike is included as a behaviorist somewhat tentatively. Looking at his entire career, which spanned 50 years of productive work in psychology, Thorndike's eclecticism appropriately groups him with the American functionalists. However, his early pioneering work on associations merits study by itself. His experiments on problem-solving behavior resulted in significant findings that were highly regarded at the time of Pavlov and Watson and are still recognized. Thorndike never intended to be a system builder, as Watson did, and his earlier, more theoretical work was later replaced by a shift to more practical problems of human learning and education (see Chapter 12).

Thorndike started graduate work at Harvard under William James and began investigating the intelligence of chickens. However, Cattell offered him a fellowship at Columbia University, and because Thorndike was able to continue his work on animal intelligence there, he accepted Cattell's offer. His doctoral dissertation, *Animal Intelligence: An Experimental Study of the Associative Processes in Animals* (1898), was expanded and published in 1911. In 1899, Columbia University took over the New York College for the Training of Teachers, and Thorndike joined the faculty of the consolidated Columbia Teachers College. He remained there for the rest of his career, pursuing educational issues, especially intelligence testing.

His earlier work on associations concerns us here. Thorndike examined problem-solving strategies in a variety of species, which he tested in puzzle boxes, various chambers designed to reward specific responses. Thorndike was impressed with his subjects' gradual acquisition of successful responses by trial-and-error learning and by accidental success. These observations led him to conclude that there are two basic principles of learning: exercise and effect. The law of exercise stated that associations are strengthened by repetition and dissipated by disuse. Thorndike's original law of effect stated that responses producing reward or satisfaction tend to be repeated, whereas responses producing punishment or annoyance tend to be eliminated. Later, he modified the law of effect to emphasize that reward strengthens associations, whereas punishment results in the subject's moving to another response, rather than weakening the association between the response and the stimulus context. Thus the earlier law of effect postulated that symmetrical reward-and-punishment feedback influences the connective bond; the later, modified version was an asymmetrical statement of the efficacy of reward and relegated punishment effects to a relatively minor role in learning. Thorndike's view of the basis of association differed somewhat from Pavlov's. First, the learning situation was under the control of the subject in Thorndike's procedure; the subject had to emit a response before receiving any reward. Second, the law of effect, or the influences of reinforcement, required recognition of the consequences of a reinforcing event by the subject. Thorndike never satisfactorily explained how reinforcement works. Because the effects presumably feed back to strengthen an associative bond between a response and a stimulus, some mechanism, or principle of realization, is needed for the subject to recognize whether the reinforcement was satisfying or not. This problem, which still plagues reinforcement theory, revolves around the need for the mediation of response-produced effects. Is some postulation of consciousness needed to deal adequately with the judgmental realization in order to act on reinforcement effects? Thorndike suggested that perhaps centers of satisfiers or annoyers exist in the brain. Although this explanation is not supported, Thorndike's principles of repetition and reinforcement, in accounting for learning, remain accepted in current research.

With the hindsight of history, we can recognize that Pavlov and Thorndike were investigating two different paradigms to produce learning, and we review this distinction later in this chapter. However, it is important to note that both Pavlov and Thorndike provided careful empirical documentation of the association process. Although neither directly intended to begin a behavioristic psychology, both contributed to the impulse that resulted in behaviorism. It was Watson who formally proclaimed a systematic context for behaviorism.

WATSONIAN BEHAVIORISM

In 1913, Watson published an article in the *Psychological Review* calling for a behavioristic psychology and changed the course of modern psychology. Watson asserted that a subject's behavior is worthy of study in itself, not for what it might reflect about some underlying state of consciousness. Although he expanded and gave coherence to the arguments favoring the study of behavior rather than consciousness, Watson did not write anything truly original. As mentioned before, the entire French sensationalistic tradition, which reduced mental content to sensory input, established an early version of behaviorism. The reduction of presumed mental events to physical correlates represents a consistent theme in the studies of the French sensationalists, as well as in the later writings of Comte, and finally in Watsonian behaviorism.

The shift from consciousness to behavior as the proper province of psychology received more immediate support from the nineteenth-century evolutionary movement. In particular, Darwin's meticulous observations supporting the principles of evolution by natural selection underscored the importance of the adaptive value of behavior. Supported also by Spencer's hypotheses of "social evolution," behavior as organismic activity came under new scrutiny. The renewed interest in the study of behavior during the latter part of the nineteenth century was immediately translated into an early interest in the value of cross-species comparisons, as we have seen in Chapter 10 from the works of Washburn, Romanes, and Morgan. Watson's emphasis on behavior rather than consciousness was a consistent step toward the development of comparative psychology, resting on the efficacy of homologous and analogous interpretations of behavioral patterns among varying species.

In addition to serving as a catalyst for several converging traditions, Watson's behaviorism provided a strong reaction to the methods of study prevalent in the psychology of consciousness. Watson rebelled against introspection as an appropriate method. Citing the difficulty of finding agreement among introspectionists observing the same processes, he argued that introspection is simply not an objective methodology, and reliance on it would spell disaster for psychology. Accordingly, Watsonian behaviorism "reestablished" the science of psychology. In discarding both the content (consciousness) and the methodology (introspection), Watson was advocating a complete reformulation of psychology.

Watson was born in South Carolina and received his undergraduate degree from Furman University. At the University of Chicago he studied under two important American functionalists, John Dewey and James Rowland Angell. Watson also studied physiology and neurology under H. H. Donaldson and Jacques Loeb and completed his PhD in 1903. Watson's early work on maze learning relied heavily on the methodological practices of physiology, including use of the laboratory rat. In 1908, Watson accepted a position at Johns Hopkins University, where his views on the possibility of an objective psychology took on systematic form as a coherent program. In 1920, Watson divorced his wife and married Rosalie Rayner, his former laboratory assistant. The ensuing scandal forced his resignation from Hopkins, and he never held another academic position. Rather, he applied his expertise to using psychology in advertising with some success, and wrote popular expositions of psychology. Accordingly, Watson's contributions to systematic psychology were completed by the middle 1920s, when he was in his early forties, an age when many scientists are only beginning their most productive period.

Watson's views centered on the premise that the province of psychology is behavior, measured in terms of stimulus and response; accordingly, psychology is concerned with the peripheral elements of stimulus and response impinging on the organism. Every response is determined by a stimulus, so that behavior may be completely analyzed by means of the causal relationship between stimulus and response elements. Watson did not deny the possible existence of central mental states, such as consciousness, but believed that because such alleged central states are nonphysical and cannot be studied scientifically, they are pseudoproblems for psychology.

Watson's view of the nature of the stimulus–response relationship—that is, association—relied primarily on the principle of frequency, or exercise, and secondarily on the principle of recency. Increasingly, he favored the conditioning reflexology of Pavlov and the puzzle box methods of Thorndike. However, Watson never fully appreciated the nature of reinforcement, and was especially skeptical of Thorndike's law of effect, which he criticized as resting on mentalistic inferences, without empirical support. Nevertheless, Watson did have faith in the principles of association as the key to psychological (behavioral) growth, although he acknowledged that his own theory of learning was largely inadequate. Accordingly, all behaviors—locomotive, perceptual, emotive, cognitive, and linguistic—are complexes or sequences of associative stimulus–response bonds.

The parsimony of Watson's proposal for psychology was most appealing. In a debate with William McDougall, later published as the *Battle of Behaviorism* (1929), Watson conceded that McDougall's call for accepting data from varieties of sources to gain a complete view of an individual has an attraction. Yet as soon as a scientist accepts data other than behavioral, the scientific clarity of the investigation begins to deteriorate. Indeed, the use of behavior, defined in terms of stimulus and response elements, gives psychology a unity because of the possibility of consensus yielded through objective observations, and this consensus provided an alternative to the introspective method of structuralism. Accordingly, Watson's system, focusing on behavioral adaptability to environmental stimuli, offered a positive, objective science of psychology, and by 1930 behaviorism was the dominant system of American psychology.

The major criticism of Watsonian behaviorism may be summarized under two points. First, this initial version of behaviorism restricted psychology by limiting behavior solely to the peripheral events of stimulus and response elements. In dismissing mental events, Watson also ignored physical, central mediation of stimulus and response bonds. He seems to have recognized the need for a more thorough elaboration of internal, central mediation by his appreciation of Pavlov. However, by the time Pavlov's views became better known, Watson had been removed from academia and was unable to pursue an integration of his views with those of Pavlov. It was left to his successors to modify the scope of behavioristic psychology by admitting the functions of central mediation, physiological as well as cognitive, to scientific scrutiny.

The second problem with Watsonian behaviorism concerns the issue of reductionism. We can probably say that in 1913 psychology lost its mind. The behavioristic strategy took those functions that had been reserved for the mind since the time of Descartes' speculation and reduced them to behavior. Behavior, in turn, was reducible to environmental stimuli and observable responses. Although Watson did not greatly elaborate on the specifics of the reduced level of stimuli and responses, the logic of Watson's approach is to suggest that behavior really reduces to physics and physiology. As noted, Watson's successors opened the behavioral system and rescued some of the discarded mental functions. Nevertheless, Watson's behaviorism was reductionistic. Carried to an extreme, such reductionism questions whether behavior per se possesses the integrity to warrant a separate and distinct science. On the one hand, if mental functions are added back to psychology, then psychology would once again become a metaphysical, not an empirical, discipline. On the other hand, if psychology is reduced to peripheral stimuli and responses, then it is equated with physics and physiology. So, although Watson's call to behavioristic psychology offered simplicity and clarity, the authenticity of a truly behavioral level of investigation remained questionable.

Other scholars, contemporaries of Watson, contributed to the formulation and acceptance of behaviorism. Like Thorndike, however, they should be considered as transitional figures between American functionalism and behaviorism. They did not intend the systematic upheaval envisioned by Watson, nor were they as committed to the theoretical implications of behaviorism. Nevertheless, their research and attitudes toward emerging behaviorism were critical to its eventual success.

Other Early American Behaviorists

Edwin B. Holt.   After completing a doctorate at Harvard in 1901 under the guidance of William James, Edwin B. Holt (1873–1946) taught at both Harvard and Princeton, but devoted most of his career to writing. The titles of his major works,

The Concept of Consciousness (1914), *The Freudian Wish and Its Place in Ethics* (1915), and *Animal Drive and the Learning Process* (1931), all reflect his major contribution to behaviorism, which was to infuse the notion of purpose or motivation in behavior for a more complete system. Holt did not accept the equation of behaviorism and reflexology inherent in the positions of both Pavlov and Watson. Instead of the reduction of behavior to constituent elements, Holt argued that behavior has purpose. Moreover, for Holt, behavior can only be understood from the perspective of the pattern of behavioral acts and sequences of acts. For the psychologist, behavior is more than the sum of stimulus–response bonds. Holt looked to other psychological models emphasizing motivational principles, such as Freudian psychodynamics and theories of instinctual drive, to examine how those views might present a more holistic context for behaviorism. One of his students, Edward Tolman, reviewed later in this chapter, followed Holt's lead and developed a comprehensive cognitive model of behaviorism.

Albert P. Weiss.   After immigrating to America as a child, Albert P. Weiss (1879–1931) studied at the University of Missouri under Max Meyer, who had been a student of Stumpf at Berlin. On receiving his doctorate in 1916, Weiss went to the Ohio State University and remained there for the rest of his brief career. His major work, *A Theoretical Basis of Human Behavior* (1925), attempted to deal with many of the complex human activities that were ignored or glossed over by Watson. Weiss concluded that psychology may best be understood as a biosocial interaction; that is, all psychological variables are reducible to either physicochemical or social levels, prompting Boring (1950) to remark that Weiss was a curious mixture of La Mettrie and Comte. However, by modifying reductionistic reflexology through consideration of socially based motivation, Weiss allowed psychology to deal better with complex forms of activity. Accordingly, the integrity of a psychological level of scientific inquiry of behavioral processes was greatly enhanced.

Walter S. Hunter.   After receiving his degree from the Chicago functionalist school in 1912, Walter S. Hunter (1889–1954) taught at several universities, then settled at Brown University in 1936. He earned a reputation as a respected researcher rather than a theoretician, and worked mainly on problem-solving behavior in mammals. Some of the behavioral tasks that developed from his experimental work, such as delayed response and double alternation behavior, were assumed to be representative of higher-order problem solving and remain in use today. Interestingly, Hunter, like other behaviorists, disliked the use of mentalistic terms so prevalent in German psychology, and proposed *anthroponomy* as a better term than *behaviorism* to replace *psychology*.

Karl S. Lashley.   Karl S. Lashley (1890–1958) was one of the few students to study with Watson during Watson's brief career at Hopkins. After completing his degree in 1915, Lashley taught at several universities before finally affiliating with the Yerkes Laboratory of Primate Biology in 1942. Lashley was a physiological psychologist, introducing the critical role of the physiological correlates of behavior. Moreover, his productive laboratory work served as a model for many psychologists, so that behaviorism became permanently linked to physiological investigation. However, it is important to contrast Lashley's physiological behaviorism with Pavlov's reflexology. Although followers of both scientists might very well have done similar experiments leading to related conclusions, their reasons for doing the experiments were different. Under Pavlov's reflexology, there was no true behavioral level of investigation per se. Rather, presumed psychological events were explained completely through physiological causes. For Lashley, however, the integrity of observable behavior was assumed, then the physiological substrates were investigated. He did not equate the psychological and physiological. Rather, depending on the complexity of the problem under study, he considered the physiological level an explanatory component of psychological events. Thus the integrity of each level was retained.

Operational Positivism

A movement that supported the success of behaviorism was initiated in physics and had wide-ranging influence in all of the sciences. This movement, generally called operationism, was a twentieth-century expression of positivism. In the United States, a Harvard physicist, Percy W. Bridgman, influenced by the work of a group of physicists centered in Copenhagen, published *The Logic of Modern Physics* (1927), in which scientific concepts were defined by the operations employed to observe them. By implication, the concept was equated with the operations, nothing more or less. Any concept that presumably could not be defined operationally was for Bridgman a pseudoproblem—that is, the concept did not have scientific value.

At the same time in Vienna, a group of philosophers was formalizing a broader version of positivism, closely linked to Bridgman's operationism. This group derived its immediate ancestry from the teachings of Ernst Mach and came to be known as the Vienna Circle of Logical Positivists. It sought to supplement Mach's views with contributions from contemporary developments in philosophy and logic. Logical positivism is a comprehensive philosophy of science. This movement essentially stressed the unity of all science because, studied by the methods of empiricism, all science is ultimately physical. Accordingly, all truly scientific issues may be examined through a common language derived from physics and expressed in terms of operationism. Until its members' dispersal in the late 1930s, the Vienna Circle remained a spirited group that aimed to unify science on the basis of the operational character of scientific problems.

The expression of operationism in psychology was an attempt to resolve the conflict between the empirical traditions of psychology and the prevailing metaphysics of the psychology of consciousness. By reinforcing a radical empirical stand within all of science, behaviorism was the sole system within psychology at that time to act as vehicle for logical positivism with its concomitant operationism. The reductionism inherent to the description of psychological events in terms of stimulus and response elements fits nicely into the movement. The movement of the logical positivists and operationists suggested a behavioristic model of psychology and, similarly, behaviorism supported the recognition of the unity of science expressed in an operational approach to sciences. The net result for psychology of this interchange of forces was the further entrenchment of behaviorism.

It is important to try to appreciate the full impact of the development of behaviorism on psychology. Behaviorism fundamentally offered the opportunity for a truly scientific psychology based on an empirical approach, just as in the physical and life sciences. By turning away from the elusive nature of consciousness, behavioral psychology permitted the study of its subject matter through a methodology that had proved successful for nineteenth-century science. Looking back on the historical development of psychology from 1870, Watsonian behaviorism was a bold attempt to reformulate and reestablish the science of psychology.

BROADENING BEHAVIORISM

After Watson's initial formulation of behavioristic psychology and the revisions by the early behaviorists, the movement began an evolution that gradually expanded the scope of behaviorism to include issues relating to the central mediation of behavior. Although the very definition of behaviorism did in fact change, one commonality shared throughout this evolution was the acceptance of an essential empirical methodology in the study of behavior. Perhaps more than Watson's preliminary analysis, it was the positivist character of behaviorism that left a more permanent legacy to psychology.

In the United States, the initial phase of the behavioristic evolution consisted of an intensive effort to build systematic structures of behavior theory. Beginning in the 1930s and lasting for approximately 20 years, eminent psychologists attempted to find a complete theoretical conceptualization for all behavioral processes. In a sense, this phase of theory building reflected an enthusiasm for behaviorism by accepting the possibility that this system of psychology could indeed constitute the definitive model for the new science. This phase of the behavioristic evolution ended with the recognition that an all-encompassing theory of behavior was at least premature and maybe impossible. However, the theory-building phase was critical for the development of behaviorism. In their attempt to formulate a general theory to accommodate the diversity of behavioral processes, these psychologists broadened the scope of the Watsonian version. Moreover, they rendered to the study of behavior a refined scrutiny that entrenched the definition of psychology in terms of behavioral processes.

In the second phase of the behavioristic evolution, the preoccupation with theory building was replaced by data collection. In response to the elusive search for a complete behavioral theory, psychologists began employing data as the guide to progressive research. In this phase, behavioral psychology took on a methodological character that was identical to that of the natural or physical sciences. In many respects, this phase of the behavioristic evolution is still continuing. However, by the 1970s another shift in behaviorism was apparent; it emphasized mini-theory or model building as well as the application of behavioral principles, especially in the development of so-called behavioral technology.

Before examining the details of the behavioristic evolution in America, we should be mindful of what was happening to European psychology during this period. Although the psychological models based on active assumptions of consciousness—such as Gestalt, psychoanalysis, and phenomenology—were European movements, the turmoil created by the volatile events in twentieth-century Europe resulted in the exportation of these views to America. In addition to bringing death and destruction, the world wars completely disrupted intellectual activity. It was no accident that one of the early revisions of Watsonian behaviorism coincided with the emigration of the leaders of the Gestalt movement, who fled the anti-intellectualism and anti-Semitism that followed Hitler's assumption of power in 1933. After the leaders of European proposals for the formulation of psychology fled to the United States, their views modified existing behaviorism to varying extents. However, the European manifestation of the natural science model for psychology—namely, Russian reflexology—remained a developing force in the states of the former Soviet Union. Reflexology exerted a major impact in the early years of American behaviorism, and the more modern expressions of reflexology continue to be an important influence.

Reflexology Expanded

Russian and Eastern European psychology accommodates a full range of theoretical issues and applications broadly based on a variety of perspectives, as in the United States. However, the pioneering work of Russian reflexology, culminating in the work of Pavlov, occupied a preeminent place in Russian psychology. Although seriously disrupted during World War II, Russian science, as rebuilt in the postwar period, supported the continuing development of reflexology.

As mentioned before, Pavlov's reduction of psychological events to physiological materialism was generally consistent with the philosophical underpinnings of the Marxist–Leninist government of the former Soviet Union. After many years of discussion and debate, Marxism–Leninism and Pavlovian reflexology were integrated into a single philosophical basis for psychology. Within this foundation, all mental activity was interpreted as the product of the physiological mechanisms of higher nervous activity centered in the brain. External, overt behavior interacts with the internal, central physiology, so that internal and external processes were considered to be two aspects of the same psychological mechanism. With harmony between science and government, and consistent with the permeation of Marxist–Leninist philosophy throughout Soviet society, the highly centralized Academy of Sciences of the former Soviet Union established research centers of reflexology that applied their research efforts to the full range of psychological issues, such as social psychology, personality, and psychopathology.

One of the more interesting developments in reflexology during the period between the two world wars began with the research of two young medical students at the University of Warsaw, Jerzy Konorski (1903–1973) and Stefan Miller (1902–1941). They became interested in the newly published Russian edition of Pavlov's *Lectures on the Higher Activities of the Brain* (1926), and their ability to read Russian gave them access to primary reports of Pavlov's ongoing research program as well as data from various Russian laboratories. Konorski and Miller argued the novel hypothesis that because Pavlov's account could not completely explain behavioral changes following the reward of certain movements and the punishment of others, there indeed may be two types of conditioning paradigms. They tested their hypothesis in a series of ingenious experiments, which led to the distinction between response-dependent reward, or avoidance of punishment (type II conditioning), and Pavlov's CS–US sequence resulting in behavior change (type I conditioning). The report of their findings to the Warsaw Division of the French Biological Society in 1928 generated considerable interest in Europe, and Pavlov himself extended an invitation to Konorski and Miller to work with him in the Koltushi Laboratory outside Leningrad (now St. Petersburg). Konorski spent 2 years with Pavlov, repeating and confirming the experimental work from Warsaw, later published as *Physiological Bases for the Theory of Acquired Movements* (1933) and in the laboratory journal of the Pavlovian Institute (1936), with an introduction by Pavlov. Because of the political isolation of Russia at that time, the details of Pavlov's research program and Konorski and Miller's revision of the two processes of conditioning went relatively unnoticed in the West. Instead, Skinner's (1935, 1938) similar distinction between Pavlovian and instrumental conditioning, published in English, preempted the earlier work of Konorski and Miller. Although differences in interpretation existed between the view of Skinner and that of Konorski and Miller, the latter researchers may be credited with the important distinction between Pavlovian and instrumental conditioning.

After his work with Pavlov, Konorski returned to Poland and systematically began to approach his major goal in reflexology—the integration of Pavlov's and Sherrington's models of neural processes. His work was halted by the German invasion of Poland on September 1, 1939, and the devastation of the country during the subsequent 6 years. In addition to the destruction of universities and research institutes, the vast majority of Poland's intelligentsia, including Stefan Miller, died during the struggle against Nazism. Konorski spent the war years in the Soviet Union, for the most part working in military hospitals in the Republic of Georgia in the Caucasus.

After the war Konorski was instrumental in the difficult task of rebuilding the Polish scientific establishment. In particular, he founded the Department of Neurophysiology of the Marceli Nencki Institute of Experimental Biology in Warsaw. In addition to carrying out a productive research program in general reflexology, the department served as a center for educating a new generation of Polish neurophysiologists. Moreover, the unique political position of postwar Poland, coupled with the research activity and personal dynamism of Konorski, provided an ideal setting for a dialogue between Western and Eastern scientists. The research direction of Konorski and his coworkers generally concerned brain physiology; in particular, the central mechanisms regulating behavior, especially instrumental conditioned reflexes. In his last systematic contribution, *Integrative Activity of the Brain* (1967), Konorski considered brain activity as a complex cybernetic system controlling activities of the organism as a whole. This work represents a complete synthesis of Sherrington's neurology and Pavlov's reflexology. Accordingly, Konorski viewed higher nervous activity as a dynamic system capable of varieties of adaptive strategies, anticipating the advances in cybernetics and information processing that occurred subsequently in the behavioral sciences. As the most famous of Pavlov's students outside Russia, Konorski followed the reductionistic strategy of reflexology. However, in addition to his rejection of a single conditioning process, his significant contribution consisted of a true interdisciplinary perspective for reflexology, and within this context, Konorski broadened reflexology to accommodate a full range of psychological issues.

Since the end of World War II, Russian reflexology has moved far beyond the study of conditioned associations. Firmly based in materialistic reductionism to the mechanisms of neural activity, the research strategy of reflexology has been employed in all types of psychological research, ranging from the problems of psychiatric disorders to the development of language. A guide for the inclusion of such widespread concern within the materialistic model of reflexology was proposed by a brilliant scientist of the interwar period, L. S. Vygotsky (1896–1934), who influenced many prominent scientists of the postwar period. Essentially, Vygotsky called for the complete application of scientific technology to further the betterment of the individual and society, but at the same time argued for the recognition of the complexity of human nature. Hence, scientific technology should serve the scientist pursuing a holistic understanding of the person. Vygotsky extended Pavlov's reflexology to higher mental functions but insisted that the reductionism of the materialistic methodology must not obscure the complexity of human mental activity.

Perhaps Vygotsky's most famous student was A. L. Luria (1902–1977), whose long career included detailed investigations of such diverse issues as the development of language and thoughts, the neurophysiology of cortical functions, and cross-cultural comparisons of sign systems. Luria's study of language tested Vygotsky's hypothesis that speech forms a critical link in the relationship between external, overt behavior and internal, symbolic thought. While extending Russian psychology beyond the traditional province of reflexology, Luria's view was also consistent with the monistic underpinnings of reflexology in that it stressed the unity of psychological and physiological aspects of experience. Luria identified four distinct and progressive stages in the developmental process of speech functions: activity initiation, activity inhibition, external regulation, and, finally, internal regulation of activity. Internal speech was the foundation of thought processes. In another area, Luria's research on the frontal lobe systems helped to isolate the localization of behavioral patterns, and his studies of recovery of function after brain damage contributed to the understanding of retrieval processes in memory. Luria's productivity and wide-ranging investigations consistently combined clinical and laboratory observations within a coherent theoretical framework of reflexology.

Studies of the neurophysiology of conditioning have continued in Russia. One area of major concern has been the orienting reflex, recognized by Pavlov as a form of external inhibition. In 1958, E. M. Sokolov wrote a classic paper (translated into

English in 1963) that related the orienting reflex to sensory thresholds involved in arousal. Through the use of a variety of physiological and electrophysiological measures, the adaptive significance of the orienting reflex has been extended to such behavioral processes as habituation and attention.

The major focus of contemporary reflexology in Russia has concerned the ongoing theme of the single, materialistic basis of psychological events. Such physicalism, in sharp contrast to idealistic or mentalist constructs, is reflected in the emphasis on measurement of neural mechanisms, especially through electrophysiological recordings. Laboratories, such as the Institute of Higher Nervous Activity and Neurophysiology in Moscow, led for many years by Ezras E. Asratyan (1903–1981), pursued interdisciplinary programs of research. In addition to the active research centers under the direction of the Russian and Siberian Academies of Sciences, research activities are found in nations contiguous to Russia. Especially active are Ukrainian and Armenian Academies of Sciences. Moreover, one of the most creative and productive centers of contemporary reflexology is found in the Georgian Republic. There, the Institute of Physiology of Tbilisi University reached notable achievement under the leadership of Ivan Solomonovich Beritashvili (1885–1974), whose name is sometimes rendered in English as Beritov. After his education in St. Petersburg, Kazan, and Utrecht, Beritashvili returned to post-revolutionary Georgia in 1919 and founded the Institute of Physiology. His various investigative programs included studies of the rhythmic nature of subcortical inhibition, the physiological properties of dendrites, the functions of the reticular activating system, and conditioning and memory.

The movement started by Sechenov, Bekhterev, and Pavlov established the principles of conditioning and evolved into a reliance on the materialism of physiology to explain psychological activity. With the disintegration of the Soviet Union and its replacement by new independent countries, scientific work entered into a period of adjustment. The successor structures of the former Soviet Academy of Sciences are still evolving, so the future direction of reflexology, and psychological research in general, within these countries remains unclear.

The American Behaviorists

As Pavlov's system in the 1930s was undergoing assimilation within Russian Soviet science, behaviorism in the United States was evolving into a theory-building phase. This phase reflected the triumph of behaviorism over the mentalistic psychology of consciousness. Moreover, the identification of psychology as a positive science, similar in approach to the physical sciences, proceeded concurrently. This period was dominated by four important scientists: Edwin R. Guthrie (1886–1959), Clark L. Hull (1884–1952), Edward C. Tolman (1886–1959), and B. F. Skinner (1904–1990). The first three proposed theories of behavior and contributed to this phase of the evolution of behaviorism; Skinner attempted an "antitheory" and marked the end of this phase.

Guthrie's Contiguity Theory.   Like Watson, Edwin R. Guthrie advocated a psychology of observable behavior consisting of muscular movements and glandular responses elicited by environmental stimuli. His theory of associations was in the tradition of Pavlov and Thorndike, asserting a single principle to account for learning. Guthrie did not accept Thorndike's reinforcement principle based on the law of effect, but rather viewed Thorndike's secondary notion of associative shifting as the basis of learning.

Guthrie received his doctorate in 1912 from the University of Pennsylvania after earlier training in mathematics and philosophy. He joined the University of Washington in 1914 and remained there for his entire career. Guthrie was not a systematic experimenter and his arguments were mainly based on general observations and anecdotal information. His major experimental work, written in conjunction with G. P. Horton, studied problem-solving behavior of cats and was published as *Cats in a Puzzle Box* (1946). His most influential theoretical work was *The Psychology of Learning* (1935; revised in 1952).

The key to Guthrie's associationistic theory lies in the single principle that contiguity is the foundation of learning. Guthrie viewed behavior in terms of movement rather than responses. By this distinction, he meant that movements are the components of larger response units, or behavioral acts. Accordingly, skilled behaviors may be viewed in terms of a gross response composed of smaller units of movements that are largely muscular. Stimuli were likewise viewed as a complex situation consisting of smaller elements. Guthrie's principle of contiguity stated that when a combination of stimulus elements is accompanied by movement, the movement sequence will recur, given the presence of similar stimulus elements. Guthrie held that learning is a pattern or chain of discrete movements elicited by both environmental and internal stimulus cues.

Because Guthrie's view of associations relied on stimulus and response contiguity, the role of reinforcement received a unique interpretation. Guthrie believed in one-trial learning—in other words, the contiguous relationship between stimulus and response elements immediately produces the associative bond at full strength. The effects of a reinforcing reward or punishment serve to feed back on the stimulus situation, altering that situation and requiring a new bond between the altered stimulus situation and movement. Thus, reinforcement provides a means of changing the stimulus context, requiring movement, and the learning proceeds within the behavior act. Extinction, or forgetting, was interpreted as the result of interference from new associations rather than the decay of stimulus-response bonds caused by the absence of reinforcement. Similarly, practice effects were not seen as affecting stimulus-movement association but rather as improving the coordination of established bonds within the gross behavioral act. In a consistent vein, Guthrie viewed drives not as causal motivational agents but rather as energizers of behavior acts.

Guthrie's arguments and interpretations influenced later behavioristic psychologists. F. D. Sheffield defended Guthrie's views and extended them to include the use of positive reinforcement as a means of refining behavior. Similarly, Virginia Voeks used carefully designed experiments to demonstrate many of the implications of Guthrie's writings. However, the stimulus sampling theory of William Estes (see later Information-Processing and Mathematical Models section) is perhaps the most extensive application of Guthrie's associationism, and statistical models of learning have generally found Guthrie's theory amenable to computer simulation of associative processes.

The major criticism of Guthrie's views may be that they are incomplete and do not deal comprehensively with complex types of learning and memory problems. However, Guthrie's seeming ability to explain, in a parsimonious way, some of the principles of more complicated systems, notably Hull's theory, constitutes his appeal.

Hull's Hypotheticodeductive Theory. Clark L. Hull's systematic theory came closest to a comprehensive treatment of behavioral issues governed by common principles. As a behaviorist, Hull centered his psychological views on habit formation, the accumulations of experiences for effective adaptation. His scientific approach was truly systematic. Recognizing the importance of observation and experimentation, he advocated a hypotheticodeductive structure to guide research. In this strategy, following the approach of Euclidian geometry, a behavior principle or formulation is first deduced from postulates and then rigorously tested. A successful test supports belief in the postulates; failure results in revision of the postulates. Hull's approach was positivist and followed a logical progression, verified through empirical demonstration.

Hull's theory was the product of a lifetime of disciplined work. Born in New York and raised in Michigan, Hull suffered from ill health, had poor eyesight, and was crippled by polio. His education was interrupted at various times because of illness and financial problems. After pursuing mining engineering at Alma College, he transferred to the University of Michigan and completed a degree in psychology. In 1918, he received his PhD from the University of Wisconsin, where he stayed for 10 years as an instructor. During that time he studied the effects of tobacco smoking on performance, reviewed the existing literature on testing, and began research on suggestion and hypnosis, the latter culminating in a widely read book published in 1933. In 1929, he was named to a research position at Yale University and began the serious development of his behavior theory. Until the end of his career Hull and his students dominated behavioristic psychology.

Hull's system is intricate and relies heavily on mathematical predictions. He made detailed modifications as his experimental tests progressed over time. The present survey attempts to highlight his views. Essentially, Hull's theory of learning is centered on the necessity of reinforcement, defined in terms of the reduction of drives arising from motivational states. The behaving organism is viewed in the context of a homeostatic model seeking equilibrium from drive forces. The core of Hull's analysis concerns the notion of *intervening variables*, described as unobservable entities employed by psychologists to account for observable behavior. Thus, from a purely behavioral perspective, Hull extended Watson's conceptualization of behavior in terms of the peripheral (S–R) events to a consideration of central, organismic factors, stimulus–organism–response (S–O–R), intervening variables. This expansion of the behavioral model had been suggested as early as 1918 by Woodworth (see Chapter 12), but it was Hull who systematically articulated organismic variables.

The chief intervening variable for learning in Hull's theory is called habit strength, ($_SH_R$), which depends on two factors for associations. The first is a contiguity principle, meaning that a close temporal relationship must exist between stimulus and reinforcement. The second principle is reinforcement itself, defined in its primary form as drive reduction, but there are also secondary reinforcements, cues that are reliably associated with primary reinforcement and take on reinforcement properties. For example, if a hungry rat is repeatedly given food for correct responses in the presence of a light, the light takes on some of the rewarding characteristics of the food. Hull attempted to integrate Thorndike's law of effect with Pavlovian conditioning, so that the basic procedure in which learning occurs is contiguity of stimulus and response under conditions of reinforcement. Habit strength ($_SH_R$) and drive (D) interact to produce what Hull referred to as reaction potential ($_SE_R$)—the "tendency to produce some reaction under the effect of the stimulus." $_SE_R$ was a theoretical concept for Hull, not synonymous with observable responses; it is the product of $_SH_R$ and D:

$$_SE_R = {_SH_R} \times D$$

Hull's intervening variables represented not only a qualitative conceptualization but also an attempt to define quantitative relationships. For example, on the basis of the above expression, little performance would be observed from a hungry but naive rat: Drive is high, but habit strength is not, resulting in a low tendency to respond. Similarly, accounting for the distinction between learning and performance, a rat with a well-established response to bar-press for food reward would not perform if it is not hungry: Habit strength is high, but drive is minimal, producing little expectation of reaction potential. To complete his framework for the intervening variables mediating performance, Hull included negative, inhibitory factors (I), resulting from fatigue and boredom, as a by-product of performance. He also included the contributions of stimulus magnitude (V)—for example, a faint versus a loud CS; the magnitude of reinforcement (K)—for example, one versus four food pellets per correct response; and the oscillating, momentary threshold of reaction for an individual subject ($_SO_R$). All of these intervening variables were related:

$$_SE_R = {_SH_R} \times D + V + K - I - {_SO_R}$$

It should be noted that this summary equation was itself articulated into more refined components as Hull's theory developed.

The entire detailed structure of Hull's system was applied to the quantification of all possible influences on the acquisition of adaptive behavior. Indeed, empirical tests, largely conducted with laboratory rats, tended to support Hull's conceptualization. This analytic approach assumed that more complex forms of behavior could be derived from these intervening variables. However, the theory as a whole was not successful after all. There were empirical discrepancies, such as the inability of the theory to deal with insightful, rapid acquisition of behavior. Hull's view stressed the importance of practice during training, producing continuous but gradual improvement during acquisition. More importantly, however, the theory fell apart in its attempt to quantify the conceptual relationships among intervening variables. As a model or guide for research, Hull's system was superb; much of our contemporary jargon to describe learning was invented by Hull. However, as the exact, definitive statement of behavior, Hull's views were probably premature, resulting in a fixed, rigid structure not amenable to the variability of human and animal behavior.

Tolman's Cognitive Behaviorism.   As a behaviorist, Edward C. Tolman developed a theory that pushed the scheme of Watsonian behaviorism toward further expansion than did either Guthrie or Hull. In his major work, *Purposive Behavior in Animals and Men* (1932), Tolman proposed a consideration of behavior that was molar, as opposed to molecular. He viewed molar behavior as a unified and complete act, which provides the proper unit for psychology. Underlying molecular elements, whether neural, muscular, or glandular processes, were not sufficient to account for the molar act. In this sense, Tolman departed from Watsonian behaviorism by opening psychology to the study of higher, cognitive processes. His approach to molar behavior was not reductionistic. In adhering to the molar level, Tolman argued that reductionism results in the loss of the purely psychological level, and explanations based upon molecular components are not adequate. Thus, for Tolman, molar behavior is more than the sum of the molecular elements.

Like Hull, Tolman originally was interested in engineering, and he received a degree from the Massachusetts Institute of Technology. He switched to psychology and finished his PhD in 1915 at Harvard. After teaching at Northwestern University for 3 years, Tolman joined the University of California at Berkeley, where he contributed considerably to the developing reputation of that institution. Tolman became known as an excellent and warm teacher. In 1950 he led the movement against the California state loyalty oath as an affront to academic freedom, and the oath was eventually discarded. The image of Tolman that comes through is of an open person welcoming new trends and ideas in psychology.

Tolman's view of psychology relies heavily on many of the premises of the Gestalt psychologists. Indeed, he used the term *Gestalt* to describe holistic, insightful learning experiences. Moreover, his conception of behavior as molar and his adoption of mental isomorphism were directly borrowed from Gestalt psychology. He used the latter construct to describe the central product of learning in terms of the acquisition of field maps that exist in the brain as cognitive representations of the learned environment.

Tolman's theoretical orientation was not as systematic in approach as that of Hull. His criticism of the reduction of psychological events to the mechanical elements of stimulus and response caused many researchers of the Hullian orientation to pause and modify their views. Tolman's laws of acquisition essentially focused on practice that builds up sign Gestalts, or expectancies. In maze learning experiments with rats, for example, he described the acquisition of place learning, inferring the acquisition of relationships or cognitive maps in the subject. Similarly, he demonstrated the expectancy of reinforcement in rats trained to one kind of reward and then switched to a more appealing food. Finally, he showed that latent learning occurs in rats, indicating that the quality of reinforcement can exert a differential effect on performance levels. In all of these experiments Tolman used cognitive explanations as intervening variables to show that behavior in organisms is governed by central, mediating processes that go beyond environmental input only.

Tolman was often criticized for his lack of specific explanations of the central mediation of cognitive learning. However, he brought to behaviorism a new perspective that departed from the sterile reductionism of molecular Watsonian behaviorism. Moreover, his repeated demonstration of performance versus learning differences clearly showed that learning is not reducible simply to stimulus-response-reinforcement elements. If he failed to offer a more comprehensive explanation, he nevertheless succeeded in justifying the integrity of molar behavior and stimulated inquiry. Tolman did not leave a systematic school of followers, as did Hull, but he anticipated the entire research theme of cognitive learning prevalent in contemporary psychology.

Skinner's Radical Positivism.   In 1950, B. F. Skinner published a paper entitled "Are Theories of Learning Necessary?" His discussion formally signaled the end of the theory-building phase of the behavioristic expansion. Skinner recognized the shortcomings of the attempt at theory building—the inadequacies of the theories and the distortion of behavioral science predicated on questionable a priori assumptions. In the place of theories he advocated a system of behaviorism guided by data. According to Skinner, theory, when psychology's progress permits it, should be confined to loose, descriptive generalizations arrived at through reliance on facts yielded by a positive scientific approach.

Skinner received his doctorate in psychology from Harvard in 1931, after an earlier interest in literature. He taught at the University of Minnesota and Indiana University before returning to Harvard in 1947. In addition to a prolific research record and influence on a generation of neobehaviorists, Skinner popularized his behavioristic principles through novels and commentaries. His novel *Walden II* has sold more than 2 million copies. He was widely known for his opinions on social structures and institutions.

Skinner's positivism consistently advocated a methodological emphasis and a return to the study of behavior defined in terms of peripheral events. He argued against speculating about central mediating agencies of behavior, whether cognitive or physiological. Rather, behavior, for Skinner, was completely subject to environmental determinacy. If the environment is controlled, behavior is controlled. For this reason, Skinner accepted the validity of exhaustive study of a single subject, because variability arises not from individual differences inherent in the organism, but rather from differential environmental contingencies.

The basis for Skinner's research was the study of operant behavior. In contrast to respondent behavior, where responses are elicited by specific stimuli, operant behavior is ongoing without any apparent stimulus. To investigate operant behavior, Skinner devised an environmental chamber where birds could engage in pecking, or rats in bar pressing. In this manner, environmental control is easier to obtain and ongoing, operant rates of responses can be readily recorded. Learning occurs when the operant behavior comes under the control of reinforcement from the environment. At first, the operant responses may be shaped by reinforcement of approximations of the desired operant character. When the refined operant is followed by presentation of the reinforcing event, the probability of the occurrence of the operant is increased. For example, if an operant is defined as bar pressing in a rat, presentation of food following a bar press increases the likelihood of more bar presses. Thus, Skinner's view of reinforcement was defined in terms of the probability of changes in the operant rate. It avoided inferences of satisfiers or annoyers, as in Thorndike's law of effect, or of drive reduction, as in Hull's theory.

Skinner clearly demonstrated the power of reinforcement by showing that characteristic response rates are obtained for particular schedules of reinforcement delivery. Similarly, he translated conditioning processes such as generalization and discrimination to a reinforcement contingency framework. Moreover, he extended the principles of operant control to a consideration of verbal behavior. Skinner used his experimental data to argue that behavior is controlled, and the critical role of the psychologist is to define the parameters of effective control for appropriate social implications.

Skinner's view of behavior has often drawn the harsh criticism of those who are offended by his mechanical conception of human nature. Skinner's view, however, has clear antecedents in the history of psychology—for example, the views of Condillac and some of the pre-Socratic scholars. A more direct antecedent is the German zoologist Jacques Loeb (1859–1924), who taught Watson at the University of Chicago. Loeb suggested a theory of animal tropism and was quite influential in the development of comparative psychology. Whether one considers Skinner's environmental determinacy or Pavlov's physiological reductionism, the net conceptualization of human activity precludes any attributes of personal freedom, self-determinacy, or the dynamics of consciousness. Skinner perhaps earned more of the scorn of critics because he articulated the social controls that are derived from the principles of operant behavior. In the spirit of positivism, Skinner argued that the humanistic characteristics of the species, which presumably set us off from the rest of living evolutionary products, are in fact an illusion, created by us over history to give us a sense of security. In fact, for Skinner, to be truly human means to be in control—to understand and use environmental contingencies to self-benefit. Skinner addressed the place of the person in terms of his own views as well as those of his critics in the following passage from *About Behaviorism*:

> Behavior is the achievement of a person, and we seem to deprive the human organism of something which is his natural due when we point instead to the environmental sources of his behavior. We do not dehumanize him: we dehomunculize him. The essential issue is autonomy. Is man in control of his own destiny or is he not? The point is often made by arguing that a scientific analysis changes man from victor to victim. But man remains what he has always been, and his most conspicuous achievement has been the design and construction of a world which has freed him from constraints and vastly extended his range. (1974, pp. 239–240)

THE ROLE OF THEORY

On leaving the theory-building phase of behaviorism, it is appropriate to pause briefly to examine the uses of theory in science so that the significance of theory building within psychology may be appreciated. Although we are here concerned with theories in behaviorism, we have surveyed many theories so far—among them Wundt's theory of consciousness and Freud's dynamic system. It is interesting to question what theories are supposed to do in the progress of science. Marx defines a theory as

> a provisional explanatory proposition, or set of propositions, concerning some natural phenomena and consisting of symbolic representations of (1) the observed relationships among (measured) events, (2) the mechanisms or structures presumed to underlie such relationships, or (3) inferred relationships and underlying mechanisms intended to account for observed data in the absence of any direct empirical manifestation of the relationships. (1976, p. 237)

Accordingly, theories should provide a framework to test existing hypotheses and generate new hypotheses.

Marx (1963) has provided a useful description of the elements of theory construction that offers three dimensions that distinguish between the arts and sciences; it is presented in Figure 15–1. Marx discussed the three components of theory construction—hypotheses, constructs, and observations—as continua ranging between art and science. The continuum of observations classifies the way a theory reduces the variation in measurement coming from the influence of stimulating conditions.

FIGURE 15–1   The elements of scientific theory construction. (Reprinted by permission of Prentice Hall, Upper Saddle River, NJ, from *Theories in Contemporary Psychology,* 1st and 2nd eds., edited by Melvin H. Marx. Copyright 1963, 1976 by Macmillan Publishing Company.)

DIMENSIONS OF THEORETICAL EVALUATION

HYPOTHESES:	Testability	
	intuitive	rigorous
ART CONSTRUCTS:	Operational Specificity	**SCIENCE**
	with surplus meaning	with explicit empirical referents
OBSERVATIONS:	Control	
	everyday (ambiguous)	experimental

For example, watching spontaneous play activity of children in a schoolyard is a less controlled observational situation than recording the magnitude of the CR upon presentation of the CS. Constructs, the major substance of explanation in theories, vary from general concepts without tight definition to explanatory mechanisms closely defined in terms of readily observable referents. For example, the libidinal energy of Freud has more surplus meaning as an explanation of human motivation than Hull's intervening variable of a drive such as hunger, defined in terms of a specific number of hours of food deprivation. The third continuum of hypotheses is differentiated by the degree of testability. For example, it is more difficult to construct empirical tests of the validity of Freud's stages of psychosexual development than it is to test a hypothesis of frontal lobe mediation of behavioral responses, as derived from Pavlov's theory of conditioning.

It is important to note the bias inherent in Marx's schema of theory evaluation. He has defined science in terms of empirical approaches based on observation. To thus evaluate Freud's largely nonempirical views is perhaps unfair because it is an open question whether a nonempirical approach can be considered scientific rather than necessarily artistic. However, these evaluative dimensions are useful in a comparison of the empirically based orientations of Guthrie, Hull, Tolman, and Skinner.

Relative to Figure 15–1, Hull's and Skinner's theories relied on a more experimental approach than did the theories of Guthrie and, to some extent, Tolman. Hull's experimental observations were dictated by the systematic implications of his hypothesis-testing strategy, whereas Skinner's positivism and reliance on the determinacy of environmental control were readily amenable to experimental investigation. The constructs of the theories of both Hull and Tolman were based on intervening variables. Yet the systems of each may be differentiated along this dimension by comparing Hull's reliance on observable operations, such as the definitions of drive or magnitude of reinforcements, with Tolman's less operationally specific notions, such as cognitive maps or expectancies. Similarly, the parsimonious theory of Guthrie allowed contiguous relationships to be defined quite specifically. Although Skinner's positivism did not admit any constructs, the question remains whether some constructs, consisting of loose assumptions about the nature of environmental control, are implied. At the very least, it appears that the discarding of central mediation in behavior offers an example of an explanatory mechanism that is an a priori assumption in Skinnerian behaviorism. Again, Hull's hypotheticodeductive theory produced rigorous hypotheses, more so than the theories of Tolman and Guthrie. Testable hypotheses are generated in Skinner's system as well, given the acceptance of preconceived notions of environmental determinacy.

The result of these comparisons indicates that Hull's theory, as might be expected, meshes most closely with a scientific approach, defined empirically. His orientation was the most structured and comprehensive, so his theory was designed to offer the most scientific framework. However, all four behavioral theories fell short in terms of the outcomes of the progression of components of theory construction. Specifically, the rigorous testing of hypotheses generated by each orientation fell short of expectations; none of them provided behaviorism with principles of all human and infrahuman activity. Accordingly, behaviorism turned away from this structure of theory building to pursue more modest goals.

POST-THEORY FORMULATIONS

The third phase of the expansion of behaviorism, inaugurated by Skinner's atheoretical positivism, led to a period of mushrooming experimentation. Indeed, with little regard to theoretical guidance, data collection appeared to have become an autonomous project without an overriding rationale. In time, research efforts took on direction, guided by the development of models with a pervasive flavor of applying the principles of behavior. Because of its applied character in this period of the behavioristic expansion, so-called neobehaviorism has also been described as neofunctionalism (see also Chapter 17).

Neobehavioristic Models

As a link to the theory-building phase of the behavioristic evolution, neobehaviorism may be classified in terms of information-processing/mathematical models of learning, neo-Hullian learning models, cognitive models, and operant models. To varying degrees these classifications are derived, respectively, from the views of Guthrie, Hull, Tolman, and Skinner.

Information-Processing and Mathematical Models.   The view of intellectual functions in terms of the intricate logic of mathematical and probabilistic relationships reflects a merger between the mathematical underpinning of Hullian theory and the parsimonious orientation of Guthrie's contiguity principle. This movement received a great impetus from the advancing technology of computerized hardware during the postwar period. The potential for quantifiable prediction of learning parameters was initially explored in efforts to simulate learning processes by studies of artificial intelligence conducted in the 1940s and 1950s. For example, the General Problem Solver, developed at Carnegie-Mellon University, used computer programs to simulate human problem-solving behavior in a variety of performance tasks. This work led to the Logic Theorist program, the product of cooperative efforts among the Carnegie group, the Massachusetts Institute of Technology, and RAND Corporation scientists, which provided a model for programs in computer simulation of human intelligence and studies of artificial intelligence.

From the early version of Estes' (1950) stimulus sampling theory that views learning as a statistical process involving the selection of stimulus elements, a wide set of applications of probability functions to predict behavior has been proposed. To define a learning problem, a strategy that started with empirically based assumptions to generate the probability of responses to form predictive learning curves was proposed (see, for example, Estes, 1964). A vast literature developed that portrays human learning in terms of an information-processing system and examines intellectual and motor functions, such as decision making and skilled practice. Moreover, this approach has been extended to the traditional psychological problems of sensory processing (see, for example, Swets, 1961).

As research progressed in the quantitative prediction of learned behavior, more sophisticated programs were developed using noncontinuous assumptions of the acquisition processes. One such program is termed the *Markov model*. In it, acquisition is viewed as a chain process, and each stage of the process may be modified by the effect of a previous trial or stage in the chain. The stimulus elements at a given stage are relatively small in number, but the sampling probabilities associated with each element change from stage to stage.

The information-processing model of learning, based on complex mathematical prediction, has advanced to the point of exhaustive analyses of complex learning processes. Studies of concept formation and linguistic development have yielded detailed views of human learning that transcend earlier theories based on the accumulation of S–R associations. Moreover, the advanced technology developed for such research has helped bridge a gap between simpler learning processes, typically observed in infrahuman subjects, and complex human intellectual activities. This link helps to integrate the neurophysiological substrates examined in infrahuman learning and the sophisticated learning models derived from the information-processing context of human learning.

The Neo-Hullians.   Hull's most famous student and later collaborator was Kenneth W. Spence (1907–1967), who spent his most productive years at the University of Iowa. The research of Spence and his many students was characterized by a concern with refining Hull's theory as well as with applying Hull's principles to varieties of behavioral processes, including an analysis of anxiety. Spence's major contribution to the theoretical basis of Hullian behaviorism was his explanation of discrimination learning (Spence, 1937, 1940). Briefly, Spence held that gradients of excitatory potential and inhibitory potential are generated around stimulus values that are reinforced and not reinforced, respectively, during discrimination training. These hypothetical gradients merge algebraically to account for observed performance during assessment of stimulus generalization. Spence and his students also investigated eyelid conditioning and found that certain levels of anxiety facilitate acquisition of that response as well as others, leading them to an examination of the role and the assessment of anxiety (Taylor, 1951, 1953). These studies are important because they represent some of the initial attempts to integrate behavioristic principles and psychopathology, an area of later intensive study.

Another important student of Hull is Neal Miller (1909–2002), whose productive career was characterized by important studies of a variety of psychological issues. His early work (see, for example, Dollard and Miller, 1950) attempted to apply a Hullian analysis to behavioral issues derived from the psychoanalytic literature. Miller's research with Dollard and others on frustration and conflict has become classic, leading to direct support for the contemporary behavior modification trend. In studies of physiological substrates Miller made significant findings concerning the relationship between reinforcement mechanisms and the control of autonomic behavior (Miller, 1969).

A third student of Hull, O. Hobart Mowrer (1907–1982), expressed the distinction between Pavlovian and instrumental conditioning in a 1947 paper. He argued that in avoidance learning the fear of the CS is acquired by Pavlovian principles, and the motor response to that fear is instrumentally acquired through the reinforcing effect of fear reduction. The CS then functions as a sign of impending shock. From this distinction Mowrer asserted a revised two-process theory involving incremental punishment and decremental reward. In incremental reinforcement, stimuli act as signs of fear; in decremental reinforcement, stimuli serve as signs of hope. Applying these principles to psychopathology, Mowrer (1960) helped prepare for the emergence of behavior modification. Subsequent refinements and interpretations of two-process learning by Schoenfeld (1950) and, especially, Rescorla and Solomon (1967) have generated many hypotheses of theoretical and clinical significance that have advanced the use of conditioning principles in behavior modification.

Contemporary research in the neo-Hullian tradition has also extended to questions concerning the physiological basis of learning. Borrowing from the neurophysiological findings of reflexology, these investigations focus on such areas as the ontogeny of learning, consolidation and retrieval processes of memory, and sensory factors of attention (see also Chapter 17). Together with the efforts of Miller and his collaborators working in human psychophysiology, they have rapidly expanded our understanding of learning processes.

Cognitive Models.   As mentioned earlier, Tolman did not leave a legacy of followers to pursue his theoretical views. Accordingly, as behaviorism expanded to include a consideration of cognitive learning, there was little of the systematic coherence that was typical of the neo-Hullians. In surveying more contemporary developments in cognitive models, then, diverse research directions are evident.

Egon Brunswik (1903–1955) developed a theory called probabilistic functionalism from his early research on perceptual constancy. Influenced by the Gestalt movement while he lived in Germany, and later by Tolman, who secured a position for him at Berkeley, Brunswik found that subjects tend to perceive consistently, despite distortions in sensory input, through a series of relative adaptive compromises to varying environmental variables, and that these adaptive compromises are self-initiated. Accordingly, Brunswik held that subjects' adaptations in perceptual and behavioral situations are relative and definable in terms of probabilities. His research approach was in contrast to the rigidly controlled behavioristic experiments that typically examined relatively few variables. Brunswik criticized such experimentation as an inadequate and distorted representation of reality. Rather, he advocated a wider sampling of variables as they actually occur in the environment. Although Brunswik's systematic theory was left unfinished because of his early death, he contributed to an acceptance of less analytical and mechanistic approaches to research that allowed cognitive behaviorism to consider the state of organismic–environmental interactions.

A second major development within cognitive models of learning came from the social psychological research of Leon Festinger (1919–1990). His theory of cognitive dissonance essentially asserted that contrasting objectives within a person's value system result in discomfort that must be resolved by adapting behavioral strategies to reduce the dissonance. Of interest is that Festinger's theory is a behavioral view holding an explanatory central mechanism with mentalistic implications. Thus Festinger offered a cognitive model that directly confronts the very basic premise of the peripheral character of Watsonian behaviorism.

Similarly, the more recent study of language processes by Noam Chomsky (b. 1928) falls into the same type of cognitive model as Festinger's theory. Chomsky, who wrote an insightful criticism of Skinner's writings on verbal behavior, argued that the acquisition of syntactical structure of language requires the existence of a mental construct that he calls the language acquisition device. Without this mechanism, Chomsky held that true language cannot emerge. Chomsky's theory is consistent with the cognitive approach of the French psychologist Jean Piaget (1896–1980), who intensively studied the development of knowledge; it also has the support of other American psychologists, such as Jerome Bruner (b. 1915), who has studied the formation of concepts in children (see also Chapter 17).

The development of cognitive models, especially those of Festinger, Chomsky, and Bruner, has been characterized by a radical departure from the initial behavioristic formulation. However, these models accept the significance of examining overt behavior as well as the methodological strategies common to other forms of behaviorism. Nevertheless, the emergence of clear mentalistic constructs has brought behaviorism almost full circle and provides confirmation of the full expansion of the behavioristic model of psychology.

Operant Models. The radical positivist approach of Skinner continues among psychologists who advocate the experimental analysis of behavior into components of environmental and reinforcement contingencies. However, in extending Skinner's initial principles, less rigid interpretations of operant behavior have emerged. In particular, operant research has examined physiological and centrally mediated motivational variables. The applications of operant principles in clinical and teaching settings have also dealt with assumptions of mentalistic constructs underlying observable responses. The *Journal of the Experimental Analysis of Behavior* and the *Journal of Applied Behavior Analysis*, both dominated by the operant approach of Skinner, show increasing diversity and eclecticism in both subject matter and methodology. Moreover, as formulations of behaviorism have evolved and become diffused, the importance of Skinner's methodological innovations has been recognized and used in varieties of laboratory and applied settings.

Applications

Behavioristic principles have wide-ranging applicability in contemporary psychology. Educational policy, military training, and advertising techniques are just a few areas that employ behavioral principles. However, one area of present concern is the application of behavioral findings in clinical and therapeutic settings. The reason for giving this movement more attention than other applications is its relevance to the treatment of mental illness, an issue central to the development of psychology.

During the 1950s and early 1960s there was widespread acceptance of a growing division in psychology between the "experimental" and "clinical" branches of the discipline in the United States. Experimental psychologists were accused of isolating themselves in laboratories, perhaps concerned more with rats than with people; clinical psychologists were seen as relying more closely on the medical attitudes of psychiatry than on any psychological models. One of the factors that helped to ease the division between the theoretical and applied branches of psychology was the advent of a behavioral model of clinical applications, commonly called behavior modification.

The antecedents of behavior modification may be traced to several attempts that related learning principles to psychopathology. In addition to applications proposed as early as Watson (e.g., Watson and Rayner, 1920), we have already mentioned the work of Miller and Dollard and of Mowrer in applying Hullian theory to clinical problems. Moreover, Skinner's notion of environmental control was tried with some success in token economies devised for the closed, controlled setting of mental institutions. However, a book by Joseph Wolpe (1915–1998), entitled *Psychotherapy by Reciprocal Inhibition* (1958), provided the catalytic event that unleashed contemporary behavior modification. Wolpe, a psychiatrist, saw the powerful potential for changing behavior through the application of principles outlined under Pavlovian and instrumental conditioning. Specifically, he took many of the principles of aversive conditioning and extinction and devised such techniques as desensitization and counterconditioning to deal with anxiety-based symptoms.

Behavior modification has generated considerable controversy and criticism, especially criticism aimed at its alleged impersonal and mechanical basis. Consistent with its place in the behavioristic evolution, behavior modification is attacked as the epitome of "mind control" and "brainwashing." However, it has been argued that anxiety reduction techniques are actually adapted to the individual, depending on the hierarchy of anxiety-provoking stimuli, defined by the person. At any rate, it would be premature to evaluate the efficacy of behavior modification per se. For our purposes, we should recognize behavior modification as an important development in the behavioristic evolution. By providing a behavioral framework of clinical application, behavior modification has served the critical function of uniting researchers and clinicians under a common model of psychological activity. Whether behavior modification proves to be a stable force maintaining that unity or simply a temporary bandwagon phenomenon remains to be seen. It has already served an important function in the development of behaviorism.

Concluding this rather involved story of the changes and expansion of behaviorism, we may say that behaviorism has approached the definitive model of psychology more closely than any other conceptualization since the 1870s. Psychology in America was not only recognized in academic and professional settings but was also firmly entrenched in the scientific establishment by the theory-building stage of the behavioral evolution during the 1930s. However, it is important to acknowledge how much has happened during the evolution of behaviorism from the time of Watson. Behaviorism as a model, or a philosophy of psychology, is currently a diffuse system subject to diverse interpretation. Behaviorists may include the radical positivists of the Skinnerian tradition, as well as cognitive psychologists who propose definite mentalistic constructs. Behaviorists may be researchers who investigate behavioral processes exclusively on an infrahuman level, or they may be clinicians preoccupied with therapeutic applications. Neobehaviorism, then, may be a consensus, rather than a system, that recognizes the importance of observable behavior. Beyond that consensus the eclecticism of neobehaviorism appears dominant, precluding further definition.

CHAPTER SUMMARY

The shift in American psychology from the essentially German emphasis on the study of consciousness to a primary focus on behavior was initiated by J. B. Watson in 1913. However, behavioristic psychology had received expression in both the French sensationalistic and British empiricistic traditions. The immediate predecessors of behaviorism were the reflexology of Russian physiology and the associationism of Thorndike. Physiological reflexology received a sound foundation with the works of Sechenov and Bekhterev, but it was Pavlov who refined the reduction of psychological events to behavioral and physiological processes within a comprehensive theory of conditioning. Watson's formulation of psychology was essentially defined in terms of stimulus and response elements. However, in attempting to rid psychology of residual mentalistic constructs, Watson's definition of psychology as solely peripheral events was too confining, and Watson's contemporaries began the process of evolving behaviorism into a more complete system. Such researchers as Holt, Weiss, Hunter, and Lashley restored critical psychological activities to behaviorism. However, it was probably the logical positivist movement, expressing an operational spirit in the unity of science, that insured the initial success of the behaviorist model.

Behavioristic psychology expanded beyond the original formulations of Pavlov and Watson. Russian reflexology continued in the tradition of Pavlov, and one of the more significant developments was found in the work of the Polish scientist Jerzy Konorski, whose goal was to integrate Pavlov's conditioning physiology with Sherrington's neurophysiology. Konorski's early work first drew a sharp distinction between the two paradigms of conditioning, and his career culminated with an insightful discussion of brain physiology supporting a cybernetic system of behavior. Contemporary reflexology in Russia and in nearby countries has greatly expanded to include a wide range of psychological and physiological problems, led by such eminent scientists as Vygotsky, Luria, Asratyan, and Beritashvili.

In the United States, behaviorism has moved through several intellectual stages. In a theory-building phase during the 1930s and 1940s, psychologists such as Guthrie, Tolman, and Hull attempted comprehensive theories of learning. Although receiving their most complete articulation under Hull, comprehensive theories were not adequate, prompting the radical positivism of Skinner. A return to data gathering followed, characterized by the development of models or mini-theories with an applied flavor. Information-processing and mathematical models of learning, neo-Hullian research models, cognitive models, and operant approaches are all examples of recent groupings of behaviorists. A major use of behaviorism has been the behavior modification model of clinical application. Contemporary behaviorism is a dominant force in psychology, but the behaviorism that has evolved is widely based, admitting a wide diversity of assumptions, methodologies, and applications.

BIBLIOGRAPHY

Reflexology

BERITASHVILI, I. S. (1965). *Neural mechanisms of higher vertebrate behavior* (W. T. Libersen, Ed. and Trans.). Boston: Little, Brown.

BERITASHVILI, I. S. (1971). *Vertebrate memory characteristics and origin.* New York: Plenum Press.

BROŽEK, J. (1971). USSR: Current activities in the history of physiology and psychology. *Journal of the History of Biology, 4,* 185–208.

BROŽEK, J. (1972). To test or not to test—Trends in Soviet views. *Journal of the History of the Behavioral Sciences, 8,* 243–248.

BROŽEK, J. (1973). Soviet historiography of psychology: Sources of biographic and bibliographic information. *Journal of the History of the Behavioral Sciences, 9,* 152–161.

BROŽEK, J. (1974). Soviet historiography of psychology. 3. Between philosophy and history. *Journal of the History of the Behavioral Sciences, 10,* 195–201.

BROŽEK, J., & SLOBIN, D. I. (Eds). (1972). *Psychology in the USSR: An historical perspective.* White Plains, NY: International Arts and Sciences Press.

COLEMAN, S. R. (1984). Background and change in B. F. Skinner's metatheory from 1930 to 1938. *Journal of Mind and Behavior, 5,* 471–500.

COLEMAN, S. R. (1985). When historians disagree: B. F. Skinner and E. G. Boring, 1930. *Psychological Record, 35,* 301–314.

KONORSKI, J. (1948). *Conditioned reflexes and neuronal organization.* Cambridge: Harvard University Press.

KONORSKI, J. (1967). *Integrative activity of the brain: An interdisciplinary approach.* Chicago: University of Chicago Press.

KONORSKI, J. (1974). Autobiography. In G. Lindzey (Ed.), *A history of psychology in autobiography* (Vol. 6). Englewood Cliffs, NJ: Prentice Hall.

KONORSKI, J., & MILLER, S. (1933). Podstawy fizjologicznej teorii ruchow nabytych. Ruchowe odruchy warunkowe. *Medyczny Doswiadczalny Spolem, 16,* 95–187.

KONORSKI, J., & MILLER, S. (1937). On two types of conditioned reflex. *Journal of General Psychology, 16,* 264–272.

LURIA, A. R. (1979). *The making of a mind. A person's account of Soviet psychology* (M. Cole & S. Cole, Eds.). Cambridge: Harvard University Press.

MILLER, S., & KONORSKI, J. (1928). Sur une forme particuliere des reflexes conditionels. *Comptes Rendus des Séances de la Société de Biologie, 99,* 1155–1157.

MOWRER, O. H. (1976). "How does the mind work?" Memorial address in honor of Jerzy Konorski. *American Psychologist, 31,* 843–857.

MOWRER, O. H. (1976). Jerzy Konorski Memorial Address. *Acta Neurobiologiae Experimentalis, 36,* 249–276.

PAVLOV, I. P. (1960; orig. 1927). *Conditioned reflexes: An investigation of the physiological activity of the cerebral cortex* (G. V. Anrep, Ed. and Trans.). New York: Dover.

SECHENOV, I. M. (1935). Reflexes of the brain (A. A. Subkov, Trans.). In *I. M. Sechenov, Selected works.* Moscow: State Publishing House for Biological and Medical Literature, 264–322.

SOKOLOV, E. M. (1963). Higher nervous functions: The orienting reflex. *Annual Review of Physiology, 25,* 545–580.

ZIELIŃSKI, K. (1974). Jerzy Konorski (1903–1973). *Acta Neurobiologiae Experimentalis, 34,* 645–653.

Operationalism

BERGMAN, G. (1954). Sense and nonsense in operationalism. *Scientific Monthly, 79,* 210–214.

BRIDGMAN, P. W. (1927). *The logic of modern physics.* New York: Macmillan.

BRIDGMAN, P. W. (1954). Remarks on the present state of operationalism. *Scientific Monthly, 79,* 224–226.

ROGERS, T. (1989). Operationism in psychology: A discussion of contextual antecedents and historical interpretation of its longevity. *Journal of the History of the Behavioral Sciences, 25,* 139–153.

SINGER, E. A. (1911). Mind as an observable object. *Journal of Philosophy, Psychology, and Scientific Methods, 8,* 180–186.

Early Behaviorism

HOLT, E. B. (1915). *The Freudian wish and its place in ethics.* New York: Holt, Rinehart & Winston.

LASHLEY, K. S. (1916). The human salivary reflex and its use in psychology. *Psychological Review, 23,* 446–464.

LASHLEY, K. S. (1923). The behavioristic interpretation of consciousness. *Psychological Review, 30,* 237–272, 329–353.

THORNDIKE, E. L. (1899). The mental life of the monkey. *Psychological Review*, Monograph Supplement, 3, no. 15.

THORNDIKE, E. L. (1936). Edward L. Thorndike. In C. Murchison (Ed.), *A history of psychology in autobiography* (Vol. 3). Worcester, MA: Clark University Press, 263–270.

THORNDIKE, E. L., & HERRICK, C. J. (1915). Watson's behavior. *Journal of Animal Behavior, 5,* 462–470.

WATSON, J. B. (1913). Psychology as the behaviorist views it. *Psychological Review, 20,* 158–177.

WATSON, J. B. (1916). The place of the conditioned reflex in psychology. *Psychological Review, 23,* 89–116.

WATSON, J. B. (1917). An attempted formulation of the scope of behavior psychology. *Psychological Review, 24,* 329–352.

WATSON, J. B. (1919). *Psychology from the standpoint of a behaviorist.* Philadelphia: Lippincott.

WATSON, J. B. (1920). Is thinking merely the action of language mechanisms? *British Journal of Psychology, 11,* 87–104.

WATSON, J. B. (1928). *Psychological care of infant and child.* New York: W. W. Norton & Co.

WATSON, J. B. (1936). Autobiography. In C. Murchison (Ed.), *A history of psychology in autobiography.* (Vol. 3).Worcester, MA: Clark University Press, 271–281.

WATSON, J. B., & McDOUGALL, W. (1929). *The battle of behaviorism.* New York: Morton.

WATSON, J. B., & RAYNER, R. (1920). Conditioned emotional reactions. *Journal of Experimental Psychology, 3,* 1–7.

WEISS, A. P. (1917). The relation between structural and behavioral psychology. *Psychological Review, 24,* 301–317.

WEISS, A. P. (1925). *A theoretical basis of human behavior.* Columbus, OH: Adams.

YERKES, R. M., & MORGULIS, S. (1909). The method of Pavlov in animal psychology. *Psychological Bulletin, 6,* 257–273.

Broadening Behaviorism

COAN, R. W. (1968). Dimensions of psychological theory. *American Psychologist, 23,* 715–722.

FORSCHER, B. K. (1963). Chaos in the brickyard. *Science, 142,* 339.

GUTHRIE, E. R. (1946). Psychological facts and psychological theory. *Psychological Bulletin, 43,* 1–20.

GUTHRIE, E. R. (1952). *The psychology of learning* (Rev. ed.) New York: Harper & Row.

GUTHRIE, E. R. (1959). Association by contiguity. In S. Koch (Ed.), *Psychology: A study of a science, Vol. 2: General systematic formulations, learning and special processes.* New York: McGraw-Hill, 158–195.

HULL, C. L. (1937). Mind, mechanism, and adaptive behavior. *Psychological Review, 44,* 1–32.

HULL, C. L. (1943). *Principles of behavior: An introduction to behavior theory.* New York: Appleton-Century-Crofts.

KELLER, F. S. (1991). Burrhus Frederic Skinner. *Journal of the History of the Behavioral Sciences, 27,* 3–6.

MARX, M. H. (1963). The general nature of theory construction. In M. H. Marx (Ed.), *Theories in contemporary psychology.* New York: Macmillan, 4–46.

MARX, M. H. (1976). Formal theory. In M. H. Marx and F. E. Goodson (Eds.), *Theories in contemporary psychology,* 2nd ed., New York: Macmillan, 234–260.

SAMUELSON, F. (1985). Organizing for the kingdom of behavior: Academic battles and organizational policies in the twenties. *Journal of the History of the Behavioral Sciences, 21,* 33–47.

SCHNAITTER, R. (1984). Skinner on the "mental" and the "physical." *Behaviorism, 12,* 1–14.

SHEFFIELD, F. D. (1949). Hilgard's critique of Guthrie. *Psychological Review, 56,* 284–291.

SKINNER, B. F. (1935). Two types of conditioned reflex and a pseudo type. *Journal of General Psychology, 12,* 66–77.

SKINNER, B. F. (1937). Two types of conditioned reflex: A reply to Konorski and Miller. *Journal of General Psychology, 16,* 272–279.

SKINNER, B. F. (1966). *The behavior of organisms: An experimental analysis.* Englewood Cliffs, NJ: Prentice Hall.

SKINNER, B. F. (1974). *About behaviorism.* New York: Alfred A. Knopf.

SKINNER, B. F. (1984). Behaviorism at fifty. *Behavioral and Brain Sciences, 7,* 615–667.

SMITH, S., & GUTHRIE, E. R. (1921). *General psychology in terms of behavior.* New York: Appleton.

SPENCE, K. W. (1937). The differential response in animals to stimuli varying within a single dimension. *Psychological Review, 44,* 430–444.

SPENCE, K. W. (1940). Continuous vs. non-continuous interpretations of discrimination learning. *Psychological Review, 47,* 271–288.

TOLMAN, E. C. (1922). A new formula for behaviorism. *Psychological Review, 29,* 44–53.

TOLMAN, E. C. (1948). Cognitive maps in rats and men. *Psychological Review, 55,* 189–208.

TOLMAN, E. C. (1949). *Purposive behavior in animals and men.* New York: Appleton-Century-Crofts, 1932; reprint, University of California Press.

VOEKS, V. W. (1950). Formalization and clarification of a theory of learning. *Journal of Psychology, 30,* 341–363.

VOEKS, V. W. (1954). Acquisition of S-R connections: A test of Hull's and Guthrie's theories. *Journal of Experimental Psychology, 47,* 137–147.

Applications:

ATKINSON, R. C., BOWER, G. H., & GROTHERS, E. J. (1965). *Introduction to mathematical learning theory.* New York: Wiley.

BRUNER, J. S., BRUNSWIK, E., FESTINGER, L., HEIDER, F., MUENZINGER, K. F., OSGOOD, C. E., & RAPAPORT, E. (1957). *Contemporary approaches to cognition: A symposium held at the University of Colorado.* Cambridge, MA: Harvard University Press.

BRUNSWIK, E.(1956). *Perception and the representative design of psychological experiments.* Berkeley: University of California Press.

BUCHANAN, R. D. (1994). The development of the Minnesota Multiphasic Personality Inventory. *Journal of the History of the Behavioral Sciences, 30,* 148–161.

CHOMSKY, N. (1959). Review of verbal behavior by B. F. Skinner. *Language, 35,* 26–58.

CHOMSKY, N. (1972). *Language and mind.* New York: Harcourt Brace Jovanovich.

COFFER, C. N. (1981). The history of the concept of motivation. *Journal of the History of the Behavioral Sciences, 17,* 48–53.

DOLLARD, J., & MILLER, N. E. (1950). *Personality and psychotherapy: An analysis in terms of learning, thinking and culture.* New York: McGraw-Hill.

ESTES, W. K. (1950). Toward a statistical theory of learning. *Psychological Review, 57,* 94–107.

ESTES, W. K. (1959). The statistical approach to learning theory. In S. Koch (Ed.), *Psychology: A study of a science, Vol. 2: General systematic formulations, learning and special processes.* New York: McGraw-Hill, 380–491.

ESTES, W. K. (1964). Probability learning. In A. W. Melton (Ed.), *Categories of human learning.* New York: Academic Press.

FESTINGER, L. (1957). *A theory of cognitive dissonance.* New York: Harper & Row.

GARNER, W. R., & HAKE, W. H. (1951). The amount of information in absolute judgments. *Psychological Review, 58,* 446–459.

MILLER, N. E. (1969). Learning of visceral and glandular responses. *Science, 163,* 434–445.

MOWRER, O. H. (1949). On the dual nature of learning: A reinterpretation of "conditioning" and "problem-solving." *Harvard Educational Review, 17,* 102–148.

MOWRER, O. H. (1960). *Learning theory and behavior.* New York: Wiley.

PIAGET, J. (1952). *The origins of intelligence in children* (M. Cook, Trans.), New York: International Universities Press.

RESCORLA, R. A., & SOLOMON, R. L. (1967). Two-process learning theory: Relationships between Pavlovian conditioning and instrumental learning. *Psychological Review, 74,* 151–182.

SCHOENFELD, W. N. (1950). An experimental approach to anxiety, escape and avoidance behavior. In P. H. Hock & J. Zubin (Eds.), *Anxiety.* New York: Grune and Stratton.

SHEFFIELD, F. D. (1965). Relation between classical conditioning and instrumental learning. In W. F. Prokasy (Ed.), *Classical conditioning: A symposium.* New York: Appleton-Century-Crofts, 302–322.

SWETS, J. A. (1961). Is there a sensory threshold? *Science, 134,* 168–177.

TAYLOR, J. A. (1951). The relationship of anxiety to the conditioned eyelid response. *Journal of Experimental Psychology, 41,* 81–92.

TAYLOR, J. A. (1953). A personality scale of manifest anxiety. *Journal of Abnormal and Social Psychology, 48,* 285–290.

TRIPLETT, R. G. (1982). The relationship of Clark L. Hull's hypnosis research to his later learning theory: The continuity of his life's work. *Journal of the History of the Behavioral Sciences, 18,* 22–31

WEIDMAN, N. (1994). Mental testing and machine intelligence: The Lashley-Hull debate. *Journal of the History of the Behavioral Sciences, 30,* 162–180.

WINKLER, R. C. (1970). Management of chronic psychiatric patients by a token reinforcement system. *Journal of Applied Behavior Analysis, 3,* 47–55.

WOLPE, J. (1958). *Psychotherapy by reciprocal inhibition.* Stanford, CA: Stanford University Press.

WOLPE, J. (1969). *The practice of behavior therapy.* Elmsford, NY: Pergamon.

Studies

BITTERMAN, M. E. (1969). Thorndike and the problem of animal intelligence. *American Psychologist, 24,* 444–453.

BORING, E. G. (1950). *A history of experimental psychology,* 2nd ed. Englewood Cliffs, NJ: Prentice Hall.

BRUCE, D. (1986). Lashley's shift from bacteriology to neurophysiology, 1910–1917, and the influence of Jennings, Watson, and Franz. *Journal of the History of the Behavioral Sciences, 22,* 27–44.

BUCKLEY, K. W. (1982). The selling of a psychologist: John Broadus Watson and the application of behavioral techniques to advertising. *Journal of the History of the Behavioral Sciences, 18,* 207–221.

BURNHAM, J. C. (1968). On the origin of behaviorism. *Journal of the History of the Behavioral Sciences, 4,* 143–151.

BURNHAM, J. C. (1972). Thorndike's puzzle boxes. *Journal of the History of the Behavioral Sciences, 8,* 159–167.

BURNHAM, J. C. (1977). The mind-body problem in the early twentieth century. *Perspectives in Biology and Medicine, 20,* 271–284.

CARMICHAEL, L. (1968). Some historical roots of present-day animal psychology. In B. Wolman (Ed.), *Historical roots of contemporary psychology.* New York: Harper & Row, 47–76.

COHEN, D. (1979). *J. B. Watson: The founder of behaviorism.* Boston: Routledge and Kegan Paul.

COLEMAN, S. R. (1985). The problem of volition and the conditioned reflex: I. Conceptual background, 1900–1940. *Behaviorism, 13,* 99–124.

DANZIGER, K. (1979). The positivist repudiation of Wundt. *Journal of the History of the Behavioral Sciences, 15,* 205–230.

FRANK, P. (1941). *Between physics and philosophy.* Cambridge: Harvard University Press.

HERRNSTEIN, J. R. (1969). Behaviorism. In D. L. Krantz (Ed.), *Schools of psychology: A symposium.* New York: Appleton-Century-Crofts, 51–68.

JONCICH, G. (1968). *The sane positivist: A biography of Edward L. Thorndike.* Middletown, CT: Wesleyan University Press.

LEYS, R. (1984). Meyer, Watson, and the dangers of behaviorism. *Journal of the History of the Behavioral Sciences, 20,* 128–149.

LOWRY, R. (1970). The reflex model in psychology: Origins and evolution. *Journal of the History of the Behavioral Sciences, 6,* 64–69.

MACKENZIE, B. D. (1972). Behaviorism and positivism. *Journal of the History of the Behavioral Sciences, 8,* 222–231.

MCCONNELL, J. V. (1985). Psychology and scientist: LII. John B. Watson: Man and myth. *Psychological Reports, 56,* 683–705.

ROBACK, A. A. (1964). *History of American psychology* (Rev. ed.). New York: Collier.

RUCKMICK, C. A. (1916). The last decade of psychology in review. *Psychological Bulletin, 13,* 109–120.

SAMELSON, F. (1981). Struggle for scientific authority: The reception of Watson's behaviorism, 1913–1920. *Journal of the History of the Behavioral Sciences, 17,* 399–425.

SCHNEIDER, S. M., & MORRIS, E. K. (1987). A history of the term "radical behaviorism": From Watson to Skinner. *Behavior Analyst, 10,* 27–39.

STEININGER, M. (1979). Objectivity and value judgments in the psychologies of E. L. Thorndike and W. McDougall. *Journal of the History of the Behavioral Sciences, 15,* 263–281.

STEVENS, S. S. (1939). Psychology and the science of science. *Psychological Bulletin, 36,* 221–263.

THORNE, F. C. (1976). Reflections on the golden age of Columbia psychology. *Journal of the History of the Behavioral Sciences, 12,* 159–165.

TIBBETTS, P. (1975). The doctrine of "pure experience": The evolution of a concept from Mach to Jones to Tolman. *Journal of the History of the Behavioral Sciences, 11,* 55–66.

TODD, J. T., & MORRIS, E. K. (1986). The early research of John B. Watson: Before the behavioral revolution. *Behavior Analyst, 9,* 71–88.

TURNER, M. B. (1967). *Philosophy and the science of behavior.* New York: Appleton-Century-Crofts.

WASHBURN, M. F. (1917). Some thoughts on the last quarter century in psychology. *Philosophical Review, 27,* 44–55.

WINDHOLZ, G. (1990). Pavlov and the Pavlovians in the laboratory. *Journal of the History of the Behavioral Sciences, 26,* 64–74.

WOODWORTH, R. S. (1959). John Broadus Watson: 1878–1958. *American Journal of Psychology, 72,* 301–310.

YAROSHEVSKI, M. G. (1968). I. M. Sechenov—The founder of objective psychology. In B. J. Wolman (Ed.), *Historical roots of contemporary psychology.* New York: Harper & Row, 77–110.

✻ 16 ✻

The Third Force Movement

European Philosophical Background
    Existentialism
        Søren Kierkegaard
        Wilhelm Dilthey
    Modern Expressions of Existentialism
        Jean-Paul Sartre
        Albert Camus
        Karl Jaspers
        Martin Buber
    Phenomenology
        Edmund Husserl
        Martin Heidegger
Existential–Phenomenological Psychology
    Maurice Merleau-Ponty
    Ludwig Binswanger
The Third Force Movement in America
    American Humanistic Psychology
        Gordon Allport
        Charlotte Bühler
        Abraham Maslow
        Rollo May
        Carl Rogers
    The Duquesne Group
Chapter Summary

We have seen that the emergence of psychology in Germany during the last quarter of the nineteenth century was presented under the conceptual expressions of a natural science model and a human science model. The reliance of the natural science model on philosophical assumptions of the essential passivity of the mind and the belief in the empirical approach to science were initially reflected in Wundt's structural psychology and later were fully elaborated in America by the behaviorists. In contrast, the human science model had diverse applications, but at the very least it accepted the assumption of mental activity and allowed methods of scientific approach other than empirical strategies only. Gestalt psychology grew out of the German active mind tradition of nonsensory consciousness and recognized the necessity of nonanalytic methods to study psychological processes. In this context, the dynamics of unconscious motivation within the psychoanalytic movement were derived from internal psychic energy and precluded the exclusive reliance on empirical methods of study.

The third force movement in psychology was also derived from the traditions of the human science model of mental activity. The term *third force* is actually a general categorization for several orientations and emphases within psychology. If psychoanalysis is considered the "first force" and behaviorism the "second force" within twentieth-century psychology, then the "third force" may be any movements that are not psychoanalytic or behavioristic. Other labels describe various expressions of the third force movement: *Existential psychology* indicates the applications of existential philosophy to psychological issues. The term *phenomenological psychology* is sometimes used to express characteristic ways of studying psychological events without resorting to reductionism. Finally, *humanistic psychology* describes the approach of a group of psychologists, mainly American personality theorists, who held a view of individuals as seeking the full development of their capacity or potential and who rejected any mechanical or materialistic explanations of psychological processes.

Although the third force movement consists of a diverse collection of psychologists and philosophers, some commonly shared points of view are evident. First, the movement clearly recognizes the importance of personal freedom and responsibility in the lifelong process of decision making to fulfill the human potential. It considers the mind to be an active, dynamic entity through which the individual expresses uniquely human abilities in cognition, willing, and judgment. Second, psychologists of the movement do not accept the reduction of psychological processes to the mechanical laws of physiological events. Rather, they see human beings as separate from other forms of life. Individuals, in the very process of defining their humanity, must go beyond the hedonistic satisfaction of physiological needs in quest of personal values and attitudes of social and philosophical significance. Thus, there is an emphasis on the self in the third force movement, which attempts to foster the development of individually defined, uniquely human personality fulfillment.

The third force movement is not a coherent system of detailed principles that are universally accepted by all followers. Rather, it is an orientation within psychology that has reacted to the inherent reductionism of moving from psychological processes to physiological bases, represented by empirical behavioristic psychology. Like psychoanalysis, the third force movement did not emerge from the academic setting of university research. Rather, its roots may be found in philosophical speculation, literary works, and clinical observations. These sources coalesced after World War II and gave expression to the third force movement in Europe and in America.

EUROPEAN PHILOSOPHICAL BACKGROUND

In the review of European philosophy contained in Chapters 6 through 9, the development of competing models of mental processes was presented in terms of the eventual emergence of distinctive active and passive assumptions about the mind in modern psychology. However, certain philosophical trends continued to develop the notion of mental activity after the initial, formal expressions of nineteenth-century psychology. Collectively, these philosophical trends of existentialism and phenomenology formed the basis of the third force movement.

Existentialism

The core of existential philosophy holds that the individual is free to define life's direction through a continued succession of choices, but that this freedom also gives the individual responsibility for the outcomes of personal decisions, so that freedom is a source of anguish and dread. Before we explore the elaboration and implications of this definition, it is important to recognize that existential themes were common to many of the philosophical views dating back to antiquity. Indeed, it may be argued that all of the superordinate models of dynamic human activity, which stressed a holistic position, were existential. Such philosophers as Socrates, Plato, Aristotle, and Aquinas taught that people are free to decide their individual fate and must also accept the consequences of their choices.

In the nineteenth century modern existentialism began to grow in literature through such notable writers as Fyodor Dostoyevsky (1821–1881) and Friedrich Nietzsche (1844–1900). Dostoyevsky was born and educated in Moscow, but in 1849 was exiled to Siberia for revolutionary activities. Upon his return to European Russia in 1859, he resumed his writing and soon demonstrated his genius as one of the world's greatest novelists. His characters from such novels as *The Idiot* (1869), *The Brothers Karamazov* (1880), and *Crime and Punishment* (1866) confronted and wrestled with the difficult decisions of defining themselves and their feelings about God, social values, and personal ideals. Nietzsche, who wrote on philosophical themes, was born in Saxony and attended the universities at Bonn and Leipzig. At age 24, he was appointed professor of classical philology at the University of Basel. His thinking on the profound issues of life led him to the conclusion that God is dead and the individual is forlorn and alone, unable to rely on God for security. Each individual must confront alone the choices in life and face the consequences of those decisions without recourse to divine reassurance.

Whereas the major themes of existentialism are vividly portrayed in nineteenth-century literature, the formal statement of modern existential principles resulted from a theological controversy surrounding the manner of knowing and experiencing God. As background to this controversy, it should be recalled that the interpretation of dynamic mental activity in the structuring of knowledge, championed by Kant, became the dominant force among the German intelligentsia. This position, known as rationalism, glorified the value of reason in finding ultimate truths. German rationalism of the nineteenth century found an articulate spokesman in Georg Hegel (1770–1831).

As a philosophy, Hegel's rationalism held that intellectual progress proceeds through a sequence in which an idea, or thesis, gives rise to its opposite idea, or antithesis, and the two synthesize into a new unity that in turn becomes a thesis, repeating the cycle. This notion developed into a form of logical argumentation termed "dialectics," which was later adopted by Karl Marx (1818–1883) and Friedrich Engels (1820–1895), who used the dialectical method to formulate their theory of socialism. For present purposes, it is important to note that Hegel's views emphasized the centrality of intellectual progress with the implication of a hierarchy of intellectual activities. Hegel's rationalism found a sympathetic audience among nineteenth-century German theologians who recognized the decline in the strength of dogmatic church authority. Hegel's rationalism offered an alternative to the traditional tenets based on faith; it ordered nature and tried to develop a science of theology based on logical demonstration. Human intellectual activities could be ordered from the primitive level of art to a mediocre level of religion to the highest level of reason and science. The position of religion was relegated to a second-rate belief suitable for second-rate minds. This interpretation was consistent with the prevailing nineteenth-century atmosphere that exalted positivist science above all forms of intellectual activity. Science was viewed as the model that all intellectual endeavors should emulate.

Søren Kierkegaard.   A strong reaction to Hegel's rationalism was expressed by a Danish Lutheran clergyman, Søren Kierkegaard (1813–1855). Western civilization had once been Christian but, Kierkegaard insisted, people had lost their faith. He took it upon himself to teach Christianity to Christians and to support the view of the primacy of faith over reason. Kierkegaard perceived the elevation of reason, represented by Hegelian rationalism, as a distortion of human experience. As he confidently put it, "It was intelligence and nothing else that had to be opposed. Presumably that is why I, who had the task, was armed with an immense intelligence" (Kaufman, 1956). Kierkegaard continually questioned the true feelings of Christians and challenged them to demonstrate more than superficial belief.

Kierkegaard was born in Copenhagen, the youngest child of an eventually successful merchant. He was raised in a strict, religious home but seems to have spent his years at the University of Copenhagen rebelling against his father and his religious views. Rejected by the Danish royal guards because of his health, Kierkegaard began seeking a place in life. Around 1835, he went through a religious conversion, which changed his life. In 1837, Kierkegaard met and fell in love with a woman named Regina Olsen. During their engagement he questioned the authenticity of his love for her. He broke off the engagement in 1841 and fled to Berlin, where he immersed himself in philosophical study and finished his first major work, *Either/Or.* He returned to Denmark and spent the remainder of his life attacking the established religious practice in his country and advocating a recommitment to Christianity.

For Kierkegaard, existence is made authentic by a total acceptance of faith. Existence is not to be studied but lived. He described three progressive levels of existence. The first is esthetic and characterizes the childhood stage of living for the moment according to the dictates of temporary pleasure or pain. Although it is an important stage, it is primitive to the extent that the individual is a detached observer of life's events, simply responding to external contingencies according to the needs of the moment. The esthetic gives way to an ethical stage that requires courage on the part of the individual, because the person must make choices regarding the values of life and accept responsibility for those choices. The highest level of existence is the religious. In this stage the individual goes beyond the social morals of the ethical stage to a choice of God, which is an act of faith. In his work *Fear and Trembling* (1843), Kierkegaard recalled the biblical story of Abraham's preparing to sacrifice his son Isaac at God's command. That moment, as Abraham lifted his knife to kill his son, captures Kierkegaard's feelings of faith. Religion is a leap into darkness, accompanied by anguish, fear, and dread. Christianity, for Kierkegaard, must be a total subjective experience directed inward by a fully committed participator with Christ, not by a spectator. Christianity, then, is absurd. Just as it made no sense for the Creator to become a creature in the person of Christ, so a profession of Christianity is unreasonable because the profession of faith runs against the grain of our rational abilities. Christianity requires faith in the unreasonable. Whereas Kierkegaard would disagree with Nietzsche's conclusion that God is dead, he would agree with Nietzsche's feeling of God as dead, because faith requires a person to forsake the security of reason and plunge into the unknown.

Wilhelm Dilthey.   Another of the earlier expressions of modern existentialism came from Wilhelm Dilthey (1833–1911), who was mentioned in Chapter 11 as an advocate of alternatives to the natural science model. He brought existential principles to psychological perspective. In 1852, Dilthey began his studies at Heidelberg, initially intending to become a divinity student, but soon turned exclusively to philosophy. After studying Kant's rationalism, Hume's empiricism, and Comte's positivism, Dilthey developed an emphasis on the historical presence of the individual human being. His teaching career took him to several German universities and eventually to Berlin, where he remained until his retirement in 1906.

Dilthey called for a "science of the spirit," as opposed to the natural sciences, to understand the historicity of human beings by discovering what is individual and particular in each person. Historical consciousness is the defining characteristic of each person. In his *Essence of Philosophy* (1907), Dilthey wrote that religion, art, science, and philosophy are all expressions of experiences lived in the world, and these experiences involve not only intellectual functions but individual goals, values, and passions as well. Accordingly, Dilthey's emphasis on lived-through experience asserts the basic individual nature of consciousness that defines existence.

The early expressions of existential philosophy, represented by Kierkegaard and Dilthey, were pursued in the twentieth century by a group of philosophers and writers who moved away from the religious perspective of Kierkegaard to more inclusive statements on the self and the psychology of the individual. Although as a group they gained some prominence between the world wars, it was in the years immediately following World War II that the existentialists exerted influence on Western intellectual life. Their call for a restructuring of human values and respect for individual dignity gained a sympathetic audience among those who had suffered the depersonalization of industrialized warfare.

Modern Expressions of Existentialism

Jean-Paul Sartre.   Perhaps the most popular existentialist of the twentieth century, Jean-Paul Sartre (1905–1980) successfully conveyed his existential themes through novels, plays, and philosophical essays. After earning his philosophy degree from the Ecole Normale Supérieure in 1929, he studied in Germany, coming under the influence of the existential and phenomenological teachings of Edmund Husserl and Martin Heidegger. Their influence was reflected in Sartre's first major philosophical work, *Being and Nothingness* (1943). His first successful novel, *Nausea* (1938), was followed by over 15 other novels, plays, and collections of short stories. Sartre was drafted as a private into the French army in 1939. Shortly afterward, he was captured by the Germans in the doomed defense of the Maginot Line, but was released in 1941. He worked in the French Resistance until the end of the war, writing and teaching in the underground. During most of his life he was aligned with leftist and communist politics, and with his long-time companion, the philosopher Simone de Beauvoir (1908–1986), he became a French institution and spokesman for various political and social causes. He refused awards for his writings, including the 1964 Nobel Prize for literature, claiming acceptance would compromise his beliefs.

Basic to Sartre's views is that existence precedes essence. In contrast to the Aristotelian and Scholastic tenet that individual existence is an expression of a general, metaphysical essence or being, Sartre asserted that existence defines the essence of an individual. In this sense, we are what we do. Our existence is not defined by what we might become, but only by what we are in actuality, the collection of our acts. For this reason it is critical that we continually move through choices, for by making decisions we define ourselves and secure personal growth. One is, then, what one wills oneself to be. We are free to choose, but we must take responsibility for our choices. The only compulsion in life is to choose.

The individual lives her or his existence and creates a personal essence. The essence of God, according to Sartre, is a product of humans, who give God existence in their minds. God is reducible to human existence. The qualitative distinction between humans and the rest of nature is our subjectivity. Sartre asserted that human subjectivity is an enormous privilege that provides great dignity, but also condemns us to the freedom of making choices. Accordingly, as individuals, we are filled with anguish. We have total and deep responsibility that rests with us every time we make a decision. For example, if we decide that we shall be truthful, that decision imposes a truthful standard on all people for us. We are forlorn. Sartre concluded that because God does not exist, we are alone and insecure, with everyone potentially possessing the freedom to make up his or her own rules of deportment, with no divinely inspired guidance. We are in despair. According to Sartre, our responsibility is to ourselves and we have only ourselves to rely on. We cannot blame God or "fate" for bad decisions; we can blame only ourselves. Thus, Sartre's psychology is based on the existential premise of the radical freedom of individual existence.

Albert Camus.   A novelist–philosopher of the postwar French existential tradition, Albert Camus (1913–1960) took as his main literary theme courage when faced with life's absurdities. Camus was born and raised in poverty in French Algeria. After a serious bout with tuberculosis in 1930, he went on to complete his studies in philosophy at the University of Algiers, although a career in university teaching was precluded because of his medical history. He became involved in theater and journalism in Algiers, and during World War II edited a clandestine newspaper in Lyon, France. Among his many works are the essay *The Myth of Sisyphus* and the novel *The Stranger*, both originally published in 1942. After the war Camus returned to directing theater and writing. He also engaged in a heated debate with Sartre over the application of communist principles to government and society. The circumstances of his death reflected Camus' sense of the absurd. Apparently undecided whether to drive or to take the train to his destination, he died in an automobile accident on January 4, 1960, with a train ticket for that day in his pocket. In his writings Camus continually placed the individual at the mercy of external forces that render the life situation absurd. He attempted to identify individual resources that might allow a person to reorient life to more fulfilling directions by exerting the courage to take control and establish a sense of purpose.

Karl Jaspers. Like Camus, Karl Jaspers (1883–1969) pursued the theme of meaning in existence and the relevance of meaning to psychology. He defined philosophy as the inquiry into freedom, history, and the possibility of meaning in existence. Jaspers studied medicine and law at four German universities prior to joining the staff of a psychiatric hospital in Heidelberg. Specializing in psychology, Jaspers joined the philosophy faculty at the University of Heidelberg in 1913, where he continued to develop his existential basis for psychology. However, because he refused to leave his Jewish wife, the Nazis harassed him increasingly during the 1930s, and by 1938 he had lost his professorship and was forbidden to publish. In 1945, when Heidelberg was liberated by the Americans, Jaspers formed a group to reopen the university and continued with that task until 1949, when he joined the University of Basel in Switzerland.

Jaspers consistently expressed his concern with human existence, which led him to suggest three stages of being. The first stage is *being-there* and places the individual in reference to the external, objective world of reality. *Being-oneself* is the stage that allows the person self-awareness of choices and decisions. *Being-in-itself* is described by Jaspers as the highest stage of existence, characterized by the attainment of the fullness of meaning. This stage is the transcendental world of individual meaning that encompasses and comprehends the totality of meaning; the individual is in effective communication with the social and physical environment, so that existence is fully defined.

Martin Buber. A final representative of modern existential philosophy is Martin Buber (1878–1965), who was born in Vienna and raised by his grandfather, a Hebrew scholar, in the predominantly Polish city of Lvov (now in the Ukraine). Buber received his degree in philosophy from the University of Vienna in 1904, and by this time was involved with the Zionist movement. He spent 5 years in Hasidic communities in Galicia studying the religious, cultural, and mystical traditions of his ancestors. Returning to Germany, he edited *Der Jude* (1916–1924) and with a Catholic and a Protestant coedited *Die Kreatur* (1926–1930). He was professor of comparative religion at the University of Frankfurt from 1923 until his dismissal by the German government in 1933. He went to Palestine in 1938 and taught social philosophy at Hebrew University until his retirement in 1951. He remained active, lecturing in Europe and in America until his death.

Buber's writings are interesting because he did not emphasize consciousness or self-awareness. Rather than "self-dialogue," Buber stressed dialogue between persons and between the person and God, as reflected in his work *I and Thou* (1923). Out of the dual contributors of a dialogue comes a unity, so that individuals define themselves in terms of other persons or in terms of God. Thus, Buber added a critical social dimension of personal growth, which complemented other expressions of self-growth in the existential framework.

Although this brief review of several existential philosophers is certainly not comprehensive, it reflects the diversity of opinion. Existentialists are atheistic as well as religious; pessimistic and optimistic; looking to meaning and relegating life to absurdity. However, they do share common ground in emphasizing the individual's quest for existence and identity. After surveying the phenomenological trend in philosophy, we will review some specific existential interpretations of psychology.

Phenomenology

In Chapter 13, the phenomenological basis of Gestalt psychology was outlined in terms of a general approach in German psychology, which was contrasted with the analytical alternative of other empirical strategies. However, in relation to the third force movement, phenomenology assumes a more critical role, both as a methodology and as an expression of essential assumptions common to many of the positions within the movement. In this context phenomenology developed in a more specific and elaborate way than portrayed as background to Gestalt psychology.

Within the approach of the third force movement, phenomenology concentrates on the study of phenomena as experienced by the individual, with the emphasis on exactly how a phenomenon reveals itself to the experiencing person in all its specificity and concreteness. As a methodology, phenomenology is open to whatever may be significant to the understanding of a phenomenon. The subject experiencing a phenomenon is required to attend to it exactly as it appears in consciousness, without prejudgment, bias, or any predetermined set or orientation. The goals of the method are:

1. The apprehension (literally, the mental grasping) of the structure of the phenomenon as it appears;
2. The investigation of the origins or bases of the phenomenon as experienced; and
3. The emphasis on the possible ways of perceiving all phenomena.

The task of the phenomenologist is to investigate the processes of intuition, reflection, and description. Accordingly, phenomena are not manipulated but, rather, are permitted to reveal themselves.

The substance of phenomenology consists of the data of experience and their meaning for the experiencing individual. Phenomenology rejects the reductionism inherent in the empirical methods of the natural sciences. Rather, phenomenology focuses on the significance and relevance of phenomena in the consciousness and perspective of the whole person.

Edmund Husserl. The founder of modern phenomenology was Edmund Husserl (1859–1938), who was born in Moravia, now a province of the Czech Republic. From 1876 to 1878 he studied at Leipzig, where he heard Wundt's lectures on psychology; in 1881 he transferred to Vienna to study mathematics. While at Vienna he came under the influence of Franz Brentano, whose act psychology became an important part of Husserl's phenomenology. Brentano sent Husserl to Halle in 1886 to study psychology with Stumpf. Accordingly, Husserl's commitment to psychology was by way of the antireductionistic views of Brentano and Stumpf, rather than Wundt's study of the elements composing consciousness. Husserl taught from 1900 to 1916 at Göttingen and then was named to the chair of philosophy at Freiburg, where he remained until his retirement in 1928.

Husserl's goal was to find a philosophy of science, and an associated methodology, which would be as rigorous as the empirical methods but would not require the reduction of subject matter to constituent elements. He distinguished between two general branches of knowledge. One branch includes those disciplines that study the person's experience of the physical world, which involve the person turned outward to the environment. Husserl described these disciplines as the traditional natural sciences. The other branch—philosophy—takes as its subject matter the study of the person's experience of herself or himself, the person turned inward. The major implication of Husserl's distinction between branches of knowledge is that psychology should resolve any differences and study the relationship of the person's inward-directed and outward-directed experiences.

For Husserl, consciousness does not exist as an abstract mental agency or a storehouse of experiences. Rather, consciousness is defined as the individual's being conscious of *something*. That is, consciousness exists as the individual's experiencing of an object. Reflecting Brentano's notion of the intentionality of the person, Husserl stated that every conscious act intends some object. To study consciousness, Husserl introduced the method of phenomenological "reduction," which is not the empirical, elementaristic approach of reducing psychological events to component parts, but a way of grasping the salient images of consciousness by penetrating the "layers" of experience. He described three types of phenomenological reduction:

1. The "bracketing" of being, which specifies relations within an experience between the individual and the object of consciousness while retaining the essential unity of the experience. For example, the experience described by "I see the dog" could be bracketed as follows:

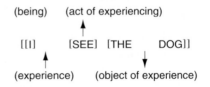

In this procedure, the processes of the experience are articulated and the unity that would be destroyed if any of the processes were isolated and examined separately is underscored.

2. The relationship of the cultural world to an immediate experience. This type of reduction recognizes the assimilation of values and attitudes that people acquire and carry with them, with the result that cultural modes exert a continual contextual set in the appearance of experiences.

3. Transcendental reduction, which leads the person from the phenomenal world of specific experiences to a level of subjectivity that rises above present reality to an integrative level of unifying experience. It is by achieving transcendental subjectivity that we live truly human existences, according to Husserl.

Thus, Husserl attempted to provide an alternative to the elementaristic reductionism of the empirical approaches of the natural science model. He employed a descriptive method that proposed to make psychological inquiry more complete through a consideration of the essential structure of experience and its objects.

Martin Heidegger. One of Husserl's assistants at Freiburg, Martin Heidegger (1889–1976), extended these interpretations of phenomenology. Born in the state of Baden in Germany, Heidegger briefly entered a Jesuit seminary, then spent 2 years training as a diocesan priest in Freiburg. There he was introduced to Brentano's dissertation on the meaning of being in Aristotle, a theme that Heidegger consistently studied throughout his life. In 1909, he began to study philosophy at the University of Freiburg and in 1914 received his degree for a dissertation entitled *The Theory of Judgment in Psychologism*. Shortly after, as a young faculty member, he became Husserl's assistant, marking the start of a productive, although tumultuous, relationship that furthered the development of the phenomenological movement. Heidegger's career from 1933 until his death was clouded by his controversial relationship with the Nazis. Certain pro-Nazi statements by Heidegger were recorded, yet his students during this period have also testified that he was anti-Nazi. After World War II Heidegger retired and made few public appearances, and he denied the more vehement accusations of his alleged collaboration.

His major work, *Being and Time* (1927), was dedicated to Husserl, but this work contains the seeds of their subsequent disagreements. Essentially, Husserl stressed the study of philosophy as an examination of consciousness, whereas Heidegger emphasized philosophy as the study of being. Heidegger wrote that people are estranged from their own being. He distinguished between *being* used as a noun and *being* as a verb. He argued that, throughout history, people have been bound to beings in terms of things or objects, but they have become alienated from being as living. Heidegger used phenomenology as a means of returning to the act of being. Phenomenology (the original Greek word means "to reveal itself") allows phenomena to be understood, if we do not coerce them into preconceived structures. Thus, for Heidegger, the essence of psychology is to study the characteristic modes of a person's being-in-the-world, for if people are estranged from their own being, they go through life alienated and psychologically fragmented, ultimately falling into a psychotic existence.

Heidegger, then, did not refer to an individual or to consciousness, because such terms imply an object. Rather, he categorized human existence by three basic, interacting traits:

1. *Mood or feeling*: People do not have moods; they are moods—we are joy; we are sadness.
2. *Understanding*: Instead of the accumulation of conceptual abstractions, human existence should be examined as the search for understanding our being. Heidegger described this search as standing open before the world so that we can internalize our confirmation of the truth or falsehood of our experience—that is, so we become an authentic self.
3. *Speech:* Rooted in the internal silence of the person, speech as language provides the vehicle for our knowledge of ourselves as beings.

Heidegger suggested that we become truly authentic only after we adjust to the concept of death and internalize the subjective meaning of death. Anxiety is the fear of nonbeing, the very antithesis of being, which is the result of an individual's unwillingness to confront death. By accepting and understanding that we are finite, we begin to penetrate the core of our existence. Thus, the uniqueness of human life lies in our understanding, however dim, of our own being.

The phenomenology of Husserl and Heidegger provided a strategy for studying the individual as an existential person. Together, existentialism and phenomenology gave philosophical substance and methodological direction to the third force movement as a psychological system.

EXISTENTIAL–PHENOMENOLOGICAL PSYCHOLOGY

As an expression of contemporary psychology, existential–phenomenological views are intimately bound up with their respective philosophical underpinnings. Indeed, the boundary separating existential phenomenology as a philosophy from existential phenomenology as a psychology is obscure. Existential–phenomenological psychology is typically an application of the philosophical principles, usually in a therapeutic, clinical setting. These principles may be summarized as follows:

1. The person is viewed as an individual existing as a being-in-the-world. Each person's existence is unique and reflects individual perceptions, attitudes, and values.
2. The individual must be treated as a product of personal development and not as an instance of generalized, human commonalities. Accordingly, psychology must deal with individual experience in consciousness to understand human existence.
3. The person moves through life striving to counteract the depersonalization of existence by society, which has led to subjective alienation, loneliness, and anxiety.
4. Phenomenology as a method permits the examination of the experiencing individual.

We briefly consider two representative psychologists of the European existential–phenomenological movement: Maurice Merleau-Ponty and Ludwig Binswanger. Although both are famous as exponents of existential–phenomenological approaches in psychology, neither can be viewed as a comprehensive system builder. Rather, both Merleau-Ponty and Binswanger reflect the attempt by psychologists to assimilate the basic philosophical tenets of existentialism so as to arrive at successful forms of treatment supporting the individual's search for authenticity.

Maurice Merleau-Ponty

Maurice Merleau-Ponty (1908–1961) received a strong background in philosophy and the empirical sciences, and taught in the most eminent French universities. In 1927, he met Sartre and began a long association that culminated in 1944 with their coediting *Les Temps Moderns*, a journal devoted to philosophical, political, and artistic issues. In 1952, he broke with Sartre over the questionable benefits of Marxist government for France and in the Soviet Union. Also in that year Merleau-Ponty was appointed to the chair of philosophy at the Collège de France, the youngest person ever named to that prestigious position.

In his most famous work, *Phenomenology of Perception* (1944), Merleau-Ponty described psychology as the study of individual and social relationships as they particularly link consciousness and nature. Reflecting the influence of Husserl, Heidegger, and Sartre, Merleau-Ponty maintained that the person is not a consciousness endowed with the characteristics that anatomy, zoology, and empirical psychology traditionally suggest. Rather, the person is the absolute source of existence. The individual does not acquire existence from antecedent physical events. Instead, the person moves toward the environment and sustains physical events by bringing those aspects of the environment into her or his existence. Psychology, then, is the study of individual intentionality. For Merleau-Ponty, every intention is an attention, and we cannot attend to something unless we experience it.

Merleau-Ponty described three major questions confronting modern psychology:

1. Is the human being an active or a reactive organism?
2. Is activity determined internally or externally?
3. Is psychological activity of internal origin, and can subjective experience be reconciled with science?

Merleau-Ponty believed that human processes cannot be accounted for by physics, nor can the empirical, positive method of physics be adequate for psychology. Rather, the primary subject matter of psychology must be experience, which is private and individual, occurring within the person and not subject to public verification and replication. Thus the proper approach of psychology is to learn the secrets of inner perception, which can be accomplished only by the descriptive methods of phenomenology.

Ludwig Binswanger

A second representative scholar of existential–phenomenological psychology is Ludwig Binswanger (1881–1966), who attempted to integrate this movement, especially the works of Husserl and Heidegger, with psychoanalysis. He was born in

Thurgan, Switzerland, and studied at the universities of Lausanne, Heidelberg, and Zurich, receiving his medical degree from Zurich in 1907. Binswanger succeeded his father in 1910 as director of the Swiss Bellevue Sanitarium, which had been founded by his grandfather.

Using Heidegger's notion of the individual's being-in-the-world (signified in German by *Dasein*), Binswanger termed his approach *Daseins-analyse*. Arguing that the reductionism of the natural science methods is inadequate, Binswanger looked to phenomenology to provide a full explanation of mental activity. Binswanger's goal was to have the therapist apprehend the world of the patient as it is experienced by the patient. He restricted his use of analysis to the present experience of the patient represented in consciousness, and he believed the analysis should reveal the structures of phenomena interpreted by each patient's individually defined context of meaning. The structures of phenomenal meaning describe each person's orientation in her or his world with respect to thought processes, fears and anxieties, and social relations.

Binswanger accepted the psychoanalytic emphasis on instinctual manifestations in early development, but maintained their importance only to the extent that they are represented in present consciousness. Accordingly, the past exists only in the present, as contributing to the design of the structure of meaning for each person. Binswanger's psychology and his application of it to psychiatry assumed that phenomenology is the critical tool for discovering the essential self of each person. This apprehension of the phenomenal structures guides the process of helping a patient modify the meanings and interpretations of living.

Both Merleau-Ponty and Binswanger represent the major focus of existential–phenomenological psychology through applications in clinical settings. Such existential themes as forlornness, depersonalization, and absurdity provide the context for accepting individual problems of existence. However, a therapist can expect to understand truly neurotic existence only by meeting individuals at their level of personal meaning.

THE THIRD FORCE MOVEMENT IN AMERICA

Like other systems of psychology imported from Europe, the third force movement in the United States has varied, eclectic expressions. Several psychologists attempted to incorporate some of the tenets and implications of the movement within existing behavioristic or psychoanalytic orientations, whereas a distinct group adhered to a strict existential–phenomenological view. However, in all expressions of the third force movement, the common view poses a contrast to the dominant, reductionistic position of materialistic behaviorism.

American Humanistic Psychology

The expression of the third force movement known as "humanistic psychology" is an eclectic grouping of American psychologists who advocated various interpretations of human personality. The term *humanistic* reflects the focus on defining a human psychology with emphases on individual existence and variability, in sharp distinction to the biological foundation of behaviorism. We shall consider several representatives of the various interpretations within humanistic psychology.

Gordon Allport.   The personality theory of Gordon Allport (1897–1967) may be classified under several systems of psychology, but it is presented here as humanistic psychology because Allport, especially later in his career, proposed a framework that was essentially consistent with the existential basis of the third force movement. In his study of personality, Allport distinguished between an idiographic approach, emphasizing the individual and associated variability or uniqueness, and a nomothetic view, stressing groups and minimizing individual differences. Advocating the idiographic approach, Allport continually stressed the uniqueness and complexity of the individual and suggested an underlying unity in personality that ultimately determines consciousness. He emphasized the self, or ego-function, in consciousness, which must be understood as present manifestations of integrated goals with an individual sense of future directions. Reflecting the eclecticism of American humanism, Allport described personality in terms of traits, or predispositions to respond, in a manner similar to Freud's instincts and Horney's needs. As the product of genetic inheritance and acquired learning, Allport's traits are mental structures that account for the consistency of a person's behavior.

Allport's notion of intentions in personality best shows his agreement with the existential–phenomenological position. This construct consists of present and future aspirations and hopes that are individually defined. In Allport's personality theory, intentions account for the continual growth process of becoming. Moreover, intentions provide the ego with unity that results in the development of personal strivings, the sense of individuality, and the attainment of self-knowledge.

Charlotte Bühler.   Born in Berlin and educated at several German universities, Charlotte Bühler (1893–1974) was a student of Külpe at the University of Munich when he died suddenly in 1915. A young scholar, Karl Bühler, who had served as an army physician in the German army earlier in World War I, came to Munich to assume supervision of Külpe's graduate students. Charlotte and Karl married in 1916 and, 2 years later, she completed her PhD. Both Bühlers contributed to the growing reputation of psychology in the exciting intellectual atmosphere of Vienna between the wars. From 1924 through 1925, Charlotte Bühler held a fellowship at Columbia University, where she met many of the prominent American psychologists of the period. On her return to Vienna with a 10-year research award, she was well on her way to establishing a reputation as a pioneer in the humanistic approach to lifespan developmental psychology.

The Bühlers' life in Vienna was cruelly interrupted by the Nazi movement in Austria and eventual annexation to Germany. Karl Bühler was briefly imprisoned, and following his release in 1939, the Bühlers went first to Norway and then to the United States. After several years taking short-term clinical positions at several places in the United States, the Bühlers moved to California in 1945, and Charlotte worked as a clinical psychologist at Los Angeles County Hospital and in a part-time academic affiliation with the University of Southern California. From 1953 until 1972, she was in private practice in Los Angeles.

Charlotte Bühler's perspective on development emphasized that healthy growth is psychologically purposive. Central to Bühler's views on personality was her belief in the importance of the harmonious balance of basic tendencies for need satisfaction, self-limiting adaptation, creative expansion, and upholding an internal order. Only the first involves a kind of passivity, and lifelong growth requires active engagement in the latter three tendencies. This conceptualization anticipated Maslow's "hierarchy of needs," described below, and Bühler insisted that this process is continuous throughout life.

Bühler was described by her contemporaries as the living embodiment of her psychological views. Bugental (1975/1976) described her as "a very real and at times a very formidable person who knew her own mind and set about doing things the way she believed they should be done. . . . She was usually on the move, active, doing, involved" (pp. 48–49). Bühler was an active collaborator with Carl Rogers and especially Abraham Maslow in fostering American humanistic psychology. She challenged young scholars and fostered their growth through her activities in the Association for Humanistic Psychology, for which she served as president in 1965–1966.

Abraham Maslow.   Another major figure in American humanistic psychology was Abraham Maslow (1908–1970), who is sometimes called the primary mover in the popularization of this approach. He evolved a view of personality that was greatly influenced by European existentialism. Maslow's position was based on a motivational framework consisting of a hierarchy of needs, from primitive biological levels to truly human experience. For example, the physiological needs of thirst and hunger must be met before the needs of safety and security are considered. When those needs are met, individuals proceed to satisfy their need for love and belongingness, then their need for self-esteem, their need for knowledge, and finally their need for beauty. The lifelong process of personal growth through progressive needs satisfaction was termed "self-actualization" by Maslow. The proper result of self-actualization is the harmonized personality, fully utilizing individual talents, intellectual capabilities, and self-awareness.

Rollo May.   After obtaining his PhD from Columbia University in 1949, Rollo May (1909–1994) worked in private practice in New York City. *Existence: A New Dimension in Psychology and Psychiatry*, a book May edited in 1958, provided one of the first introductions to the potential for existential principles applied to psychotherapy and personality theory. In the first two chapters of *Existence*, May wrote a detailed argument supporting the notion that existential interpretations of human activity provide a needed direction for psychological inquiry; that is, psychology requires a complete understanding of human experience as experienced in terms of uniquely human issues of willing, choosing, and developing.

Carl Rogers.   Perhaps the most popular of the humanistic psychologists, Carl Rogers' (1902–1987) writings on clinical applications are much admired. His "client-centered therapy" holds that the therapist must enter into an intensely personal and subjective relationship with the client, acting not as a scientist or a physician, but as a person interacting with another person. For the client, counseling represents an exploration of strange, unknown, and dangerous feelings, which is possible only if the client is accepted unconditionally by the therapist. Thus the therapist must attempt to sense what the client feels as he or she moves toward self-acceptance. The result of this empathic relationship is that the client becomes increasingly aware of authentic feelings and experiences, and her or his self-concept becomes congruent with the totality of existence.

Rogers' views of personality are basically phenomenological in that he focuses on the experiencing self. The person is seen as existing initially as part of the phenomenal field of experience, and the conceptual structure of the self must become differentiated from the overall field by the acquisition of self-knowledge. The self, then, consists of organized and consistent concepts based on perceptions of the characteristics of the "I" or "me" and perceptions of the relationships of the "I" to others. Once the conceptual structure of the self is known and accepted, the person is truly free from internal tensions and anxieties.

This brief overview of the positions of Allport, Bühler, Maslow, May, and Rogers is intended to show their relationship to the third force movement. Humanistic psychology is primarily a clinical application of a psychology of the individual. Although it accepts the importance of physiological and instinctual influences on personality, humanistic psychology emphasizes individual growth to reach experiences of total realization of the vast potential of personal resources. This goal is achieved by the phenomenological appreciation of self-knowledge.

The Duquesne Group

The most consistent expression of existential–phenomenological psychology in America has come from psychologists centered at Duquesne University in Pittsburgh. Many of the writings of European scholars have been republished through Duquesne University, which initially sponsored publication of current research in the *Review of Existential Psychology and Psychiatry*. Since the early 1970s, the Psychology Department at Duquesne has sponsored the *Journal of Phenomenological Psychology*. As the most active center of existential–phenomenological psychology in America, the Duquesne group represents a rather unique orientation within the prevailing eclecticism of American psychological academia.

The inspirational force of the Duquesne group has been Adrian van Kaam (b. 1920), originally from the Netherlands, who is a member of the order of priests that founded Duquesne. He advocated a revision of psychology based on the principles of existentialism, away from the confining reductionism of natural science models and methods. Having studied with leaders of the American third force movement, such as Rogers and Maslow, van Kaam started an institute at Duquesne designed to explore the development of spirituality. He directed this institute until 1980.

The call for more phenomenological emphases in psychological research is consistent with the definition of psychology as a truly human science. A former member of the Duquesne group is Amedeo Giorgi (b. 1931), who was trained as an experimental psychologist at Fordham University. Giorgi argued for a more open approach to psychology in his 1970 work *Psychology as a Human Science*. He concluded that psychology should have as its subject matter the human person who "must be approached within a frame of reference that is also human, i.e., one that does not do violence to the phenomenon of man as a person" (pp. 224–225). Although a description of research activities of the Duquesne group is beyond our present scope, it is important to recognize that this orientation in American psychology brings the benefit of diverse perspectives on the nature of psychological inquiry.

As we conclude this chapter, it is interesting to note the similarity in the influences of the third force movement and psychoanalysis as systems of psychology. The clearest expressions of each had European origins, and their impact in America has been largely through clinical applications. Both systems lack an empirical base, limiting their appeal to mainstream American psychology. Moreover, both systems are characteristically fragmented in their contemporary expressions. However, the third force movement, unlike psychoanalysis, never had an accepted reference figure, a role provided by Freud in psychoanalysis. Indeed, the philosophical foundation of the third force movement consists of a collection of varied writings, ranging from literary works to comprehensive systems of human existence. Translated into American psychology, the third force movement influenced psychological views, especially in therapeutic applications, but did not become a serious alternative to the dominant behavioristic establishment.

CHAPTER SUMMARY

The third force movement in psychology evolved from the active model of mental processes. Firmly grounded in the principles of existential philosophy, this movement focuses on the individual in quest of identity, values, and authenticity. The nineteenth-century writings of such figures as Kierkegaard, Nietzsche, and Dilthey formed the background for the view of the person as alone and dehumanized. The twentieth-century works of Sartre, Camus, and Jaspers offered further expression to the basic state of anxiety and absurdity in human existence. The methodological writings of Husserl and Heidegger contributed to the development of phenomenology as a means of investigating the holistic character of human experience. The combined existential–phenomenological psychology was an application of a new orientation in clinical settings, represented in Europe by such psychologists as Merleau-Ponty and Binswanger. In America, the humanistic viewpoints of Allport, Bühler, Maslow, May, and Rogers agreed, to varying extents, with the European movement, and a center of existential–phenomenological psychology emerged at Duquesne University. The third force movement is largely a fragmented orientation within contemporary psychology. Although it did not generate a comprehensive alternative to behavioristic formulations, the third force movement has exerted an impact on clinical applications, especially in therapeutic efforts.

BIBLIOGRAPHY

Primary Sources

ALLPORT, G. W. (1947). Scientific models and human morals. *Psychological Review, 54,* 182–192.

ALLPORT, G. W. (1955). *Becoming.* New Haven: Yale University Press.

BINSWANGER, L. (1963). Freud and the Magna Carta of clinical psychiatry. In J. Needleman (Ed.), *Being-in-the-world.* New York: Basic Books.

BINSWANGER, L. (1963). Freud's conception of men in the light of anthropology. In J. Needleman (Ed.), *Being-in-the-world.* New York: Basic Books.

DOSTOYEVSKY, F. (1970). *The idiot* (E. M. Martin, Trans.). London: Everyman's Library.

HEIDEGGER, M. (1949). *Existence and being.* Chicago: Henry Regnery.

HODGES, H. A. (1944). *Wilhelm Dilthey: An introduction.* London: Routledge.

HUSSERL, E. (1962). *Ideas* (W. H. B. Gibson, Trans.). New York: Collier.

KAUFMAN, W. (1955). *The portable Nietzsche.* New York: Viking Press.

KAUFMAN, W. (Ed.). (1956). *Existentialism from Dostoyevsky to Sartre.* Cleveland: Minden Books.

KIERKEGAARD, S. (1954). *Fear and trembling and the sickness unto death* (W. Lowrie, Trans.). Princeton, NJ: Princeton University Press.

KOCKELMANS, J. (Ed.). (1967). *Phenomenology: The philosophy of Edmund Husserl and its interpretations.* Garden City, NY: Doubleday.

MASLOW, A. H. (1962). *Toward a psychology of being.* Princeton, NJ: D. Van Nostrand.

MASLOW, A. (1966). *The psychology of science: A reconnaissance.* New York: Harper & Row.

MERLEAU-PONTY, M. (1962). *Phenomenology of perception* (N. C. Smith, Trans.). New York: Humanities Press.

MERLEAU-PONTY, M. (1963). *The structure of behavior* (A. Fisher, Trans.). Boston: Beacon Press.

ROGERS, C. R. (1951). *Client-centered therapy: Its current practice, implications and theory.* Boston: Houghton Mifflin.

ROGERS, C. R. (1955). Persons or science? A philosophical question. *American Psychologist, 10,* 267–278.

SARTRE, J. P. (1956). *Being and nothingness.* (H. Barnes, Trans.). New York: Philosophical Library.

TILLICH, P. (1952). *The courage to be.* New Haven: Yale University Press.

VAN KAAM, A. (1966). *Existential foundations of psychology.* Pittsburgh: Duquesne University Press.

Studies

BOSS, M. (1962). Anxiety, guilt and psychotherapeutic liberation. *Review of Existential Psychology and Psychiatry, 2,* 173–195.

BRODY, N., & OPPENHEIM, P. (1967). Methodological differences between behaviorism and phenomenology. *Psychological Review, 74,* 330–334.

BUGENTAL, J. F. T. (1963). Humanistic psychology: A new breakthrough. *American Psychologist, 18,* 563–567.

BUGENTAL, J. F. T. (1975/1976). Toward a subjective psychology: Tribute to Charlotte Bühler. *Interpersonal Development, 6,* 48–61.

CARDNO, J. A. (1966). Psychology: Human, humanistic, humane. *Journal of Humanistic Psychology, 6,* 170–177.

CORRENTI, S. (1965). A comparison of behaviorism and psychoanalysis with existentialism. *Journal of Existentialism, 5,* 379–388.

FRANKL, V. E. (1963). *Man's search for meaning.* New York: Washington Square Press.

GAVIN, E. A. (1990). Charlotte M. Bühler (1983–1974). In A. N. O'Connell and N. F. Russo (Eds.), *Women in psychology: A bio-bibliographic sourcebook.* New York: Greenwood Press, 49–56.

GILBERT, A. R. (1951). Recent German theories of stratification of personality. *Journal of Psychology, 31,* 3–19.

GILBERT, A. R. (1970). Whatever happened to the will in American psychology? *Journal of the History of the Behavioral Sciences, 6,* 52–58.

GILBERT, A. R. (1972). Phenomenology of willing in historical view. *Journal of the History of the Behavioral Sciences, 8,* 103–107.

GILBERT, A. R. (1973). Bringing the history of personality theories up to date: German theories of personality stratification. *Journal of the History of the Behavioral Sciences, 9,* 102–114.

GIORGI, A. (1965). Phenomenology and experimental psychology, I. *Review of Existential Psychology and Psychiatry, 5,* 228–238.

GIORGI, A. (1966). Phenomenology and experimental psychology, II. *Review of Existential Psychology and Psychiatry, 6,* 37–50.

GIORGI, A. (1970). *Psychology as a human science: A phenomenologically based approach.* New York: Harper & Row.

KRASNER, L. (1978). The future and the past in the behaviorism-humanism dialogue. *American Psychologist, 33,* 799–804.

KWANT, R. (1963). *The phenomenological philosophy of Merleau-Ponty.* Pittsburgh: Duquesne University Press.

LANGUILLI, N. (1971). *The existentialist tradition.* Garden City, NY: Doubleday.

LUIJPEN, W. (1960). *Existential phenomenology.* Pittsburgh: Duquesne University Press.

MACLEOD, R. B. (1947). The phenomenological approach to social psychology. *Psychological Review, 54,* 193–210.

MAY, R. (Ed.). (1958). *Existence: A new dimension in psychology and psychiatry.* New York: Basic Books.

MCCLELLAND, D. C. (1957). Conscience and the will rediscovered. *Contemporary Psychology, 2,* 177–179.

PERVIN, L. A. (1960). Existentialism, psychology and psychotherapy. *American Psychologist, 15,* 305–309.

SCRIVEN, M. (1965). An essential unpredictability in human behavior. In B. Wolman & E. Nagel (Eds.), *Scientific psychology.* New York: Basic Books, 411–425.

SEVERIN, F. T. (Ed.) (1965). *Humanistic viewpoints in psychology.* New York: McGraw-Hill.

SMITH, D. L. (1983). The history of the graduate program in existential phenomenological psychology at Duquesne University. In A. Giorgi, A. Barton, & C. Maes (Eds.), *Duquesne studies in phenomenological psychology* (Vol. 4). Pittsburgh: Duquesne University Press, 257–331.

SONTAG, F. (1967). Kierkegaard and search for a self. *Journal of Existentialism, 28,* 443–457.

STRASSOR, S. (1963). *Phenomenology and the human sciences.* Pittsburgh: Duquesne University Press.

STRASSOR, S. (1965). Phenomenologies and psychologies. *Review of Existential Psychology and Psychiatry, 5,* 80–105.

STRAUS, E. (1966). *Phenomenological psychology.* New York: Basic Books.

STRUNK, O. (1970). Values move will: The problem of conceptualization. *Journal of the History of the Behavioral Sciences, 6,* 59–63.

✵ 17 ✵

Contemporary Trends

Postsystem Psychology
Learning, Motivation, and Memory
    Theoretical Perspectives on Conditioning
    Biological Predispositions
    Neuroscience and Learning
    Cognitive Processes
Perception
Developmental Psychology
    Cognitive Development
    Psycholinguistics
    Lifespan Development
Social Psychology
Personality
International Perspectives: Modern Asian Psychoogy
    India
    China
    Japan
Chapter Summary

POSTSYSTEM PSYCHOLOGY

Some of those same forces that led to the intellectual ferment reflected in the existential and humanistic roots of the third force movement described in Chapter 16 also had an impact on the social changes that marked the 1960s and 1970s. Higher education in the United States became more accessible and expanded exponentially. The expanded opportunities for women, in particular, brought both talent and creativity to psychology's research agenda. For obvious reasons, psychology was at the center of these changes within the university arena as well as in the increasingly broadened definition of research. By the turn of the twenty-first century, psychology is interactive with other disciplines as one of many perspectives contributing to the advancement of our understanding of ourselves, and has given rise to entirely new areas of investigation, such as cognitive science and neuroscience.

As psychology moved beyond the middle of the twentieth century, its one hundredth anniversary as a recognized independent discipline, and into the twenty-first century, a transition was evident. Specifically, the psychology that emerged from the period of identifiable, contrasting systems of psychological inquiry evolved toward a greater emphasis on data collection, toward psychology's empirical roots. This transition did not occur all at once, with universal rejection of strict adherence to particular systems. Rather, there was a trend toward investigation of particular issues, which indicated a specific research strategy; the systems themselves were less likely to dictate the issues of importance. Some limited influences from earlier systems of psychology remained and were represented by psychologists who place varying emphases on the underlying philosophical bases of one or more of the systems. Contemporary American psychology may be described as behavioristic only in the broadest sense that accepts observable behavior as a primary, but not exclusive, source of data. Such "watered-down" behaviorism does not prevent psychologists from pursuing research questions beyond the limited scope of traditional behaviorism, in ways that would probably make Watson recoil. Likewise, in the applied sphere, clinical psychologists may value the techniques and research approach of behavior modification, but such views do not preclude their using aspects of the more psychodynamic orientations.

Accordingly, contemporary psychology is characterized as a discipline composed of various areas of study, which might include traditional research psychology issues of learning, perception, development, social activity, and personality. Research efforts in certain of these areas sometimes reflect the earlier dominance of a given research strategy derived from one of the systems. For example, current advances in learning have resulted from studies based in neurophysiology consistent with Pavlovian reflexology and behaviorism in general. The area of developmental psychology has accumulated significant findings from studies based upon the mentalistic assumptions of cognitive approaches and psycholinguistics consistent with the traditions of Gestalt psychology and views emanating from the human science model. However, in most of contemporary psychology, the approach is eclectic, avoiding exclusive commitment to any given systematic framework. Specific issues guide the strategy and direction of research. In this sense, contemporary psychology may be characterized as an empirical, but not a completely experimental, science. The methodological focus of psychology confirms the tradition of sense validation of psychological events—that is, an empirical approach—but further restriction of empiricism in psychology is not universally accepted.

An additional trend in contemporary psychology concerns the tendency toward redefining substantive areas of study. This has occurred by either specializing within psychology or joining part of traditional psychological content with another discipline. New specializations have often evolved because of the demands placed on psychologists for changes in functional roles. Industrial and organizational psychology, community psychology, and sports psychology are examples of specializations defined by new problem areas in which psychologists have found appropriate research issues and applications. Current trends also tend toward inter- and multidisciplinary studies, as opposed to exclusive specializations within psychology. The breakdown of traditional disciplinary barriers as well as the recognition of methodological commonalities has brought two or more disciplinary approaches together to address a given problem. This tendency toward interdisciplinary affinity has been accelerated by advances in the technical sophistication of scientific inquiry, making traditional disciplinary-bound approaches seem outmoded and inadequate. Perhaps the best example of this redefinition of traditional disciplines has occurred in the emergence of the research areas of "cognitive science" and of "neuroscience." Psychology forms an integral part of both interdisciplinary areas. Other specialized research and clinical topics have been similarly defined. For example, Miller (1983) described this intersection of traditional disciplines when he defined the field of behavioral medicine as the "integration of relevant parts of epidemiology, anthropology, sociology, psychology, physiology, pharmacology, nutrition, neuroanatomy, endocrinology, immunology, and the various branches of medicine and public health, as well as related professions such as dentistry, nursing, social work, and health education" (pp. 2–3). In the intervening years, with advances in research against cancer and HIV, this field has expanded almost exponentially (see also Cohen & Herbert, 1996).

Another important trend in this postsystem period has been the increasing "internationalization" of psychology. Immediately after World War II, the United States emerged as a dominant power not only in political and economic terms, but in the intellectual and academic spheres as well. European and Asian universities and research centers were in ruins, so that young scholars from these continents came to American universities to study, bringing back to their countries a particular American perspective, which included American advances in psychology. In the intervening years, these academic and research infrastructures have been restored, and as we enter the twenty-first century, clearly identifiable influences can be described in terms of a triad. In particular, the Americans continue a leadership role in psychology as well as other areas of study, and Asian and European players have assumed coequal places. The Japanese have assumed the lead in Asian science, benefiting from significant government and industry support for research and development, which are viewed as national assets of the greatest importance. Similarly, the economic power of the European Community has fed financial resources for research centers throughout the continent. While scholarly support has fostered the desired goal of unity among the subcultures of European nations, it has also resulted in the emergence of scientific leadership. In this day of instantaneous communication through electronic transference of data, collaboration among scientists approaches a truly international flavor, which has benefited psychology and related disciplines.

In surveying the major areas of contemporary psychology, we attempt to present representative trends in research developments rather than comprehensive reviews of specific fields. The interested student may find more detailed surveys of the contemporary research literature in many general textbooks available in each area of modern psychology. For specialized accounts, consult specific review journals, most notably the *Annual Review of Psychology*, *Psychological Bulletin*, and *Psychological Review*. In a very unscientific classification of the distribution of topics addressed in review articles published in the *Annual Review of Psychology* during the last part of the 1990s, from 1996 through 2000, the relative comparison of areas of psychology reveals interesting trends. A total of 90 articles were classified. The traditional area of learning, motivation, and memory reflected the fertile territory of neuroscience and cognitive science, with 26% of the articles falling within this general area. The second most represented area, with 22% of the total, consisted of review articles on the applications of psychology in schools, health delivery systems, community agencies, and similar institutions. The traditional areas of social psychology and developmental psychology comprised 17% and 12%, respectively. Articles dealing with methodology, statistical inference, and theoretical aspects of assessment made up 8% of the total reviews. Personality theory and applications in psychopathology make up only 6%; the dominant area of nineteenth century psychology—perception—comprised only 5% of the review articles. As mentioned earlier, this classification was arbitrary, but seems to reflect the balance of the traditional areas of psychological inquiry as the distinctions between psychology and related disciplines is blurred in contemporary research and application.

LEARNING, MOTIVATION, AND MEMORY

Theoretical Perspectives on Conditioning

Variations derived from the neobehavioristic formulations continue to guide investigations of learning processes. Although these models do not claim to replace the grandiose designs of the neobehavioristic theories, they serve a cohesive function, binding together lines of empirical research.

The modern statement of the two-process theory of Pavlovian–instrumental interactions in conditioning, elegantly stated by Rescorla and Solomon (1967) and summarized in Chapter 15, gave rise to much research that may collectively be labeled "transfer of control" studies. Essentially, such experiments demonstrate that stimuli with associative value from Pavlovian conditioning can modify instrumentally maintained responses. The data from these experiments showed that more than a simple stimulus-response relationship may be learned during instrumental conditioning, and behavior may ultimately be controlled by two stimuli: the predictive, Pavlovian CS and the instrumental reinforcing stimulus. Experiments reported by such investigators as Hearst and Peterson (1973), Overmier and Bull (1970), and Rescorla and Wagner (1972) confirm the potency of this relationship. The significance of these studies lies with the evidence that organisms do not simply learn to associate responses with stimuli; rather, they learn relationships among environmental stimuli, and these relationships are capable of exerting a powerful influence on various types of responses. Moreover, these studies have provided behavioral evidence in support of the neurophysiology of learning (Rescorla, 1988).

Another postsystem interpretation of incentive motivation was proposed by Bindra (1972, 1974), who discarded the Hullian constructs of habit and drive described in Chapter 15. Instead, Bindra proposed that an organism learns a contingent relationship between two stimuli, such that the presentation of one stimulus evokes the other. These stimuli are in turn represented in a central motive state, according to Bindra. If one stimulus is presented, the second stimulus is anticipated, and if the second stimulus has incentive value for the organism, then specific behaviors will be emitted. In this view of incentive motivation, there is no need for general drive motivation, as in Hull's system, but only for specific motivational states related to the incentive stimuli. The existing inhibitory mechanisms of the central nervous system are sufficient to accommodate the sensory-motor coordination of Bindra's model. He postulated three categories of sensory-motor relationships: regulatory, consummatory, and instrumental mechanisms. Thus, Bindra held that learning is not the acquisition of stimulus-response associations, but rather acquisition of relationships between stimuli as well as between stimuli and the environment.

The third extension of behavioristic formulations of learning processes was the model of Bolles (1967, 1970), who followed in the tradition of "cognitive behaviorism" started by Tolman (Chapter 15). Bolles suggested two types of expectancy in Pavlovian and instrumental learning. The first, similar to that described by Bindra, involves stimuli that predict the occurrence of other biologically important environmental events; the organism learns an expectancy as the result of the relationship between stimuli. The second type of expectancy concerns the learning of the predictive relationship between the organism's own responses and the consequences of those responses. Both types of expectancies occur during Pavlovian and instrumental conditioning; the second type is predominantly involved in instrumental training. To the two types of learned expectancies, Bolles suggested an additional, innate expectancy that imposes constraints, or limits, on a subject's ability to learn. For example, Bolles invoked the concept of species-specific defensive responses (SSDR) to explain avoidance behavior. When frightened, mammals will either freeze or flee. Bolles viewed the SSDR of freezing and flight as innate expectancies because of the subject's expectation that such behavior would successfully remove the source of fear. Thus Bolles integrated both acquired and innate activities within a motivational model based on expectancies.

Biological Predispositions

As reviewed in Chapter 15, one of the weaknesses of early American behaviorism, in its total reliance on environmental determinacy, was its deemphasis of any consideration of the biological inheritance of the organism other than the recognition that an organism is equipped with sensory and motor abilities to acquire experiences. In contrast, Pavlov's reflexology relied on a physiological reductionism to explain psychological events, giving neurophysiological mechanisms a critical role. Neither of these positions, however, placed much emphasis on the role of specific response patterns that might be innate, yet not directly reducible to physiological mechanisms.

The works of such renowned ethologists as Lorenz and Tinbergen, cited earlier in connection with the psychology of William McDougall, established the importance of biological limitations on behavior. Laboratory investigations of such events as the delay of reinforcement and autoshaping have pointed to the importance of the survival value of learning processes. Such factors as the response repertoire of a species and stimulus salience must be included in any comprehensive model of learning. Thus, instinctual patterns, evolutionary background, and social ecology contribute to the acquisition of responses in organisms.

A representative, postsystem model of learning that emphasized biological inheritance focused on the concept of preparedness (Seligman, 1970; Seligman & Hager, 1972). According to Seligman's interpretation of an organism's evolutionary history, members of a given species may be prepared, unprepared, or counterprepared to associate certain stimulus and response relationships. The ease of acquisition and resistance to forgetting are related to this biologically determined dimension of preparedness. This notion of preparedness for learning has been related to other processes besides simple conditioning, such as language acquisition and phobic neuroses.

An additional area of research in the biological bases of simple learning and motivation deals with the reconsideration of the nature of motivational systems (see Brehm & Self, 1989). In particular, studies have moved away from a focus on neural organization of response patterns to an examination of peripheral activity in sensory control of reinforcement effects. These findings have suggested that organisms acquire representations of reinforcers, which are embedded in the individual motivation systems (White & Milner, 1992). Technical advances allow the study of neurotransmitter systems as well as the manipulation and assay of peptide systems that were largely unknown until relatively recently. Data from behavioral, anatomical, and chemical studies are recognized as critical to a comprehensive view of motivation (see Wise & Rompre, 1989).

Neuroscience and Learning

As described in Chapter 15, the tradition of Russian reflexology has consistently explained learning in terms of physiological reduction. As mentioned in Chapter 15, the investigation of physiological correlates of learning in the United States was initially pursued in the programmatic efforts of Lashley. He influenced a generation of students at several universities before assuming the directorship of the Yerkes Laboratory of Primate Biology in Orange Park, Florida. Lashley was long interested in brain research and developed many of the standard laboratory procedures and experimental designs currently used in physiological psychology.

Since World War II, American research into the neurophysiological basis of learning has mushroomed in a variety of directions. With the demise of the nonphysiological interpretations of traditional behaviorism, many researchers initially turned to the prevailing rationale of Russian reflexology and viewed behavioral psychology as ultimately reducible to the mechanisms of physiology. In addition to intensive study and mapping of functions in the cortex, postwar research employed lesioning and chemical implantation techniques as methods of extirpation to examine subcortical structures and sensory-motor pathways. These methodologies permitted the study of the interactive functions of various neural structures and allowed the recording of many electrophysiological indices of variables measuring acquisition and memory retrieval.

Two major areas of research that began to evolve a more innovative approach to the learning process involved split-brain preparations and state-dependent learning. Both research programs view learning in terms of information processing, as evidenced by the complicated nature of the transmission of neural fibers (see also Gluck & Myers, 1997). The split-brain technique, pioneered largely by Nobel laureate Roger Sperry (b. 1913), attempts to identify neural fiber projections by separating hemispheric input and measuring the effects on learning acquisition and retention. Research groups (e.g., Gazzaniga, 1967) reported impressive evidence of both deficits and excesses of learning, which depended on such factors as the nature of the task, the response requirement, and temporal and sequential factors. The split-brain technique seems to provide an appropriate model for learning and, especially, memory processes. A second major area of research, state-dependent learning, offered an interesting direction in the use of drugs as a tool to facilitate our understanding of acquisition and memory retrieval. Essentially, state-dependent learning studies have indicated that in order for an organism to retrieve a certain set of information, its central nervous system must be in the same physiological state as it was during acquisition. Conversely, disruptions of memory retrieval may be produced by drug-induced differences in organismic states between acquisition and retention testing. Split-brain and state-dependent research both take the approach of isolating functions to study how the intact brain deals with the myriad of information in the organism at any given moment.

Perhaps the most exciting trend in contemporary investigations of learning concerns the study of the neurochemical basis of acquisition, storage, and retrieval of information. Studies of the role of RNA in memory storage led to a consideration of the changes in proteins in the metabolic processes that accompany learning. Investigations of gene expression in several brain structures offer the possibility of direct assessment of neural changes following acquisition, which is described as long-term potentiation (see Martinez, 1989; Matthies & Derrick, 1996). Studies of the role of epinephrine and norepinephrine, hormonal secretions of the adrenal gland, have suggested mediating chemical changes paralleling behavioral changes (e.g., Everitt & Robbins, 1997). Moreover, neural circuitry seems largely responsible as the mechanism whereby a nonspecific chemical change translates into specific reinforcing activity. Although research has not yet progressed to a definitive description of neurochemical storage of information, this direction represents an approach that may lead to the extreme reductionism of psychological processes to neurophysiological and neurochemical elements (see Anokhin & Rose, 1991; Davis & Squire, 1984; Rosenzweig, 1996). A significant area of creative research involves the study of how the brain is able to change its structure and function as a result of experience. Through elegant and sophisticated experiments, investigators have measured changes in neurons through an array of concomitant changes in factors from the learning of new responses to aging to stress (Kolb & Whishaw, 1998).

Cognitive Processes

A final area of current research in learning, motivation and memory, termed *cognitive processes*, concerns broadly defined areas that relate to all those specializations within psychology that deal with explanations of the organization of thinking. "Cognitive science" provides a unifying theme that integrates data collected in disciplinary studies from psychology, anthropology, philosophy, computer science, and neuroscience. In the tradition of Tolman's purposive behavior, and following the neobehavioristic study of human information processing and mathematical models, cognitive psychology includes such global classes of behavior as perception, memory storage and retrieval, categories of social and developmental variables, and social attitudes and traits. In addition, recent studies of animal cognition have suggested such cognitive abilities as time discrimination in rats (Church, 1978), self-awareness in pigeons (Epstein, Lanza, & Skinner, 1981), and cognitive representational processes in invertebrates (Roitblat & von Fersen, 1992). Whereas some reviewers (e.g., Premack, 1983) caution that cognitive processes defined in humans and in animals may not reflect comparable mechanisms, the infrahuman studies show distinctive behaviors and patterns that are not easily accommodated by more traditional conditioning models of learning.

Research on concept formation, decision making, judgments, and attitudes collectively points to entire complexes of activities that fall under the scrutiny of experimental methodologies. Along with advances in neurophysiology and sensory physiology, new techniques are rapidly evolving to measure physical substrates of cognitive processes. For example, Hillyard and Kutas (1983) have reviewed research advances in the use of electrophysiological event markers during stages of various cognitive processes, from selective attention to language processing. Cognitive psychology seems to be emerging as a central explanatory framework for many behavioral activities (e.g., Carpenter, Meyake, & Just, 1995). Although they descended from early theoretical perspectives, contemporary studies of cognitive processes are bound together more by a consensus on issues and methods than by an all-encompassing explanatory and predictive model.

Cognitive science has become a dominant force in contemporary psychology, linking the traditional psychological concerns in learning and memory with other disciplines that investigate thought processes. Moreover, Wellman and Gelman (1992) advanced the view that children as young as 3 or 4 years of age possess a "theory of mind" that explicitly structures their mental world, which challenges more traditional perspectives on cognitive development such as Piaget's theory (discussed later). Quite recent attention has been directed to the accuracy of memory retrieval (Koriat, Goldsmith, & Pansky, 2000; Wenzlaff & Wegner, 2000), which in turn has supported a coherent model of memory accounting for neurological and brain imaging data (Rolls, 2000). Hunt (1989) reviewed prevalent models in cognitive models and argued that the database has advanced to the point that a new paradigm is needed to accommodate new frontiers of research into reasoning, language, and problem solving.

PERCEPTION

Perception is psychology's oldest and most traditional area in terms of the formal expression of psychology as an independent discipline in the nineteenth century. Although the early studies of the psychophysicists and the basic tenets of structural psychology were surveyed for their historical importance, many of the methodological and substantive issues of these movements remain critical in modern psychology. Moreover, the Gestalt movement, which derived its initial formulations from perceptual processes, raised many questions that have current interest in thinking and problem solving.

Recent developments in perception research have distinguished between static and motion perception, with the latter emphasizing perception of an event or events over time. Advances in equipment and measurement techniques, along with the emergence and acceptance of an information-processing model of cognition, have given traditional perceptual research a central place in contemporary psychology. In particular, issues such as sensory detection, filtering, and attention have relevance to those models of learning that view the person in terms of the organization and mediation of sense information (see Haber, 1978). Accordingly, studies of perception have complemented the study of learning processes by focusing on the sensory part of the sensory-motor relationship. Moreover, the relationship between developmental variables and the intersection of perceptual, behavioral, and cognitive maturity defines a promising area of current research (Bertanthal, 1996).

The traditional issues of depth perception and pattern vision have been expanded to include varieties of performance variables. For example, initial work by Pettigrew and his associates (Pettigrew, Nikara, & Bishop, 1968) led to a physiological model of depth perception based on neural differences from cell to cell in the receptor-field locus of area 17 of the visual cortex, when mapped separately from each eye. Although the specifics of the Pettigrew model have been challenged, the neurophysiological techniques developed provide a means to resolve this traditional problem in perception (see DeValois & DeValois, 1980).

The study of perception has been historically linked to specific systems of psychology, and perceptual data have been used to support or refute various formulations, from attention to higher cognitive processes (Kinchla, 1992). Although this linkage has occurred more directly with the structural, Gestalt, and phenomenological systems, all of the twentieth-century systems had interpreted perceptual studies in line with their underlying assumptions. Accordingly, the postsystem period in psychology has freed the study of perception from preconceived assumptions attached to specific systems. In the 1950s textbooks in perception typically began with an introduction to classical psychophysics with overtones of structuralism, or they introduced students to basic Gestalt principles, or reiterated the Lockean assumptions of radical behaviorism. However, by the 1970s perception was defined as an empirical study, devoid of specific assumptions, and this data-based strategy has been apparent in recent research efforts (e.g., Hersh & Watson, 1996). In addition, the integration of various interdisciplinary approaches has afforded research into applied settings that provides insights of a broader perspective (Egeth & Yantis, 1997; Feng & Ratnam, 2000).

DEVELOPMENTAL PSYCHOLOGY

Cognitive Development

Perhaps the dominant model in developmental psychology is derived from cognitive interpretations. Although other approaches are recognized and accepted, it is the cognitive approach, intimately linked to language development, that has shaped the direction of developmental research. The dominant figure in this field has been Jean Piaget (1896–1980). After receiving his doctorate in zoology at age 22, Piaget embarked on a career that centered on the question of how people learn. He considered himself a philosopher concerned with the issue of knowing, as his later work on epistemology and logic amply testify. His methods of study were unorthodox compared to the standards of contemporary empiricism. Indeed, his theory of cognitive development was largely based upon his observations of his own children. Nevertheless, Piaget's influence has been tremendous and his reputation rivals that of Freud in terms of individual contributions to psychology during this century.

Piaget's view of cognitive development posits four distinct periods of intellectual growth that characteristically organize the child's interaction with the environment. Although the rate of intellectual growth may differ from child to child, Piaget maintained that this sequence of development is followed by all children:

1. *Sensorimotor period* (birth to 2 years): This stage is nonverbal and involves the child's initial experiences with environmental relationships, which become internalized in a rudimentary fashion by organization imposed along dimensions of meaning, intentions, causality, and symbolic value.
2. *Preoperational period* (2 to 7 years): During this phase, the child acquires language and deals with time relations, past and future as well as present.
3. *Concrete operations period* (7 to 11 years): At this stage, the child grasps abstract notions represented by complex qualitative and quantitative relations.
4. *Formal operations period* (11 to 15 years): In this final phase of intellectual growth, the child acquires understanding.

Piaget published over 50 books and monographs during his 60 years of active research. In his later years, he concentrated on the issues of the logic underlying the acquisition of knowledge. Although he is best known for his theory of cognitive development, Piaget consistently studied knowledge per se. The potency of the structures of mental development and organization impressed him to argue that education and teaching need not be manipulative but rather should provide the child with opportunities to invent and discover.

With the impetus of Piaget's synthesis of the development of intellectual abilities, the entire range of complex human learning and memory processes received closer attention within developmental psychology. For example, research in concept formation, involving the classification of multiple events or objects into a conceptual category, has been guided by a model of information processing focusing on the critical functions of input, output, and feedback. In this model, conceptual learning is seen as dependent on the learner and on the importance of individual decisions that evaluate stimulus characteristics and environmental contingencies. Moreover, conceptual learning requires a more dynamic interpretation of the complex issues of memory storage and retrieval. That is, the selective attention of the learner to the varying saliencies of stimuli involves flexibility of memory processes.

The emphasis on individual differences in complex learning processes has led contemporary psychology to suggest that intellectual abilities may be formulated within a personally devised *cognitive style,* a term that describes a person's learning strategy or approach to intellectual tasks. Research efforts have attempted to specify characteristic mental strategies. This emphasis on cognitive styles, or the individual imprint on learning strategy, is reminiscent of the trait theories of intelligence proposed in the nineteenth-century British views of Francis Galton and his followers (see Chapter 10). Trait theory was eventually overshadowed in the United States by the advent of Watsonian behaviorism and its successor movements. These views favored a more concrete and restricted definition of intelligence in terms of quantitative stimulus-response associations as reflected by overt performance. It is intriguing to consider that psychology's study of intelligence in the last hundred years has come full circle and research is focused on such dynamic aspects of human intelligence as creativity (e.g., Sternberg & Lubart, 1996).

Contemporary issues in cognitive development include efforts to integrate the traditional frameworks of Piagetian views and rigorous experimental psychology so that more complete models of early development can address motor, cognitive, social, and linguistic variables within the context of the behaving individual. This goal attempts to avoid the pitfalls involved in research that focuses on a stage or phase of development, or is constrained by concern with a single variable, while losing sight of the entire person. For example, recent studies have offered a developmental perspective on social interactions by looking at long-term effects of early experience on later developmental patterns (Cairns & Valsiner, 1984). In summary, two trends evident in contemporary psychology are also seen specifically in cognitive development. Specialization has segmented broad categories of traditional research (e.g., child psychology) to accommodate more refined concerns; at the same time, research is drawing increasingly from interdisciplinary resources (Brainerd, 1996; Flavell, 1996).

Psycholinguistics

Perhaps no other area in psychology benefited more from the genius of Piaget than the study of language. The dominance of the traditional behavioral model of psychology through the first half of the twentieth century had left the study of language in a relatively sterile state. Specifically, behaviorism emphasized the associations between words, and verbal learning was largely viewed as the aggregate of these associations. Indeed, the methods of verbal learning up to the 1950s were essentially unchanged from the approach used by Ebbinghaus late in the nineteenth century (see Chapter 11).

Piaget's theory of cognitive development offered refreshing insights into the development, structure, and use of language. Psycholinguistics may be broadly defined as the study of communication and the characteristics of the persons communicating. The actual shift in research direction to a consideration of the syntax and organization of language was prompted by an article by George Miller that appeared in 1962 in the *American Psychologist*, entitled "Some Psychological Studies of Grammar." This paper introduced the clearly mentalistic constructs of Noam Chomsky, who remains a pioneer in psycholinguistics. Chomsky referred to the developmental necessity for a "language acquisition device" as a mental mechanism to account for the onset of a child's ability to deal with grammar. During the 1960s and 1970s, the study of language development was completely recast. Contemporary psycholinguists portray the child as possessing innate mechanisms for interpreting and organizing the auditory stimulation of speech from the environment. The child's acquisition of grammatical syntax reflects an individual sense of language, permitting the child to mediate the linguistic environment.

Psycholinguistic theory points to the major function of language as the conversion of the varieties of ideas, conceptions, and thoughts into sentence structures. The rules of grammar operate on semantic units to produce a competence in expression. Researchers have extended the range of psycholinguistics by asserting that language is basic to understanding, problem-solving behavior, self-perception, and social relationships. Psycholinguistics, then, focuses on semantics—or the underlying meaning of words, other signs, and sentence structure—and psychologists have designed assessments of semantic value (see, for example, Osgood, Suci, & Tannenbaum, 1957).

Recent trends in psycholinguistic research have emphasized language processes within a comprehensive psychological context. As such, language as an expression among modes of communication assumes a critical role. Investigations of such issues as semantic memory, sentence comprehension, and word processing, including underlying meaning, study contextual variables such as word sensitivity, semantic references, and concept categories (see Foss, 1988; Carpenter, Meyake, & Just, 1995). Moreover, the importance of both biological and cultural determinants of language development and use has generated considerable research in several disciplines. Seen in this light, psycholinguistics and communication in general are best examined through an interdisciplinary approach, merging the approaches of the behavioral sciences, anthropology, sociology, computer science, and philosophy (see also McKoon & Ratcliff, 1998).

Lifespan Development

Traditional developmental psychology has focused on early experience, perhaps because of the compelling and obvious need to educate and socialize children. Such an emphasis has historically been reinforced by theoretical frameworks that view childhood as a period when the critical determinants of adult behavior are acquired. Systems as diverse as behaviorism and psychoanalysis have suggested, for different reasons, the importance of experiences in early development and their profound effects on subsequent maturation. While not ignoring or even de-emphasizing early development, lifespan developmental psychology has recently attempted to describe and explain development as a continual, comprehensive process from conception to death.

One important by-product of this more balanced investigation of lifelong development concerns contemporary interest in the study of aging, a long-neglected topic in psychological research (e.g., Birren & Fisher, 1995).

With the conceptualization of lifespan development, various interpretations have suggested a pluralistic sequence of development that results in critical periods of growth during life. These critical periods tend to generalize their effects across age periods. In other words, developmental functions of specific behavioral changes, such as language acquisition, psychological and biological changes in adolescence, and adult career decisions, may have different patterns of transforming behavior. This rather complicated picture of development has led to the study of lifespan profiles of influences that result from behavioral changes. The profiles, in turn, are designed to show not only individual growth but also how growth patterns interact with biological, environmental, and social determinants. Research in lifespan development includes the investigation of such issues as social development, family constellation, personality, and learning and memory (see Schultz & Heckhausen, 1996).

In this area, as in other contemporary areas of psychology, research efforts are combined because of a common orientation rather than because of a common theoretical heritage. Honzik (1984) categorized contemporary empirical research in terms of age differences, longitudinal changes, precursors of later development, biographical studies, and life satisfaction at a later age. Further, she defined significant developmental areas as health, temperament, intelligence, and issues related to self-concept, self-esteem, and altruism. Within these approaches to the lifespan, there is clearly an emphasis on multidisciplinary study, especially considering current, more comprehensive treatments of the aging part of the lifespan continuum (Baltes, Staudinger, & Lindenberger, 1999).

The study of aging in the context of lifespan development has practical as well as theoretical significance. With the numbers of people reaching old age increasing, society has yet to deal effectively with problems that have immense physical, psychological, and sociological importance for the aged. Psychology has only recently started to generate substantial research on aging, and these initial studies have clearly indicated the often traumatic and largely misunderstood changes that occur. Of theoretical interest is the extent to which the aging process is consistent with earlier, antecedent stages of development. Questions relating to the adjustments in lifestyle that accompany old age suggest the uniqueness of this stage of life, yet the individual's ability to make such adjustments depends on his or her lifelong experiences. Clearly, the investigation of the psychology of aging will provide a major research field for developmental psychology.

SOCIAL PSYCHOLOGY

Social psychology studies the behavioral processes, causal relations, and products of interactions among people and groups. Social activities may be viewed from three perspectives: individual contributions, interpersonal relations, and group behavior. The obvious importance of the social nature of human experience has been recognized since the time of antiquity. The historical antecedents of contemporary social psychology found expression, along with psychology in general, during the nineteenth century. In particular, Comte's positivism viewed the study of social structures and institutions as the most positive of sciences, and he viewed sociology as the culmination of intellectual progress. Darwin wrote on the social character of the evolution of humans, and Herbert Spencer attempted to devise a theory of social evolution. By the beginning of the twentieth century, the influences of Darwin and Spencer had led to the prevailing view that human social activities, in terms of origins as well as articulation, are governed by inherited instincts. The instinctual basis of social behavior was the dominant theme in McDougall's attempt to present a systematic account of social psychology in his textbook written in 1908 (see Chapter 12). However, McDougall's reliance on instinct to explain social processes ran counter to the environmental determinism of early behaviorism, which soon became the dominant American system of psychology. In 1924, Floyd H. Allport published his *Social Psychology*, in which social processes were presented in better conformity with behavioristic principles by avoiding instinctual explanations in favor of what he called "prepotent reflexes," or impulses modified by conditioning. In addition, Allport's book was the first treatment of social psychology that relied entirely on experimental evidence rather than on less controlled observational approaches.

Following Allport's precedent, social psychology has developed a broad base of experimental data. However, just as American behaviorism continually extended its study beyond the narrow confines of Watson's formulations, so, too, did social psychology gradually modify both its content and its methodology. Specifically, social psychology was greatly influenced by the field theory of the Gestalt movement and, to a lesser extent, by phenomenology, so that social psychology evolved into one of the broadest areas of contemporary research. Social psychologists have also studied social influences on individual behavior, investigating such topics as social imitation and learning, attitude and motive development, and social roles. The area of interpersonal relations encompasses the study of social status and communication, and theoretical interpretations have borrowed from other areas of psychology, ranging from stimulus–response learning to cognitive dissonance. The study of groups has concentrated on the development of participation, the formation and maintenance of groups, and the structure and management of organizations.

After World War II, research in social psychology grew tremendously, examining such issues as power, leadership, and social persuasion. For example, Milgram's (1963) classic work on obedience and conformity identified critical variables of social control. Social psychology has evolved into an interdisciplinary study, extending its scope to include cultural, anthropological, and moral questions. The work of cultural anthropologists, such as Margaret Mead's (1949) analysis of social rites in "primitive" societies, was integrated into a more comprehensive social psychology. Similarly, the survey techniques of sociology were employed by social psychologists to examine the development of racial attitudes (see, for example, Pettigrew & Campbell, 1960), and the findings were subsequently used to foster modification of those attitudes during the upheaval and social changes of the 1960s.

Recent studies in social psychology reflect the unsettled theoretical nature of this field. More than in any other area of contemporary psychology, the conceptual basis of social psychology appears to be rapidly evolving, perhaps as the result of the many recent strides at the empirical level with a focus on sophisticated designs (e.g., Kenny, 1996). The disagreements over strategies of study have been summarized within an investigation of social motivation in a review by Brody (1980). Essentially, Brody posed the distinction between phenomenological (defined broadly as nonanalytic) and antiphenomenological approaches in social psychology. A decision about the very basic assumptions of psychological processes seems especially compelling for social psychology, which has as its subject matter the elusive quality of social interactions. It is interesting to note that the dilemma of choosing between phenomenological and nonphenomenological assumptions about social activities, still unresolved, essentially represents the same basic issue with which psychology has struggled since its modern inception in the 1870s.

Nevertheless, on an empirical level, research has generated creative new studies of social interactions. Investigations of group tasks and group problem solving have isolated critical roles played by participants and have analyzed the nature of cooperation and compliance. The use of "games" to examine social influences on resolving conflicts and dilemmas has frequently been reported (see Dawes, 1980) and has provided a means for measuring such social characteristics as leadership, competition, trust, and obedience. Similarly, studies of environmental influences, investigated through the generation of models of social enrichment and deprivation, have provided evidence for a multidimensional reconsideration of individual social background (e.g., Schlenker & Weigold, 1992). The application of these results to the study of not only groups but also formal organizations is an area of growing attention (Harris Bond & Smith, 1996; Snyder & Stukas, 1999). Finally, attribution of perceived causality has become a major research field, with a natural affinity to cognitive, motivational, and personality research. Contemporary social psychology is a very active field, drawing on interdisciplinary resources as it moves toward theoretical coherence.

PERSONALITY

Historically, the study of personality has often served as the vehicle for development of specific systems of twentieth-century psychology. The most obvious example of a personality theory expanding into a system of psychology is psychoanalysis. Further, the close, mutual benefits between a general system and specific implications for personality may be seen in the relationship between Gestalt psychology and field theory, as well as between behavioristic learning theory and behavior modification techniques. Moreover, the phenomenological movement essentially defines psychology itself as the study of the individual personality. Thus personality has offered, and continues to represent, one of those fundamental areas of psychology providing distinctions about human nature among the basic assumptions that compete to guide the approach to psychological inquiry.

Perhaps the most important development in personality research during the contemporary postsystem period of psychology has been the emphasis on the empirical study of personality. The empirical approach, with its requirement of operationally specific variables and tightly controlled observations, reflects the success of neobehaviorism, as this system is most amenable to empirical strategies. The closest approach to behaviorism, of course, concerns the therapeutic application of learning theory in behavior modification (see Chapter 15), wherein personality is literally reduced to learning principles. However, even less extreme approaches conform to the accepted standards of empiricism and are aligned to varying extents with a behavioristic posture.

An empirical approach that has gained wide recognition concerns the orientations collectively called factor theories of personality. One by-product of this perspective on personality is an emphasis on testing and the assessment of personality. Using the statistical procedure of factor analysis to identify common dimensions emerging from many tests, factor theories attempt to identify characteristic traits in personality that not only are of descriptive value but can also be used in the prediction of personality development.

A representative major figure in contemporary factor theories is Hans Jurgen Eysenck (1916–1997). He was born in Germany but spent most of his career at the University of London. Eysenck views personality as composed of a bodily sense and divisions that function as intellectual, affective or emotional, and motivational or striving. In his research, he has identified two fundamental variables of personality: introversion-extraversion and neuroticism. The first is interpreted much as Jung initially proposed, and Eysenck has reported evidence to support the existence of this dimension. Personality highly rated on the neuroticism dimension is characterized by inferior performance in each division of personality, and especially in lowered motivational levels. Eysenck's work is noteworthy because, without accepting a completely behavioristic orientation, he has nonetheless developed an empirically based factor theory that appears to assess quantitatively the dynamic theories of personality.

Factor theories and the study of personality assessment remain major thrusts in contemporary personality research. Various assessments ranging from the measurement of intelligence to the use of projective tests have contributed detailed descriptions of personality. Of interest is the use of tests designed for one purpose and used for another. For example, studies have used the Minnesota Multiphasic Personality Inventory (MMPI) as a general assessment tool for predicting outcomes of varieties of intellectual and performance tasks.

Recent themes in personality research seem influenced by interdisciplinary influences prevalent in other areas of contemporary psychology, particularly cognitive science (see Mischel & Shoda, 1998). Moreover, the framework for personality theory as it influences issues of psychopathology must accommodate the dramatic advances made in neuroscience, from brain imaging studies to neurochemical bases of observable dysfunction. Personality research is presently most active where attempts are made to broaden the empirical basis that was ignored during the period of dominant systems of psychology.

INTERNATIONAL PERSPECTIVES: MODERN ASIAN PSYCHOLOGY

In Chapter 1, alternative intellectual and religious traditions from non-Western cultures were outlined to underscore that, although psychology as an independent discipline emerged from a focused Western perspective on human experience, other cultures had important contributions in dealing with the subject matter of psychology. Although cognizant of the varying traditions, the international character of scientific inquiry is diminishing these differences. That is, in reviewing more recent developments in Asian psychology, we should be mindful that contemporary trends in psychology in Asian countries are quite similar to modern trends in psychology found in Western countries. With the significant governmental investment in science that occurred after World War II in the United States and the former Soviet Union, the two superpowers in politics and economics created spheres of influence in science as well. Both countries opened their universities to students of their respective Asian allies and, by the 1970s, to each other. The models of psychology in both the United States and Russia, although differing in emphases, are founded upon the same rationale as are the European models of psychology. Coupled with the information explosion and increased access to information, an international database of psychology is universally available; access to it depends solely on the availability of the technology needed to retrieve it.

Thus we should not expect contemporary psychology in Asia to be very different from psychology in the United States. Given the survey of the rich traditions of the East in Chapter 1, contemporary Asian psychology as an identifiable discipline is somewhat paradoxical in that it does not rely on indigenous traditions, but rather reflects the Western tradition. Although Asian psychology is not devoid of its native Eastern heritage, that influence is subtle, and the preponderance of Asian psychology follows the same direction as the rest of international psychological inquiry. This review of more recent developments in Asian countries attempts to highlight some of these subtleties.

India

Three centuries of British influence on the educational systems of India, as well as the tradition of sending promising youths from the subcontinent to England for their education, resulted in a systematic imposition of Western thought, including psychology. In 1916 at Calcutta University, N. N. Sangupta became the first professor in the department of psychology. He later went to Lucknow in northern India, where he started a psychology laboratory in 1929. By 1925, Mysore University in southern India also offered a psychology curriculum. The Indian Psychoanalytic Society was founded in 1922, followed 3 years later by the organization of the Indian Psychological Association, which publishes the *Indian Journal of Psychology*. Since the beginning of Indian independence, psychological practitioners have been required to be certified or licensed. India and, especially, China have fewer psychologists in relation to total population than any other country where psychology is recognized or organized.

In recent years there has been renewed interest in the application of yoga in psychology. As mentioned earlier, yoga was a dominant philosophy of ancient India, dating from the Upanishads. Yoga is a system of self-discipline and reflection used to help a person obtain self-knowledge. As taught by the ascetic philosopher Patanjali (ca. 150 B.C.) in his yoga-Sutras, the goal of yoga is to seek independence of the self from all mental context. Achieving this end permits a person to apprehend directly and with certainty the reality and essence of the self. Psychologists have viewed yoga in terms of its implications for behavior therapy, psychophysiological control, and cognitive development.

China

Earlier in the twentieth century, psychology was taught at several universities, and a significant proportion of the professors had been trained in the United States. The first psychology research laboratory was founded at Beijing (Peking) University in 1917, and the first independent psychology department was established at Nanking University. The Chinese Psychological Association was started in 1921 with Zhang Yaoxiang as its first president. Because of their training in the United States, Chinese professors required translations of American textbooks. Also, Chinese psychological journals provided summaries of current American experimental work. At the same time, other behavioral disciplines, especially sociology (Huang, 1995), prospered in China.

When the Japanese invaded five northern provinces of China beginning in 1937, all research activity stopped, not only for the duration of the invasion, but also during the civil war, which lasted until the victory by the Communist forces in 1949. Contact with the West virtually ended then, and early efforts to revitalize psychology were influenced by Soviet advisors who tended to propose models of reflexology (see Chapter 15). The Chinese Academy of Sciences was reopened in 1950, and by 1956 an Institute of Psychological Research was established under the academy's biology section, which perhaps reflected the influence of the Soviet advisors. At any rate, the major role for psychology in the early years of the People's Republic of China was in teacher training, so that teachers' colleges often had the most active departments. In 1955, the Chinese Psychological Association was refounded with Pan Shu, who was Director of the Psychology Institute of the Chinese Academy of Sciences, as its president. During this period the nature of psychology as the study of social relations was expressed in a dialectical approach. This study also attempted to justify a natural science model for those aspects of human experience that are clearly biological.

The Cultural Revolution of the 1960s was a time of great social upheaval, and psychology and psychological research were early targets for attack from the most radical elements. Consciousness as an area of study was condemned as class-determined, and psychological research was denounced as metaphysical and bourgeois. The Chinese Psychological Association was again abolished and its four journals ceased publication. Scientists and professors were often sent to work camps or reeducation centers.

With the normalization of Chinese life in the early 1970s, psychology began to revive. Several national conferences were held in the late 1970s, but psychological study is still largely limited to applications in educational psychology. China's long-range planning to revitalize and upgrade the university system will certainly benefit psychological research and education. Until that is achieved, however, the impact of psychology as a formal disciplinary study is marginal at best.

In summary, psychology in China has been subjected to the turmoil that has characterized all aspects of Chinese society during most of the twentieth century. Little of either the Western models of psychology or the indigenous heritage of Confucian thought has prospered. In fact, it appears that contemporary psychology, in common with other disciplines, is starting a careful process of recovery and re-building in China.

Japan

Historically, both Korea and Japan were recipients of Chinese cultural achievements, but in importing Chinese religion, philosophy, and literature, the Japanese impressed a clearly native imprint as they assimilated selected aspects of China. Japanese legend teaches that its sacred islands were created by the gods who gave birth to the first emperor, who was succeeded in unbroken lineage by the present emperor.

Japanese society in the feudal period (lasting from about the year 1000 until the reassertion of imperial authority at the accession of Emperor Meiji in 1868) was rigidly divided into castes. The emperor was largely a figurehead, and real power lay with the shogun, who emerged usually after a power struggle involving fierce fighting and political intrigue. The shogun and his immediate descendants were able to hold on to power for only relatively brief periods before another challenge would begin the struggle again. The contenders for the shogunate involved lords of various ranks whose wealth came from land, peasants, and slaves. Each lord was supported by a class of warriors, called samurai, who numbered more than a million men at various periods in feudal Japan. They followed a rigid code of behavior based upon loyalty, courage, and great sensitivity to personal dignity and honor. The actual work of the country was performed by classes of artisans, peasants, and merchants. There was also a very large class of slaves, almost 5% of the population, who were criminals or people born into, or sold into, slavery. The workers were heavily taxed and were required to donate given periods of labor to the local lord or the state. As in China, the basic social unit was the family, and the first lessons of loyalty and respect were taught in the family context.

The oldest religion in Japan, Shinto, was based upon ancestor worship and had a rather simple creed of respect for tradition with some nationalistic rites and prayers. Shinto did not provide a formal priesthood, elaborate rituals, or a detailed moral code. Aside from requirements for occasional prayers and pilgrimages, little was demanded of the believer. In 522, Buddhism was imported from China and was remarkably successful, seemingly meeting religious needs not accommodated by Shinto. However, the version of Buddhism that succeeded in Japan did not contain the original Buddhist emphasis on agnostic belief and a rigid moral code. Buddhism in Japan became a positive affirmation of belief in gentle gods. With the observance of duty to ritual and the living of a virtuous life of obedience, those who suffered in this life could expect relief in the anticipation of a better lot in the next incarnation. This version of Buddhism fit well into the kind of social control that characterized the hierarchical structure of Japanese society. This, in turn, bolstered the nationalistic aspirations of the society as well.

Confucianism was introduced to Japan in the sixteenth century and provided the first real impetus to and framework for learning. The great Confucian teacher and essayist Hayashi Razan (1583–1657) was widely recognized as a scholar and won converts from Buddhism and the newly introduced Christianity. Although the first Japanese university was founded in Kyoto in the eighth century, a true commitment to higher learning did not emerge until the seventeenth century with the advent of the Tokugawa Shogunate (1603–1867). In 1630 at Yedo, Hayashi Razan started a school for government administration and Confucian philosophy, which later became the University of Tokyo. Thus, Confucianism succeeded in uplifting the intellectual climate and appreciation of learning in Japan. Kaibara Ekken (1630–1714) was perhaps the most famous Confucian philosopher in late feudal Japan. A renowned teacher who emphasized the unity of the person within the environment, he advocated virtuous living to achieve harmony with nature. Japan soon became a center of Confucian study, with rival schools of interpretation.

In terms of specific applications of Confucian thought, Soho Takuan (1573–1645) viewed the individual as a microcosmic reflection of the universe; thus, personal discipline can lead to control of external events. Baigan Ishida (1685–1744) suggested that the mind is physically based and sensitive to environmental inputs. Almost reminiscent of Locke, Ishida taught that the contents of the mind are environmentally dependent, so that personality change accompanies change in the input. Ho Kamada (1753–1821) suggested a total of 14 emotions and proposed a psychological code based on virtuous living to attain personal happiness. Accordingly, Japanese philosophy of the late feudal period was rich in psychological interpretations, many of which were as sophisticated as any views propounded in Europe during the same time period.

The Japanese borrowed liberally from other cultures, especially the Chinese, but restated these imported positions and views to conform to their social and national character. Despite recurring internal strife, limited natural resources, and calamitous earthquakes, the Japanese built a society that eventually accepted the Confucian emphasis on scholarly study. As Japan rapidly moved from a feudal to an industrial society in the late nineteenth century, it built a high-quality educational system based on a deep commitment to learning.

The transition in Japanese society from a feudal to an industrial organization during the latter part of the nineteenth century was truly remarkable. The successful industrialization of Japan was confirmed by the spectacular victories of the Japanese over the Russians during the Russo-Japanese War of 1904–1905. Japanese industrialization retained some of the traditions of Japanese philosophical teachings. Loyalty, affiliation, and family strength were all woven into the structure of Japanese industrial organization. Very clear attitudes toward productivity and education were inculcated into Japanese social values, providing a unique social psychology on a national scale that has served Japanese society well in this century.

Perhaps because of its smaller, more homogeneous population that accepted the utilitarian and functional value of psychological research, the development of modern psychology has fared much better in Japan than in China. Moreover, Japan's close relationship with the United States, imposed on the Japanese by the American victory in World War II, drew the recovery of scholarly activity close to American research directions. Today Japan ranks as a leader in psychological research, and Japanese journals provide a respected and invaluable part of the database of psychology.

The founding of Western models of psychological inquiry in Japan usually counts Yujiro Motora (1858–1912) as Japan's first experimental psychologist. Born in Osaka, he attended Boston University and then received his doctorate under G. Stanley Hall at Johns Hopkins University in 1888. Upon his return to Japan, he became Japan's first professor of psychology at the University of Tokyo and founded a laboratory there. He continued the research that he had started with Hall on dermal sensitivity, and published three books on general and systematic psychology. Motora's successor at the University of Tokyo was Matataro Matsumoto (1865–1943), who had received his PhD at Yale in 1898. He then went to Leipzig to work with Wundt and returned to Japan in 1900. He founded the psychology department and laboratory at Kyoto University and finished his career at the University of Tokyo. Matsumoto referred to his system of psychology as "psychocinematics," or mental works, which was a type of psychophysiological control wherein he studied experimentally the conditions of mental power over bodily motion. Curiously anticipating later developments in Zen psychology, this work led Matsumoto to an association with the Aeronautical Research Institute of the University of Tokyo, where he worked in human engineering psychology.

Kwanichi Tanaka (1882–1962) was instrumental in the introduction of Watsonian behaviorism into Japan. Tanaka publicized and advocated the type of objective methods proposed by Watson. As in the United States, the rigid formulation of the original version of behaviorism was modified and made more flexible to accommodate the data of consciousness and purpose. For example, Koichi Masuda (1883–1947) proposed an early version of animal cognition with his interpretation of animal behavior in terms of consciousness. Similarly, Ryo Kuroda (1890–1947) argued that behavior and consciousness are two aspects of the same experience and are complementary rather than contradictory.

Gestalt psychology was introduced to Japan by Kanae Sakuma (1888–1970), who received his initial education in Japan and then studied in Berlin with Köhler and Lewin. Applying Gestalt principles to the development of language, Sakuma was one of the first psycholinguists. Similarly, after studying in Berlin in 1925 and 1926, Hiroshi Hayami introduced the phenomenological tradition of Husserl as providing more direct access to experience.

Perhaps clinical applications best exemplify the attempt to integrate Eastern and Western traditions in psychotherapy pioneered in Japan. Shoma Morita (1874–1938) argued that the reaction and undue attention to neurotic behavior often exaggerate the problem and result in a vicious cycle. Morita offered a therapeutic alternative that borrowed from a distant version of Buddhism termed Zen Buddhism (Barrett, 1956). Like other Buddhist traditions, Zen is antirationalistic, but it seeks knowledge solely by intuition and interpretation rather than by reliance on traditional Buddhist writings. The goal of Morita's theory was to seek harmony with the universe, not to fight or resist the universe, as taught in Western philosophy. Accordingly, the person simply accepts his or her condition in an attempt to reduce the anxiety associated with undue attention to the condition. Morita employed a four-stage procedure beginning with the patient's yielding to the anxiety and ending with the patient's preparing to return to everyday existence.

This model was developed more fully in the Zen psychology of Koji Sato (1905–1971), a professor of psychology at Kyoto University. Originally influenced by Gestalt psychology, Sato later turned to psychoanalysis and clinical psychology. During the 1950s, he became interested in Morita's work and spent the remainder of his career extending Zen teachings to psychotherapy. Essentially, meditative Zen techniques use physical adaptations in posture and breathing to achieve mental serenity and clarity through the realization of the harmony and integration of the person and the universe. Zen techniques are methods of psychophysiological control that feed back on the mental state to produce an internal sense of well-being. Sato and his teachings in Zen psychology were recognized by Western therapists, such as Karen Horney and Carl Rogers. Zen was a major vehicle in introducing Western psychologists to Eastern thought.

Japanese psychology, in contrast to Chinese, has enjoyed widespread acceptance and prosperity in both Japan and the international community. It is a credit to the industry of Japanese scholars that they were able to recuperate from the devastation and losses of war and the subsequent restructuring of Japan. Interestingly, the relationship with American psychology that predated World War II may have facilitated the rebuilding of Japanese psychology along eclectic lines, a theme common to the traditions of both Japan and the United States.

It appears that contemporary psychology has moved into a phase that characteristically rejects the systems period. Such a development is surely beneficial to the extent that it justifies psychology as a truly open-ended science, without rigid, preconceived assumptions and biases. However, this development must also be qualified, because in rejecting the systems, psychology has substituted a definition of science that places faith in empiricism, especially in the experimental method. Psychology in this sense is aligned with the natural science model of inquiry. Although adherence to this model varies from area to area within the discipline, a general consensus that the natural science model is the optimal approach represents in itself a set of assumptions about the nature of human activity.

CHAPTER SUMMARY

Current trends within psychology are reflected by representative developments in the areas of learning, motivation and memory, perception, development, social psychology, and personality. In addition, from the end of the nineteenth century, when contact with the West became routine, psychology enjoyed relative success in Asia. Indeed, we can point to Japan as a contemporary leader in psychological inquiry in all areas, rivaling the productivity of the United States and Europe. In all areas we see a clear shift away from adherence to the systems of psychology and toward a greater reliance on the data collection of an empirical approach to psychological issues. In general, psychology is guided by a direction best described as eclectic. Although models integrating the diversity of data have emerged, especially in the areas of learning and developmental psychology, the remaining areas of contemporary psychology remain at an empirical level with no universally accepted theoretical views apparent. Such a state is beneficial because empiricism provides psychology with a framework of open-ended study. However, empiricism, especially when articulated as the experimental method, also carries assumptions that ultimately commit psychology to a natural science approach, to the exclusion of other methods of inquiry.

BIBLIOGRAPHY

COHEN, S., & HERBERT, T. B. (1996). Health psychology: Psychological factors and physical disease from the perspective of human psychoneuroimmunology. *Annual Review of Psychology, 47,* 113–142.

MILLER, N. E. (1983). Behavioral medicine: Symbiosis between laboratory and clinic. *Annual Review of Psychology, 34,* 1–31.

Learning, Motivation, and Memory

ANOKHIN, K. V., & ROSE, S. P. R. (1991). Learning-induced increase of immediate early gene messenger RNA in the chick forebrain. *European Journal of Neuroscience, 3,* 162–167.

BINDRA, D. (1972). A unified account of classical conditioning and operant training. In A. H. Black & W. F. Prokasy (Eds.), *Classical conditioning II: Current research and theory.* New York: Appleton-Century-Crofts, 453–481.

BINDRA, D. (1974). A motivational view of learning, performance, and behavior modification. *Psychological Review, 81,* 199–213.

BOLLES, R. C. (1967). *A theory of motivation.* New York: Harper & Row.

BOLLES, R. C. (1970). Species-specific defense reactions and avoidance learning. *Psychological Review, 77,* 32–48.

BREHM, J. W., & SELF, E. A. (1989). The intensity of motivation. *Annual Review of Psychology, 40,* 109–131.

BRUCE, D. (1985). On the origin of the term "neuropsychology." *Neuropsychologia, 23,* 813–814.

CHURCH, R. M. (1978). The internal clock. In S. H. Hulse, H. Fowley, & W. K. Honig (Eds.), *Cognitive processes in animal behavior.* Hillsdale, NJ: Erlbaum.

DAVIS, H. R., & SQUIRE, L. R. (1984). Protein synthesis and memory: A review. *Psychological Bulletin, 96,* 518–559.

DUNN, A. J. (1980). Neurochemistry of learning and memory: An evaluation of recent data. *Annual Review of Psychology, 31,* 343–390.

EPSTEIN, R. (1987). Comparative psychology as the praxist views it. *Journal of Comparative Psychology, 101,* 249–253.

EPSTEIN, R., LANZA, R. P., & SKINNER, B. F. (1981). Self-awareness in the pigeon. *Science, 212,* 695–696.

EVERITT, B. J., & ROBBINS, T. W. (1997). Central cholinergic systems and cognition. *Annual Review of Psychology, 48,* 649–684.

GAZZANIGA, M. S. (1967). The split brain in man. *Scientific American, 217,* 24–29.

GLUCK, M. A., & MYERS, C. E. (1997). Psychobiological models of hippocampal function in learning and memory. *Annual Review of Psychology, 48,* 481–514.

HEARST, E., & PETERSON, G. B. (1973). Transfer of conditioned excitation and inhibition from one operant response to another. *Journal of Experimental Psychology, 99,* 360–368.

HILLYARD, S. A., & KUTAS, M. (1983). Electrophysiology of cognitive processes. *Annual Review of Psychology, 34,* 33–61.

HUNT, E. (1989). Cognitive science: Definition, status, and questions. *Annual Review of Psychology, 40,* 603–629.

KOLB, B., & WHISHAW, I. Q. (1998). Brain plasticity and behavior. *Annual Review of Psychology, 49,* 43–64.

KORIAT, A., GOLDSMITH, M., & PANSKY, A. (2000). Toward a psychology of memory accuracy. *Annual Review of Psychology, 51,* 481–537.

MARTINEZ, J. L., & DERRICK, B. E. (1996). Long-term potentiation and learning. *Annual Review of Psychology, 47,* 173–203.

MATTHIES, H. (1989). Neurobiological aspects of learning and memory. *Annual Review of Psychology, 40,* 381–404.

OVERMIER, J. B., & BULL, J. A. (1970). Influences of appetitive Pavlovian conditioning upon avoidance behavior. In J. H. Reynierse (Ed.), *Current issues in animal learning: A colloquium.* Lincoln: University of Nebraska Press, 117–141.

RESCORLA, R. A. (1988). Behavioral studies of Pavlovian conditioning. *Annual Review of Neuroscience, 11,* 329–352.

RESCORLA, R. A., & SOLOMON, R. L. (1967). Two-process learning theory: Relationships between Pavlovian conditioning and instrumental learning. *Psychological Review, 74,* 151–182.

RESCORLA, R. A., & WAGNER, A. R. (1972). A theory of Pavlovian conditioning: Variations in the effectiveness of reinforcement and nonreinforcement. In A. H. Black & W. F. Prokasy (Eds.), *Classical conditioning II: Current research and theory.* New York: Appleton-Century-Crofts, 64–89.

ROITBLAT, J. L., & VON FERSEN, L. (1992). Comparative cognition: Representations and processes in learning and memory. *Annual Review of Psychology, 43,* 671–710.

ROLLS, E. T. (2000). Memory systems in the brain. *Annual Review of Psychology, 51,* 599–630.

ROSENZWEIG, M. (1996). Aspects of the search for neural mechanisms of memory. *Annual Review of Psychology, 47,* 1–32.

SELIGMAN, M. E. P. (1970). On the generality of the laws of learning. *Psychological Review, 77,* 406–418.

SELIGMAN, M. E. P., & HAGER, J. L. (Eds.) (1972). *Biological boundaries of learning.* Englewood Cliffs, NJ: Prentice Hall.

STERNBERG, R. J., & LUBART, R. I. (1996). Investing in creativity. *American Psychologist, 51*, 677–688.

WENZLAFF, R. M., & WEGNER, D. M. (2000). Thought suppression. *Annual Review of Psychology, 51*, 59–91.

WHITE, N. M., & MILNER, P. M. (1992). The psychobiology of reinforcers. *Annual Review of Psychology, 43*, 443–471.

WISE, R. A., & ROMPRE, P. P. (1989). Brain dopamine and reward. *Annual Review of Psychology, 40*, 191–225.

Perception

BARTENTHAL, B. I. (1996). Origins and early development of perception, action, and representation. *Annual Review of Psychology, 47*, 431–459.

DEVALOIS, R. L., & DEVALOIS, K. K. (1980). Spatial perception. *Annual Review of Psychology, 31*, 309–341.

EGETH, H. E., & YANTIS, S. (1997). Visual attention: Control, representation, and time course. *Annual Review of Psychology, 48*, 269–297.

FENG, A. S., & RATNAM, R. (2000). Neural basis of hearing in real-world situations. *Annual Review of Psychology, 51*, 699–725.

GIBSON, J. J. (1970). *The ecological approach to visual perception.* Boston: Houghton Mifflin.

HABER, R. N. (1978). Visual perception. *Annual Review of Psychology, 29*, 31–59.

HERSH, I. J., & WATSON, C. S. (1996). Auditory psychophysics and perception. *Annual Review of Psychology, 47*, 461–484.

JOHANSSON, G., VON HOFSTEN, C., & JANSSON, G. (1980). Event perception. *Annual Review of Psychology, 31*, 27–63.

KINCHLA, R. A. (1992). Attention. *Annual Review of Psychology, 43*, 742–71.

PETTIGREW, J. D., NIKARA, T., & BISHOP, P. O. (1968). Binocular interaction on single units in cat striate cortex: Simultaneous stimulation by single moving slit with receptive fields in correspondence. *Experimental Brain Research, 6*, 391–410.

Development

BALTES, P. B., REESE, H. W., & LIPSITT, L. P. (1980). Life-span developmental psychology. *Annual Review of Psychology, 31*, 65–110.

BALTES, P. B., STAUDINGER, U. M., & LINDENBERGER, U. (1999). Lifespan psychology: theory and application to intellectual functioning. *Annual Review of Psychology, 50*, 471–507.

BIRREN, J. E. (1983). Psychology of adult development and aging. *Annual Review of Psychology, 34*, 543–575.

BIRREN, J. E., & FISHER, L. M. (1995). Aging and speed of behavior: Possible consequences for psychological functioning. *Annual Review of Psychology, 46*, 329–353.

BRAINERD, C. J. (1996). Piaget: A centennial celebration. *Psychological Science, 7*, 191–195.

BRIM, O. G., & KAGAN, J. (1980). Constancy and change: A view of the issues. In O. G. Brim & J. Kagan (Eds.), *Constancy and change in human development*. Cambridge: Harvard University Press, 1–25.

CAIRNS, L. B., & VALSINER, J. (1984). Child psychology. *Annual Review of Psychology, 35,* 553–577.

CARPENTER, P. A., MEYAKE, A., & JUST, M. A. (1995). Language comprehension: Sentence and discourse processing. *Annual Review of Psychology, 46,* 91–120.

DEESE, J. (1970). *Psycholinguistics*. Boston: Allyn & Bacon.

DENNIS, M. (1985). William Preyer (1841–1897) and his neuropsychology of language of acquisition. *Developmental Neuropsychology, 1,* 287–315.

ELLIS, H. C. (1978). *Fundamentals of human learning, memory and cognition* (2nd ed.) Dubuque, IA: William C. Brown.

FLAVELL, J. H. (1996). Piaget's legacy. *Psychological Science, 7,* 200–203.

FOSS, D. J. (1988). Experimental psycholinguistics. *Annual Review of Psychology, 39,* 301–348.

GLUCKSBERG, S., & DANKS, J. (1975). *Experimental psycholinguistics*. Hillsdale, NJ: Erlbaum.

HONZIK, M. (1984). Life-span development. *Annual Review of Psychology, 35,* 309–331.

JARVIK, L. F. (1975). Thoughts on the psychology of aging. *American Psychologist, 30,* 576–583.

MCKOON, G., & RATCLIFF, R. (1998). Memory-based language processing: Psycholinguistic research in the 1990s. *Annual Review of Psychology, 49,* 25–42.

OSGOOD, C. E., SUCI, C. J., & TANNENBAUM, P. H. (1957). *The measurement of meaning*. Urbana, IL: University of Illinois Press.

PHILLIPS, J. L. (1975). *The origins of intellect: Piaget's theory* (2nd ed.). San Francisco: W. H. Freeman.

PIAGET, J. (1926). *The language and thought of the child*. London: Routledge.

PIAGET, J. (1958). *The growth of logical thinking from childhood to adolescence*. London: Routledge.

PIAGET, J., & INHELDER, B. (1969). T*he psychology of the child*. London: Routledge and Kegan Paul.

PREMACK, D. (1983). Animal cognition. *Annual Review of Psychology, 34,* 351–362.

SCHULZ, R., & HECKHAUSEN, J. (1996). A life span model of successful aging. *American Psychologist, 51,* 702–714.

SNYDER, S. H. (1984). Neurosciences: An integrative discipline. *Science, 225,* 1255–1257.

WELLMAN, H. M., & GELMAN, S. A. (1992). Cognitive development: Foundational theories of core domains. *Annual Review of Psychology, 43,* 337–375.

Social Psychology

ALLPORT, F. H. (1924). *Social psychology*. Boston: Houghton Mifflin.

BRODY, N. (1980). Social motivation. *Annual Review of Psychology, 31,* 143–168.

DAWES, R. M. (1980). Social dilemmas. *Annual Review of Psychology, 31,* 169–193.

HARVEY, S. H., & WEARY, G. (1984). Current issues in attribution theory and research. *Annual Review of Psychology, 35,* 427–459.

HARRIS BOND, M., & SMITH, P. B. (1996). Cross-cultural social and organizational psychology. *Annual Review of Psychology, 47,* 205–235.

KENNY, D. (1996). The design and analyses of social-interactive research. *Annual Review of Psychology, 47,* 59–86.

MEAD, M. (1949). *Male and female: A study of sexes in a changing world.* New York: Morrow.

MILGRAM, S. (1963). Behavioral study of obedience. *Journal of Abnormal and Social Psychology, 67,* 371–378.

PETTIGREW, T. F., & CAMPBELL, E. Q. (1960). Faubus and segregation: An analysis of Arkansas voting. *Public Opinion Quarterly, 24,* 436–447.

SCHLENKER, B. R., & WEIGOLD, M. F. (1992). Interpersonal processes involving impression regulation and management. *Annual Review of Psychology, 43,* 133–168.

SNYDER, M., & STUKAS, A. A. (1999). Interpersonal processes: The interplay of cognitive, motivational, and behavioral activities in social interaction. *Annual Review of Psychology, 50,* 273–303.

Personality

EYSENCK, H. J. (1953). *The structure of human personality.* New York: John Wiley.

MISCHEL, W., & SHODA, Y. (1998). Reconciling processing dynamics and personality dispositions. *Annual Review of Psychology, 49,* 229–258.

International Perspectives

BARRETT, W. (1956). *Zen Buddhism: Selected writings of D. T. Suzuki.* Garden City, NY: Doubleday.

BROWN, L. B. (1981). *Psychology in contemporary China.* Oxford: Pergamon.

CHIN, R., & CHIN, A. L. S. (1975). *Psychological research in Communist China.* New Haven: Yale University Press.

COLEMAN, D. (1981). Buddhist and western psychology: Some commonalities and differences. *Journal of Transpersonal Psychology, 13,* 125–136.

HUANG, SU-J. (1994). Max Weber's *The religion of China*: An interpretation. *Journal of the History of the Behavioral Sciences, 30,* 2–18.

MARX, M. H., & HILLIX, W. A. (1973). *Systems and theories in psychology,* 2nd ed. New York: McGraw-Hill.

MURPHY, G., & MURPHY, L. B. (1968). *Asian psychology.* New York: Basic Books.

NAKAYAMA, S., & SIVIN, N. (Eds.) (1973). *Chinese science: Exploration of an ancient tradition.* Cambridge, MA.: MIT Press.

NEEDHAM, J. (1970). *Clerks and craftsmen in China and the West.* Cambridge, U.K.: Cambridge University Press.

ORLEANS, L. A. (Ed.) (1980). *Science in contemporary China.* Stanford, CA: Stanford University Press.

PETZOLD, M. (1984). The history of Chinese psychology. *History of Psychology Newsletter, 16,* 23–31.

ROSENZWEIG, M. R. (1984). U.S. psychology and world psychology. *American Psychologist, 39,* 877–884.

❉ 18 ❉

Epilogue

The Systems of Psychology: An Integration
    The Mind: Dualistic Activity versus Monistic Passivity
    Sources of Knowledge: Self-Generative versus Sensory
    The Basis of Psychology: Mentalism versus Materialism
    The Acquisition of Knowledge: Internal Mediation
        versus External Association
The Problem of Science
Conclusions
Chapter Summary

The subject of this book has been the vast development of intellectual thought about the nature of humanity, a topic first systematically explored by the Greeks and subsequently elaborated through a gradual but steady focus on psychology as an empirical discipline. For the most part, the development of psychological inquiry since Greek antiquity has been intimately involved with the history of philosophy. Indeed, the central psychological issues debated in the nineteenth century concerned the philosophical basis of psychological study. The assumptions underlying the definition of psychology as well as the proper methodological approach of psychological inquiry are essentially philosophical matters. They address fundamental questions about the nature of people, how they know their environment, how they think, and how they interact with each other. All formulations of psychology ultimately rest on the answers to these questions.

This book opened with a statement recognizing the diversity of contemporary psychology. Psychologists work in many different applied settings, performing in a variety of roles. Even within the halls of academia, contemporary psychology is somewhat difficult to identify. Psychological research and teaching take place in departments of psychobiology, cognitive science, organizational management, and social relations. Psychology appears to be evolving toward greater diversification rather than a cohesive unity. The survey in Chapter 17 of contemporary trends in the traditional research areas of psychology may reflect a consensus of approaches to research issues in specific areas, but it does not indicate agreement about psychology as a unified discipline. Rather, the only major point of agreement appears to be a general consensus that contemporary psychology is an empirical discipline.

At the very least, the systems of psychology developed in the twentieth century offer a reasonable description of how psychology attained its diversity. The systems phase of psychology's development was a necessary part of psychology's evolution. It demonstrated the difficulty of defining psychology as a science and of placing psychology within science. Because the empirical expression of science forms the major commonality among the contemporary areas of psychological inquiry, it is appropriate to update the story of psychology's evolution in Western thought by examining the relationship between psychology and science. However, before addressing that issue, we shall compare the systems of psychology using some basic philosophical assumptions.

THE SYSTEMS OF PSYCHOLOGY: AN INTEGRATION

It is curious that the major twentieth-century systems of American psychology were preceded and succeeded by periods best described as functional. Both the earlier functional period and contemporary neofunctionalism take an eclectic attitude toward specific issues of study. Just as the Greek Sophists abandoned the search for a superordinate framework to guide psychological inquiry and instead sought specific, limited models to contain their utilitarian speculation, both functional periods of twentieth-century psychology have eschewed theory building. During the earlier functional period, the avoidance of systematic overviews for psychology was a reaction to the sterility of the orthodox structural psychology of Wundt and Titchener. The reorientation away from theory and toward eclectic issues and research in contemporary neofunctionalism appears to be a reaction to the futility of the intervening systems phase of twentieth-century psychology. Although the earlier functionalism provided a transition to the systems phase, and to behaviorism in particular, it is premature to ascribe a similar, transitional role to contemporary neofunctionalism. It is certainly tempting to draw a parallel between the two functional periods and speculate that the forces of the *Zeitgeist* are building up to a new phase for psychology, for which the present neofunctionalism is an entrée. However, the historian is on dangerous footing when interpreting the present, so the parallel must remain questionable and tentative.

It is the intervening movement between the two functional periods that concerns us here. Specifically, the evaluative dimensions for considering the mind and its activity, used in Chapter 9 to compare the major traditions in philosophy, are employed below to compare and contrast Gestalt psychology, psychoanalysis, behaviorism, and the third force movement. Before proceeding, two qualifications are in order. The first reiterates what was stated in Chapter 9—namely, that the selection of the evaluative dimensions is arbitrary. Other important dimensions of comparison could be considered and would be informative. The four dimensions offered in Chapter 9 and below represent the kinds of comparisons that may provide some closure on the diversity of the systems of psychology. The second qualification is the reminder that there was diversity within the systems themselves. There was, for example, a Gestalt overview and a general psychoanalytic theory, but within each system, as we have seen, different scholars offered variants of the general scheme. Similarly, behaviorism as a system evolved from a rigid formulation to a more open acceptance of various interpretations, so that Watson's behaviorism was quite different from Tolman's behaviorism. Perhaps most diverse was the third force movement, with its contributors coming from very different backgrounds, including philosophy, science, and literature.

The Mind: Dualistic Activity versus Monistic Passivity

This dimension of evaluation essentially contrasts mind–body dualism with monism. Specifically, a dualistic position holds that the mind is a necessary agent of psychological processes, and the mind functions as an active determinant of psychological outcomes. Mental activity is not synonymous with bodily functions, so that the mind is not reducible to the physical bases and mechanisms of the body. Conversely, materialistic monism holds that all psychological processes are ultimately reducible to bodily or physical processes; therefore, there is no need to speculate about the existence of other agents of psychological activity. The single living entity of the body fully accounts for human experience.

Perhaps the most striking and explicit exponent of dualism among the systems of psychology is psychoanalysis. According to the psychoanalytic position, the major determinant of psychological activity is the largely unconscious forces, or psychic energies, of a characteristic sexual and aggressive nature. For psychoanalysis, the goal of personality is to seek equilibrium and harmony among the forces emanating from the unconscious. The reliance on the mental agency of unconscious personality relegates the physical aspects of the person to a secondary role. Rather, overt behavior and even conscious mental processes have symbolic value beyond their actual representations. The contents of observable behavior and consciousness are manifestations of unconscious forces, so that the bodily functions of the individual assume a reactive stance to the energy forces of unconscious personality. Thus in the psychoanalytic system there is not only an implicit acceptance of a dualistic position but also, within the dualism, an emphasis on the mental, or psychic, aspect over the physical.

Although not as well articulated as the dynamics of the psychoanalytic position, there is also a consensus for an implied dualism among the various writers of the third force movement. In particular, those points of agreement, focusing on the critical nature of decisions, the personal responsibility for individual decisions, the recognition of individual dignity and integrity, and the nurturing of personal freedom for psychological growth, assume the existence of a dynamic mental agency that is neither synonymous with nor reducible to the physical aspect of the body. The extent of the dualism varies within the third force movement with different writers. Certainly, the phenomenological method was developed to study precisely the dynamics of mental acts without the reductionistic limitations of the analytic methods of the physical sciences, which would, if imposed, destroy the mental acts. Rather, the very need for phenomenology rests on the acceptance of a separate, mental kind of activity that is different from physical activity.

The views of the Gestalt movement fall between a completely dualistic position and a monistic assumption. The early formulations of the Gestalt writers, based on their research on perceptual processes, tried to avoid dualistic implications. When possible, they attempted to rely on explanations of phenomena through acquired experiences. Their principle of isomorphism was invoked to provide a physical basis of perceptual phenomena. However, the inadequacies of isomorphism as a physiological explanation and the extension of Gestalt principles to field theory together moved Gestalt psychology closer to an admittedly dualistic position.

Behaviorism, of course, is the major proponent of monism, a single, physically based psychological process. The most extreme positions on monism within behaviorism were the radical view of Watson and the thorough physiological reductionism of Pavlovian reflexology. The readmission of limited dualistic views, through proposals for mental constructs, provided the major factor in the evolution of behaviorism after Watson and Pavlov. Moreover, the diversified views of contemporary behaviorism, ranging from neurophysiological to cognitive types of interpretations, differ in their acceptance of mental activity that is not directly and immediately reducible to underlying physical causes.

The dimension of dualism-monism helps to discriminate among the four major systems. For psychology, the primary implication for acceptance of one or the other assumption lies in the nature of the psychological event that is studied. A dualistic position tends to minimize the significance of observable behavior and conscious thought processes, focusing instead on the inner dynamics of mental activity. Conversely, the monistic position elevates observable, physical behavior as the primary data of psychology. Interestingly, formal psychological study has produced more extreme positions along this dimension in the last hundred years than in all the previous periods. In the philosophical traditions up to the nineteenth century, mental activity, expressed in the German tradition originating with Leibniz, could be contrasted with mental passivity, consistent with the Lockean empirical tradition. The twentieth-century systems produced the behavioral tenet that specifically denied the mind's role in psychology. Accordingly, the dimension of mental activity versus passivity sharply contrasts dualism and monism. The latter position requires a rejection of any need for the concept of the mind, a view that reverts to the position of French sensationalistic philosophy.

Sources of Knowledge: Self-Generative versus Sensory

Another dimension of evaluation concerns the ways in which people acquire knowledge of themselves and their environment. Among the philosophical movements of pre-nineteenth-century psychological thought, this dimension essentially contrasted the empirical position of sensory dependence with the rational thesis of self-generated knowledge—that is, knowledge as the product of dynamic activity. In the twentieth-century systems of psychology, the empirical attitude continued to dominate one side of the dimension, and the notion of internal knowledge was extended.

It was primarily within psychoanalysis that the nature of internally generated knowledge was elaborated beyond the confines of the rationalism derived from Kant and the German tradition. Freud's initial formulation of psychoanalysis showed an appreciation of the writings on unconscious strivings of the will by such nineteenth-century German philosophers as Schopenhauer and von Hartmann. Freud's notion of unconscious motivation, based on psychic energy, added a new interpretation and qualification to the meaning of self-generated knowledge. Specifically, the dynamics of the unconscious are largely unknown to the individual, yet each person's conscious thoughts and other experiences (such as dreams) are structured by unconscious energy forces. Accordingly, the definition of knowledge in Freudian psychoanalysis must be qualified—that is, mental activity is self-generated but largely unknown to the individual and certainly not rational. This qualification of self-generated knowledge was further expanded in Jung's views. According to Jung, we inherit specific conceptual frameworks, stereotypes, and mental structures through the personality construct of archetypes. Again, this "knowledge" is not rational, nor is it understood by the individual, yet such thoughts are present in personality and are self-generated, according to Jung.

Within the third force movement there is a clear reliance on self-generated knowledge. Indeed, one major commonality among the varied contributors to this movement is the insistence on inner, reflective, and deliberate mediation of thought processes as the unique human experience. While acknowledging the person's relationship with the environment and accompanying sensory sources of knowledge, the existential–phenomenological position clearly defines the person–environment relationship as a dynamic interaction. Accordingly, the individual's role in interactions with the environment is not reactive or passive, but rather active and constantly seeking to exert control over the environment so that, in turn, personal actions may be self-governed. Within the positions of the third force movement subjective knowledge is a product of individuals acting on environmental sources of knowledge, and the personalized contribution to the relationship with sensory knowledge is the higher, uniquely human level of knowing.

Perhaps because of its general consistency in appreciating the notion of psychological phenomena, the Gestalt movement shared some of the views on the sources of knowledge advocated within the third force positions. The Gestalt movement relied on the interaction between the perceiving individual and the sensory input of environmental stimuli. Accordingly, the Gestalt principles may be interpreted as a compromise between an empirical basis of sensory knowledge and an active mediation that results in the self-generation of knowledge. The Gestalt movement described the person as predisposed to receive sensory information in characteristic ways. As stated earlier, the major difficulty with this compromise between sensory dependence and inner determination of knowledge lies with the precise manner of accounting for how the interaction is achieved—that is, whether a mental agency or an entirely physical explanation is appropriate. As the Gestalt principles were extended beyond sensory and perceptual issues to the field theory of personality, the basis of knowledge became increasingly obscured by the implicit dependence of the individual on interactions with the environment. More reliance was placed on individual initiative to account for field dynamism.

The empirical position of exclusive dependence on sensory experience as the source of knowledge is the foundation of behaviorism. The basic premise of both the Watsonian formulation and Pavlovian reflexology placed the organism within a radical empirical view of acquiring all knowledge through experience with environmental events. Although this view still finds acceptance among behaviorists who seek to find the mechanisms of learning processes in neurophysiological explanations, the evolution of behaviorism has produced moderation of extreme environmental determinism as well. The initial questioning of the extreme behavioristic position occurred in response to the inadequacies of Thorndike's explanation of reinforcement through his law of effect. Further, reluctance to discard all possibility of subjective mediation led Tolman and later psychologists to offer a cognitive interpretation of behavior, a movement that has a counterpart in recent Russian views, such as Luria's study of language. However, despite the moderation of extreme environmental determinism, behavioristic psychology placed the primary source of knowledge in the acquisition of environmental events.

Sources of knowledge serve as a viable comparative tool because all four major systems differ from one another along this dimension. Moreover, the issue of empiricism as the dominant expression of scientific inquiry comes into clear focus under the scrutiny of this dimension. Specifically, the acceptance of knowledge derived from sources other than the environment makes empiricism untenable.

The Basis of Psychology: Mentalism versus Materialism

A direct implication of the dimension contrasting dualistic and monistic conceptions of the individual is the issue of the physical, materialistic basis versus the psychic, mentalistic basis of psychological processes. The acceptance of either assumption involves perhaps the most basic decision about the definition of psychology. We have seen representatives of both positions among the ancient Greek scholars. The Ionian physicists and the later biologists searched for the basic physical substance responsible for life. Conversely, the teachings of Socrates, Plato, and Aristotle concluded the necessity of some nonphysical, spiritual, life-giving entity that transcends the physical nature of the body and the environment. The Greek notion of the soul was Christianized through the efforts of Saint Augustine and, later, the Scholastic philosophers. This interpretation prevailed through the beginnings of science during the Renaissance. Indeed, Descartes defined psychology as the study of the mind in dualistic contrast to the study of physiology. The philosophical traditions that developed after Descartes essentially differed in their position on mentalism versus physicalism. The German tradition accepted the psychic character of an active entity independent of bodily processes; the French tradition generally advocated the opposite position and relegated all psychological and physiological processes to the materialism of the body. The British empirical tradition attempted to forge a position between these extremes by acknowledging the existence of the mind but ascribing to it the passive role of reacting to environmental input. Although various British empiricist scholars held different views of the exact extent of mental activity–passivity, the empirical view prior to the nineteenth century at least nominally accepted the dualistic assumption.

Mentalism dominated in the systems of psychoanalysis and the third force movement. Both positions were logical descendants of the German philosophical tradition of mental activity, and the psychology of both movements is not reducible to physical processes or mechanisms. The Gestalt movement is also grounded in dualism and mentalism. Given the dynamics of person–environment interactions, a mentalistic assumption underlies Gestalt principles. Although Gestalt psychology is not as dependent on mental activity as psychoanalysis or the third force movement, the empiricistic emphasis of the Gestalt principles alone is not sufficient to account for the dynamics of person–environment interactions.

The most materialistic system is behaviorism. Watson's views were an extension of traditional British empiricism, carrying the logic of empiricism to a final conclusion: If the mind is passive and reactive, and knowledge is derived from the sense information originating in the environment, then there is no need for the construct of mind in psychology. Mentalism interferes with the making of an objective psychology. However, when later behaviorists joined Watson's empiricism to Pavlovian reflexology, the implicit physical assumptions of the latter position transformed empiricism within psychology to materialistic empiricism. That union of empiricism and materialism marked a critical juncture for psychology and a triumph for the natural science approach. By removing mentalism from psychology, despite later efforts by the neobehaviorists to rescue mental constructs, behaviorism took on an attraction as an objective science. Herein lies the justification for infrahuman experimentation; without mentalism, the differences among species of animals is one of complexity, not of quality.

The Acquisition of Knowledge: Internal Mediation versus External Association

A final dimension of evaluation concerns the manner of acquiring knowledge. Intimately related to the other three dimensions, assumptions about the acquisition of knowledge may be contrasted as the dynamics of mental organization or the mechanics of associations. The systems of psychoanalysis, the third force movement, and Gestalt psychology depend on various expressions of inner activity, ranging from the innate forces and concepts of psychoanalysis, to the internal characteristics of growth and responsible decisions of the third force movement, to the inner organization of mental activity of Gestalt psychology. In all three systems the acquisition of knowledge is influenced and structured according to forces or patterns arising from within the individual. In contrast, behaviorism relies on mechanical principles of association based on the contingencies of environmental events to explain the acquisition of knowledge.

To summarize briefly, it is interesting that these representative dimensions of critical evaluation in psychology, which successfully discriminated among the pre-nineteenth-century philosophical views, also served as an effective discriminative tool for the twentieth-century systems of psychology. This observation confirms that the critical issues of psychology were not resolved during the systems phase. Indeed, it may be suggested that the systems drew sharper contrasts, because the formal application of diverse assumptions to explicit systems of psychology produced even greater fragmentation within psychology in general. As both the specific descriptions of the systems and the eclectic flavor of contemporary neofunctionalism indicate, the major point of agreement is the acceptance of some version of empiricism—which takes us to the relationship between science and psychology.

THE PROBLEM OF SCIENCE

There was a striking parallel between psychology's development as an independent discipline and the development of empirical science itself, dating back to the origins of modern psychology during the Renaissance. By the nineteenth century, empiricism had demonstrated its benefits in the physical sciences by successfully generating new knowledge with utilitarian applications. The carefully controlled methods of empirical investigation justified a faith in scientific study to improve society and improve the quality of life. Accordingly, the methods of biology, chemistry, and physics offered the optimal model for psychology to emulate. Copleston (1956) has argued that the rise of empirical science is one of the major intellectual accomplishments of the post-Renaissance world, and this period is remarkable because of the enormous advances in empirical discoveries. Moreover, the empirical sciences nurtured the development of the applied sciences, or technologies, with beneficial consequences for our industrialized civilization.

In contrast, the development of organized inquiry outside of empirical science has not prospered as much. Speculative study largely deteriorated to personal accounts. Without empirical verification, it is difficult to offer convincing arguments and win acceptance. For example, within the twentieth-century systems of psychology, the psychoanalytic movement underwent a marked fragmentation brought about by the contributions of divergent scholars who did not conform to any common form of rigorous empiricism. Similarly, despite the development of the phenomenological method, the characteristic diversity among writers of the third force movement has made it difficult to find specific points of universal agreement. This situation offers further support of empiricism, to the point where empiricism and science are generally equated. As a result, empiricism has become the dominant perspective of contemporary psychology, gaining almost universal acceptance. There seems to be widespread agreement that scientific advances are optimally produced and conveyed under the procedures of empirical verification; other forms of inquiry do not appear to offer the compelling attraction of empiricism.

When the twentieth-century systems were contrasted along the dimension of mentalism versus materialism, one of the important developments in modern behaviorism was seen to be the link between empiricism and materialism, brought about through the union of Watson's formulations and Pavlov's reflexology. Materialistic empiricism was, in turn, reinforced by the logical positivism of the Vienna Circle (Chapter 15), which provided a philosophy of science to bolster an objective, behavioral psychology. By relying on the semantics of logical positivism, behaviorism was able to define its subject matter operationally and presumably discard, once and for all, the metaphysics of mentalism.

In evaluating the union of materialistic empiricism, it is important to consider the possibility of nonmaterialistic empiricism. Examining the works of John Locke, the founder of modern empiricism in psychology, we should recall that Locke did not discard mentalistic activities. Acknowledging the dependency on sensory input, he nevertheless recognized two ways of knowing: associations and reflection. The latter process consists of the mental activity of compounding ideas, which represents a mental function. Subsequent refinements within the British empirical tradition, such as the proposal for mental induction by John Stuart Mill, served to separate empiricism and materialism.

This survey of the twentieth-century systems of psychology dramatically underscores one of the major implications of materialistic empiricism: Behaviorism is clearly set apart from the other formulations of psychology. Expressed succinctly, behaviorism, with its reliance on materialistic empiricism, has evolved a definition and methodology of psychology that contrast sharply with other systems. Although the phenomenologists recognized the need to devise a nonmaterialistic empirical method, the difficulty in applying their procedures resulted in an obscurity and elusiveness when compared to the readily quantifiable methods of objective empiricism. Accordingly, the evaluation of the systems leads to the dichotomy of either accepting or rejecting the underlying materialism of behaviorism.

A second implication of the materialism of empirical behaviorism may be seen in contemporary neofunctional trends and concerns the logical conclusions of consistent investigations; namely, that a purely psychological level of analysis, having an integrity in itself, becomes lost in the application of materialistic empiricism to its ultimate end. The distinction between psychological processes and underlying physical explanations is blurred, resulting in the equating of psychology with physiology or other underlying levels, such as cellular or neurochemical biology. By studying psychology as defined through materialistic empiricism, the ultimate conclusion is the rather startling implication that psychology may not be necessary. Consequently, we can observe contemporary trends toward identifying psychology in terms of an interdisciplinary subject matter, reflecting this inherent reduction, such as in psychobiology or in neuropsychology. Whereas these areas of study may indicate an appropriate scientific approach to given issues by circumventing the artificiality of disciplinary barriers, such labels also identify the vulnerability of psychology equated with materialistic empiricism.

In considering the question of psychology's place within empirical science, it is informative to re-examine the contrasting models of Wundt and Brentano, offered over a century ago. Essentially, Wundt, and later Titchener, proposed a model of psychology that had a similarity to materialistic empiricism. Although they recognized the necessity of a mental construct, they argued that the contents of the mind could be reduced to the elements of sensations. However, this analytic model of psychology ultimately led to a reduction of the sensations to their corresponding stimuli. The integrity of psychology itself was lost in Titchener's analysis, so that psychology was logically reduced to physics. The sterility of Titchener's model for psychology's development resulted in the complete failure of his structural psychology. In contrast, Brentano proposed an open-ended model of empirical psychology. His less articulated views recognized a distinctive psychological area of inquiry. Certain psychological events are phenomenal and are destroyed if reduced. Unfortunately, Brentano's act psychology has never been developed to its fullest extent. Certainly, his thoughts influenced both the Gestalt and the phenomenological movements, but the full impact of his nonmaterialistic empiricism has not been explored systematically.

Of interest in the recent neofunctional trends is the growth of certain areas of psychology that seem to accept an implied nonmaterialistic empiricism underlying their research approach. In particular, the study of psycholinguistics and cognitive views of learning, as well as certain trends in social psychological research, suggests a reaction to materialistic empiricism. Although these developments grew out of certain neobehavioristic implications, it is probably no longer correct to label as behavioristic such areas as psycholinguistics and cognitive psychology, as they rely on modest mentalistic overtones in their empirical approach. An expansion of these areas to a systematic and comprehensive framework for psychology in general is premature at this time. However, these developments offer an indication that empiricism may be broadened to include appropriate mentalistic as well as materialistic assumptions. At the very least, it seems that Sperry's (1995) observation that psychology may be in the midst of a Kuhnian paradigm shift is certainly compelling.

CONCLUSIONS

The history of psychology offers a fascinating reflection of the evolution of intellectual thought in general. Because its traditional subject matter is human activity, psychology's past reflects the larger view of the course of Western civilization. For this reason, psychology's development cannot be separated from the evolution of all knowledge. Moreover, as students of psychology, we must accept and tolerate the dissonance, contradictions, and inconsistencies in the history of psychology, for such factors have been present in the often turbulent history of Western civilization. From the turmoil of disagreement and controversy comes greater clarity of the issues, and knowledge is advanced.

In Chapter 2, Comte's description of the historical progress of civilization was cited, and it was noted that he regarded ancient Greek thought as the transition between a reliance on theological explanations and a view that looked either internally to the person or externally to the environment for causal explanations. The philosophical studies of the ancient Greeks identified basic issues of psychology, focusing on the necessary assumptions about the nature of human activity. These critical issues, which the Greek scholars did not resolve, still baffle psychologists. Can human beings explain psychological activity in terms of physical matter only, or is some proposal of mental life necessary? The progress of Greek thought led to the development of the concept of soul, as represented in the comprehensive philosophies of Plato and Aristotle. Despite the almost 2,500 years since the flowering of Greek thought, very little of truly original quality has been added. Changes, modifications, and reinterpretations have been offered, but essentially science as we know it today is a study based on an Aristotelian framework of knowledge. Indeed, Scholastic philosophy, reaching a pinnacle under the genius of Saint Thomas Aquinas, marked the resurrection of civilization after centuries of social deterioration and provided a reintroduction to Aristotelian philosophy, interpreted in the light of Christianity.

The modern age of empirical science began with Descartes, whose interpretation of knowledge was based on the Aristotelian system. The philosophical justification of empiricism, as well as the first statements of how knowledge is acquired by the association of ideas, was introduced by Hobbes and Locke. From their writings, the possibility of an empirical science of psychology was explored. However, the empirical strategy of psychology was not universally accepted, and rival conceptualizations were proposed. One tradition, centered in France, rejected the need for a psychology, presenting the modern monistic argument by reducing mental activity to the elements of sensory physiology. Alternatively, the tradition that began with Leibniz was inspired by the Greek concept of the activity of the soul, and he proposed a psychology determined by the activity of the mind. This tradition culminated in the rationalism of Kant, and mental activity was the prevailing theme in German philosophy well into the twentieth century.

Nineteenth-century psychology inherited the competing models of psychology. It was the empiricist framework that propelled psychology into a separation from philosophy, physics, and physiology, so that by the 1870s psychology started to gain recognition as an independent discipline. However, even within the empiricist orientation there were disagreements about the scope and methods of psychology. As we have seen, Wundt and Brentano disagreed over the type of empiricism, and their argument essentially involved the issue of mental versus materialistic empiricism.

From this survey of the origins of psychology, we see that the history of psychology can hardly be described as a smooth, even flow of progressive developments. The new science of psychology inherited some violent disagreements over the most fundamental assumptions of the discipline. On the basis of psychology's past, the subsequent turmoil of psychology's first century was easily predicted. The systems phase of twentieth-century psychology attempted to deal with basically different conceptualizations of the nature of psychological activity. The systems phase, however, did not produce the definitive model of psychology. Behaviorism, the dominant system in the United States, evolved so drastically that it is barely recognized now as a consistent system. Rather, behaviorism dissolved into an eclectic attitude emphasizing empiricism. As the systems phase of twentieth-century psychology was preceded by a functional psychology, so too has it been succeeded by a neofunctionalism. Accordingly, we must conclude that contemporary psychology is deficient as a theoretical discipline. The major agreement of contemporary neofunctionalism lies with the consensus that psychology is an empirical science, which is itself an atheoretical statement. Thus we must reserve judgment about psychology's theoretical future and await the forces of the *Zeitgeist*.

On an applied level, we can safely conclude that psychology has been successful over the last century. The empirical developments in psychology have added to our knowledge of very different areas, from psychopathology to advertising to interethnic understanding. In this sense, the functional character of psychology has produced results. Moreover, using the criteria of the utilitarian and the eclectic, we may feel confident about the future of psychology.

We started this inquiry into psychology's past by noting the diversity and apparent confusion of opinions in contemporary psychology. It was not our purpose to resolve the disparity. It was our aim, rather, to clarify the confusion by using the knowledge of history to discover where the present myriad of views on psychology originated. To survey the present state of psychology quite simply, psychology is an active and exciting discipline, despite its failures, regressions, and false starts. This statement readily admits that psychology is not an easy discipline to study. The student must cope with some very basic decisions before moving on to systematic investigation of the issues. However, such dissonance is perhaps appropriate, for unlike other disciplines, psychology has as its subject matter the most complex of questions to answer—namely, why are we what we are, and why do we do what we do?

CHAPTER SUMMARY

The scope of this book is summarized in terms of the basic issues that have historically confronted psychology. The four systems of psychology—psychoanalysis, Gestalt psychology, the third force movement, and behaviorism—have been compared along four critical dimensions: mental dualism versus monism, self-generative versus sensory sources of knowledge, mentalism versus materialism, and internal mediation versus external association in the acquisition of knowledge. The evaluation points to the relationship between psychology and science, and in particular, the problems resulting from a reliance on materialistic empiricism. Psychology as a theoretical discipline has suffered from the disagreements and controversies of the first century of its existence. Yet in its first hundred years, psychology has been successful as an applied science.

BIBLIOGRAPHY

General Sources

COPLESTON, F. (1956). *Contemporary philosophy: Studies of logical positivism and existentialism*. Westminster, MD: Newman Press.

GIORGI, A. (1970). *Psychology as a human science*. New York: Harper & Row.

KOCH, S. (Ed.) (1959). *Psychology: A study of a science, Vol. II: General systematic formulations*. New York: McGraw-Hill.

SPERRY, R. (1995). The future of psychology. *American Psychologist, 50,* 505–506.

TURNER, M. B. (1967). *Philosophy and the science of behavior*. New York: Appleton-Century-Crofts.

Glossary

The following terms and concepts are defined in the context of their use in this book. In selecting items for this glossary, one goal was to include terms and concepts derived primarily from disciplines other than psychology. The discipline of psychology evolved from philosophy, theology, and the natural sciences, whose terminology may not be familiar to the student of psychology. This glossary therefore concentrates on definitions of terms drawn from other disciplines that are appropriate to the history of psychology. Italicized words within each definition refer to terms and concepts defined separately in the glossary. Numbers in parentheses at the end of each definition refer to chapters in which the terms are elaborated.

Act psychology. In general, those versions of psychology that emphasize the unity and cohesion of individual interactions with the environment and recognize the multifaceted levels of human experience. In particular, the act psychology proposed by Brentano, Stumpf, and the Würzburg school contrasted the integrative unity of human experience with the elementarism of Wundt's *structural psychology*. Consistent with the German philosophical tradition of *mental activity*, Brentano especially argued that the psychological act is intentional, and those methodologies that are rigidly *analytical* result in the destruction of the act under study. A truly descriptive approach to psychology must be *empirical* yet at the same time deal with the phenomenal character of psychological acts (11, 13, 16).

Analysis. The general strategy of study, or methodology, that seeks to explain psychological events in terms of contributing parts or underlying elements. The experimental method, as applied in the *natural sciences* and in some models of psychology, is an analytic method. Such methods are usually *reductionistic*; they may also be described as elementaristic, *atomistic*, and *molecular* in character. Analytic methods are in contrast to views of psychological events in terms

of unity and *phenomenal* quality, which require a holistic or a *molar* strategy of study (9, 11, 18).

Analytic psychology. The label given to Jung's modification of Freud's *psychoanalysis* (14).

Associationism. The view that interprets higher mental processes as resulting from combinations of *sensory* and/or mental elements. A reliance on associationistic processes was an outcome of *empirical* models of psychology, because associations provided a *mechanism* of environmental adaptation and learning. Among the explanations for the formation of associations, the principles of *contiguity*, *contingency*, and *similarity* were most prominent in the British philosophical tradition of *mental passivity*. The quantification of association principles was realized in Pavlov's theory of conditioning, adopted by the behaviorists (7, 15).

Atomism. The philosophical view that complex events can be *reduced* to component elements. Applied to psychology, atomistic views support the *analysis* of experience into constituent parts—for example, an idea reduced to stimulus-response associations. Moreover, an atomistic framework admits that little is lost in the reductionistic analysis, so that the simpler components completely explain the complex psychological event (2, 6, 7, 11, 15).

Behaviorism. The system of psychology that admits as its subject matter overt, *observable*, and measurable behavior. In its most rigid form, offered initially by J. B. Watson and later by B. F. Skinner, behaviorism denies the admission of traditional issues of mental events. Contemporary behaviorism has evolved to a broadly based *eclectic* system of psychology, which emphasizes to varying extents the study of behavioral processes that may be mediated by nonobservable *mechanisms* or agencies (12, 15, 17, 18).

Buddhism. A religion or philosophy that originated in India with Buddha (sixth century B.C.) and spread throughout Asia. Buddhism generally prescribes a life of reflection and self-denial that will enable the individual to reach a level of bliss and release from the bonds of earthly desires (1, 17).

Confucianism. A system of ethics originating with the Chinese philosopher Confucius (ca. 551–478 B.C.), which emphasized social values, individual loyalty, and family ties (1, 17).

Consciousness. The personal awareness of subjective experience at any point in time. In general usage, consciousness has meant the individual's total awareness of past experiences and future aspirations, as well as ongoing self-knowledge, and this usage implies active self-reflection. Specific definitions of consciousness have ranged from global meanings, such as William James's interpretation of consciousness as continuous and transcendent of time, to Freud's limited view of consciousness as confined to distorted reflections of the more active and encompassing *unconscious* (6–9, 11, 12, 14, 16).

Constructs. In models and theories, explanatory devices that tend to be only distantly related to specific *empirical* referents. For example, the notion of *consciousness* is a construct because it is used to explain several psychological processes, but it is not directly *observed*, nor is it defined in terms of specific observable and measurable events. Constructs are often contrasted with *intervening variables*, with the former having less *observational* reference than the latter (16, 18).

Contiguity. A general principle of *associations* stating that two or more events occurring together in time tend to be associated and retained together. The British philosophers Hume, Hartley, and James Mill gave contiguity a primary role in accounting for the acquisition of associations; other philosophers, most notably J. S. Mill and Brown, argued that principles in addition to contiguity (e.g., *contingency* and *similarity*) were needed to explain associations. More recently, Pavlov's conditioning theory has advocated the temporal relationship between the unconditioned stimulus and the conditioned stimulus as the primary determinant of successful acquisition, and Guthrie's learning theory emphasized contiguity as the central principle of association (7, 15).

Contingency. The principle of association referring to the extent of the dependent relationship between two or more events that accounts for the association of the events. Although contingency was recognized by the British *empirical* philosophers, this principle has received attention in more recent revisions of Pavlovian conditioning theory that stress the contingent, predictive value of the conditioned stimulus in relation to the unconditioned stimulus, such as in acquisition training through the delayed conditioning procedure (7, 15).

Cosmology. The branch of *metaphysics* that studies the total universe and the general properties of nature in terms of ultimate principles. Those early Greek scholars who attempted to find the basic substance of life in the physical environment may be described as cosmologists. Modern astronomers who search for ultimate theoretical explanations of the origins and workings of the universe continue the tradition of cosmological study (2, 4, 10).

Deduction. The *logical* process or sequence of reasoning involving a progression from a known principle or premise to an unknown; from the general to the particular. Deductive reasoning is a complement to *inductive logic*. Systematically presented by Aristotle, deductive reasoning assumed a dominance in the methodology of *Scholasticism*. Its value was later questioned as *empiricism*, based primarily on *induction*, assumed importance in the rise of *Renaissance* science (2, 4, 5, 10).

Determinism. In psychology, the doctrine or philosophical assumption that a given psychological event or process is completely governed by specified factors, usually beyond individual control. For example, the Roman Stoics resigned themselves to the belief that all of life's events are determined by fate, independent of individual desires or intentions. Similarly, contemporary operant conditioning theory accepts the possibility that complete control of environmental events will lead to perfect control of behavior, reflecting a deterministic position. Complete determinism is in opposition to views emphasizing personal freedom, individual variability, and free *will*. The issue of determinism occupies an important role in the historical development of psychology and in the expressions of contemporary systems (2, 3, 9, 15, 18).

Dialectics. In general, any extended, detailed *logical* argument in reasoning. In particular, the nineteenth-century philosopher Hegel devised a dialectic method of logic, proposing that an event or an idea (thesis) gives rise to its opposite (antithesis), leading to a reconciliation of the opposition (synthesis). Historical progress is explained by repetitions of the cycle, and Hegel's dialectic method was adapted by Marx and Engels to explain changes in society and in nature (3, 16).

Dualism. Any of the philosophical assumptions underlying psychology that accept the position that human beings possess two basic aspects, mental and physical. Since postulated by the ancient Greeks, dualistic positions have consistently dominated Western preconceptions of human psychology. The modern development of psychology was spurred by the dualism of Descartes, who proposed that physiology is the study of the physical and *material* body; psychology, the study of the nonphysical immaterial mind. Dualism is in contrast to *monism*, which postulates only a single physical or mental aspect of human existence. As a recurring theme in psychological inquiry, dualistic positions are also represented in such twentieth-century systems as *psychoanalysis* and the third force movement (all chapters).

Early Middle Ages. The period lasting roughly from the removal of the imperial capital from Rome (476) until the eleventh century, during which western Europe was torn by war, disease, and ignorance. The ancient great cities of the Roman Empire were largely abandoned, and European life became predominantly rural. Intellectual life first stagnated, then regressed to the point of almost complete eradication. The social fabric became feudal and the sole international or intertribal institution of any authority was the Church, headed by an increasingly powerful papacy (4).

Eclecticism. An attitude in psychology that supports the selection of positions and interpretations of psychological issues from various diverse systems. The resulting system attempts to blend the valued interpretations picked up from other theories into a harmonious, consistent perspective on psychology. The prevailing theme giving unity within an eclectic selection typically involves some limited goal of explaining psychological processes. For example, the ancient Greek Sophists were eclectic in their attempt to eschew the search for an all-encompassing principle of life and settled instead for a view that bonded together natural, physical events only. Similarly, the twentieth-century American *functionalists* were eclectic to the extent that they abandoned the search for a theoretically coherent psychology of *consciousness* in favor of gathering *empirical* data of an applied value (2, 12).

Empiricism. A philosophy of *science* that accepts experience as the sole source of knowledge. As a result, *sensory* processes constitute the critical link between the environment and subjective knowledge, and *observation* through the senses becomes the standard criterion for the validity of empirical science. Scientific empiricism and psychology developed together in post-*Renaissance* Western thought. Empirical psychology received its initial comprehensive expression within the British philosophical tradition, and subsequently, in the latter part of the nineteenth century in Germany, two empirical models competed for the definitive framework of psychology. Twentieth-century psychological systems have differed primarily in their commitment to empiricism (1, 7, 9, 11, 18).

Epistemology. The branch of *metaphysics* that studies the origins, characteristics, modes, and limits of knowledge. Aristotle's human psychology was basically epistemological because his views on mind and body were mostly descriptions of how we acquire knowledge. Piaget's developmental psychology is a modern example of epistemology because Piaget was ultimately concerned with knowing and how we know (2, 4, 11, 16, 17, 18).

Essence. A philosophical issue derived from the Greek scholars, especially Aristotle, who viewed all living and nonliving objects as manifestations of some defining property or characteristic common to all similar objects. As applied to humans, each person has an individual *existence*, but all people share in the common essence of the *soul*. The adoption of the Greek concept of essence into Christian thinking by the *Scholastic* philosophers of the late *medieval* period resulted in the very definition of psychology as synonymous with the Christian goal of perfection of the essence shared by each person—namely, eternal salvation of the soul. Thus, for the Scholastics, essence precedes existence. In the nineteenth and twentieth centuries this Scholastic notion of essence was seriously challenged by the philosophy of existentialism, reflected in the third force movement within psychology (2, 4, 16).

Evolution. A process of orderly development and growth. Within psychology, evolution implies the contemporary systems that tend toward *monistic* assumptions, such as *behaviorism*, and accept that human beings are phylogenetically continuous with the rest of living nature. In general, Darwin's theory of natural selection forged an inseparable link between evolutionary data and psychology (10).

Existence. In the Aristotelian and *Scholastic* sense, the individual expression of each object *observed* in nature. For people, existence is the individual state of being that gives expression to the universal essence shared by all people. Existential philosophy challenged the Scholastic conception by proposing that individual existence, the act of being, defines a person's *essence*, so that existence precedes essence (2, 4, 16).

Faculty psychology. The view of the mind or of mental processes that holds that human psychology is derived from a number of mental abilities or specific mental agencies, such as memory, reason, and the *will*. Although a justification for faculty psychology may be found in ancient Greek thought, the more modern expression evolved within the German philosophical tradition of *mental activity*. The emphasis on mental predispositions, exemplified in Kant's categories, gave rise to a distinct proposal that the mind has functions that underlie similar mental activities. Contemporary expressions consistent with faculty psychology include trait theories of intelligence and personality (2, 8, 10, 15, 17).

Functionalism. An attitude that has dominated American psychology during most of the twentieth century. Functionalism emphasizes and values the utilitarian and applied aspects of psychological activities, as opposed to describing psychological *structures* and contents. Philosophically supported by American *pragmatism*, varying degrees of functionalism may be ascribed to all systematic expressions of twentieth-century psychology in America, because all of the schools, including those imported from Europe, were subjected to criteria of applicability and usefulness (12, 17).

Geocentric, or **Ptolemaic, system.** A system of the universe holding that the earth is the fixed center around which all heavenly bodies revolve. This position was systematized by the astronomer Claudius Ptolemy (ca. second century) of Alexandria in Egypt and was essentially accepted by the early Christian philosophers, such as Saint Augustine, and the later *Scholastics*. The earth-centered system was not seriously challenged until Copernicus proposed the *heliocentric* alternative (4).

Gestalt. A German word literally meaning shape or form. As used in psychology, Gestalt implies any of the unified patterns or *structures* that make up experience and have properties that cannot be *reduced* to the component parts or elements of the whole, so that the unity of the whole is more than the sum of the parts. Gestalt psychology, which can be readily traced to the German philosophical tradition of *mental activity*, advocated an emphasis on psychological events as *phenomena* that cannot be reduced without loss of the integrity and unity of the event (8, 13, 15, 18).

Great man theory. Interpretation of historical progress suggesting that significant events of historical and social importance occur because of the efforts of outstanding persons. This position is in contrast to the *Zeitgeist*, or "spirit of the times," interpretation (1, 18).

Hedonism. In psychology, the view that individual activity is governed by the seeking of pleasure and the avoidance of pain. For example, the Epicurean philosophy of ancient Rome advocated ethical values based on hedonistic principles; in contemporary psychology, the role of *reinforcement*, especially as expressed in Thorndike's law of effect, provides an example of hedonistic implications (3, 6, 16).

Heliocentric, or **Copernican, system.** A system of planetary organization that holds that the sun is the center of the universe, and all heavenly bodies revolve around the sun. Moreover, the turning of the earth on its axis is responsible for the apparent rising and setting of the sun. Championed by the Polish astronomer Copernicus, the heliocentric position initially argued from the parsimony of logic against the prevailing *geocentric*, or *Ptolemaic*, view. Copernicus's heliocentric system was successful in challenging the Ptolemaic system that was supported by the authority of the Church (4).

Hinduism. The varied indigenous systems of Indian philosophy that teach that the person should seek to move from the level of specific individuality to the level of unity and harmony with the universal (1).

Humanism. Those trends in Western thought that tended to view individual people in terms of their dignity, ideals, and interests. Humanistic themes throughout history have elevated the value of human intellectual powers and downgraded *deterministic* interpretations of life, whether arising from theistic or environmental control. Humanistic attitudes may be found in the development of the concept of the rational *soul* in Greek scholarship, in the art and literature of the *Renaissance*, and in the *humanistic psychology* of the contemporary third force movement (2, 4, 11, 16).

Humanistic psychology. A label given to a group of mostly American psychologists within the third force movement who have devised eclectic criteria for individual growth, applied primarily in clinical settings. They hold that each individual is capable of a truly psychological level of well-being, characterized by self-fulfillment and a complete integration of subjective goals, desires, and expectancies within an honest *perception* of reality (16).

Human science model. In general, a series of assumptions about the definition and the methods of psychology, advocating recognition of the complexity of human motivation and dynamic activity and suggesting that human psychology is qualitatively different from other forms of life. Moreover, the human science model is open to several strategies of methodology, all within an open-ended definition of *empirical science*.

The human science model is in contrast to the *natural science model*, which defines a psychology of observable activity in a relatively restricted sense and fails to differentiate the types of psychological events emanating from various species, instead seeking to model psychology on the methodology of the natural or physical sciences (11, 18).

Hypotheticodeductive approach. A methodological approach in *science* that may be *logically* or *empirically* based and that involves a series of initial principles that are tentatively accepted and subsequently tested for all implications before their final inclusion in a general theorem. The Greek mathematician Pythagoras provided an early example of the logical rigor of this method; in contemporary psychology the empirical use of this approach is seen in the systematic *behaviorism* of Hull (2, 15).

Idiographic. Descriptions of psychological events and processes from the perspective of the singular individual, in contrast to *nomothetic*, which emphasizes group or normative description. An idiographic approach is a characteristic approach of *humanistic psychologists* (9, 16, 17, 18).

Individual psychology. The term used to describe Adler's modifications of Freudian *psychoanalysis* (14).

Induction. The *logical* process or sequence of reasoning involving the progression of inference of known principles to some general statement covering all instances applicable to the principle; reasoning from the particular to the general. Inductive logic is the complement of a *deductive* progression in logic. Induction forms the logical basis of *empirical* methodologies in science, because conclusions about particular *observations* are tested for generalizations to cover all possible cases of similar observations (2, 4, 5, 10).

Innate ideas. A philosophical assumption that the mind is born with content. The innate content of the mind may be specific, such as Descartes' suggestion that each person is born

with the knowledge of God or Jung's notion of the archetypes of the collective *unconscious*. The view that the mind is predisposed to certain modes of knowing, such as the position of Kant and, more recently, *Gestalt* psychology, is consistent with belief in innate ideas and, more generally, the doctrine of *nativism* (8, 9, 11, 13, 14, 18).

Interactionism. The philosophical interpretation of mental and bodily processes suggesting that the mind and body, although separate entities, influence each other. This view contrasts with *parallelism*, which asserts no interaction, but rather processes that grow in the same direction yet are independent. A contemporary example of interactionism is *psychoanalysis*, which holds the psychic energy of the *unconscious* mind exerts dominant direction over all human processes, including bodily responses (6, 7, 8, 9, 11, 13, 18).

Intervening variable. A relatively specific process or event that is assumed to link directly *observable* events. For example, a Pavlovian-conditioned *association* may be used as an intervening variable to account for the relationship produced between a conditioned stimulus (CS) and a conditioned response (CR) following appropriate acquisition. Both the CS and the CR are observable events, and the conditioned associative bond is directly inferred from these events. Intervening variables are usually contrasted to *constructs*; both devices are used as explanatory *mechanisms*, but intervening variables have more direct *operational*, *empirical* referents than constructs (15).

Introspection. In general, an individual's reflection or contemplation of subjective experience. Recorded introspective reports abound in literature, with perhaps Saint Augustine's *Confessions* being the most famous example. In a specific sense, introspection was the experimental method used by Wundt for the study of psychology. Within his *structural psychology*, introspection became a highly controlled method by which a trained psychologist could presumably study the contents of immediate experience (3, 5, 11).

Logic. The study and method of correct reasoning. Logic as systematized by Aristotle contains the criteria for the validity of arguments derived through orderly, sequential processes of *deduction* and *induction*. Although the *empirical* methods are logical, not all logical methods are empirical, because logical arguments may be exclusively based in rational abstractions, as indeed was the case prior to the post-*Renaissance* emergence of empirical *science* (2, 4, 5, 9, 18).

Materialism. The philosophical position that matter is the only reality and that all objects and events, including psychological processes of thinking, *willing*, and feeling, can be explained in terms of matter. Materialistic assumptions are often equated with physicalism, because the latter holds the similar view that psychological events are based on the physical mechanics of bodily processes. Materialism is opposed to those views of psychology that stress mentalistic *constructs* (2, 4, 11, 15, 18).

Mechanism. A philosophical position that assumed the systematic operation of physical and mental processes to produce all psychological experiences; also referred to as a mechanical view of psychology. Usually, a mechanical interpretation accepts that bodily mechanics in particular underlie all psychological events, precluding the need for mental *constructs*. A belief in mechanism is in contrast to *vitalism*, which insists on the need for some living agency distinct from physical mechanics. A mechanical view of learning is inherent in contemporary conditioning theory, which interprets *associations* as accounted for and explained by sensory-motor relationships in the nervous system (2, 9, 18).

Medical model. An approach to psychological problems or deviancy that adapts the strategy of physicians and proposes that *behavioral* manifestations are symptomatic of some underlying cause. For example, *psychoanalysis* interprets overt activities as important only for what they reflect of unobservable, largely *unconscious* psychodynamics. A medical model approach to psychology may be contrasted to a behavioral model, which values *observable* activity as the critical approach to treatment (14, 15).

Medieval period. The epoch in European history existing between the *Early Middle Ages* and the *Renaissance* and lasting approximately from 1000 to 1500. This period was characterized by social and political dominance of the papacy, the emergence of the nation-states of Europe, and the gradual revival of scholarship. *Scholasticism* was the primary intellectual achievement of medieval Europe (3, 4).

Mental activity. The core of assumptions underlying the psychology that dominated the German philosophical tradition. This view basically holds that some agency, such as the mind, is separate and distinct from the body and is responsible for the higher psychological processes of thinking, *willing*, and perceiving. The mind is active and dynamic, and, to varying extents, the mind generates knowledge and is not entirely dependent on environmental input for its contents. Contemporary psychological views that emphasize mental activity include *psychoanalysis*, the third force movement, and, to a limited extent, *Gestalt* psychology (8, 9, 11, 13, 14, 16, 18).

Mental passivity. The basis for the *empirical* psychology of the British philosophical tradition, in which the mind is viewed largely as a reactive receptive agency, and the contents of the mind are dependent on environmental input. Mental passivity justified the study of psychological processes in terms of the *observable* events of the environment as the substance of *sensory* processes. Moreover, the acquisition of knowledge about the environment is valued for its role in assisting the adaptation of the organism. Mental passivity is the converse of mental activity, which posits the mind as acting by its own abilities on input from the environment. Mental passivity is implicit in *behavioristic* psychology in general (6, 7, 9, 11, 12, 15, 17, 18).

Metaphysics. The branch of philosophy dealing with the ultimate explanations and first principles of being or reality (*ontology*), the nature and structures of the universe (*cosmology*), and the study of knowing (*epistemology*). Metaphysics and *empirical* psychology have often been set in opposition in the history of science, because the development of *empiricism*, based on *observation*, was viewed as essentially replacing metaphysical explanations of psychological events with demonstrated facts (2, 16).

Molar behavior. The view of total behavior defined in relatively large units, emphasizing behavior as unified and purposive. Molar behavior is contrasted with *molecular behavior*, which tends to lead to *atomism* and *reductionism*. Tolman exemplified a molar approach in *behaviorism* when he incorporated some of the *phenomenological* emphases of *Gestalt* psychology into behaviorism (15).

Molecular behavior. Behavior defined through the collection of small segmented units, such as muscular or glandular activities. The *logic* of *atomism* in molecular interpretations of behavior leads to the reduction of units of behavior to the neurophysiological or neurochemical levels of *analysis*. Molecular behavior is in contrast to *molar behavior* (15).

Monadology. The philosophy of Leibniz, who postulated the existence of "monads," defined as life-giving entities that are ultimate units of life. Monads essentially provide the agency of activity in the world. The human *soul* is the most active monad. As the founder of the German philosophical tradition of psychology, Leibniz gave an active imprint to the direction of this tradition, leading to the emergence of a psychology based on the assumption of dynamic, self-generating *mental activity* (8, 9).

Monism. Any of the philosophical assumptions underlying psychology that admit to only a single substance or principle of psychology, usually in the *materialism* of the body. Monistic systems of psychology reject the mental activity of *dualistic* positions. The growth of monism has paralleled the development of *empirical* psychology itself, so that materialistic monism is the predominant perspective in contemporary psychology, expressed in the teachings of neobehaviorism and *reflexology* (2, 6, 7, 9, 15, 17, 18).

Nativism. Specifically refers to the doctrine of *innate ideas* and is used in psychology to indicate any inherited ability, predisposition, or attitude. Nativism is in contrast to *empiricism*, and is represented in such diverse contemporary constructs as Jung's collective *unconscious*, *perceptual* predispositions of *Gestalt* psychology, and Chomsky's language acquisition device (all chapters).

Naturalism. The philosophical position that the natural world as we know and experience it is the only certain reality. Standards of ethics are derived from the lawful relationships in nature. If God or other supernatural forces exist, such influences are not responsible for the direction of human activities. Naturalism is a recurrent theme in Western psychology, from the early Greek explanations of life by specific natural events to Spinoza's equation of the forces of God with the forces of nature (2, 5).

Natural science model. In general, a set of assumptions about the definition and the study of psychology that supports the notion of psychological events as *materialistically* or physically based *observable* processes. These assumptions translate to a methodological *empiricism* that is essentially the same as that used to study such sciences as biology, chemistry, and physics. The natural science model stands in contrast to the *human science model*, which sees psychological activity in human beings as qualitatively different from other forms of life (9, 11, 18).

Nomothetic. Used to describe psychological events and processes in terms of general laws that tend to apply to group or normative standards. A nomothetic emphasis contrasts with an *idiographic* approach, which stresses the individual rather than the group (9, 16, 18).

Observation. The deliberate act of examining particulars of an event through *sensory* awareness on the part of the observer. Observation may involve direct sensory experience of an event under scrutiny or may employ instrumentation that serves as a medium between an event and the observer's sensory processes. Observational methods, which form the core of *empirical science*, may range from rather informal descriptions to formal controlled procedures, such as the experimental method. In psychology, observation is the critical dimension in the definition of psychology's subject matter. For example, a process not directly observed, such as the mediation of id energy by the ego in *psychoanalytic* theory, may be readily distinguished from directly observed events, such as the magnitude of a conditioned response in conditioning *reflexology* (1, 2, 4, 7, 9, 11, 18).

Ontology. The branch of *metaphysics* that studies the ultimate nature and relations of being. Ontology seeks to discover the abstractions that define a thing to be what it is. Those philosophical speculations that proposed the existence of an immaterial *soul* as the ultimate life-giving element are examples of ontological study (2, 3, 4).

Operationism. The scientific view that requires the definition of a scientific event in terms of the identifiable and repeatable procedures that produce the event, and nothing more. As a formal doctrine, operationism grew out of the logical *positivism* movement of the early twentieth century, which attempted to rid scientific issues of surplus meaning and pseudoproblems. Adapted to psychology, operationism advocated the definition of psychological events in terms of the procedures required to produce *observation* of such events. For example, hunger may be operationally defined as the motivational state that results from 24 hours without food (2, 5, 11, 15, 18).

Paradigm. In *science*, a model or pattern that accommodates all forms of diversity and variability related to a given issue. For example, if the association of ideas is viewed as synonymous with conditioning, the model of conditioning serves as a framework to explain all forms of *associations* (1, 11, 18).

Parallelism. A general interpretation of mental and bodily processes asserting that mind and body are independent entities functioning separately but in parallel. As an explanation of *dualism*, parallelism is in contrast to *interactionism*, which stresses the mind acting on the body and vice versa. A contemporary example of parallelism is the *Gestalt* psychologists' assertion of psychophysical parallelism through their principle of isomorphism, which suggests a dynamic correspondence between the excitation in the physical brain field and a perceived field of experience (6, 7, 8, 9, 11, 13, 18).

Perception. Any experience that is primarily dependent on *sensory* input but has content and organization usually derived from previous experience or predisposition. Perception is typically interpreted as a cognitive process, in contrast to *sensation*, which is usually defined as sensory experience only. The exact distinction between sensory processes and perceptual processes is not clear and varies with diverse models of psychology; as a result, the two terms are often used interchangeably or to imply different levels of complexity along the same dimension. The study of perception is one of the fundamental areas of psychological inquiry, and has provided critical issues for all systems and theories throughout psychology's history (9, 11, 13, 17, 18).

Phenomenology. A methodological approach to psychology and other disciplines that focuses on the unity and integrity of events and experiences. Phenomenology may be informal to the extent that it is an attitude of study that allows free expression to the various ways that events appear to the observer, enabling the observer to apprehend the integrity of an event as going beyond its component elements. The *observational* approach of Purkinje's physiological research is an example of informal phenomenology. An example of systematic, formal phenomenology is Husserl's method of specific procedures of observation (9, 10, 11, 13, 16, 18).

Phenomenon. Literally, that which appears. In psychology, phenomena are usually described as events that are experienced as unified and unanalyzed. The view of psychological experience as phenomenal contrasts with assumptions that hold experience to be capable of *analysis* into components. As an example of the study of phenomena in psychology, the *Gestalt* psychologists accepted the principle that *perception* of environmental objects is an experience that is not reducible to *sensory* elements, but rather consists of a whole process of person–environment interactions that produce the integrity and unity of experience (10, 11, 13, 16).

Phrenology. An attempt in the eighteenth and nineteenth centuries to relate specific mental abilities or traits to the size and skull contours of brain areas where particular capacities were assumed to reside. Essentially, phrenology tried to establish a physical basis for the prevailing philosophical view of *faculty psychology*. However, the movement was ridden with quackery, and subsequent neurophysiological research showed that phrenology was completely untenable (10).

Platonism. The collective philosophical views based on the writings of Plato. For psychology, Platonic belief stressed the unreliability of *sensory* knowledge and the inherent evil of bodily passions; only the wisdom of the human *soul* can provide the key to truth, knowledge, and understanding. Revived interest in Plato's views during the ascendancy of the Roman Empire, termed Neoplatonism, led to the assimilation of Platonic thought into Christian teachings, primarily through the writings of Saint Augustine (2, 3).

Positivism. The philosophical systems that consider knowledge as derived exclusively from *sense* experience, rejecting all *theological* and *metaphysical* sources of knowledge. Popularized in the nineteenth century by Comte, positivism asserts that scientific study must be centered on *observation* and avoid speculation. Positivism and *empiricism* are essentially compatible because both rely on the experiencing observer for the data of science. In the twentieth century, a movement called logical positivism placed a more radical emphasis on observation through a proposal for the unity of all sciences to be achieved by operationally defining true scientific issues (2, 7, 9, 10, 11, 15, 18).

Pragmatism. The American philosophical view, initially formulated by William James and Charles Peirce, that asserts the interpretation of the truth and meaning of concepts in terms of the practicality and utility of results. Pragmatism forms the intellectual justification for *functional* approaches to psychology (7, 12).

Psychoanalysis. A system of psychology, initially developed by Freud and later modified by others, based on the notion of *unconscious* motivation. Psychoanalysis also refers to the therapeutic activities, mainly free association and dream analysis, that are a product of the Freudian system and deal with the symbols and behavioral manifestations of underlying unconscious conflict (14).

Psychophysics. The study of relationships between the physical properties of environmental stimuli and the intensity of *sensory* experience. Historically, psychophysics emerged as a movement that immediately preceded the formal recognition of psychology as an independent discipline in the 1870s. Psychophysicists developed innovative methodologies that have successfully survived the last hundred years of psychology (10).

Rational psychology. Those psychological systems and theories that assume the existence of a mind or *soul* having such characteristics as immortality and spiritual aspirations.

In this sense, the *Scholastic* psychology of Aquinas and Descartes are examples of rational psychology because both views accepted the essential features of a human soul created and nurtured by God. Rational psychology is also used to describe those *dualistic* interpretations that stress *mental activity* as providing knowledge, independent of *sensory* input. In this sense, rational psychology is similar to *faculty psychology*, the psychological views arising out of the German philosophical tradition, as exemplified in the writings of Kant and Wolff (8).

Reductionism.   Any scientific method that explains complex processes or *observations* in terms of simpler, underlying elements. Such *analyses* accept that the complex level may be completely understood at the simpler level. Reductionism is opposed to all of the *phenomenological* approaches. The *reflexology* interpretation of *associations* as the product of the relationships of conditioning components is an example of reductionism. Reductionism is an inherent part of many applications of *empiricism*, especially those that stress *operationism* (9, 11, 15, 18).

Reflexology.   The view that psychological processes can be explained by the biologically based *associations* of *sensory*-motor relationships. Modern reflexology received a firm basis in the neurophysiology of Sherrington and later was developed systematically by Pavlov and his successors (10, 15, 17).

Reformation.   The sixteenth-century movement that initially attempted to correct abuses within the Roman Catholic Church, but later disputed doctrinal matters as well, resulting in the establishment of Protestant sects. The Catholic Church attempted to recoup its losses by a Counter-Reformation that reorganized Church practices and clerical discipline (4).

Reinforcement.   The principle of learning asserting that positive or rewarding events facilitate acquisition of and negative or punishment events inhibit acquisition of an *associative* bond. In Pavlovian conditioning, the unconditioned stimulus serves as the reinforcing agent; in instrumental conditioning, the consequences of a response serve as the reinforcement. Behaviorists disagree as to the specific impact of reinforcement on learning processes, but all generally accept the necessity of some agent of reinforcement for learning to occur (15).

Renaissance.   Literally "rebirth"; used to describe the revival of art, literature, and scholarly pursuits during the fourteenth to sixteenth centuries in Europe. Starting in Italy, the Renaissance spread throughout Europe and resulted in the elevation of interest in humanity per se and a fascination with human intellectual capacities, largely at the expense of concern for the spiritual aspects of life (4).

Rhetoric.   The study of effective use of words in oral and written communication. Considered a basic subject in the academies of ancient Greece, rhetoric assumed a prominent place in the curricula of the *medieval* universities (3).

Scholasticism.   The system of Christian philosophy based on the essential teachings of Aristotle. Originating in the late medieval universities and culminating in the writings of Saint Thomas Aquinas, Scholasticism succeeded in elevating human reason, in addition to faith, as a source of knowledge by Church authorities. Scholastic philosophy produced a *rational psychology* that viewed reason and *will* as the ultimate sources of psychological processes (4).

Science.   In its most general sense, the acquisition of knowledge, or knowing. However, the term has evolved to mean the systematic study of the natural world, primarily through methods based on *observation*. With the rise of *empiricism*, logical observation assumed a critical characteristic of science, and for psychology, empiricism has dictated many of the assumptions underlying the definition of the science of psychology. Those methods of controlled observation produced a *natural science model* of psychological inquiry; a *human* *science model* was also proposed, involving an open-ended, less rigid form of empirical study (1, 9, 11, 18).

Sensation. The basic unit of experience made up of input from the senses. Sensation is properly distinguished from *perception* in that the former is an unanalyzed element of the latter, although the terms are often used interchangeably. Sensory processes have offered challenging issues that discriminate among the varied systems of psychology (9, 11, 13, 17, 18).

Similarity. The principle of *association* referring to the extent to which a specific event recalls another event that it resembles along some dimension. Long recognized as a fundamental principle by associationists of the British *empiricist* tradition, similarity retains its importance in contemporary conditioning theory. For example, Osgood's transfer surface is a quantitative model that predicts the strength of associations based on the dimension of similarity of stimulus and response elements of verbal associations. Moreover, the basic learning processes of stimulus generalization and Pavlov's views on irradiation result from responses made to the similarity dimension of a stimulus (7, 15).

Skepticism. The philosophical belief that all knowledge must be continually questioned and that the process of intellectual inquiry begins with doubt. A skeptical attitude challenges the validity of knowledge that is given on the basis of some authority. Historically, *empiricism* was supported by a skeptical attitude on the part of scientists who declared that existing knowledge is questionable and tenuous until demonstrated through *sensory observation* (2, 5).

Soul. Regarded as the life-giving entity of living beings, and of people, the soul is viewed as the immortal and spiritual aspect of a person, having no physical or material existence, but accounting for the psychological processes of thinking and *willing*. The soul is perhaps the oldest subject matter of psychology, with the very name of the discipline derived from the Greek *psyche*. From the initial search for some essential common basis to all of life, Greek scholars eventually postulated the concept of soul, which was systematized in Western thought by Aristotle. This concept was eventually Christianized and emerged intact through *Scholasticism* to post-*Renaissance* Europe, at which time Descartes suggested the mind–body *dualism*, with psychology as the study of the former and physiology the study of the latter aspects of human experience. The concept of the soul in psychology was not seriously challenged until the nineteenth and twentieth centuries with the rise of *materialism* in *empiricistic science* (2, 3, 4).

Structural psychology. (Also known as **content psychology.**) The system of psychology that defined its subject matter as the study of immediate experience in the *consciousness* of the normal adult mind. Moreover, psychology was to use as its exclusive methodology the highly controlled procedure of introspection by a trained observer. Largely invented by Wundt and championed in the United States by Titchener, structural psychology was limited in both its definition of psychology and its method of inquiry. From its very inception, structural psychology's limitations were recognized by critics who argued that the study of immediate experience produced observations of *sensations* based on the physical properties of stimuli. Under such constraints, psychology was vulnerable to *logical reduction* to physics. Structural psychology was largely a force against which alternative models reacted. By 1930, structural psychology had ceased to be a viable conceptualization of psychology (11, 12, 13).

Theology. The study of God and the relationship of God to the universe. In contrast to knowledge of God based on faith or revelation, theology uses the rationality of human intellectual abilities to inquire about God. Formally presented by Aquinas in the *Scholastic* movement, systematic theology has logically argued for the necessity of a first principle (an impersonal God, at the very least) that may be described as the "uncaused cause" or the "prime mover." Under the dominance of Scholasticism, Western psychology and theology were virtually synonymous. Another later, *rationalistic* systematization of theology was developed by the nineteenth-century followers of Hegel, against whom Kierkegaard reacted (2, 3, 4, 16).

Topology. The branch of mathematics that studies those dimensional and abstract properties of geometric figures that remain constant even when under distortion. Lewin used the analogy from topology to describe the relationships of person–environment interactions (13).

Unconscious. A general term used to describe those levels of psychological activity that are not within a person's awareness or *conscious* accessibility. Emphasized in nineteenth-century German philosophy, the unconscious received interpretations ranging from its being responsible for unconscious strivings to suggestions that it was capable of subthreshold psychophysical *sensory* detection. However, it was Freud who built an entire system of personality on unconscious motivation through his model of energy exchange. The unconscious tends toward primarily *psychoanalytic* interpretation in contemporary psychology (8, 10, 14).

Vitalism. The philosophical position that views life and psychological processes as caused and maintained by a living force or agency, separate and distinct from the physical *mechanisms* of the body. Most *dualistic* assumptions about psychology are vitalistic, ranging from traditional theories of the dynamic *soul* contained in Aristotelian and *Scholastic* philosophies to contemporary expressions in the third force movement, emphasizing individual definition of *existence* and the importance of the *will* (2, 4, 9, 11, 16, 18).

Will. In general, the motivational capacity to pursue goals and aspirations voluntarily. Within the Christianized concept of the *soul*, the will and the intellect were viewed as the primary mental functions. In this context, good impulses were pursued and evil desires were inhibited to achieve human perfection. Certain suggestions of the will as irrational and *unconsciously* determined provided the philosophical bases of Freud's concept of id energy as the principle of motivation. More recent formulations have questioned the existence of the will and the notion of freedom in personal motivation (e.g., Skinner), and these views are consistent with *materialism* (2, 3, 4, 8, 11, 14, 15).

Zeitgeist. Literally, "spirit of the times." An interpretation of historical trends suggesting that the intellectual and social forces of a given period create a momentum for progress and produce individuals to express the changes within the times. This interpretation of historical developments is in contrast to the *great man* interpretation (1, 18).

Name Index

Abélard, Pierre, 52, 57–60, 70
Abraham, Karl, 232
Abu ibn Sina (Avicenna), 46
Adams, John, 107
Adler, Alfred, 218, 224, 229, 230, 232, 234, 236–238
Agassiz, Louis, 185
Albertus Magnus, 52, 59–61, 70
Alcmaeon, 19, 32
Alexander (the Great), 5, 24, 25, 27
Allport, Floyd H., 311, 323
Allport, Gordon, 278, 291, 293–295
Ambrose, 42
Anaxagoras, 22, 23, 32
Anaximander, 18
Anaximenes, 18
Angelico, Fra, 65
Angell, Frank, 163
Angell, James, 179, 194, 195, 200, 201, 248
Anokhin, K.V., 304, 320
Anrep, G.V., 245, 272
Anthony, 42
Antiphon of Athens, 22
Aquinas, Thomas, 52, 60–64, 70, 71, 169, 280, 338, 348
Aristotle, 16, 24, 27–33, 37, 40, 41, 58–63, 70, 72–74, 169, 280, 283, 287, 330, 338, 340, 341, 348, 349
Asratyn, Ezras E., 256, 270
Augustine, 34, 42, 43, 48, 50, 51, 61–63, 164, 330, 343, 347
Avenarius, Richard, 159, 167, 168, 176
Averroës, 60

Bach, Johann Sebastian, 119
Bacon, Francis, 72–75, 77, 79, 87, 106
Bacon, Roger, 52, 59, 70
Bain, Alexander, 102, 115, 117, 135–139, 187
Baldwin, James, 196, 200
Baltes, D.B., 310, 322
Basil, 42
Beethoven, Ludwig van, 119
Bekhterev, Vladimir Michailovich, 239, 242, 256, 270
Bell, Charles, 141, 144, 156
Benedict, 46, 54
Beneke, Friedrich Eduard, 118, 128, 130, 135–138
Bentham, Jeremy, 113, 114
Bergson, Henri, 159, 174, 176, 185, 207
Beritashvili, Ivan Solomonovich (Beritov), 256, 271
Berkeley, George, 102, 109–112, 115, 116, 134–139
Bernard of Clairvaux, 54
Bernheim, Hippolyte, 221
Bertanthal, B.I., 306, 322
Bindra, D., 301, 302, 320
Binet, Alfred, 164, 167, 182
Binswanger, Ludwig, 278, 289, 290, 294, 295
Biran, Maine de, 89, 97, 98, 100, 101, 134–138

Birren, J.E., 310, 322
Bishop, P.O., 306, 322
Bismark, Otto von, 119, 120
Black, Joseph, 104
Bolles, Robert C., 302, 320
Boniface VIII, 64
Bonnet, Charles, 89, 94, 95, 100, 134–138
Boring, Edwin G., 2, 12, 14, 109, 165, 166, 177, 180, 187, 192, 208, 250
Bose, George, 121
Boyle, Robert, 79, 107
Boylston, Zabdiel, 104
Bradley, James, 104
Brainerd, C.J., 308, 322
Brehm, J.W., 303, 320
Brentano, Franz, 12, 159, 169–178, 190, 205–207, 213, 216, 219, 222, 230, 286, 287, 334, 335, 338
Brett, G.S., 12
Breuer, Josef, 222, 223
Bridgman, Percy, 251
Broca, Pierre-Paul, 143
Brody, Nathan, 312, 323
Brown, Thomas, 102, 112–114, 134–139, 339
Brunelleschi, Filippo, 65
Bruner, Jerome, 268, 274
Brunswick, Egon, 267, 274
Bryan, William Jennings, 196
Buber, Martin, 278, 283, 284
Buddha, (Siddhartha Gautama), 7, 8, 339
Bühler, Charlotte, 278, 291–294, 296
Bull, J.A., 301, 321
Burt, Cyril, 181

Cabanis, Pierre, 89, 96, 97, 100, 134–139
Cairns, L.B., 308, 323
Cajal, Santiago Ramón y, 142
Calkins, Mary, 179, 198, 201
Calvin, John, 68, 79, 183
Campbell, E.Q., 311, 324
Camus, Albert, 278, 283, 284, 294
Carpenter, P.A., 305, 309, 323
Carr, Harvey, 179, 195, 200, 201
Cattell, James McKeen, 179, 192, 196, 201, 203, 246
Charcot, Jean Martin, 221, 223, 242
Charles of Anjou, 61
Charles II, 80, 103, 106
Chomsky, Noam, 268, 274, 309, 345
Chuang-tze, 11
Church, Russell, 305, 320
Cicero, 36
Clement, 40
Clement V, 64
Clement VII, 64, 68
Coan, R.W., 134, 139
Cohen, S., 300, 320

Colbert, Jean Baptiste, 80
Comte, Auguste, 16, 17, 72, 89, 98–101, 114, 117,
    134–138, 168, 170, 247, 250, 311, 335, 347
Condillac, Étienne Bonnot de, 89, 93–98, 100, 108,
    111, 134–138, 240, 262, 282
Confucius, 9–11, 339
Constantine, 41
Copernicus, Nicholas, 52, 57, 69–71, 73, 75–77, 151,
    157, 159, 342
Copleston, Frederick, 13, 51, 82, 101, 116, 130, 177,
    332, 337
Corneille, Pierre, 90
Cronan-Hillix, William, 134, 139
Cyrus, 5

da Gama, Vasco, 6
d'Alembert, Jean Rond, 90
Darius III, 5
Darwin, Charles, 70, 82, 104, 115, 140, 152–158, 160,
    180, 181, 191, 193, 194, 247, 311, 341
Darwin, Erasmus, 104, 152, 154, 155
da Vinci, Leonardo, 65
Dawes, R.M., 312, 323
de Beauvoir, Simone, 283
Defoe, Daniel, 103
Delabarre, Edmund Burke, 200
Democritus, 18, 32, 123
Derrick, B.E., 304, 321
Descartes, René, 72, 83–89, 93–97, 100, 105, 106,
    109, 110, 118, 122, 123, 240, 242, 249, 330, 340,
    343, 349
DeValois, K.K., 306, 322
DeValois, R.L., 306, 322
Dewey, John, 179, 192–194, 200, 201
Diderot, Denis, 90
Dilthey, Wilhelm, 159, 173, 174, 176, 207, 278,
    282, 294
Dix, Dorothea, 220
Dominic á Guzman, 54
Donaldson, H.H., 248
Donatello, 65
Dostoyevsky, Fyodor, 280, 295
Dryden, John, 103
Du Bois-Reymond, Emil, 141, 142, 156, 162, 192, 242

Ebbinhaus, Hermann, 159, 167, 176, 178, 198, 308
Eccles, John, 144
Edwards, Jonathan, 109, 183
Egeth, H.E., 306, 322
Ehrenfels, Christian von, 159, 173
Ekken, Kaibara, 317
Elizabeth I, 78
Empedocles, 20, 32
Engles, Friedrich, 73, 281, 340
Epicurus, 34, 37, 38, 42, 50, 51
Epstein, R., 305, 321
Erasmus, Desiderius, 68, 70, 71
Estes, William, 250, 268, 274
Euclid, 21, 59, 75, 258
Euler, Leonhard, 119, 121
Everitt, B.J., 304, 321
Eysenck, H.J., 313, 324

Fahrenheit, Gabriel, 119
Fechner, Gustav T., 128, 140, 147–150, 156–158, 167
Feng, A.S., 306, 322

Festinger, Leon, 267, 268, 278
Fisher, L.M., 310, 322
Flavell, J.H., 308, 323
Flourens, Pierre, 143, 156
Foss, D.J., 309, 323
Francis of Assisi, 54
Franklin, Benjamin, 104, 183
Frederick of Hohenzollern, 119
Fredrick (the Great), 90, 95, 119, 124, 130
Freud, Sigmund, 121, 129, 170, 190, 193, 214,
    218–238, 250, 263, 264, 291, 329, 338, 343,
    347, 350
Fromm, Erich, 218, 235–237

Galileo, Galilei, 70, 72, 75, 76, 79, 80, 87, 106
Gall, Franz Josef, 142, 143, 156, 221
Galton, Francis, 114, 140, 154–157, 181, 196,
    203, 308
Galvani, Luigi, 141
Gärtner, Josef, 121
Gazzaniger, M., 304, 321
Gellman, S.A., 305, 323
Ghiberti, Lorenzo, 65
Ghirlandaio, Domenico, 65
Gilbert, William, 78
Giorgi, Amedeo, 293, 294, 296
Goethe, Johann Wolfgang von, 119, 148
Goldsmith, M., 305, 321
Golgi, Camillo, 142
Gorgias, 22
Gralath, Daniel, 121, 141
Gray, Stephen, 104
Gregory XIII, 36
Guericke, Otto von, 119
Gutenberg, Johann, 67
Guthrie, Edwin K, 239, 256–258, 264, 265, 273, 274

Haber, R.N., 306, 322
Hager, J.L., 303, 322
Hall, G. Stanley, 179, 185, 192, 193, 200, 201, 204,
    224, 318
Halley, Edmund, 104
Harris Bond, M., 312, 324
Hartley, David, 102, 111, 112, 115, 117, 135–138
Hartmann, Eduard von, 118, 129, 130, 134–138, 160,
    167, 329
Harvey, William, 79
Hearst, E., 301, 321
Heckhausen, J., 310, 323
Hegel, Georg, 280
Heidegger, Martin, 288, 293, 297–300, 305, 306
Helmholtz, Hermann von, 140–142, 145, 148, 150,
    151, 156–158, 162, 165, 166, 199, 241
Helvétius, Claude Adrien, 89, 96, 100, 134–139
Henry VII, 68
Henry VIII, 68
Heraclitus, 19, 26, 32
Herbart, Johann Friedrich, 118, 127, 128, 130,
    135–139, 160
Herbert, T.B., 300, 320
Hering, Ewald, 159, 166, 176, 199
Hersch, I.J., 306, 322
Herschel, William, 104
Hillyard, S.A., 305, 321
Hippocrates (the mathematician), 21
Hippocrates (the physician), 19, 20, 32, 240

Hobbes, Thomas, 102, 106, 107, 111, 115, 135–138, 335
Holmes, Oliver Wendell, 185
Holt, Edwin, 189, 239, 249, 250, 270, 272
Honzik, M., 310, 323
Hooke, Robert, 79
Horney, Karen, 218, 232–234, 236–238, 291, 319
Horton, G.P., 257
Hull, Clark L., 239, 256, 258–260, 262, 264, 266, 267, 270, 273, 275, 343
Hume, David, 102, 110–112, 115–117, 126, 135–138, 168, 245, 282, 339
Hunt, E., 305, 321
Hunter, John, 104
Hunter, Walter, 239, 250, 270
Hunter, William, 104
Husserl, Edmund, 170, 172, 207, 208, 278, 283, 286–288, 294, 295, 347

Innocent II, 58
Ishida, Baigan, 317

James, Henry, 188
James, William, 82, 97, 98, 167, 179, 184–189, 192–194, 198, 200, 201, 203, 246, 249, 347
Janet, Pierre, 221
Jaspers, Karl, 278, 284, 294
Jastrow, Joseph, 200
Jefferson, Thomas, 107, 181
Jerome, 42
Jesus, 39–42, 50, 282
Julius II, 65
Jung, C., 218, 224, 230–232, 236–238, 313, 329, 338, 343, 348
Just, M.A., 305, 309, 323
Justinian, 45, 49

Kamada, Ho, 317
Kant, Immanuel, 96, 118, 124–131, 134–138, 147, 160, 166, 168, 187, 194, 206, 207, 219, 236, 280, 282, 329, 341, 343, 348
Katz, David, 166, 167
Kenny, D., 312, 324
Kepler, Johann, 70, 72, 76, 77, 79, 87
Kierkegaard, Søren, 278, 281, 282, 294, 298, 350
Kinchla, R.A., 306, 322
Kleist, E.G. von, 121
Koffka, Kurt, 173, 200, 208–210, 216, 217
Köhler, Wolfgang, 173, 205, 208–210, 212–214, 216, 318
Kolb, B., 304, 321
Konorski, Jerzy, 253–258, 270–272
Koriat, A., 305, 321
Kolb, B., 304, 321
Kraemer, Heinrich, 55
Krölreuter, Josef, 121
Kuhn, Thomas, 3, 15, 71, 334
Külpe, Oswald, 164, 174–177, 206, 207, 217
Kuroda, Ryo, 318
Kutas, M., 305, 321

Ladd, Georg Trumbull, 200
Ladd-Franklin, Christine, 179, 198, 199, 201
LaFontaine, Jean de la, 90
Lagrange, Joseph Louis, 90, 100
Lamarck, Jean-Baptiste Pierre, 152, 153, 157

La Mettrie, Julien Offroy de, 89, 95, 96, 100, 134–138, 240, 250
Lange, Carl, 82, 186
Lanza, R.P., 305, 321
Lao-tze, 9
Laplace, Pierre Simon, 92, 100
Lashley, Karl S., 239, 250, 251, 270, 272, 303
Lavoisier, Antoine, 92, 100
Leeuwenhoek, Anton van, 79
Leibniz, Godfried Wilhelm, 77, 118, 122–124, 127, 130, 134–138, 219, 236, 328, 345
Lenin, V.I., 242
Leo III, 48
Leo X, 65, 70
Leo XIII, 61
Lewin, Kurt, 214–217
Lindenberger, U., 310, 322
Linnaeus, Carolus, 121
Livy, 36
Locke, John, 93, 102, 107–112, 115–117, 122, 134–139, 181, 183, 197, 240, 306, 328, 333, 335
Loeb, Jacques, 262
Lombard, Peter, 60
Lorenz, Konrad, 192, 302
Lotze, Rudolph Hermann, 118, 128–130, 135–138, 166, 170, 196
Louis XIV, 80, 89, 91, 92
Louis XV, 89, 92
Louis XVI, 97
Louis XVIII, 97
Lubart, R.I., 308, 320
Lucretius, 36
Luria, A.L., 255, 270
Luther, Martin, 2, 3, 68, 79

Mach, Ernst, 159, 167, 168, 176
Machiavelli, Niccolo, 73
Madison, James, 107
Magendie, Francois, 141, 144, 156
Malpighi, Marcello, 79
Malthus, Thomas, 153
Martin V, 64
Martineau, Harriet, 99, 101
Martinez, J.L., 304, 321
Martland, Charles, 104
Marx, Karl, 73, 281, 340
Marx, Melvin H., 134, 139, 263, 264, 273
Mary (Queen), 107
Maslow, Abraham, 278, 292–295
Masuda, Koichi, 318
Mather, Cotton, 55
Matthies, H., 304, 321
Matsumoto, Matataro, 318
May, Rollo, 278, 292–294, 296
McDougall, William, 179, 190–193, 200, 201, 203, 248, 302, 311
McKoon, G., 309, 323
Mead, Margaret, 311, 324
Medici, Lorenzo de, 65
Mencius, 11
Mendel, Gregor Johann, 153
Mendeleyev, Dimitri, 241
Merleau-Ponty, Maurice, 278, 289, 290, 294–296
Mesmer, Franz Anton, 121, 220, 221
Meyako, A., 305, 309, 323
Meyer, Max, 250

Michelangelo (Buonarroti), 65
Milgram, S., 311, 324
Mill, James, 102, 113, 115, 116, 134–138, 248
Mill, John Stuart, 99, 102, 113, 114, 116, 117,
   135–139, 191, 245, 333, 339
Miller, George, 309
Miller, Neal, 266, 267, 269, 274, 275, 300, 320
Miller, Philip, 121
Miller, Stefan, 253, 254, 271
Milner, P.M., 303, 322
Milton, John, 103
Mischel, W., 313, 324
Mohammed, 45–47
Molière (Jean Baptiste Poquelin), 90
More, Thomas, 68
Morgan, Lloyd, 154, 157, 247
Morita, Shoma, 318
Mo Ti, 11
Motora, Yojiro, 318
Mozart, Wolfgang Amadeus, 119
Mowrer, Herbert O., 267, 269, 272
Müller, Georg Elias, 159, 166, 167, 176, 199
Müller, Johannes, 141, 144, 150, 156, 162, 241
Münsterberg, Hugo, 179, 188–191, 198, 200–203

Napoleon (Bonaparte), 94
Nencki, Marceli, 243, 254
Newton, Issac, 70, 72, 77–79, 83, 87, 103, 122, 145
Nietzsche, Friedrich, 280, 282, 294
Nikara, T., 306, 322

Ohm, Georg, 147
Olsen, Regina, 281
Origen, 40
Osgood, C.E., 309, 323
Overmier, J.B., 301, 321

Pan Shu, 327
Parmenides of Elea, 19, 26, 32
Pansky, A., 305, 321
Pascal, Blaise, 79
Patanjali, 315
Paul of Tarsus, 40
Paul III, 70
Pavlov, Ivan Petrovich, 144, 194, 212, 239, 242–249,
   251, 253–256, 259, 264, 267, 269, 270, 272,
   277, 301, 302, 328, 330, 331, 348
Pearson, Karl, 181, 182, 202
Peirce, Charles Sanders, 179, 187, 188, 199, 200,
   202, 347
Peterson, G.B., 310, 323
Pettigrew, J.D., 306, 322
Pettigrew, T.F., 311, 324
Philip IV (the Fair), 64
Piaget, Jean, 268, 307, 308, 322, 323, 341
Pillsbury, W.B., 12
Pinel, Philippe, 220
Plato, 16, 24, 26, 27, 32, 38, 39, 41–43, 50, 58, 61,
   83, 84, 280, 330, 338
Plotinus, 38, 42, 50
Polo, Marco, 8
Polybius, 36
Premack, D., 305, 323
Priestley, Joseph, 90, 104
Protagoras, 22

Purkinje, Jan, 145, 146, 151, 156, 157, 164, 166,
   207, 347
Pythagoras, 20, 21, 23, 32, 127

Racine, Jean Baptiste, 90
Rancurello, Antos, 12, 178
Rand, Benjamin, 12
Ratcliff, R., 309, 323
Ratnam, R., 306, 322
Rayner, Rosalie, 248, 269, 273
Razan, Hayashi, 317
Reid, Thomas, 102, 112, 113, 117, 134–138, 198
Rescorla, Robert A., 267, 275, 301, 321
Robbins, T.W., 304, 321
Rogers, Carl, 278, 292–295
Roitblat, J.L., 305, 321
Rolando, Luigi, 143
Rolls, E.T., 305, 321
Romanes, George, 154, 157, 247
Rompre, P.-P., 303, 322
Roosevelt, Franklin, 224
Rose, S.P.R., 304, 320
Rosenzweig, M., 304, 321
Rousseau, Jean Jacques, 90
Rush, Benjamin, 184, 203

Sachs, Hans, 232
Saint-Simon, Comte de, 98
Sakuma, Kanae, 318
Sanford, Edmund Clark, 193, 200
Sangupta, N.N., 314
Sartre, Jean Paul, 278, 283, 289, 294, 295
Sato, Koji, 319
Schlenker, I.D., 312, 324
Schlosberg, Harold, 197
Schoenfeld, W.N., 267, 275
Schopenhauer, Arthur, 118, 129, 130, 134–138,
   160, 329
Schule, Karl Wilhelm, 90
Schulz, R., 310, 323
Scripture, Edward Wheeler, 200
Sechenov, Ivan Michailovich, 239, 241, 242, 256,
   270, 272
Self, E.A., 303, 320
Seligman, Martin E.P., 303, 320, 321
Shoda, Y., 313, 324
Sheffield, W., 257, 273
Sherrington, Charles S., 143, 144, 156, 157, 177, 212,
   241, 254, 255, 270, 348
Shih Huang-ti, 8
Skinner, B.F., 239, 254, 256, 261, 262, 264, 268, 270,
   273, 274, 305, 321, 339
Smith, P.B., 312, 324
Snyder, M., 312, 324
Socrates, 23, 24, 26, 27, 32, 280
Sokalov, E.M., 256, 272
Solomon, Richard L., 267, 301, 321
Spearman, Charles, 181
Spence, Kenneth W., 266, 274
Spencer, Herbert, 140, 154, 156, 181, 247, 345
Sperry, Roger, 304, 334, 337
Spinoza, Baruch, 72, 81–83, 86, 87, 118, 122, 186
Sprengel, Konrad, 121
Sprenger, Jacob, 55
Spurzheim, J.G., 142, 221

Staudinger, U.M., 310, 322
Stern, William, 182
Sternberg, R.J., 308, 322
Stukas, A.A., 312, 324
Stumpf, Carl, 159, 170, 172, 173, 176, 205, 207–209, 211, 213, 216, 219, 250, 286
Suci, C.T., 309, 323
Sullivan, Harry Stack, 218, 234, 236, 237
Swets, J.A., 266, 275
Swift, Jonathan, 103

Takuan, Soho, 329
Tanaka, Kwanichi, 318
Tannenbaum, P.H., 309, 323
Taylor, Janet, 266, 275
Thales, 18
Thomson, Godfrey, 181
Thorndike, Edward Lee, 179, 196, 197, 201–203, 239, 246–248, 257, 259, 262, 270, 272, 276, 330
Thurstone, L.L., 181, 182
Tinbergen, Niko, 192, 302
Titchener, Edward Bradford, 159, 161, 163–167, 169, 175–178, 189, 195, 199, 204, 326, 334, 349
Titus, 40
Tolman, Edward C., 189, 213, 239, 250, 256, 260, 261, 264, 267, 270, 274, 276, 302, 327, 330
Tschirnhaus, Ehrenfried von, 119

Urban VI, 64

Valsiner, J., 308, 323
van Kaam, Adrian, 293, 295
Varro, 36
Verrocchio, Andrea del, 65
Virgil, 36
Voeks, Virginia, 257, 274
Voltaire (Francois Marie Arouet), 90, 119
von Fersen, L., 305, 321
Vygotsky, L.S., 255, 270

Wagner, R., 301, 312
Washburn, Margaret, 179, 199, 202, 204, 247
Watson, C.S., 306, 322
Watson, John B., 144, 191, 192, 194, 195, 239, 240, 245, 247–250, 252, 258, 260, 262, 268, 269, 270, 272, 273, 275–277, 299, 318, 327, 328, 331, 333, 339
Watson, Robert I., 3, 15, 133, 134, 139
Watt, James, 104
Weber, Ernst Heinrich, 128, 140, 146–148, 156, 157
Wegmer, D.M., 305–322
Weigold, M.F., 312, 324
Weiss, Albert P., 239, 250, 270, 273
Wellman, H.M., 305, 323
Wen Wang, 9
Wenzlaff, R.M., 305, 322
Wertheimer, Max, 205, 208–210, 214, 216, 217
Whishaw, I.Q., 304, 321
White, N.M., 303, 322
William of Champeaux, 57
William III, 103, 107
Wise, R.A., 303, 322
Wolff, Christian von, 118, 124, 130, 134–138, 160, 348
Wolpe, Joseph, 269, 275
Woodworth, Robert S., 164, 179, 197, 201, 202, 258
Woolman, John, 183
Wundt, Wilhelm, 98, 148, 159, 161–166, 169, 171–178, 186, 188–190, 192, 194, 196, 199, 200, 205–207, 211, 212, 216, 217, 242, 263, 286, 318, 326, 334, 335, 349

Yang Chu, 11
Yantis, S., 305, 322
Young, Thomas, 144, 148, 150, 156

Zarathustra, 5, 6
Zeno, 37
Zang Yaoxiang, 315
Zwingli, Urich, 68

Subject Index

Act psychology, 159, 169–172, 175, 176, 189, 190, 218–220, 332–334, 338
America, psychology in, 183, 184. *See also* Functional psychology
American Psychological Association (APA), 12, 80, 163, 192, 198, 210
American Psychological Society (APS), 80
Analytic psychology, 230–232, 236–238
Animism, 16, 17
Apperception, 165, 166
Appetite, 26. *See also* Will
Applied psychology, 182, 183, 188–190, 200, 201, 240, 252, 253, 268, 269, 298–301. *See also* Functional psychology
Artificial Intelligence (AI), 265, 266
Associations, mental, 30, 31, 93–95, 97, 106–116, 118, 128, 135–137, 154, 155, 163–165, 196, 197, 212, 239–249, 252–277, 308, 309, 328–330, 338, 339, 344. *See also* Learning processes
Astronomy, advances in, 69, 70, 75–78, 104, 105, 119, 121, 342
Atomism, 18, 38, 39, 95, 122, 123, 168, 169, 338, 339, 345
Attention, 122, 165, 256

Behavior, 100, 189–195, 215, 216, 239–277, 327, 328, 339, 344
Behaviorism, 100, 167, 168, 189–195, 200, 201, 206, 210–216, 239–277, 299–305, 311, 318, 325–332, 335, 344
Bell-Magendie Law, 141
Biological orientation of ancient Greek psychology, 16, 19, 20, 32
Brain, physiology of, 140–146, 211, 212, 241–245, 253–256, 270, 271
British monarchs, 68, 78, 103, 106
Buddhism, 1, 7, 8, 316, 317, 319, 339
Byzantine Empire, 44, 45

Categories, mental
  Aristotle, 30, 31
  Aquinas, 61–63
  Leibniz, 122, 123
  Kant, 124–126, 141, 147, 219, 220, 282, 286, 287, 331
  Peirce, 187, 188
Catharsis, 231
Causality, 16, 17, 29, 30, 37, 99, 110, 113–115, 124–127, 148, 149, 189, 206, 207, 247–249, 251, 252
Censorship, church and state, 48, 54–57, 63, 64, 67–70, 75, 76, 85, 86, 92, 93
Chemistry, advances in, 90, 92, 104, 119, 121, 161
Chicago, University of, and functionalism, 179, 193–195, 200, 201, 247–250

Chinese traditions, 1, 8–11, 315, 316
Christianity, 34, 36, 37, 39–51
Church councils, 41, 64, 170
Clinical psychology, 155, 220–237, 268, 269, 289–293
Cognitive processes, 163–165, 210–212, 216, 252, 253, 260, 261, 267, 268, 279, 305–309, 328, 330. *See also* Learning processes
Cognitive science, 267, 268, 305–309, 329
Columbia University, and functionalism, 179, 195–197, 200, 201, 246, 247
Common sense psychology, Scottish, 111, 112, 116, 134–138, 184, 190, 191
Comparative psychology, 152–154, 190, 191, 195, 247–249
Conditioning, 194, 195, 212, 241–247, 253–256, 301–305, 330, 331. *See also* Learning processes
Confucianism, 1, 9, 10
Consciousness. 38, 39, 75, 76, 84, 85, 97, 98, 108, 122–125, 134–138, 186, 187, 194, 195, 207, 212, 240, 242–249, 279, 334–336, 339. *See also* Mind; Self-reflection; Soul
Content psychology. *See* Structural psychology
Copernican revolution, 52, 69–71, 151, 152
Cosmology, 18, 19, 29
Counter-Reformation, 67, 68, 118, 119
Crusades, 34, 49–52
Cybernetics, 267

Dark Ages, 43–51
Defense mechanisms, 225, 227, 235–237
Depth perception, 109, 150. *See also* Vision
Determinism, 37, 39–41, 61–63, 76, 77, 81, 82, 108, 129, 340
Developmental psychology, 192, 193, 224–228, 268, 269, 307–310
Drive, 224–228, 232–234, 236, 237, 258–260, 301–305
Dualism, 22–32, 38–43, 46, 57–63, 82–87, 89, 93–97, 100, 101, 107–111, 115, 118, 122, 123, 137–139, 186, 187, 194, 195, 205, 327, 328, 334–336, 340

Eclectic orientation of ancient Greek psychology, 16, 21, 22, 32
Effect, Law of. *See* Hedonism
Elements, mental, 163, 168, 286, 287
Emotion, 163–166, 186, 187, 266–268
Empiricism, 2, 59, 60, 72–79, 105–116, 119, 121, 124–127, 129, 130, 135–138, 169–176, 184–187, 207, 208, 218–220, 228, 236, 237, 247, 251–253, 258–260, 263–265, 298, 299, 312, 313, 325, 328–330, 332–336, 341
English writers, 52, 103
Enlightenment, French, 89, 90
Epicureanism, 34, 38, 42, 50

Essence, 27–32, 40, 62, 63, 283–285, 341
Evolution, 70, 82, 95, 140, 151–156, 160, 180, 181, 194, 200, 341
Existence, 27–32, 40, 62, 63, 283, 285, 341
Existentialism and existential psychology, 278–285, 288–297
Experience, 105, 144, 145, 163–166, 283–285
Experimental method, 2, 159, 160, 167, 168, 228, 237, 257, 313
Extirpation, method of, 143–145

Faculty psychology, 61–63, 124–127, 187, 188, 341
Feudalism, 35, 46, 48–51
Fiber psychology, 96–98, 100, 101
Field theory, 214–216
French monarchs, 48, 61, 64, 80, 89, 91, 92, 97
French writers, 92
Functional psychology, 172, 179–204, 206, 213, 214, 326, 336, 341

Geocentric theory of planetary motion, 69–71, 75, 76, 342
German artists and writers, 119, 145
German monarchs, 90, 95, 118–120, 124, 130
Gestalt psychology, 167, 172, 173, 175, 188, 200, 205–216, 219, 260, 267, 279, 306, 311, 318, 326, 328–332, 334, 336, 342
Great man model of history, 2, 3

Hedonism, 38, 83, 95, 106, 113, 224–227, 246–248, 258–262, 279, 301–304, 342
Heliocentric theory of planetary motion, 69–71, 75, 76, 342
Hinduism, 1, 6, 7
Hormic psychology, 190–192
Humanistic orientation of ancient Greek psychology, 16, 22–24, 32
Humanistic psychology, 278, 279, 290–293, 342
Human science model, 159, 168–176, 206–208, 278, 279, 341, 342
Hypnotism, 121, 221–223, 242, 258

I-Ching, 9
Ideologists, 97, 98
Indian traditions, 1, 6–8
Individual psychology, 229, 230
Innate ideas, 26–28, 42, 43, 83, 84, 93, 94, 122–127, 137–139, 166, 219, 230–232, 328–330, 342
Inquisition, 54, 55, 75, 76, 85, 86, 220
Instinct, 190–192, 302, 303, 311
Intelligence, 59, 60, 154–156, 181, 182, 196, 197, 241, 242, 305–309
Introspection, 42, 43, 164–166, 193–195, 196, 197, 242, 247–249, 343
Ionian physicists, 18, 19, 32, 240, 330
Islam, 5, 34, 45–47, 51
Isomorphism, 212, 219, 328
Italian Renaissance artists, 52, 55, 56, 65–67, 70

Japanese traditions, 298, 316–320
Journal of the History of the Behavioral Sciences, 12
Just noticeable difference (jnd), 148, 149

Latin writers, 36
Learned societies, 72, 80, 81, 90, 92, 95, 104, 163, 184, 192, 198, 210

Learning processes, 30, 31, 62, 63, 93, 94, 106–116, 183, 184, 186–192, 194–201, 205, 209–214, 241–271, 298, 301–305, 319, 338, 339
Limen, 148, 149. *See also* Threshold
Logic, 28, 29, 36, 57–63, 73–79, 106–111, 114–116, 124, 160, 251, 252, 280–282, 340, 343, 344
Logical positivism. *See* Positivism

Materialism, 18, 19, 42, 43, 89, 93–97, 99, 100, 109, 114–116, 127–130, 134–139, 146–151, 241, 247–249, 253–256, 279, 280, 330, 331, 344
Mathematical orientation of ancient Greek psychology, 16, 17, 20, 21, 32
Mechanism, 38, 75–79, 81, 83–87, 93–97, 99, 100, 106, 127–130, 159, 160, 196, 197, 224–228, 241–245, 261, 262, 280, 281, 328–331, 344
Memory, 30, 31, 60, 62, 63, 82, 93, 94, 106, 110, 125, 126, 167, 188, 189, 248–271, 301–305. *See also* Learning processes
Mental activity, 37, 89, 118, 122–130, 134–139, 188–190, 205–207, 211, 212, 219, 220, 267, 280, 328–331, 344
Mental illness, 50, 142, 143, 220, 221, 226–228, 288–290
Mental organization, 210–212, 219, 220. *See also* Categories, mental
Mental passivity, 37, 89, 102, 105–116, 118, 122, 123, 134–139, 241, 280, 328–331, 344
Metaphysics, 28–32, 39, 46, 57–64, 99, 100, 124–127, 159, 161, 163, 164, 339, 341, 345, 346
Middle Ages, 43–51, 52–64, 67, 344
Mind, 1, 42, 43, 81–87, 92–101, 105–116, 122–130, 134–139, 159, 160, 184–187, 190, 191, 210–212, 219, 220, 241, 244–245, 247–249, 255, 267, 325–332
Mind-body. *See* Dualism
Monadology, 122, 123, 130, 137, 219, 345
Monasticism, 42, 46, 48, 54–56
Monism, 81–83, 87, 137, 138, 184–187, 327, 328, 336, 345
Motivation, 96, 97, 184–187, 190, 191, 197, 214, 215, 229, 230, 243–245, 249–251, 298, 301–305

Nativism, 206, 207, 336, 345. *See also* Innate ideas
Naturalistic orientation of ancient Greek psychology, 16–19, 32
Natural science model, 159, 161–168, 175, 176, 345
Neoplatonism, 34, 38, 39, 42, 43, 50
Nervous system, 95, 96, 140–146, 163–166, 210–212
Neurophysiology, 140–146, 150, 151, 241–245, 303, 304. *See also* Brain, psychology of
Neurosciences, 303, 304
Nonsensory mental events or consciousness, 111, 112, 174, 175, 206, 207, 278, 279
Nous, 22, 23

Observation, 2, 17–22, 59, 60, 72–79, 90, 92, 95, 99–101, 163–166, 171, 172, 193–195, 206–208, 240–243, 247–252, 256–265, 313, 321–332, 335, 336, 346
Operationism. *See* Positivism

Papacy and the popes, 36, 41, 42, 63–71, 170
Pax Romana, 34–37, 39, 40
Perception, 92–101, 109, 127–130, 146–152, 163–176,
    205–212, 219, 220, 267, 298, 306, 319, 330,
    331, 346
Persian kings, 1, 5
Persian traditions, 1, 5, 6
Personality, 214–216, 224–228, 298, 312, 313, 319
Phenomena and phenomenological psychology, 171,
    172, 205–208, 278, 279, 285–290, 293, 294,
    328–330, 346, 347
Philosophies, 92, 93
Phi phenomenon, 208, 209
Phrenology, 142, 143, 221
Physics, advances in, 28, 29, 90, 92, 104, 105, 119,
    121, 159
Physiology, advances in, 73–81, 90, 92, 104, 105, 114,
    119, 121, 140–146, 152–154, 159, 241–245, 298,
    302–304
Pneuma, 18
Positivism, 16, 17, 79, 89, 98–101, 114, 167, 168,
    170, 240, 251, 252, 256, 258–262, 311,
    332–334, 347
Pragmatism, 179, 184–187, 200, 347
Prescriptions of psychological issues, 3, 133,
    134, 139
Primary qualities, 76, 109, 112
Prussia, and the rise of modern Germany, 119, 120
Psychoanalysis, 218–237, 253, 279, 326–332, 336,
    347
Psycholinguistics, 268, 298, 299, 308, 309
Psychophysical parallelism
    Bain, 115
    Leibniz, 122, 123
    Wolff, 124
Psychophysics, 140, 146–151, 155, 156, 167, 169,
    195, 347
Psychosexual stages, 224–227
Psychotherapy, 50, 55, 220–224, 226, 227, 269, 270,
    288–290
Ptolemaic, 69, 70, 342

Rationalism, German, 124–130, 135–137, 159, 160,
    280–288, 335, 347, 348
Reason, 26, 28–32, 37–39, 42, 43, 45, 46, 57, 60–71,
    81–87, 110, 111, 124–127, 130, 135–137
Reductionism, 92–101, 111, 113, 134–139, 163–166,
    167, 168, 205–208, 213, 241, 242, 243–245,
    247–249, 253–256, 258–265, 279, 282–288,
    304, 326–332
Reflexes and reflexology, 115, 194, 213, 214, 239,
    241–245, 253–256, 270–272, 327, 328, 348
Reformation, 3, 52, 67, 68, 71, 119
Reinforcement, 243–247, 254, 255, 258–269, 266,
    267, 301–304, 348. *See also* Hedonism
Religious orders, 48, 49, 54, 55, 59, 61, 68, 75, 83,
    93, 96, 169
Renaissance, 52, 56, 57, 65–67, 70, 220, 332, 348
Roman emperors, 34, 36, 45, 50
Roman Empire, 34–41, 43–45, 50, 51
Roman philosophies, 34, 37–39, 42, 43, 50, 51

Schisms
    Eastern, 48
    Papal, 54, 64
Scholasticism, 46, 52, 60–64, 67, 72, 76, 83, 93, 169,
    335, 348
Secondary qualities, 76, 108, 112
Self, 84, 98, 112, 118, 127–130, 198, 230–232, 233,
    283, 284, 292, 293, 307, 308
Self-reflection, 93, 108, 122, 123, 134–139
Sensation, 21, 22, 26, 30, 39, 43, 62, 63, 74, 82, 84,
    93–98, 100, 105–116, 118, 122, 124, 140, 141,
    144–151, 164, 167, 172, 173, 194, 206–211,
    240, 349. *See also* Perception
Sensationalism and sensory physiology, 89, 93–98,
    100–102, 118, 122, 123, 132–139, 240, 241,
    347, 328–330
Shintoism, 316, 317
Skepticism, 22, 75, 83, 110–112, 168, 349
Social psychology, 100, 298, 310–312, 323, 324
Sophists, 21, 22, 32, 189, 326
Soul, 23–32, 37–43, 46, 60–64, 128, 230–232, 349.
    See also Consciousness; Mind
Stoicism, 34, 37, 38, 40, 50
Structural psychology, 159, 161–166, 168, 174, 175,
    180, 188, 190, 200, 205, 206–207, 212, 213,
    216, 242, 278, 334, 349
Subjective report, methods of, 145, 146

Taoism, 9
Testing, mental, 154–156, 181, 182, 196, 197
Theology, 40–43, 56, 57, 60–64, 70, 122, 123, 183,
    280–282
Third force movement, 278–294, 325–332
Threshold, 146–150. *See also* Limen
Two-factor theory of mental ability, 181, 182
Two-process theory of conditioning, 254, 267, 301

Unconscious, 96, 123, 129, 130, 160, 190, 219–237,
    279, 328, 329, 350
Universities, 52, 54–61, 69, 70, 104, 106, 110, 113,
    119, 121, 122, 124, 127, 128, 130, 142, 144–147,
    150, 162, 163, 166–170, 172, 174, 175, 179, 181,
    182, 184, 185, 187–200, 206, 208–210, 214, 222,
    241–243, 246, 248, 250, 251, 253, 257, 258, 260,
    261, 265–267, 284, 286, 291–294, 318, 319
Upanishads, 6, 7, 315
Utilitarianism, 113, 183, 184

Vedas, 6, 7
Vienna Circle. *See* Positivism
Vision, 109, 145, 147, 150, 151, 208, 211, 212, 216,
    306

Weber's Law, 147–149
Will, 30, 62, 63, 93, 97, 106, 126, 129, 164, 165, 190,
    279, 350
Women in American psychology, 179, 197–199
Würzburg School, 159, 174, 175, 205–207, 216

Zeitgeist model of historicity, 2, 3, 160, 336, 350
Zen Buddhism, 319